Alfred Thayer Mahan

Rear Admiral Alfred Thayer Mahan

ALFRED THAYER MAHAN

The Man and His Letters

by
Robert Seager II

NAVAL INSTITUTE PRESS
ANNAPOLIS, MARYLAND

Naval Institute Press
291 Wood Road
Annapolis, MD 21402

First Naval Institute Press paperback edition published in 2017.
ISBN: 978-1-59114-592-9 (paperback)
ISBN: 978-1-68247-213-2 (eBook)

Library of Congress Catalogue Card No. 77-74158
ISBN: 0-87021-359-8

⊗ Print editions meet the requirements of ANSI/NISO z39.48-1992
(Permanence of Paper).
Printed in the United States of America.

25 24 23 22 21 20 19 18 17   9 8 7 6 5 4 3 2 1
First printing

FOR MY MOTHER

Helen Adeline Hales Seager
Lieutenant, Army Nurse Corps, 1942–1945

Contents

CONTENTS

Preface

This is not, and could not be, a definitive biography of Rear Admiral Alfred Thayer Mahan—not when some 70 per cent to 75 per cent of his personal and professional letters remain secreted in various attics or archives or have been destroyed. It is only as definitive as an analysis of his 2,900 surviving letters, his diary for April 1868 to September 1869, his numerous speeches and position papers, and his 20 books and 137 articles permit.

It is certainly not the story of a swashbuckling naval officer. Save for a few minutes at Port Royal, South Carolina, on November 7, 1861, Mahan never heard a gun fired in anger. Only in the pages of his books did he experience combat. It is the portrait—warts and all—of a historian, strategist, tactician, philosopher, Episcopalian, theologian, diplomat, imperialist, mercantilist, capitalist, Anglophile, patriot, Republican, racist, Social Darwinist, journalist, polemicist, naval reformer, adviser to presidents and legislators, teacher, academic administrator, social climber, egoist, introvert, swain, husband, and father. Mahan remains one of the few military figures in American history whose brain power was his main shield and buckler. He read good books and wrote better ones. He was an intellectual in uniform, and his busy pen was mightier than his sheathed sword.

As a seagoing naval officer, however, Mahan was a disaster. He was an indifferent seaman. Indeed, he feared and hated the sea, its storms, its moods, its loneliness. But as a propagandist for sea power, especially as it was represented by the U.S. Navy in the years 1890 to 1914, he was a genius. He thoroughly disliked the Navy, notably the U.S. Naval Academy, and many naval officers disliked him. At best, his "service reputation" was mixed. His personal battles, literary and professional, were frequent and intense. Yet, he made the Naval War College what it is today, and *The Influence of Sea Power Upon History*—perhaps the most powerful and influential book written by an American in America in the nineteenth century—had much to do with resurrecting the U.S. Navy from its post-Civil War grave and giving it the professional ballast and theoretical direction that helped guide it to victory in 1898, in 1918, and in 1945.

This account of Mahan's life and work is based largely on primary-source materials in *Letters and Papers of Alfred Thayer Mahan*. Save for the fact that he has modernized spelling, punctuation, and capitalization, the author permits the admiral to speak, sometimes at length, in his own words. Thus, readers can judge for themselves whether the biographer has been faithful to the historical record with which he worked. To a large extent, every reader can become his own biographer of Mahan by perusing *Letters and Papers* and by reading Mahan's books and articles, most of which have recently been reprinted.

Mahan's research methods would not pass muster in a modern Ph.D. seminar in historiography. For this reason, the author's rather traditional approach to the writing of biography borrows neither from the admiral's highly selective choice and arrangement of facts (he called the process "subordination"), nor from similar methods embraced these days by those "New Left" historians who see conspiracy lurking everywhere in history. Since the author is not a "Cliometrician," the book also has the advantage or disadvantage, depending on one's point of view, of not having been written by a computer. Further, it is not an exercise in the "psycho-history" that is currently the rage in the history departments of some universities. True, Mahan was a complex person in a psychological sense, as are all human beings, but no attempt has been made to stretch him out on a couch and subject him to psychological analysis. Since he died in 1914, it seems a bit late for that.

To balance and supplement opinions of the controversial and contentious officer presented herein, students of Mahan and the New Navy should have another look at William D. Puleston's solid *Mahan* (1939) and at William E. Livezey's excellent *Mahan on Sea Power* (1947). Charles C. Taylor's episodic *The Life of Admiral Mahan: Naval Philosopher* (1920) is also worth rereading. Because the account presented in this study does not attempt to re-create in detail the history of the "From-Sail-to-Steam" Navy in which Mahan served, or the international diplomacy of the turbulent period in which he lived, the reader should examine various recent monographs and biographies that pertain importantly to those subjects. Among them are studies by T. A. Bailey, S. F. Bemis, W. R. Braisted, D. J. Carrison, O. J. Clinard, G. T. Davis, F. R. Dulles, K. J. Hagan, W. R. Herrick, P. Karsten, R. W. Leopold, A. J. Marder, D. W. Mitchell, E. E. Morison, R. G. O'Connor, G. C. O'Gara, E. B. Potter, R. Spector, H. and M. Sprout, D. F. Trask, and R. S. West. Here the reader is given only enough of the historical background to make Mahan's views on particular naval and diplomatic events intelligible.

At the same time, students of the U.S. Navy and its role in the nation's diplomacy should be wary of efforts to apply quotations from Mahan's teachings to the strategy and tactics of the Cold War and of the continuing American-Soviet military confrontation. Modern-day geopoliticians can "prove" almost anything they wish by citing carefully selected chapters and verses from Mahan's numerous works.

In most instances, however, were Mahan alive today, he would not understand what these earnest people were talking about. He saw twentieth-century naval tactics as an extension of the tactics used by armies of the eighteenth and early nineteenth centuries. Tactical analogies between infantry units and ships of the line, and between cavalry and frigates, fascinated him. He frequently blurred the distinction between strategy and tactics. He felt that developments in the technology of weapons had little effect on the operation of the immutable "principles" on which, he was certain, the "art" and "science" of war were based. He thought, for example, that HMS *Dreadnought* was far too costly a weapon for what she was worth tactically. War over the sea and under the sea played no role in his thinking. "Some years will probably elapse before 10,000 men can cross the British channel, aviating," he wrote in 1911. The very idea smacked of Jules Verne. Similarly, he had no conception of amphibious warfare. The future of the submarine, he argued, was uncertain, more dubious than that of the submerged mine. The naval applications of wireless telegraphy largely escaped him. He could barely cope with the logistical implications of coal as a motive power for fleets, much less with the potentialities of diesel fuel. Naval guns capable of firing projectiles 18,000 yards boggled his mind. He was, in fine, a man from the Age of Sail. Until the end of his days he believed in the efficacy of tight blockades, control of the "narrow seas," and broadside-to-broadside combat fought in traditional eighteenth-century sailing-ship formations. He never wavered in his conviction that the seizure and exercise of "command of the sea," his chief strategic principle, could be achieved only by decisive surface-fleet actions. He was a devotee of the "Big Battle."

Marxist historians find him an easy target to bracket and sink since he was a bourgeois capitalist-imperialist who rejected socialism with almost the same passion that he embraced a literal interpretation of the New Testament. They have more difficulty with the fact that he feared and opposed the growth of trusts and monopolies in America's turn-of-the-century domestic economy with equal fervor. On the other hand, they may be pleased to learn that much of what Mahan published after his retirement from the Navy in 1896 was written for the royalties involved.

He is one of very few historians in the United States, then and since, who actually made substantial amounts of money with his pen.

Royalties aside, Mahan was without peer as a diplomatic historian-journalist of the era in which he lived. As well as any American of his time, he understood the balance of power that existed in Europe and the Far East before World War I; and he saw the relationship that the Monroe Doctrine and the Open Door policy had to the European alliance system. Most importantly, he saw that the Royal Navy and the U.S. Navy were, together, America's shield against the aggressive policies of Germany and Japan in the early-twentieth century.

He also had a firm grasp of the administrative needs of the Navy, and, at considerable risk to his professional career, he led the way in advocating that the office of chief of naval operations be established. His rejection of the unrealistic doctrine of "freedom of the seas" in wartime was less than popular on Capitol Hill in the years 1890 to 1917; but the notion that "free ships make free goods" was abandoned with alacrity by nations and navies when hostilities began in 1914 and again in 1939. If Mahan was a disbeliever in the presumed virtues of peace, arbitration, and disarmament, so too were millions of his fellow Americans.

In the opinion of this writer, Alfred Thayer Mahan's thoughts and professional attitudes reflected shifting combinations of genius and mediocrity, varying degrees of awesome prescience and stultifying rigidity. But because he was both a complicated and an influential human being, future students of his life will likely take issue with the assessment of him presented in these pages—if for no other reason than that their own biases and perceptions, and the times in which they write, will differ markedly from this author's. In the history of historiography, that is the way it has been, is, and should be.

Robert Seager II
Baltimore, Maryland
April 1977

Acknowledgments

The author is indebted principally to Alfred Thayer Mahan II, grandson of the admiral, who encouraged this volume in many ways and who made available family letters, diaries, and scrapbooks. He is also much in the debt of Doris D. Maguire, who edited with him the three-volume *Letters and Papers of Alfred Thayer Mahan* on which this biography is substantially based.

Special thanks for assistance are due the author's former colleagues in the Department of History of the U.S. Naval Academy, Paolo E. Coletta, E. B. Potter, Neville T. Kirk, Michael Jasperson, and the late Robert W. Daly. Professor Clark G. Reynolds of the U.S. Merchant Marine Academy was also helpful, as were Professors William D. Donahoo of the University of Baltimore, Tristram P. Coffin of the University of Pennsylvania, Mark R. Peattie of The Pennsylvania State University, Raymond G. O'Connor of the University of Miami, Merle Rife of Indiana State University in Pennsylvania, and Lawrence C. Allin of the University of Maine. Professor Kenneth J. Hagan of the U.S. Naval Academy read the entire manuscript and made valuable suggestions for its improvement.

Commander Richard A. Smith, RN, who knows much more about naval guns and gunnery than he does about American football, aided the author in understanding the ordnance aspects of the all-big-gun ship controversy and Mahan's role in it. Frank Uhlig, Jr., editor of *Naval Review*, provided a great deal of sound advice. Professor Henry H. Simms and the late Professor Foster Rhea Dulles, both formerly of The Ohio State University, contributed much to the writer's early understanding of Alfred Thayer Mahan. The late Henry W. Mattfield, headmaster of the Virginia Episcopal School in Lynchburg, and the late Edward H. Zabriskie of Rutgers University in Newark, New Jersey, first introduced him to history and the writing of it.

The patient and skillful support given the author by the library staff of the University of Baltimore went far beyond the call of duty. Ann Haynie Green, Joan Pasterfield Burns, and Robert B. Pool II were extremely solicitous and energetic in this regard. University of Baltimore staff members E. Drusilla Chairs, Theresa V. Gross, Diane M. Jackiewicz, and Kay Auman Windsor also assisted the author in a variety of ways. A grant from the University of Baltimore Educational Foundation helped him with the cost of preparing the manuscript for press.

Important support was received from Dean C. Allard of the Naval Historical Center of the Department of the Navy, Anthony S. Nicolosi, curator of the Naval Historical Collection at the Naval War College, Rear Admiral John D. Hayes, USN (Retired), Marion Sherman Borsodi of the Nimitz Library of the U.S. Naval Academy, Colonel David E. Schwulst, USMCR (Retired), former deputy director of the U.S. Marine Corps Museum, Quantico, Virginia, Lillian R. Rasmus of Peekskill, New York, Virginia T. Mosley of Tenafly, New Jersey, and N. M. Getty of the Groton School in Massachusetts. *The New York Times Book Review* published an "Author's Query" about Mahan which led to interesting discoveries.

Mary E. Mangelsdorf of the Seamen's Church Institute of New York, the Reverend Halsey M. Cook, rector of Old St. Paul's Episcopal Church in Baltimore, Maryland, Lynn Leonhardt of Hauppauge, New York, William Ashe Bason of Raleigh, North Carolina, and Charles S. Gosse II of New York City assisted the project in special ways.

Helen Lewis Parker (Mrs. Harry B.) Wilmer of Annapolis, a direct descendant of the Reverend Milo Mahan's stepdaughter, Mary Lewis Parker, remembers "Cousin Alfred," read parts of the manuscript, and, on occasion, graciously provided the author with anecdotes, good conversation, and supper. Other Mahan and Evans descendants, direct and collateral, who assisted the study are John Mahan Brooks, Alfred T. Mahan III, Marion O. (Mrs. Lyle Evans) Mahan, Caroline S. (Mrs. Chester M.) Carré, Rosalie Evans (Mrs. Van Vechten) Burger, Evelyn Evans (Mrs. John B.) Wright, and Charlotte Bushnell Watson.

Mary Veronica Amoss, senior manuscript editor of the Naval Institute Press, did a superb job in splinting the author's fractured syntax and excising his ambiguities. She also instructed him in the proper use of the Queen's English, and showed him better ways to organize and present the material to the reader. Her help was invaluable.

Nevertheless, any factual, literary, and interpretative errors that remain in this account of Mahan are the author's own. His opinions of the admiral and the navy in which he served are not necessarily shared by Mahan's living descendants, the contemporary U.S. Navy, the U.S. Naval Institute, or Doris D. Maguire.

Caroline Parrish Seager, the author's wife, did most of the back-breaking work on this book. It was she who transcribed most of Mahan's manuscript letters, typed the book manuscript several times, corrected proof, and compiled the index. Through this servitude, six years of it, she took care of Thrasy, Quincy, and Matthew, and made our homes in Baltimore, Maryland, and Wakefield, Rhode Island, pleasant places in which to study, edit, and write. For all practical purposes she is the co-author of this volume, as she has been of other of the writer's books and articles over the years.

Alfred Thayer Mahan

I

Mr. Midshipman Mahan
1847-1859

Please tell me in your next letter whether you keep my letters. If you do not, return them to me instead of destroying them, as I have no doubt that twenty years from this time these mute but faithful transcripts of my every thought and feeling will amuse me much if they serve no better purpose.

Alfred Thayer Mahan to Samuel A'Court Ashe, January 1, 1859

Profuse recourse to letters simply turns over to the reader the task which the biographer has undertaken to do for him. Perhaps the biographer cannot do it. Then he had better not undertake the job. A collection of letters is one thing, a biography another; and they do not mix well when a career abounds in incident. Letters are material for biography, as original documents are material for history; but as documents are not history, so letters are not biography. . . . It is no fair treatment to tumble at the reader's feet a basketful of papers, and virtually say, "There! Find out the man for yourself."

Alfred Thayer Mahan, *From Sail to Steam*

A biography of Rear Admiral Alfred Thayer Mahan, Philosopher of Sea Power, one of America's best known and most influential naval officers, a biographer himself, might well begin with the observation that in addition to twenty books and 137 articles, Mahan wrote more than 10,000 letters during his lifetime. Some 2,900 of these have survived, many of them "mute but faithful transcripts" of his "every thought and feeling," and all of them "material for biography," since "original documents are material for history." But whether they have merely been tumbled haphazardly at the reader's feet here—"There! Find out the man for your-self"—each reader must judge for himself. Whatever the judgment is, however, it should be kept in mind that this complicated, aggressive, con-tentious, and brilliant man produced in 1890 perhaps the most influential book written by an American in America during the nineteenth century—*The Influence of Sea Power Upon History.* And since the admiral came firmly to believe that his intellect, his love of history, and his ability to make sense of history and write it were inherited from his father and his uncle, the influence of Dennis Hart Mahan and Milo Mahan on Alfred Thayer Mahan was significant. At least Alfred thought so. He called it "inherited aptitude." But first things first.

Alfred Mahan was born on the grounds of the U.S. Military Academy at West Point, New York, on September 27, 1840. He died in his seventy-fifth year, on December 1, 1914, at the Naval Hospital in Washington, D.C. In the intervening three-quarters of a century, he was seldom far removed from government service, the government payroll, or govern-ment property. He was truly Government Issue.[1]

The first of six children, he was born into the household of Dennis Hart Mahan, Dean of Faculty and Professor of Civil and Military En-gineering at West Point, and Mary Helena Okill Mahan, his wife, a professor of great Christian faith. Dennis was the son of an Irish immi-grant, John Mahan, who settled in Norfolk, Virginia, early in the nine-teenth century. There he followed, rather ineffectually it would seem, the trades of carpenter, contractor, and realtor. His most important con-tribution to his adopted country was the fathering of two intelligent and prominent sons. Dennis, child of his first wife, Mary Cleary Mahan, was born in 1802; Milo, child of his third wife, Esther Moffitt Mahan, was born in 1819. By the time Dennis went off to West Point in 1820 as a cadet, John had already imparted to him something of the haughtiness and self-confidence of the Old Dominion's comfortable gentry. Like his father, Dennis became a professional Virginian. Immigrant John (né Mahon) affected it; Norfolk-born Dennis absorbed it. Thus the family in which Alfred grew up considered itself to be Virginian, Southern, and eminently superior. It also professed Episcopalianism and Anglophilism, Dennis Mahan's Roman Catholic and Irish roots having conveniently withered somewhere along the way.[2]

In 1824 Cadet Mahan, D. H., a short, skinny, taciturn, and intense young man, was graduated first in his class at West Point, commissioned second lieutenant in the Army, and assigned to the Corps of Engineers.

Almost immediately, however, he was reassigned to West Point as Assistant Professor of Mathematics for the academic year 1824–1825. Lieutenant Colonel Sylvanus Thayer (from whom Alfred got his middle name) was then in the eighth year of his restorative superintendency of the Academy, and it was through the interest and influence of the "Father of West Point" that Dennis was ordered to the school's faculty and then, in 1825, to France to continue his study of military engineering and fortifications, the subjects in which he excelled as a cadet. In 1830, Colonel Thayer brought him back to West Point to teach, and in 1836 Professor Mahan repaid the superintendent's confidence in him by publishing his classic *Field Fortifications*, a study based on his research in Europe. Two years later Dennis was promoted to Dean of Faculty, a post he held until his death in 1871. The year after his elevation to the deanship, he married Mary Helena Okill of New York City, a devout, fundamentalist Protestant lady of unknown denominational antecedents.

In 1847, when Alfred was seven, the elder Mahan published his seminal *An Elementary Treatise on . . . the Rise and Progress of Tactics*. In this brilliant book, and in classroom lectures on the subject over the years, Dennis Mahan made known to hundreds of cadets who passed through his classes—among them Pierre G. T. Beauregard, Ulysses S. Grant, Ambrose P. Hill, Thomas J. Jackson, William T. Sherman, Philip H. Sheridan, James E. B. Stuart, and George H. Thomas—the works and ideas of the great Swiss strategist and tactician, Antoine Henri, Baron de Jomini (1779–1869). Jomini fought as a general officer in the French army under Napoleon (a genius in Professor Mahan's opinion) and in 1838 wrote his *Précis de l'Art de la Guerre* (translated into English as *Study of the Art of War*). Mahan borrowed directly from Jomini when he told his West Point students that "war in its most extensive sense may be regarded both as a *science* and an *art*. It is a *science* so far as it investigates general principles . . . and an *art* when considered with reference to the practical rules for conducting campaigns, sieges, battles, etc." To Jomini and D. H. Mahan, the basic principles of military tactics were viewed as unchanging and timeless. They were natural laws pervading the universe, a rational, mechanistic, arithmetically logical universe of the sort conceived by the philosophers of the eighteenth-century Enlightenment. Chief among these "laws" was the military doctrine of concentration, the concept of maneuvering one's own force in such manner as momentarily to bring its maximum power against an inferior section of the enemy's strength. The trick, as Jomini and his disciples saw it, was to defeat weaker segments of the enemy's force in sequential detail.

As will be seen, Alfred was also destined to become a careful student of Jomini's thoughts, although not by way of his father's books and pamphlets on the subjects of fortifications and tactics. Surprisingly, there is no evidence that Alfred Mahan ever read any of D. H. Mahan's books. Nor, in spite of his great respect for his father and his strong sense of pride in family, did he ever number his father among those men he later identified as having had a major influence on the evolution of his own ideas—ideas that sought to apply Jomini's principles of strategy and tactics in land warfare to fleet deployments and actions at sea. True, father and son went to the same Jominian well; but they went separately and with different buckets.

There is, on the other hand, considerable evidence that Alfred read the books written by his Uncle Milo Mahan, his father's half-brother, and was much influenced by them. At age seventeen Milo had mastered ancient Greek so well that he was hired to teach the subject at the Episcopal High School in Alexandria, Virginia. There, in 1838, he experienced a profound conversion to the Anglo-Catholicism of the Oxford Movement. With financial assistance from Dennis, he continued theological studies. Following parish work in Jersey City, New Jersey, and Philadelphia, he joined the faculty of the General Theological Seminary of the Episcopal Church in New York City. In 1860 he published his scholarly *A Church History of the First Three Centuries*. The book, rooted in original Greek and Latin sources, went through five editions, several reprintings, and was for half a century the standard work in its field.

Milo was also the author, in the 1860s, of two curious books that sought to prove the truths of Christianity and to demonstrate the way God's cosmos works in Pythagorean terms. A close student of Greek mathematician-philosopher Pythagoras (B.C. 582–504?), he was fascinated by the Pythagorean notion that all relationships in the universe could be explained in numerical terms and by arithmetical formulae. In his *Palmoni; or The Numerals of Scripture* and in *Mystic Numbers*, he tried to apply mathematics to Christian doctrine. Specifically, he attempted to demonstrate that the numbers found scattered through Scripture were put there by God as clues to the fact of His creative handiwork, as well as to reveal the truth that the universe, a rational entity, was permeated with laws, principles, and concepts whose numerical values had discoverable mathematical relationships. Like the Enlightenment philosophers and Henri Jomini, like his half-brother Dennis and his nephew Alfred, the Reverend Milo Mahan searched for, and became certain he had found, the origin, behavior patterns, and relationships of the transcendent principles (all

[4]

capable of numerical designation and manipulation) that both pervaded an orderly universe and proved that orderliness. The peculiar philosophical system he devised, if not his mathematical rationalizations of it, came significantly to influence the formulation of Captain Alfred T. Mahan's philosophy of history. It seems clear, therefore, that within the Mahan family circle Alfred owed a greater intellectual debt to his uncle than to his famous father.[3]

These weighty intellectual matters and influences lay far in the future of the handsome little boy who grew up on a busy Army post in the 1840s, in a house full of books dealing with war, and in a military environment never much more complicated than faith in and obedience to "Duty, Honor, Country." His day began with the sound of bugles and marching feet. Indeed, one of his first recollections, at the age of eight, was the return of the West Point garrison from the Mexican War. It was a proud and heroic moment, complete with brass bands and dazzling fireworks.

Nevertheless, little is known of Mahan's early life. He scarcely mentioned the West Point period in his autobiography. He left behind no revealing account of his early feelings about his parents, or about his younger sisters and brothers, save his embarrassment that his sister, Mary (1842–1891), was retarded. In a letter dated November 21, 1858, he confessed her plight to his Naval Academy friend, Samuel A'Court Ashe:

> You do not probably know, that, although I have a sister . . . she has in consequence of early sickness, which attacked her brain, been backward both mentally and physically, and is now no more, if as much, as a child of twelve, nor will she probably ever be more. We have all of us long hoped that as she grew older the cloud that had settled on her mind would gradually clear off, and leave her, as she was before her sickness, one of the brightest, of what I can say without boasting, is a remarkably talented family.

It is not known whether Professor Mahan's reputation at West Point as a parade-ground martinet carried over into the private life of the Mahan family. Probably not. Alfred recalled that his father always had an eye for "pretty young women," a propensity his eldest son inherited, and that he loved flowers and all "young things, from young girls to puppies and kittens." He probably had a soft side. He was, however, a man of unbending moral principle, and this he conveyed to Alfred.[4]

When Alfred was twelve years old he was packed off to St. James School, a Southern-oriented, Episcopal boarding school for boys in Hagerstown, Maryland. His devout, Bible-reading mother prayed God that he would become a clergyman. Much to her disappointment, but happily for Poseidon and Clio, he became instead a naval officer and a historian. He also became in adult life a prominent lay Episcopalian, and was active in Episcopal Church affairs all his days. Religion was always an important force in the molding and expression of his personality and character. It was a major influence in the later formation of his military and political ideas as well as of his philosophy of history. It seems fairly certain, then, that together with Duty, Honor and Country, young Mahan was raised at West Point on heavy doses of Protestant salvationism and biblicism. These props seem to have carried the Mahans through such tragedies as the mental condition of daughter Mary and the death of daughter Helen in 1846 at the age of two. Family prayers were a daily event. Sundays were grim, barely endurable. As Mahan's daughter Ellen later recalled, "He had suffered much in his youth from the abnormal amount of piety required on that day."[5]

Alfred was also the recipient of religious tracts sent him regularly by his maternal grandmother, Mary Jay Okill (1786–1859), an estimable woman who conducted a seminary for young ladies on Barclay Street in New York City. In the earliest Mahan letter that has survived, the seven-year-old lad laboriously thanked his grandmother Mary for "your books [which] I enjoyed very much especially Agathos. I liked the tent on the plain Agathos or the whole armour of God, the story of Jonah teaches me that man cannot fly from God." Nor did Mahan ever so fly—at least not far or for long. The religious faith of his youth remained with him until his death.[6]

If he was not exactly the Huckleberry Finn of the Hudson, he seems to have had a reasonably pleasant childhood. He had the usual friends and interests. He teased his young brother Fred; he badgered his parents for fireworks with which to celebrate the Fourth of July; and, like all little boys, he craved candy, toys, and animal books.[7]

One of his playmates, William Whitman Bailey (1843–1914), later Professor of Botany at Brown University, remembered Alfred and his family as they were in the early 1850s. It is the only such recollection known to have survived:

> Next north of my old house, on Officers' Row, lived Professor D. H.
> Mahan, to whom the Academy owes much of its distinction at home
> and abroad. In my mind's eye I can see him very distinctly. I always
> felt considerable awe for him, but was in and out of his house almost
> like a son of his own. He and his wife, the best of good women, loved

flowers. They maintained a well-kept garden. . . . Near the fence that separated our great yards, drooping over our gate, but in Mr. Mahan's, was, and I think is, one of the finest of many fine elms on the Point. Ah! me!, how much of sunshine and of shadow I have known beneath it. Mr. Mahan had a very large weeping willow back of his house. Up and down the garden paths used to parade with his drum, Fred A. Mahan, now Major of Engineers. He was an unappreciated expert on that military instrument. Prof. Mahan always had some few civilian pupils, I think, whom he used to teach in a class-room he had built for that purpose. When after leaving West Point I used to return in vacations, I often stayed at the Mahans, I fear beyond reasonable limits. When I think that upon them I had no claim whatever, I wonder at their polite endurance. They never showed any annoyance, but I am quite sure I must have been a trial, and had moments, in correspondence, of sharp remorse. I owe to Mrs. Mahan very many little points of culture, sweetly indicated, against which I should otherwise have awkwardly stumbled. What an exemplary family it was, exhibiting every Christian grace and virtue. The sons—I might say, the children —were all my intimate friends. I rejoice over the name of Alfred as if it were my brother's. It is long since I have met any of them. I can recall when the author of the *Life of Nelson* was a youth, with "Smiling morning face," and much actuated by the sea-tales of Cooper. With him I recall scaling the steep rocks near the new dock and searching for "ten-penny-silvers" (whatever they were!) among the cliffs. I fancy that elsewhere Alfred has been more successful than I in up-turning treasure. At least I devoutly hope so.

Mahan remembered one incident of his association with the Baileys. In 1852 his grandmother planned a trip down-river to New York with the Bailey family. Reaching the West Point pier, the party discovered that two steamboats, the *Armenia* and the *Henry Clay*, were taking passengers and that they were to race one another. Mary Jay Okill, who was returning to her seminary duties in the city, asked her young grandson which vessel to board. He advised the *Armenia*, since the name "Henry Clay" was not politically a popular one in the Mahan household. The Baileys, perhaps Whigs, took the *Henry Clay*. Unhappily, during the race down the Hudson the *Clay* caught fire and was burned. Eighty passengers died, among them young William Bailey's mother, father, and sister. He alone in the family survived.[8]

This tragedy notwithstanding, Mahan recalled "these happy hours that only childhood knows" almost solely in terms of his reading. In fact, he later made much of the point that he virtually read himself into the U.S.

Navy. He devoured the stirring sea tales of James Fenimore Cooper and Frederick Marryat. He poured over back issues of English publisher Henry Colburn's *United Service Magazine*, bound copies of which he found in the Academy library. In Colburn's journal he read the reminiscences of British naval officers who had fought gloriously and heroically (so they claimed) through the great wars against the tyrant Napoleon. In the family library, alongside works on military history, he discovered and read such serialized trash for boys as *Leaves from My Log Book*, by "Flexible Grommet" and *The Order Book* by "Jonathan Oldjunks." But was it trash? Mahan did not think so, then or later:

> Upon the whole is not the trash the truest history? perhaps not the most valuable, but the most real? If you want contemporary color, contemporary atmosphere, you must seek it among the impressions which can be obtained only from those who have lived a life amid particular surroundings, which they breathe and which colors them— dyes them in the wool.[9]

What was not acceptable reading in Dennis Hart Mahan's sternly anti-abolitionist household was Harriet Beecher Stowe's *Uncle Tom's Cabin*, published in 1852. "My father took it out of my hand," Mahan recalled, "and I came to regard it much as I would a bottle labelled 'Poison.'" It was partly to give Alfred a better appreciation of the South, its genteel life, its aristocratic customs, and the "peculiar institution" that was slavery, that Virginian Dennis H. Mahan sent his son down to St. James School in slave-owning Maryland.[10]

Unfortunately for the Mahans, father and son, St. James' was a disappointment. Whatever its value as an Episcopal training school, whatever its function as a proper environment for the incubation of Southern Gentlemen, its curriculum was sadly deficient in science and mathematics. Or so thought engineer Dennis Mahan. In June 1854, after two years in Hagerstown, Alfred was removed from the institution and entered in Columbia College in New York City. When he arrived at Columbia in late September 1854 the boy had just turned fourteen.

The choice of Columbia was not random. It was arranged that Alfred would live in the home of his Uncle Milo on Twentieth Street, between Ninth and Tenth Avenues, while attending the college. Milo had recently married (in August 1853) Mary Griffitts Fisher Lewis, an attractive widow with five children, two of whom were girls about Alfred's age. The boy immediately contracted his first serious case of puppy love, the object of his affection being Uncle Milo's step-daughter Elizabeth Lewis,

Courtesy The Reverend Halsey M. Cook

Milo Mahan

Courtesy Helen Lewis Parker Wilmer

Elizabeth Lewis

then about fourteen years old. She was called "Libbie." She was a beautiful child, possessed of jet-black hair, porcelain-white skin, and finely wrought facial features. Although he thought of this lovely young lady as his "cousin by marriage," he was enamored of her until well into his senior year at the Naval Academy. It was Libbie who graced him with his first romantic kiss.[11]

Milo Mahan had been appointed, in 1851, Professor of Ecclesiastical History at the General Theological Seminary, a position which had brought him to New York City from St. Mark's parish in Philadelphia and which also permitted him the financial luxury of acquiring a ready-made family of six. Milo's churchmanship at this time was decidedly Anglo-Catholic, the result of his deeply emotional encounter with the Oxford Movement while he was teaching at the Episcopal High School. He remained a contentious, if not always entirely orthodox, High Church-man throughout his subsequent career. More importantly, he was an excellent historian, and when Alfred joined his household in the fall of 1854, he was already at work on his magisterial *Church History*. Milo had decided that the facts of history should be assembled and organized in such manner as to reveal "that living flow of events in their natural order by which history explains and justifies itself."[12]

From his Uncle Milo, young Alfred derived a love of history, a sense of order in history, some notion of historiographical technique, and an appreciation of the highly introspective salvationist theology of Anglo-Catholicism. It was this High Church Episcopalianism that he carried with him to Annapolis in 1856 and throughout his life. He never had much use for pentecostal Protestantism of the hell-fire-and-brimstone sort and he avoided it whenever he could. Until his untimely death in 1870, the Reverend Dr. Milo Mahan was Alfred's spiritual mentor.[13]

Two years at Columbia College were enough for Alf. He was still under the influence of Flexible Grommet and Jonathan Oldjunks. The sea still beckoned. Armed with a letter of recommendation from Charles King, President of Columbia, whom he had come personally to know, he sought out and subsequently secured from Representative Ambrose S. Murray of New York an appointment to the Naval Academy in Annapolis. Family tradition has it that Alfred's initiative in the matter and his decision to join the Navy were exercised over the stern disapproval of Dennis Mahan. "My entrance into the Navy," wrote Mahan in 1906, "was greatly against my father's wish. . . . he told me he thought me much less fit for a military than for a civilian profession, having watched me carefully. I think myself now that he was right. . . . I believe I should have done better elsewhere."[14]

If Dennis Mahan did disapprove, he nonetheless permitted Alfred the use of his name, reputation, and station in life when the lad went to Washington in January 1856 to seek an appointment to the Academy. The boy spoke personally with Secretary of War Jefferson Davis, who had been three classes behind Dennis Mahan at West Point. Davis arranged the matter with Congressman Murray, neatly, politically, and behind the scenes. It should be recalled that Dennis Mahan also urged his second son, Frederick Augustus, into West Point in 1863, and saw his third son, Dennis Hart, Jr., into Annapolis in 1865. His was, purely and simply, a military family. All three Mahan sons served in the armed forces until retirement. Further, if the father had truly disapproved Alfred's choice of career, that would have ended the matter. In the Mahan home at West Point, an order was an order was an order.[15]

Courtesy Alfred Thayer Mahan II

Frederick Augustus Mahan

So it was that Alfred Thayer Mahan, aged sixteen, departed the benign household of Milo Mahan and the company of his pretty young step-daughters after two pleasant years, and entered the intensely competitive masculine society that was the U.S. Naval Academy. He reached Annapolis on September 30, 1856, and took the oath of office as acting midshipman on October 2. He was not an obscure person when he arrived at the Academy. Two faculty members, Henry H. Lockwood and William F. Hopkins, were former West Pointers who knew Mahan's father well; and both the superintendent, Captain George S. Blake, and Captain Thomas T. Craven, who became commandant of midshipmen during the academic year 1858–1859, were well acquainted with the distinguished Professor Dennis H. Mahan. Nonetheless, Mahan suffered a severe attack of mental depression ("melancholia," it was called in the nineteenth century) on his arrival at the Academy, but gradually he shook this off and got down to the serious business at hand.[16]

Because he had had two years of college-level work at Columbia, he was permitted to skip the fourth class year. He was placed directly in the third (sophomore) class, with those men who had entered in September 1855 and would be graduated in June 1859. Mahan thus joined a class that had already been winnowed from 49 to 28 (it graduated but 20 of the original number), had collectively endured its period of plebe hazing, and had already formed its friendships and cliques. According to a sketch of his career later prepared in the Bureau of Naval Personnel, Mahan's class standing, which he had earned by applying for and passing an advanced placement examination, was "by special arrangement" and was "the only occasion on record of that concession being made." The privileged Mahan was therefore something of a marked man with his classmates. Nevertheless, it appears that he and his roommate for the year 1856–1857, Roderick Prentiss of Indiana, got on well.[17]

No letters from his first year at the Academy have survived. And only three from his second year. One of these last, written to Elizabeth Lewis, pictured a happy, successful, and confident midshipman. At this time he was particularly fond of his roommate, Thomas Starr Spencer of Pennsylvania, and of classmate Samuel A'Court Ashe of North Carolina. "You can form no idea what a nice class we have," he reported to Libbie, "my affection seemed to be wrapped up in them, and I believe the same is the case with the greater part of them." Life at sea, he added, having just returned from the 1857 summer cruise to the Azores in the *Plymouth*, "is the most happy careless and entrancing life that there is. In a stiff breeze when the ship is heeling well over there is a wild sort of delight that I never experienced before. . . . I long for next summer when I will again be on the ship and have all of them [classmates] along with me too." One brief trip to sea and Mr. Midshipman Mahan had become Marryat's Mr. Midshipman Easy.[18]

Mahan did have, however, one bad experience at the Academy during the 1857–1858 school year. On December 5, 1857, while serving as midshipman officer of the day, he was charged with permitting another midshipman to secrete "a bundle under the stairway" of the OD's office. The bundle, as it turned out, contained tobacco, contraband cargo at the Naval Academy in those days. Commandant of Midshipmen I. F. Green learned of the incident and demanded of Mahan the name of the blockade-runner. He reported that Mahan "declined positively to give me the desired information thereby nullifying his usefulness as Officer of the Day—exhibiting contumacy and a total unfitness for any position of trust or responsibility in the government of the Academy." The matter was carried to Superintendent Blake. Mahan explained to Blake that he was an innocent victim of circumstances, that he did not wish to "involve the gentleman in trouble." He pleaded that "I was totally ignorant of the contents of the bundle, and that I refused to inform on the gentleman through ideas, perhaps mistaken ones, of honor." Blake replied that Mahan's explanation was "insufficient," and that the young man was in open defiance of Academy regulations. Unless Mahan supplied the name of the contraband-carrier to Commandant Green, this was a direct order, he would be dismissed from the Academy. "I am willing to believe that you are not fully sensible of the danger of the ground you have assumed and to give you an opportunity to recede from it," said Blake. A shaken Mahan replied immediately that "the consequences of dismissal from a *Government* institution are too heavy to be lightly encountered, and with the full consent of the gentleman implicated, and indeed by his request, I am prepared to answer all questions addressed me by Captain Green." On this basis the crisis was resolved; and on the morning of December 8 Mahan called at the superintendent's office and "acknowledged in the fullest manner his sense of error, admitting that he had been entirely wrong and that nothing of the kind should ever again occur." It was to Mahan an object lesson in what was Duty and what was Honor and what the Navy insisted upon when the two abstractions came into conflict. Duty first.[19]

The summer of 1858 arrived without further unpleasantness and once again Mahan went on the scheduled training cruise for midshipmen. Thanks to bad weather, it was an extremely rough voyage in the *Preble*, so rough that Mahan's closest friend, Sam Ashe, afflicted with chronic seasickness, decided to leave the service and take up the study of law in his native North Carolina.[20]

It was on that same cruise that Mahan first unburdened himself to Ashe. He told Ashe that the day of traditional naval heroes, men like Stephen Decatur, was over, that distinction through personal daring would be difficult if not impossible to achieve, and that he "proposed to win renown in his profession through intellectual performance." This remark, clairvoyant though it was, was naive. The U.S. Navy in the nineteenth century was scarcely a home for budding intellectuals. On the contrary, a person interested primarily in "intellectual performance" clearly belonged someplace else. It was this fact that lay at the root of many of Mahan's problems as a naval officer for the next forty years. He was generally too bright and too inquiring of mind for most of the officers with whom he came in contact. He was, Ashe recalled, "the most intellectual man I have ever known. He had not only a remarkable memory but also a capacity to comprehend and a clarity of perception." Unfortunately, Mahan also knew this and, because he had little desire or ability to conceal his intellectual superiority, he was often resented by his peers in the service. From the very outset of his career Alfred Thayer Mahan found himself in the wrong profession for the wrong reasons at the wrong time. In general, the operational Navy and those who ran it bored him.[21]

His career problems began at the Naval Academy during his first class (senior) year. The Academy in those far-away days was little more than a trade school; and not a very good one at that. Mahan made no secret of the fact that the curriculum in no way challenged him intellectually and that, with little sustained effort, he could excel at the rote memorization and factual regurgitation that the various courses required. Without extending himself, he finished second in his class academically. He could easily have stood at the top of the class, but he chose not to alter his cram-a-little, loaf-a-lot approach to his studies. He had, in sum, a supreme contempt for the intellectual and academic demands of the Academy. Therefore, he spent much of his time reading good history and cheap novels, sometimes two or three of the latter in a week, writing long letters to family and friends, and flirting with the Annapolis ladies. He read Jean Froissart, Henry Lytton-Bulwer, and Walter Scott and filled other available hours reading such pulp fiction as Charles James Lever's *Charles O'Malley; or the Irish Dragoon.* As he boasted to Sam Ashe: "If your friends are surprised at the length of my letters tell them that an acting midshipman is too lazy to study, and, not able to read more than two novels a week, must write. . . . [Midshipman] Cenas can't discover my secret for having so much time to spare. It is a simple one. Make it!"[22]

One of the local belles would occasionally encourage Mahan to take the head of his class, a feat which almost everyone at the Academy and in Annapolis knew he could accomplish if he tried. One evening he told Miss Anne ("Nannie") Craven, daughter of the commandant, that the courses in his first class year were so numerous and boring that he "preferred to let everything go."

"But does that not affect your standing?" Nannie asked.

"No," replied Mahan, "I think not in the long run."

"So you are going to take one, are you?"

"Oh, no," answered Mahan, "two."

"But why don't you study and take one?" she persisted; "you can do it if you try."

"Indeed, how do you know?" Mahan asked.

"Oh, I know you can very well, you can stand one easily if you try; I have heard professors and I have heard officers say so."[23]

Flattery "coming from such sweet lips" would rouse Mahan to a 4.0-level of performance for a week or two, but he would invariably return to his pulp novels, his reading of history, and his letter-writing. Further, academic success only created tensions with his plodding classmates, and during his first class year 1858–1859 he already had more than enough difficulties in that realm. Stern letters from home demanding that he improve his academic standing were not received gratefully or answered graciously. "I . . . told them so for the first time in my life, for I think I am now old enough . . . at least not to be talked to as a child." Nor did the Lawrence Literary Society at the Academy absorb Mahan's considerable intellectual energies. Its lecture program was dull and ill attended, and Mahan, after a period of loyal support, finally stopped going. "Lectures as a rule are a grand bore," he concluded.[24]

The same could have been said for the interminable fundamentalist sermons preached weekly by Academy Chaplain George Jones. Few things at the institution outraged Midshipman Mahan more than the froth-at-the-mouth religion compulsorily purveyed in the Academy chapel by "Old Slicky" Jones in 1858 and 1859. Not that Mahan was irreligious. Quite the contrary. He thought a great deal about his religion, read the Bible carefully and devotedly, and corresponded with his Uncle Milo on fine points of theology. It was just that Mahan, a "high church Episcopalian," had profound distaste of glorious visions of a pie-in-the-sky afterlife and of "what looks like an effort to bully you into religion." As he told Ashe:

> They make Religion be abhorred
> That round with terror gulf her,
> And think no word can please the Lord
> Unless it smell of sulphur.

Mahan felt that a man "who is religious because he fears to go to hell is as despicable as one who remains irreligious because he fears the world's opinion." On the contrary, his own idea of the "loveliness of religion" was "the thought of a being who shows His love less in the physical comforts of this life, than in sympathy for our sufferings, and I believe that the great God would rather have us look on Him as a friend than as a benefactor."[25]

This was not the official view of God at the Naval Academy in 1858 and 1859, and Mahan was forced to sit through numerous sermons and lectures which attempted to blast him into repentance and salvation. His reports on these grim experiences were consistent. Chaplain Jones, an "intolerable old poker," was variously "delightfully and successfully stupid," was filled with "rant and cant," and generally was "getting more and more stupid every day." Mahan attempted to endure the anti-intellectual religiosity of the chapel services by sleeping through them or by thinking of other things. He derived enormous pleasure when the services were somehow interrupted. Indeed, the high point of his religious career at the Academy came on Sunday, December 5, 1858, when a small dog wandered into chapel and began barking. "Despite the utmost efforts that I could make my risible muscles became rebellious beyond control. . . . during the remainder of the time I was in agony, for in my place decorum of manner is most necessary and I could not attain to it."[26]

Nor was Mahan enthusiastic when a group of civilian professors and officers formed a Bible Society for the voluntary study of the Scriptures. Mahan immediately began to organize among his classmates an opposition society called "The Grand Anti-Biblical Corruption Society." When this effort failed, he retreated to a position of detached ridicule, observing that the bootlicking "Sunday-school scholars" who joined or attended the Bible Society were simply playing grade-point-average politics with the faculty and staff members who had launched the holy venture. "I wonder," he remarked of one meeting of the group, "how much bootlicking and hypocrisy were mingled with true religious feeling present. I was of course absent."[27]

Nonetheless, in the interests of his own service image and reputation at the Academy, Mahan occasionally played the salvation game. When Mrs. George S. Blake, the wife of the superintendent, told Mahan's mother that she wanted the lad to help her lead the responses in chapel, Mahan was so instructed and meekly complied. "I am obliged now to go through the motions in church," he confessed. On the other hand, he frankly told Joseph E. ("Holy Joe") Nourse, Professor of Ethics, that the simplistic little religious tracts that Nourse insisted on handing out to midshipmen did more harm than good because "of the ridicule they excited, for bad as the fellows are usually, they are devils so far as religion is concerned when just out of Old Slicky's hands." Yet Mahan stood first in Nourse's course in Moral Science and, on the eve of his graduation, he managed to convince the school's Academic Board that he was truly one of God's own sulphur-sniffing children:

> I passed one in Moral Science [he boasted to Ashe], and read a most comforting discourse on the "Rules for Moral Conduct" before the Naval Academic Board which I sincerely hope they will lay to heart for the good of their spirits. It's a fact, it was so much like one of Slicky's sermons that I came near snuffling while I delivered it and half expected to hear an almighty tarnation oath arise from the Academic Board and wing its way to hell.[28]

To overcome the boredom of Naval Academy religion and to transcend the monotony of the less than rigorous academic program, Midshipman Alfred Thayer Mahan spent a great deal of his time ineffectually pursuing almost every eligible young lady in Annapolis, a "miserable little town" that he otherwise despised. Miserable town or not, there were some very pretty girls resident there and Mahan fell deeply "in love" with several of them. At times he was madly infatuated with two or more of them simultaneously. He would fall in love with one young lady one week, be down on her the next (for some imagined slight), be in love with another the following week, and be back in love with the first one the week after that. It usually took little more than a pleasant smile and a bit of flirtatious parlor conversation from a lady to convince Mahan that he was "head over ears in love" all over again. He admitted his "fickleness" in these matters and the "moral impossibility for me to love a woman three months. . . ." His "smitations" were thus invariably of short duration. "A very violent one lasts about two months, a moderate one three," he remarked with a laugh. Indeed, he noted that "of all the kind fairies who attended my nativity, I bless the one most who bestowed on me the gift of 'Inconstancy.' "[29]

The fact of the matter was that at the age of 18 Mahan was exceptionally shy and socially introverted in the company of women. His pursuit of the local ladies was extremely tenuous, so much so that it was often not recognized as pursuit by the ladies themselves. He was fearful that he did not have the personality or gift of small talk that would enable him to compete successfully with other young men for a lady's attention, and that "the more I go into ladies' society the more convinced I am that it is not my proper sphere and I am going to quit it as soon as possible." When he was alone for a moment with one of the Annapolis belles he managed to converse easily and naturally, even a bit flirtatiously; but when other midshipmen crowded in, as invariably they did, he was certain he did not show comparatively to advantage. His mother sensed his awkwardness in this regard and urged him to get out more into female society, a suggestion which Mahan felt "will rather knock the studies wild, which will not suit Father." At the same time, Mahan rationalized that it would be "foolish . . . to want to fall in love while a midshipman." For this reason he resisted an attempt by his grandmother to match him with one of the young ladies in the seminary she ran in New York when he visited there during his Christmas leave in December 1858. As he told Ashe, he had a "vague dread of the women" and this made it very difficult for him to enjoy their company.[30]

With all his bashfulness and trepidation, Mahan still managed to spend a great deal of time in the Annapolis parlors of the Misses Anne Craven, Julia Kent, Anna Franklin, Lucy and Ellen Kate Brewer, Anne and Mary Esther Gill, and Clara Adams, who was from Baltimore but often visited friends in the town. At various times he proclaimed to Ashe his great love for Julia, Anne, Mary Esther, and Clara. Among the four Anne Craven was the principal local object of Mahan's affection during his first class year. He was in and out of love with her at least three times between 1858 and 1859. Daughter of the respected Commandant of Midshipmen, "Nannie" was an attractive teen-age girl. Mahan described her as "a beautifully formed woman; no angles, everything is beautifully full and rounded." She was also an accomplished practitioner of the Victorian mating game who never for a moment let Mahan or any of the other midshipmen who frequented her parlor know precisely where they stood with her. This ambiguous tactic completely confused the inexperienced Mahan as he twirled helplessly around her beckoning finger. The closest he came to success in his unrequited pursuit of Miss Nannie was her tentative agreement, later withdrawn, to let him write to her after his graduation; she consented to this only after he had made it clear that he would write to her "just as I would to a sister." His revolving-door love for her he confessed only to his friend Sam Ashe.[31]

So too was it with Julia Kent and all the others. They were much too experienced and elusive for the bashful young man from West Point, New York. Consistently rebuffed by the ladies, Mahan took refuge in a world of romantic fantasy, in the thought that what he was really looking for in a woman was someone like Lucy Dashwood, a cardboard heroine in Charles James Lever's romantic war novel, *Charles O'Malley*. "I am in love with her character," he confided excitedly to Ashe. "Would that if there were a war I might find one such woman to love myself." Certainly, none of the unobtainable real-life Annapolis girls could compete with the fictional, love-starved Lucy Dashwood, whose chief function in life was to swoon romantically at the feet of her Irish dragoon.[32]

At the same time, Mahan also decided, defensively it would seem, that what he wanted in a woman was a combined sweetheart and sister relationship. The early death of his sister Helen and the mental condition of his sister Mary left "nothing to fill that place which every man should have filled." He longed, he told Ashe in November 1858, "for a sister whenever I see a girl I like much; it is strange how strongly this feeling has taken possession of me in late years." He thought that either Nannie Craven or Mary Esther Gill might serve as surrogate sisters, a notion that became increasingly attractive to him as it became clear that neither lady was likely to succumb to his awkward romantic blandishments.[33]

Given his failures among the Annapolis ladies, Mahan turned back to the safety and predictability of his earlier love, the beautiful Libbie Lewis, his "cousin by marriage" who still lived with his Uncle Milo in New York. He told Ashe that Libbie could not, however, fill the role of a sister in his life "owing to my having been in love with her and its being an understanding between us that we were in love, though both had too good sense to make an engagement of it." Nevertheless, in November 1858 a lonely Mahan resumed correspondence with Libbie and began arranging his Christmas leave so as to see "*her* whom I was so much in love with when I came to the school, and who came so near making another impression on me last summer." His campaign carefully planned, he spent two days with her in New York in late December of that year and at last achieved a genuine romantic success about which he could boast to Ashe:

> At first I was constrained, thinking that she had changed toward me, but the instant that we were alone, we were standing up, I passed my arm around her waist and she, as she used formerly to do, leaned against

me, resting her head on my shoulder as confidingly and affectionately as before. Whether I kissed her or not you may imagine. . . . When I left her to come to the Academy, she was as far as I can judge a woman in feelings, a child almost in form and guilelessness. Now she is a full grown woman, but guileless as ever, and extremely beautiful. That she is all my own yet is as plain as the sun at noon day. . . . if I am as constant as she my fate in this life is fixed. Between sixteen and eighteen I was not, how it may be afterwards I cannot say. That she will feel towards me as she does now, unless I change toward her, she has shown satisfactorily. A love that lasts from sixteen to eighteen will surely last after that age, and then too she has all along thought that I had ceased loving her.[34]

Elizabeth Lewis was no Lucy Dashwood; but she would do until something better came along. While he continued to profess his love for her, Mahan turned again to the nearer-at-hand Annapolis ladies during the spring of 1859, after indulging briefly in a harmless romantic fantasy involving Libbie's sister, Maime, then living in Wilmington, Delaware, as the wife of the Reverend Stevens Parker, Rector of St. John's Episcopal Church there. But he soon decided, wisely, that he would "try my luck with Miss Nannie a little longer." Unfortunately, and as might be expected from one so naive and inexperienced in matters of the heart, Mahan made the tactical error of boasting to Nannie about his "New York flame." He spent the next month trying to repair the damage. "I have laid out my plans on paper," he told Ashe, "so as to have them clearly before me, as Napoleon did on his campaigns and I am going to follow them out consistently and see what the result will be. . . . My impression is that once succeed in destroying the belief in another flame of mine and my chances are very good."[35]

Actually, Mahan's "chances" with Nannie Craven were non-existent. And when he invited Libbie down to a Naval Academy soirée in mid-February 1859 and she was unable or unwilling to come, that love also died. Out of sight, out of mind. He took Julia Kent to the dance instead, because "she takes compassion on my bashfulness." They had a fine evening together. By the time of his graduation in June 1859, Libbie, Nannie, Julia, Clara, and all the others had faded into the background of his excitement and eagerness to get to sea and play the role of Mr. Midshipman Easy on a full-time basis. As he explained to Ashe:

Although ladies' society makes me temporarily feel in good spirits, I do not expect fully to enjoy myself again until I get to sea. I am more at home on a ship than anywhere else; my health and spirits are always good and the very air of the sea inspires a man with a sort of "insouci-ance" that all the ladies in God's world can not give. . . . I don't want to live ashore. There is a buoyancy in the sea air that elevates me, and as it can be accounted for chemically by the greater quantity of oxygen it contains, I guess my feelings do not arise from romance.

His belief in the chemical advantages of life at sea as a substitute for women in arms soon changed.[36]

Any analysis of Mahan's personality, any insight into the professional dimensions of his subsequent naval career, must turn in part on his roman-tic frustrations, on his hair-trigger temper, on his sense of intellectual superiority, and on his pride of family. All these factors were important in the formation of his character; and all contributed to his tense personal relations with his Academy classmates. It is not too much to suggest in this regard that his career at the Naval Academy was a disaster, one that colored his attitudes toward the U.S. Navy for the rest of his life.

It began harmlessly enough. On or about October 15, 1858, shortly after classes resumed in the fall of his third and final (first class) year at the Academy, Mahan put his classmate Midshipman Samuel Holland Hackett on report. Hackett, who had been Ashe's roommate, was the "Second Captain" of the "Gun Crew" that Mahan commanded as "First Captain."[37]

Raised as he had been midst the spit, polish, and precision of the West Point Corps of Cadets, Mahan returned to the Naval Academy in Sep-tember of 1858 determined to exercise his authority as First Captain in shaping up his Gun Crew along the strict lines followed at West Point. He therefore announced flatly to his crew at the beginning of the school year that things in his tiny command (fifteen men) were going to be different, that breaches of discipline in ranks, particularly talking, reading, and skylarking, would be instantly reported. This would apply to all midshipmen in his crew, regardless of class. In sum, the stated regulations of the Naval Academy were to be enforced on all hands. Further, he made it clear that he expected his Second Captain, S. H. Hackett, to emulate him and conscientiously carry out his orders in this respect.

The upshot of the matter was that Sam Hackett told Alf Mahan to go straight to hell. Classmates did not report classmates. He bluntly in-formed Mahan that he would report whom he wanted, if he wanted, and when he wanted, particularly on the issue of talking in ranks, a wide-spread practice at the institution. Just what happened next is not entirely clear. But someone in Mahan's Gun Crew talked in ranks, Mahan knew it, and ordered Hackett to report it. Hackett flatly refused to report the violation, and Mahan put him on report for willful disobedience. Mahan's version of the incident was this:

> Hackett has willfully misconstrued my language when I warned the crew that I should report strictly, and says that it was as much as saying to the fourth class in the crew that they were the scum of the first class. So that doing a thing which was right and without doing which I would have been entirely wrong, is twisted and perverted. But I feel, I said when I heard this, "If they chose to be such fools let them and be damned to them." . . . [Hackett's] professed cause for falling out with me is that I showed a want of confidence in him by making him report when Second Captain of Crew. Had Hackett told me that, when I asked him if there had been talking, I would have told him that I had no intention to make him report but that I would rely upon his honor to report any delinquency not manifestly excusable. . . . Hackett did not do me the justice to state his complaint, had he done so I would have satisfied him that my course was not intended to show, or caused by, any distrust of him. But as he has given me no reason, he goes in with the rest of the crew—"stopped speaking because reported."[38]

Midshipman Mahan, First Captain of the First Gun Crew, had decided to reform the military appearance and bearing of the Naval Academy all by himself. Compared with the snap, discipline, and rigid sense of honor and personal integrity of the cadets at the Military Academy, the midshipmen at Annapolis were admittedly a relaxed and casual group. Downright sloppy. For the edification of former Midshipman Ashe, Mahan frequently made comparisons between the two service institutions, and always to the disadvantage of the Naval Academy. "I would rejoice to see the whole Navy imitate" the cadets, Mahan declared. As a reward for his efforts to bring the Navy up to snuff, most of Mahan's crew and several of his classmates "stopped speaking" to him.[39]

However correct Mahan was in reporting Hackett, whatever the loftiness of his motives, or the logic of his sense of rightness and righteousness, his course of action in the Hackett Affair was fraught with practical difficulties. First, it was already a tradition at the twelve-year-old Naval Academy (as it remains to this day) that first classmen did not ordinarily put other first classmen on report, and certainly not for such minor infractions as talking in ranks. Mahan sharply challenged this intra-class understanding. Secondly, Mahan's position on reporting his classmates was, by his own admission, less than consistent. As he confessed to Ashe, with reference to a breach of discipline by roommate Thomas Spencer, "I only deviate from it when I see a person getting a great many demerits and there is no absolute necessity for a report. Thus I know Spencer was reading in ranks today. I did not look at him purposely, for I had had already to spot him once in the day, and Borchert had had to do the same in the morning for visiting." The reportorial act was therefore somewhat arbitrary, a point which Mahan seems not to have appreciated, and one that left him in an ambiguous moral position.[40]

It should be pointed out, too, that Mahan was invariably outraged when he himself was put on report. He could scarcely comprehend it, for instance, when a lowly fourth classman (plebe) reported him for hazing. And once, when reported for improperly visiting another midshipman's room during study hours, he angrily carried his case directly to the Commandant of Midshipmen. He lost.[41]

The Hackett Affair split the class of 1859 to its core. Within a few weeks two implacable factions had emerged—a majority group of midshipmen who would not speak to Mahan, and a minority group who remained friendly with him. A few earned Mahan's contempt by steering neutral courses, even though neutrality included normal social inter-course. As this division occurred, Mahan consulted his father as to what his own attitude should be, and was firmly counseled to cut off all those who had rejected him. "Stand up to your work bravely, my dear boy," the father advised his troubled son, "and always in the tone of a high-minded Christian gentleman, and then let the consequences take care of themselves. Your own reputation will be unsullied." His father's firm support throughout the crisis was a source of great comfort and pride to Mahan. He was also pleased to learn from his mother, who visited Annapolis in early November 1858, that Commandant of Midshipmen Craven "was greatly gratified at the course I had been pursuing here this year." On the other hand, he was hurt to observe one after another of his classmates join the opposition. "Schoonmaker and Butt have fallen out with me for reports," he told Ashe. "That damned little Butt annoys me a great deal, for he proved a tyrant to the 10th crew while he had it temporarily." By November, and by his own generous count, Mahan was still on speaking terms with but nine of his classmates.[42]

As his class reputation sank in the waters of the Severn River, Midshipman Mahan became increasingly convinced that his position was not only morally correct, it was entirely salutary insofar as overall military discipline at the Naval Academy was concerned:

> The good effects of discipline are very perceptible [he wrote Ashe];
> our company drill is the best I have ever seen here. . . . Not a man will
> talk now when he sees my eye on him, for he feels a spot coming. . . .

> Father is delighted, as you may suppose, at my conduct and with his warm approval and such friends as Billy [Claiborne], Cenas and Borchert the rest of them may go to hell. I take it very easily now. The drill is acknowledged on all hands to be vastly superior to last year's and its defects could be altogether remedied if all the [crew] captains would do as we few have [done] and Lockwood would give us some three or four weeks of constant drill with companies.[43]

His solution to the problem of disaffection was stubbornly to wait until his enemies showed enough "manliness" to accept the correctness of his position and abjectly apologize to him. "Of course the offer must come from them and come as a request coupled with an apology," he insisted. He would then decide whether to accept their obeisances. Needless to say, no long lines formed for his ablutionary rite and Mahan continued putting his classmates on report, particularly personal enemies like Midshipman Roderick S. McCook. At the same time, he came firmly to believe that the crisis with his classmates had greatly strengthened his character. "After all," he boasted in March 1859, "it did require a great deal of moral courage to meet that trial, and like many another, now that the conflict is over, I shudder to look back on it, though I feel proud in the conquest as much over myself as over others. I can rely upon my own force of character now, for it has been tested."[44]

The force of his character aside, Alfred Thayer Mahan was a lonely young man during his final year at the Naval Academy. Under the best conditions, the introverted midshipman did not easily make friends, male or female. Nor were the depths of the friendships he did make very great. Instead, he was destined to go through life sustained by little more than an ever-shifting number of casual acquaints, people who passed hurriedly through his life like shadows on a screen. It is probably correct to say that he expected too much of mere mortals and that he was a very private man. As his daughter Ellen recalled: "My father was essentially 'The Cat That Walked By Himself'. . . . Friends of his own were practically nonexistent." Nevertheless, Mahan often complained to Sam Ashe, perhaps the nearest to a real friend he ever had, that he had no friends, nor had he the ability to make them. "I cannot remember the time that I ever cared for two persons," he confessed.[45]

Mahan defined friendship in a way too theoretical and idealistic for most of his contemporaries to understand, and he expected too much from such relationships. For example, he thought of his friendship with young Ashe largely in terms of brothers-in-arms. Indeed, the reader of Mahan's moving description of Nelson's death at Trafalgar, and the dying admiral's final faltering conversation with Captain Thomas Hardy, will grasp something of Mahan's conception of the love of one man for another. It was the love, rooted in trust, that existed among Lord Nelson's ships' captains, among his loyal and devoted "band of brothers." Mahan firmly believed that personal associations formed at West Point and Annapolis "must be far more lasting and deep than those made elsewhere, for here we are from every cause brothers, our association, our hopes, our profession all the same." Unfortunately for Alfred Mahan, none of his personal associations, naval or other, were ever that sort. He remained "The Cat That Walked By Himself" to the end of his days, putting people on report all the way.[46]

There was thus something almost pathetic in Mahan's desperate reaching out by mail to Sam Ashe for friendship and approval, as his personal life at the Naval Academy became more complicated and difficult in 1858 and 1859. In a typical letter the young midshipman put his hoped-for relationship with his former classmate in these terms:

> I lay in bed last night, dear Sam, thinking of the gradual rise and growth of our friendship. My first visit even to your room is vividly before me, and how as I went up from there from night to night I could feel my attachment to you growing and see your own love for me showing itself more and more every night. After all, what feeling is more delightful than that of loving and being loved, even though it be only man's love for man. . . . But, dear Sam, my own dearest and warmest friend, although years must change the character of my love for you, I think I can promise you that you will ever be first, and never less than second, in my heart. I do not think that your love for me equals mine for you, for if you did, I think you would, like me, recall those little things, nothing in themselves, everything as showing affection and regard. But I have schooled myself to be content as far as I can with my share, and the knowledge that I am now your dearest friend.[47]

Mahan's loneliness also took the form of insisting that Ashe not correspond with the Hackett group at the Academy, that he demonstrate his affection in regular correspondence and affirmation, and that he accept on faith and love Mahan's analysis of the internal politics of the class of 1859. In return for this expected constancy, Mahan kept Ashe posted on Academy gossip, on his own romantic and academic progress, and on the social life of Annapolis. Occasional sexual references gave Mahan's letters to Ashe an *entre nous* masculinity. Mahan gleefully reported his own modest moral debauches, which consisted mainly of smoking cigars.[48]

A major theme in the letters he wrote to Sam Ashe from Annapolis understandably concerned his own personal hatreds and vendettas, as he became increasingly sealed off from the internal camaraderie of the Yard. Some of these youthful aversions he carried with him throughout his naval career. Save for Ashe, he did not keep up with any of his classmates in the years ahead. Those who had formed what Mahan always called the "cabal" against him were dismissed with absolute contempt. Samuel H. Hackett, Edmund G. Read, Roderick S. McCook, Samuel W. Averett, and Norman H. Farquhar were among this group. He was completely (and incorrectly) convinced that of the first classmen in his crew, "not one of them will leave his name behind him. They will never excite confidence enough in their abilities to give them the chance of the doubtful reputation of a tremendous defeat." Similarly, he became increasingly contemptuous of his roommate, "Fan" Spencer, the "very nice fellow" of the year before. Academically, Spencer was not the brightest person in the world, and he made the additional mistakes of maintaining liaison with Mahan's enemies and participating in Sunday School activities and in the Bible Society. Both of these latter activities were voluntary for midshipmen, and both were discreditable in Mahan's eyes. He therefore decided that Spencer was a worthless cuss who would end up disgracing the service, and would probably lose a ship at sea. "I abominate him as a man, and shan't come within ten feet of him after I graduate if I can help it," he said of his future shipmate in the *Congress*. Also, Mahan had little respect for Lieutenant Samuel P. Carter, an officer instructor at the Academy, a man with whom he again came in contact in the Far East in 1867. Carter received Midshipman Mahan's disapprobation because he too was connected with the Bible Society, influenced Spencer in that direction, and had a sense of humor of the kind that led him to serve cotton-filled doughnuts to visiting midshipmen as a practical joke. Very funny. Carter was definitely below the salt at Mahan's table of good opinion.[49]

Midshipman William Thomas Sampson, later Mahan's candidate for hero status at the Battle of Santiago (1898), was two classes behind Mahan at the Academy and was a member of his crew from 1858 to 1859. Mahan was much impressed with him. He continued speaking to Alfred during the Hackett Affair, and frequently took his professional questions to him. "He had none of the tricks of the popularity hunter, and he suffered for it," Mahan recalled.

Also at the Academy in 1858 and 1859 was Second Class Midshipman Winfield Scott Schley of Maryland, who later fought Mahan over issues concerning the Naval War College and became one half of the famous

Sampson-Schley controversy in which Mahan participated so vigorously on Sampson's behalf in the years 1898 to 1901. One year behind Mahan at the Academy, Schley was a leading figure in a group of midshipmen called The Pelicans, a band of irreverent pranksters from which the unpopular Mahan was excluded. Nevertheless, Mahan was both amazed and amused by Schley's humorous and imaginative antics and by the great pleasure he seemed to derive from standing near the foot of his class academically. Schley himself later recalled that he "held pleasure and holidays in higher esteem than plodding study, which was more interesting in some such ratio as the square of the distance separating us from books." Put another way, the dashing Schley was almost everything Alfred Thayer Mahan was not. Popular, athletic, a great story-teller, a natural leader of men, he was supremely confident socially, danced beautifully, was a great favorite with the ladies, and had an ebullient sense of humor. He later proved himself as confident in combat as he was able in Navy Department political in-fighting. There is no certain evidence that Mahan particularly disliked Schley during their midshipman days together—Mahan's violent hatred came later. There is, on the other hand, much evidence that Mahan was relegated to the periphery of the Naval Academy-Annapolis society in which Schley excelled. In the kind of world in which Schley moved and flourished, Mahan was ever the outsider looking in.[50]

At the heart of Mahan's problems at the Naval Academy, and at the root of his later unpopularity among his service peers, was his ill-concealed vanity. The fact of the matter is that he considered his appearance, his mentality, his morality, and all his own works, ideas, and attitudes to be vastly superior to those of the common run of mankind, particularly that segment of mankind he observed in attendance at the Naval Academy. He could neither understand nor tolerate anyone who disagreed with him. Such people were either perverse or malevolent. Samuel W. Averett, for example, who had a distinguished career as a Confederate officer and who was a prominent postwar educator in Virginia, was dismissed for holding "ideas [that] will never change and . . . are radically wrong." Midshipman Roderick Prentiss, who was killed in action at the Battle of Mobile Bay, was deemed unsuited to be color bearer at graduation exercises in 1859 because Mahan thought him "insignificant looking." The office of color-bearer, said Mahan, "should be filled by the finest looking midshipman in the Academy." That person, of course, was Mahan himself. At slightly over six feet, one inch, in height, he was enamored of his own stature and good looks. He thought it positively humorous that Midshipman Gilbert C. Wiltse was slightly cross-eyed.

Mahan could not resist the temptation to laugh at the mistakes of others. He was incapable of laughing at his own. A half-century after leaving the Academy, he admitted in his autobiography that his mastery of marlinespike seamanship never progressed beyond tying a few simple knots. Ashe also recalled that his friend "was not apt as a sailor man." But Mahan could not bring himself to admit this inadequacy at the time. Indeed, on one occasion, when teased by his classmates about his awkwardness in seamanship, he angrily instructed Ashe "if you hear any such damned lies, don't believe them." He did not take criticism lightly or easily, then or ever. In fine, Alf Mahan was convinced that he was without question the most able and intelligent midshipman at the Academy, and that he came from a "remarkably talented family," which "for talent and character . . . [was] far above the ordinary run of mankind that I have usually met. . . ." He thought, too, "that the whole family think more of me than any other one member in it."[51]

Having regaled Sam Ashe with such egocentric observations over a period of several months, Mahan finally summed up his own virtues in these words:

> I hope you are not thinking "that Mahan's a damned conceited ass." I fear I am, Sam, but it's not my fault. In the last few years I have had far fewer kicks and far more compliments than enough to turn a poor middy's head. Regarded throughout the Academy as the smartest man in the class, and the prettiest girl in Annapolis wanting to know why I won't pass one, as she did to-night; told frequently of my good looks and complimented sometimes by ladies in society, to my great annoyance really, and which I always slue over as quickly as possible, although I have the greatest contempt for my vanity, yet I cannot escape knowing that they only tell me the truth. . . . In fact, to acknowledge my true estimate of myself, I think I am very good-looking, very talented, and a favorite in society, and with more moral *character* than nine-tenths of the midshipmen in the school, and I also feel that I would give anything if to this were added in its highest degree the Christian virtue of humility. I do not, however, think that my self-conceit, a quality which you will remember I have always owned up to, is disagreeably conspicuous.[52]

Unfortunately for Mahan, his enormous conceit was quite conspicuous, and disagreeably so, at that. Miss Nannie Craven pointed to it as his greatest fault and Mahan cheerfully agreed that she was right. Even his mother hedged on the point, saying that her son was not conceited "in the ordinary meaning of the word," whatever that meant. Mahan's classmates were more direct. As Midshipman Walter R. Butt, one of the smallest men in the class, put it to Midshipman Silas Casey of Rhode Island, a hulk of a man, "By Jove, Casey, I wish I was as strong as you. If I would not pound that Mahan!" Mahan affected people that way.[53]

It was his youthful sense of superiority, compounded in part by his loneliness and rejection, that led Mahan to give vent to a number of extremist political statements during his final year at the Academy. Actually, he was not particularly concerned with national politics at this time. His surviving letters of the period reflect little interest in the heated issues that stimulated the rapid onrush of the Civil War. To be sure, he had no use for the ultra-abolitionists. His father had taught him the danger of abolitionism. He accepted the existence of slavery uncritically and, given his family background and training, his view of the American Negro was predictable. Negroes were "niggers" and "darkies." Nothing more. He was only casually aware of the possibility of civil war. But, while his racial sympathies lay with the South, he was not convinced, as were some of his Virginia classmates and Annapolitan lady friends, that all Virginians were automatically the Chosen of God. "Virginians are liable to the infirmities of our common mortality," he conceded.[54]

What he did exhibit was a contempt for American democratic processes, a view that seems to have been indirectly related to his continuing bitterness over the Hackett Affair. To be sure, he was convinced that those of his classmates who had cut him off were his professional and moral inferiors. And he believed, further, that school officials had shown shocking weakness and indecisiveness in their unwillingness to support vigorously and publicly his insistence on obedience to Academy regulations. Such flabbiness of performance would not have occurred, he felt, in the highly disciplined Royal Navy, the fine navy in which the fictional Mr. Midshipman Easy had served. He also saw far too much political influence rampant in the U.S. Navy of 1859. Like most under-educated and overly impatient college students, he related this observation to what he believed was a fundamental sickness permeating American society. The country was sliding rapidly toward ruin and only stern authoritarian measures could halt the decay:

> These ideas and feelings [he told Ashe] are the product not of our individuals, but of our lamentable national institutions and government, and ideas. Oh, Sam! say what you please, a republic is the damndest humbug ever created for times when war is even a bare possibility.

> Until the reign of peace, good-will to men comes, mankind must be subject to mankind, and for the preservation of the State this subjection must be absolute, perfect—a principle, a creed. England's greatness arises from this fact, the idea of obedience to the powers that be is born, bred and nourished in an Englishman from his cradle to his grave, and see their glorious navy. . . . And our God damned American independence forbids us to cultivate the great virtue that alone will save us in the hour of danger, obedience—passive, unresisting obedience.

Certain that the lack of passive obedience in the national character ensured that the United States would be "thrashed at first" in its next war, Mahan was determined to do what he could as a naval officer to stave off the impending doom. Specifically, he would dedicate his career to upholding the virtues of the warrior. As he assured Ashe, "By God, I'll make my inferiors obey me."[55]

Half-baked though these observations were, they were not views that Mahan confided only in his letters to Sam Ashe. They were opinions he expressed freely and frankly in the social parlors of Annapolis, much to the distress of some of his listeners:

> Despotism—every great man that ever lived had the nature of a despot. I must have spoken very strongly on the subject, for the lady said, "Mr. Mahan, you frighten me; what a tyrant you will be." And in my nature I feel no sympathy for the oppressed mutineer, no matter if his officer felled him on the quarter deck and made him lick up his own blood; if he made any reply I would hang him as high as Haman. I suppose you think I have been savage enough for once, but I assure you I speak but the truth. And you must bear a little more if it help you to learn another trait in my character.[56]

Mahan was not, nor did he ever become, a "tyrant." His daughter Ellen recalled that "his sense of justice made it impossible for him to be tyrannical." He did, however, later support his wife's "tendency . . . toward the autocratic" when it came to raising their three children. She was Mahan's executive officer. As Ellen put it: "We must do as she said, and we did. . . . by the time I became aware of her in relation to myself the rule of the house had become 'Few orders, absolute obedience.' " It would seem, then, that Mahan's wife, not Mahan himself, later ran the home like a ship of the Royal Navy. No mutineers permitted.[57]

One final attempt was made to straighten out Alfred's tense relationships with his classmates prior to his graduation in June 1859. In May, much to Mahan's embarrassment, his father wrote Superintendent Blake from West Point requesting that the men who had fallen out with Mahan be asked flatly why they had adopted their course of action. As Mahan reported the incident, his father wanted the reasons for the explosion in the class of 1859 "distinctly known, lest on going away they should say that it had been for a reason that would reflect on my character." Blake obligingly called the men to his office and asked them if Mahan's reporting of Hackett and other first classmen was indeed at the root of the difficulty. They all denied "having any such reason as my reporting," said Mahan. The only reason they gave was Mahan's "manner," a manner that was "reserved and averse to cultivating a general acquaintance among my classmates." Mahan rejected their explanation. "I believe it is all humbug as regards my manner," he wrote, "such a charge need give me no concern even though literally true. To say the least, it is strange that all this was not found out before this year. Hereafter my course is plainly to act as though that crowd had no existence." As he explained his final position on the Hackett matter to Ashe:

> I have already forgiven them I hope, not as a Christian, an offender, but as a man [forgives] a child. I can never forget it, and years of sternly tried friendship must lapse ere I can look with affection on those who deserted me in the hour of need. What infatuation can possess those fellows I cannot conceive. Not one of them would dare go to any Army officer and say "Am I right?" for he would be treated as a fool. They must feel they are wrong.[58]

And there the matter rested at the time of Mahan's graduation and promotion to the rank of passed midshipman. He had failed in his relations with his classmates; he had cut less than a dashing figure in the parlors of Annapolis; and he had begun to suspect that he was no seaman. But he had convinced himself that he was a wholly superior human being —in mind, body, and morality. Thus armed, he began a thirty-seven-year career in the operational U.S. Navy. It was destined to be a stormy passage.

II

The Civil War
1860-1866

Let us examine it in the light of history. . . . In what way did . . . preparation for war contribute to the outbreak? What trained soldiery, what fortifications on either side, that in any way affected the determination to fight? The remote cause of the war was slavery; the immediate occasion popular emotion, fervid nationalism, patriotism, truly or falsely so-called, aroused on either side.

Alfred Thayer Mahan to the Editor, *The New York Times*,
August 31, 1914

During his last months at the Academy the unhappy Mahan busied himself, as did all graduating first classmen, with arranging his orders to sea duty. The ideal scheme was to get up a "party" of three or four classmates and secure joint assignment to the same vessel. Mahan and his two closest associates in the Hackett Affair, Hilary Cenas and Henry B. Claiborne, came to constitute such a party. First, their attempt to gain assignment to the sloop *Levant* failed—which was just as well since she was lost with all hands in the Pacific in 1860. Actually, Mahan preferred the *Iroquois*, a speedy, shallow-draft steam vessel mounting 13 guns which in the "war that any moment may now bring on us" would be particularly effective "around in harbors and on cutting out expeditions that will give me the exciting sort of service that I most crave." There was also the additional advantage that "such ships as she will be more likely to make prize money than any other." But in June 1859 he and his party were ordered to the frigate *Congress*, an antiquated 50-gun vessel with a complement of 480 officers and men.[1]

With some prospect of civil war in the offing, Mahan was encouraged to think in terms of rapid promotion to lieutenant. "Mr. Mahan, you will be a lieutenant before you can turn around," Superintendent Blake had assured him. This hopeful prognosis was in part the result of a shortage of officers in that rank brought about by the long-overdue pruning of the officer list by the famous (or infamous) Retiring Board, 1854–1855. From a career standpoint Mahan thus began his service in the *Congress* at a particularly advantageous moment in American naval history. With him went Cenas and Claiborne. Also in the *Congress* party were Fan Spencer, Mahan's detested roommate, and Gil Wiltse, one of the less brilliant members of the class and one who had openly consorted with Mahan's enemies during the Hackett explosion. But considering the personal bitterness through which Mahan had recently passed and the understandable unwillingness of the Navy Department to adjust its personnel assignments to petty undergraduate hatreds, it turned out to be a reasonably congenial group. Attached to it was Jefferson A. Slamm, Sam Ashe's roommate in Annapolis. Slamm had flunked out of the Academy and was then serving as master's mate in the *Congress*. Other officers in the ship whose service paths Mahan would later cross were William A. Kirkland and John N. Quackenbush.

Passed Midshipman Mahan was appointed aide to the commanding officer of the Brazil Station, Commodore Joshua Sands, who flew his broad pennant in the *Congress*. At general quarters he was assigned the charge of the Powder Division. Captain Louis M. Goldsborough commanded the vessel. She was designated flagship of the station, to which there were also assigned three brigs, a small steamer, and a store vessel. Goldsborough's son, young John Goldsborough, served as his father's clerk. He soon became a drinking companion of Mahan's and the other passed midshipmen on board the ship.[2]

Mahan later wrote a lengthy account of his two-year cruise in the *Congress*, the salty details of which need not detain us here. Only three personal letters of this period have survived. One was written to Captain Goldsborough putting two crew members of the *Congress* on report for "direct and repeated disobedience of orders from me," orders that had to do with talking in the market boat to shore one morning. Another was a travelogue letter to Sam Ashe in which, among other things, Mahan boastfully confessed to getting "very drunk" in Rio in celebration of his twentieth birthday. The third, actually written after the *Congress* had returned home, indicates that Mahan's excursions ashore, particularly in Montevideo, were socially pleasurable. He met a number of English and

American families resident there and was entertained in their homes. He managed also to fall briefly, hopelessly, and joyfully in love. This time with Clara Villegas, a dark-eyed Latin beauty of Montevideo whom he called his little "duck," and whom he never forgot. Twenty-five years later, when his eye for the ladies was "perhaps more critical and no longer leads to my heart and fancy by electric wire," he recalled that "some of the beauty I once saw in Montevideo might still waken the fire in the ashes."[3]

His passion for kilowatt Clara aside, it is important to recall that Mahan was out of the United States during the traumatic political events of 1859–1861 that finally brought on the Civil War. The news of these crises at home traveled slowly to Rio de Janeiro and Montevideo, the main cruising stations of the *Congress*, and the seriousness of the events was sometimes clouded in delayed transmission. The crew of the vessel did, nevertheless, begin to divide along sectional lines. Leading the Southern war hawks were the two U.S. Marine Corps officers, Captain Robert Tansill and Second Lieutenant T. S. Wilson. At the head of the Unionist fire-eaters was Passed Midshipman Gil Wiltse, "a plucky fellow, but with an odd cast to his eyes and a slight malformation, which made his ecstasies of wrath a little comical." Mahan later described himself at this juncture of the North-South debate as a "doughface," or as one of those who "between the alternatives of dissolving the Union and fighting one another, were longing to see some third way open out of the dilemma." He recalled that in June 1861, when orders came directing the *Congress* to return to Boston and in the same mail came news of the Confederate firing on Fort Sumter, "the doughfaces were set at once, like a flint. . . . Every voice but one was hushed, and that voice said 'Fight.'" Mahan was ready to do just that. Later he remembered that for the concept of "The Union" he had an "almost idolatrous veneration." Based "equally upon interest and sentiment [it] is one of the reminiscences of my youth which thrills me even now."[4]

When the *Congress* reached Boston, Mahan's closest friends, Cenas and Claiborne, refused to take the oath of allegiance to the United States. Together with Tansill and Wilson, they were arrested and placed in Fort Lafayette where they remained as prisoners of war until exchanged. Both later fought in the Confederate States Navy. Wiltse remained in the *Congress* and Spencer was detailed to the New York Navy Yard as a drill instructor. He soon after resigned his commission and sat out the war. John Goldsborough became a lieutenant in the U.S. Marine Corps, having "outlived all secesh tendencies, even his quondam unwillingness to fight against Virginia." As he explained it: "You see, Mahan, when I got home, I found how they were going, got disgusted, and concluded just to let all the *States* go to hell!"

Mahan's own family was faced with difficult decisions of this sort, as were tens of thousands of other American families. The pro-Southern sympathies of Uncle Milo Mahan were so strong and ill disguised that he was finally forced to resign his professorship at General Theological Seminary in New York in 1864 and move to the pastorate of St. Paul's Episcopal Church in Baltimore. There he remained until he passed away in 1870. Professor Dennis Hart Mahan was also sorely tried. His intense love for his native Virginia, which he had visited as recently as the summer of 1860, was equalled only by his dismay as he watched such old Army and West Point friends as P. G. T. Beauregard and Robert E. Lee resign their commissions and go south. But he stuck with the Union.[5]

On August 31, 1861, the Union now disintegrated, Passed Midshipman Mahan was promoted to lieutenant, the usual examinations having been waived. "This is a grand time for young officers," he crowed. Less to crow about was the fact that he was assigned to the *James Adger*, a 17-gun, schooner-rigged, paddle-wheel merchant steamer which had been hastily purchased and armed by the government. She was then lying in New York. He was only in this unlikely craft for ten days—just long enough to write his famous "mystery ship" letter of September 9 to the Department of the Navy and to have a sharp run-in with the merchant marine crew still on board the vessel. This last occurred when two members of the vessel's black-hole gang took it upon themselves to saunter ashore, as was (and is) the custom of merchant mariners, without young Mahan's permission. Lieutenant Mahan stopped them on the pier, became embroiled in a heated argument with the civilian chief engineer, and won his point that the *James Adger* was now a naval vessel and would be run like one.[6]

The "mystery ship" letter to Assistant Secretary of the Navy, Gustavus V. Fox, suggested that the raider CSS *Sumter*, commanded by the intrepid Rafael Semmes, might be lured to her destruction by being enticed to attack a Union war vessel camouflaged to look like a harmless, unarmed merchantman. This ruse would obviate the need to deploy a full squadron, better employed on blockade duty, to track down and destroy the elusive *Sumter*. Mahan offered to lead the enterprise which, even were it to fail, would cost the Navy only "a useless ship, a midshipman and a hundred men." While the concept was tactically sound, there was a distinct Marryat quality to it. Mahan himself admitted that it might "appear rash or even hare-brained." Whatever its virtues, the plan died aborning. The letter to Fox was never answered. Lieutenant Mahan was, however, thinking large and heroic thoughts; and he was also spoiling for combat. *Nos Morituri.*[7]

From the *James Adger* Mahan was sent as first lieutenant to the *Pocahontas*, "one of the prettiest gunboats in the United States Navy." This single-screw, brig-rigged, 11-gun vessel of 694 tons carried 173 officers and men and was lying at the Washington Navy Yard when Mahan went on board. Great things were planned for the little ship. Indeed, in early October, as Mahan explained her movements to C. S. Newcome, his friend in Montevideo, the *Pocahontas*

> went down the river . . . expecting to be concerned in a hell of an attack at Matthias Point, a position of considerable importance in the river. The plans were laid—4000 troops to come—the navy all ready to start, and I turned in prepared to conquer or die next day . . . and woke up sold. I go to windward of the balance of the officers, most of whom turned in with their clothes on; but I stripped and got my natural rest. The troops didn't come. . . . [Nevertheless] you need not be discouraged, I think, at the lack of enthusiasm that appears on the surface— the people have settled down to the war as a matter of course and as a necessity to win future prosperity, and I verily believe it might be carried on for fifty years without creating a growl.[8]

It was also in the *Pocahontas*, commanded by Percival Drayton, that Mahan participated in the combined Army-Navy operation against Port Royal, South Carolina, on November 7, 1861. Unfortunately for the would-be hero, his ship was delayed by heavy weather on her trip south from Hampton Roads. She arrived late at the scene of combat, made a couple of passes at Fort Walker, and sustained thereby minor damage to her upper rigging. After the battle was over and the fleet was seeking anchorage, the *Pocahontas* added confusion to jubilation by colliding ingloriously with the *Seminole*, an act that caused more damage to both vessels than had the Confederates.[9]

The embarrassing performance at Port Royal was something of a harbinger of Alfred Thayer Mahan's combat record for the remainder of the Civil War. Put succinctly, his wartime duty stations invariably placed him where the fighting was not. The only enemy guns he ever heard fired in concert and in anger during forty years as an active-duty naval officer were those of the subsiding Confederate batteries in Fort Walker in November 1861. He did, however, experience other collisions at sea. Several.

Following the Battle of Port Royal, Mahan and the *Pocahontas* spent the next ten months poking their respective noses into every river, cove, and inlet from Georgetown, South Carolina, to Fernandina, Florida, sustaining thereby the vital in-shore work of the South Atlantic Blockading Squadron. News of the progress of the shooting war reached the blockaders ten days to two weeks after the events. To Mahan, the real war seemed far away, as indeed it was.

But it was during this tedious period that Mahan became a belated convert to abolitionism. When he first saw field-hand slavery in South Carolina he became an instant abolitionist. As he said in his autobiography: "It was my first meeting with slavery, except in the house servants of Maryland. . . . and as I looked at the cowed, imbruted faces of the field-hands, my early training fell away like a cloak. The process was not logical; I was generalizing from a few instances, but I was convinced." Better late than never.

On the other hand, Mahan told his British readers years later that the nation did not wage the Civil War "for the abolition of slavery, still less for equal rights of citizenship." As a "contemporary and partaker, I can affirm this as a general tone though there was a strong minority of abolition sentiment." Similarly, American readers were assured that the "remote cause of the war was slavery; the immediate occasion [was] popular emotion, fervid nationalism, patriotism, truly or falsely so-called, aroused on either side." What Mahan really felt on the origins, purposes, and racial dimensions of the Civil War cannot therefore be known with certainty. What is clear is that he always believed in the "great superiority . . . of the white over the negro." He was certain, too, that Asiatics were racially superior to the American Negro. In a racial field of three, the black man finished third.[10]

Mahan's monotonous life as a South Atlantic blockader was pleasantly interrupted when he was assigned, in September 1862, to duty on the faculty at the Naval Academy. For safety's sake, the Academy had been moved northward, to Newport, Rhode Island, for the duration of the war, and there Mahan remained until October 1863. Again, no personal letters have survived this period of his career. In his autobiography we learn only that his effectiveness as a teacher of marlinespike seamanship was humorously dismal, and that he sailed as first lieutenant in the *Macedonian*, the obsolete vessel (mounting in her battery four fake "Quaker" guns) which took the midshipmen on their practice summer cruise to

Europe in 1863. It is known that he was generally disliked by the midshipmen with whom he came in contact at Newport. He was simply not the popular type and never would be.[11]

From a career standpoint Mahan's brief service in the *Macedonian* was extremely useful in that she was commanded by Lieutenant Commander Stephen B. Luce, an officer who later played such a decisive role in Mahan's professional life. Another of the ship's officers was Lieutenant William T. Sampson, a favorite of Mahan's when they were midshipmen at the Academy. Mahan got along exceptionally well with both men while they were together in the *Macedonian*. The voyage also permitted Mahan to visit Paris, travel overland on a sightseeing jaunt, and rejoin his ship at Cadiz. All in all, these were "pleasant months" in Newport and in the *Macedonian*, even though an old Naval Academy enemy, Tecumseh Steece, class of 1861, was also on the Academy staff at that time. Forty-five years later Mahan still had little good to say of Steece, who died on active duty in July 1864. The old Annapolis hatreds lingered long.[12]

The thirteen-month tour at Newport was pleasant indeed. Mahan discovered that the Rhode Island beer was excellent. More importantly, he again fell desperately in love. This time with a woman, somewhat older than he, who was a resident of the fashionable summer colony at Newport. She was, unfortunately, married. Nonetheless, the lady gave Mahan enough encouragement to fuel an unrequited love that lasted, on and off, for the next seven years. Her name is not known.[13]

From his peaceful and romantic interlude in Newport, Mahan was rudely "exiled" back to the war in October 1863, or to that phase of the war off the Texas coast where they also served who only rolled and pitched. In this duty Mahan pitched, rolled, and wallowed for five boring months as first lieutenant in the little steam sloop *Seminole*, 9 guns, stationed on blockade off Sabine Pass and Galveston. It was "the end of nowhere." Indeed, Mahan recalled his experience in the West Gulf Blockade Squadron as miserable duty, "desperately tedious." Morale in the vessel was terrible. "I have never seen a body of intelligent men reduced so nearly to imbecility as my shipmates then were," he remembered. In April 1864 the unhappy *Seminole* "was recalled in mercy to New Orleans." At that place Mahan vigorously attempted to join the shooting war by getting himself transferred to the *Monongahela*, then engaged in the relatively "sociable blockade" that was Mobile. His attempt failed. Classmate Roderick Prentiss was ordered to the *Monongahela* instead and was killed aboard her in August 1864 at the Battle of Mobile Bay. Mahan was leading a charmed life.[14]

During his lonely exile in the *Seminole*, Mahan again gave serious thought to his religious and theological principles. He had gradually recovered from his outrage against the kind of hell-fire religion preached at the Academy by "Old Slicky" Jones. In a letter (or letters) now lost, he wrote his Uncle Milo from the *Seminole* asking specifically how he could best influence the men under his command toward spiritual goals; he also wanted Milo's opinion on whether or not the Bible should be taken literally. In a letter dater October 3, 1864, after Mahan's detachment from the *Seminole*, Milo answered the first question quite simply, leaving aside the more controversial issue of whether a naval officer should feel any spiritual responsibility or obligation for enlisted men under his command. He told Alfred to set a Christian example for his men, to lead "a quiet consistent life accompanied with as much of courtesy, gentility and consideration in dealing with your men as the nature of the Service will allow."[15]

The question about the Bible was more difficult to answer, especially since by 1864 Milo had reached a point in his own thinking that was both unorthodox and rationalist. His rationalist views were implicit in his attack on John William Colenso, Anglican bishop of the diocese of Natal, South Africa, in a book written in 1862 and titled *The Spiritual Point-of-View, or The Glass Reversed. An Answer to Bishop Colenso.* In this work, Milo took the heretical Colenso to task for questioning the historicity of the Pentateuch, for laughing at the contradictory arithmetical and numerical references in the Old Testament, and for denying that the Bible, which was being cited by Christians in the United States to sustain the noxious institution of human slavery, was divinely inspired. Milo agreed that there were indeed grave historical and scientific difficulties inherent in Scripture. He accepted the fact that the Pentateuch abounded in "half truths." But, as mentioned earlier, in answering Colenso's specific attack on the numerology of the Old Testament, Milo devised an elaborate cosmological system, neo-Pythagorean in substance, that was later to find its way into his nephew's philosophy of history.

In his *Palmoni; or The Numerals of Scripture*, published in 1862, and in *Mystic Numbers*, published posthumously in 1875, Milo posited the existence of an orderly, rational, and arithmetical universe. Such a universe, because it was rational and orderly, clearly revealed the hand of God in its creation and movements. Further, those movements were explicable in terms of the "divine" numbers that permeated it, numbers whose relationships God intended man to discover. Milo also argued, somewhat ambivalently, that since the Old Testament contained numerous "half truths" it could not be taken literally in a scientific sense; it should, however, be accepted literally in a psychic sense. He explained this dichotomy to his nephew, urging him at the same time to postpone judgment in the matter until he was older, wiser, and more sure of himself:

> As to your questions about *belief*—whether the words of the Bible are to be taken *literally or not*—it is well to understand the distinction between *implicit* and *explicit* faith. . . . The Bible is most instructive when received in this temper. . . . Where a particular question comes up, a difficulty of any kind, it is well enough to examine it, and turn it over in the mind, and find a solution if possible; but if a thoroughly satisfactory solution cannot be found, then *do not accept a half solution*; rather, let the matter rest—turn to other subjects; in short, wait till the solution comes of itself. With this general maxim, I am of course an advocate of the closest, most exact, most *literal interpretation* of Scripture. In many cases such interpretation obliges one to receive "a hard saying," and to admit things as true which we cannot reconcile to facts as they commonly appear. . . . Still, if the Bible is authority at all, it must be authority chiefly in those things in which reason or self will at first rebel against it. . . . Things happen to us constantly which prove either that *God* rules, or else that *chance* rules. But if I must choose between chance and God, to solve the mysteries of life, it is certainly reasonable to refer things to God of whom I can form *some* idea, rather than to chance of which I can form *no* idea whatever. . . . A belief of this kind leads one, I think, to the habit of observing facts and accepting them, whether we comprehend them or not; and, in the same way, it leads us to take Scripture simply as it is, without over-anxious efforts to make everything in Scripture plain.[16]

Whether this satisfied Alfred's curiosity about the Bible is not known. But in the years ahead he seldom mentioned the Old Testament as a basis for his faith. There were too many "hard sayings" in it. On the other hand, he never doubted or challenged the exact language of the New Testament in supporting or explaining the highly traditional theological beliefs that came to dominate his religious life after the Civil War. More to the point, it seems clear that he read his uncle's books. As will be seen, the philosophy of history he outlined in his presidential address to the American Historical Association in 1902 drew significantly on some of the cosmological views contained in the works of Milo Mahan.[17]

As important as was Milo's influence on Alfred's subsequent intellectual development, it is not likely that his uncle's protracted war with Bishop Colenso was uppermost in his mind when he received orders, dated February 18, 1864, detaching him from the accursed *Seminole*. In May 1864 he was assigned as first lieutenant in the *James Adger*, the vessel in which he had briefly served in 1861. She was at this time attached to Rear Admiral John A. Dahlgren's South Atlantic Blockading Squadron based at Port Royal, South Carolina. Compared with the isolated and sunbaked West Gulf Squadron, this was truly a "sociable blockade." In July 1864 Mahan was detached from the *James Adger* and assigned temporarily to the command of the double-ended, side-wheel steamer *Cimarron*, a 4-gun vessel engaged in close-in blockade support. Three months' duty in the *Cimarron* led, in October 1864, to his appointment as ordnance officer of the squadron.

From a career standpoint, his service on Dahlgren's staff was by far the best duty Mahan enjoyed during the Civil War. It permitted him to be present at the victory celebrations attendant on the capture of Savannah in December 1864 and on the surrender of Charleston in April 1865, and to meet and greet the commanders of Sherman's March to the Sea, several of whom studied under his father at West Point and inquired after "Old Dennis."[18]

There is some indication, however, that Mahan's performance as ordnance officer of the South Atlantic Blockade Squadron did not entirely please Admiral Dahlgren. Several trenchant letters to Mahan from Fleet Captain Joseph M. Bradford, and from Dahlgren himself, seem to attest this. On February 18, 1865, following one particularly pointed order to Mahan (dated February 15) relating to an overdue inventory of ordnance stores in the squadron, Dahlgren transferred Mahan back to the *James Adger*. This transfer was effected on May 6, 1865. Meanwhile, the war had ended.[19]

The *James Adger* was then briefly assigned to convoy duty in the Gulf of Mexico, it being thought that there might still be danger to American shipping in those waters from Confederate cruisers that had not learned of the surrender of Lee's army in Virginia. This cruise took Mahan to Haiti. There he contracted malaria and was invalided home to West Point for two months' leave in June 1865. In that same month he was also promoted to the rank of lieutenant commander, but only after personal agitation with the Navy Department on the subject. Throughout July, August, September, and October of 1865 Mahan regularly reported to the Chief of the Bureau of Navigation and Detail, Captain Percival Drayton (the job was later held by Captain Thornton A. Jenkins) that he was unable, by reason of a very slow recovery, to return to active duty. In each report he requested an extension of his sick leave. His infirmity did not, however, prevent his making a trip from West Point to Newport in mid-July to visit friends. As he informed Drayton from Newport on July 23, he was "gaining strength gradually" but was "not yet able to do duty."[20]

In mid-November 1865 the Navy finally decided that Mahan was well enough to return to active duty; and as if to punish him for his five inactive months ashore he was assigned as executive officer of the iron side-wheeler *Muscoota*, a double-ended, schooner-rigged, paddle steamer, mounting eight guns. She was then lying in Man of War Harbor at Key West, Florida. It was an assignment back to hell. Mahan always remembered his nine and a half months in the bedbug-ridden junk heap that was the *Muscoota* as the most disagreeable duty of his career. As he told his mother, his orders to the vessel were "the most distasteful that ever reached me."[21]

He joined the ship on December 29, 1865. Her commanding officer, Commander Thomas Pattison, came on board two days later. The crew of approximately 160 enlisted men and 15 Marines was in a state of fractiousness bordering on mutiny. Morale was non-existent. The *Muscoota*, detailed as part of a naval build-up in the West Gulf designed to uphold the recently rediscovered Monroe Doctrine by persuading the Emperor Maximilian and his French army of occupation to leave Mexico, was in no condition to fight anything or anyone. In more ways than one, she symbolized the Navy's sudden and tragic decline into helpless inadequacy after the Civil War. As a naval arm of the Monroe Doctrine, a policy about which Mahan later wrote at length, the *Muscoota* was a cruel joke.

No Mahan letters have survived the period of his grim duty in the *Muscoota*, but the log of the vessel for the period from 1865 to 1866 has survived. It consists of a dreary record of desertions, fighting, disobedience of orders, neglect of duty, profanity, drunkenness, and violations of various naval regulations, along with Mahan's notations of punishments (often solitary confinement on bread and water) meted out. Indeed, Mahan was almost constantly in attendance at summary and general courts-martial. On the other hand, there is no evidence that his voluntary service as chaplain of the *Muscoota*—he conducted divine worship every Sunday morning—in any way improved the behavior of the crew, although he undertook to bring all hands speedily to God. He later boasted that he had saved two souls in the disorderly crew, a spiritual harvest so modest that it would seem to suggest that even the Creator had all but abandoned the unhappy vessel. About the best that can be said for the power of Mahan's prayer was that he remained healthy when fever struck the vessel. Amusements aboard the ship were few, and seldom transcended the level of dressing the ship's dog in "soldier clothes" and otherwise tormenting the beast.

Ten days (in August 1866) at anchor off Brazos, Texas, represented the only tangible support the *Muscoota* gave Secretary of State William H. Seward's anti-Maximilian policy in Mexico. But even this modest contribution to American diplomacy was interrupted by an epidemic of "bilious fever" which swept through the crew in mid-August. Three men died, including the ship's surgeon. By August 20, 1866, some eight officers and more than eighty men were down with the malady. The *Muscoota* was no longer operable as a fighting ship. A volunteer crew from the *New Berne* had to be put aboard her, and she was sailed back to Pensacola Bay and into quarantine. So ended Mahan's first effort personally to sustain the Monroe Doctrine. In this particular area of American foreign policy his pen proved far mightier than his sword.[22]

Mahan was detached from the *Muscoota* on September 7, 1866, two and a half months before the agony of the sorry vessel was mercifully ended by act of decommissioning at Portsmouth, New Hampshire, on November 20, 1866. As was his custom, he went directly from Portsmouth to West Point for a well-earned leave. No sooner had he reached home, however, than he undertook to instruct Captain T. A. Jenkins, the new Chief of the Bureau of Navigation and Detail, in how to do his job. Specifically, he told Jenkins that if he was to be assigned again by the bureau as a first lieutenant afloat, "my position during five years back," he would need at least two weeks' notice properly to prepare himself to take the berth and get the vessel ready for sea. Such lead time was particularly important to an executive officer, Mahan argued, explaining to Jenkins why this was so. He further informed the bureau chief that he was representing the views of other officers as well as himself in the matter. He concluded his unsolicited lecture to Jenkins with the hope that he would not be assigned again to duty "for two or three months." Not surprisingly, the unimpressed Captain Jenkins had the outspoken Lieutenant Commander Mahan back on active duty within a month, ordering him to temporary ordnance duty at the Washington Navy Yard. It can thus be assumed that Mahan's first venture into the thickets of naval administrative reform was something less than a gigantic success.[23]

During much of the fall of 1866 Mahan suffered a serious attack of depression. He felt friendless, frustrated, and lonely. His were feelings, he later said, "of the nature of agony while they last—the heart crying bitterly for that which it has not, nor can have." His work at the yard did not interest him. Nevertheless, while stationed briefly in Washington he learned that the *Iroquois*, captained by Commander Earl English, was being outfitted in New York for deployment to the Far East, and that she would sail to Japan, via Brazil, South Africa, and the East Indies. Her mission was to support the opening of treaty ports in Japan in January 1868 and otherwise encourage and protect American merchant shipping in China, Japan, and the Philippines. When Mahan learned her itinerary and mission he applied for assignment to her as executive officer. He received his orders to the *Iroquois* on December 5, 1866, and reported on board on New Year's Day 1867. Unfortunately, he somehow managed to lose his orders and suffered the embarrassment of having to write Jenkins for a duplicate copy. So began Lieutenant Commander Mahan's unhappy 33-month cruise in the *Iroquois*.[24]

With his assignment to the *Iroquois* a new career chapter opened for Mahan. The Civil War was over. It was a war in which he had gained two ranks although he had seen no real combat. The ships in which he had served were scarcely prides of the U.S. Navy or any other navy. He ended his war service in a state of complete boredom. Then came malaria, followed by a near nervous breakdown. He had made no close friends during the conflict. The women to whom he had been attracted were either unattainable or unavailable. He was a lonely man, unsure whether he should even remain in the service.

On balance, the Civil War was not a glorious experience for Alfred Thayer Mahan. About the best he could say for it in later years was that its outbreak helped him prove his historical arguments against national disarmament and international arbitration. "When the people of two nations are antagonistic," he would frequently argue, "because of clashing interests, the peace can only be kept by force; like a policeman arresting two brawlers. As regards absence of armament making for peace, I always say: Look at our North and South in 1861. Never were two communities less ready, but they fought all the same, because interests clashed." It was also Mahan's dilemma that he never came to a firm and final conclusion on just why the war was fought. He was convinced only that the blockade established by the Navy along the Confederate coast had been the most important factor in assuring Union victory; that, together with the fact that in all war "numbers and money will eventually tell, as in our Civil War."[25]

III

With God in the *Iroquois*
1867-1869

I am going to begin keeping a journal soon which will be a sight to see, though it is not my intention that any mortal being save myself shall lay eyes on it. It will be a dark book indeed. My most hidden acts will be written in it. My only reason for not doing it is the fear lest all my precautions may be of no avail and the book be seen by some other.

Alfred Thayer Mahan to Samuel A'Court Ashe, March 25, 1859

True to his word, Mahan finally began keeping a daily personal journal during his cruise to the Far East in the *Iroquois*, 1867–1869. Half of it has survived. While it is not necessarily "a dark book indeed," it is a highly personal account of Mahan's thoughts, fears, temptations, and frustrations during the twenty-seventh and twenty-eighth years of his life. As an insight into the personality of Mahan it is without equal. The primary purpose of keeping the diary he made quite explicit: "I hope and pray that the system of self-examination thus attempted may be successful to the health of my soul, and to the glory of God." But it reveals much more of the man than this.[1]

Mahan and his earlier biographers have provided accounts of the cruise of the *Iroquois* in Japanese waters, details of which are available elsewhere. Suffice it to say here that the vessel participated actively in protecting and advancing American interests in the newly opened treaty ports in Japan, landed armed parties to effect this end when necessary, and helped to maintain order ashore during the Japanese civil war attendant on the restoration of the Meiji.[2]

A major dimension in any understanding of Alfred Thayer Mahan during his tour in the *Iroquois* is the fact that the future historian and philosopher of sea power became deathly afraid of the sea. Certainly he was during his service in the Far East. And there is no evidence that he ever wholly transcended this fear. Little of this terror was suggested in his letters home, although he did once confess to his mother that two or three rolls of the *Iroquois* during a gale just out of New York "almost terrified me." For home consumption, for the edification of his friends, and for the readers of his autobiography, Mahan's striving against the angry elements was invariably portrayed in heroic terms:

> You can hardly conceive the fearful splendor of such scenes—the wind roaring; the rain pouring pitilessly on you—the pitchy darkness, which prevents your seeing two feet from you; the vivid blue lightning, blinding you and yet showing every yard and rope clear as at the noonday; the ship rolling heavily from side to side, water smashing with each lurch—every now and then a sea coming on board; officers shouting, a few men replying and working like beavers; and many half stupified with amazement and awe—it is worth seeing; wonderful and grand to remember, but very trying to go through. . . . I prayed very earnestly and tried to bring my mind to face the thought of death near at hand—for we all believe our position to have been most critical.

Nor was Sam Ashe, in whom he confided much, ever told of the fear that possessed his friend whenever he put to sea. Mahan told him only that "I have some apprehensions of the cyclones at this somewhat boisterous season," but also reassured him that "I think I am justified in venturing with trust in Him who spreadeth out the heavens and ruleth the raging of the sea. I was fortunate in being able to receive the Communion this morning."[3]

On the other hand, Mahan's diary entries show that he was exceptionally nervous, irritable, depressed, sleepless, and queasy of stomach each time the *Iroquois* left harbor, that he was inclined to want alcohol during these periods to help bolster his courage, that he prayed with great fervor when faced with the necessity of going to sea, and that his fear of rough weather, real and anticipated, was always intense. When actually at sea, he was terrified. His diary is strewn with evidence of a fear so overpowering that one wonders why it was that he remained in the Navy. Something of this can be seen in the following at-sea observations scattered throughout the diary:

> Little annoyances have made me break out. . . . Shortish with everybody. . . . Had I not better discontinue drinking altogether? . . . I tried today to do my duty manfully and seeking His help out of fear. . . .

I have been very very anxious and troubled; yet by God's grace I have been enabled to bear up against my fears and depression. I have prayed earnestly and sought, having asked for peace with God, to give myself to my duties. . . . Have been more than usually anxious and fearful to-day, but this certainly is an alarming and dangerous coast to stronger hearts than mine. . . . God sustained me wonderfully through the gale, but . . . the reaction from the gale and this evil cowardice has made me fretful and . . . I get sick with fear, unable to attend to duty—yet not unable if I pray and strive. . . . Cowardice and lack of trust in God have been my worst tempters. . . . We have had much bad weather and I am so anxious; my mind seems half broken down by the strain. If I could only get out of the service how glad I would be to go. . . . I am depressed and irritable. I wish if it please God I might soon get home and get some rest from the unending ship and winds. I can scarcely keep down my murmuring because I am so frightened. . . . More anxiety tonight running through a passage of which little is known ex-cepting that dangers do exist, badly laid down probably. Here was where I thought I would enjoy cruising. God pity my weakness and anxiety; may it lead me to closer affiance with Him. . . . Today I have been weakhearted and depressed. My constant fearfulness still pursues me. . . . It is not the real danger but the constant fear that oppresses me. . . . It was raining so hard that I knew I could not relieve [the watch]. The weather is very bad. May God help me; it seems as though my nerves were going to give way under the pressure. I shall not be able to endure much more.

Mahan remained in the Navy and he endured; but there is no evidence that he ever again found going to sea a romantic and swashbuckling occupation—as he thought during his midshipman days it would be. In-deed, throughout the remainder of his career he attempted to avoid or postpone assignment to sea duty whenever the prospect reared its head.[4]

His fear of the sea was hidden in part behind a facade of outrage and annoyance with his fellow officers and with the crew of the *Iroquois* when something went wrong on board the vessel. Outwardly a perfec-tionist, inwardly unsure of himself, Mahan accepted minor shipboard mishaps with little grace and with even less sense of humor. He knew, of course, that he was no great seaman. "I am not very smart in this sort of work," he confessed, "but I hope I may do fairly." Still, when a "ter-ribly mortifying blunder" was made in handling sails, a fairly common occurrence in the *Iroquois*, Mahan was "greatly incensed." And he was not successful in controlling his temper at such frustrating moments. On one occasion he lost his temper at "an awkward mistake—and . . .

punished a number of men among whom was the blame of the mistake."
He considered his embarrassments in these instances to be among the
"great many trials of small kind" designed by God "to humble me."
Humble, Mahan was not. "I am neither humble nor willing to be humbled," he frankly admitted. He did, however, understand his limitations
as a practical seaman. Thus, when an awning collapsed one day, he "felt
it was in good degree owing to my own stupidity [and] I was terribly
vexed and mortified." On another occasion he sent out one of the ship's
cutters at dusk to search for an American merchantman reported aground
nearby; but he absent-mindedly neglected to provide the boat with a
compass. He acknowledged that this was a "wretched lack of foresight,"
a neglect that "caused me a great deal of self-reproach and anxiety."
Similar errors, accidents, and oversights—sloppy boat-handling, misplaced
gear, failure to get the vessel under way neatly, a clumsy performance
in anchoring the ship, the snapping of the main-topmast, slowness in
working the guns—incensed the perfectionist Mahan. One day he "found
a pail of slops sitting in the steerage, got very angry and made a considerable row. Was very surly, irritable, and somewhat unjust about this
time." In another instance the short-fused executive officer

> was much annoyed and angered at finding some more men on the sick
> list; this tried me a very great deal. I fought on the verge of defeat
> against my impatience and escaped not without a fall. Called a man a
> fool in my impatience, about another thing at the same time. . . . My
> troubles came on me at one o'clock; furling sails we did very badly
> and the *Oneida* beat us. I was very irritable during the early part of the
> afternoon, so much as hardly to be able to control myself at all. . . .
> My great trouble today has been my excessive irritability. . . .[5]

When, by Mahan's demanding standards, things went well—a reading
of his diary suggests that this was seldom—he cheered triumphantly.
Even when such routine operation as loosing sails was done successfully,
it earned a happy comment in his personal journal. He was particularly
pleased when the *Iroquois* beat the other vessels in the squadron in the
sail-furling contests and the longboat races occasionally held to occupy
the American crews and introduce an element of excitement and competitiveness into an otherwise boring existence on the station. These little
successes were good for Mahan's ego and his disposition and he regarded
them as personal victories. "The fortune of the day seemed to change
about this time," he remarked at the end of one particularly good day.
"Got the hammocks down, etc., then furled sails in doing which we made

remarkably good time, about which I boasted. Then painted ship rapidly and successfully. Temper and patience therefore have not been greatly tried this afternoon." And later: "I furled sails today at one o'clock by signal from the *Shenandoah*, beat her badly and crowed over it."[6]

Even though he agonized over what he conceived to be the daily mismanagement of the vessel by Captain Earl English, and privately berated himself for his own small contributions to such mismanagement, Mahan thoroughly disliked English's penchant for daily drills and exercises of the practice-makes-perfect variety. He found these make-work sessions useless and tedious, often because he feared something might go wrong that would show him in a bad light. In fine, he hated the "pottering housecleaning" that was the fate of a station ship confined most of the time to port. At the same time, he recognized that there was not enough useful work on board the *Iroquois* to keep the polyglot crew busy and out of trouble. "The fact is plain—we have not ordinarily aboard ship sufficient work to breed habits of application to it."[7]

Nor did the man who titled his autobiography *From Sail to Steam* have much interest in the "steam" part of the Navy between 1867 and 1869. There were frequent malfunctions of the Fulton engines mounted in the *Iroquois*, as there were in the steam plants of almost all the steam-and-sail vessels of the period. Steam propulsion was scarcely an exact mechanical science in the years following the Civil War. But Mahan went a bit far on one occasion when he "rejoiced at hearing of the defects of our boilers," a remark designed to annoy Captain English. He had no confidence in the *Iroquois*' engines and little use for her engineering officers. He expressed his views on this subject "very plainly" in the wardroom, in his letters to Ashe, and to his parents. "Our machinery," he complained, "is in very bad order. . . . Incredible is it not that a ship after being over a year at home should be sent away in such condition?" Other professional questions of a technical sort interested him not at all.[8]

Part of his disinterest in the operational Navy and his boredom with the routine of daily shipboard life can be traced to his conviction, an attitude that became progressively more pronounced during the *Iroquois* cruise, that he was really wasting his time in the service; and that there were more important and interesting things to do in life than being a naval officer. His existence in the *Iroquois* had reduced itself, he felt, to "trifling details" and "uncongenial professional duties." His time was "very harassingly run away with."[9]

To bring some order, direction, purpose, and useful activity into an otherwise stultifying existence, Mahan sat down on August 7, 1868, and carefully "drew up a plan for the day in order to save time and avoid the distraction from a multiplicity of pursuits." The plan set aside large blocks of time designated for secular and sacred reading, for study, for prayers and meditation, and for exercising, eating, drinking, and going ashore. Naval duty as such was confined to little more than two hours per day. From his point of view, that was about all the effort that the job of executive officer of the *Iroquois* was worth.[10]

Increasingly, therefore, Mahan felt the need for activities much more intellectually stimulating. As he expressed it in his diary in July 1868:

> I found myself perplexed by my pretty strong conviction that the employments to which I am forced are a waste of time, and by the opposite fact that I am bound to obedience and submission. . . . Felt depressed and vexed at the business on hand, and most severely the kind of work that I have to do, with [the] capacity I feel for much more intellectual work. My tendency was to despair, hardly an exaggerated word in view of my keen feelings of how, humanly speaking, I had thrown myself away.

Feeling as he did, he spent much time "cudgelling my brains for plans for that future that may never be." Obviously, he expected too much of the Navy, although he might later have appreciated the kernel of truth in the waggish observation that the U.S. Navy was a wondrous machine designed by geniuses to be run by idiots. Mahan was no idiot. And that was the basis of his problem as an officer in the Navy.[11]

The problem caused him to invest his spare time—a commodity in plentiful supply on board the *Iroquois*—in reading and studying. His secular reading centered on history, particularly the works of John Lothrop Motley, Leopold von Ranke, and François Pierre Guillaume Guizot. Mixed with this was a dash of naval biography. He also read Thackeray, Longfellow's translation of Dante, and Tennyson. On a lesser literary level he read the popular novels of the day, some in French, others in Spanish. He referred to these novels as his "promiscuous reading," and felt a certain guilt in spending his time in such frivolous literary pursuits; such reading, he noted, "always disagrees with me and makes me a little sick." As part of a self-improvement program, and as an act of self-discipline, sometimes as penance, he regularly set aside time for the study of Greek, French, and Spanish. French and Spanish went well; Greek he could not master. "I am almost disheartened at the look of the verbs," he complained. His letters home contained requests that books be sent to him on the station. He also asked for the *New York Semi-Weekly*

Times and *The Army and Navy Journal*. If he was nothing else, the executive officer of the *Iroquois* was a dedicated reader.[12]

That Mahan spent a great deal of time in his tiny cabin reading, studying, and meditating was not unrelated to the fact that he was unpopular with his fellow officers. While he occasionally felt "anxious to try and get closer relations with the younger officers," he was never able to break through to them. He had "an inordinate longing for men to speak well of me," and he tried on occasion to impress his good qualities on others; but basically he was a lonely and isolated person. Indeed, his Anglophilia was such that he was usually more at ease in the wardroom of British ships on the station than in the wardroom of the *Iroquois*. "My manner is very bad to subordinates," he decided, "sneering and cynical. I must be very unpopular."[13]

He was. The chatty diary kept by Marine Lieutenant Michael Gaul when he served in the *Iroquois* does not mention Mahan at all. The first lieutenant might as well have been on the planet Mars. Mahan's isolation was partly because he had no patience with, respect for, or toleration of the humor, gossip, and "entirely worldly" conversation that permeated the *Iroquois* wardroom and the other wardrooms in the squadron. Only three of the ten officers in the *Iroquois* were over thirty; none was married. They were all profane, lascivious, high-spirited young men who had just been through a war and who thoroughly enjoyed drinking, fornicating, gambling, and gossiping. They were, in truth, entirely normal. Mahan did not feel comfortable in their presence. Their earthy conversations were too frequently "of a kind that I would rather not have joined." He objected to their recitations of "scandal," to "speculative conversations that are *not* productive of good," and to gossip about the sexual misdemeanors ("acts of impurity") of various officers in the squadron. Still, Mahan could not always resist the temptation to pass along salacious information himself, and he occasionally listened to wardroom gossip "without disapproval, with interest—with satisfaction."[14]

He took no part, however, in gambling on the intra-squadron boat races, a widespread practice on the station. The frequent use of profanity by officers and men annoyed him greatly. "The swearing etc. is very offensive and very wanton on board here," he informed his mother, "and I sometimes feel inclined to attempt the strong hand with it—but I hesitate; the step would be very full of personal annoyance—not only an unpopular step but one difficult to carry out." He considered talk about sex particularly improper. When the conversation of the officers turned to "sanitary precautions against syphilis," a major health problem in the squadron, Mahan branded the discussion "unsavory." The "morals of factory girls," and those of "Charlestown Navy Yard girls," were also "unclean subjects and to be avoided." He opposed the legalization of prostitution, a favorite topic of wardroom debate in Yokohama and Hong Kong, and preferred not to discuss the subject. "The conversation sometimes took rather an objectionable form," he remarked on one occasion, "which I did not want to smile at, and yet found it difficult to avoid." In general, Mahan cut a dour conversational figure in the wardroom and seems to have enjoyed "a jolly laughing time" there only in relief at not having to put to sea or when coming in from sea.[15]

Whatever his prim public views on questions sexual, the fact of the matter was that during his cruise in the *Iroquois* Lieutenant Commander Mahan thought a great deal about women, about sex, and about marriage. The end pages of his diary were decorously covered with the neatly lettered given names of numerous young ladies of his acquaintance. Women were very much on his mind. He frequently confessed to "abominable lustful thoughts that at times assail me," and was often "tempted to lust," and to harboring "sensual thoughts to which I do not earnestly close my ears." The fact was that "impure" and "gross" reveries frequently "assaulted" him and were most disturbing to him. So too was the realization that he would sometimes awaken in the morning "with a tendency to soft and sensual thoughts" which "tempted slightly to impurity." From these temptations, thank heavens, he was "speedily delivered by God's grace." Letters from home "tended to put me in a little flutter, by their mention of the other sex. No doubt nature claims her own of me. How will it result?"[16]

It resulted, ultimately, in marriage to Ellen Lyle Evans, of Philadelphia and New York, in June 1872. Meanwhile, uppermost in his mind was the married woman (he called her the "Nonpareille") he had met in Newport in 1862. In October 1868, while his ship was at sea between Hiogo-Kobe and Nagasaki, he explained to Ashe the continuing, though somewhat tenuous, hold she had on him:

> I confess candidly I prefer men in the general to women; perhaps a little on the sour grape ground, for though I am told I am good looking, I don't think I take with the sex. There are some few, foremost among them the Nonpareille, whom I am devoted to, and think charming. Nothing I like better than to be with them; but as I have friends among men, so I have among women, each individual tub standing on its own bottom, with little reference to sex—save perhaps in one. I think I still love her, as I once did passionately. But when you come to a simple question of sex, on the whole commend me to men.

As the trip wore on, Mahan thought more and more of his "Nonpareille." By February 1869, when he was in Hong Kong, he confessed in his diary that "I have spent some time today thinking of her. I wonder whether God does mean to let me be truly, purely faithful to her—without sin or offence in His eyes. There is something very sweet to me in the thought. Yet not free from taint of self."[17]

Mahan was, indeed, "truly, purely faithful to her" while he was in the *Iroquois*. There is certainly no suggestion in his journal that he was in hot pursuit of the few eligible young Western ladies resident in the foreign colonies of Yokohama, Hong Kong, Shanghai, Kobe, Nagasaki, or Manila—as he had vigorously chased the young women of Annapolis a decade earlier. He did not dance. He was still shy and awkward in the presence of women, and he participated infrequently in social activities ashore involving them. Generally, he avoided the company of females. "Have remained aboard all day, hardly moving out of the cabin, and so free from many of my temptations," he wrote in March 1869. His attitude toward women in general remained fashionably patronizing. As he told his teen-age sister Jenny: "I have fancied a good many girls a little, in my time; quite as much I imagine as some men have women to whom they proposed and I have little faith in first or very early loves. I have heard too many men laugh over their early fancies and rejections not to feel regret when I see them come to anything." Mahan would wait. As he explained to his mother from Yokohama in April 1868:

> All the women in town are married, which is rather a recommendation to my taste. I rather like ladies society, and for a perhaps strange reason, it disenchants me. While condemned to my messroom society they become enveloped in a misty atmosphere of I know [not] what fascination; those ashore I know, who are sweet and pleasant, become half angels. Association naturally dispels illusion to some extent . . . all "charm" in the literal sense of the word vanishes; and I think my mind and temper is more healthful in consequence. Does this sound conceited? It feels so a little, and affected. But I will humble myself to acknowledge that I have felt charm which endured association. Such cannot exist for many women at any time, for more than one at once; except when debarred from their society.[18]

When Mahan went ashore in Japan and China he did so usually to play billiards, take long walks, ride horseback through the surrounding countryside (in Yokohama he bought his own horse for $50), have dinner, attend church, buy souvenirs, or visit briefly with various British and American families in their compounds. He did not frequent the local houses of prostitution, or generally deport himself in any manner other than that of an officer and a gentleman. When he got gloriously drunk, as he frequently did, it was decently effected in the relative privacy of the wardroom of one of the American or British warships in the harbor. He made no spectacle of himself ashore.[19]

Instead, he used many of his hours ashore carefully to observe the country and the people and to gather the material that went into his delightfully descriptive letters home. He had a sharp eye for internal Japanese politics, and his letters from Hiogo describing some of the events of the Japanese civil war, 1867–1868, were unusually perceptive for the time and place. This is not to say that Mahan liked or respected the Japanese. Although he agreed that many of them were quaint, he thought them a ludicrous race. He thought, too, that they lacked the martial virtues necessary to national greatness. But so did many American naval officers in 1940 and 1941. "It is a very small race—and nearly beardless, which tends to make them appear like boys playing at soldiers," he noted.

This attitude could be traced in part to the fact that Mahan in 1868 fully accepted the body of convictions that later in the century came to be called the "white man's burden." "Are a pack of savages to stand in the way of the commerce of the world?" he once asked in reference to Britain's seizure and exploitation of Aden. The imperious British way of doing things abroad fascinated him. He was particularly impressed with the precision, efficiency, and appearance of the British army and naval units he encountered in various places around the world, and with the general tone, organization, and administration of the British Empire. The mild case of Anglophilia that he had contracted at the Naval Academy became between 1867 and 1869 a serious disease from which he was destined never to recover. "When compared with our penny policy there is something grand in the display England makes," he remarked. Conversely, he was appalled at the low quality of the American ministers and consuls sent out to the Far East by the administrations of Andrew Johnson and Ulysses S. Grant.[20]

Ironically, at the time he was keeping his diary, Mahan appears to have had a better appreciation of internal Japanese politics than he did of the political agonies of his own distracted country. Indeed, he was as far removed from the political and social problems of Reconstruction as he had been from those related to the onset of the Civil War. His main source of information on Reconstruction in the South was Sam Ashe who was struggling to make a living as a lawyer in Wilmington, North Carolina. Seen through the eyes of Ashe, all Radical Republicans were

"Black," and President Andrew Johnson was a "scoundrel" beneath contempt. As he commiserated with Ashe:

> I feel deeply how annoying and trying the present state of affairs at home must be [to] you; as in some measure it is to us all. I am not myself desirous of bolting the entire negro [question]—and hope, somewhat sanguinely, that the ultraism of the Radicals may work our deliverance. But I have no faith in the Democratic party. We must all pray for the best, and comfort ourselves with the thought of the land which is very far off—but where these accursed political mongerings will have no place.

On the other hand, Mahan had no respect for that "arrogant pride of family . . . latent in a very large proportion of Southerners"; nor, when pressed by foreigners, could he really explain to them the difference between Democrats and Republicans at home. But as a naval officer, he thought it improper publicly to denounce the president of the United States. In sum, Mahan was apolitical at this stage of his career. He knew very little about American domestic politics and he generally sought to avoid "loud-mouthed" political discussion in the wardroom, not always with success.[21]

The complex problems of Radical Reconstruction in the South, insofar as he understood them at all, he viewed narrowly in terms of the personal difficulties of his old friend Sam Ashe. The letters Ashe wrote to Mahan from North Carolina in 1866 recounted the political and economic disasters the defeated and occupied state was experiencing and, more specifically, the desperate financial situation in which the Carolinian found himself. Mahan responded instinctively and generously to Ashe's plea for assistance, thanks to an ample annual salary as a lieutenant commander of $2,343. In late 1866 or early 1867 he sent Ashe $500, which was accepted as a loan. In October 1869 he wrote Ashe from Hong Kong offering the struggling young lawyer an additional loan of $500 "or even more" and refusing "any such usurious interest as 8 per cent" on the transaction. "If you wish," he wrote, "I will consent to receive the same interest as I should otherwise have got." Ashe certainly needed these loans. They helped him keep body and soul together until his law practice, launched in Wilmington in January 1867, began to pay. By January 1870 the lawyer was beginning to fare somewhat better. "Your ultimate success I have not doubted," Mahan assured him, "but in the complicated and embarrassing state of things that have so long excited at home, particularly in the South, I did fear that a longer time would elapse before you saw your way clear." The loans, totaling several thousand dollars, were re-paid in May 1875 and in May 1879, at Mahan's urging, at a time when Mahan himself was desperately in need of money. "Without any expensive habits," he confessed to Ashe, "I have never been able to hold on to money further than to keep myself out of debt."[22]

It is well that Mahan maintained his friendship with Ashe by mail since it is clear from his journal that he made no close friends in the *Iroquois*. He variously characterized his fellow officers as weak, inconsistent, lazy, unreasonable, incompetent, loudmouthed, and uncooperative. Their presumed derelictions of duty were promptly reported to Captain English, a man whom Mahan also detested. Tension in the *Iroquois* wardroom was never far below the surface. But mostly Mahan reserved his disgust, harassment, and venom for Lieutenant Arthur H. Fletcher. Just why young Fletcher was chosen by Mahan as chief whipping boy of the *Iroquois* wardroom is not clear. It may have had to do with Fletcher's alleged agnosticism—this at a time when Mahan was searching tirelessly for God. Whatever the reason, Mahan alternated between attempting to save Fletcher's soul ("I gave my afternoon mainly to the writing up of an argument for our faith which I intend for Fletcher") and hounding him professionally. Fletcher could do no right. Mahan considered him "a miserable officer . . . trying to his superiors" and was quite certain that he had "never sailed with a person so thoroughly disagreeable to me as he is." As the cruise wore on, Mahan's feelings toward the hapless Fletcher became "bitterly wicked"; indeed, to Mahan's mind Fletcher was "more and more foolish as time passes over his head." The fact that Mahan signally failed to convert Fletcher to "our faith," meaning Mahan's version of High Church Episcopalianism, may have had something to do with his constant hazing of the young officer. Fletcher, in turn, had no love for Mahan.[23]

Fortunately for Fletcher, Mahan had other shipboard personal dislikes which absorbed some of his boundless critical energies. Specifically, he developed and maintained a pronounced antipathy toward his skipper. Captain English was a precise, no-nonsense, by-the-book naval officer. He was also a perfectionist who demanded speed and snap in the carrying out of his orders. Mahan, however, considered him highly authoritarian, petty, provoking, possessed of poor taste, and unnecessarily meddlesome in the daily business of the executive officer. More to the point, Mahan bitterly and loudly expressed his negative opinions of English in the wardroom, on deck, ashore, and to virtually anyone who would listen. Free speech of this sort was not highly appreciated in the Navy. There were thus several "unpleasant scenes" between the captain and his executive officer, and Mahan, on occasion, was barely able to control his considerable temper in English's presence. It was a tense situation at best. Indeed, Mahan described English as "the most provoking person for a superior that I have ever known," a man given to "authoritarian discourses," who "thinks he knows more than anyone else extant." That he knew more about handling a ship than did Mahan, the latter did not deny. There was no criticism of Captain English's skillful seamanship.[24]

There was, however, much criticism by Mahan of Rear Admiral Stephen C. Rowan, senior officer of the American squadron in the Far East. Mahan thought Rowan a peculiar and secretive figure, particularly in his habit of concealing operational plans from the captains and officers of the squadron until the last minute.[25]

Toward the enlisted men in the *Iroquois* Mahan was sharp, demanding, short-tempered, and often unreasonable. Not that the crew deserved coddling. It was a fairly typical naval crew of the post-Civil War period. Only about one-quarter, or 58, of the men were American. Most of the rest were Irish, followed in numbers by Germans and French. Almost every European nation was represented. A scattering of Negroes, Orientals, and mixed-bloods of one sort or another completed the international potpourri. Desertions were common. Drunkenness was a major problem. Theft, insubordination, and fighting were of constant concern to the officers. The frequent movement of enlisted men from one ship to another in the squadron, as the result of desertions, expired enlistments, and sickness (usually smallpox), added still another element of crew instability. Mahan complained periodically of the "shorthandedness of the crew and consequent difficulty of doing anything properly."[26]

Not surprisingly, Mahan spent a great deal of his waking time participating in courts-martial proceedings, as the officers of the *Iroquois* struggled to maintain order and discipline in the ship. At one point, according to Michael Gaul, the situation deteriorated to near-mutiny. This occurred when one of the midshipmen overheard the use of profane language on deck one evening. Failing to identify the culprit, he ordered the entire crew to stand sea watches when the vessel reached Hong Kong the next day. As Gaul reported the denouement:

> Last night the captain had the men standing sea watches and toeing a seam on the quarterdeck all the watch. In the midshipman who is the cause of all this coming on board, he was hissed by all the watch. Later in the night all the watch laid down and would hardly get up. In the morning it seemed as though the crew were just about ready for mutiny

and only needed a leader. During the day, however, overtures were made by both parties and efforts were made to find out the offending person and a clue was found.[27]

The fractious crew of the *Iroquois* was seldom in fighting trim. "The men are a little restless and unsettled after their liberty," Mahan remarked on one occasion. "I want very much to see exercise, etc., resumed thus we may break them in again." He was genuinely grateful when the liberty boat returned from shore with only a few incapacitated drunks aboard. Usually the entire liberty party had to be poured back into the ship.[28]

Mahan had little patience with crew malingering. On more than one occasion he "suffered a good deal from nervousness today, imagining and anticipating trouble with the crew of some kind." He was often "fretted and worried by the misconduct of the men." He frequently spoke "very harshly and angrily" to the enlisted rates and was quick to "put a man in irons for disrespect which I think was just enough." He was "very much irritated by a piece of neglect of duty on the part of a subordinate." He also had to be constantly alert to the presence of liquor in the crew quarters. It was the powder that could blow the ship apart at any time. To this incendiary condition was added Mahan's own violent temper. "My temper snappish as it is apt to be on deck," he confessed; "and I forget that men have feelings that can be hurt by sneers, etc."[29]

Mahan's temper was indeed quick and towering. It was one of his least desirable characteristics and it was a weakness that he was destined to carry throughout his naval career. He was, he told his mother, "prey to violent fits of wrath at times which almost invariably overcome me." His temper was "very bad when balked—childishly so almost"; in fact, "the more I reflect on my temper the more convinced I am that my natural disposition, speaking only humanly, is most abominable." As he confessed in his diary:

> Lack of patient and meek submission is the main cause [of] my sins of the tongue . . . against my superior officers. . . . This lack of patience is a most insidious [fault] of mine. It appears so very absurd and mistaken what my superiors have ordered—that it cannot be wrong to characterize and complain of them. Now thinking coolly I know the folly of this. . . . It is my great and besetting sin I verily believe [one] that will beset me through life.

This unprofessional shortness of temper contributed to his sense of "aloneness" and to his feeling of "great isolation" in the *Iroquois*. He found life in her "often hard to bear—and it weighs on me more—for that I cannot feel sure that I am in earnest desirous of doing what I should do."[30]

It is not unlikely that Mahan's nearly complete personal estrangement from the officers, crew, and captain of the *Iroquois* was due also to his vanity. This, like his temper, was still a major factor in his personality, as it had been during his unhappy days at the Naval Academy. It had not subsided much since 1859. It was, however, somewhat better concealed than it had been a decade earlier. More importantly, Mahan had come to recognize it as a fault in his character and was attempting to treat it as such. At least he was perceptive enough to notice in the mirror that his personal appearance had atrophied a bit and that the young midshipman of 1859 who considered himself the handsomest of all men had become the lieutenant commander of 1868 who was "beginning to show the marks of time a little on my face—wrinkles and creases are making their appearance." By the time he was thirty-five, he was nearly bald.

Personal appearance aside, in his daily professional relations with his fellow officers he continued to insist that "I *will* have my own way," and he admitted that "I am very fond of hearing my own thoughts." He knew that his "vain thoughts are terrible to think of." Criticism or censure by another officer produced an instant explosion. "The whole thing is I lack humility, to submit my self-will to others," he allowed. The problem was indeed his highly developed sense of selfness:

> I build day dreams of good done, convincing words spoken, victorious arguments, souls turned to God—by me, me the central figure of the whole. I am harsh, overbearing, and sneering to offenders, men in many cases whose faults are akin to my own . . . my thoughts wandered much, and a good deal to those fancied interviews and conversations in which self is always the chief center and object of interest. . . . One of the greatest faults that I have recently noticed in myself is the intense "self"-ishness of my thoughts. It is continually of myself, my ship, my thoughts, my experience, that I am in fancy speaking; not only in fancy but in fact I want to talk a great deal too much [about my] own self.

Unfortunately for the unhappy Mahan, he was so sealed off, so excluded from the normal society of the *Iroquois* that he had few opportunities to talk with others about his favorite subject—himself; or about much of anything else. Only occasionally, and in wardrooms not his own, was he able to indulge in such happy subjects as "self glorification as to my performances when a midshipman." Mostly, he talked to himself in his diary, lonely conversations, at best.[31]

It was Mahan's aloofness and boredom, his feeling of professional inadequacy, his disinterest in the Navy, his fear of the sea, his sexual frustration, his theological dilemmas (about which more later), and his desire
to be accepted into the society of the squadron that turned him simultaneously to God and to liquor. To put the matter flatly, Lieutenant Commander Alfred Thayer Mahan had a drinking problem while he was
serving in the *Iroquois*. It was one that he overcame; and it seems never
to have troubled him again in his career or in his life. But in the *Iroquois*
it was a distinct problem, or so he said at the time.

His drinking was related to his constant feeling of nervousness and to
his occasional bouts with severe depression. That he was frequently tense
and nervous is a fact made clear by his diary. He was most nervous when
faced with the distasteful prospect of putting to sea, but the feeling was
more or less constant. In any event, he was often "nervously uncomfortable and somewhat irritable," a condition that often caused his skin to
erupt. Nervous headaches plagued him. "I have found myself," he said,
"very subject to nervousness and excitability, a frequent trouble with me
when business presses." Nervousness impelled him to drink and drinking
made him nervous. It was a vicious circle.[32]

His nervousness, tension, and fear not infrequently gave way to periods
of deep despondency and melancholia—to what he called his "brown
study." He had experienced these bouts with melancholia before—in 1856
when he entered the Academy and again at the Washington Naval Yard
in 1866. They were "of the nature of agony while they last." He thus
complained often of his "low spirits," his "depressed and bad humor," his "gloomy, unhappy mind," his "general lassitude and depression,"
the fact that his mind was "in a very unhealthy state," and his tendency
to fall into "one of my despondent, cheerless frames of mind." These
dark moods came upon him every few months and would last as long
as a full week. "The dull cheerlessness and despondency still hangs to
me," he wrote in January 1869. "I dread everything, all sorts of contingencies. I am a slave in the matter." It particularly worried him that he
was indentured to alcohol:

> This morning I again lay in bed late still feeling much under the
> weather, and oh I am so dreadfully depressed. It seems to me as though
> things were getting almost hopeless for me. That miserable after dinner
> excess of drinking and smoking that has been so frequently committed
> —darkening all my hopes of heaven—benumbing all my physical ener-
> gies and leaving me as I now am in a state of morbid depression. Re-
> solves so broken—so dishonored. What shall I do?

What Mahan tried to do during his tour in the *Iroquois* was frankly to recognize that he *had* a drinking problem, to regulate his intake, and to relate his vows not to drink to his daily communion with God. He did a great deal of praying in the gloom of his hangovers. And hangovers he had—many of them. "Have been unstrung all today," he lamented on one occasion.[33]

That he understood his weakness there is no doubt. His diary is filled with his recognition of it. He rejoiced and praised God when he got through a day without a drink or kept a vow not to drink; he made excuses for himself when he broke a vow, and he berated himself sharply when he succumbed knowingly to temptation. The fact of the matter is that Mahan could not hold his liquor. It made him sick and irritable and it inflamed an already hair-trigger temper. He was also convinced that drinking impeded his path toward salvation, if for no other reason than it left him in such sad shape that he could not properly say his prayers. As he stated this particular problem:

> Yesterday made a second excursion up to the Moon Temple; drank on the trip so as to feel it a little but not so as to be sin. But unfortunately I did not stop here, but drank more and elsewhere not having made any vow, so when I came to my prayers, I could not clear my head well. I sinned in drinking too much. This morning I am of course suffering for my sins. I do not feel any poignant sorrow, but I trust I shall be enabled yet to strive without either undue despondency or presumption.

"Wrong wrong!" he exclaimed on another occasion. "Drank some whiskey and so could not pray."[34]

One of his approaches to his dilemma was to make solemn, formal vows not to drink. First he tried stopping for a week at a time. After some initial success with abstention on a week-to-week basis, he backslid. Then he tried, "as a corrective to drinking," a plan to "vow each day at noon for 24 hours not to drink excepting at meals, unless visiting or receiving visits from foreign officers." But since the British, French, Prussians, and Danes all maintained naval squadrons on the Asiatic Station, this self-imposed prohibition was something less than onerous. In any event, Mahan drank on. In late November 1868, while at sea, and while quite upset by "anxious carefulness and nervousness about the ship's prospects," he "meditated a great deal" about his drinking, asked God for "guidance and grace," and finally devised an elaborate scheme to deal with the situation:

My idea is to resolve—Not to drink any more until the ship is ordered to return to the United States—excepting in company—meaning thereby when I am invited out to dine, or have to ask others to see me—and leaving scope for an occasion like the going home of a ship—or a birthday. And when dining out to limit myself to the pint bottle [ale] and two glasses of sherry. But not to drink on excursions, or from fancied fatigue. The late gale was probably as severe a trial of my physical endurance as I am likely to undergo. My object is to prevent the flesh from becoming master of the spirit.

In spite of the liberality of this proposed arrangement, Mahan soon slid backward. For this reason, a New Year's resolution, dated January 1, 1869, which he titled "Rules for My Life," included another "Rule for Drinking" that limited him to "a glass of sherry before and a pint bottle at dinner." This resolve, like most New Year's resolutions, lasted less than a month. Indeed, on the very day that he determined to reduce his intake he was "persuaded . . . that I have been mistaken in some of the restraints which I have in days past proposed to lay upon myself; the character of St. Paul's denunciations of bondage to elements and mere fleshly wisdom has caused this. Is not the Temperance stand of New England of this type?" By late January 1869 Mahan's exercise in controlled temperance had gone by the board, broken during a trying moment at sea when he suffered his usual fear and anxiety and turned again to the surcease that he found in alcohol.[35]

Additional pressures of the sort that impelled Mahan to fear, drink, mental depression, and spiritual lamentations were brought to bear on him when he was appointed acting commanding officer of the *Iroquois*. This occurred at Hong Kong on February 19, 1869, as the result of a shake-up that recalled Admiral Rowan to the United States and elevated Earl English to acting command of the squadron. Mahan remained in his billet until May 1869 when the *Iroquois* returned to Japan. Later that month, he fell seriously ill with malaria. He was hospitalized in Nagasaki during most of June and part of July, an event that led to the cancellation of his orders to the *Ashuelot* as commanding officer. Released from medical confinement, he returned to Yokohama in mid-July and was assigned as commanding officer of the *Aroostook*. He remained in that broken-down hulk until she was sold in Yokohama in September. Shortly after the sale, he departed for home. Thus, during his final five months in the Far East, he was never entirely well.

His promotion to the temporary command of the *Iroquois* in February 1869 inflated his ego and caused him to take generous stock of himself as a naval officer. As he wrote in his diary in March 1869:

I do not think I have been a bad first lieutenant—my captaincy is too recent. I used to reproach myself a great deal with the infrequency of my inspections of certain parts of the ship; yet I do not think that very marked fault really existed. Orders were good, the ship was essentially clean though not up to a model kitchen. Things were allowed and encouraged to go along by themselves as far as possible. I certainly did not come up to the conventional idea of an executive officer—puttering round every job, interfering, faultfinding, managing and controlling everywhere. It is open to doubt which system is best. Of one fault I cannot clear myself and that is procrastination. I do put off—put off continually—and without sufficient cause.[36]

What Mahan learned as commanding officer of the *Iroquois* was that he was even more isolated from shipboard society, if that were possible, than he had been as her executive officer. "I wonder how the old hermits stood it," he asked. In sum, he experienced what thousands of naval officers before and since have known as the "loneliness of command." He certainly wanted the command, however, and had angled successfully for it with Captain English. He liked the power and leverage that went with the job and the relaxed regime in port that a commanding officer enjoyed. "The quiet life of a commanding officer in port does not present the same difficulties and trials as an executive billet," he observed. At the same time, he began better to appreciate his former skipper's insistence on absolute precision, and, like English, he was extremely upset when something went awry. "This afternoon the crew were exercised with the sails," he wrote. "I appreciated better than before the annoyance Captain English must have felt when things went wrong." More importantly, the sudden responsibility of command, combined with a Lenten vow, caused him to cut down substantially on his drinking. Nevertheless, he remained fearful of the sea and his "anxiety as commanding the vessel engrosses my mind even from my prayers." His temporary command produced no new confidence in his ability as a practical seaman. On one occasion, returning to Yokohama Harbor from target practice outside, having first prayed God for help, he managed to bring the *Iroquois* back into the busy anchorage without colliding with anyone. For this feat he was terribly pleased with himself. "Vanity excited," he wrote.[37]

Ironically, Mahan's struggle with Demon Rum was successfully terminated by the breakdown of his health in May 1869. The condition of his body was always a major concern to him and in his diary he carefully detailed his numerous physical ailments. Actually, he was something of a hypochondriac. While in the *Iroquois* he complained regularly and variously of dyspepsia and rheumatism. His feet hurt. He suffered the discomfort of sleeplessness, and he endured periods of sheer fatigue. Diarrhea plagued him. He occasionally complained of a feeling of clamminess. He discovered that brandy, taken medicinally, did little to relieve the symptoms or pain of these maladies. Quite the opposite.[38]

But mostly Mahan suffered digestive upsets and stomach disorders; he may well have had ulcers. Certainly, the conditions for ulcers were present—constant fear, tension, and frustration, indifferent shipboard food, and too much liquor. The stomach of a goat would have rebelled under such assault. He had a major stomach upheaval in July and August 1868, another flareup that October, and a violent attack in August 1869 just before leaving the station for home. His mood was much depressed by "that wretched gnawing at my stomach which is of late no stranger to me." At one point, in near despair, he asked rhetorically, "Can a person be gay with a constant belly ache?" Treatment with opiates by the ship's doctor brought only temporary relief. His liquor intake, however, decreased substantially during these painful attacks. Such were the fringe benefits of a bad stomach to Lieutenant Commander A. T. Mahan.[39]

Between these bouts with stomach disorders he suffered, in May 1869, a return of malarial fever. It was this illness that removed him from the decks of the *Iroquois* and landed him in hospital in Nagasaki. Later he was moved to a hotel there, where he spent a month convalescing. During this period there was, of course, no drinking at all. This, too, was a fringe benefit of malaria.[40]

Mahan's uncooperative stomach and his second major bout with malaria put an end to his drinking problem. And while he did not swing violently to the other extreme and become either a crusading teetotaler or prohibitionist, there is no evidence in his letters or papers that he ever again felt unsure of his basic self-control in the matter of liquor. He remained a moderate social drinker most of the rest of his life, always alert, however, to the dangers of alcoholism. His glancing brush with the disease was very educational.

Throughout the many vicissitudes of his unhappy time in the *Iroquois*, the thoughts that most occupied the mind of Alfred Thayer Mahan were God, Christianity, and Anglicanism. As even a casual reading of his letters and his diary suggests, the years from 1867 to 1869 were years of spiritual odyssey. Special hours were set aside for daily prayer and meditation and for sacred reading. Each diary entry was, to a certain extent, an exercise in spiritual self-examination, spiritual self-criticism and, occasionally, spiritual self-flagellation—in the manner of theologian Richard Hurrell Froude, who was a member of the Oxford Movement and whose own diary and other works Mahan read and admired. He wrestled thoughtfully and oft-times unequally with the problems of eschatology, biblical criticism, salvation, and redemption; and most frequently with the nature and reality of personal sin and behavior as these relate to separation from or approaches to the Godhead. Formally untrained in theology, determined to educate himself in the discipline and thereby more swiftly and easily commune with God, Mahan took on heavy study assignments while he was on board the *Iroquois*. It was this intellectual task, together with frequent outward manifestations of a self-conscious religiosity, that further set Mahan apart from his shipmates, increased his sense of isolation, and imparted to him a moralistic primness unusual in a red-blooded young American naval officer on the morally permissive Asiatic Station. Mahan took not a little pride in being thus different from the other officers in the squadron. When his friend Theron Woolverton once told him that "the only accusation made against my Christian character was that I was over-scrupulous," Mahan was "pleased and, I fear, elated." Or, as he put it while reading Richard C. Trench, *Notes on the Parables of Our Lord*:

> Have been meditating somewhat upon the parable of the Pharisee and Publican. Who the Publican may be in the case I don't know, but I do see that in myself there has been much thought of my not being as other men are—adulterers or drunkards or unjust. And when I think of it I see how many phases of that and kindred faults of self-gratulation or exaltation through comparison with others; I wish the sense of their multiplicity and embarrassment might convince me of the human impossibility of overcoming and so in some measure work their cure.

He had a high opinion of his own morality and his spirituality, even as he confessed that his self-satisfaction in recognizing his superiority was in itself sinful.[41]

Mahan's practice of religion between 1868 and 1869 was highly visible. He went ashore to church and to prayer meetings whenever possible. He organized, participated in, and frequently conducted, as lay reader, Sunday services on board the ship. "Give unto Thy servant wisdom and grace that Thy word read and preached by him may be blessed to his hearers and that he may receive the reward of a faithful minister," he prayed. Not infrequently, he conducted a private service—usually the Ante-Communion—for himself in his cabin. He encouraged the enlisted men to attend church and otherwise seek clerical guidance. In 1867 he joined and commenced to support what is now known as the Seamen's Church Institute of New York; indeed, it was Mahan who suggested the present name of the organization in 1904. He tithed regularly and, in 1868, contributed funds to the furnishing of the Episcopal Church of the Atonement in Tenafly, New Jersey. This particular beneficence interested him so much that he briefly "resolved to try and stop drinking in order to save money for the building a church at Tenafly (N.J.)." He was at all times and in many ways a busy Christian. He was a bit hungover at times, but he was never at a loss for work to perform in the vineyards of the Lord.[42]

In spite of this dedication to God's work, he strongly opposed compulsory attendance at Protestant church services on board the *Iroquois*. He had seen enough of such ecclesiastical compulsion at the Naval Academy and knew perfectly well that the long-range effect of such spiritual tyranny was negative. At the same time, he bemoaned the fact that so few of the officers and crew turned out for the voluntary Sunday services, and he rejoiced on those rare occasions when more than a handful of men appeared. The Royal Navy did not do much better in this regard. In 1867 Mahan attended the Christmas communion service aboard HMS *Rodney*, then at Hiogo, and the congregation consisted of only five persons, including himself and the celebrant. He was stunned. After all, the *Rodney* had a crew of more than 700 officers and men.[43]

Further, Mahan had not recovered from his aversion to the burning-sulphur histrionics and homiletics of "Old Slicky" Jones at the Naval Academy. He continued to have no use for "violent and ranting language" in sermons or for the "extempore prayers" offered during unstructured religious services he attended ashore. The emotional, pentecostal approach to God was not his.[44]

Instead, Mahan's main highway to God in 1868 and 1869 was paved with highly personal self-criticism, self-examination, self-abnegation, and with nearly constant prayer and meditation. This was the main concern of his diary; and it was the primary reason he kept such a journal in the first place—to measure daily his spiritual progress or decline. As a celestial score card, however, the diary reflects Mahan's feeling that he seldom broke par. His "sins" as he conceived and listed them, were numerous and dark. They included, in no special order, temper, vanity, gluttony, intemperance, profanity, conceit, failure to lead others to God, laziness, fear, inattention at prayers, desultory meditation, lack of religious fervor, contempt for others, injudicious conversation, procrastination, sensuous thoughts, insincerity, self-satisfaction, late rising, reading of French novels, backbiting, and lack of attention to shipboard duty. For deliverance from these and his other presumed spiritual weaknesses, he vigorously prayed

God—just as he also prayed God for good weather, for coming safely and successfully to anchor, for guidance while serving on courts-martial, and for direct assistance in accomplishing the simplest and most mundane of his daily professional tasks. The executive officer of the *Iroquois* was almost constantly at prayer.[45]

No human being could possibly be or become what Mahan demanded of himself. So intense at times was his daily program of self-flagellation that it literally fatigued him. "I discontinued the practice of self-examination during last week in order to rest myself," he wrote in June 1868. "I thought I would intermit my self-examination for a time but it does not pay," he wrote on another occasion. In fine, the discipline and machinery of self-examination became almost as important to him psychologically as the hoped-for spiritual result. No wonder he drank. By the self-imposed rules of the debilitating game he was playing with God, there could be no winners—only losers.[46]

The motive underlying Mahan's search for God through self-purification, was, of course, his thirst for immortality. He thought a great deal about eternal life on his voyage to the Far East in 1867. His "desire for a better country" was always a strong one. Thus when he learned that his 14-year-old sister, Jenny, then a student at Bolton Priory School in Pelham, New York, had become confirmed in the Episcopal Church he was ecstatic. He assured her that

> You in your turn will learn the deep pleasure of hearing that [one] whom you love dearly has embraced the same hope which you yourself have; you will know then how I am now rejoiced that the sister whom I love dearly but from [whom] on earth I must be much separated, and from whom death must soon part me here, is striving for the heaven where no sorrow or parting shall ever be known. While in that heaven the love and presence of God shall be our great delight and happiness, it is not forbidden to rejoice in the company of those dear to us. I most earnestly thank God for the goodness which He has shown us all, in leading you to Him. As He has begun so I trust He will finish the work.

Before reaching the station, he had decided that he would make use of his months of relative inactivity on board the *Iroquois* to test himself, to earn salvation by undergoing

> a discipline of doubt and uncertainty of myself. . . . The discipline of doubt, the bearing one's own burden is the very hardest to me, and I can see how very tempting Romanism must be to a mind so constituted.

> Not that I feel inclined to seek that refuge—I feel now too strongly convinced of the necessities of those inward struggles, in order to realize purification of the heart.

He felt, too, that his personal key to salvation turned importantly on his effort and ability to bring others to God as he himself made his own way to Heaven. He was convinced that he had been "the instrument in His hands of bringing two souls to confess themselves His servants" while serving in the *Muscoota* and he wished to repeat that modest missionary triumph in the Far East. As he told Ashe, it was his fervent hope that "it may please God to have chosen me to be of some use to Him" in the task of converting others. When, on one occasion, he learned that several Chinese in Shanghai whom he had helped proselytize had finally been converted to Christianity, Mahan was beside himself with joy: "I cannot analyze my feelings," he wrote, "it seems to me that there is a mixture of exaltation, gratification in the hope that altogether I have not lived for nothing." Success in such ventures proved elusive for Mahan. "Oh, that I might simply work out my own salvation in fear and trembling, but were in no way bound to strive and do anything for others," he moaned after one notable failure.[47]

To prepare himself better to do God's work, to discipline himself, to understand better and master the Christianity which he would espouse for the uplift of others, and to resolve his own theological doubts and uncertainties, Mahan undertook an intense program of sacred reading during his imprisonment in the *Iroquois*. Several hours a day were budgeted for this activity. Within the framework of Protestant source materials his tastes were catholic. He corresponded with his Uncle Milo at St. Paul's Episcopal Church, Baltimore, on theological questions and asked him to recommend readings in religion. While Mahan's correspondence with his beloved uncle has not survived, it is known that Milo sent Alfred various books and suggested that he read certain others. The specific titles of Milo's recommendations are not known. But they likely included some of the works Mahan mentioned in his diary as daily reading. It is known that he subscribed to the *Church Journal*, founded and edited by Milo and three of his General Seminary faculty colleagues, and that he read *The Churchman*, another Episcopal periodical. It is known, too, that he read and studied Edward M. Goulburn, Richard C. Trench, James A. Froude, Joseph Butler, Michael F. Sadler, Jeremy Taylor, Edward Putnam, Robert Leighton, Timothy Dwight, Ernest Renan, Henry Alford, Samuel Smiles, John R. Seeley, and Frederick W. Robertson. In other words, Mahan read a broad range of works in nineteenth-century Protestant theology, Church history, and Christian apologetics.

Not all of this study was a joy. While he found Seeley's biography of Christ "powerful and to the point," he regarded Butler's *The Analogy of Religion* as virtually incomprehensible. He "wavered over Renan's *Apostles*, very much irritated by his apparent unfairness." Indeed, the shock of reading Renan's rationalist views on Christianity actually drove him to "a little sherry and bitters, my vow having expired." At the same time, he found almost all of his theological reading heavy-going, tedious, and abstruse, and he was distressed to discover that if often put him fast to sleep. There were exceptions. He considered Edward Goulburn's *Thoughts on Personal Religion* the most satisfying tract he read while on board the *Iroquois*. Years later, in 1896, he said that it was "the book which more than any other has affected my spiritual life. . . . it lies unseen among the foundations of my best thought." He was also much influenced in later years by Seeley's *The Expansion of England* (1883) —more so perhaps than by his *Ecce Homo: A Survey of the Life and Works of Jesus Christ* published in 1866. Nevertheless, he invariably preferred "religious or other study" to the boredom of his daily professional duties.[48]

Mahan attempted to synthesize his religious reading into a working personal theology of salvation. One conclusion he reached was a certainty that "the priest, ministerially, absolves; that in the absolution pronounced, absolution is actually received, *through him*, by the believing penitent." As an Anglo-Catholic he accepted in part the Roman view of "priestly absolution." He was convinced, however, that a "corrupt view" of the matter had sprung up in the Church of Rome in that Rome encouraged the penitent to "regard the minister as the source of the power" to absolve, rather than teaching that God worked through the priest as a chosen instrumentality in the absolution process. Mahan was also critical of the Roman Church's "tendency to idolatry," and of the historical claims of the Bishop of Rome to spiritual and administrative primacy within Christendom. Notwithstanding these opinions, Mahan was not anti-Catholic. He had little patience with standard Protestant attacks on the presumed abuses and corruption of the Roman clergy.

He saw little at issue in the faith-versus-works salvationist arguments which had long separated Protestants and Roman Catholics. He thought instead that God's grace was transmitted to men through both channels. "I know the grace of God is not to be bought with money," he noted, "but I also know God is not unrighteous to forget your works that proceed of love." Accepting as he did the view that "absolution, benediction, baptism, Communion are all among His mysterious benefits which he dispenses by the instrumentality of men," mainly the ordained clergy, Mahan had no quarrel with Roman teaching on the role of the priest in the sacramental system. Indeed, he seems to have had more confidence in the sacramental road to salvation than in salvation through prayer alone:

> When we claim, as we justly do, that the prayer of a righteous man has power with God, we claim far more than we do in Priestly Absolution. For the prayer is an actual power orginating (by the working of the Holy Spirit but still) originating in the man; dependent in some measure on his sanctity a personal, not an official power. But the power of Absolution is simply official; not inherent but derived; therefore not dependent upon the priest's holiness. He is but the channel, though a lively one, through which the grace of God passes to man. And in all ordinary cases through such channel it must pass.[49]

Mahan had much greater difficulty with the Old Testament as a revealed source of truth than with either Roman Catholic or Anglo-Catholic theological doctrines. The more he read it, and read commentaries upon it, the more uncertain he became as to its historicity, its organic relationship to the New Testament, and its usefulness to him as a spiritual guide. He agonized over such dilemmas as the importance of Hebrew circumcision to the salvation of Christians. He found contradictory statements in the Old Testament which he attempted semantically (and unsuccessfully) to reconcile. He replayed the historical dates and numbers game of the Pentateuch, a problem to which he had been introduced by Milo Mahan's attack on Bishop Colenso. And it was apparently while he was serving in the *Iroquois* that he read his uncle's *Palmoni; or The Numerals of Scripture*. In any event, he agreed with his kinsman in Baltimore that the arithmetic of the Old Testament did not always scan. Having read E. M. Goulburn and been made aware of the arguments of Charles Darwin and Alfred Russel Wallace (or what Mahan vaguely called "the discoveries of science"), he knew, as did Milo, that the Genesis story of a six-day Creation culminating in Adam as the first man on earth was simply not tenable. But he attempted to salvage the crucial (to him) doctrine of Original Sin, weakened by the demise of the Adam and Eve allegory, by suggesting that there had existed on earth a pre-Adamic race of sinless men. This was not a satisfactory solution, as Mahan himself seemed aware. Darwin had seriously undermined the doctrine of Original Sin, and Mahan, search as he might, found no way adequately to shore it up.

So confused and uncertain of himself did he become in his quest for biblical certainty that he withdrew from shipboard discussions about the relationship between science and religion. He decided that in wardroom conversations "in which the attitude of science and religion towards one another" were discussed, it was "well to hold one's tongue." He came also to avoid all conversations "in which religious matters were touched upon" because "these are dangerous and too apt to trench into irreverence." Nonetheless, he wrestled heroically with the logical contradictions inherent in the Free Will-versus-Predestination dichotomy, and concluded, in a somewhat unimaginative way, that "the truth of God's predestination—not incompatible with His justice—lay in this very thing, viz: that with some He employs such dealings as *should* lead to repentance, with others, the elect, such as He knows *will* lead to it. In all cases the will of man is free." Mahan realized, too, that the parables were interpretively elastic and that one could read into them almost anything he wished. On one occasion he delighted himself by producing what he thought to be a new and improved interpretation of the parable of the laborers in the vineyard. It was a game with Scripture that any number could play.[50]

Much if not most of Mahan's theology remained fairly traditional—this in spite of (or because of) his questing study and meditation on board the *Iroquois*. The Virgin Birth, the Passion, the Resurrection of Jesus Christ were articles of faith he did not question. The centrality of Christ in the daily life of a professed and professing Christian, and the emulative dimension of the worship of Christ, he accepted without demur. He seemed unaware of, or disinterested in, the debate then beginning in Christian scholarly circles on the relationship between the historical Jesus and the theological Christ. He did, however, understand the difference between the Gospels as history and biography and the Epistles as doctrine; but he was not prepared to commit himself to M. F. Sadler's view "that to separate the doctrine from the history—to base the appeals upon the doctrine—to form the character of the believer upon the doctrines—to subordinate the historical recollection of Christ's life and death to the reflection upon, and self-application of, certain abstract doctrines, is contrary to God's plan as indicated in His Word—and therefore wrong." Mahan, instead, saw the doctrine as superior to the history since the history recorded in the Bible was often contradictory in a factual sense.

[71]

The Devil was a very real being to Mahan, the means by which he explained his sins, weaknesses, and lapses—especially when he broke his vows pertaining to drinking. He frequently brooded about the "Irreparable Past" and wondered whether he could ever square his morally overdrawn account with God. His view of immortality also remained traditional: "We are here in the state of struggle for the crown . . . we are now in the vineyard to labor. The reward and the crown are to come hereafter." He believed that all manner of men would eventually be saved, although he was just as certain that a class structure existed within the salvation process:

> In asserting that God's Word does not mention an inner peculiar church . . . is not meant to imply that there are not in the church those who are real children of God—and others who are not—because the Scripture distinctly teaches that such divers classes do exist.

He neatly worked himself around the much too democratic (for a naval officer) notion that "the last shall be first and the first last" with the convenient, more comfortable, and more conservative counter-quotation that "many are called but few chosen." He was convinced that "different capacities" characterized men. This belief permitted Mahan to accept as he found it the sharp social stratification in American society of the middle-nineteenth century and the similar gradations manifested in the Navy's officer corps.[51]

In the final analysis, Mahan attempted to solve the multiple problems of his personal loneliness, his professional boredom, his religious uncertainties, his missionary obligations as a practicing Christian, and his conception of himself as a miserable sinner by trying to convert Theron Woolverton to Christianity—or, more accurately, to Mahan's version of Christianity. The Woolverton Project filled many of his waking hours and thoughts in 1868 and 1869 and became a consuming passion, almost unnatural in its intensity.

Theron Woolverton, Canadian-born, entered the Navy in July 1862 as an Assistant Surgeon and was promoted to Passed Assistant Surgeon in September 1865. He was serving in that rank in the USS *Monocacy* on the Asiatic Station when Mahan came to know him in 1868. All available evidence points to the fact that Dr. Woolverton was a discouragingly normal young man, a joyous participant in the world of wine, women, and song. As Mahan put it, "his confession of the great habit of sin indulged by him has weighed upon my mind and heart very much." Woolverton was also a member of the *Monocacy*'s officers' mess, which Mahan considered the most debauched mess in the squadron. They were, he said, "hard drinkers and dissipated and used to wonder and laugh at the quietness of our mess . . . His [Woolverton's] mess and his associations on shore became objects of my cordial detestation." To make matters worse, or more challenging to Mahan, the fun-loving *Monocacy* was commanded by Samuel P. Carter. Mahan thoroughly disliked Carter when they were both at the Naval Academy, and when the two met again in the Far East ten years later that dislike was intensified. To rescue Woolverton's soul from the eternal damnation that the *Monocacy*'s wardroom seemed to promise was a missionary challenge Mahan could scarcely resist. Indeed, "when Woolverton came before [me] as a man possibly interested in religious matters . . . my heart from this reason but more especially from a sudden warm human affection went out to him." Dr. Woolverton *must* be saved.[52]

Woolverton's candidacy for salvation dated from March 1868 in Yokohama. There he and Mahan first met, liked each other, and rode horseback together daily for several weeks as they scouted the surrounding countryside. A few weeks later, in early May, Mahan happened to be on board the *Monocacy*, found her officers in the wardroom "over their wine," and engaged Woolverton in casual conversation. He later explained this pregnant moment to Sam Ashe:

> His manner was very cordial to me that evening, a sort of repressment marking it, and he drew me into his room to lend me—a volume of sermons! I was rather astounded, but recalled that I had heard him spoken of as religiously inclined, and my heart went out to him instantly. You cannot know, Ashe, how dreary it sometimes is to feel that all around you are utterly indifferent to what you would fain have the dearest of all things to yourself. . . . So I thought "I have found sympathy at last" . . . he had got my affection now, and you will understand how doubly impossible it was for me to go back from him, when I found his *claim* upon my regard. You will agree with me, I think, in looking upon my love for him as exceptional in its origin. I am so convinced of it that I hope it may please God to have chosen me to be of some use to him. He is a real good fellow, but we have hardly a taste in common, and I think could have messed together for years, without more than ordinary chumship, had he never been a communicant of *"the* Church."[53]

Woolverton, it seems, had been recently confirmed into the Anglican communion "under one of those transitory impulses" at Capetown during the *Monocacy*'s voyage out to the station. But he had quickly reverted to type and was "utterly at sea as to faith—and careless as to practice" when Mahan generously took over the direction of his spiritual welfare in May 1868. Mahan discovered, too, that Woolverton had even "taken to rationalist reading" and had abandoned prayer. "Excited and somewhat uncomfortable" by the prospects of effecting so difficult a conversion, fearful that a personal estrangement might result from too vigorous a religious approach to his new-found friend, Mahan consulted the Anglican missionary in Yokohama on the "propriety or advisability of my attempting to interfere in the matter." Urged by Dr. Charles Lee to unlimber all available persuasive and theological artillery, Mahan promptly unleashed a spiritual blitzkrieg designed to bring the wayward Woolverton speedily to God. This involved praying constantly for Woolverton, writing him religious letters, worrying about his soul, urging him to attend church services ashore, lending him religious tracts to read, and generally badgering him to seek God. When Woolverton seemed to respond to his importunities, Mahan was elated; when Woolverton seemed to shy away from the intense pressure, he was "anxious and depressed and morose," and was driven to drink. "My hopes of a friend are evidently dashed and that is wounding," he wrote at one low point; "but yet more the danger is, that failing that, I may run into the extreme of indifference to his spiritual welfare as far as I can influence it by prayer or consideration."[54]

Mahan was distressed and frustrated that the intelligent and rationalist Woolverton did not respond readily to his simplistic arguments for Christianity:

> I am now as doubtful of my ability to do the slightest good in that case, as I was before hopeful. His own intellectual ability, the fact that I can only bring forward long and old arguments, etc. etc. . . . . I have longed for wisdom of word, for the power of appeal, for the human gift, and have relied too little upon the power of the truth, upon the simple preaching of the Cross of Christ. My arguments are old and simple, folly indeed to the wise, to the acute reasoner; but in so far as they are truly of God, all powerful in their simplicity—Jesus Christ is the same yesterday, today and forever.[55]

Of enormous personal concern to Mahan was his fear that he might fail to convert the casual Woolverton and bring him, penitent, to the Lord's Table. He recognized that his ego was bound up in his missionary assault on the young surgeon; and he was distressed lest failure in that direction damage his own prospects for salvation. For this reason he was inclined at times to proceed cautiously. "His case is a serious trial to my faith," Mahan confessed. He also recognized, within a month of the conversation in May 1868 on board the *Monocacy*, that he had done about all he could be expected to do with Woolverton's soul, and he began to wonder whether "is it not time that it became me to practice self-discipline and withdraw my strenuous interest—into which so large a human element enters—and therefore so liable to perversions from self?" Before he had answered that question the *Monocacy* departed Yokohama for Shanghai, an event that the disappointed Mahan celebrated by getting gloriously drunk. As he blearily and sadly looked back on the failure of his first campaign to capture Woolverton's soul for Christ he remarked in mid-June 1868:

> He is gone now; for good or for ill the work of the past month is done, to be done no more forever. It has been a time of trial to me. . . . I saw my friendship prized less than that of others. Even my faith was tried. . . . I was hurt by neglect on his part; I do know that I sought very much his love, perhaps to the injury of my desire to see him God's. . . . I will also hope that my dear friend Woolverton may be blessed through my prayers and imperfect endeavors, though God in His wisdom . . . hath refused me to seek His fruit as my own.[56]

But Woolverton was not destined to escape the ecclesiastical embrace of Alfred Thayer Mahan so easily or for long. Indeed, Mahan was certain that the wayward surgeon would never fully elude his missionary grasp. "Those whom I love are not likely to." Letters between the two men were exchanged, Mahan receiving one in August 1868 that "from pleasure and interest has upset me as I was three months ago." When the two young officers met again early in September at Kobe, Mahan resumed his hot pursuit of the surgeon's soul. Meanwhile, Woolverton had suffered another moral lapse and was again "running pretty much the old course." Mahan consequently shifted his tactics, attacking Woolverton's disinterest in religion "on intellectual grounds, appealing more to reason than to the heart." This ploy also failed, and when the *Iroquois* and *Monocacy* parted company again in late September Mahan characterized Woolverton's continued resistance to conversion as his "principal sorrow."

> I cannot conceal from myself [he wrote] that his evident lack of sympathy with me wounds me deeply. I do not doubt his regard for me; but I am sure he would, and does much prefer other companionship and that of a kind to me distasteful.

Woolverton, he concluded sadly, was nothing less than a "terrible lady killer" who was quite willing to compromise himself in matters sexual.[57]

During their next separation, from October 1868 to March 1869, and during those that followed, Mahan kept abreast of Woolverton's movements, behavior, and spiritual life through letters and through occasional reports from Sam Hayes, another of the *Monocacy*'s crew, whom Mahan described to Ashe as having "about as large a hold upon my heart as anyone I know of, though I don't often hear from him."[58]

In March 1869 Mahan again encountered Woolverton on the station, this time at Hong Kong; and once again he resumed his crusade to save the surgeon from himself and for God. He felt that Woolverton would be much more likely to come willingly and meekly to the Anglican Communion Table "now that the attractions that Yokohama presents are gone." By this time Mahan had come to link Woolverton's salvation closely with his own, an act which lent additional urgency to his continuing missionary campaign:

> I am still much concerned for W., not for God's sake only, but much for the love I bear him. I cannot reconcile myself to the thought that he should again go back and forsake his God and separate himself from that Body to which with all my faults and sins, I hope God yet finds me bound by a living union. I feel more keenly that he would thus separate himself from *me* than from Christ.

Bound up with Mahan's somewhat confused notion of union with Woolverton in God was his awareness that his affectionate concern for the former had a distinctly non-theological dimension. "Have had some sickish mortified feelings concerning W's general neglect of me," he confessed in mid-May 1869. "My affection is too much of the earthy—and my fine thoughts about seeking not his affection but welfare may dissipate into a very self-seeking affection if I be not wary and prayerful." But together with his "earthy" affection for the medic was his absolute conviction that his faltering attempts to redeem Woolverton's elusive soul were sanctioned, indeed sanctified, by God Himself. "I believe my object is good," he wrote, "my plan sanctioned by God's Word." It was his duty, he felt, to take care of "the spiritual welfare of those around me," even though "the discouragement I have met with has inclined me to think that it is not God's will that I should do more than watch for my opportunities now." He did not feel, however, that such watchful waiting would "stand the test of the Bible," and he was constantly fearful that Woolverton's soul would somehow slip through his nervous fingers. "I must lose much if he forsakes Christ," Mahan worried. Indeed, when Woolverton was temporarily out of range Mahan searched for other souls to save. Almost any soul would do.[59]

To Mahan's heartfelt and heart-rending importunities Woolverton responded only casually. He was apparently bored by the earnest Mahan, he continued to sin, and he even recited to Mahan the range and details of his peccadilloes. Mahan was stunned and disgusted by such candor. On one occasion, probably no more serious than a drunken visit by Woolverton to a Japanese whorehouse, Mahan was "embittered by remembering how Woolverton had gone astray." He therefore insisted that his strenuous efforts on behalf of the surgeon should at least be rewarded by some show of moral decorum on Woolverton's part. After all, Mahan was neglecting his own spiritual welfare out of concern for Woolverton's and was being driven to drink in the process. On the eve of his departure from Hong Kong for Swatow, he summed up his frustration:

> Woolverton has recently been the immediate cause of my principal trial. . . . I find that I am always thinking of Woolverton—in church it is the friend who kneels beside me that my thoughts are following, rather than Christ's real covenanted presence. . . . Certain it is that my prayers are more controlled, more satisfying when he is not with me— yet I feel as though I were not doing wrong. Is it a delusion? . . . I do believe that these warm human affections, being ordained by God, sanctified by His Son, are not wrong when the subject of them endeavours to refer them to God. . . . I am well aware myself that there enter two motives into my conduct: one the desire to have him my friend in sympathy as well as affection; the other is weaker, yet I hope real—a wish to see him Christ's.[60]

When the two officers parted company again at the end of March 1869, it was clear that the lonely and despondent Mahan had still not delivered his sin-loving friend to Christ. But when they met again briefly in Nagasaki in mid-May, Mahan felt that he had made progress. His "dearly loved friend," a "professed sceptic," was now "trying to live a holy and Christian life." As usual, Mahan was nervous and excited in Woolverton's presence. Again he drank too much in his "strained affection" for Woolverton and in his concern that this meeting might be the last time he would see his friend on the station. Woolverton, for a change, was "very sweet and affectionate" throughout the Nagasaki visit. The two men even agreed to pray for each other—Woolverton praying for Mahan's conquest of Demon Rum. So well did the three-day visit in Nagasaki go that Mahan suddenly feared that his own "sins have taken such hold upon me that I cannot look up to the blessed hope of eternal life with those whom I love." He now wanted nothing less than to spend eternity in heaven with Theron Woolverton.

So it was that he assiduously prayed God to bring Woolverton into active communion with the Episcopal Church: "Oh, my God, wilt thou not take him off my mind. Were he only a communicant. If Thou wouldest but [lead] him to the Holy Table—it seems to me I might feel easier." He worried that Woolverton and the *Monocacy* were returning to the flesh pots of Yokohama. "Poor boy. I trust that God really has him in his care." Nevertheless, the brief encounter in Nagasaki had been something of a spiritual and emotional triumph for Mahan. It seemed that he had found a true friend at long last:

> My mind really seems to be getting unhinged with regard to him—so earnest is my wish to see him a communicant—and so foolish and weak the personal affection I feel for him—desiring to have him about me. Noonday prayers were, so to speak, earnest but harassed by mental fatigue caused by anxious thought in this matter; and very especially do I find my mind weary and nervous from the lack of society around me.[61]

Not until late July 1869 did Mahan see Dr. Woolverton again. This time it was in Yokohama—after Mahan's serious illness and hospitalization, and after he had left his acting command of the *Iroquois* and assumed command of the gunboat *Aroostook*. It was the last time the two men, the intense missionary and the happy heathen, met on the station. Once again Mahan noted that "falling in with W. has upset me again." More significantly, Woolverton had recently enjoyed another moral debauch ashore that "greviously distressed" Mahan and caused him to solicit aid from Sam Hayes in joint prayer for Woolverton's soul. The more Mahan brooded, the more he badgered Woolverton about the surgeon's "sad declension;" and the more he became "fearful and tearful about Woolverton; heartsick at thinking of his fault which even now sickens me to remember." It was clear, too, that the unrepentant Woolverton was soon to depart the station (before Mahan himself could leave), and that tentative plans to return home together in the same steamer, via Europe, would have to be scrapped. Indeed, Woolverton's relief arrived in Yokohama on July 27 and Mahan was distressed, filled with "sickness and a despondency," at parting from "one whom I dearly love." When Woolverton finally left Yokohama on July 29, bound for California, Mahan was crushed. "All the afternoon I have been fighting my dullness and depression—and I see that my concern is now become grief at separating from my friend rather than regard for his welfare. . . . My dear dear friend may God bless you and bring you into the fold of Christ's Holy Church."[62]

Unhappily, Mahan was destined to suffer one more blow from Dr. Woolverton. Soon after the surgeon's departure from Yokohama Mahan learned that Woolverton had lied to him. Instead of visiting with Mahan aboard the *Aroostook* on the eve of leaving the station, as he had promised, Woolverton had slipped ashore and spent the day there pursuing the ladies. He then told Mahan that he had been too busy with his official duties and with the task of updating his log to keep their appointment. Mahan was quite "wrathy," and was upset that "frankness don't seem a characteristic of his." He did not "question his attachment to me—I have only given him more than I get in return—a common enough chance in life." But the longer he thought about Woolverton's casual disinterest in him the angrier and more upset he became:

> I think it shows that his regard for me is not overpowering. It is natural to think that for a "dear dear" friend one would manage to squeeze out a few moments to say goodbye even at the expense of a flirtation. The apparent lack of frankness grieves me most. It seems as though he were aware I would not be pleased at his neglect of myself. My duty though seems plain—"though the more I love you the less I be loved."

The unrequited dimension of his relationship with Woolverton was now clear to Mahan. And while he continued to harbor "anxious fears" lest Woolverton "fall again," he came also to understand that he "had of late too much become presumptuous in a fancied claim I had upon God in virtue of my long and earnest continued prayers for W." None of these prayers had had any effect. Worse, Mahan soon learned that Woolverton had fallen among dubious companions in California. He finally became convinced that Woolverton "does not show any amount of affection for me. I am hurt—and grieved both—by him." He had failed God and self. Miserably.[63]

Mahan's concern for the soul of the departed Woolverton was partially submerged in a glow of anticipation as his own detachment from the station drew near, and in the planning of a sight-seeing trip home via Europe. His health was still poor and he hoped that it would remain poor enough to ensure the receipt of early orders home. "I am tempted to wish and even to keep myself sick in order to accomplish that end," he confessed. He was, after two long years, thoroughly disenchanted with life on the station; and with Woolverton gone there was little emotional or redemptive reason for him longer to remain there. His captaincy of the decrepit *Aroostook* was certainly a dead-end job professionally. Indeed, the Navy Department had decided to sell the vessel in Japan rather than risk sailing her home. For this reason Mahan was bound to the ship only until she could be disposed of. Throughout July and August 1869 he waited impatiently for someone to buy the old gunboat and release him from the purgatory of her command. He wanted desperately to go home. On September 18, 1869, the *Aroostook* was sold; and on September 21 Mahan, armed with a six-month leave, left Yokohama. A last-minute urge to pursue the feckless Woolverton to California was resisted and he returned home alone.[64]

IV

Elly and the *Wasp*
1870-1875

I shall not say very much about her who seemed to me, even before I loved her, and while I was seeking others, to be the woman in a thousand that Solomon could not find. You have in the house the best likeness of her that I have seen—certainly not a great beauty, she is very fair in my eyes. In her character, which has drawn me from the first, and finally, almost despite myself, won me, there is certainly, far more evidently than in most, generosity, truth, and loyalty—ingenuousness amounting to simplicity yet without taint of "greenness"—and above all, sincere and practical religious principle. . . .

Alfred Thayer Mahan to Mary Okill Mahan, August 15, 1871

It was a leisurely trip home from Yokohama. Mahan traveled in the British passenger steamer *Glencartney* via Hong Kong and Calcutta, thence overland to Bombay, on through the recently opened Suez Canal, and reached Marseilles on December 17, 1869. There he discovered that the steam sloop *Juniata* was in port, visited briefly with his friend Sam Hayes, who was her first lieutenant, and learned from Hayes that his younger brother, Passed Midshipman Dennis Hart Mahan, Jr., was at Nice on board the frigate *Sabine*. A quick trip to visit Denny turned into a six-week romantic siege. Mounted from his room at the Grand Hotel, the operation was designed to win the heart and hand of "Nonpareille," his Newport flame. The lady happened to be wintering in Nice. Her husband had died and she was free. But she turned Mahan down. He described his severe disappointment to Ashe:

Absence seems to have done its work on her, and it is too evident to me after this daily intimate acquaintance of a month—that the regard she now has for me is no real . . . [thing]. . . . I have been a good deal harassed in my mind, owing to my meeting with and continued attachment to [her] . . . a feeling as you may suppose distasteful to my relatives. I presume things of this sort are continually occurring in the histories of human life, yet to the one concerned they each seem peculiar in themselves; and I so find myself incapable of imagining any one equal to her in loveableness and fascination. The effect upon me personally however is bad—for I have no occupation requiring my mind to leave what is perhaps a very morbid condition. If ever a man needed praying for, I do just now; for I am in sore straits to do right—even to know what is right. The best hope for me—humanly speaking, would be to form some stronger and more natural attachment, but is it possible? This is the only one of her sex I ever desired to possess, to call my very own.[1]

Mahan attempted to overcome his confusion and his disappointment in love with a sight-seeing trip to Rome. He found St. Peter's Basilica "wonderfully grand" and the Vatican "bewildering in its extent." He was surprised to discover that he enjoyed the paintings and statues since his "artist like proclivities" had earlier earned the contempt of "old Seager," Professor of Drawing at the Naval Academy. He traced this reaction to his inherent "keen, almost sensuous sense of the beautiful that has been my mark and another would say my bane" and noted, his recent romantic rejection in mind, that "having only once found perfect or nearly perfect beauty in life, the result has been a disastrous constancy." Nevertheless, Mahan did not fully enjoy his two-week Roman adventure. He found the city to be "filthy, disgustingly so," and he objected to the profusion of " 'expurgated' heathen columns and obelisks every few squares." The fact of the matter was that he could not get his mind off his ladylove and onto the wonders of antiquity. As he confessed to Sam Ashe: "I think the engrossing of my mind so much and so unhappily with a present mundane interest has tended to deaden very much the pleasure derivable from old and imaginative associations. The mind can hold but one interest at a time."[2]

Following brief visits to southern Italy, the south of France, Paris, London, and the Royal Navy installation at Spithead, Mahan took passage from Liverpool in mid-May in the British steamer *Russia* bound for New York. It was a pleasurable crossing. He threw himself into the society of the ladies on board the vessel, and in so doing he gradually worked himself out of his romantic depression. It was on this trip that he met Grace Evans of Philadelphia, aunt and entrée to the lady he eventually married,

Ellen Lyle Evans. He reached West Point at the beginning of June and enjoyed a family reunion.[3]

By mid-July 1870 Mahan found himself in the distasteful position of having to think anew about resuming his boring career. His six-month leave, which began in November 1869, had been extended by his request in March 1870 for an additional six months. He confided to Ashe in July that he had no desire whatever "to return to my active profession" and noted that he was "perfectly satisfied to remain ashore as long as the Navy Department may see fit to permit me." A glance at the Navy Register told him, however, that he could not expect to be left alone for long since "almost every one seems on duty of some kind and not a few at sea." But before the duty-assignment axe again fell, he planned to visit Sharon Springs, New York, in the Adirondacks, in July and August to take the sulphur baths and ingest the sulphurous waters. This therapy, he and his doctor felt, would rid him of the remaining "unpleasant traces" of the various Far Eastern maladies he had contracted. Sharon, he pointed out, was also the most popular of New York's summer spas, and he hoped to "find there some friends." He especially craved female companionship, since he found no woman who could be said to have a "passionate attachment" to him. He therefore decided, with not a little rationalization, that he was not much interested in or "greatly attracted by the general crowd of the fair sex."

On a less romantic level, he also planned a trip to Baltimore in October to discuss religion and theology with his Uncle Milo. Prior to his departure for Sharon, throughout the month of June, he remained at West Point and read. In preparation for his conversations with Milo, he studied the theological doctrines of Emanuel Swedenborg and engaged in other religious reading. And he brought himself up to date on the contemporary history of his politically distracted and racially-torn country. His view of Reconstruction was still very close to that held by Ashe. "We have a nigger cadet here at the Point," he reported to his North Carolina friend. "People are much disgusted but very quiet about what may seem to you poetical justice."[4]

The visit to Sharon Springs did indeed produce "some friends," most notably Miss Ellen Lyle Evans, aged nineteen, whose family summered there. Her aunt, Grace Evans, whom Mahan had met on board the *Russia* in May, introduced him to her niece. This budding friendship was interrupted in late August when Mahan was ordered to special ordnance duty in Pittsburgh, Pennsylvania. From a career standpoint, Pittsburgh was the boondocks and Mahan was "hurt" by so miserable an assignment. Nevertheless, it was far preferable to sea duty. Typhoons on the Monongahela were rare.

Scarcely had he reported to his duty station in western Pennsylvania when he learned that his Uncle Milo had died unexpectedly on September 3. Granted one month's compassionate leave, an emotionally crushed Mahan hastened to Baltimore for the funeral. Milo's death was an "irreparable" loss to him. "I am quite at a loss," he lamented, "to know to whom to turn for the advice and information that I used to get from him in matters of theological, rather than religious, interest—and during my last cruise I had accumulated several points upon which I wished instruction." Perhaps it was in theological deference to his beloved uncle that Mahan promptly abandoned his study of Swedenborgianism. He decided that the doctrines of the eighteenth-century Swedish scientist, theologian, and theosophic seer were at best speculative, "singularly illogical and specious in pleading." The departed Milo Mahan, convinced that through mathematical endeavor he had discovered the numerical keys to Scripture, to history, and to the universe, would certainly have approved his nephew's rejection of the highly emotional and psychic view of a heavenly New Jerusalem with which Swedenborg claimed direct personal and physical contact.[5]

While in New York for a day on his way to Milo's funeral, Mahan encountered the officer charged with the duty of general detailing in the Navy. Asked casually by the latter how he liked his assignment to Pittsburgh, an angry Mahan "spoke openly" upon "such a hurt." The officer smiled and responded: "Well, if you find it too hard for you just let me know." Mahan did precisely that, telling the detailer that he had "strong personal reasons for desiring to remain in or near New York" during the coming winter. However, soon after his return to West Point from Baltimore he received two offers of service, neither of which would have kept him in or near New York. One was to accompany a naval canal-surveying expedition to Nicaragua; the other was a teaching post in the Department of Astronomy at the Naval Academy. He had no more desire to rot in the jungles of Central America than he had had to wither on the social vine that was Pittsburgh. Four days' duty at Fort Pitt had been quite enough. Nor did he have any particular love or nostalgia for the Academy or for sleepy little Annapolis. He respectfully turned down both offers. Indeed he was

> determined to do my best to make friends in my own region of the country, that I may not find myself quite alone in my latter days; and I shall, if persevering, at least have the opportunity of getting in love.

... I do not pretend to conceal from myself that ... that certain vague unquietness that from time to time disturbs me is due to the unnatural state that celibacy undoubtedly is.

Put simply, Mahan was determined to stay in New York City and search for a wife. Almost any wife would do, so long as he could "feel at least some of that passionate emotion which once so stirred the very inmost of my nature." To facilitate his search for a mate, the thirty-year-old Mahan specifically requested assignment to the New York Navy Yard, pointing out to his superiors that "I have never since my entrance into the service, save a short month, had any experience of this class of duty." He did not inform the Navy, as he did Ashe, that "I shall, I think, be willing to go to sea" in return for "one winter" of romance. In any event, the request was granted and on November 11, 1870, he reported to Rear Admiral Melancthon Smith at the New York Navy Yard in Brooklyn.[6]

Ensconced thus in New York, Mahan began in earnest his pursuit of a suitable wife. Within a month he had settled tentatively upon Ellen Lyle Evans, daughter of Mr. and Mrs. Manlius Glendower Evans, whom he had met at Sharon Springs in July. Glen Evans, a Philadelphia business-man, had recently moved his family to a house at 13 Washington Square North, in New York. His was an economically comfortable and socially respectable but not wealthy clan. Indeed, Evans was wiped out in the Panic of 1873 and forced to flee to Pau, in the south of France, in an effort to make his severely reduced means stretch further. His daughter Ellen, called "Elly," was not a rich *femme fatale*. She was, Mahan con-fessed to his mother, "certainly not a great beauty," though "very fair in my eyes." It was her character, generosity, truth, loyalty, "ingenuous-ness amounting to simplicity," and "above all [her] sincere and practical religious principle" that gradually won Mahan to her, "even before I loved her, and while I was seeking others." Like Elizabeth Lewis, she was no Lucy Dashwood.[7]

Mahan's pursuit of Elly was neither eager, rapid, nor torrid. Quite the contrary, he loafed along after her like an overloaded sloop tacking up-wind. She was quite a bit younger than he, eleven years, and her mother felt that she was far too young, inexperienced, and unsophisticated to proceed rapidly in such matters. Little did the lady know that Lieutenant Commander Alfred Thayer Mahan was, at the age of thirty, equally naive and unsophisticated; or that all of his earlier experiences in the realm of love and romance had ended in disaster and frustration. In this sense it was a good match. Young Elly had had no experience at all with men and Mahan had had no luck at all with women. They came together by default. Certainly, Mahan's surviving letters to Ellen Evans can scarcely be called "love" letters. They breathe no fire or passion. It was as though Mahan were negotiating an insurance policy, which, in a manner of speaking, he was.[8]

Barely had this negotiation commenced when Mahan was ordered to the steam merchantman *Worcester* at Boston. Chartered by the Navy as a relief ship, speedily commissioned and staffed, packed with 7,500 barrels of foodstuff, and riding well below her Plimsoll mark, the *Worcester* was dispatched to France at the beginning of March 1871 to relieve the famine said to be raging there as a result of the Franco-Prussian War. Needless to say, Mahan did not share his government's humanitarian sense of urgency in the matter. "I don't particularly fancy my orders," he told Sam Ashe.

As were most of Mahan's seagoing experiences, the impromptu voyage of the *Worcester* was a blend of the ludicrous and the disastrous. Her engines failed shortly out of Boston and the ship wallowed eastward under sail, "about as fast as an old woman going to market." When the engines were finally repaired and set in motion, a boiler tube burst killing four of the crew and seriously injuring seven more. "We were all near eternity," Mahan reported to Elly. "Had this happened at night—with hatches down—or had the shell of the boiler given, instead of the tubes, the casualties might have included half the ship's company." This tragedy was followed by heavy gales and intermittent squalls of hurricane force. The vessel was pounded nearly to pieces by her own antiquated engines and she ingloriously ran out of coal upon reaching the English Channel. Mahan was convinced that only "God's goodness" finally brought the ill-fated *Worcester* to port on April 4. Further, the ship's company discovered on arrival at Plymouth that there was no famine in France and that their cargo was to be sold on the open market in London. Within the next few weeks some forty men deserted the accursed ship. Nevertheless, throughout these embarrassments, gales, and difficulties Mahan portrayed himself, in his letters to Miss Evans, as the brave, unflappable, detached, highly competent naval officer at sea, admitting to her only that "this four months cruise has given me more trouble than an ordinary one of two years."[9]

No sooner had he arrived in England than he began planning to meet her at Sharon Springs during the coming summer. "Our doctor says I ought certainly to visit Sharon," he assured her. He found it "tantalizing" to learn from her that she too was anticipating a visit to the spa. Meanwhile, he spent his shore leave visiting English cathedrals and American acquaintances. At the same time be began instructing young Elly in his views of women (clearly inferior to men) and Low Church Episcopalians (well below the salt). "I prefer my own friends to think my own way—an amiable weakness."[10]

The *Worcester* got back to Boston on July 21, 1871. Mahan was distressed to learn that she was not immediately to be decommissioned and himself speedily detached. He told Ashe that while he hoped not to have to go to sea again right away, "it is quite possible I may have to." In any event, he would not have enough time to attend Ashe's wedding on August 10 to Hannah Emerson Willard in distant North Carolina. Instead, he would use the few days of leave he could arrange to go to Sharon Springs "for the benefit of the air and waters." To accomplish this, he managed to talk Admiral Charles Steedman into giving him a brief leave. But when he routinely applied to Steedman from the Pavilion Hotel in Sharon for an extension of the leave, he was instructed by telegram to direct his request to the Navy Department. He wrote Captain James Alden in Washington explaining that "I have good medical authority for saying it is very desirable that I should remain here until at least September 1st, and had I imagined there would be any difficulty I should have asked a survey; but I deemed I should have sufficient time."[11]

The time was needed for his pursuit of Ellen Evans. Steedman's unexpected telegram, received on August 12, had thrown him into a panic since Elly seemed to him to be ready to accept a proposal of marriage. On leaving West Point for Sharon Springs in early August Mahan told his mother that he wished he "loved Miss Evans sufficiently to ask her for my wife." The wish suddenly became father to the act. He explained to his mother, "a few days here with her decided me." As the wags of Sharon Springs put it:

> Elly had a big Mahan,
> Whose teeth were white as snow.
> Everywhere that Elly went,
> Mahan was sure to go.

Fearful that he might be snatched from her side by the U.S. Navy in the person of Captain Alden, Mahan impetuously proposed marriage to Elly on Sunday, August 13, 1871. Her acceptance would bring with it an extended leave of absence for marriage and honeymoon.

The proposal of marriage came upon the young lady with "utter suddenness," so sudden that two days later Mahan was uncertain what her "ultimate decision" would be. It would seem that Mahan's groundwork

for the question was neither properly prepared nor particularly sophisticated, since her initial reaction gave him concern "lest she should not
love me enough—joined to a distrust of her own constancy." But if Elly
was unsure of herself, her mother was not. She informed Mahan that
there would definitely be no engagement; further, that while her daughter
was twenty years old she was "yet too young with her character" to
make such a decision for herself. In addition, Glendower Evans was ill
at the time, so ill that he was to be told nothing of the proposal at all.
Just as Mahan's parents had earlier opposed his pursuit of his "Nonpareille" because of her experience and maturity, so Ellen's parents now
opposed her connection with the older Mahan on substantially the same
grounds. The Victorian mating dance, as practiced in New York in 1871,
had specific ground rules relating to age.

Mahan, meanwhile, informed his own mother that little passion was
involved in his proposal decision. He merely admired Elly's character,
recognized that "faults doubtless she has," and claimed only that he was
"deeply attached to her." He was "not entraîné by that mad wild instinct,
dignified by the name of love, which I have known of old." His judgment, he noted, "was formed in friendship—love came later." The immediate problem, however, had little to do with the depth or degree of his
love for her. It was to convince the senior Evanses that having an impe-
cunious naval officer in their family as a son-in-law would not be a blow
to their social status and pretensions. Annual pay for lieutenant commanders on shore duty was $1,875; at sea it was $2,343. While this was a
comfortable income for the times, Mahan would never be rich. In urging
his mother to meet the Evanses and take up his cause among them, he
explained that "personally I believe few men would be more acceptable
to Mrs. E. though my profession and means will doubtless to a mother
seem objections. The only thing to be urged is that a large share of my
sea service is done." Unfortunately for Mahan, it was not.[12]

As soon as Glendower Evans was well enough (in October) to pass
an opinion on the matter he made it quite clear that there was no engagement, formal or informal, and that as far as he was concerned there would
never be one. He had no personal objection to Mahan; it was just that
he considered "the wife of a Navy officer as little better than a man's
widow." Indeed, he persisted in this view until Elly's own importunities
caused him to change his mind early the following year. Meanwhile,
however, the pace of the romance had slowed from a trot to a walk.
Mahan was detached from the *Worcester* on August 14 and placed on
waiting orders. He lingered with Elly and her mother at the Springs until
the end of the month and then returned to his home at West Point. He

was neither engaged, assured, rejected, faced with sea duty, nor assigned to any duty. His life, personal and professional, was becalmed.[13]

On September 16, 1871, tragedy struck the Mahan household at West Point. On that day Professor Dennis Hart Mahan committed suicide by leaping into the paddle wheel of a Hudson River steamer. He had suffered severe mental depression for over a year. When the Board of Visitors of the Academy recommended in 1871 his compulsory retirement from the West Point faculty something snapped in the proud man's mind, even though President Grant had assured him that the board's recommendation would not be accepted. By the beginning of September his dark moods had become morbid. It was while on a trip to New York City to see a physician about the problem, a trip urged by his family, that Dennis Mahan, "in an instant of acute insanity," ended his useful life.

The startling fact of his father's suicide led Mahan through many "seasons of great apprehension" in fear that he had inherited a family disposition to mental illness and depression that might lead him also to self-destruction. He too had experienced periods of great mental depression while in the *Iroquois* and on several occasions prior to that, and the suicide of his father upset him severely. Within a year and a few days the two men whom Mahan most loved and respected, his uncle and his father, had suddenly departed the face of the earth. There was also the fact of the retardation of his sister Mary. For a generation that subscribed to the "bad seed" theory of mental health it was enough to give Mahan serious pause.[14]

A compassionate leave, followed by a brief assignment to temporary duty at Cold Spring, New York, permitted Mahan to oversee the settlement of his father's estate and to move his mother to Elizabeth, New Jersey, where she took up residence with her widowed sister, Jane Leigh Okill (Mrs. John J.) Swift. Mahan's sisters, Jane Leigh, then 19, and the invalid Mary, age 29, accompanied their mother to the new home at 21 Broad Street in Elizabeth. In mid-January 1872, Mahan himself was assigned to the Receiving Ship *Vermont* in nearby New York. There he resumed his quest for the hand of Elly during the remainder of the winter.

He also kept a sharp eye on the Navy Register to make sure that there were no errors in his record. In February 1872 he discovered that his brief sea service in the *Worcester* had not been properly credited. He insisted that this oversight be corrected. He wanted no more sea duty than was absolutely necessary.

By early May 1872 the Evanses had given their reluctant consent to Elly's marriage. Mahan promptly applied for a six-month marriage leave to commence on June 1. He got three months. On June 11 he and Ellen

Lyle Evans were finally married, and in early September he attempted to parlay that quiet event into a three-month extension of his leave, "or if possible to the end of the year." Three additional months were granted, subject to his standing for examination for the rank of commander during the leave period. In mid-September he left Long Branch, New Jersey, where he and his bride were living temporarily, proceeded to Washington, took a simple examination on basic seamanship, ship-handling, and navigation, and was promoted to commander, effective November 20. This promotion raised his pay to $2,800 (sea) and $2,240 (shore). He also certified himself physically qualified for sea duty. All that sulphur at Sharon Springs had done its work well.

For the benefit of the detailing officer in the Navy Department, he drew up a careful reckoning of his service to date: nine years and ten months at sea, and but three years and four months on shore. What influence these revealing statistics were supposed to have on the crusty Captain Daniel Ammen in the Bureau of Navigation is not clear. If they were designed to soften Ammen's heart toward the bridegroom with regard to imminent sea duty, they failed. On December 11, 1872, Commander Alfred Thayer Mahan was ordered to the command of the *Wasp* at Montevideo, Uruguay. Since officers' wives were permitted to join their husbands on the South Atlantic Station at this time, it was decided that Elly would accompany him to Uruguay. It was the best "sea duty" Mahan ever drew, mainly because it involved spending so little time actually at sea.[15]

Mahan and his wife, she being two months pregnant, left New York on December 23 in the British steam packet *Douro* and arrived at Montevideo in early February. On February 15, 1873, he reported to Rear Admiral William Rogers Taylor, commander of the South Atlantic Station, and on the 17th, in company with Commander John N. Quackenbush, the *Wasp*'s departing commanding officer, he inspected the ship and crew. "All was found satisfactory. The Crew was exercised at the guns and gave evidence of good instruction." That accomplished, Mahan formally took command of the vessel.

The following week he wrote to the Secretary of the Navy requesting permission for Elly to live with him on board the ship. Pending receipt of such permission from the department (a permission that Secretary George M. Robeson subsequently denied), Admiral Taylor authorized the proposed housing arrangement afloat. Accordingly, Mahan requisitioned a table cloth and linen covers for his cabin furniture and otherwise made his quarters fit for a lady. Meanwhile, the Mahans searched for and found more spacious quarters ashore at 222 Calle de San José, in Montevideo. But when yellow fever broke out in that city early in April 1873, driving all foreign warships (American, British, Italian, French, Spanish, and Brazilian) to the safety of Colonia, Uruguay, Mahan took the pregnant Elly and the wife of another *Wasp* officer along in the *Wasp*. On only two occasions during the next two years was he separated from his wife for more than a short time; once for a period of three weeks in September and October 1873 and again for the same length of time in December 1874 when the *Wasp* was ordered upriver to show the flag at Asunción, Paraguay. It was ideal "sea duty."[16]

Mahan's surviving correspondence of the 1873–1875 period is largely of the official sort associated with the daily operations of an American naval vessel on a foreign station beset with war, fever, revolution, uncharted waters, and the necessity constantly to protect American merchant shipping. Problems and activities relating to stores, requisitions, personnel changes, inspections, ship repairs, gunnery practice, charting, and operations related to showing the flag in the waters of Brazil, Paraguay, Uruguay, and Argentina occupied the body of these letters. All showed Mahan in the light of a competent commanding officer who was a stickler for operational detail, a devout votary of naval regulations, and a critic of the seakeeping capabilities of the broken-down vessel that he commanded.[17]

The 212-foot *Wasp* was, indeed, a disgrace to the U.S. Navy. British-built and operated under the name *Emma Henry*, the 1,000-ton, wooden, side-wheel steamer had been captured during the Civil War while running the Union blockade. Confiscated by the government for such un-neutral (although profitable) behavior, she entered the Navy in June 1865 as the *Wasp*, a proud American naval name for so miserable a tub. She mounted one 30-pounder Parrott rifle and two antiquated 24-pounder smoothbore howitzers. Mahan reported that the vessel had been compelled to live a "hand to mouth" existence for nearly seven years, had clearly "reached the limit of her endurance," and was generally so patched, mechanically crippled, and otherwise obsolete as a fighting ship that the Navy Department should either treat her to a complete overhaul or remove her from service. The bits-and-pieces-replacement approach to keeping her in commission no longer sufficed. Indeed, her new captain complained regularly to the squadron commander and to the department that the *Wasp* lacked essential equipment, suffered leaky boiler tubes, housed malfunctioning machinery, possessed a foul bottom, leaky hull, weakened masts, and ship's boats (so necessary for charting surveys) that would barely float. Her two smoothbores were in such poor shape that they failed in an attempt to fire the usual commemorative salute to the flag on July 4, 1873. Fortunately the ubiquitous Royal Navy came to the rescue. HMS *Pylades* "very courteously fired a salute of twenty one guns at noon." Bloody decent of her.[18]

The polyglot crew of the *Wasp* was not much better than the leaky ark in which they served. There was a constant turnover of enlisted men, many of whom were foreign-born. They were recruited in the waterfront bars and brothels on the station for one-year tours and then discharged ashore again in Rio de Janeiro, Montevideo, and Buenos Aires with a few American dollars in their pockets. Many native Americans also chose to be discharged in the ports on the station when their own enlistment periods terminated. There were the usual desertions as well as typical recruitments on the station. Indeed, one such recruit, soldier of fortune Richard Lloyd, was a deserter from the revolutionary Uruguayan Army and, after serving three days in the U.S. Navy, had to be returned bodily to his previous employers.

So low was enlisted pay in the Navy of the 1870s and so frustrated did Mahan become in trying to recruit and retain competent engineering personnel at near-starvation wages that he gratuitously informed the squadron commander on one occasion that the *Wasp* was "entirely propelled by steam" and that unless something was done about replacing skilled mechanics "serious embarrassment" could result. On another occasion he informed his superiors that "there have been no instructions in Signals during the past quarter; it being thought not desirable, owing to the constant changing of the Crew and the short time for which they enlist." His pleas for three-year men recruited in the States were not answered. He therefore instructed his officers to be particularly diligent in training the one-year men who were shipped on board in Montevideo and other foreign ports. They were, said Mahan, "literally ignorant of difference between breech and muzzle; which make all instructions of an Officer using technical terms, gibberish to them."[19]

Nevertheless, Commander Mahan somehow managed to keep the decrepit *Wasp* moving hither and yon on her appointed rounds. The main job of the vessel was to "protect American interests." These included providing transportation to U.S. diplomatic officials, boarding merchant vessels flying the American flag to verify nationality and to ensure their compliance with American neutrality laws and regulations, evacuating and otherwise protecting American citizens endangered by war, revolution, or disease, and coming to the aid of distressed American merchantmen. This last did not, however, include steaming some 250 miles from Montevideo to the mouth of the Paraná River in May 1874 to pull the American bark *A. C. Bean* off a mud bank; not when commercial tugs were available nearby. "It would have cost the Government $800 in coal alone to make the trip," Mahan declared.[20]

By far the greatest amount of time and energy spent by the *Wasp* and her crew during the period of Mahan's command was devoted to charting operations. From November 30, 1873, to July 31, 1874, the *Wasp* was principally engaged in a survey of the coast and of the coastal and estuarial waters between Montevideo and nearby Flores Island in the Rio de la Plata. Some 70 square miles were surveyed; 900 to 1,000 miles of soundings were run; and over 40,000 casts of the sounding lead were made. Submerged wrecks and other obstructions were charted and the nature of the bottom was noted. Tedious and unromantic work, this, but very useful to international navigation. "These are not data of much interest except to ourselves," wrote Mahan, "but may serve to show the exhaustive character of the work." The duty had the additional advantage of permitting officers and men to return at the end of each work day to Montevideo where Mahan and several of his officers maintained their wives.[21]

The very nature of this unpredictable work caused Mahan (and Quackenbush before him) frequently to run the *Wasp* aground and to discover submerged rocks and reefs by the unhappy device of running onto them. No wonder the hull of the *Wasp* constantly leaked; and no wonder Mahan bitterly complained that the worn-out ship's boats, the "eyes" of a survey vessel, were not equal to the triangulation tasks assigned them. The *Wasp* was often forced to survey nearly blind. Nevertheless, it is normally the business of a ship to float and Mahan often had to explain to his superiors when, where, and how he got his ship aground; and how it was that he collided with a lighter at the ship's anchorage in Montevideo.[22]

More embarrassing than any of this was the time, in June 1874, when he somehow managed to get the *Wasp* trapped in Mañá Dry Dock at Montevideo for ten days because the caisson of the dock could not be moved when the ship was ready to leave. In a blistering letter to J. M. Muñoz, agent for the dock, Mahan expressed both his embarrassment and his outrage:

> When the idea was first entertained of putting the *Wasp* on this dock, I inquired as to its dimensions and the depth of water on the sill—this latter being stated at fourteen feet. I venture to say that it would not have occurred to any naval man, unless he had had my present unfor-

tunate experience, to inquire whether the caisson could be moved at ordinary low water in the river—I did not inquire, and the information was not given me. In this ignorance I entered the dock, and now find myself unable to leave. The urgency of my leaving is nothing to the point. I wish the ship to go out. . . . and the only hindrance to our leaving is that the managers cannot open the gates. . . . I feel the loss of time to be an injury to me, and to the Service which I represent. . . . this defect can be remedied, and . . . the failure to do so must be an injury to the interest and reputation of the dock.

Mahan struck back at the recalcitrant Mañá Dock by demanding of the company $28.00 demurrage for the incident. Whether or not this fine was ever paid is not known. But one is struck with the thought that Alfred Thayer Mahan may be the only commanding officer in the history of the U.S. Navy rendered hors de combat by a dry dock.[23]

These minor technical problems notwithstanding, Mahan served the nation and the Navy well during his two-year tour in the *Wasp*—primarily as a sensitive, thoughtful, and objective reporter of the confused political and martial events that swirled around him in 1873 and 1874. History was clearly being made in southeastern South America at that time, and Mahan carefully recorded for his superiors what he saw and understood of it. His reports and letters represent Mahan at his descriptive best; they might also be said to have presaged his later emergence as a practicing professional historian. Indeed, it was in September 1874 in Montevideo that he worked up and delivered (to what audience is not known) his first formal lecture on a historical subject. He titled it "Naval Battles," and Elly reported to Mahan's mother that "he has worked so much on it that it has quite upset him and he is feeling nervous and dull." The serious reading of history that he had commenced in the *Iroquois* in Yokohama apparently continued when he was in the *Wasp* at Montevideo. With no particular plan or conscious goal in mind, Mahan was becoming a historian.[24]

Most of the South American political and diplomatic difficulties on which he reported so skillfully to his superiors stemmed from Paraguay's disastrous war against Brazil, Argentina, and Uruguay in the years 1865 to 1870. This conflict was followed by Brazil's lengthy occupation of Paraguay, a Brazilian intervention in the Uruguayan civil war of 1870 to 1872, a serious threat of war between Argentina and Brazil in 1874, and a major revolution in Argentina which began in October 1874 and was still under way when Mahan was detached from his command and departed the troubled scene in January 1875.

On most of these confused and confusing events, certainly those within his range of observation, Mahan commented with precision and insight. He reported facts and rumors, clearly separating the one from the other. For the information of the station commander and of American diplomats accredited to the affected nations, he digested and analyzed conflicting newspaper accounts of events. These, together with summaries of his personal conversations with participants and other observers, he relayed to his superiors. And since the strategic key to the area was the control of the head of the Rio de la Plata, which in turn controlled access to the Uruguay, Paraná, Paraguay, and Pilcomayo rivers, as well as to the rich and extensive hinterlands they drained, Commander Mahan paid particular attention to the movements and armaments of European and Latin-American warships operating on those important interior waterways.

He also kept an eye on the behavior of Spanish naval vessels on the station, especially when the *Virginius* affair of October 1873 seemed momentarily to threaten a Spanish-American war. This crisis began when a Cuban-owned vessel of that name, illegally flying the American flag while transporting recruits and munitions to support revolutionaries in Cuba, was captured on the high seas by a Spanish war vessel. Passengers and crew, some American nationals among them, were taken to Santiago, Cuba, where they were summarily tried and executed by Spanish authorities. American public opinion was outraged. President Grant ordered a naval mobilization at Key West in preparation for war. But passion subsided when the illegal character and mission of the *Virginius* became known, and flickered out altogether when Madrid paid indemnity to the families of the executed Americans. It was just as well that peace prevailed because the naval mobilization produced little more than a sorry array of rotting hulks scarcely capable of carrying war to the weakest of enemies. Such was the frightful condition of the U.S. Navy in the 1870s.

Nevertheless, Mahan carefully reported the presence and armament of the Spanish gunboats *Narvaez* and *Ceres* in Montevideo in late December 1873 "in case the present difficulties with Spain should lead to war," and noted that "there are no other Spanish vessels of war so far as I know upon this coast." In fine, he served the South Atlantic Squadron as a one-man Office of Naval Intelligence in the area of the Rio de la Plata. At the same time, particularly when he was out of communication with civilian diplomatic authorities, he was enough of a skilled diplomat to recognize that he had to handle potentially explosive political situations (as well as ceremonial functions) with great delicacy and dignity. This he invariably did. He was particularly adept at those exercises in gunboat diplomacy up jungle rivers—"showing the flag"—that turned on who first saluted whose flag, when, and with how many guns. The South Americans could be quite sticky about such protocol.[25]

It should be pointed out in this regard that Mahan's personal participation in showing the flag from Buenos Aires and Montevideo to Asunción left him with an abiding contempt for Latin-Americans in general and for Latin-American political, military, and diplomatic processes in particular. "One thing appears lamentably certain," he noted on one occasion, "that loyalty, whether civil or military, is not to be found among the Argentines—no man can depend on any other man's truth; you cannot count upon any man's position tomorrow."[26]

Whether Mahan mixed socially with these "backward" Latins while he and Elly lived in Montevideo is not known. The little evidence that has survived relating to his personal life in 1873 and 1874 seems to indicate that, with a pregnant woman in the house, he stuck fairly close to home.

On August 6, 1873, Elly had her baby, Helen Evans Mahan, who for a short time was called "Kitten." Elly nursed the infant herself, employing Uruguayan maids, Carolina and Pepa, to handle the more disagreeable of the baby-tending chores. The Mahans nearly suffocated the child with love and attention. All household activity seems to have centered on the infant rather than on social diversions in Montevideo. Elly reported from time to time to Mahan's mother in Elizabeth, New Jersey, that she and her husband gooed and cooed over "Kitten" and spent many of their waking hours playing with her. Indeed, Elly revealed in October 1874 that her otherwise very proper husband "lies on the floor for her amusement and lets her pull him about, slobber over him, and do anything she wishes and does not mind it a bit. The only thing he objects to is having his whiskers pulled, but now that she has learned it she never touches them except when she is loving him." Mahan delighted, too, in singing hymns to the baby. "Art thou weary, art thou languid, art thou sore distressed?" he would croon to her. He alternated this hymn with another of his favorites, "On the other side of Jordan, in the sweet fields of Eden." To this musical indoctrination in Sunday-school Christianity Helen Evans Mahan could respond with little more than a gurgle. Whether she was "sore distressed" or not is not known. Certainly she had every possible attention.

Proxy godparents selected to participate in the child's baptismal ceremony were Mary S. Hoskins, wife of Thomas R. Hoskins, the Anglican clergyman and English schoolmaster in Montevideo, and Dr. Henry Lau-

Courtesy Alfred Thayer Mahan II

Mahan and daughter Helen in Montevideo, Uruguay

rie. For reasons not clear, Mahan insisted that the child be baptized on St. Matthew's Day (September 21, 1873) even though he was taking the *Wasp* upriver to Asunción at the time and could not be present at the ceremony. That rite accomplished, Mahan noticed that "the baby's eyes are very blue. I think slightly out of line, though no one else does. . . . Mouth will be rather large I think." But, in their letters home, both parents agreed that the child was well dispositioned, although Mrs. Hoskins later recalled Mahan's remark, when Helen was being especially fretful one day, that "children are not a good investment."[27]

[97]

The Mahans attended church regularly in Montevideo. Indeed, Alfred gave his wife for their second anniversary on June 11, 1874, a Bible "of such large type as she can use all her days—if she lives to be old." He also conducted divine services on board the *Wasp* when the vessel was under way on Sundays, as had been his habit on board the *Muscoota* and the *Iroquois*. And on at least one occasion he wrote his mother a lengthy and detailed letter on the doctrine of Eucharistic adoration. His religious and theological life remained full, if his social life was not. Nor was there a steady stream of social news from home. Both he and his wife were therefore flustered to learn that Mahan's brother Dennis had become engaged to a Miss Jeannette Brodie. Since they did not know the lady at all (Elly scarcely knew Dennis) they knew not quite how to phrase their good wishes to her. They need not have bothered. Denny eventually married another woman.[28]

When Mahan was away from home in the *Wasp*, Elly kept close to her rooms. "I never go out," she told her mother-in-law, "except for a visit semi-occasionally, and a walk daily, so when my boy is away I stupify. Baby, my darling little Helen, is my one comfort." Instead, Elly usually sat at home and made clothes for the baby and flannel underwear for her absent husband. Even when the commander was home, the Mahans did not often sally forth to take advantage of the theater, opera, or other events of Montevideo.[29]

Lieutenant Commander Charles O'Neil, executive officer of the *Wasp*, did. He and his wife Mary were quite active in the busy cultural and social life of Montevideo, even though Mary O'Neil also had a new baby to tend. O'Neil's daily journal for 1874 does not mention the presence of the Mahans at any of the numerous and varied social events he attended ashore. On the contrary, he noted only two exchanges of parlor visits between the two couples during their year together in Uruguay. He did, however, record the fact that Mahan preached "very good little sermons" on board the ship; and reported, further, that all hands were delighted on Ascension Day (May 14) 1874 when Mahan decreed "no work today" and conducted brief services for the crew instead. It was piety of this kind that probably persuaded O'Neil to invite the Mahans to stand as sponsors at the baptism of his son, Richard Frothingham O'Neil, by the Reverend T. R. Hoskins on September 16, 1874. But aside from these infrequent associations, the Mahans and the O'Neils had little connection with each other in Montevideo. During this period Mahan remained "The Cat That Walked By Himself."[30]

Mahan's surviving letters, papers, and official reports do not reveal the facts that Elly and little Helen were on board the *Wasp* for a week in April 1874 while the vessel was out surveying, that on three occasions in May and July 1874 Mahan "took a holiday" ashore with his family and sent O'Neil out in the *Wasp* to conduct the surveys, a risky delegation of authority, or that the *Wasp*, Mahan in command, collided with an Argentine warship, "doing slight damage," during a storm off Buenos Aires on November 3, 1874. Such are the difficulties of reconstructing the activities and movements of so private a man and so obscure (in 1874) a naval officer as Alfred Thayer Mahan.

Nevertheless, it is known that Mahan's single attempt to entertain "the quality" of Buenos Aires ended in disaster. O'Neil recorded the event, which took place on November 10, 1874: "Fine day but a little rough. Capt. Mahan had a party of ladies on board to visit H.M. Ship *Amethyst* but all got seasick." Mahan, it would seem, was socially accident-prone, and in the years ahead he and his wife were seldom very comfortable in elaborate social situations. Elly did not enjoy formal entertaining or going forth into Society, and Mahan had little difficulty adapting himself to her introversion. They were thus destined to lead a very quiet existence socially–in a Navy Officer Corps that was highly social. This penchant for privacy probably did not help his career.[31]

Mahan's orders detaching him from the *Wasp* were dated October 26, 1874. Not until Christmas Day, however, did Commander William A. Kirkland, Mahan's old shipmate in the *Congress* and future shipmate in the *Chicago* (1894–1895) finally arrive in Montevideo to relieve him. On January 2, 1875, the change of command was effected, but not before Mahan had apprised Kirkland of the fact that the *Wasp* was something less than seaworthy:

> I have to state that there are several holes in the midship section of the vessel–under machinery and boilers and below the water line–which are now covered with inside patches, shored down; and there are also several other spots in the same neighborhood badly corroded by galvanic action–similarly patched and protected, from inside. . . . The keelsons, under each boiler, are badly corroded. As regards the qualities of the vessel, she is unfit for outside [ocean] service . . . she is very uneasy and rolls heavily. There is nothing further of any importance to state as regards her.

Except that she was a hopeless piece of naval equipment. But that was now Commander Kirkland's problem.[32]

The Mahans sailed from Montevideo for Bordeaux in the steamer *Potosi* on January 7, 1875, Rear Admiral William E. Le Roy, then commander of the station, having given Mahan permission to return home via Europe. In 1874 Glendower Evans and his wife Ellen had moved from New York to the more economical and salubrious clime of the Basses Pyrénées department of southwestern France. There, at "Villa Lebre" on Avenue Trespoey in Pau, the senior Evanses hoped to find health and happiness at rock-bottom prices. And there Elly arranged a visit so that they might see their new grandchild. Upon his arrival in Bordeaux on February 7, en route to Pau, Mahan requested, and received, a leave of absence for six months with permission to remain abroad during the leave period. It was his plan to remain in Pau until the end of March, escort Elly and the baby on a visit to Paris and London, and sail for home at the end of April.[33]

The crossing in the *Potosi*, with stops at Rio, the Canary Islands, and Lisbon, was pleasant. According to Mahan's letters to his mother, baby Helen was much the center of shipboard attention and, daughter of the sailor that she was, learned to "walk with ease" even when the ship was rolling heavily. She had also mastered singing the first line of the Uruguayan national anthem, "marking the cadence with her finger—a great entertainment to the bystanders." Since the Mahans had not been able to persuade Carolina, the nurse they had in Montevideo, to accompany them on the voyage, they had to do the babysitting themselves, a duty they shared with willing fellow passengers. They had not been inclined to engage the services of a new nurse, having decided "that we would not undergo the expense of taking a stranger—the chance of such an one being seasick—or flirtatious—a frequent difficulty—making her practically useless to us."

So it was that Mahan roamed the ship with his admittedly spoiled daughter, read back issues of *The Churchman*, and complained that many of the leaders of his beloved Episcopal Church were becoming too liberal in their interpretations of Scripture, too permissive in their attitudes toward theology, and too low in their churchmanship. To correct the problem of biblical interpretation, which he now considered largely a matter of semantics, he suggested that "the English language is singularly imperfect and should be promptly amended by a mixed congress of philologists and theologians." He was pleased to note, however, that a recent congress of the Episcopal Church had at least endorsed the doctrine of Eucharistic adoration, "as commonly understood. . . . it appears to me we have reason to be devoutly thankful for the action—upon the whole—of so large a body of fallible men."[34]

That weighty Anglo-Catholic matter having been suitably settled in Mahan's mind, the family proceeded to Pau, where they spent February and March 1875 with the Evanses, and where all hands participated in the further spoiling of the precocious Helen. They were two pleasant, relaxing, and restful months—even though they were enjoyed at the reduced leave-of-absence pay rate of $190 per month.[35]

V

Naval Reformer
1875-1880

It is scarcely necessary to say to you that holding such language touching the Secretary as I have here would expose me to severe punishment. That I use it may therefore prove to you how urgent I think the need is, and how deep my conviction of the deplorable condition in which the Navy now is.

Alfred Thayer Mahan to Samuel A'Court Ashe, December 27, 1875

Mahan and his wife reached Elizabeth, New Jersey, in May 1875. The voyage home from Liverpool was far from pleasant, Elly having suffered a miscarriage when the vessel encountered heavy seas. Nor did the immediate future of his naval career give much cause for optimism. His leave of absence on reduced pay would continue until late August, and the sad fact of the matter was that Alfred Thayer Mahan was broke. Only by moving his family in with his mother in Elizabeth was he able to make ends meet during the summer months of that year—this and the willingness of Sam Ashe to repay the loans Mahan had made him between 1866 and 1868. It was embarrassing to have to ask Ashe for these monies but Mahan was desperate. To explain his sudden need for them, he created a fanciful story about the cost of transporting Elly to his next duty station abroad; so imminent did he represent this departure to be that he urged Ashe to borrow the money to repay the loans. Nearly twenty years in the U.S. Navy and Commander Mahan was reduced virtually to begging from his family and friends in order to survive. He was encouraged only to learn that "promotion goes briskly on," although he was "sorry to say it used to be due to retirements but now to deaths."[1]

It was during the impoverished summer of 1875 that Mahan became appalled at what he observed, heard, and read about events taking place in the United States. The Panic of 1873, which had driven Elly's parents to France "mainly from economical motives," had spawned the great depression of that decade. In addition, the thoroughly corrupt and discredited Grant administration clung doggedly to power. The Navy Department, under the incompetent Secretary George M. Robeson, was permeated with corruption, scandal, and pork-barrel political influence.

The racial and political excesses of Radical Reconstruction in the South presented no prettier picture—at least not on the canvas that Captain Ashe, late of the Confederate Army, painted for his friend Mahan. Indeed, Mahan had been home scarcely two weeks when he wrote Ashe that

> the whole country is groaning under the burdens laid upon us by the ignorance and oppression of Congress, and the frauds induced by that same oppression. I trust earnestly that both North and South may be approaching deliverance from their bondage—by the awakening of the people at large to the fact that they are being robbed and swindled and misled by the men of their choice.[2]

It was in this mood that Mahan entered briefly, although effectively, into the ranks of the naval reformers. Specifically, he became a reformer through the importunities of Democratic Senator Augustus Summerfield Merrimon, of North Carolina, a political associate and law partner of Sam Ashe. It was Ashe, himself a leading figure in the movement to return North Carolina to white rule, who brought Mahan and Merrimon together. The senator, in turn, suggested that Mahan might write a position paper on the "necessities of the Navy." In considering the execution of this commission, Mahan admitted to Ashe that "I have some ideas—but before putting them down I should like to talk them over with one or two officers within my reach. Naval policy throughout the world is at present in a very unsettled, transition, state—and doctors differ greatly in the courses they advise." Nevertheless, he entered into a confidential political alliance with Merrimon at a time when his own state of mind was decidedly hostile to the service in which he had spent two decades. In congratulating Ashe on the birth of his second son, he confessed that "but for my profession I should desire a son, but the fear that he would want to enter the Navy dampens my ardor."[3]

Visits to Elly's kin in Bar Harbor, Maine, and in Chestnut Hill, Pennsylvania, in July and August 1875 afforded Mahan time to study the matter further and to think about using Merrimon as a means of getting an evaluation of the weaknesses of the Navy, and a criticism of Robeson's lax administration of the Navy Department, before a larger audience than Sam Ashe.

In August, at his own request, he was assigned to duty at the Boston Navy Yard, beginning September 1, 1875. Thus he finally got back on the Navy payroll—at $3,000 per annum "and no allowances." He was, however, provided with quarters, at cost, in the yard. More importantly, it was his observations of the chicanery in the pork-barrel-ridden Boston Yard that propelled Mahan finally and decisively into the ranks of the naval reformers. In October of that year he also joined the U.S. Naval Institute, a professional organization of officers and others dedicated to the advancement of the Navy and the naval profession. It had been founded in 1873.[4]

Thus girded for battle, in December 1875 Mahan joined in the attack on Secretary Robeson and on the corruption he saw all around him in Boston. A letter to Ashe dated December 27 breathed shock and outrage. "There is little doubt that the Navy is rapidly getting into a most deplorable condition and that the fault lies largely with our present Secretary," he wrote. Although he had studied the matter but a short time, and lacked certain and "positive knowledge of things of which I shall speak," he was nonetheless convinced that theft, "barefaced bribery," and the criminal destruction of compromising documents and evidence characterized Robeson's administration of the Boston Navy Yard and of other naval installations. The Navy, he assured Ashe, was "undergoing very serious demoralization and injury" because of Robeson's "corrupt use of his office to promote political, personal and pecuniary gain." President Grant was no better. The only solution and salvation for the nation and the Navy was "to get rid of the Secretary," and that could only be done by exposing his "corruption and malfeasance in office." To advance and hasten this exposure Mahan began sending Ashe summaries of confidential documents from the Boston Yard which he thought exposed Robeson and his political henchmen. In so doing, he urged Ashe to bring this sensitive material to the attention of Senator Merrimon. Meanwhile, he looked forward with hope and anticipation to a coming investigation of the Navy Department headed by Washington C. Whitthorne, a Democrat from Tennessee and Chairman of the House Naval Committee.

In joining secretly with an anti-administration movement to depose Robeson, Mahan harbored no illusions on what such underground activity might do to his own career in the Navy:

It is scarcely necessary to say to you [he told Ashe] that holding such language touching the Secretary as I have here would expose me to severe punishment. That I use it may therefore prove to you how urgent I think the need is, and how deep my conviction of the deplorable condition in which the Navy now is. I shall therefore ask you when you have made such use of this letter as you may judge fit, and safe to me, to destroy it. If desirable any notes could be taken from it, but let the authorship drop. I trust I am not so deficient in courage or principle as to shrink from standing by any assertion I may make; but in this case I have, from lack of positive proof, confined myself purposely to indicating directions in which corrupt practice is supposed to exist, and means possibly of unearthing it. The discovery of such action on my part might hurt me deeply and could do no possible good. . . . I confide this to your hands, being conscious that intense and long hidden indignation at the maladministration of the service is my principal motive—personally, I have little to gain or to lose except as my interests are wrapped up in the Navy.[5]

This sudden concern and indignation were indeed "long hidden," since nothing in Mahan's surviving correspondence in the period 1870 to 1875 indicates that he had been brooding excessively over maladministration or any other problem in the Navy. On the other hand, there is substantial evidence to indicate that he was thoroughly bored with his profession and had no high regard for it. At best, he accepted the Navy as it was, disliked the life style it demanded, and thought frequently of leaving it. He certainly had no firm convictions that related the Navy to the diplomacy of the United States or to the projection of American power abroad. If anything, he was a confirmed isolationist—as was the vast majority of Americans in the 1870s. Indeed, he told Ashe that the "late Cuban flurry" with Spain in 1873 over the *Virginius* incident had "partly had [as] its aim" the attempt of the Grant administration to divert "the dreaded investigations of Congress from the points where real corruption and dishonesty lie hidden." It was, he said, a "foolish and purposeless row."

Mahan was, however, distressed to learn in 1875 and 1876 that the military leadership of the operational Navy had gradually lost power, leverage, and influence to civilian administrators within the Department of the Navy during the Grant administration. But he related this decline to nagging intramural debates on rank and status within the officer corps and to political corruption throughout the land, not to his personal or philosophical concern over a weakening of traditional American military virtues in the years immediately following the Civil War. The Mahan of 1876 was neither extreme nationalist nor militarist. He was only casually interested in international affairs. Thus, while he harbored an "intense desire" to see the Christians drive the Turks out of Europe, and hoped that Britain would "get a good thrashing" if she intervened in the Serbian War of 1876 on the Ottoman side, his view was born of a theological, rather than a diplomatic, reflex. He had no wish to enhance his own social station by enhancing the power and glory of the Navy or the international prestige of the United States. He had no psychological or ideological need to become a naval reformer or otherwise to emerge from the quiet obscurity of a career which, after twenty years, was something less than brilliantly distinguished. On the contrary, he had much to lose and little to gain by being identified with the anti-Robeson crusade. Mahan simply believed that the Eighth Commandment should govern the administration of the Department of the Navy. This, and a number of niggling little intra-service concerns that were more personal than profound, launched him into the naval reform movement of 1876.[6]

These motives became apparent as Mahan commenced a letter-writing campaign in early 1876 to mobilize opinion for naval reform. Few of these letters have survived, and it is not known to whom most of them were addressed. But it is clear that Mahan went directly to the political leadership in the opposition Democratic party in making his views known. He was certainly in correspondence with Senator Merrimon, and he used his father-in-law's personal connection with Thomas F. Bayard to reach that senator from Delaware. "I am determined during the coming months to do my utmost to remedy, and to bring to light the evils under which we suffer," he confided to Ashe. "I know that you too are as desirous of seeing honesty get the upper hand as I am." Visor down, lance at the ready, sun reflecting on white armor, "Sir Alfred" thus rode out to do combat with Secretary Robeson, with Isaiah Hanscom, Chief of the Bureau of Construction, with contractor Thomas H. Eastman, and with Commander J. N. Quackenbush, calling loudly for a congressional investigation of the entire Navy as he galloped.

With little hard evidence in hand, he charged that Robeson, Hanscom, and Eastman (a Naval Academy graduate of 1856) were thieves, pork-barrel operators, and worse: "What a stench there is," he noted, "in the mere thought that party intrigues should be mixed up with the question of building sound ships and doing good work in a Navy Yard." He was even willing to close down the yards if that would stop the corruption therein. "If they are to continue however a football for local politicians I should be reconciled to their discontinuance." He argued that the only solution to the evil of hiring Navy Yard workers and foremen for their political loyalty and voting performances, rather than for their competence as shipbuilders, was to place naval officers in charge of the yards and thus remove, root and branch, the corrupt civilian influence from the establishments. The commandants of the yards must wholly control the yards.[7]

He also took up the complicated case of Commander Quackenbush, the man whom he had relieved of command of the *Wasp* in February 1873. On orders from the department, Mahan in November 1873 had helped gather facts on Quackenbush's alleged drunkenness and incompetence on board the *Wasp*, which led to that officer's dismissal from the service in 1874. This survey convinced Mahan that his predecessor in the *Wasp* was a "drunken, disreputable and incompetent blackguard," a man of "very bad character." In 1874, however, President Grant accepted a Navy Department recommendation to reduce Quackenbush's dismissal to six years' suspension; and in 1875 there was an attempt within the department, abortive, as it turned out, to return Quackenbush to the active duty list. It was this attempt, which Mahan attributed to a "highhanded act of the Secretary of the Navy, or President," that nearly gave Mahan apoplexy. He immediately alerted Senators Merrimon and Bayard, pointing out the unconstitutionality of the proposed restoration. As he explained it to Merrimon, through Sam Ashe, "the Department reconsidered its action and restored him; in other words took a citizen, and made an officer of him 'without the advice and consent of the Senate'; if desirable I could give some clue to facts in this case." Mahan did. Whether this representation actually did Quackenbush in cannot be determined. It is known only that his suspension of 1874 stood.[8]

Somewhat less personal to Mahan than the Quackenbush case, but no less indicative to him that corruption and administrative confusion were rampant in the Navy, was the famous (or infamous) line-versus-staff controversy that had raged within the service since the Civil War. The issue was whether the Navy's physicians, marine engineers, paymasters, construction engineers, and similar "staff" personnel should have ranks, promotion patterns, and perquisites equal to those enjoyed by regular deck, or "line," officers—especially those line officers who had been trained at the Naval Academy and were expected actually to fight the ships of the Navy in combat. Put another way, the alumni of the old sailing Navy were slow in making provision in the officer corps for the new, essentially civilian, professional skills needed in the steam and steel Navy that emerged during and after the Civil War. In March 1871, for example, doctors, engineers, and paymasters were given "assimilated rank" in the Navy as captains, commanders, lieutenants, and so forth, the rank depending in part on the extensiveness of their prior civilian training and experience rather than solely on their length of service in the Navy. That legislation also gave these staff officers the same ranks in grade as those enjoyed by line officers who had entered the service as many as six years earlier. This was the so-called "six-year rule." The time differential was intended to reflect the fact that professional training ashore in medicine, bookkeeping, and steam or construction engineering had professional value equal to the six years of duty (at the Academy and at sea) that midshipmen served prior to being commissioned lieutenants. It was a complicated rank and seniority issue, and Mahan, who thought the whole business a bore when he was in the *Iroquois* and had long sneered at the function of staff officers, now took a personal, emotional, and generally conservative position on the question:

> So much rank has been given to the staff [he complained to Ashe] as they are now called, i.e., doctors, paymasters and engineers, that it is difficult to find officers of those corps who, being sent aboard ship, are not senior to the first lieutenant (now executive officer). . . . Thus, for example, a surgeon enters the Navy at the same time as I do, when he reaches that position on his list which makes him rank with Commander, he ranks not with me but with Commanders who entered the Navy six years before me. The trouble is more felt in the lower grades because they come in contact and collision with the first lieutenant who, as I observed, is too often their junior.

He was convinced that some sort of conspiracy was afoot among the staff officers to do away with the office of first lieutenant (executive officer) in naval vessels, even though the senior (first) lieutenant was, historically and actually, second in command. He also thought it presumptuous of these lesser staff beings to want to call themselves "Captain" or "Commander" rather than "Surgeon" or "Paymaster." But mostly Mahan was outraged over the rumor that staff officers were on the verge of demanding the "right" to share "the cabin with the commander of the ship." This was too much. As he told former Midshipman Ashe:

> The obvious objections to this will, in part at least, suggest themselves to you, who have some familiarity with the conditions of sea life—the constant vigilance required of a Commander while Captains of the Pay Corps are snoring away below, in bad weather and ticklish navigation; and who will realize that the Commander must have some place where he can privately reprimand, investigate, receive official visits; etc.; hold

confidential communications with ministers, etc. . . . . For after all, the
Navy exists simply as a military body for fighting purposes, and as for
the incidental duties of sea going, surveying, holding quasi diplomatic
relations in certain cases—protecting commerce and American interests;
in all these it is the line officer who acts, thinks, is responsible; and the
other bodies are merely adjuncts, necessary adjuncts as is the ship itself
—but plainly and simply and essentially subordinate.[9]

Having thus relegated naval surgeons, paymasters, and engineers to his
pantheon of minor imps and devils (along with Low Church Episcopalians, Latin-Americans, and most of his Academy classmates), Mahan
eagerly awaited Representative Whitthorne's coming investigation of Secretary Robeson's alleged maladministration of the Navy. His own chance
officially to participate in this pending exposé came when he was included
among those few officers who were invited to respond in writing to certain questions on the state of the Navy posed by the House Committee
on Naval Affairs. The opportunity to testify was apparently arranged by
Senator Merrimon.

Mahan's lengthy testimony, incorporated in a letter to Whitthorne
dated March 21, 1876, was at one and the same time courageous, thoughtful, forward-looking, backward-looking, tendentious, professionally controversial, and politically foolish. It did, however, sum up the essence of
the case for naval reform in the mid-1870s.

Mahan plunged into the line-versus-staff controversy by roundly damn-
ing the six-year rule, calling attention to pay inequities benefitting staff
officers, and defending the need for the continuation of the first lieutenant
berth in combat vessels. He supported the case for the first lieutenant,
whom he regarded as chief of staff to the commanding officer in combat,
with references to German military staff policy and by citing historical
situations chosen from single-ship frigate actions in the War of 1812, as
described by James Fenimore Cooper in his *History of the Navy of the
United States*. History, Mahan found, had its practical uses. He admitted,
however, that the Navy of 1876 needed a severe pruning of its aging and
often incompetent senior line officers. "If old officers are not retired in
peace, it will be found necessary to do so when war breaks out. How
many of the senior officers of the Navy in 1861 did duty afloat during
the war?" he asked rhetorically. These men should be retired into the
civil service and the foreign service to make room for younger officers
who were trapped in grade. Further, Mahan felt that a more rational system of selection and promotion of able younger officers, based on rigorous
examinations and searching annual fitness reports, should be instituted.

Much of Mahan's testimony hit at the noxious influence of the civilian Secretary of the Navy over the several Navy Yards (ostensibly administered by the Bureau of Yards and Docks), and the related incidence of pork-barrel political corruption at those facilities. He called for a reform whereby naval commandants, appointed by the bureau, would run the yards strictly as military establishments. These commandants, along with civilian naval constructors, would serve three-year tours. Save by court action and for cause, the commandants could not be removed by the Secretary during their terms of office. The routine hiring and firing of yard workers, the appointment and removal of foremen, the supervision of work parties, and the inspection of stores in the yards should all be handled by boards of naval officers responsible directly to the commandant. Mahan frankly admitted that from a theoretical standpoint the removal of the commandants of the yards from the direct and immediate control of the civilian Secretary of the Navy was wrong in Constitutional terms. "*Generally* the commandant and other officers should be removable by the Secretary, at discretion. Practically, I think [the change] necessary at this time." In other words, the problem was George Robeson; and getting Robeson out of office was more important at the moment to Commander Mahan than were the Constitutional niceties involved.

Mahan shied away from suggesting to Whitthorne's Committee (as he had in confidential letters to Ashe and others) that civilian naval contractors were also generally a dishonest breed. He confessed that "I do not know enough to make my opinion of much value," but thought it evident "that when the bureau which makes the contract also makes the inspection, and can also release from the contract, there is room for fraud." Similarly, he hedged a private statement he had made earlier to Ashe that to control rampant corruption the entire navy yard system might well be abandoned, or the yards reduced in number.

Less inhibited was his caustic professional comment on the reasons for the inferiority in speed of American naval vessels, compared with those built for the Royal Navy in England. These performance differentials he blamed squarely on the inefficient bureau system by which the service was administered, and on the incompetence of the Navy's engineers, a group of staff officers for whom he had had the highest contempt since his days in the *Iroquois*:

> This deficiency is attributable to the inferior character of the engines, as the speed under sail is generally good. Without expressing any definite opinion as to the precise cause of this inferiority, I give it as my opinion that the engineer corps of the Navy must take the discredit.

As far as my experience goes, our ships are good sea-boats; when navy-yard built, well constructed; and of good speed under sail, if given the wind. . . . There can be no doubt [however] that the present bureau system is incompatible with the harmony of design essential to the production of a first-class vessel.

To Mahan, speed was the major concern in ship design since, like most senior officers of his day, he still thought of naval strategy in terms of coastal defense and commerce-raiding. For this last task, so important in the War of 1812, speed and more speed had to be coaxed from the sails and engines, and more efficiency should be demanded of the engineers. But he felt that the Navy's administrative structure, dating from 1842, was incapable of achieving the "harmony of design" that might rectify matters, so poorly spelled out were the duties and roles of the several overlapping and virtually independent bureaus. As for the coastal-defense function of the Navy, "vessels intended mainly for the attack and defense of ports may be constructed with less care for speed," he held, "and more single aim at invulnerability, and theoretical perfection of ordnance, both as regards range and penetration."

It must be kept in mind that Mahan in 1876 considered himself something of an expert in ordnance. For this reason his comments to the Whitthorne Committee on the relationship between speed, armor, armament, and tactics, as these applied to the new steel and steam navies then building throughout the world, are revealing. True, they were more analytical than clairvoyant, and they looked backward to Trafalgar rather than forward to Tsushima or Jutland. But he clearly asked the right questions:

In the matter of armament, and perhaps of armor, I find myself at variance with men for whose opinion I have the highest respect. Still, I must say I feel that, in the eager effort to reach a theoretical maximum of accuracy and penetration, people have lost sight of the conditions of ocean warfare. The sea is now as restless as of old, our ships perhaps less steady; they will no longer carry canvas in action to steady them. Of what use is it to carry a gun that will pierce an indefinite number of inches of solid iron at great range, when, from the motion of the ship, you have scarce a chance of hitting your mark at that distance? It may be that ships will hereafter fight at long range, but I think they will find it necessary to close, much as of old. If they do, and are unarmored, it appears to me that we have reached in guns the useful limit of weight and range. Moreover, I hold there has been yet no fair test of the wisdom of reducing greatly the number of guns and throwing your whole weight of battery in a few pieces. A ship which has two guns has far greater chance of losing half her battery by an unlucky shot than one with twelve. The modern theories on this subject have not been tested by a number of well-fought actions under various conditions of wind and sea. Our experience of the last war, outside of monitors, was more in the nature of passing inland forts, than of a stand-up fight between antagonists till one yielded. Our success depended rather on the steady working of engines than upon the safety of the battery. These remarks of mine do not bear upon the subject of smooth-water fighting, as I said at first. In applying them to armored vessels it is to be asked, can you get the speed with the armor? If you can, of course you must carry heavier guns.

Thirty years later Mahan was still arguing these points and criticizing those who demanded ship and ordnance designs consistent with the concept of the all-big-gun battleship. He saw no reason to change the opinions he had held in 1876 just because the British had the bad manners to put HMS *Dreadnought* in commission in 1906.

To consider the pressing problems of guns, armor, and architecture, and to answer difficult design and construction questions during a period of rapid technological change in naval building, Mahan joined with other naval officers of the period in proposing the creation of a high-level "Board of Admiralty" whose job it would be to recommend the classes, designs, sizes, numbers, armament, construction, operational life spans, and ultimate disposition of all the vessels of the U.S. Navy. He visualized a fighting force of approximately one hundred modern vessels, each with a combat life of fifteen years. These would replace the thirty-three rotting wooden cruisers and eighteen obsolete Civil War iron monitors still deemed capable of putting to sea. Under Mahan's plan, each of the six existing Navy Yards would build one new vessel a year to replace the six oldest ships in service. The six displaced ships would thereupon rotate into a ready reserve fleet. As for the new vessels, "the work upon them would keep the yards moving at an easy rate, preventing the deterioration of disuse. Nothing destroys like rust." In calling for a Board of Admiralty, Mahan was recommending nothing less than the abandonment of naval administration by the eight overlapping and uncoordinated bureaus. In fine, he demanded honesty, efficiency, rationality, centralization of mechanical and theoretical planning, and coordination of the administrative function throughout the naval establishment. In these recommendations, ones that he supported throughout the remainder of his career, he was well ahead of his time. He was not, of course, alone in his advocacy of these changes. Captain Stephen B. Luce, his shipmate in the *Macedonian*, was by all odds the acknowledged leader of the reform movement of the 1870s. Mahan was a tardy recruit to an existing cause.[10]

Had Mahan stopped on the high professional note of administrative reform, or limited his remarks to the Whitthorne Committee to the areas of his technical competence and professional knowledge, he might not have experienced the career difficulties that were soon visited upon him. But he chose instead to attack Secretary Robeson personally. In so doing, he called attention to political corruption in the yards, blamed it on the Secretary, and accused Robeson of hampering "the power of command-ing officers . . . by general orders, by instituting boards, more or less as a check upon the commander. This is precisely wrong. . . . It is the policy of a weak man." He charged, too, that "the present Secretary" was im-properly "moving toward crippling the executive officer on board" and was in other ways unfit for his job. He undoubtedly indulged in this blunt criticism in the foolish expectation that his testimony would be kept secret. It was not.[11]

Following the controversial statement he made to the Whitthorne Com-mittee on March 21, 1876, a confidential copy of which he entrusted to Ashe ("don't let it go out of your hands"), Mahan turned to the writing of several position papers on the line-versus-staff controversy, especially emphasizing his displeasure with the six-year rule. He also made plans to write an "exhaustive" pamphlet during the summer of 1876 that would "hasten a rightful settlement." By mid-April, however, he had tired of the protracted struggle and was reduced to little more than hoping that by "quiet tenacity, right will prevail."[12]

While waiting for right to prevail, he saw fit to lecture the in-competent Secretary on the matter of proper procedure in the court-martial trial of Seaman Charles Dotty, which took place at the Boston Navy Yard in April. On the 26th of that month, Robeson demanded a revision in the final decision of the court, over which Mahan was presid-ing officer, and asked that a board of medical officers take additional testimony on the alleged insanity of Dotty. Although Mahan had not handled the trial particularly well, the Secretary's request for additional testimony was in clear violation of existing naval regulations on the sub-ject, and Mahan pointed this out to him in no uncertain terms. He also treated Robeson to a gratuitous tour through the bibliography of the printed military and naval law pertaining to the situation.[13]

Still another threat to the Navy's besieged officer corps appeared in May 1876 in the form of legislation introduced by Democratic Representative Henry B. Banning of Ohio, and supported by Whitthorne, to reduce the size of the officer list for reasons of economy. Mahan immediately unlimbered his pen and protested to Sam Ashe. The proposed cut was, he charged, entirely political, and was obviously related to the coming presidential campaign; further, it would save the government less than $50,000 per year. To base the number of naval officers on the number of Army officers, as Banning would have it, was simply "fallacious":

> A commander, for instance, commands a ship with one to two hundred men—he has the rank of Lt. Col. But how different the duties, how far greater the naval responsibility! in times of peace. Not a heavy gale of wind, not a night's intricate navigation, not a delicate question of interfering for the protection of American citizens that does not throw greater responsibility upon the naval man than the soldier has to bear in the course of a year. On the other hand, as we have greater numbers we have individually far less pay.

Mahan was quite willing that naval officers "bear our share of the suffering of the times," but he thought the Banning legislation "sweeping" and "unwise" and felt that some of the economy measures of Whitthorne, his hero of the past February, were "novel" and "crude." At the same time, he assured Ashe, that "as regards reduction of the Navy, while I think its personnel not too large for the needs of a war, yet I don't want you to think that I want to raise a howl because *I* am going to be hurt."[14]

Actually, Mahan was about to be rendered impoverished again. To his "great astonishment" and professional embarrassment, the Whitthorne Committee published in June the answers that Mahan and others had given its questions back in March. "None of us anticipated publicity, and I expect some have opened their minds very freely," he worried. A friend in Washington wrote to inform him that his letter to Whitthorne had "excited considerable comment" in the Navy Department, but the informant was not sure whether Robeson had seen it or not. Nevertheless, Mahan expected the worst. "I imagine it will be useless for me to apply for the command of the European fleet immediately," he said facetiously.

Still, he was confident that the final report of the Whitthorne Committee would show Robeson's administration of the Navy to be "lawless and wasteful." For this reason, he was both surprised and disappointed to learn that the lengthy investigation had not turned up "proof of direct personal corruption" by the Secretary. At no time, however, did he exhibit any desire to "wade through all the testimony" himself. Had he done so, he would have recognized the accuracy of the committee's judgment. Innuendo is not fact.

Given the outcome of Whitthorne's probe, it could scarcely have been a great shock to Mahan to discover in July 1876 that, because of the projected sharp reductions in naval appropriations, he was slated to be included among those officers who would be removed from active duty and placed on waiting orders at $2,300 annual pay. He began to suspect that his sudden visibility in the reform movement would result in the further punishment of furlough from waiting orders. That blow fell in August. "My fears as to my position have proved too well founded," he lamented. "I was detached about a week ago, and within the last two days the Secretary's order has appeared reducing our leave pay by one half. This makes my yearly income $1150 after twenty years in the service." Bad as this was, it was not as bad as the $10.00 to $15.00 per week earned by the average American industrial worker at the time.[15]

Mahan blamed his sudden economic misfortunes squarely on the Republican Secretary and on a Democratic Congress unwilling "to trust a man [Robeson] of such doubtful character with money on the eve of an election." Robeson, Mahan charged, had been very astute in choosing the officers to be slaughtered. Indeed, he had arranged the list of lambs so "as to make it impossible to prove that he was actuated by hostile feeling to any one"; but Mahan had no doubt in his own mind that he was being persecuted for his role in the reform movement. As he confided to Ashe: "it seems unfortunate that the men most eager for reform have been the very ones to suffer—but a man who is not prepared to undergo some inconvenience has small claim to credit and I do believe Mr. R. has been well exposed." He could only hope that the coming elections would "give Mr. Robeson the effective showing up which he richly deserves." Meanwhile, with no temporary civilian job in prospect, Mahan began planning to flee to France with his wife and child and live there with his in-laws.[16]

The disputed and irregular Hayes-Tilden election of 1876 was the first presidential contest in which Mahan took a profound interest. He was in the ambivalent, if not contradictory, position of wanting to see Grant and Robeson humbled and the Republican party win the election. He was delighted, therefore, when the "purer" Rutherford B. Hayes won the GOP nomination over the likes of such dubious political figures as James G. Blaine, Roscoe Conkling, Levi P. Morton, and Benjamin H. Bristow. Although the Republicans had brilliantly presided over the decline of the Navy after the Civil War, Mahan felt that the "currency question will incline me to favor the Republicans. Hayes is hard money."

Mahan, it is clear, was no incipient greenbacker, populist, silverite, labor-
ite, or agrarian reformer. His tenuous identification with naval administrative reform in the mid-1870s was about as reformist as he ever became.
He strongly opposed the eight-hour-day movement; he accepted female
and child labor; and he took a conservative stance on various domestic
economic and banking issues. The thought of female suffrage horrified
him. On the other hand, he opposed the crude Republican tactic of wav-
ing the "bloody shirt" of the Civil War in the presidential elections of
the 1870s. He was, in fine, a capitalist without capital who was generally
comfortable in the Republican party, corrupt though it had been under
Grant and his henchmen.[17]

While waiting for Hayes to win the election in November, Mahan
cast frantically about in an effort to secure a full-pay, active-duty assignment, even if it meant going to sea. A request made on August 30 for
command of the new steam sloop *Essex* (obsolete the day she was
launched) was turned down in Washington. In October he was assigned
temporary duty on a board convened for examination of the class of 1877
at the Naval Academy. During this service in Annapolis—he conducted
the examinations in theoretical and practical navigation—Mahan learned
that the headship of the Department of Gunnery at the Academy was
soon to be vacated by Commander James O'Kane. He let Rear Admiral
Christopher Raymond Perry Rodgers, Superintendent at the Academy,
know that he very much desired the post. Rodgers obliged him and, on
December 4, he received orders to that berth, effective January 1, 1877.
Meanwhile, during November, he involved himself in an acrimonious
exchange of letters with William C. Church, editor of *The Army and
Navy Journal*. Church had turned down an unsolicited article by Mahan
that attacked the assimilated-rank status of staff officers. "These staff gentlemen I believe deserve ridicule," Mahan told the editor, "not so much
for their attempt to gain the military titles (though that is absurd, being
a virtual confession of inherent inferiority to the line) as for their unwarranted assumption of them." In a second article, he condemned the recently adjourned House of Representatives for having reduced the number of active-duty officers, supposedly for reasons of economy. Editor
Church rejected that controversial piece as well.[18]

The final shock to Mahan was Commodore Daniel Ammen's unexpected letter of December 7, 1876, notifying him that his orders to the
Naval Academy were "hereby annulled. By direction of the Secretary."
On the previous day, the Republicans had completed the preliminary
phases of their theft of the disputed presidential election. Samuel J. Til-

den was fraudulently counted out of the race, and Hayes the Pure seemed assured of victory. The Robeson crowd in the Navy Department thereupon hastened to settle old scores with the naval reformers, and one such score was with the outspoken Commander Mahan.

Ammen, Chief of the Bureau of Navigation and a personal friend of President Grant, was merely a stagehand in this sorry drama, but it was to him that Mahan formally protested on December 11:

> I am confident that the Bureau will suspect me neither of ignorance of professional propriety, nor of presumption. Knowing, however, that the first orders were issued by reason of the request of Rear Admiral C. R. P. Rodgers, not through my own solicitation; and having been informed by him that he was as unprepared as myself for their revocation, I have an uneasy feeling that the sudden change will seem to imply a serious reflection upon me, as a man, or as an officer. . . . I venture to ask, and certainly trust, that the Bureau will inform me what reasons, if any, derogatory to me have prompted this change; or if there be none that it will enable me to state the fact with certainty to my fellow officers, and to the world that knows me.

Ammen lamely replied on December 13 that by "inadvertence of the Office of Detail, the nomination was not presented to the Secretary in advance of the issue of orders, and when so presented, was disapproved of and necessarily annulled by the Office of Detail." Thus, Mahan received the same shoddy treatment from Robeson that the outgoing Republican administration was then visiting upon Tilden and the hapless Democrats in the Electoral Commission appointed to adjudicate dubious returns from several states. One wonders why Mahan remained a lifelong Republican. But orders were orders; and Commander Mahan had no recourse but to apply for, and receive, a one-year leave of absence from the Navy, with permission to depart the country. Elly was three months pregnant, and on an annual salary of $1,150 he could make ends meet only by moving in with her parents in France.[19]

The period of enforced economic exile in France was mercifully short. In March 1877 Rutherford B. Hayes, who had lost the election by 250,000 popular votes but managed to win it in the stacked Electoral Commission, became President of the United States. His Secretary of the Navy was Richard W. Thompson of Indiana, a man so ignorant of naval affairs that he was allegedly surprised to learn that ships were hollow. But at least Thompson was honest. He approved Ammen's recall of Mahan from Pau on June 27 and his assignment to the Naval Academy as head of the Department of Ordnance and Gunnery, effective September 1.[20]

Meanwhile, during the spring of 1877, Mahan traveled extensively throughout southern France, delighted to have "the ocean between me and my friend Robeson." On this trip he took copious notes and collected photographs with a view toward writing a "couple of magazine articles, afterward a small book" on the history of the region. Research in the city library of Pau brought the completion of the work—which *Harper's Magazine* promptly rejected. Lippincott, the great Philadelphia publishing house, saw "literary merits" in the manuscript but would undertake its publication in book form only were Mahan personally to finance the venture. This risk Mahan was unwilling and unable to undertake.[21]

His disappointment in the matter was undoubtedly assuaged by the birth of his second daughter, Ellen Kuhn Mahan, in Pau on July 10, 1877, and the receipt of his belated orders to the Academy the following day. Actually, he and Elly had despaired of having more children after her miscarriage at sea in May 1875. "An only child is too much happiness in one venture," he had earlier confided to Ashe. So there was much joy in the Mahan household when "Nellie" made her appearance. His financial circumstances were also momentarily eased when Congress passed a deficiency bill which raised Mahan's furlough pay to $2,300. On August 23 the happy family of four departed Liverpool on board the White Star steamer *Germanic*. Mahan reported for duty at the Academy on September 4 and Elly and the children joined him there in early October, following a visit with her kin in Philadelphia. They were quartered in a "large and fairly commodious house, one of a row begun and partly finished in 1859 just before my graduation." Mahan was at last back on the Navy payroll on full pay ($3,000), income enough to afford a servant.[22]

There was little else to recommend the Academy to Mahan as a duty station. He did not like the place when he was a midshipman, and in 1878 he still recalled with bitterness his controversy with his classmates in 1858 and 1859. "Bitter as was the isolation I passed through then, it was less bitter than yielding my convictions would have been," he wrote. Also, he had been an unpopular and not overly successful teacher at the Academy when the institution had moved to Newport during the Civil War. He discovered, too, on his return to Annapolis in 1878, that while he was nominally the head of the Department of Ordnance and Gunnery all drills in gunnery were handled personally by Superintendent C. R. P. ("Alphabet") Rodgers and the Commandant of Midshipmen, Silas W. Terry, who, like two small children playing at war, enormously enjoyed firing off the antiquated guns with which the midshipmen practiced. Mahan found Admiral Rodgers to be "an able man, of very polished and elegant manners, etc, but very fond of running everything himself. . . . the kind of man who *will* have his own way." Mahan had no disposition to "waste my patience and strength fretting against such when he is my superior." Nor did Mahan kick any harder against the traces when Fox-hall A. Parker replaced Rodgers as Superintendent in 1878. Parker was "an able and amiable man" who ran a "slack" ship and was "still a victim of his old infirmity," drink. His appointment, said Mahan, "shows the recklessness of the present Administration that they should send as head of a school of this kind a man who, it is well known, *will* get drunk from time to time." But Mahan did not let it bother him.[23]

Instead, Commander Mahan settled into the comfortable routine of a Naval Academy officer-instructor with not much to do. It was a boring, though pleasant, existence marred only by the fact that in June 1880 little Nellie contracted "malarial fever" and nearly died. He participated in the professional activities of the Naval Institute (then fallen on difficult times), enjoyed the company of his wife and children, visited with his kin, entertained midshipmen in his home, taught his classes, and served on the Academic Board and on various temporary boards of inquiry dealing with cheating and other breaches of honor by the midshipmen. He studied the curriculum with a view to reforming, stiffening, and otherwise improving it, and he investigated instances of hazing among the midshipmen. Hazing at the Academy had become brutal, senseless, and physical in the late 1870s and early 1880s and Mahan properly con-demned it as playing no useful role in the education of naval officers. Needless to say, his condemnation did little to correct the situation.[24]

More pleasantly, Mahan came to know Midshipman Tasuka Serata, who later became a vice admiral in the Imperial Japanese Navy. Serata, class of 1881, was one of four Japanese nationals who were then being trained at Annapolis under an agreement with Japan concluded in 1868. Academically brilliant, devoutly Christian, and socially sophisticated, Serata was there as a result of the American opening of Japan in the 1850s and 1860s. This, it will be recalled, was the naval and diplomatic action in which Mahan had participated while serving in the *Iroquois*, an experience that led him, for the rest of his life, to fancy himself as a leading authority on Japanese history and American-Japanese relations. In 1913 Mahan wrote a highly eulogistic recollection of Serata as an introduction to Commander K. Asami's biography of the vice admiral, which was published in 1914.[25]

But the most important professional event in Mahan's otherwise un-eventful tour at the Naval Academy during the years 1877–1880 was his authorship of an article, "Naval Education," that placed third in a competition sponsored in 1878 by the U.S. Naval Institute. The competition grew out of the fact, Mahan admitted, that since "the Institute was growing feeble we determined as a last resort to offer a money prize for an Essay on the subject of Naval Education." True, there were only ten entries in the contest; but Mahan's article, though hastily and awkwardly written, was a creditable piece of work that marked his initiation into that small fraternity of American officers who fight best with their paragraphs. It also assuaged a literary ego wounded by earlier failures with *Harper's Magazine*, Lippincott, and *The Army and Navy Journal*. As he put it to Ashe, "the idea seized me of ventilating some of my ideas by this means." He continued to ventilate for the next thirty-five years.[26]

His essay, "Naval Education," had a distinctly reformist orientation. It called for higher academic standards at the Academy and for modernizing the curriculum, particularly in the areas of engineering science, applied physics and chemistry (ordnance), and naval architecture and construction. Technical knowledge of this kind could only produce better combat naval officers; and combat, after all, was what education at the Academy was all about. "History does not countenance the idea that an untroubled assurance of peace is a guarantee that war will not come," he wrote. Further, Mahan urged a strengthening of the curriculum in English, law, foreign languages, and naval tactics, advocated a program whereby, beginning in their second class (junior) year, midshipmen would concentrate their studies on specific disciplines. He especially pleaded that the time had come for the Navy to "recognize clearly . . . certain classes of men in the service whose particular capacity lies in brain work or aptitude for mechanical science." Indeed, at the time Mahan wrote his article, Ensign Albert A. Michelson, class of 1873, a member of the Department of Physics and Chemistry, headed by Commander William T. Sampson, was completing the important experiments that first measured the velocity of light. But the Navy of 1878–1879 had little patience with such impractical "brain work," and the brilliant young Michelson soon left the Academy and the naval service. Mahan concluded his plea for educational reform with the thought that "any scheme of education is defective that makes no effort to help the learner to believe in and to depend upon God."[27]

These casual years at the Naval Academy afforded Mahan additional opportunity to ruminate at leisure on the state of the nation and the Navy. He considered the aged Secretary Thompson to be a complete, if honest, old fool and a "worthless" administrator. He was useful to the service only in that "his incumbency will relieve us of some of the odium that

Robeson's rascality brought on us." On the other hand, he had great hopes for a young Republican representative, Benjamin W. Harris of Massachusetts, who was soon to play a major role in launching the New Navy, and for Representative Whitthorne whom he met socially in 1878 and liked. "He is not a polished man . . . [but] likely to be in the main a good friend and useful man for the Navy." Indeed, he would rather see the Tennessee Democrat head the important House Naval Affairs Committee than any Republican he could think of. "Some very sound ideas are developing in the House Committee," Mahan wrote in June 1878. These were ideas that had to do with building a modern steam and steel navy, ideas of a naval renaissance that Whitthorne was vigorously to champion in the 1880s:

> I learned [the] other day that he [Whitthorne] had formed a very favorable opinion of me, due simply to my letters at the time of Robeson's troubles—which naturally strengthens my convictions that in the long run it is more profitable to speak boldly and honestly than to have an eye ever to policy. It may possibly be that my opinions may have as much weight as can be due them, when presented to him. Be that as it may, I am constitutionally so that no advantage can repay me for stifling my sense of right. . . . There is not much merit when a man is thus constituted; it is simply a choice of evils, suffering or humiliation.

Nevertheless, Mahan had learned an expensive lesson from the public attack he had made on Robeson in 1876. His attack on Secretary Thompson was therefore cautious and private. "You will see the propriety of not letting these private opinions of mine get out," he warned Ashe. "I shall never, I hope, be backward in resisting wrong when called on; but I don't want to get into trouble by *gratuitous* expressions of opinion."[28]

It may have been for this reason that he confined to his private correspondence in 1880 his opinions on the need for a vigorous building program. This he related in turn to the need for a dominant American presence in the Gulf and Caribbean, specifically at the Isthmus of Panama—a view endorsed by President Hayes and other prominent Americans who were beginning to visualize the commercial advantages of a more aggressive economic foreign policy. At this time, however, Mahan was no imperialist or expansionist. On the contrary, he remained an isolationist. But he was a realistic and pragmatic isolationist, and he saw that the Navy might benefit from events transpiring at the isthmus. Thus news that French interests were planning the construction of a canal at Panama brought this firm statement in May 1880:

The country, and the Navy too, have looked on with some unconcern—for the prospect of foreign entanglement seemed so remote; and few of us favored an attempt to compete with the iron clad navies of foreign powers. A strong defensive force for our coast lines; offensive operations to be directed mainly against an enemy coast. The gradual decrease of the materials of the Navy was regretted mainly because it deprived officers of the amount of sea service desirable to keep their hands in. Now the Canal at the Isthmus may bring our interests and those of foreign nations in collision—and in that case—which it is for statesmen to forecast—we must without any delay begin to build a navy which will at least equal that of England when the Canal shall have become a fact. We have for such a purpose *no* navy; it would probably be safe to say we have not two iron-clads worthy in armor or guns to stand alongside those of Turkey or Spain. To control at the Isthmus we must have a very large Navy—and must begin to build as soon as the first spadeful of earth is turned at Panama. That this will be done I don't for a moment hope, but unless it is we may as well shut up about the Monroe Doctrine at once. Our millions of men can't get to or be fed at the Isthmus except by sea; but a popular Government will never dare to spend the money necessary to prepare.[29]

Mahan had no great confidence that either a Democratic or Republican administration in Washington would or could wrench the people of the United States from their small-navy convictions or lift the Navy from its embarrassing rank of twelfth among the world's navies. As the election of 1880 approached, he worried also that the Bland-Allison Silver Purchase Act, passed under Democratic auspices and over the veto of President Hayes in February 1878, would inflate American currency to the point of severely weakening the economic integrity of the nation. He felt, too, that the Democrats were less likely to be as generous as the Republicans in the matter of naval officers' pay; and he was appalled at the corrupt antics of the Tammany Hall Democrats in New York.

But Mahan was not an automatic Republican. On the contrary, he was fearful in 1880 that the GOP would nominate some thoroughly low-class person like Blaine, Grant, or Conkling for the presidency. Should that be the case, Mahan would prefer Thomas F. Bayard, if the Democratic party would but have the good sense to nominate him. He realized, however, that Bayard's "secession speeches before the war would injure him with too many Republicans" to make his victory likely. He particularly worried that if a Democratic administration headed by Bayard or anybody else came to power "*we* [naval officers] . . . will find many officers who left the service in 1861 placed over our heads." While Mahan had no use for the excesses of Radical Reconstruction, or for the "bloody shirt" political tactics of the GOP in the 1868–1880 period, he had even less use for those American military and naval officers who had deserted the old flag in 1861 to fight for the Confederacy.[30]

So it was that the Democratic party which "always contrived to alienate" Mahan, again alienated him in 1880 on the sound-money issue and on the military-loyalty question. In the presidential election of that year Mahan voted for James A. Garfield, wholly without enthusiasm and with "no faith in Garfield's strength of character." The twentieth president, although tainted with scandal, was simply the lesser evil, the greater being General Winfield Scott Hancock of Pennsylvania, the Democratic nominee. Hancock lost by the slim margin of 7,000 votes in more than 9,000,000 cast. He lost the key state of New York thanks to "the stupidity or treachery, whichever it is, of Tammany—to which Hancock's defeat is probably due. . . . the N.Y. politicians thought the national game up after Indiana and so dropped the national contest to secure their special personal aims in the city." Or so Mahan thought. The Republicans regained control of the House for the first time since 1874. Close as the final result was, Mahan felt that "after eight years of Grant I could not understand people wanting any more soldiers for some time and I did not, and do not, see any reason to believe that Hancock had any more or as much capacity as Grant. The latter was a coarser but I think an abler man; and both were utterly unfitted by previous education for the place. There was some excuse for our failing to see this prior to Grant, but none to my mind since."

A high point of the election for Mahan was the sober orderliness of the great crowds that thronged Herald Square and Times Square in New York City, "where the returns were being shown by calcium lights." As for the political future, Mahan told Sam Ashe:

> I hope the Democratic party will now identify themselves with some other policy than the protection of the Southern states from Governmental interference. We think that a pretty dead issue. Civil service reform, revenue reform looking ultimately to free trade, and dollars *worth* dollars, that was my old idea of the Democratic party—and when those ideas are identified with any party I will be so too.

But, as it turned out, Mahan never voted for a Democratic presidential nominee. He was a potential Democrat only in his letters to Sam Ashe and only between elections.[31]

VI

A Career in Stays
1880-1885

I respectfully, but very earnestly, ask that I may be relieved from the command of the Wachusett *and ordered home. . . . The* Wachusett *is probably the worst Commander's command in the service. . . . I have borne it long enough [and] I shall be deeply grateful for relief.*

Alfred Thayer Mahan to William C. Whitney, May 15, 1885

On July 3, 1880, Mahan was detached from the Naval Academy and ordered to report to Commodore George H. Cooper at the Navy Yard in New York (Brooklyn) as navigation officer. It was as though he had been assigned to the USS *Trivia* on an extended cruise to nowhere. Seldom has the U.S. Navy buried one of its good minds in a job so thoroughly mechanical. For three years Commander Alfred Thayer Mahan devoted his time and professional energies to routine tasks that could have been handled by a competent clerk. This is not to say that he objected to this waste of his intellectual talent. On the contrary, he seems to have enjoyed his immersion in pointless make-work at the Brooklyn Yard. "These details may seem trivial," he wrote on one occasion, with reference to the width of signal flags, "but, if the observing of them ensures better and more uniform results, they are worth attending to; and their very triviality gives force to [my recommendations] . . . for it is not probable that they will be carefully watched." Certainly, minor concerns such as these required no brainpower and they permitted Mahan to turn to more important tasks—the writing of his first book and the raising of his children. And, dull as it was, the Brooklyn Yard was shore duty.[1]

During this three-year period he and Elly and the children rented a house on 11th Street, just off Fifth Avenue, within a short walk of the

Hotel Hanover, on East 15th Street, where Elly's mother, Ellen Kuhn Evans, and her Aunt Margaret Evans had come to reside after the death of Manlius Glendower Evans in Pau in 1879. The 11th Street house was wholly inconvenient to Mahan's job. It required an hour's commutation each way by ferry to Brooklyn. Only the rent was right. "My means compel me to live about 2½ miles from the Yard," he complained to Ashe. But it was on 11th Street, on February 12, 1881, that Lyle Evans Mahan was born. He was the third and last child of the Alfred T. Mahans, and was destined to go on to Groton School, to Columbia College (class of 1902), and to a successful law practice in New York City. The period 1880–1883 was a time for family.[2]

During the early 1880s Mahan commenced the instruction of his children in history, literature, and theology. They were never sent to regular Sunday School since Mahan "greatly distrusted the abilities of the average teacher" found in such places. Instead, he taught his children their prayers and their catechism at home. He wrote young Ellen's confirmation instructions himself. The children were "expected to read our Bibles regularly and to pray night and morning; and what he expected of us he did himself." Mahan personally conducted family prayers every morning after breakfast which, like lifeboat drills, "lasted exactly five minutes." The children were also taken to Episcopal church services at the earliest possible ages. Mahan would attend these himself, on some Sundays as often as three times. Still, the religious regime imposed upon his own children was not nearly so rigorous as that imposed on him during his adolescent days at West Point. After church the Mahan children were permitted to play games and read secular books, their father maintaining that "Sunday was a day of recreation and rest, as well as of worship, and that it was instituted for these two purposes." To be sure, the children were taught to tithe, as Mahan himself did throughout his life. "He early taught us to tithe what money we received," Ellen recalled. "He would tell us about the poor little Indians or Chinese until we longed to help; the rest was easy." They were taught also instantly to obey, a reaction encouraged by firm parental hands applied to soft bottoms.[3]

Mahan instructed his children in a Christian theology of a rather traditional sort, filled as it was with warnings of the wiles of an ever-scheming and ever-present Satan, with admonitions always to "pray and watch and struggle." He insisted on regular Bible-reading and pure moral thought, assuring his children that these exercises would bring "the gift of the Holy Ghost" and otherwise guarantee their personal salvation.

Further, the children were taught to eschew bad grammar and those who used it, and to read only those books "which are well written with good language and worthy thoughts." From time to time, when he was away at sea, he would draw up and send to them lists of suitable books which he insisted they must read. "If you do not like them at first," he admonished, "make up your mind that it is a *duty* to thus get the knowledge of them, the liking will follow." Aside from the Bible, he particularly recommended the works of Washington Irving as being instructive and uplifting (perhaps because his grandmother, Mary Jay Okill, had known Irving personally), and he suggested the reading of Shakespeare and Milton. While he admitted that he personally did not care for the works of the famous Englishmen, he noted that "if I had kept reading them as I have the Bible I might have learned to love them."[4]

Strictly forbidden his daughters were books and stories in popular magazines that suggested, even with Victorian indirectness, that sex existed. And for Helen and Ellen Mahan it probably never did. Thanks to their father, both ladies went through life unpursued, unsullied, and unmarried, closely monitored (until his death in 1914) by a stern head of house who considered sex to be a human weakness. Ellen, for example, felt it necessary to ask her father's permission to read certain doubtful books until she was over twenty years of age. One such book, *A Blameless Woman*, she was permitted to read only with Mahan's firm warning, "Remember, she isn't a blameless woman." Ellen later wrote that "Somehow, I think I must have suspected that." Other treatises on the forbidden subject were denied the children outright.[5]

Meanwhile, Mahan's naval career moved forward at the New York Navy Yard with all the precision, direction, excitement, and speed of a sailing ship in stays. Assisted by Lieutenants Edward W. Bridge and Franklin J. Drake, Mahan supervised the procurement, testing, and installation of navigational equipment in ships of the Navy. This equipment included compasses, binnacles, taffrail logs, running lights (and the various oils burned therein), flags, fathometers (lead lines), chronometers, and such navigational tools as charts, books, and mechanical drawing instruments. The duty required daily correspondence with various ships' chandlers in New York, with the Bureau of Navigation in Washington, and with G. H. Cooper and John H. Upshur, the two commandants of the Brooklyn yard during his tour there. It was correspondence of a highly technical nature, and it revealed Commander Mahan as an efficient, conscientious, thorough, cost-conscious, and dedicated naval technician. His attention to detail was profound. Indeed, he "polished up that handle so carefullee" and otherwise performed menial tasks so well, that it could later have been his own advice to young naval officers to

Stick close to your desks and never go to sea,
And you all may be Rulers of the Queen's Navee![6]

He was particularly fascinated with the testing of various new inventions thought suitable for use in the naval service. On one occasion he urged upon his superiors "an appliance," invented by his subordinate, Lieutenant Drake, "for taking bearings more easily and accurately by night as well as day." But mainly he tested various designs and improvements in ships' lanterns and reported on the quality and types of oil that produced optimum results in specific kinds of lamps. Seldom has an American naval officer so selflessly or for so long a period of time dedicated himself to the relative advantages and disadvantages of lard oil, whale oil, and coal oil for shipboard illumination—all this three years after John Wanamaker had installed electric arc lights in his store in Philadelphia. In 1883 the *Trenton* became the Navy's first ship to be fitted with similar illumination.[7]

Indeed, Mahan suggested to his superiors in March 1882 that the Age of Electricity had truly dawned. He urged the Bureau of Navigation to place suitable textbooks dealing with the subject on board all ships and in the libraries of all shore stations. When asked, however, whether he had considered "the application of Electricity to Torpedo Warfare," he admitted that he had but cautiously insisted that that problem belonged "to the Bureau of Ordnance, and has not [been] gone into . . . in the present examination."[8]

Clearly, Mahan had learned, after twenty-five years in the Navy, not to stick his neck out unless absolutely necessary. He had also learned that a commander on his way slowly up the rank ladder (he was in that grade for thirteen years) was not expected to make decisions that required personal judgments. In one instance, for example, he was severely criticized for authorizing the expenditure of $8.46 for plotting instruments needed at the last minute to get a ship to sea on schedule. The employment of such common sense was not encouraged in the Navy in 1883. For this reason Mahan was inclined to submit to his superiors the responsibility for making final decisions on even the most niggling matters. Better stupidly safe than sensibly sorry.[9]

Given so much daily paper-shuffling between the Bureau of Navigation in Washington and the navigation officer at the yard in New York, and given, too, the mass of picayune administrative detail that was carried out at the Brooklyn yard by order of the bureau, it is not surprising that the eagle-eyed clerks in the bureau occasionally caught Mahan in a minor administrative error. When this occurred, and it was infrequent, Mahan responded as any career officer might: he accepted full blame for the mistake. This was honorable. It was expected of gentlemen. But he would then proceed to exculpate himself by the time-honored device of blaming the error on a subordinate, often a civilian employee at the yard. Only on rare occasions during his service in the New York Yard did he flatly admit a mistake without providing an extenuating circumstance.[10]

At the same time, it should be noted that Mahan spent these three otherwise non-productive years at the New York Navy Yard studiously investigating ways and means for the Navy to do its business more efficiently and more economically. He had witnessed at first hand the waste and inefficiency at the Boston Navy Yard during the Robeson administration of the Navy Department, and he was determined that such sloppiness would not be repeated at Brooklyn—at least not on his watch. He was therefore constantly recommending to his superiors small ways in which time, money, and equipment might be saved. "I would respectfully submit to the consideration of the bureau," he wrote Cooper on June 13, 1881,

> that we have on hand here a considerable quantity of old brass, and it is probable that an arrangement could be made with the Bureau of Steam Engineering or Construction, to cast binnacles for us in the Yard. . . . It has also occurred to me, though the matter is beyond my own province, that there must be a good many bronze smooth bore howitzers now becoming useless, and the Bureau might perhaps obtain by negotiation with the Bureau of Ordnance the binnacles to be cast at the Washington Navy Yard, where bronze founding has been so long carried on.

Needless to say, this suggestion was too obvious and reasonable to command Cooper's interest.

Undeterred, Mahan pushed on. He paid careful attention to comparative prices for goods and services, insisted on the delivery of quality merchandise, monitored costs, suggested centralized purchasing, and recommended coordination of the manufacturing and distribution of items such as flags and bunting, that were then being produced in several Navy Yards. He also forwarded to his superiors numerous suggestions for effective cost accounting as well as proposals for efficient inventory accession, control, and management. It can be said without hesitation that during his tenure as navigation officer at Brooklyn, the yard there, certainly the part of it that came under his direct purview and responsibility, was run honestly, economically, and efficiently. The taxpayer got his money's worth and Mahan got the satisfaction of knowing that the flag of cost-effectiveness was nailed firmly to the yard masthead.[11]

Nowhere was Mahan's capacity for tedious efficiency better displayed than in his exhaustive testing of the stitching used in the manufacture of bunting into various flags, signal hoists, national ensigns, and special pennants used in the fleet. The question he addressed was whether the cost factors involved justified shifting from hand to machine manufacture. To be sure, Elias Howe and Isaac M. Singer had invented, perfected, and marketed the common sewing machine some forty years earlier. But the Navy was slow in getting around to a formal recognition of that event, and Alfred Thayer Mahan spent the better part of two years in Brooklyn testing sewing-machine performance. Thus, while others in the Navy and the Congress were beginning to worry about the complex problems inherent in converting an antiquated wood, sail, and smooth-bore navy into a modern fighting force of steel and steam and rifled guns, Mahan sat happily in the New York Navy Yard counting stitches and testing threads. They also serve who only sit and sew. Specifically, he wrote detailed recommendations on how best to save an inch or two of bunting in the manufacture of various flags, while conducting elaborate tests of the tensile strength of different grades of thread supplied to the Navy by its chandlers. At best it was idiot work. Nonetheless, Mahan asked the Bureau of Navigation in March 1882 to give him the "benefit of any suggestions or warnings" as he launched his thread-testing program. "The field," he confessed, "is a new one to me." New or not, the commander finally decided that hand-sewn flags were superior in quality and durability to those produced by sewing machines. The Age of Singer was not yet destined to dawn in the U.S. Navy.[12]

Another of Mahan's duties at the New York Yard was to supervise the manufacture of sets of foreign national ensigns supplied to American warships bound overseas. Appropriate foreign flags were normally flown at the foremast, as a gesture of courtesy, when American men-of-war visited foreign ports. Unfortunately for the conscientious Mahan, and perhaps symptomatic of America's diplomatic isolation in the early 1880s, the Bureau of Navigation did not have the foggiest notion of the correct design of some foreign flags, particularly those of several of the Latin-American countries. Some of the flags (the Mexican and the Spanish) being issued to American naval vessels in 1881 and 1882 were of faulty design; others (the Paraguayan and the Peruvian) had been out of stock for years and could not be supplied at all; still others (the Brazilian, for example) showed inaccurate color combinations, proportions, and color shadings. The *Book of Flags* issued by the bureau in 1876 was filled with errors.

Mahan thus began preliminary work on a new edition of the *Book of Flags*, assigning to Lieutenant Drake the task of drawing correct designs and accurate coats of arms. When the bureau was unable to tell him, for instance, what the national ensigns of Guatemala, El Salvador, Santo Domingo, and Haiti were supposed to look like, Mahan went directly to the New York consulates of those states and asked. Research in primary source materials, this. He discovered in May 1882 that the current Guatemalan flag had been in existence for "five or six years—without coming to the knowledge of the Bureau." As he wondered aloud to Upshur, "I suppose that our ships rarely go to Guatemalan ports." He also learned that while the designs of the Honduran and El Salvadorian flags he had on hand in Brooklyn "are in some cases not quite accurate there will be no occasion to meddle with such serviceable flags as may now be on hand." It would be too expensive to make the corrections needed. Why bother? Few American warships called in Central American ports, anyway.[13]

If Mahan recognized that the Bureau of Navigation could not even keep up with the correct designs of foreign flags, he recognized even more clearly that the Navy as a whole was in a frightful condition during these same years. There were, to be sure, stirrings of the birth of what would be called the New Navy, but Mahan seems not to have had much hope between 1880 and 1883 that its conception had been effected or that its delivery would be normal. Instead, he had only to look at the New York Navy Yard and be utterly depressed. He complained that his own office was understaffed and that he needed at least four civilian workers "to meet the growing needs of the office," rather than the three allotted him by a cutback decision on September 15, 1882. When in that same month the Navy decided that it would implement the federal legislation passed in 1882 to create the eight-hour work day (applicable only to workers employed at government installations) by cutting wages 20 per cent from that paid for the earlier ten-hour day, Mahan protested that he could neither recruit nor retain competent workers at the lower wage. He believed that a man had the inherent right to choose to work ten hours a day for $3.00 rather than eight hours for $2.40.[14]

If there were not enough civilian workers at the yard to suit Mahan, there was not much else there that pleased him either. The yard had no lighter in which to move stores and equipment easily and efficiently around New York Harbor. Staten Island was a world away. There was but one tug available. Much to his embarrassment he discovered that the Navigation Office of the yard had no navigational charts of New York Harbor and no charts of Long Island Sound or the coast of New England. The dry dock was jury-rigged. As he described it in April 1883: "I will mention in this connection that, besides the gates, there are at the outer end of the dock some five hundred tons of pig iron needed to keep the bottom of the dock down against the upward pressure of the water." No copy of the U.S. Naval Institute's *Proceedings* had been received at the yard since 1877, and the professional library there was wholly inadequate. Mahan attempted to straighten out the mess and he was constantly putting through book-order requisitions for basic historical and technical texts.[15]

All this was indicative of the sorry state of the Navy as Mahan saw it in the early 1880s. It is well to point out, however, that his critical views of the situation were revealed only to Sam Ashe and to a few other confidants. The briefly aroused naval reformer of the mid-1870s was now a chastened career officer, ensconced in a pleasant if boring shore job, studiously bent on avoiding public controversy. Indeed, even Secretary Thompson had, by January 1881, come to have some redeeming merit in Mahan's eyes. While he had "done much harm from either ignorant or willful neglect to urge upon the country the worthlessness of most of our vessels," he had rendered a personal service (just what is not known) to Lieutenant Dennis H. Mahan, the commander's younger brother.[16]

On only one known occasion during his tour at the New York Navy Yard did Mahan sound off publicly to the Secretary of the Navy. On April 20, 1881, he wrote the new Secretary, William H. Hunt, pointing out the arithmetical fact that the Naval Academy was graduating far too many midshipmen annually and that most of these young men could never hope to reach the rank of commander. He correctly noted that but ten commanders and six lieutenant commanders retired, resigned, or died each year, whereas the Academy was graduating more than seventy passed midshipmen in the class of 1881 alone. Some of these men would have to wait ten years before being commissioned ensign. The Royal Navy, he argued, admitted but twenty-five new midshipmen annually to sustain the needs of an officer corps numbering 50 admirals, 150 captains, 200 commanders, and 600 lieutenants, much larger than that of the U.S. Navy. "Contrast the proportions with ours," he asked Hunt:

> For the good of the service, and for the sake of the young men who,
> during their thoughtless age, are preparing for themselves a manhood

without hope or future, I solicit your attention to this matter. The measure proposed by them, that they should receive their Ensign's commission two years after graduation, is the merest palliative. It will not help them in their road to the higher grades . . . it will simply beguile them, through a little more money, to remain in the Navy till too late to make their way outside. It is, however, manifestly beyond my province to suggest what is to be done.[17]

Mahan had no solution to the officer glut save the obvious one: build more ships. But to what purpose? In response to what presumed national need? The Mahan of 1880 to 1882 embraced no imperialist solution to the problem of too many officers for too few ships. His understanding of and interest in American diplomacy in the early 1880s did not transcend his belief that control of an isthmian canal by a European power would not be in the interest of the United States and its Monroe Doctrine. He felt that such control would be fraught with danger, even with future war—a war the unarmed nation could not hope to win. "To control at the Isthmus we must have a very large Navy," he had warned Ashe in March 1880. But he went no further than this in explaining the need for more warships. Indeed, at this point in his career he thoroughly distrusted such advocates of a muscular foreign policy as Secretary of State James G. Blaine. At the same time, however, he warmly approved Secretary Hunt's and Secretary William E. Chandler's advocacy of the building of a modern steam and steel navy, if not the foreign-policy rationalizations with which that advocacy was accompanied.

The expansion of American commerce into overseas markets interested Mahan not at all in these years. The acquisition of American colonies abroad was a thought that apparently had never entered his head. Only gradually did he come to embrace the arguments that were being developed in Congress in 1880 to 1883 that related national economic well-being and national power to the existence of sea power—arguments that he himself so effectively synthesized, publicized, and championed in the 1890s. Bogged down as he was in pedestrian jobs in Annapolis and New York from 1880 to 1883, it is not surprising that he had not evolved a world view of the nation and its Navy. On the contrary, he was as much concerned with the domestic political and economic corruption he thought would be inherent in the construction of the first ships of the New Navy as he was with the arguments concerning economic foreign policy and national security being advanced for their building. He expressed his ambivalence in this regard to Ashe in December 1882:

Immersed as our people are in peaceful and material pursuits, the military establishment is necessarily one of our lesser interests. . . . Practically we have nothing. Never before has the Navy sunk so low. . . . it is not too much to say we have not six ships that would be kept at sea in war by any maritime power. . . . The urgency is great; and although the horde of robbers that surround the treasury and Congress will make it necessary to have caution in guarding the expenditures, yet they must be made and made very freely if the Navy is to be maintained.

He thought that Secretary of State Blaine's "reckless" meddling and muddling in 1881 in the War of the Pacific (1879–1884), which pitted Chile against Peru and Bolivia, had been fraught with danger. "We could not have controlled Chile's men of war," he noted. He knew that Spain, "a near and troublesome neighbor," possessed naval forces far superior to those of the United States. But while he hoped "that the Democrats may do something for rebuilding the Navy," he saw "no chance" of anything really happening until after the 1884 elections. The only ray of hope he could detect was that Secretary Chandler was "doing well, wiping out all the old figureheads."[18]

By August 1883, as he prepared to take command of the *Wachusett* at Callao, Peru, Mahan had gradually shifted and sharpened his position and was beginning to show real enthusiasm for the naval building program launched by President Chester A. Arthur and Secretary of the Navy Chandler in 1882. This initiative by the administration that came to power after Garfield's assassination in September 1881 produced, in 1883, legislation authorizing the U.S. Navy's first modern steel vessels—the protected (but unarmored) cruisers *Atlanta*, *Boston*, and *Chicago*, and the dispatch boat *Dolphin*. The cruisers were small (3,189 to 4,500 tons), slow, and vulnerable. But they represented the beginning of the New Navy and their authorization persuaded Mahan to deny that the construction of such vessels need necessarily be expensive or corruption-laden—a denial made full in the face of the fact that President Arthur's past reputation as Collector of the Port of New York in the 1870s was anything but snow-white. Nevertheless, Mahan's new position was that the nation must undertake immediate naval preparation for possible future war, now that European nations had solved most of the design problems associated with steam and steel warships:

The present time is very favorable [he told Ashe in mid-August]; it is possible after twenty years of experiments, mainly by foreign nations, the results of which are known to us, to build a fine fleet, of such numbers as may be judged necessary, and equal to performance and wants now well understood; a fleet that shall be superior ship for ship to the same kind of vessels elsewhere. This was our old policy. . . . the cheapest way of having a small navy capable of expansion is to have a full corps of capable combatant officers, with a sufficient nucleus of trained seamen attached to the flag. Such a leaven would quickly leaven the lump —though unfortunately we have no lump, no merchant service, whence to train seamen. This, of course, is partly a plea for my own prospects; but only slightly so, for I am so heartily disheartened by our history of the past fifteen years that I have left in me no expectations except to do my duty as I may best, and trust that the Lord will look out for me. The country cares nothing for the service nor will care, *I* think, till irremediable disaster in that quarter has overtaken it. It will then be too late for that time.[19]

It would be convenient to argue that Commander Mahan's conversion to advocacy of the New Navy was related primarily to "a plea for my own prospects," or to some similar self-serving economic or professional need he may have had. But far more important to him than these concerns was his interest in solving the problem of the overproduction of U.S. officers and his recognition of the fact that technical breakthroughs in warship design had at last been accomplished by foreign naval architects. Purely personal considerations ranked low on his scale of rationalizations for a respectable naval capability. He was already high on the commanders' list in 1883, virtually certain of promotion to captain in 1885, unless, he told Democrat Ashe facetiously, "your side of the House follow Robeson and reduce our numbers still farther." His "own prospects" were therefore assured.

He had come to feel, too, that a New Navy of modest size would absorb the officer surplus, thanks to abolition of the policy at Annapolis that distinguished between cadet midshipmen (line) and cadet engineers (staff). "This in time will result in the line officers being qualified to run the engine, and in having not more than one or two, instead of four to six Engineers. . . . With the further change of making the paymaster from the line officers and so having him a combatant instead of a non-combatant officer will further reduce the necessary personnel."[20]

Mahan's belated endorsement in mid-1883 of the various technical arguments for the New Navy can therefore best be traced to his reading and writing of history. He had much time for this while serving at the Brooklyn yard. It was during his leisurely tour there that he read William F. P. Napier's classic *History of the War in the Peninsula*. This multi-volume work transported him immediately into "a new world of thought" that made him "appreciative . . . of the military sequences of cause and effect." It also encouraged him to try his own hand at military history; specifically, to undertake the research and writing of his first book, *The Gulf and Inland Waters*, when unexpectedly asked to do so. This volume was published in June 1883 as part of Charles Scribner's Sons hastily conceived and executed series *The Navy in the Civil War*.

The book was not his greatest or most brilliant work. It was little more than a straightforward account of selected Civil War naval operations. In it there is no suggestion or hint of his later sea-power hypothesis; and since his publisher insisted on speed, it was put together in less than five months of weekend and evening work. Some of the writing and research was done on his Navigation Office job, when the Navy's cosmic concern with lard oil and flag bunting permitted. Major changes and additions were still being made at the galley-proof stage in late May.

Mahan's primary motive in writing *The Gulf and Inland Waters* was probably the $600 he received for the job from Scribner's. As the always-economically-embarrassed officer confessed to Ashe: "As I wanted the money I consented with great misgivings as to whether I could do justice to the subject, but believing I would probably do as well as another who would accept the same time [limit]." In addition to the money involved, the book was very important to Mahan's career in that it established him as a competent naval historian—a fact that led directly to his appointment to the faculty of the new Naval War College in 1885. The study also convinced him that U.S. naval power had ensured victory in the ideologically and constitutionally just cause he felt was the Civil War. Most interestingly and importantly, he saw that Union naval control of the Gulf, of Mobile Bay, and of the Mississippi and Red rivers had in a very real way brought the Confederate enemy to ruin. "Of course I don't pretend to believe that I have no bias," he admitted; "I only claim I did my utmost to speak the truth."[21]

To get at the "truth" of what he regarded as a "just war," Mahan corresponded with as many of the participants on both sides as the short time at his disposal allowed. He consulted the "voluminous material now accessible, both Union and Confederate." He personally interviewed several of the participants, mastered the reminiscences on the subject then available, and in April 1883 made a quick trip to Washington to consult relevant materials in the War Record Office. "When in Washington I spent two days overhauling the records of the Vicksburg Campaign in hopes of getting what you have just given me," he told former Con-

federate artillery officer, M. M. McDonald, one of his eye-witness correspondents. He hastily prepared the several operational maps included in
the volume. By and large, *The Gulf and Inland Waters* was a tour de
force which gave Mahan an appreciation of the historical value and the
potential of American naval power. It also gave him confidence in his
ability to write history. As he explained his writing problem to his eleven-
year-old daughter, Helen:

> First I will be careful to have everything right, no mistakes; next that
> everything shall be very clear, the sentences arranged that the reader
> shall easily understand; and then I will cut out all the big words I can and
> put short strong English words in their place. To do this Papa had to
> write over and over again, and keep changing words he had written. . . .

Having produced *The Gulf and Inland Waters* in record time, it was
probably a form of professional justice that permitted Mahan, as one of
his final acts at the New York Navy Yard, to order 60 copies of his own
book for placement in post and ships' libraries. At $1.00 each.[22]

Soon came the warm glow of authorship and the realization that he
had done a creditable piece of work. From all over the country came
letters of praise and congratulations from officers, friends, kinsmen, and
strangers. From his old friend of *Iroquois* days, Dr. Theron Woolverton,
he heard: "I admire your deliberate style very much. You couldn't help
but express your conviction that in any well regulated universe, the 'Executive' ought to control, could you?" Sam Ashe reprinted sections of the
book in his *Raleigh News* and pronounced the work "very remarkable"
considering the "short time allowed for its preparation." He felt, too, that
"you did well to avoid attempts at fine writing. The historical style of
frozen fact is alone calculated to give a book life." The reviews were
also good, the *Chicago Tribune* remarking that the "author's style is simple and direct, and plainly shows that he has conscientiously followed
the official reports, which have been supplemented and connected by
information gathered from actors on both sides in the events described."
The Army and Navy Journal liked its "frankness and general fairness"
and noted that the author's "narrative is throughout picturesque and instructive." Classmate S. D. Greene thought Mahan had told the story
"wonderfully well . . . and such will be the verdict of all fair-minded
men." Even in ex-Confederate military and naval circles generous things
were said about the volume. Mahan was particularly pleased to hear from
James Russell Soley, the distinguished naval historian who had served as
civilian Head of the Department of English, History, and Law at the

Naval Academy when Mahan headed the Department of Ordnance there. Author of *The Blockade and the Cruisers* in the Scribner's series, Soley wrote from the Navy Department in Washington that "everybody here speaks highly of it and seems to be thoroughly pleased with it." Mahan had shown his service colleagues that he could write solid naval history and do it under forced draft.[23]

Happily, the Department of the Navy had not yet arrived at the classic position it took in 1893 regarding Mahan's scholarly pursuits, a position which declared that it was not the business of naval officers to write books. Instead, it held up his assignment to sea duty for three months so that he might complete his study. This thoughtful delay, however, cost Mahan command of the desirable steam sloop *Juniata*, then in Bombay, from which Commander George Dewey had been recalled because he was suffering from a liver abscess. The steam sloop *Swatara*, repairing in New York in July 1883, was another command possibility since it was now certain that Mahan would have to go to sea. While this vessel was being considered for him, Alfred was temporarily assigned to a mixed civilian-military review board appointed to determine whether a railway bridge should be constructed across the Thames River near New London, Connecticut. This duty permitted him to visit with his family then spending the summer at the "reasonably cheap" Plimpton House in nearby Watch Hill, Rhode Island, a delightful seaside resort "not frequented by expensive people who run prices up."

Mahan naturally hoped that he would be ordered to a ship on the North Atlantic Station, "which would have allowed me to see my family some time." But this was not to be, and for his ill fortune in this respect he blamed Dewey "who after having one of the best ships allowed our grade, given him a year ago, from which he returned after a severe illness, has had sufficient favor with the powers that be to cut me out. It is not precisely a grievance, yet I feel that . . . I had the better claim." Claim or not, Dewey got the new steel dispatch boat *Dolphin*, still under construction, and was assigned to the desirable North Atlantic Station. The dour Mahan was banished to the *Wachusett* ("though a smaller ship . . . a good one," he said, without conviction) on the distant South Pacific Station. He felt, however, that it would not be more than an eighteen-month exile. He was slated for promotion no later than the spring of 1885 and officers as senior as captain did not command junk heaps like the aging and obsolete *Wachusett*.[24]

So it was that Commander Alfred Thayer Mahan bid his wife goodbye (it was their first extended separation in eleven years of marriage), kissed adieu his three children, aged ten (Helen), six (Ellen), and two (Lyle), and made a $200 monthly allotment from his annual sea-duty salary of $3,500 to support them all in his absence. He departed New York on August 20, 1883, for Callao, Peru, on a mail steamer to Panama, then across the isthmus on the American-owned railroad which ran parallel to the canal the French were attempting to build, and finally on to Peru by steamer. On September 9 he reported at Callao to Rear Admiral Aaron K. Hughes, commander of the South Pacific Station, and on the same date relieved Commander Frederick Pearson on board the *Wachusett*. He inspected the third-rated, wooden sailing-steam vessel and found her to be "in a satisfactory condition." It was one of the great overstatements of Mahan's life.[25]

The *Wachusett*, built in 1861, sister ship of the *Iroquois*, was one of a five-vessel American group grandly called the "Pacific Squadron." The primary function of the squadron for several years past had been to protect American life and property during the War of the Pacific. By the time Mahan reached Callao, the war was in its fifth and final year. Chile was everywhere victorious. Bolivia had lost her nitrate-rich coastline, Peru had ceded to Chile her southern nitrate province of Tarapacá, and a Chilean army of occupation was ensconced in Lima. Peru was in nearly as bad shape as the *Wachusett*.

The vessel was, in Mahan's words, an "old war-horse, not yet turned out to grass or slaughter, ship-rigged to royals, and slow-steamed." She had been in continuous operation for nearly five years without a yard overhaul. Indeed, she had last been outfitted for a limited six-month cruise which, when Mahan joined her, had already extended to nearly a year. As her new captain soon discovered, her hull and deck timbers were rotten, several frames were broken, she carried a permanent port list, and her two boilers were worn out. By constantly having "first one, then the other" of her boilers patched, the *Wachusett* could make all of 8 knots "in smooth water" under steam. Her two 11-inch and four 8-inch smoothbore guns, "respectable 20 years ago—are absolutely obsolete—and beyond them she has nothing." Her boats and gig were in frightful condition, and the ribs on her capstan were so badly worn that the anchors could be raised only with the greatest difficulty. The equipment in the *Wachusett* was equally antiquated, not worth the powder it would have taken to blow it up. Not that an explosion could have been effected had Mahan ordered it. He discovered that 75 per cent of the ship's fuses were defective. Her powder was in such poor condition that it could only be trusted for blank firing; and both powder and shot were in such short supply that target practice for the quarter October-December 1883 consisted of firing "one round only." There were no gunnery-training manuals. The ship's fire-extinguishing equipment was inoperative. Her papers were in such disarray that Mahan himself, while puttering around one day, "accidentally discovered" her 1881 log books and medical records on "some rarely used shelves" and belatedly forwarded them to the Bureau of Navigation. In sum, the noble *Wachusett* would have had difficulty doing combat with a Staten Island ferry. Even the ship's three cats were "very stupid." They "don't catch any rats and don't even seem to know what a rat means when they see one," Mahan reported to his "darling Miss Nellikin."[26]

The sad condition of the vessel was regularly reported by Mahan to his superiors, in tones increasingly shrill as absolutely nothing was done to rectify the situation, and as his tenure of command stretched toward two long, frustrating, boring, and homesick years. On May 15, 1885, he finally exploded, telling the Secretary of the Navy that "the *Wachusett* is probably the worst commander's command in the service. . . . I have borne it long enough [and] I shall be deeply grateful for relief." Needless to say, relief was slow in coming. Meanwhile, Mahan's reputation back in the department in Washington became that of a crank and a chronic complainer. Whatever might be said of naval officers writing books, it was clearly not their business so bluntly to call attention to the state of their leaky commands.[27]

The *Wachusett* also had personnel problems. Her authorized complement of 145 enlisted men was never filled. Indeed, Mahan could find among the ship's papers no record of just what her official complement was supposed to be. That information was in Washington. Replacements for enlistments expiring on the station could not be secured, so low was the Navy's pay scale. Crew vacancies ran as high as 15 to 25 per cent of the total during Mahan's period of command. Because the Chinese immigration act of 1882 prohibited the shipping of Chinese nationals on board the *Wachusett* or any other U.S. naval vessel, that source of cheap and readily available maritime labor had been closed to American warships.

Similarly, officer turnover during Mahan's two-year command was heavy. In December 1884 he reported to Secretary Chandler that "during my command . . . I shall have changed, at odd times, every line officer but one, nearly every staff officer and a large proportion (45 per cent), of the crew." It was these "disorganizing conditions" that persuaded him to request changes in the paragraph of *Navy Regulations*, 1876, that denied ensigns the classification and duty of watch officers. Specifically,

Mahan suggested to Chandler in September 1884 that the wording of the paragraph "be so far modified as to give some discretion to commanding officers. . . . if for no other reason in order that Ensigns might begin to bear responsibility, at an age certainly none too young." But while this sensible suggestion received the endorsement of Rear Admiral Upshur, then commander of the station, it remained an idea whose time had not yet come in the Navy.[28]

Whatever the value to the Navy of employing aging ensigns as watch officers, Mahan was generally blessed with competent junior officers during his service in the *Wachusett*. Among these was Ensign Hugh Rodman, who had the poor grace years later to reveal that his commanding officer had managed, in broad daylight, on a smooth sea, to crash his vessel into another ship which "without question had the right of way." Rodman recalled this glorious moment in Mahan's career as a practical seaman:

> It was our duty to keep clear. We were under sail before the wind, steering north; she was on the port tack heading about W.S.W. and was sighted broad off our starboard bow, distant several miles. Yet we collided with her and were badly damaged, and all hands called to abandon ship, though this was later found to be unnecessary. There was never a court-martial of any kind, but when one of our officers, who was something of a wag, was asked the reason of the collision, he answered, "Why the Pacific Ocean wasn't big enough for us to keep out of the other fellow's way."

Perhaps this event had something to do with the unseaworthiness of the unlucky *Wachusett*. It is probably more accurate to maintain, however, that the ship was a wreck before Mahan wrecked her.[29]

During the first half of his tour Mahan saw little national purpose being served by his lonely service on the distant station. He held a cynical view of the politics and politicians of the Latin-American banana republics in which he was supposed to "protect American interests," and noted that there were precious few Americans in Peru for him to protect, anyway. As he bitterly wrote Ashe from Callao in July 1884:

> You are not unacquainted with the general facts of the war between Chile and Peru; as our country seems to consider it has some business with them we are pretty nearly tied down to [this] stretch of coast. . . . The air is rife with expected strife and revolution and the American squadron which, *pace* the Monroe Doctrine, has the fewest interests and fewest people to protect is tied down to this place. We have here

three out of the five ships composing it. . . . Luckily Mr. Blaine is not yet President so we will not probably interfere beyond taking refugees on board if necessary; but if that magnetic statesman were in office I fancy the American diplomats would be running around in the magazine with lighted candles. . . . the question of landing troops in a foreign country is very delicate. I trust it may be avoided. I don't know how you feel but to me the very suspicion of an imperial policy is hateful; the mixing our politics with those of Latin republics especially. Though identified, unluckily, with a military profession I dread outlying colonies or interests, to maintain which large military establishments are necessary. I see in them the on-coming of a "strong" central government . . . perhaps a subversion of really free government. . . . In our war, the Union was with me at first a sentiment; it became the expression of a condition in which large military establishments would be unnecessary. Having opposed secession I have no mind to see the country travel towards a like catastrophe via colonies or the Monroe Doctrine. . . .[30]

This was Mahan's last recorded anti-imperialist statement. It was rooted in homesickness, loneliness, a passing impulse to sustain his friend Ashe's states' rights views, a personal hatred of James G. Blaine, a particular and long-standing antipathy to Latin-Americans and a slowness to recognize the potential of the Navy as a tool of imperialism. These roots were soon to wither. Within a few months he experienced a Damascene conversion to imperialism.

It is well to emphasize again that A. T. Mahan was a convert to the proposition of building a respectable naval force on grounds other than that the New Navy was needed to support a nascent policy of American imperialism. In his mind, in 1883, the well-being of the Navy was important without reference to expansion. It had saved the Union during the Civil War. If for no other reason than that it was an institution worth preserving. It also commanded his loyalty because he had given his life to it and because he reluctantly continued to serve in it. It galled his professional ego that it was a laughingstock all over the world. But the imperialist use of the Navy was an idea that occurred to him only later —in March and April 1885 when he saw the decisive role it played in foreign policy during the disorders in Central America, and as he continued the preliminary reading and thinking that led, in May 1885, to his full appreciation of the influence of sea power on history.

Meanwhile, he continued to grouse about his situation in the *Wachusett*. He considered the gathering of naval intelligence, a function insisted upon by the Navy Department, no better than a wasteful exercise in reporting the obvious to the meddlesome. He persisted in sneering at the turbulent Latin-Americans. Chile, he said, "now leaves Peru to govern itself, a feat she is as capable of performing as my boy of three years old." But he drank in from afar the beauty of the Latin women ("I have not got beyond my delight in a pretty face and dark Spanish eye"). Through all his frustrations he hoped against hope that Grover Cleveland would win the election of 1884—certainly he prayed that former Secretary of State Blaine would not win:

> Hoping for his defeat [he explained to Ashe], I trust that the return of the Democrats to power will be signalized by the development of a policy approaching the old platform of the Democratic party of days gone by. The strict construction of the constitution, the jealous maintenance of the rights and powers of the states, freed from what from my point of view was the erroneous "right of secession," the vigilant limitation of the central government to simply what is granted it by the Constitution; this is my dearest political wish. You may think of Daniel come to judgment but, leaving aside the effect of immaturity upon previous views, you will recognize that one may hold a principle strongly and yet think it must be waived, under some conditions, temporarily. Even the Constitution might be violated to save the country, as an operation may be risked to save from death though with but one chance in ten in its favor. I also long for free trade. But the great issue now is between centralization and the reverse, I think, and for this reason, quite outside of the question of his honesty, I dread to see Mr. Blaine in the presidential chair. With his strong, aggressive, unscrupulous character, and instinct for meddling, I fear the central power would grow in his hands like the papacy in the hands of Hildebrand.[31]

At the very moment that Mahan was worrying about power in the hands of a Blaine or a Pope Hildebrand, the power of control over his distasteful career was passing into the capable hands of Stephen B. Luce. Luce, the Navy's leading exponent of continuing professional education for naval officers, had recently realized his greatest dream—the establishment of the Naval War College at Newport, Rhode Island. Authorized by Secretary Chandler on October 6, 1884, and placed under the supervision of the Bureau of Navigation, the postgraduate school had as its purpose the training of career officers in the rapidly changing and closely interrelated fields of naval strategy, tactics, and technology. By 1885 the building program that would produce the New Navy was conceptually and technologically well advanced. Indeed, within fifteen years (1885–1900), the long-moribund U.S. Navy would grow in relative size from twelfth to third among the world's navies. But how the modern steam-driven, steel-hulled ships with their rifled cannon should be fought, how they would relate to a broad naval strategy, and how the strategy eventually selected would in turn influence national foreign-policy aspirations and planning, remained unanswered questions. The Naval War College, the educational and philosophical nerve center of the New Navy movement, was founded to help wrestle with these issues.

Strategy, tactics, technology. As will be seen, these were to be the college's main curricular concerns. Or at least they were among the areas of study recommended by Commodore Luce in his report to Secretary Chandler dated June 13, 1884. Because of the all-important technological dimension, it seemed reasonable that the college be attached in some way to the Navy's experimental Torpedo Station at Newport. One must understand the academic connection between the college and the Torpedo Station because there soon arose much intraservice bitterness and misunderstanding (a bitterness to which Mahan contributed and a misunderstanding he shared) as to the proper curricular balance between the two institutions. Suffice it to say here that the Naval War College was not established as an ivory-tower retreat primarily for the study of naval history, although founder Luce had a lively appreciation of the "science" of history as a basis for contemporary naval decision-making. Instead, it was authorized by the Department of the Navy to teach a variety of courses "supplementing the torpedo course." Naval history was to be but one aspect of this supplement. Naval technology was to be a major concern.[32]

On July 22, 1884, Luce wrote to Mahan inviting him to join the faculty of the new institution (after Lieutenant Commander Caspar F. Goodrich had declined the honor), instruction at which was scheduled to begin in the fall of 1885. The invitation issued out of a meeting, arranged by Secretary Chandler, between Luce and the bureau chiefs, at which the staffing of the college faculty was discussed. At this meeting Montgomery Sicard, chief of the Bureau of Ordnance, sarcastically remarked: "Well, Captain Luce, I have quite half a dozen young officers among my gunnery officers who can teach all the war you want." Luce patiently explained that the faculty he needed must be composed of officers whose interests, skills, and capabilities far transcended competence in gunnery alone. Mahan was the kind of person he had in mind. He knew something about ordnance and he knew some history. The upshot of the meeting was that the Secretary approved Mahan's detachment from the *Wachusett* and his assignment to the new college.[33]

In choosing Mahan, Luce had turned to one of the few officers on active duty who had clearly demonstrated his ability (in *The Gulf and Inland Waters*) to undertake serious historical research, to condense and coordinate mountains of factual material, to write acceptable prose, and to do all this under considerable pressure. Luce therefore asked Mahan to prepare and deliver a series of lectures at the college on naval history, naval tactics, and the evolution of tactics. The invitation, however, did not reach the distant Mahan until September 4, when it caught up with him at Guayaquil, Ecuador.

Marooned as he was on the *Wachusett*, heartsick for hearth and home, depressed and melancholic, Mahan leaped at the invitation to join the War College faculty. It was his ticket home. In his reply to Luce, eagerly accepting the appointment, he admitted that he knew very little about the subject involved, but noted that he had begun immediately to scour local libraries for possible materials. Also, he pointed out that he had "perhaps some inherited aptitude for the particular study," and added, his homesick soul filled with anticipation, that

> I take it the subject you propose to me involves an amount of historical narration, specially directed toward showing the causes of failure and success, and thus enforcing certain general principles. Whether to this is to be added any attempt at evolving systems of tactics applicable to modern naval warfare, I don't understand. . . . The report of the [Luce] Board speaks of the course as supplementing the torpedo course. . . . As to preparation here, it is impossible. I have worked through the library and find little material and less that is first-rate. I can go through it all in a few weeks. Besides, I should have to give my whole mind to the matter, which in command of a ship is impossible. No man is able to serve two masters. . . . I ought to go home at once and be given till at least next summer to get up the work. . . . Meantime, while waiting to hear from you, I will work up what is at hand as though the matter were settled. If you say come—I should wish to go home at once and be put on special duty. I should be actually on duty and could not long live on leave pay. . . . As regards the general service aspect of the matter —I have now three years as commander and will have a total of thirteen —the ship is worn out and ought to go to San Francisco now; but if they choose to hold on to her longer, the executive [officer] is quite capable. For my own professional good, nothing more is to be made out of her.

Luce informed Mahan on September 30 (the letter reached him in late October at Callao) that whatever his feelings of inadequacy in the matter, the commander of the *Wachusett* was very much wanted for the War College post. More to the point, he had urged the Navy Department to expedite reassignment. Mahan replied dejectedly on November 5 that he had been hopeful "that that next mail would bring my detachment and enable me to take tomorrow's steamer for home"; he assured his mentor, however, that "my only impatience, believe me, is to be able to get to work with undivided attention if I am to go to work at all."[34]

While waiting for Luce and the department to rescue him from the wretched *Wachusett*, Mahan set about accomplishing whatever preliminary reading he could manage in nearby Lima. He took leave from the ship in November 1884. It was during that month, while reading Theodor Mommsen's *The History of Rome* in the small library of the English Club in Lima, that he stumbled onto the great historical insight that so radically changed his professional life, so thoroughly revolutionized the study of naval history, and eventually made his name a household word during America's imperialist period. He later identified that awesome moment of discovery as a sudden gift from God:

> He who seeks, finds, if he does not lose heart; and to me, continuously seeking, came from within the suggestion that control of the sea was an historic factor which had never been systematically appreciated and expanded. For me . . . the light dawned first on my inner consciousness; I owed it to no other man. . . . I cannot now reconstitute from memory the sequence of my mental processes; but while my problem was still wrestling with my brain there dawned upon me one of those concrete perceptions which turn inward darkness into light—and give substance to shadow.[35]

It should be noted that this account of the origin of his great insight was written in 1906 and 1907, at a time when an aging Mahan was deeply involved in a renewed search for religious certainty. When he first reported his discovery to Luce, six months after the "light dawned" on him in Peru, he indicated no special communion with the Creator—only with Mommsen. As he explained his concept and the probable scope of his future research and writing to his benefactor on May 16, 1885, following a deployment of the *Wachusett* northward to Central America:

> I had at one time [November 1884] the main features more or less arranged in my head, but preoccupation with the concerns of the ship, and the hot weather latterly, have somewhat driven them out, left them a little vague. As far as I can remember, and can now gather in a hurry from scanty notes made, I meant to begin with a general consideration

of the sea as a highway for commerce and also for hostile attacks upon countries bordering on it, dwell upon principal commercial routes—then consider sources of maritime power or weakness—material, personnel, national aptitude, harbors with their positions relative to commercial routes and enemies coasts. I proposed after to bring forward instances, from ancient and modern history, of the effect of navies and the control of the sea upon great or small campaigns. Hannibal, for instance, had to make that frightful passage of the Alps, in which he lost the quarter part of his original army, because he did not control the sea. What a mass of reading must go to this. I read 2½ volumes of Mommsen in this one view. . . . I proposed next to study great campaigns . . . Alexander, Caesar, Hannibal, etc., partly to clear up my own mind on great questions of strategy, but mainly perhaps to seek out any parallelism between the weapons or branches of land forces and those of the sea, if any hints can be drawn as to their use. The inevitable "Ram, Gun and Torpedo" would come in here. On the subject of naval tactics I own I am awfully at sea; but in a study like the above I should hope for light.[36]

It would seem, therefore, that within six months of the revelation that came to him at the English Club in Lima, Mahan had modified any thought of centering his forthcoming lectures at the War College on tactics or on the relationship between ordnance and tactics. He would, however, search for tactical principles of land warfare that might be applied to the sea, an enterprise apparently suggested to him by Luce. But mainly he had come to focus his interest on the broader and far more significant concept of the influence of sea power upon history.

Regarded in hindsight, it appears that he was never much interested in the "Ram, Gun and Torpedo"; nor did he ever really master the tactical implications of the complex new naval weapons that emerged between 1885 and 1914. Rather than tackle that subject, he preferred to spend the major part of his career as a historian immersed in the maritime milieu that he best understood—the Age of Sail. He remained happily anchored in that age, selectively documenting his sea-power hypothesis from its chronicles, as it became less and less relevant, technologically and tactically, to understanding the realities of twentieth-century naval warfare. As will be seen, it was this backward-looking emphasis that led him to some of his later personal and professional difficulties in and out of the Navy.

Nevertheless, by March 1885, four months after Mommsen had introduced him to the theory of sea power, Commander Mahan had begun the final stages of a conversion to anti-isolationism and to the notion, as he told Ashe, that "the surest way to maintain peace is to occupy a position of menace." This change of heart was clearly influenced by his experiences in Panama and in El Salvador during the wars and revolutions there in March and April of 1885. In truth, he was beginning to see the outlines of a larger and more complicated world, one that included potential foreign threats to America's commercial and strategic position at the Isthmus of Panama and one that would eventually demand a modern navy second only in size to Great Britain's. He still visualized naval strategy largely in terms of commerce-raiding and coastal defense; and he saw enormous political difficulties in bringing the nation, especially the Democratic party, to a pro-Navy stance. But while he was not yet an enthusiastic imperialist, he was moving inexorably in that direction early in 1885, especially with regard to the logic of an Anglo-American connection:

> I think that our geographical position will make war with us unlikely, but the surest deterrent will be a fleet of swift cruisers to prey on the enemy's commerce. The great need of such ships are speed and coal stowage. . . . They should be able to fight their equals in size because running away is demoralizing. This threat will deter a possible enemy, particularly if coupled with adequate defense of our principal ports. My theory, however, is based on the supposition that we don't have interests out of our own borders. If we are going in for an Isthmian policy we must have nothing short of a numerous and thoroughly first class, iron clad navy—equal to either England or France. To this I would add, throw overboard the Irish vote (if you dare) and pursue a policy not of formal alliance but of close sympathy, based on common ideas of justice, law, freedom and honesty, with England.

Mahan was still not convinced that Southern Democratic politicians like his friend Ashe fully understood the national psychological implications of the sad condition of the Navy in the mid-1880s, and the need for a naval renaissance. "If we are made to go from port to port in ships which are a laughing stock," he wrote, "knowing that we are, must be, laughed at behind our backs by men too civil to say an unpleasant word to our faces, you cannot expect that our pride and self respect will escape uninjured. Either we must continue to suffer, or we must steel ourselves to indifference—become shameless in fact." And although he was out of the country and had not voted, he was delighted that Grover Cleveland had won the recent election. "I have not been so thoroughly glad of any result since [Horace] Greeley was defeated in 72. . . . I felt as regards Greeley and Blaine little short of terror, believing the former to be an honest lunatic . . . the latter far more insane, except so far as dishonesty is bad policy and somewhat crazy." The question immediately at issue was the future of the service under Cleveland and the new Secretary of the Navy, William C. Whitney.[37]

It is not surprising that Mahan by 1885 had returned to his conviction, first expressed when he served in the *Iroquois* in the Far East, that the British, whatever their other faults, ran a navy and an empire as both should be run. While he was on the South Pacific Station he saw again their neat and modern ships, met and fraternized again with their sophisticated and mannerly officers (among them Bouverie F. Clark, commanding HMS *Sappho*, later a frequent correspondent), used their fine clubs ashore, and communed with Mommsen in their library in Lima. When, for example, Midshipman F. E. Coley of the *Wachusett* died of typhoid fever at Callao in December 1883, it was a British admiral who helped with the funeral arrangements, a British chaplain who performed the final rites, and a squad of British midshipmen who stood at attention at the grave in Callao's Protestant Cemetery as young Coley was lowered to his rest. The British, Mahan had long since concluded, were a civilized race. England, he wrote, "is like every nation, selfish but in the main honest; and the best hope of the world is in the union of the branches of that race to which she and we belong."[38]

Armed with the main outline of his great scheme of historical interpretation, certain of the need for a "union" or "close sympathy" of the English-speaking peoples, Commander Mahan launched a veritable drumfire of letters pleading with his superiors to order him home so that he might get on with the business of writing naval history. His letters to Luce were filled with similar pleas. Those to the departing Secretary Chandler and to the station commander, Admiral John H. Upshur, emphasized the hopeless condition of the *Wachusett* and urged her immediate removal from the station. He insisted to Luce that he would need at least a year to prepare his first set of lectures for War College students and at least three years to write a book examining the influence of sea power on history. "I think too in the quiet evolution of a book I am stronger than in the teacher's chair, but you must decide what is best—except the one original condition as to time. But if you can, do get me ordered home, I have applied by this very mail." So insistent did Mahan's importunities in this regard become that he felt constrained, in June 1885, to assure Luce that "I do not want you to think that I was using the College as a means of escape. I should not have asked you to interfere had I not felt that I was not needed here." In spite of what he told Luce he was indeed using the college as a means of escape. All evidence points to that fact.[39]

Further, events in Central America in March 1885 showed that Mahan and the *Wachusett* were needed exactly where the Navy Department had placed them. But before these events intruded, his letter-writing campaign and Luce's assistance had borne fruit. In early January 1885 the department issued orders for the vessel's recall to San Francisco in March. Mahan learned of this decision in mid-February and was overjoyed. It appeared for a moment that he had escaped his purgatory at last. But on March 16 there occurred in Panama a revolution against the Colombian government that clearly threatened American lives and property as well as the nation's treaty right of transit at the isthmus. All redeployment orders for the *Wachusett* were suddenly cancelled. The onrush of political events in South and Central America involving American interests there pinned the *Wachusett* to the station for five more months. Mahan almost exploded in his frustration over this unexpected turn of events, even though he had the assurance of outgoing Secretary Chandler in January that he would certainly be assigned to the War College, once it was convenient for the service to detach him from the *Wachusett*. Two months later it was not convenient.[40]

The department's original plan was to have the *Wachusett* return to Mare Island from Callao in March 1885 by way of Topolobampo, Mexico—at which place the vessel was to stop and take a series of soundings on the bar. Topolobampo was to be the western terminus of a proposed railroad across Mexico, and the development of its harbor facilities and navigational system was being anticipated by the Navy. On January 28 orders to Mahan to tarry at Topolobampo for surveying duty were dispatched. He received these directives on March 5 and went immediately into a blue funk. He told the department that the *Wachusett* was far too unseaworthy for such tedious duty, that she carried no surveying instruments, that he was short of necessary line officers to carry out the assignment, and that the ship's boats were "old and poorly adapted for this work." The whole enterprise would be a waste of time and effort. He assured the department that the proposed American and Mexican Pacific Railroad line had "never been fairly begun; and there seems no doubt that it is *not* approaching completion." He asked that his orders in the matter be revoked. They were.[41]

Meanwhile, Mahan became involved, in February 1885, in the Santos case in Ecuador. While this involvement also threatened to hold the *Wachusett* to the station and further postpone Mahan's departure for home, it demonstrated clearly the use of naval power to "protect American interests."

Julio Romano Santos, an Ecuadorian by birth, left his native land in 1865 and went to the United States to seek his education and his fortune. He resided in America from 1865 to 1879, attending the University of Virginia and serving briefly there as a tutor in mathematics. On July 6, 1874, he became a naturalized American citizen. He returned to Ecuador in 1871 and in 1874 on personal and business visits; in April 1879 he returned on a third visit to participate in a family commercial venture under the company name, Santos, Hevia Hermanos. He subsequently maintained that it was always his intention to return to New York to head a branch office of the firm. But the fact was that he had lived continuously in Ecuador for five years when he was arrested and imprisoned early in 1884 for allegedly participating in a revolutionary uprising against the Ecuadorian government led by General Eloy Alfaro. While the evidence that he cooperated with the so-called "Alfaroist Rebellion" was shaky, he was nonetheless slapped into jail and his personal property to the value of $5,000 was confiscated. The arresting officer, General Reynaldo Flores, was brother-in-law to José Placido Caamaño, president of Ecuador. To keep him out of range of American assistance, the Ecuadorian government regularly moved Santos from jail to jail, each worse than the last.

During his period of residence in Ecuador, 1879–1884, Santos had refused service in the National Guard and had eschewed other public employment, consistently arguing that he was an American, not an Ecuadorian, citizen and no longer subject to the government of the land of his birth. These refusals had not been contested at the time by Ecuadorian authorities. Indeed, the government of Ecuador conceded that Santos had been a naturalized American citizen, but it held that his residence in Ecuador for so long a time had resulted in the forfeit of his acquired citizenship under the terms of Article II of the American-Ecuadorian Treaty of Naturalization of 1872. That article read: "If a naturalized citizen of either country shall renew his residence in that where he was born, without an intention of returning to that where he was naturalized, he shall be held to have reassumed the obligations of his original citizenship, and to have renounced that which he had obtained by naturalization." It was a question of *intention*. But to make matters more complicated, the treaty had expired in 1883.

These facts Mahan ascertained soon after the *Wachusett* was ordered to Bahía, Ecuador, on January 28, 1885, to protect Santos from the wrath of the Ecuadorians. He arrived there on February 9. "Great interest here in Santos Case," wired Secretary of State Frederick T. Frelinghuysen on that date, "two resolutions passed in House." In his most workmanlike and precise fashion, Mahan interviewed and took a deposition from Santos in his prison cell, collected other depositions from the prisoner's business associates, communicated with members of his family, spoke personally with President Caamaño, and gathered all other available facts and documents in the case from the American consular agent at Bahía, E. T. Goddard. These he skillfully summarized in a letter to Secretary Chandler dated February 17, 1885. The information was sent also to Martin Reinberg, the American Vice Consul at Guayaquil, with the expectation that he in turn would communicate with the State Department as well as with Horatio N. Beach, the American Consul General at Quito.

At this point, with the *Wachusett* scheduled to depart the station for San Francisco in early March, Mahan preferred to express no formal or personal opinion on the claim of Santos that he was an American citizen and was entitled therefore to the protection of his adopted land. Someone else would have to worry about that little detail after Mahan had gone. Mahan informed Chandler only that "Mr. Santos' life is not in the slightest danger, and the presence of a ship of war in Guayaquil is not in the least needed at present. If tried, the trial must take place in this province [Manabi], not in Guayaquil." With that observation, Mahan departed for Paita [Payta], Peru, to coal and to await further orders. Privately, however, he asked Sam Ashe: "How far and for how long should a naturalized citizen be permitted to return and live in his native land and claim U.S. protection, especially in countries like the S. American republics to whom revolution and political turmoil is inbred and ineradicable?" On February 22 he reported to Chandler from Paita that he had telegraphed Admiral Upshur at Valparaiso that "Santos was not condemned to death and that the presence of the ship was not needed." There the Santos matter rested, insofar as Mahan was concerned, until mid-May. Meanwhile, Upshur ordered the *Wachusett* to Coquimbo, Chile, for one final show of the flag there prior to her departure for Mare Island.[42]

On March 6, 1885, Mahan finally left Callao bound for San Francisco. On the day before his departure he heard from Thomas Adamson, the Consul General at Panama, that Charles L. Belden, the American Consul at Buenaventura, Colombia, had been made a political prisoner. Would he please look into the matter on his way north? Fortunately, as he shaped course for that port, Mahan learned by telegram that Belden had been released and had left the town, and that the American Consulate had been taken over by a trustworthy Colombian national. Since "the place is so wholly insignificant . . . I saw no cause to depart from my orders." Thus the *Wachusett*, manned by a skeleton officer complement, lumbered northward toward Panama. Indeed, before the ship left Callao, Admiral Upshur stripped her of all but four of her qualified watch officers, all but one of her remaining line officers, and all but one of her junior officers. Such cannibalization of personnel was common on all foreign stations at the time. The undermanned *Wachusett* nonetheless steamed to Panama Bay without incident, arriving there on the evening of March 17.[43]

Unfortunately for Mahan's haste to get home, fighting had broken out in the streets of Panama City the previous day. There being no U.S. warship in port at the moment, the American Consul had requested Captain R. F. Blackburne of HMS *Heroine* to land a British party to protect the station and telegraph facilities of the American-owned Panama Railroad Company in the town, and the *Heroine* had "kindly" complied. Mahan's first act was therefore to put an armed party ashore on March 18 to relieve the British party. "I cannot see there is cause for any serious apprehension," he told Secretary Whitney, "though the precaution is well until things become more settled." He saw with equal clarity, when he visited on board the *Heroine* a few days later, that Blackburne's daughter was a "very showy girl of striking appearance." No mere revolution could dim his eye for a pretty face.

On March 19 Mahan received two communications from the Navy Department. One ordered the *Wachusett* to La Unión, El Salvador; the other detached his last remaining line officer. He protested to Secretary Whitney on March 22 that Consul Adamson wanted the ship to remain in Panama Bay to protect the railroad station and that the detachment of Lieutenant William F. Low would leave the *Wachusett* with but three watch officers, two of whom were down with fever. The ship also had to take coal. He pointed out, further, that the vessel was in no condition to undertake extended operations and that "if, unfortunately, this ship should be delayed here by the unsettled condition of affairs on the Isthmus and in Central America, it would be further desirable that an assistant surgeon and some junior line officers be sent to her." He dashed off a bitter letter to Luce on March 23 to the effect that the decrepit *Wachusett* was being discriminated against by a stupid and inefficient department. He was not sure now when he would reach San Francisco.[44]

The fact of the matter was that the department had been caught with its ships down in March 1885, in that it was suddenly and simultaneously faced with two separate crises involving American treaty rights and the protection of American lives and property in Central America. The first of these was the Panamanian revolution of March 16 against the central government of Colombia. This uprising sought political independence. During the ensuing confusion, however, the insurgent forces obstructed the operations of the American-owned railway and threatened American lives. Under a treaty concluded in 1846 with the Republic of New Granada, as Colombia was then called, the United States had the right in such circumstances to intervene militarily to maintain freedom of transit. This the American government did without hesitation in March and April 1885. While the Colombian government struggled to collect and dispatch sufficient forces to put down the revolt, an American expeditionary force of 750 seamen and Marines, commanded by Commander Bowman H. McCalla, was transported from New York by the ships of Admiral James E. Jouett's North Atlantic Squadron and was landed at Aspinwall in mid-April. The Americans quickly and forcibly reopened the railway transit, restored public order, captured the revolutionary leaders, and handed a stabilized situation over to Colombian national forces, which finally arrived by sea from Buenaventura on April 28. By mid-May the Americans had withdrawn from the isthmus.[45]

Mahan participated in none of these stirring events, save initially to occupy the railroad-telegraph station at Panama City at the southern terminus of the railroad on March 18. At that juncture in the proceedings, the most violent of revolutionary disorders centered across the isthmus at the Aspinwall end of the railroad. By March 27, Mahan could therefore report from Panama Bay that the situation in his sector was quiet and that he was ready for sea—ready to show the flag at the scene of the second Central American crisis.[46]

This had occurred in February 1885 when President Justo Rufino Barrios of Guatemala unilaterally proclaimed a federal union of all the states of Central America and grandly appointed himself commander-in-chief of the combined military forces of these five states. Unfortunately for the pompous Barrios, neither Nicaragua, Costa Rica, nor El Salvador was particularly enthusiastic about being absorbed into Guatemala by proclamation. They decided instead to join together and fight rather than permit Guatemala's dictator to become the dictator of all Central America. Only Honduras supported the pretensions of Barrios. In late March, Barrios and his Honduran ally invaded El Salvador. But on April 2 he was killed in battle and the little war soon sputtered to an end. Two weeks later it was formally concluded.

On March 17 Whitney wrote to Mahan explaining at length American policy in the area. Certain that "hostilities are likely to take place which will endanger the lives and properties of citizens of the United States," Whitney ordered the *Wachusett* to cruise the El Salvadorian coast and "such other points on the coast of Central America as you may deem advisable in order to protect American interests." Specifically, Mahan was instructed to take particular care lest Guatemalan forces or Guatemalan agents in the capital city of San Salvador interfere with the submarine cables of the American-owned Central and South American Telegraph Company. Since these written instructions did not reach Mahan until April 8, long after Whitney's telegram of March 19 ordering the *Wachusett* to the troubled area, and since, further, Mahan was detained in Panama Bay until March 28 by the crisis there, the *Wachusett* belatedly undertook the support of American policy in El Salvador during the period March 28–April 8, on the basis of little more than her captain's instinct and common sense.[47]

That common sense promptly told Mahan that the *Wachusett* needed coal to support anything anywhere. Her bunker capacity enabled her to steam but 1,500 miles in smooth water. More to the point, there was virtually no coal to be had at any price between Acapulco, Mexico, and Panama City, a distance of 1,400 miles. He hoped, therefore, that Whitney would "recognize the embarrassment" the *Wachusett* faced on the Central American coast, given her wholly inadequate steaming radius. "Unless favored by wind," she could go but half the distance between Acapulco and Panama and "have just coal to reach either end." Thus was the question of adequate coaling stations abroad first brought forcefully to the attention of Alfred Thayer Mahan. A steam navy without well-placed coaling stations overseas was no navy at all, a point Mahan never tired of emphasizing in his books and articles. Failing to find coal at Corinto, Nicaragua, he did manage to pick up thirty-four tons of the precious fuel at La Unión in El Salvador. This small amount enabled him to proceed up the coast to La Libertad on April 6. It also enabled him to run the *Wachusett* aground on April 5 when leaving La Unión. The shock to the ship was slight, however, and Mahan, who was personally conning the vessel, did not "think any serious harm had been done, though I cannot of course speak positively."[48]

He was much more positive in reporting the political quiet he observed at Corinto, La Unión, and La Libertad. On April 5 he learned that Barrios and his army had been defeated by the Salvadorians and their allies. The following day, from La Libertad, he reported good order reigning throughout El Salvador and "great disorder . . . throughout Guatemala." He also found that the cable between La Libertad and San

José de Guatemala had been cut; and since he could not "afford the coal to steam back and forth from San José merely to cable," he was effectively isolated from communication with Charles Hall, the American Minister in Guatemala City.

While trying to establish that contact, Mahan finally received Whitney's written instructions of March 17. This prompted from him a telegram and a letter to the Navy Department in which he reported his coaling and communications difficulties, the death of Barrios on April 2, the eruption of civil war in Guatemala, the Nicaraguan invasion of Honduras, and the disorderly retreat of the Guatemalan-Honduran army from El Salvador. He also mentioned Mexico's diplomatic support of the anti-Barrios coalition, and the impending invasion of chaotic Guatemala by the victorious allies. He reported no injury or threat to any American citizen in all this confusion. Moreover, he concluded that "it is unusual for foreigners to suffer directly from the conflict of parties in these revolutions. Of course they are indirectly sufferers, but the people generally know it don't pay to molest them." At the same time, his brief experience in La Libertad did teach him to be wary of the opinions of American diplomats abroad. As he told Whitney: "From my observation I have come to a general conclusion that our diplomats generally sympathize with the country in which they live."[49]

Having decided to his own satisfaction on April 10 that the Central American war was for all practical purposes over, Mahan resumed his agitation with the department to order him home. Immediately. He was pleased to report, however, that the presence of the *Wachusett* was thought by some on the scene to have had "an effect upon the relations of the other Central American States toward Guatemala." He could think of no government policy statement capable of exercising the same "pressure, which a ship of war is the exponent of, upon the [diplomatic] negotiations between the late belligerents." Power came out of the barrel of a gun, even guns as antiquated as those mounted in the decrepit *Wachusett*. Nevertheless, the *Wachusett* was using five tons of coal a week (the equivalent of fifty miles' steaming) merely to distill her drinking water. That being the case, it was obviously time for the vessel to proceed to Mare Island. She had shown the flag. Her job was done.[50]

The *Wachusett* was still not destined to return home. On May 2 she was ordered back to Panama City and arrived on May 11. There, to his great distress and outrage, Mahan learned that the vessel had again been ordered south to Guayaquil for another look at the nagging Santos case. So upset was Mahan at this turn of events that he wrote Luce offering to withdraw from the War College faculty. It seemed to him that he would never get home. He was bone tired. He had had no opportunity for study or reading. And there would simply not be enough time, if ever he did get home, to work up the lectures. "If the Department felt an interest in the College," he told Luce, "I cannot understand the refusal to order me home." When Luce informed him that his lectures at the college had been postponed from the fall of 1885 to the fall of 1886, that he would have no interim teaching duties, and that he would therefore have a full year for study and writing after his expected return, Mahan was mollified. But he made no secret of his feeling that the department was discriminating against him:

> The longer I stay here being made a handy billy of, the less fit I shall be for work. The *Hartford* was allowed to go junketing to the islands and I kept here with a broken down ship for work; now after nearly four months between Guayaquil and Guatemala I am sent to the former place at the worst time of the year, while two ships that were in Chile for two months of the time remain in Panama.

The more he meditated on his situation the more convinced he became that he was the victim of a conscious conspiracy of delay on the part of the department. He was certain that official assurances to Luce that the *Wachusett* would soon be ordered to San Francisco "cannot be in the least depended on." Not only was the department filled with liars, it was also an inefficient agency staffed by fools. "Do what they may otherwise—it is the sheerest trifling to assign me to such a work and keep me at this mere routine jog."[51]

Such was Mahan's gloomy frame of mind on the eve of his scheduled return to Guayaquil early in May, to carry there various State Department letters and instructions on the Santos affair for the American Consul General. On May 5, Cleveland's new Secretary of State, Thomas F. Bayard, wired Consul General Beach in Ecuador: "We hold Santos's citizenship fully established and not debatable, and expect treatment accordingly. *Wachusett* will return soon Guayaquil bearing full instructions." The ominous words "treatment accordingly" meant but one thing. The Ecuadorians must bring Santos to a fair and speedy trial American-style, or release him—or else. This tough talk led quickly to negotiations in Washington on May 15 and 16 between Bayard and Ecuadorian Minister Antonio Flores, in which it was resolved that Santos would be released if the Americans would remove their warships from the coast of Ecuador. Mahan, of course, did not know of this arrangement until later.

Although the mind of his government was made up to force the issue as early as May 5, he was determined not to go back to accursed Ecuador without a struggle. To this end he dug deeply into the legal background of the Santos case. He read carefully the State Department dispatches he was to convey to Beach in Quito, found among the ship's papers a copy of the American-Ecuadorian Naturalization Treaty of 1872, and consulted various treatises on international law that he found in the ship's library and on shore. This research had nothing to do with the influence of sea power upon history; it had only to do with the influence of a home-sick Mahan on the Department of the Navy, an influence that was ultimately persuasive enough to head off the return of the *Wachusett* to Ecuador.

His scholarly summary of the Santos situation to Whitney on May 14 raised the basic question of whether the gentleman was indeed a bona fide American citizen and thus entitled to protection. Article III of the Treaty read: "A residence of more than two years in the native country of a naturalized citizen shall be construed as an intention on his part to stay there without returning to that where he was naturalized. This presumption, however, may be rebutted by evidence to the contrary." Mahan admitted to the Secretary that it was "perhaps indiscreet for a commander in the Navy to make any comment upon a State paper signed by the eminent man who now is head of the Department of State"; but he noticed in one of Bayard's instructions to Beach that there was a misreading of Article III. Bayard had pointed out to Beach that "two years residence in Ecuador *may* create a presumption [on the part of Ecuador] that their citizen intends to remain there." Mahan argued, instead, that the expired U.S. accord with Ecuador, "contrary to all other naturalization treaties furnished to this ship," did not read *may*, but held clearly that "a residence of more than two years in the native country *shall be construed* as an intention to stay there without returning to the country where he was naturalized."

The "plain English" of this clause convinced the commander that Ecuador had a good case. He was not impressed with the truth of the depositions he had taken from Santos and his friends in February 1885 at Bahía. In these, all hands had sworn solemnly that, despite his residence in Ecuador from 1879 to 1884, Santos had always intended to return to his adopted country. But "not a step homewards was taken by himself," Mahan noted. The deponents were liars.

Because his view of the Santos matter contradicted that of Secretary Bayard, it seemed obvious to the commander that the Department of

State in future years had better let naval officers entrusted with carrying out American foreign policy abroad know exactly what was expected of them in various situations:

> I cannot but think it would be well to let naval officers generally know the terms of the decision of the Secretary in this, and other cases resembling those in which they may be called to act. Special examples do so much to clear up general principles. I feel this just now the more, because I should have fallen, as far as the authorities furnished the ship guided me, into the opposite decision; and at one time it seemed possible I might have to act on my own judgment.[52]

Whatever the legal and semantic details of the Santos affair, Mahan had certainly had enough of the sorry business. "I respectfully, but very earnestly, ask that I may be relieved from the command of the *Wachusett* and ordered home," he pleaded to Whitney, "when the government of Ecuador has acknowledged the American citizenship of Mr. Santos, either by releasing or bringing him to fair and open trial for his alleged offence." Again, he informed the Secretary that the ship was badly undermanned, that the crew would surely wilt in fever-ridden Guayaquil ("one of the sickliest cities in the world"), and that the vessel had already more than done her duty for the fatherland. To these arguments he added the observations that steaming Panama City was unhealthy for his officers and men, that the ship was barely able to function, and that political stability had returned to the Isthmus of Panama.

The reopening of his verbal bombardment of the Navy Department produced results. On July 18, four days before Santos was released from prison, the *Wachusett* was withdrawn from her projected mission to Guayaquil. The *Iroquois*, Commander Yates Sterling, was sent in her stead with orders to bring Santos to Panama. And on July 23 Whitney ordered the benighted *Wachusett* and the impatient Mahan to proceed from Panama to San Francisco.

So it was that in early August 1885 Mahan at last reached Mare Island. He had completed, almost to the day, the normal two-year tour at sea expected of all officers at the time. He had not been discriminated against by Chandler or Whitney. Nor was he the victim of a department conspiracy. He had simply been required to do his full two years at sea—like any other officer. As for the miserable *Wachusett*, she was mercifully decommissioned in September. The decommissioning inspectors found her efficiency to be "exceptionally high." Indeed, the report of the Board of Inspection was "very complimentary" to Mahan. The vessel had survived a collision, a grounding, and a voyage to the frontier of American imperialism under Commander Mahan; and he had brought her safely home gracefully to die.[53]

But since the first session of the War College was scheduled to begin on September 4, Mahan had returned too late to make any contribution to the historic opening of the institution. He was not officially detached from the *Wachusett* until August 24. For this reason, he wrote Luce, "pray do not expect anything in the way of lecture or instruction from me this year. It would be worse than useless, probably harmful to what I would call 'prestige' if it were not an assumption that I have any."[54]

VII

The Naval War College
Sea Tactics and Navy Politics
1885-1889

The result I think, in the present state of the naval mind, will be to sink the study of the Art and Conduct of War and substitute for it the treatment of development of material—to teach how to build and equip ships and naval weapons, not how to use them in war. I am possibly biased, for the step taken by our late Secretary [Whitney] has been to turn me out without a word of acknowledgement after two years of hard work, and to give my place to a junior, but I know that during my incumbency I had to resist a constant pressure to introduce these questions of construction and mechanical appliances and thus crowd to one side the discussion of the problem of war.

Alfred Thayer Mahan to William H. Henderson, March 18, 1889

In October of 1885 Mahan officially joined the faculty of the infant Naval War College at Newport, Rhode Island, an institution already the subject of considerable controversy among naval officers. Just what the college was supposed to do, or be, was still very much up in the air when Mahan arrived on the scene.

Languishing in the *Wachusett* on the distant South Pacific Station, he had played no role whatever in establishing the college. Moreover, its founder, Stephen B. Luce, had apparently told him very little about the background of the school, its educational mission, the compromises that had to be made to get it started, or the contradictions lurking in the report of the so-called "Luce Board" that had recommended its commencement. Further, Captain Luce, the Navy's leading scholar and intellectual in the late 1870s and early 1880s, as well as its most visible reformer, had himself contributed to the confusion. In his various arguments for the founding of the school he left the impression that what he had in mind was something in the nature of a "post-graduate course," an extension of the Naval Academy curriculum "for the study of the Science of War, Ordnance, and International Law, and such cognate branches of the three grand divisions as may be determined upon." But the board which he headed, appointed by Secretary Chandler in May 1884 to study his proposal (Commander William T. Sampson and Lieutenant Commander Caspar F. Goodrich also served on the body), recommended in June 1884 the creation of a college with a broader mission.

The report of the Luce Board visualized an institution at which the postgraduate student officer would study "the great naval battles of history, even from the earliest times, which illustrate and enforce many of the most important and immutable principles of war." He would, in addition, study international law and diplomacy and he would benefit from "a more extended course in mechanics, gun construction, etc." The *et cetera* included "electricity in its application to torpedoes, chemistry in its application to explosives, metallurgy in its relation to ordnance, and steam as a motive power." The Luce Board thus suggested that there would be a mixed theoretical and practical course of study. On the one hand, the student would study military and naval history, modern strategy and tactics, diplomacy, international law, and modern languages. On the other, he would immerse himself in the nuts and bolts of ordnance, torpedoes, hydrography, and "practical exercises afloat." All of this was to be crammed into a few brief weeks. From a curricular standpoint, therefore, the new Naval War College began life as a contradiction in terms. Indeed, during the months between July 1884 and March 1885, when he was writing to Mahan in Latin America about the college, Luce found it difficult to explain to the skipper of the *Wachusett* what the course of study was actually supposed to emphasize. Was it naval history, strategy, and tactics? Or was it ram, gun, and torpedo? Or a bit of both? Or both and more?

No one was certain in 1884, least of all Mahan. Secretary Chandler sold the idea of the college to Congress in February 1885, largely with the argument that the curriculum would supplement the technical engineering and ordnance studies being carried out at the Navy's Torpedo Station in Newport. But Luce, in his capacity as the first president of the college, informed the handful of students comprising its initial class, in September 1885, that the "War College is not . . . for post-graduate study merely, as that term is generally understood, but for the higher and much more comprehensive purpose of a greatly advanced course of professional instruction" involving studies of naval history, strategy, and tactics. It seems likely, therefore, that the mission of the institution was kept vague enough to command the broadest possible support for it within the service. If so, it was a tactical compromise that produced a great deal of intra-service misunderstanding and tension in the years ahead.

Ordnance officers and other technicians within the New Navy were pleased with the Luce Board's recommendation that the college be placed on Coaster's Harbor Island at Newport, close to the scientific and engineering faculties and facilities of Harvard University and the Massachusetts Institute of Technology in nearby Boston. They hoped to draw on these outside academic resources, and they noted with approval that the course of study at the school would be geared to the experimental work of the Torpedo Station situated on Goat Island in Narragansett Bay. As the Luce Board had pointed out, "the Torpedo Station is already at this place, and it would be possible to extend its facilities that the instruction in physical science might be given." At the outset, those officers in the Navy most interested in the development of gun, ram, and torpedo saw no threat in Chandler's explanation to Congress that the college would complement the work of the Torpedo Station by "adding to an extent never hithertofore undertaken the study of naval warfare and international law and their cognate branches." While these "cognate branches" were not well defined, few officers (or legislators) could fault Chandler's clinching argument that "very little expense" would be incurred in launching the small facility at Newport, and that from an educational standpoint the combined Torpedo Station and War College operation would do much to meet the "constant change in the methods of conducting naval warfare, imposed by the introduction of armored ships, swift cruisers, rams, sea-going torpedo-boats, and high power guns, together with the more rigid methods of treating the various subjects belonging to naval science."

Actually, the first mistake made by Luce and Chandler was to situate the institution in Newport. Presumably it was done for reasons of economy and for the purpose of permitting the students easy access to the vessels of the North Atlantic Squadron for "practical exercises afloat." But from an administrative standpoint it was a disastrous decision. The Torpedo Station, dedicated to the study, manufacture, construction, and testing of "automobile" torpedoes and other explosives, was under the management of the Bureau of Ordnance. The new War College, dedicated to curricular uncertainty, was placed under the Bureau of Navigation. Since the two bureaus were often locked in mortal combat, administrative infighting at Newport was almost certain to become intense. Further, the *New Hampshire*, a training ship for apprentice seamen, administered by the Bureau of Equipment, was berthed at Coaster's Harbor Island. Thus the Navy clustered at Newport three separate training facilities, administered by three different bureaus. The subsequent struggle among them for *lebensraum* was bitter.[1]

The first session of the college in 1885 was academically unimpressive. To get the project under way at last, Luce hastily slapped together a three-week program, presented in September, that had little rhyme or reason. The nine student officers present were treated to several lectures in general naval history and tactics by Luce, and to various lectures in military history and international law by faculty members James Russell Soley and Lieutenant Tasker A. Bliss, U.S. Army. Volunteer guest lecturers, four in number, including two obscure Civil War generals, spoke briefly on unrelated military and naval topics. It was a weak beginning, but at least it was a beginning.

Most importantly, it gave Luce an opportunity to set the academic tone and direction of the place, to stamp on it his personal concept of what its true mission should be. As he saw it, this mission involved nothing less than elevating naval history to the level of a science. In a lecture, later published under the title "On the Study of Naval Warfare as a Science," he told the students in September 1885:

> Naval history abounds in materials whereon to erect a science . . . and it is our present purpose to build up with these materials the science of naval warfare . . . . there is no question that the naval battles of the past furnish a mass of facts amply sufficient for the formulation of laws or principles which, once established, would raise maritime war to the level of a science. Having established our principles by the inductive process, we may then resort to the deductive method of applying those principles to such a changed condition of the art of war as may be imposed by later inventions or by introduction of novel devices. . . . Hence, to elevate naval warfare into a science, as we now propose doing, we must adopt the comparative method . . . we [must] co-ordinate the study of naval warfare with military science and art. That is the theory on which we are now to proceed. . . . For having no authoritative treatise on the art of naval warfare under steam . . . we must, perforce, resort to the well-known rules of the military art with a view to their application to the military movements of a fleet, and, from the well-recognized methods of disposing troops for battle, ascertain the principles which should

govern fleet formations. . . . *It is by this means alone that we can raise naval warfare from the empirical stage to the dignity of a science.*

This goal was crystal clear to Luce, so clear that he carefully repeated the remark to the college's students and staff in September 1886. But it may not have been what Congress, the Department of the Navy, or Secretary Chandler had in mind in 1884 when the institution was established. The search for historical laws and principles had little to do with the speed, range, and launching mechanisms of self-propelled torpedoes, or with how much shell would penetrate how much armor plate at what distance. Nor is it likely that many officers at the Torpedo Station or anywhere else in the Navy had heard of English historian Henry Thomas Buckle (1821–1863), the man from whom Luce drew his staunch conviction that all human activity and progress was regulated by the operation of discoverable scientific laws. Nevertheless, this is what Luce believed, together with the idea that the infantry and cavalry tactics of the past were applicable to the naval warfare of the future.

Armed with these convictions, Luce began planning the curriculum for the 1886 session. It emphasized extensive lectures on naval history, tactics, gunnery, and hygiene, with spot lectures on military (land) strategy and tactics and on U.S. coastal defense. Mahan was scheduled to give the lectures on naval history and naval tactics under steam. The latter, however, was a subject on which Luce had already delivered himself at length in 1885 in an address at the college (repeated in 1886 and later published) titled "On the Study of Naval History (Grand Tactics)." In this presentation he told the student officers and faculty members that naval "victory had generally been with that leader who had the skill to throw two or more of his own ships upon one of the enemy. That is one of the most valuable lessons of naval history and . . . is one of the fundamental principles of our science." In this lecture he also called attention to the works of various military and naval historians worthy of study, not the least of whom was General Henri Jomini, the Swiss theorist whose tactical insights had influenced Mahan's father forty years earlier. "The existence of fundamental principles, by which all the operations of war should be conducted, has been placed beyond doubt by the researches of Jomini," Luce declared.

Given his certainty of the existence of the "science" that was naval history, and of the "fundamental principle" that was the achievement of tactical concentration in fleet actions, it is not too much to say that the War College which Mahan finally joined in 1886 had taken on something

[164]

of the intellectual complexion of its founder. Luce had already determined the mission of the college insofar as the study of naval history and tactics was concerned; he had already decided that the "principles" governing military and naval tactics were opposite sides of the same theoretical coin and should be treated as such in the classroom; and he had virtually selected the authors Mahan would read as he prepared his own lectures on the subject during the winter of 1885–1886.

Like any properly disciplined naval officer reporting to a new duty station, Mahan accepted the college and its commander much as he found them. Certainly, he was aware of Luce's views on history as science and on the functional interchangeability of military and naval tactics. Not surprisingly, therefore, his mentor's concept of the mission of the War College soon became his, as did many of Luce's views on naval history and tactics. However, the larger idea of the influence of sea power on history, derivative though it was, Mahan considered his own. At least it was not Luce's.[2]

Prior to beginning the studies that would occupy the rest of his life, Mahan rented an apartment for his family at 2 East 15th Street in New York City and then joined Elly and the children in Bar Harbor, Maine, for a month's vacation. In mid-October he travelled to Washington where he passed an examination for promotion to the rank of captain. "You may remember," he told Ashe, "that when you and I entered the service Captain was the highest grade to be reached—and the period for getting it was virtual old age. I have been more fortunate, by a good deal, than I then expected." A main concern was that his new uniforms would not prove too costly. For, as usual, Mahan was broke—his sea pay of $3,500 per annum as a commander in the *Wachusett* was identical with that of a captain in a shore billet. His promotion did not make him richer by a single dime.[3]

In his conversations and correspondence with Luce in October 1885 it was decided that he would remain in New York to commence research on the lectures he was to deliver at the college during the 1886 session. It made sense, he explained, "to place myself where I can find the best material for my intended book" on sea power. There were also family and economic considerations. Elly did not want to leave New York or remove her children from "surroundings wholly familiar." Her widowed mother, who also lived at 2 East 15th Street, wished her to remain nearby; she even agreed to help subsidize the Mahans' living expenses in the city. "A stay in the city has been made pecuniarily possible to me," Mahan informed Luce, "which I did not expect when I left it." So it was that from October 1885 until August 1886 Mahan enjoyed in New York what in effect was a paid leave of absence from the U.S. Navy. Technically, he was under Luce's orders during this period; but practically he was a free agent.[4]

During his ten-month sabbatical, much of which he spent in the Astor Library in New York and in the New York Lyceum, Mahan worked on two separate sets of lectures. The first of these dealt with contemporary naval tactics. They were brought together in mid-1886 in an unpublished manuscript titled "Fleet Battle Tactics." This was a curious document at best and Mahan barely mentioned his authorship of it in his autobiography save to note that it might well have been "postponed." The second set of lectures, the product of his beginning research in naval history, became the essence of his seminal *The Influence of Sea Power Upon History, 1660–1783*, published in 1890, which brought worldwide fame to him and to the War College.

During the late fall and early winter of 1885–1886 his reading was of such a general nature as to contribute to the preparation of both series of lectures. Gradually, however, in January and February 1886, it became more specialized and more directed to his two distinct tasks. To get at the problem of devising a handbook for officers that would explain the basic procedures for conducting naval tactics under steam, he turned to the works of Jomini, especially to the general's six-volume *Critical and Military History of the Campaigns of the Revolution from 1792 to 1801* (1820), and to his *The Summary of the Art of War* (1836). This line of inquiry was probably suggested by Luce, who himself was wrestling with the problem of the application of land tactics to war at sea.

On the other hand, Mahan's reading of L. L. La Peyrouse Bonfils' *History of the French Navy* and Henri Martin's three-volume *A Popular History of France From the First Revolution to the Present Time* served a different function in that these books provided factual support and historical illustrations for his idea about the influence of sea power on history, the insight he had stumbled upon a year earlier in the pages of Mommsen while serving in the *Wachusett*. Put another way, Mahan's study of Bonfils, Martin, and others served mainly to illuminate a general historical theory of sea power he already held. His reading of Jomini, Admiral Sir George Elliot, Admiral Sir Charles Ekins, General Sir Edward B. Hamley, and Charles Louis, Archduke of Austria, helped him to develop a preliminary theory of modern naval tactics, a subject about which he knew virtually nothing in 1885. The lectures on tactics were written first, set to paper in April and May 1886; those on sea power were written later, being composed at Bar Harbor during the summer of 1886.[5]

Mahan's chief difficulty with the lectures on naval tactics under steam was that there was very little literature on that highly technical and speculative subject and there were no historical illustrations upon which to rely. Except for the confusing Battle of Lissa between the Italians and Austrians in July 1866, there had been no fleet actions between steam-driven ironclads mounting rifled guns and equipped with bow rams. And while at Lissa the opposing fleets had steamed boldly into battle in traditional formations (the Austrians in line abreast, the Italians in line ahead), the engagement had quickly degenerated into a general melee featuring sporadic close-range gunfire and mutual attempts to ram. Further, the larger and more powerful Italian fleet was defeated in this tactically chaotic exercise. About the only lesson to be learned from Lissa was that the ram could occasionally be a lethal piece of ordnance. It is not surprising, therefore, that Mahan overlooked the battle entirely in preparing his lectures for delivery at the college in 1886. It did not fit his growing conviction, derived in part from Luce (and in part from his Uncle Milo), that there existed in the universe certain basic "laws" or "principles," the discovery and application of which would govern the handling of steam vessels in combat.[6]

To make these tactical matters more difficult to analyze, the "automobile torpedo" had made its appearance since 1866, ship speeds had increased appreciably, gun ranges had lengthened, and naval armor had become heavier and less pervious to shell and ram. There was, in sum, no obvious point at which Mahan might commence a study of modern naval tactics. For this reason, he had little choice but to rely on the successful tactical maneuvers (he soon regarded them as "principles") of British combat commanders during the Age of Sail—men such as Howe, Rodney, Jervis, and the incomparable Horatio Nelson.

Chief among these principles was the idea of firepower concentration, i.e., the device (some called it a "science," others thought of it as an "art") of maneuvering a fleet under sail in concert and in such manner as to bring the larger number of ships and guns to bear on the smaller number. This idea, more easily conceived than accomplished, was of uncertain practical applicability to the fast new steam and steel warships being built by the world's navies in the 1880s. Nevertheless, Mahan undertook to apply it to the naval war of the future. Essentially, then, he returned to the tactics of the Age of Sail, the age in which he himself had been trained and in which he had held command at sea, if not command in actual combat.

To the concentration of firepower used by ships in the Age of Sail, Mahan added elements of the tactics of land warfare used in the Napoleonic Wars. This allowed him to take into account the greater speeds of the new ships and the fact that their movements in combat were not subject to the vagaries of the wind. He especially drew upon Napoleon's rapid deployment and movement of infantry and cavalry, as this technique was explained by Jomini in his *The Summary of the Art of War.*

Jomini, it will be recalled, preached the strategic doctrine that successful war turned on the capture and possession of an enemy's major military points, not necessarily his capital city. He emphasized the tactical importance of concentrating superior numbers of troops (or firepower) in combat; conversely, he preached the avoidance of pitched battles between armies or units of equal strength. Most importantly, he advocated speed such as provided by cavalry and the swift movement of infantry and horse-drawn artillery to achieve momentary firepower concentration in the field against an inferior segment of the enemy force. The idea was to destroy the enemy's armies piecemeal by preventing their junctures (concentrations). Constant, daring, and rapid movement of forces was best calculated to accomplish this, as Bonaparte had frequently demonstrated. Thus the destruction of the enemy army in the field, rather than the occupation of his territory, or the siege and seizure of his cities, was the strategic key to victorious warfare. Once his armies had been destroyed, his collapse would follow in train.

Mahan followed in Jomini's train. He came to see a combat relationship between a fleet's ram vessels, its torpedo boats, and its fast ships of the line (battleships) in much the same way that Jomini viewed the relationship of cavalry to the main body of an army. It was essentially an argument and exposition from historical analogy; but how else could someone in the years 1885 and 1886 explain the manner in which modern steam and steel fleets were to concentrate their firepower on an enemy?

This was the question that plagued him as he began his research on "Fleet Battle Tactics" in November 1885; indeed, it continued to plague him even as he began committing his tentative answers to paper in early April 1886. At the outset of his labor, and after a cursory reading of Jomini's *Summary of the Art of War*, he told Luce that his "principal use of Jomini" would be merely "as a *model* possibly suggestive of *manner* of treatment." Since he was not yet convinced that Jomini held the master key to all naval tactical locks, he also read the existing biographies of the great captains of the Age of Sail, studied Sir Charles Ekins' respected *Naval Battles* (1828), and scanned such speculative works as Admiral Sir George Elliot's *A Treatise on Future Naval Battles and How to Fight Them* (1885). Ekins assured him, for example, as had Luce earlier, that "in no case has a victory been won over a fairly equal force where the ignorance of the one commander-in-chief, or the skill of the others, has caused the strength of the fleet to be dispersed and has spread the attack over the whole, instead of concentrating it against a part." So instructed in the historical argument for concentration, Mahan immersed himself in all of the available secondary sources on the subject he could find, working "to the top of my present capacity, between four and five hours a day." As he settled to his task, he was amazed to discover that "the naval *history* of the world is for the most part, so far as records go, confined to the period between 1660 and 1815." He was persuaded as well that while "the tactics and nautical conditions of those times are of the past. . . . the lessons and incitement of the part played by fleets remains."

Not until early January 1886, however, did he hit upon the idea that his best prospect of making a lasting contribution to the theory of modern naval tactics was to "keep the analogy between land and naval warfare before my eyes." This pregnant thought seems not to have come directly from the pages of Jomini or from the letters of Luce. It came to him from Army Lieutenant Tasker A. Bliss. Perhaps it came to him from Luce by way of Bliss. The precise origin and transmission of the idea is not known.

What is known is that Bliss had been brought to the War College faculty by Luce in 1885. He had heard and admired Luce's two principal lectures in September of that year—"On the Study of Naval Warfare as a Science" and "On the Study of Naval History (Grand Tactics)"—and had himself lectured on military (land) history, strategy, and tactics at the college during the brief session in 1885. At the time he corresponded with Mahan during the winter of 1885–1886 he was expanding and honing those lectures for presentation at the 1886 session. But whether or not he was the natural parent of Mahan's belief in the "analogy between land and naval warfare," the fact remains that his suggestion about historical analogies turned Mahan to Edward B. Hamley's *The Operations of War Explained and Illustrated* (1866), to Admiral J. Penhoat's *Elements of Naval Tactics* (1879), and, most significantly, back to a more thoughtful consideration of Henri Jomini. "I am now reaching a point at which I think the books of other writers on kindred subjects will be more suggestive to me than they would have been three months ago," he remarked.[7]

By January 22, 1886, Mahan had tentatively solved the problem of how best to treat modern naval tactics. He reported his solution to Luce:

> *Now* I believe myself to have a good working knowledge of most, of all the important, naval campaigns of the years 1660–1815, and the tactics

of the various battles. Of course the question thrusts itself forward: under all the changed conditions of naval warfare of what use is the knowledge of these bygone days. Here I am frankly still a little at sea how to point my moral. . . . For instance strategy, as distinguished from tactics, will have plenty of illustration; the advantages and disadvantages of the possession of sea power and its effects upon specific campaigns must always possess useful lessons. Ships will no longer tack nor wear; but they must turn round sometimes; and I fancy that some thought expended upon the difficulties and confusion that may be thrown into an enemy's line or other order by forcing them to a change of order in action will have some fruit in the consideration of naval tactics in action; and I believe that knowledge of the great battles between sailing fleets will help in the solution of the problem. There will too always remain the great naval lessons . . . of the preponderance gained by activity, promptness, watchfulness, care, foresight and attention to details. . . . I think [these are] most true relatively to an army, land force. The admiral will not, nearly as far, make or mar as the general. By February 1st I expect to begin with Jomini, etc. and, having naval conditions constantly before my mind, I shall hope to detect analogies.[8]

Well said. But when Sam Ashe asked him a week later how he could possibly evolve "from the history of wooden ships and 24-pounders lessons that would be useful for ironclads and modern implements," Mahan waffled a bit:

[The] greatest difficulty lies in the fact that all naval history hitherto has been made by ships and weapons of a kind wholly different from those now in use. How to view the lessons of the past so as to mould them into lessons for the future, under such differing conditions, is the nut I have to crack. To excogitate a system of my own, on wholly a priori grounds, would be comparatively simple, and I believe wholly useless. We are already deluged with speculations and arguments as to future naval warfare, more or less plausible and well considered; but I don't see any use in my adding to that clack. I want if I can to wrest something out of the old wooden sides and 24-pounders that will throw some light on the combinations to be used with ironclads, rifled guns, and torpedoes; and to raise the profession in the eyes of its members by a clearer comprehension of the great part it has played in the world than I myself have hitherto had.[9]

Hot on the trail of historical analogies that would make these cloudy matters clear, Mahan pushed the writing of his lectures on tactics to a conclusion, pausing only to gain "a more intimate acquaintance with past

Naval History and also with the general theory of war, and especially the value of different kinds of orders in Grand Tactics." Since he knew little about recent developments in naval weaponry and was bored by the subject, he secured from the Office of Naval Intelligence the latest data on foreign experiments with naval guns, rams, and torpedoes. Indeed, he explained to Luce that he had undertaken "the consideration of modern vessels, weapons, etc. . . . to deduce from them the necessary orders and plans of battles" only because the subject would be the one "most demanded" by the reader and because the absence of such considerations would "provoke naval criticism." He was conscious of the fact that if he confined himself solely to naval history, "the College would be blamed for not keeping me to things that were useful." By April 24 he had written his way past the tiresome business of "weapons, etc." and had experienced "a first glimmering of how to hitch on the history of the past to the theory of the present." The harness finally linking the two was Jomini's analysis of the effectiveness of infantry firepower concentration (supported by cavalry flanking movements) during the battles of the Napoleonic Wars.

On May 1, 1886, he mailed the manuscript of his "Fleet Battle Tactics" to Luce, noting that it still lacked consideration of where to place torpedo boats in the battle formation, the best formation for close action, the "merits and defects of various defensive, or offensive-defensive orders," and "how to avoid and how to force action." He told his mentor that the two lectures which comprised the paper were all that he planned to do on the subject at the forthcoming session of the college. "The first parts of my course relating to naval history, etc. are yet untouched, though prepared for," he complained. He would therefore turn to that far more congenial task.[10]

Mahan's study on fleet battle tactics under steam is an interesting and controversial document, interesting in its naïveté, controversial in its heavy reliance on historical analogy. The neat battle diagrams accompanying the text, detailing fleet combat formations, ship evolutions, and gun ranges, theoretically spelled victory after victory for the emerging New Navy. Beginning with the assumption that the fleet which has "confidence in its artillery power will refuse *close* action, ram and torpedo, until it has either obtained, or lost hope of obtaining, odds in its favor by first injuring the opponent with its guns," or what "Jomini calls the defensive-offensive," Mahan maintained that future naval battles would be fought much as they had been under sail, new weapons notwithstanding. He considered the torpedo, owing to its slowness, to be an ineffective weapon.

The usefulness of the ram was also limited. Fleets would thus still be maneuvered and fought as they had been by Lord Nelson, in such manner as to concentrate the guns of the many ships on those of the few. Future battles would not, however, be fought broadside to broadside from line-ahead formations. Because of the greater ranges and the fore-and-aft firing capability of rifled guns, fleet actions of the future would likely be joined, and would be fought at the outset, in line abreast or echelon formations, since these deployments best adapted themselves to the achievement of maximum firepower concentration from the forward and after guns of the new steam-driven battleships. As the action began to develop, the battle line would wheel, turn, and perform various precise, complex, and opportunistic geometric evolutions designed either to secure, maintain, regain, or increase its concentration of fire ("the essence of scientific warfare") on selected enemy units, which would be sunk one by one. It was this vision of rapid offensive movement and selective firepower concentration that Jomini had clarified in Mahan's mind. "The essence of my system," said Mahan, "lies in adopting a formation which while good for artillery fire, distinctly contemplates a change which the enemy cannot foreknow; and which lends itself to such a change by its elastic character." Easier said than done.

The great rifled guns and the armored battleships that carried them were, thought Mahan, the ultimate keys to victory. The smaller ram vessels and torpedo boats, about which he admitted he knew little, were secondary weapons. They were to be positioned safely behind the main battle line and ordered to stay there until the enemy had been badly mauled or was in flight. At this juncture, like Jomini's spirited cavalry, they would swoop down on the troubled scene to harass the collapsing or collapsed enemy flanks, annoy enemy vessels that might be milling about in confusion, and dispatch crippled stragglers.

At no point in his "Fleet Battle Tactics" did Mahan indicate anything but a pessimism about the tactical usefulness of the ram and the torpedo. The rifled gun was king. At no point did he contemplate the possibility of a disorderly melee, as the Battle of Lissa had been. On the contrary, the battles of the future would remain controlled, orderly, and precise. But at no point, either, did he lose sight of the human factor in the outcome of war at sea. As he put it:

> Battles are won because one side is less numerous, or less efficient, or one leader is less skillful than the other. . . . We must assume throughout a highly drilled fleet. Perfection is our aim, and we must be granted reasonably perfect ships, reasonably drilled and commanded, to achieve

it. . . . the machines will do their work, if the men have had practice enough to gain confidence and to reduce the errors due to the personal equation. . . . You cannot as a rule count upon what [the enemy] may choose to do, though . . . knowledge of the personal character of the enemy's admiral, and of the efficiency of his fleet, are legitimate elements in your plans, as they were in Nelson's.

In retrospect, it would seem that by following the arrows and dotted lines on Mahan's classroom battle plans, almost any War College student could instantly become a modern Nelson. Further, the impression is gained from "Fleet Battle Tactics" that the enemy fleet, searched out and lured skillfully into battle by a superior American force, was expected to sit more or less dead in the water—docilely accepting concentrated fire, watching in awe a series of beautifully executed parade-ground exercises —while it was being decimated in detail by the firepower of the entire U.S. line. Like Jomini's infantry battles, Mahan's naval engagements were expected to end with the total annihilation of the enemy force, the torpedo boats and rams standing down at last on the enemy vessels still afloat to put them out of their misery. This portrait of the wholly decisive big battle was an appealing one in a larger strategic sense, especially when Mahan saw such happy results issuing from a proper understanding of the "laws of war," the "art of war," and the historical "truths" implicit in both.

With most of this scenario Luce agreed. Still, he laced the pages of Mahan's manuscript with technical criticisms, most of them offered in an attempt to strengthen the author's imperfect grasp of recent developments in ship design and ordnance. Nevertheless, he pronounced the manuscript "in the main, satisfactory." He informed his protégé, however, that he had invited Lieutenant Commander William Bainbridge Hoff (class of 1864) also to deliver a series of lectures on the subject of naval tactics during the September 1886 session of the college. This news caused Mahan to comment, with some relief it appears, that "it would be a distinct advantage to the course to have the subject treated by another as well as myself." In 1884 Hoff had published a book on the subject, *Examples, Conclusions, and Maxims of Modern Naval Tactics*, which Mahan thought weak, but which he read while writing his own lectures. For reasons not clear, Mahan did not lecture on naval tactics at all during the 1886 session of the college. Hoff did. Instead, Mahan spoke on naval history, especially the general influence of sea power on history.[11]

Of great value to the U.S. Navy were Mahan's lectures at Newport on sea power and the numerous books and articles which later grew out of them. These have endured, whereas his "Fleet Battle Tactics" disappeared from sight almost instantly. Certainly, he had a much easier and more enjoyable time with the preparation of these lectures than with his awkward tactical exegeses. Indeed, as his reading and research progressed during the fall and winter of 1885–1886, he began to see that his theory of the influence of sea power on history could be documented. La Peyrouse Bonfils' *History of the French Navy* convinced him that he was on the right track.

As noted before, the dominant role of sea power in history was not an original idea with Mahan—he never claimed that it was. His initial demonstration of the concept was drawn almost entirely from secondary sources. Still, he had hold of a thought that was potentially of great importance to the emerging New Navy. The significance of this he clearly understood, and his anticipation and excitement increased as the supporting pieces of selected historical evidence fell into place—or were made to fall into place. He worried, however, that his intellect might be in decline and that his 45-year-old brain might not be equal to the great challenge. He wrote Ashe in mid-January 1886:

> I find alas, that I am of an age where the brain is not in as good working order as it was. Accustomed work and strain I think the brain stands long and well, but not the taking up a new thing and pressure of an exceptional kind and degree—such at least is my present experience. I am somewhat fearful of failure, but am resolved not to break myself down straining after the impossible, if it prove so. My general health fortunately is very good.

By January 22, nine days later, both the underlying theory and the organizational formula for his subsequent naval histories, virtually a synopsis of them, had taken final shape. His excitement was understandably intense; his mind had truly seized the "thunder" of a great idea:

> With regard to my own course of lectures [he told Luce] my ideas have not yet attained the precision which I would like to throw into any reply to you. In a general way they are these: I think to begin with a general consideration of the sea, its uses to mankind and to nations, the effect which the control of it or the reverse has [had] upon their peaceful development and upon their military strength. This will naturally lead to . . . a consideration of the sources of Sea Power, whether commercial or military; depending upon the position of the particular country—the character of its coast, its harbors, the character and pursuits of its people, its possession of military posts in various parts of the

world, its colonies, etc.—its resources, in the length and breadth of the word. After such a general statement of the various elements of the problem, illustrated of course by specific examples—the path would be cleared for naval history. There are a good many phases of naval history. I have been led, and I think upon the whole happily led, to take up that period succeeding the peace of Westphalia, 1648, when the nations of Europe began clearly to enter on and occupy their modern positions, struggling for existence and preponderance. I have carefully followed up this period both in respect of naval history and the general struggles of Europe; for it has seemed to me . . . that the attempt to violently separate the naval history from that context will be something like . . . Hamlet with all but the part of Hamlet left out. I have nearly finished, within a week's work, this general consideration down to 1783. . . . Whether I can accomplish anything more, in the matter of naval history of other epochs, this year, I cannot say. . . . I am working to my full capacity—and have to feel that that is less than it was. . . . I would like this letter, however, to be confidential—in case any of my thunder should turn out *real* thunder.[12]

Mahan did not immediately push on to harness his *"real* thunder." He paused, instead, to finish his "Fleet Battle Tactics." Throughout February and well into March he was ill, a recurrence of malarial fever "apparently due to Panama." During this five-week period he "tried head work from time to time but in vain." He was further slowed in his work by his attempt to secure, through a private bill referred to the House Committee on Pensions, an arrears payment of the pension his mother received as an Army widow. Her circumstances, he confided to Ashe, "have altered a good deal since [her husband's] death and the matter is one of some consequence to her." Ashe, whom President Cleveland had appointed Postmaster of Raleigh (the income "will be a comfortable addition for you," Mahan noted) obliged his old friend with a letter of support addressed to Representative William H. H. Cowles, of North Carolina, a member of the committee. And so the matter was arranged.[13]

In spite of these medical and family interruptions, by early May 1886 Mahan had accumulated more than 400 pages of notes for his lectures on sea power. Convinced that his mind was "well stocked" with the "quite voluminous" material, he planned to write the lectures during the summer at Bar Harbor, Maine, where his mother-in-law rented a house. It was a delightful place to work. "I think I shall have no great difficulty in finishing," he told Luce. Meanwhile, he borrowed from various officers and Navy libraries a collection of standard references to carry with him to Maine. Soley was helpful in this regard. Francis M. Ramsay, Superinten-

dent of the Naval Academy, was not. "It is a pity but only an inconvenience," said Mahan, "not a disaster." The real "disaster" with Ramsay
came later. Once he reached Bar Harbor, he promised Luce, he would
"tie myself down wholly to the historical discussion, which I think I have
pretty well in my head." The pledge was kept. The matter of the influence of sea power upon history, about which more will be said in the next
chapter, was accomplished in broad outline in June, July, and August of
1886.[14]

No sooner had Mahan settled his family in Maine for the summer and
plunged into his writing than he learned that Luce, who had been promoted to rear admiral, had been detached from the college, effective
June 18, and ordered to the command of the North Atlantic Station. He
went immediately to Newport to consult with his mentor and it was
arranged between them that Mahan would succeed Luce as president of
the college. He received no formal assignment to the post. He recalled
that he "simply fell into the presidency as a first lieutenant does into
command after the captain's removal." When he returned again from Bar
Harbor to Newport in late August it was as the second president of
the fledgling institution. Elly and the children joined him there in October, when quarters for him and his family were finally provided.

The Naval War College in 1886 was no place of beauty or comfort.
Originally the Newport Almshouse, it was as poor a facility for an educational institution as it was for the poor who had recently inhabited it.
Renovation was still under way when Elly and the children arrived
that fall. This necessitated the family's fleeing their living quarters after
breakfast so that classes might be held in the same rooms. The building
itself was cold and sparsely furnished. The three children were bathed in
front of the dining-room fireplace in tubs modestly screened from the
rest of the room and heated with rubber tubing connected to the steam
valve of a nearby radiator. Such was Mahan's grasp of practical steam
engineering. Equipment was scarce. Mahan moved the single study lamp
the Navy provided from room to room at night. Nonetheless, his daughter Ellen remembered the old Newport Almshouse "as the one place in
all the world that was most like Heaven," and Mahan reported to Ashe
in early October that while the place "somewhat tried" his wife and himself, it had the economic advantage of being "entirely out of Newport,
indeed in the very opposite direction from the fashionable quarter." It
had better views and breezes than Newport proper, to which Coaster's
Harbor Island, site of the college, was joined by a causeway. Indeed, he

could look "straight down the narrow entrance through which, over a hundred years ago, D'Estaing sailed in with the French fleet under the fire of the English batteries." If nothing else, it was historical. It was also in Newport during these pleasant years that Mahan's favorite dog, "Jomini," was born and raised. As Ellen Mahan recalled, "friends of mine said he *looked* like my father. I can see what they meant, the dog intent on his own thoughts, as the man was on his. I, too, soon learned, when walking with my father and 'Jomini,' to be intent on *my* thoughts also."[15]

The session opened on September 6, 1886, with twenty-one students and five staff lecturers, including Mahan. The *Tennessee*, Luce's flagship, was conveniently in port and her officers attended the first ten days of the session. Luce insisted that the ships and men of his command be used by the college for "practical work." This involved employing the *Tennessee*'s steam launches for simulated ramming exercises on Narragansett Bay. While these evolutions were not too relevant to the problems of fleet tactics in the mid-1880s, Mahan felt that they "would lighten the monotony of constant lectures." It was also highly important that the college give its hard-headed critics the impression that it was interested in down-to-earth training. For this reason, in his annual reports for 1886 and 1887 to the Chief of the Bureau of Navigation, John G. Walker, who was most friendly toward the college, Mahan asked that he be provided with two specially constructed small boats to be used for practice ramming maneuvers. After 1887 he dropped the point.[16]

The fact of the matter was that the curriculum that Luce designed for 1886 was sharply oriented toward the strategical, the theoretical, and the historical. It featured no fewer than eighteen lectures by the brilliant Tasker Bliss on military (land) strategy and tactics, a dimension of the course that required some defense within Navy circles. Mahan provided the justification:

> Two objects are aimed at by this. First, to enlarge the knowledge of sea officers in the matter of conducting such expeditions as may be feasible with forces landed from a fleet alone; familiarizing them with the best approved methods and expedients of modern armies. . . . The second object may be stated thus. . . . It is reasonably thought that the broad study of land warfare . . . will materially aid the sea officer to correct conclusions as to the best use of the yet untried weapons.[17]

This glancing reference to the possibility of amphibious operations, stimulated perhaps by Mahan's experience in Panama in 1885, was about as close as he ever approached to that dimension of warfare. The projection

Francis M. Ramsay at his desk in the Bureau of Navigation

and maintenance of naval power ashore was not a problem with which he came to grips.

What he did anticipate was strong and active opposition to the War College as an ivory tower for the theoretical study of war. And although the 1886 session went extremely well ("My own lectures . . . met with a degree of success which surprised me and which still seems to me exaggerated," Mahan rejoiced), he immediately met opposition. Led within the Navy by Francis Ramsay and Winfield Scott Schley, it called attention to the institution's lack of practical studies, argued that its operation was too expensive for what the Navy was getting out of it, demanded that it be moved to Annapolis and attached to the Academy as a postgraduate course, and held that the facility at Newport for training apprentice seamen badly needed the space the college was occupying on Coaster's Harbor Island. It was even suggested by some critics, not facetiously, that the student-officers at the college did little more than spend their time flirting and dancing with the fashionable belles of the Newport summer colony. Others contended that in the interests of administrative, economic, and curricular efficiency the college should be consolidated with the Torpedo Station on nearby Goat Island. Taken together, the arguments were not without merit.

These criticisms reached Congress, especially the ears of Representative Hilary A. Herbert of Alabama, Chairman of the House Naval Affairs Committee. The result was that the Naval Appropriations Bill for fiscal 1887–1888 contained no money designated specifically for the college. Mahan went to Washington in an attempt to change Herbert's mind in favor of funding the college, but he did not succeed. More than that, he was appalled to discover that Herbert, "a man so influential upon the interests of the Navy had no apparent conception of the necessity for studying the Art of War"—and this with modern steam and steel ships at last in prospect. As he told Ashe, the House budgetary action was "a great pity, for in the absence of modern ships which we cannot effectually overcome for three or four years more, the time of officers cannot be better spent than in preparing, even theoretically, to use them to the best advantage when they are built." A major purpose of the War College was to organize and apply "systematic pressure" to ensure that preparation.

Fortunately, Commodore Walker, with Secretary W. C. Whitney's approval, managed to shift funds around within the Navy Department budget and this fiscal legerdemain allowed the college to limp along through the 1887 session. It "was run on a vacuum," Mahan recalled. Warning signals, however, were clearly flying and these became disaster signals in the autumn of 1887, when Luce and Whitney had a bitter personal falling-out over American fishing rights in Canadian waters. Indeed, as early as October 1886 Mahan had alerted Ashe to the possibility that the influential Carolinian might soon have to use his good offices with the North Carolina congressional delegation in Washington if the attacks on the college became more direct, or if money for its proper support did not soon begin to flow. He knew that "there was disposition, even among the friendly, to enhance the importance of the College by dwelling upon electricity, steam ordnance, and other studies dependent upon the mechanical and physical sciences, as being part of the service it might do the Navy." He was determined, however, to keep such practical concerns out of the college curriculum, even if it meant antagonizing erstwhile friends of the institution. In later years he recalled the opinions he had held on this matter in 1886:

> It appeared to me that once impress upon the College that [practical] characteristic, it would inevitably predominate over the study of Warfare, because the disposition, alike of the Navy and of the age, is to

insist upon material perfection as the chief end of military effort. Consequently, the only way to preserve the College at all, for its particular end, was resolutely to put away all thought of the material of the service; and this discardment destroyed also at once the argument for removal [of the College] to Annapolis, the result of which would have been the inevitable strangulation of the younger and weaker institution by the older and stronger, much as a mother suffocates a baby by overlying.

It was this view, correct in retrospect, coupled with Mahan's unwillingness further to compromise on the curriculum, that would virtually destroy the college in 1889. In 1887, however, he was still willing to attempt compromise.[18]

He realized, of course, that as its president he would have to defend his concept of the college as an institution dedicated to the theoretical and historical study of the art of war. He came also to see in 1887 that he could best parry the critical thrusts of Ramsay, Schley, and Herbert by relating the curriculum in some manner to the real world of American politics and foreign policy. Consequently, during that year's session he lectured on the strategic features of the Caribbean Sea and the Gulf of Mexico. This lecture, revised and published in 1897, as well as his lectures on naval history, "met with great approval." In his annual report to Walker in October 1887 he linked the school's curriculum to the question of the Isthmus of Panama and the French presence there. "The consideration of the results of an isthmian canal," he argued, "is designed to familiarize the minds of officers with the great issues that are maturing in the waters of Central America; the importance of those regions from the point of view of military control, if not in war; and also incidentally to awaken attention to the close connection between the commercial and naval interests of a country." This emphasis was not hastily trumped up merely to allay criticism of the college. It issued naturally from his recent conversion to imperialism, a conversion that began with his experiences in Central America in the *Wachusett* and matured during the research and writing of his lectures on naval history at the War College. As he recalled a few years later, "the study of the influence of sea power and its kindred expansive activities upon the destiny of nations had converted me; and my new faiths, thus originated, colored the first of my writings, as they have continued to do the rest."[19]

It cannot be known whether hitching the War College curriculum to the nascent imperialist urges of the United States during the 1887 session helped Mahan's cause or hurt it. Certainly it was politically more astute to relate the business of the college to the problems of an isthmian canal than to Admiral Howe's breaking of the French line at the Battle of the Glorious First of June in 1794. It was during that session that Lieutenant William McCarty Little joined the staff and set up the course on naval war games (*kreigspiel*) that became an important practical facet of the curriculum in the years ahead. Further, 75 of the 146 lectures given at the college in 1887 dealt with topics practical, tactical, and operational; 71 addressed issues strategical, theoretical, and historical. Clearly, then, Mahan made a major effort during the college's third session to counter the attacks of those who argued that the curriculum was largely irrelevant to the practical needs and concerns of the New Navy.

Nevertheless, he had small confidence that a better-balanced curriculum alone would mollify the anti-college brotherhood. At the close of the 1887 session, again an extremely successful one from his point of view, he began actively to lobby for the upcoming Naval Appropriations Bill, the one that would determine the fate of the college in fiscal 1888–1889. He wanted that legislation to include a specific budget item for the institution. Enlisting the assistance of such solid citizens as Sam Ashe, John C. Ropes (who had twice been a guest lecturer at the college), and Henry Saltonstall of Massachusetts, Mahan got his version of the importance and uniqueness of the school to the ears of no fewer than a dozen prominent representatives and senators during the early months of 1888. In January of that year he again went to Washington to buttonhole various legislators and naval officers on the desirability of a separate budget for the college. In spite of the fact that he managed to lose or misplace important letters of support to members of the North Carolina delegation supplied him by Ashe, his two-week immersion in the seedy world of Washington politics went well.

As might have been expected, he got nowhere with Herbert, failing entirely to shake the Alabama Democrat's arguments against the college on economy grounds. This caused the able legislator to be placed on Mahan's black list as "an impossible man; naturally obstinate and proud of being so—honest but pigheaded to a degree." He did, however, manage to get from Secretary Whitney a firm commitment that he would not oppose a separate budget for the War College during the committee hearings—even though the Secretary had come to the personal view that "he did not favor the College as a separate institution." This promise was a major political breakthrough and Mahan smelled the sweet scent of victory. It now mattered less that Whitney "had absolutely no appreciation of the necessity for systematic study of Warfare." It was enough that he had assured the captain that "I will not oppose you, but I do not authorize you to express any approval from me." Mahan was delighted. As he told Ashe, "while using influence to gain a hearing . . . I am relying mainly upon the goodness of the cause and the quality of our work. People smile now-a-days when one expects to win because his cause is good; but I prefer to look to that, and my anxiety is lest I may be led into any crookedness to further what I believe a good object." In fact, so decent a hearing did he receive in Washington that he began worrying that "overconfidence may ruin us at any moment."[20]

To all who would hear him out, in Washington and elsewhere, Mahan's message was the same: the Naval War College must be preserved, protected, and sustained as the only theoretical military-naval institution in the world at which the art, principles, and strategies of war were studied without reference to the technological and scientific development of the machines of war. Its consolidation with the Naval Academy, the Torpedo Station, or any other naval training command would mean its certain death. Senator Eugene Hale of Maine and Representatives W. C. Whitthorne of Tennessee, Joseph Wheeler of Alabama, William L. Scott of Pennsylvania, and William Elliott of South Carolina were a few of the legislators who heard Mahan's sermon in 1887 and stayed to pray.[21]

By June 14 Mahan was convinced that he was home free. In the House Naval Committee he counted 10 of the 13 votes in favor of a separate appropriation for the War College within the Navy's 1888–1889 budget. True, Herbert's opposition remained "sustained and strenuous." But at this juncture a confident Mahan was more worried lest the Republican presidential nominating convention in Chicago the following week draw supporters of the college away from the capital at the very moment the appropriation measure was scheduled for debate and vote. "Attendance is so irregular now vigilance is needed lest defeat be incurred even by very superior numbers." Happily, all went well. The measure was successfully reported out of committee and was passed by the House. It was then sent to the Senate and was referred to the Appropriations Committee.[22]

At this point Mahan's dream suddenly collapsed. Secretary Whitney marched into the Senate Appropriations Committee and suggested amendments to the House legislation which, in Mahan's view, defeated "the entire purposes of the College." Specifically, Whitney recommended, for reasons of economy and administrative efficiency, that the War College and the Torpedo Station be consolidated, that the combined facility be located on Goat Island under the command of the officer in charge of the Torpedo Station (who happened to be Caspar F. Goodrich), and that the War College building be turned over to the apprentice seamen's training program. That function, it will be recalled, was administered by the Bureau of Equipment headed by Schley. Whitney asked also that he be authorized to make these administrative changes at his early convenience. Meanwhile, he recommended that the college be given a budget of $10,000 to carry it through the coming session. Much to Mahan's distress, Congress accepted this arrangement. Soon after, in late July 1888, the Secretary issued a press statement explaining his position. In this release he argued that

> the Torpedo School grew up first as a school for the education of officers supplemental to the Naval Academy. . . . Then the new College started, where courses of lectures were delivered on miscellaneous subjects, again covering instructions supplemental to that of the Naval Academy. A channel less than half a mile wide flows between these two institutions, and Congress is asked to provide for each separate and distinct institution for line officers—making three altogether: the Naval Academy, the Torpedo School, and the War College. . . . The bill provides that two of these shall be consolidated. I have favored the War College in each of my annual reports, but I do not deem the present arrangement wise or sensible, and have not seen any other person understanding the matter who does.

To give further point to his sudden anti-War College attitude, to add insult to injury as it were, Whitney, on August 1, ordered that the planned fourteen-week course scheduled by Mahan to begin on August 6, 1888, be reduced to three months. "In view of the fact," he said, "that during the last year's course less than an average of two lectures per day were delivered, including Saturday and Sunday, the Department feels that the interest attached to the course will not be impaired by condensing the course into a shorter period." Mahan had to make the necessary curricular adjustments on five days' notice.

He was livid with rage. Seldom had his considerable temper been so aroused. He was stunned by Whitney's double-cross. The Secretary's press statement, he felt, lacked candor. The Torpedo School was already overburdened with instruction and could not possibly absorb that of the college. In the previous session, the lectures had averaged fewer than two a day only because "several days were given to practical exercises with the fleet." But it was mainly upon Whitney's character and personality that Mahan poured his wrath:

> I do think [he exploded to Ashe] that common fairness and decency demanded that, before thus upsetting my work, he should have asked whether I had any good reasons to urge against the step he was about

to take. . . . Now, understand I have no objection to the Secretary overruling me; I object to his overruling me *unheard* in a matter immediately under my charge. . . . You will also believe me when I tell you that my administration here has commanded the approval of the Navy, converted opponents into friends. . . . I have worked a doubtful experiment up into full professional favor. . . . Whitney is considered by men in the Navy able to judge as one of the strongest men in the Cabinet; but he is corrupt (politically) in the use of patronage and I gather that in that respect the Navy is worse than it has ever been in my time. . . . in this respect he is as bad or worse than Chandler or Robeson.

The comparison of Whitney with Robeson was unworthy of Mahan. But such was the degree of the latter's anger and disappointment in August 1888. Actually, Whitney was an honest, strong, and effective Secretary of the Navy. He was not politically corrupt. He had done much to support and develop the emerging New Navy. On the other hand, Mahan simply could not understand or accept a viewpoint that differed from his own on the subject of the Naval War College. His ego was too wrapped up in the well-being of the struggling institution. For this reason he moved quickly from understandable anger to interpreting Whitney's behavior as part of a conspiracy.[23]

He had been done in, he finally decided, by that old Pelican Club member of his unhappy Academy days—the handsome, debonair, and popular Winfield Scott Schley. He had been disenchanted with Schley for thirty years. Schley's naval career, quite unlike Mahan's, had been brilliant, dashing, and much in the public eye. The former Pelican, now Chief of the Bureau of Equipment, was determined to bring Coaster's Harbor Island under the control of his bureau and establish there a shore-based training station in the college facility. The training ship *New Hampshire*, tied up at Newport, was entirely inadequate for this purpose. Schley saw no professional good coming out of the War College, and, during the financially lean session of 1887, refused to approve vouchers submitted by Mahan to pay for coal to heat the drafty old almshouse. Moreover, since there was no separate budget for the War College and the Navy Department did not have funds to cover all maintenance costs, Schley supported a proposal within the department in 1887 to force the institution's staff officers to defray minor maintenance expenses out of their own pockets. Touched in the sensitive nerve that was his wallet, Mahan did not become any more enchanted with Schley.

It is not surprising, then, that in 1888 he saw a Whitney-Schley conspiracy against the War College where there was none. "I will not ask you to believe, what I believe but do not know," he told former Midshipman Ashe, "but which is commonly believed in the Navy, that the Secretary is largely influenced by a man named Schley—whom you may remember—who has never achieved more than a second-rate reputation, if that, among his brother officers." The whole thing, he told Luce, had been at "the instigation of Schley."[24]

Mahan understood that "military propriety prevents my working against or answering" the Secretary. Directly, that was. But nothing prevented him from saying again, and saying publicly, what he thought the War College should be. Still outraged over the Whitney-Schley counterstroke against him, he chose the opening of the fourth annual session of the college, on August 6, 1888, to deliver an ill-considered and uncompromising attack on those in the Navy who equated in importance the development of the weapons and machinery of war and the theoretical and historical study of the art of war. And to make sure that all hands got the message, he personally paid for the reprinting and distribution of the speech in pamphlet form after its appearance in the December 1888 issue of the U.S. Naval Institute *Proceedings*.

He admitted in his angry address that the Luce Board had confused the issue in 1884 by suggesting that the college might play a "postgraduate" role in the education of Naval Academy graduates. That phrase was "unfortunate." He then launched into his own understanding of what the founders had really intended the institution to be:

> It is to be said, then, that the War College does not propose to devote its energies to the question of the material and mechanical development of the Navy, except in a secondary and incidental manner. . . . If his [the military seaman's] ship will make a certain speed, she may, for all he cares, be driven by a tallow-candle; if his gun will do so much work, it may, so far as he is concerned, be made of pasteboard. . . . Speaking broadly, it may be said that the true aim is to promote, not the *creation* of naval material, but the knowledge how to *use* that material to the best advantage in the conduct of war. . . . [our object] is the study and development, in a systematic, orderly manner, of the art of war as applied to the sea, or such parts of the land as can be reached from ships.

He argued further that the materialistic and scientific spirit of the times threatened to reduce the warrior as artist to the warrior as mechanic and to deprive him of those "rarer qualities—intuition, sagacity, judgment, daring, inspiration—which place great captains among creators, and war itself among the fine arts." He was also certain that the greatest master of the art of war, the first Napoleon has . . . laid down the principle that to become a great captain the soldier must study the campaigns of Hannibal, Caesar, and Alexander. . . . In short, the great warrior must study history. I have wished to bring out this point clearly, if briefly, for there is a very natural, though also very superficial, disposition in the Navy, at present, to look upon past history as a blank book so far as present usefulness is concerned. . . . valuable lessons may be derived . . . from the study of those wars . . . in which the naval preponderance of one nation has exercised an immense and decisive effect upon the issues of great contests both by land and sea; in which, if I may so say, the Navy has been a most, perhaps the most, important single strategic factor in the whole wide field of a war. . . . I will sound again the note of warning against that plausible cry of the day which finds *all* progress in material advance, disregarding that noblest sphere in which the mind and heart of man, in which all that is god-like in man, reign supreme; and against that temper which looks not to the man, but to his armor.

Further, he again felt it necessary to defend his belief that there was a close relationship between the conduct of land warfare and that of war at sea. This connection he related to the logistical requirements of all modern navies, specifically to America's need for overseas coaling stations and ammunition depots if the nation and its Navy intended to play a major political role at the Isthmus of Panama. There were also the purely intellectual advantages of these relationships: "Even if history had not shown that the principles of strategy have held good under circumstances so many and so various that they may be justly assumed of universal application, to sea as well as to land, there would still remain the fine mental training afforded by the successive modifications that have been introduced into the art of war by great generals."[25]

None of this public scolding and pleading had one whit of influence on William C. Whitney. He had little interest in the "fine mental training" the college might provide the Navy. He therefore went straight ahead with his consolidation plan, even though Mahan instructed J. G. Walker that merging the college with the Torpedo Station would mean the certain demise of the former.

Ironically, the 1888 session was academically the best that the beleaguered school had experienced, at least from the standpoint of its president. The faculty was excellent. The curriculum was imaginative, well integrated, and carefully thought through. W. McCarty Little again lectured on war games, an innovation borrowed from the Germans. Young Theodore Roosevelt, fresh from Harvard and author of a good monograph on the naval history of the War of 1812, lectured on that tragic conflict. Mahan himself lectured on naval history, on fleet battle tactics, and once again on the strategic features of the Caribbean and Gulf. Attending the Caribbean lecture was George Sydenham Clarke, the British army officer with whom he corresponded frequently in the years ahead. Said Clarke of his first encounter with Mahan: "The subject—the Gulf of Mexico and the Caribbean Sea in their strategic relations to the United States—was treated with consummate ability. A new light seemed to be thrown upon the whole question of naval warfare; confused pages of naval history took form and order; great principles stood forth clearly revealed."

But whatever the teaching skills of its outspoken president, it was clear that the days of the War College, as Mahan conceived it, were numbered. The Cleveland-Whitney administration simply would not support the school to the degree Mahan considered essential. The class of student-officers was thus decreased from twenty-one in 1887 to fourteen in 1888. Further, these fourteen warm bodies were a docile and unimaginative lot, scarcely worth the time and energy of their teachers. Mahan described them to a British correspondent, Royal Navy Commander William H. Henderson: "The officers are under orders; they have nothing else to do for the time; they listen with the attention of men who are trained to obey orders, and when we reach the stage of setting problems of war, and requiring theses, they will be equally docile." In addition to providing a student body comprised of *lumpen proletarians*, Whitney had shortened the course of study. Consolidation with the Torpedo Station loomed. The building would soon pass into the hands of Schley. An attempt by Mahan to interest the British United Service Institution, a professional association of officers, in the fate of the sinking institution failed. "So much importance is attached here to what you do in England," he informed Henderson, "that such an endorsement might avert our fate." There was no endorsement, in spite of Mahan's assurance to Commander Henderson that the Royal Navy was "the only one in truth in which I feel a strong kindred interest."

Desperately, he wrote to various American officers thanking them for their past support and asking their aid against Whitney's nefarious consolidation scheme. He even considered mobilizing the Newport Town Council against the pending consolidation and, through Republican Senator Nelson Aldrich of Rhode Island, bringing its voice to bear on the Cleveland administration. But by mid-November 1888 all efforts to save the institution had apparently failed, and Mahan was "too fagged in both mind and body" to carry on the fight much longer. He was beaten. Only the incoming Republican administration could rescue the dying college.

> Nothing [he told Luce] will change Whitney's intention except a degree of power and influence which I do not expect from Newport. Conciliation and procrastination are our only hope now—for though I do not expect to prevent his moving us out, the longer it can be delayed the less established will Schley's arrangements be, and the more possible the restoration by a new administration. . . . I think with patience we shall come out all right; but I would not even propose a Board to consider the matter until the Secretary begins to move, then it may serve for delay. Had the present [Democratic] Administration continued, then our hope was in a Board; now it is in Aldrich's restored influence and the general consent of the Navy.

The decision, then, was to lie low, to hope that Bureau Chief Walker might be able to "work to undo the wrongs of this year," and to pray that the new Republican administration, which would take office in March 1889, would harken to Senator Aldrich's representations against the consolidation and the removal of the school from Coaster's Harbor Island.[26]

The election of Benjamin Harrison to the White House in November 1888 gave Mahan hope that the college might still be salvaged. Harrison was certainly no great statesman, but Mahan voted for him. "It is curious," he confided to Democrat Ashe, "that though upon the whole favoring your ticket and platform, the desire to get rid of Whitney influences my hopes about the election." His continued "horror and loathing" of James G. Blaine almost made a temporary Democrat out of Mahan in 1888 since he was also "against the high tariff and the consequent concentration of wealth and power in the hands of a protected few" that the GOP supported. But his hatred of the double-crossing Whitney was far greater. Thus when Blaine was passed over for the Republican nomination Mahan had no difficulty backing the lackluster Harrison. Mahan remained a Democrat between elections.

In this instance his political hopes were not dashed. He was delighted with Harrison's appointment of General Benjamin F. Tracy of New York as Secretary of the Navy. He was willing to abandon temporarily the fight for the college and await the smoother seas the new secretary might provide after March 1889. Tracy, one of the great nineteenth-century Secretaries of the Navy, soon proved to be a man after Alfred Thayer Mahan's own heart.[27]

In the meantime, Mahan was fearful that if he angered Whitney further by continued opposition to consolidation he might well be shipped off to sea before the Cleveland administration left office. This became a possibility when he discovered shortly after the election that the steam sloop *Richmond* did not have a captain. The news shook him. He felt that were the command forced on him it would be unjust, "seeing how many have been ashore years longer than I." At the same time, he knew that he would have "no solid ground for complaint" if Whitney decided to exile him to sea. For this reason, he told Luce that "I should certainly like quiet kept until the *Richmond*'s captain is ordered." Quiet was kept, and America's emerging Philosopher of Sea Power, to whom sea duty was a form of cruel and unusual punishment, managed to tiptoe past the *Richmond* crisis.[28]

His eagerness to stay out of Whitney's line of fire did not extend to his dealings with the U.S. Naval Institute or with those who edited its *Proceedings*. Asked by Charles R. Miles, Secretary of the Institute, for permission to publish some of the theoretical lectures he and others had given at the War College, Mahan flatly refused. He considered the *Proceedings* to be completely dominated by the materials and mechanics tribe in the Navy, and he feared that if the lectures were published therein for all to read there would be little incentive for student officers to seek assignment to the college to *hear* the lectures and to discuss them with the lecturers. To print them in *Proceedings* would undermine the college; it would be casting scholarly pearls into smelly shops and engine rooms. As he explained to Miles:

> If the instruction of the War College is printed in the *Proceedings* on an equal footing, as of course it must be, with the mass of matter dealing with all sorts of mechanical and physical problems, it will be swamped by them—it will receive rare and desultory attention. It is now thought, practically, more important for a naval officer to know how to build a gun, to design a ship, to understand the strength of materials, to observe the stars through a telescope, to be wise in chemistry and electricity, than to have ingrained in him the knowledge of the laws of war, to understand the tactical handling of his weapons, to be an expert in questions of naval policy, strategy, and tactics. This is, I think, all wrong; but it can be set right, not by printing our work, however good it be, among a lot of papers on matters considered more important, but ony by an *organized effort of the Government* to create and disseminate a system of naval war. The College is such an organized attempt.[29]

Secretary Whitney had no such vision of the War College. On January 11, 1889, a few weeks before leaving office, he finally ordered it moved to Goat Island. There it was consolidated with the Torpedo Station, and the two were placed jointly under the command of Commander Caspar F. Goodrich. The War College building was transferred to Schley's Bureau of Equipment for use as a training facility for apprentice seamen. The following day, January 12, Mahan was exiled; not to sea as he had earlier feared, but to the farthest point in the continental United States to which Whitney could contrive to send him—specifically, to Washington Territory, there to select a site for a naval base on the northwest coast and to "ascertain the principal lines of defense for the waters of the Pacific Coast north of the 42° parallel of latitude." It might as well have been an assignment to plan the naval defense of Timbuktu.

Naturally, Mahan was bitter. He was assuaged only by the hope that his friend Goodrich, member of the founding Luce Board, staunch supporter of the college and a former lecturer there, might have a helpful say in its future. He was more certain, however, that the Bureau of Ordnance would somehow manage to circumvent Goodrich and snuff out the little intellectual life left in the college. He suspected that Goodrich's successor in the post would be someone "who looks upon the Navy rather as a school of mathematics and technology than a fighting machine." Nevertheless, he informed Luce and Walker that while the consolidation order was "simply ruinous," he would "take no hand in any effort to undo it." He had had enough. He was still outraged, he told Henderson, that Whitney had seen fit "to turn me out without a word of acknowledgment . . . and to give my place to a junior." Just the same, he was persuaded that he had fought the good fight to preserve "the study of the Art and Conduct of War." To the very end he had resisted "a constant pressure to introduce . . . questions of construction and mechanical appliances and thus crowd to one side the discussion of the problem of war." His was a victory Pyrrhic.[30]

So Pyrrhic that the U.S. Navy, in its wisdom, shipped the contentious Captain A. T. Mahan off to the salmon streams and pine barrens north of Seattle. There he would end the decade of the 1880s as he began it— testing thread and lard oil at the Brooklyn Navy Yard—only this time he would use his considerable talents to take bottom soundings and measure potable water flow. Nothing like a lead line well swung or a water pump well primed to sharpen an agile mind.

VIII

The Influence of
Sea Power Upon History
1888-1890

When I was first asked to lecture on Naval History at our War College, I proposed to myself at once the question: "How shall I make the experience of wooden sailing ships, with their pop-guns useful in the naval present?" The first reply was: "By showing the tremendous influence Naval Power, under whatever form, has exerted upon the Course of History"; the second, as I went on with my studies was: "By showing that the leading principles of war received illustration in the old naval experience, just as they did in land warfare under all its various phases during the past twenty-five centuries." The present work is the outcome.

Alfred Thayer Mahan to William H. Henderson, May 5, 1890

Mahan's duty as chairman of the Northwest Navy Yard Site Commission commenced on November 30, 1888, and he began preliminary work on the assignment early in December. This was interrupted in late December when he came down with a severe case of "debility and commencing parotitis"—in a word, mumps. It was, reported J. R. Tryon, the Navy surgeon in New York who diagnosed and treated him, uncertain when he would be able to travel. Because of this, his formal detachment from the War College did not occur until January 12, 1889, and the commission did not depart Washington for Seattle until later that month. Supported by a $5,000 appropriation (much too small Mahan later argued), the commission was on the ground in Washington Territory from mid-February through the third week of March. On March 24 it departed Portland, Oregon, for the east. During the five months that followed it wrote its lengthy report. Mahan was thus out of the mainstream of naval affairs for only three months. It was a short exile. By early April 1889 he was back on the East Coast. July was spent in Bar Harbor on annual leave. In August he was ordered to the War College for a week of lectures on naval strategy and on the strategic features of the Gulf and Caribbean. At the conclusion of that brief stint, he returned to Maine. It was almost as though he had never been away.[1]

While Mahan was rusticating on distant Puget Sound, Secretary Benjamin F. Tracy responded positively to requests by Luce and others that the college be separated from the Torpedo School and returned to its former quarters on Coaster's Harbor Island. To help this project along, the recently elected Republican Congress appropriated $100,000 for a new War College building in March 1889. Actual construction was delayed for eighteen months by an acrimonious debate over whether the structure should be erected on Goat Island (then Army property) or on Coaster's Harbor Island. Still, the fact was that within a few months after he took office Secretary Tracy gave promise of undoing most of the damage wrought by Whitney and Schley. Certainly it was his intention to set the college back on the track laid down by Luce and Mahan. Indeed, in the fall of 1889 he ordered Mahan to the duty of supervising the construction of the new building when that time came.[2]

Prior to leaving New York for Puget Sound, Mahan had begun to search for a publisher for his lectures on naval history. These, he felt, were almost ready for the printer, lacking only a concluding chapter and some minor revisions to correct inadequacies of style. Elly had carefully typewritten the entire manuscript on the second-hand machine Mahan had bought for her when they first arrived in Newport in 1886. As she completed her task, Mahan tinkered with his prose. By October 1888 he considered the job finished. It will be recalled that he had already decided against burying any part of his manuscript in the matériel-oriented journal that was the U.S. Naval Institute *Proceedings*. For this reason he sought a commercial publishing house.

Because Charles Scribner's Sons had brought out his *The Gulf and Inland Waters* in 1883, Mahan turned in that direction first, pointing out to the firm that his new manuscript embraced a wholly original concept. "I do not myself know any work that covers the idea," he affirmed. Scribner's considered the book and rejected it—on the grounds that it was far too technical and specialized to appeal to most readers. Mahan then began circulating it among other commercial publishers, all of whom turned it down.

Through these early disappointments he had the constant support and encouragement of his wife and of Stephen B. Luce. The latter, retired from the Navy in February 1889, very much wanted to see the lectures published because such publication would allow Mahan to "unload an immense amount of material," and get the subject off his chest and out of his mind. Completion of the book would permit him to return to the more urgent and practical task of solving the problems of fleet tactics under steam. This enterprise Luce considered much more important to the image and future of the struggling War College, and to the Navy in general, than the publication of Mahan's historical lectures. Further, it would better serve Mahan's future career. Luce, of course, had no way of knowing that Mahan's concern with coordinating the potentialities of the ram, gun, and torpedo into a grand tactical system was far less than his interest in the broader subject of the influence sea power had had on history.[3]

The continuing search for a publisher was necessarily put aside when Mahan, recovered from his bout with mumps, boarded the train in late January 1889 for his trip to Puget Sound. The Site Commission consisted of Captain Mahan as senior officer, Commander Colby M. Chester, and Lieutenant Commander Charles H. Stockton. Richard Kern, a civilian, served as clerk to the commission. The Navy Department's charge to the commission was clear: it was to select a suitable site for a new navy yard north of the 42nd parallel, taking into account its naval and military defensibility. It was not to consider or speculate on the necessity or wisdom of acquiring or building such a yard. That concern properly belonged to Congress.

Prior to his departure for the northwest, Mahan drew up and submitted a list of twenty questions addressed to various political figures, businessmen, and newspaper editors resident in the region. These were designed to produce a body of basic factual information on the natural resources, population, skilled labor supply, climate, standards of living (wages, prices, rents), birth and death rates, manufacturing facilities, communications, and the costs of shipbuilding materials at various possible sites.

Once on the scene, the Mahan Commission went deeply into the more technical problems of topographical surveys, bottom soundings, core borings, land prices, available acreage of potential sites, anchorage room, tidal flow, and the presence of fresh water. In all this the commission did a thorough and accurate job. It paid particular attention to the naval and coastal artillery defenses that each possible site would require. The duty was not exciting, certainly not earth-shaking in import. But it was scientific and thoughtful work, and Mahan was not averse to time-consuming detail. He enjoyed chugging about on Puget Sound in the lighthouse tender *Manzanita* looking at various sites. It was his kind of sea duty.

By mid-March the commission had settled on a wooded, 1,752-acre property at Point Turner in the Port Orchard area—the location of the present naval installation at Bremerton—and recommended that the proposed yard be situated thereon. The value of the land was estimated to be $33,129. John F. Pratt, a civil engineer attached to the U.S. Coast and Geodetic Survey office in Seattle, was given the task of doing a detailed topographical and feasibility analysis of the selected site. The sum of $1,500 was allotted to this phase of the study. Indeed, the Coast and Geodetic Survey, especially in the persons of Pratt and B. A. Colonna, was extremely helpful to the commission throughout its labor. Mahan was pleased with its cooperation, although at times his patience with Colonna wore thin. The Survey was not pleased with Mahan's somewhat eccentric suggestion that Puget Sound be renamed.[4]

The U.S. Navy could only have been pleased with Mahan's careful attention to the handling of his $5,000 budget. Since it was but half of what Mahan thought it should be, he spent it like a poor widow living on a pension. Every cent was carefully accounted for. Every expenditure was monitored. Indeed, he discharged Richard Kern at the end of June 1889 so that the salary saved thereby would see the commission through the writing of its final report. The cost of a few small items he absorbed out of his own pocket. "There is so much bother about these small sums," he complained to Chester, "that I have let my own go; not from liberality, but because of the trouble."

Such generosity was unusual for the penurious Mahan. Nevertheless, he had strong feelings about the sanctity of government property and money, perhaps because he had seen so much corruption in and around the Navy in the 1870s. Recalling that he would not even allow her to use government pencils, his daughter Ellen said of him: "It appeared that Uncle Sam's property was to be treated as the apple of one's eye and that what might be overlooked, in the case of one's [own] property, was a great offense if 'Government Property' was involved. On this subject my father was adamant." He was certainly adamant about balancing the Site Commission's budget. On September 9, 1889, his careful accounting of funds showed $53.69 of the $5,000 appropriation remaining. When the commission was dissolved on September 30 his final reckoning showed that the government owed him $1.05. He solemnly billed the Treasurer of the United States for this amount. He liked keeping things neat.[5]

As soon as the commission returned to the East Coast in early April 1889 it set about writing its report recommending the purchase and development of the site at Port Orchard, "the citadel of Puget Sound." Each member wrote a part of the document. Chester did the complicated map work, and Mahan coordinated and edited the several parts. An unforeseen last-minute discrepancy on how many gallons of potable water flowed hourly and daily from Lake Kitsap was discovered after the galley proof had been corrected and returned to the printer. Mahan hastily checked the figures, accepted Pratt's more recent and lower estimate of the flow, and prepared a correction slip for insertion in the finished volume. "The civil engineers may be pleased at our error if they hear of it," he confided to Chester.[6]

More interesting to Mahan than the rate of water flow at Lake Kitsap was the question of whether broader military arguments for a naval base in the Pacific northwest should be incorporated into the commission's final report. This point had not been emphasized in the commission's charge. Whitney insisted only that "due regard to the commercial and naval necessities" be kept in mind in selecting a site. But Mahan, embryonic naval theorist that he was, could not resist inserting some comment on the subject into the finished manuscript.

San Francisco, he pointed out, was too far distant from Puget Sound properly to sustain a naval defense of the northwest in time of war. "It must be remembered, too, that a slight injury . . . may unfit a modern warship for a place in the order of battle until it is repaired. This is not a question of building ships; ships must now be built in time of peace. It is a question of establishing a base of operations, without which our military position on the northwest coast cannot be maintained." Further, "as regards the military question, the Commission does not think that Puget Sound can be made impregnable except by the presence of a naval force equal to that brought against it." The United States, he noted, must come to grips with the necessity of maintaining in Puget Sound a fleet capable of parrying a hit-and-run attack on the Seattle-Tacoma area by units of the Royal Navy operating from bases in Vancouver. To build a naval yard on the sound and not have it supported by such a mobile force would be foolhardy.

Mahan also responded to a request by the Office of Naval Intelligence to draw up a memorandum on "the strategic character and important military features of the N.W. Coast." This report embodied his "personal views only, not as a member of the Commission—still less conjointly with any one else." Unfortunately, this study has not survived, although something of the general thrust of it was conveyed to Colby Chester in a letter dated October 18, 1889. Suffice it to say that Mahan thought the Puget Sound area generally defensible from attack by an enemy fleet, given sufficient coastal batteries and supporting U.S. warships.

Chester, incidentally, had ten days earlier brought to his attention a magazine article by Major General John Gibbon from which Mahan drew "some hints for a strategic study of the N.W. Coast which I have promised the Intelligence Office." Gibbon had recently traveled Puget Sound by steamer, had met Mahan there while conducting a personal study of the area, and had noticed some of the same geographic and naval advantages Mahan had noted. Gibbon's article commented favorably on the Port Orchard (Point Turner) anchorage, praised the relative ease with which the entrances to the harbor and its main interior points might be made defensible, and made particular mention of where defensive artillery might best be situated. While it is doubtful that Mahan learned anything new from the Gibbon piece, the Intelligence Office might have. Such was the undeveloped state of the art of naval intelligence in 1889.[7]

All in all, Mahan was more than satisfied with his report on the Site Commission. He knew it would be criticized by some, as indeed it was. Specifically, the choice of Port Orchard immediately triggered protests from business and commercial interests in Seattle and Tacoma. Not surprisingly, some naval officers preferred an expansion of the existing San Francisco facility and questioned the wisdom of having a yard in the distant northwest at all. Others criticized the technical arguments on which the choice of Port Orchard was based. Mahan brushed aside all these criticisms, pronounced his labors good, and suggested that autographed copies of the commission's report be deposited in the libraries of the Navy Department, the War College, and the Naval Academy. "We are bound to undergo criticism," he told Chester, "but I must say that I am so well satisfied at the thoroughness of our efforts that I feel able to bear any." He noted, too, that the commission to select a new yard site on the Gulf Coast, sent out simultaneously with his own, had spent more money than had his group, had been unable to reach a unanimous decision, and had in the end produced a split-vote recommendation—two for Pensacola, one for New Orleans. Mahan, Stockton, and Chester were unanimous in their choice of Port Orchard; they had worked harmoniously together; and they had managed their budget precisely.

In the final analysis, however, congressional criticism of the Port Orchard site, principally from disappointed Oregon politicians, necessitated the appointment of a second Northwest Site Commission in 1890. This redundant group selected the exact spot earlier chosen by Mahan and his colleagues. But the delay was such that it was not until September 1891 that the Navy finally took possession of Port Orchard for a naval station. By this time Mahan had achieved worldwide fame for his *Influence of Sea Power Upon History* and was basking in the adulation of the moment. The Port Orchard experience was behind him.[8]

No sooner had he returned from Washington Territory than he resumed his search for a publisher for his War College history lectures. In this task he was principally assisted by Luce and Soley, by William McCarty Little, and by writer John S. Barnes. The last was an acquaintance from his Naval Academy midshipman days who had resigned from the service and become a successful author and critic. Throughout August and September 1889, while on leave at Bar Harbor and lecturing for a short time at Newport, Mahan continued "writing and polishing on the book at all my spare moments." Simultaneously, he finished the final draft of the Puget Sound report.

During these months he sought also to secure backing from private sources with a view toward personally financing the publication of his sea-power manuscript if a commercial publisher could not be found. To this end he wrote several wealthy men, among them J. Pierpont Morgan, begging for financial assistance and, in a moment of depression, "offering to surrender all property in the work myself." Morgan pledged $200 toward the publication costs, cautiously making his offer contingent on Mahan's raising the remaining $2,300 thought necessary to see the lengthy manuscript into print. To this fund Mahan himself pledged $100, and John S. Ropes, a former War College lecturer, guaranteed a similar amount. John Barnes favored this approach, agreed to contribute to the fund, and offered to dun his friends in Mahan's behalf. To make the project more appealing to possible investors, Mahan secured promises from within the services to purchase the book in bulk lots. In response to his importunities in the matter, the Department of War—thanks in part to the intercession of Tasker Bliss—agreed to take 100 copies; J. G. Walker of the Bureau of Navigation agreed to purchase 50 copies for ships' libraries; and Caspar Goodrich promised to buy 100 copies for use at the Naval War College. This last purchase, Mahan argued, would permit the course of history lectures at the college to be "much compressed."[9]

Mahan was convinced that it was the duty of the government to "help to get such works out" because they were "essential to the college and . . . congenial to its aims." Nevertheless, he continued to search for a commercial publisher for the 185,000-word manuscript. Harper's Brothers, like Scribner's, turned him down, although the firm's manuscript reader thought well of the work. A letter from Mahan to Benjamin F. Stevens in London, in search of a British publisher, failed to elicit interest from that sector of the English-speaking world. At this point the prospective author was filled with despair. As he told Luce on September 21:

> With these efforts I purpose giving up the effort. I wish to publish for I am naturally a teacher and would like to increase my audience; but I don't care for it enough to continue applications which have to me all the appearance (doubtless mistakenly) of personal solicitation for a favor. . . . I cannot go on entreating people to spend money for me. . . . I believe the book to be, in the main, good and useful—and am therefore ready to work hard at its proper presentation, if a publisher turns up. . . . But I am not willing . . . to go on begging publishers. It both distracts, vexes and hinders me in my other work.[10]

During the last week in September 1889 James R. Soley found a publisher for the disconsolate Mahan. The intermediary in the transaction was Soley's personal friend, James W. McIntyre, a New York "selling agent" of Little, Brown and Company of Boston. Soley urged Mahan to send McIntyre a copy of the manuscript. This he speedily did, representing it to McIntyre only as a "conscientious piece of work." McIntyre, however, immediately saw the importance of the study and urged his employer, John Murray Brown, owner of Little, Brown and Company, to publish it. At McIntyre's suggestion, Soley then prepared for Mahan a letter of introduction to Brown and instructed him on how best to approach the well-known publisher. Armed with this letter, Mahan went to Boston to sell Brown on the idea of publishing the manuscript. A few days later he told Luce how he had handled this crucial interview:

> By Soley's advice I dwelt upon the fact that it was *popular* and *critical*; both of which are very true. In the historical treatment [at the War College] I had the probable knowledge of officers before my eyes and aimed above all at simplicity and coherence; while in recasting I have remembered the public, and endeavoured to make nautical maneuvers clear by the avoidance of technical terms, and very minute though simple description of difficult or complicated actions of bodies of ships. There is not a single-ship action in the whole work. As for critical, I have expressed opinions and given reasons on all sorts of subjects.

The upshot of Soley's assistance, McIntyre's intervention, and Mahan's persuasiveness, was John Brown's willingness to read the manuscript. That did it. By mid-October Brown had "undertaken to publish the book," and a jubilant Mahan was already urging Luce to "promote the sale of the book by recommending it, for upon the pecuniary result depends of course the continuance in another series of the history to Trafalgar." He also continued working to ensure that the Army and Navy purchased no fewer than 250 copies.[11]

At this moment of triumph Mahan was distressed to learn that John R. Seeley of Cambridge University, a British historian of considerable reputation, had published in the September 1889 issue of the *Journal of the Military Service Institution of the United States* an article titled "War and the British Empire." This piece was based on Seeley's "The Empire," an address before the Aldershot Military Society on April 24, 1889. It "so epitomized the general drift of my book on Naval History," Mahan worried, "that I at once forwarded it to the publishers who are now examining my manuscript." He was fearful that publication of his own study would be stopped. But fortunately for the ego of Mahan, the welfare of the Navy, and the considerable profits that the book earned his firm over the years, Brown decided to push ahead with the captain's manuscript. Unlike his counterparts at Scribner's and Harper's, John Murray Brown mixed considerable literary imagination with his commercial instincts.

With the Seeley threat behind him, Mahan entered upon the dreary servitude of reading and correcting the galley of *The Influence of Sea Power Upon History, 1660–1783*, even as he began planning the sequel that would carry his story forward to the year 1812. Little, Brown and Company "kicked" at the expense of including the large number of plates illustrating naval actions that Mahan insisted had to accompany the text, and kicked so hard that the author agreed to pay out of his own pocket the added cost of printing them. This came to $200 for twenty-five plates. But at last the chore was done, and during the first week of May 1890 *The Influence of Sea Power Upon History* was published. Priced expensively at $4.00 a copy, it was dispatched to the reviewers for its builders' trials while the author nervously awaited their verdict.[12]

As Mahan himself knew, and as the appearance of Seeley's article had again reminded him on the eve of the publication of his book, *The Influence of Sea Power Upon History* was not an original piece of work from either an intellectual or conceptual standpoint. It was a skillful synthesis of the ideas of others. Some of its concepts went back to the ancient Greek historian Xenophon, who observed in the fourth century B.C. that control of the sea played an important role in the outcome of land wars. Much more recently than Xenophon, and far more relevantly, Commander Robert W. Shufeldt, USN, writing in the late 1870s, had anticipated

Mahan's argument (developed at length in *Influence*) that there was a direct connection between America's commercial expansion, her national power and security, and the existence of a powerful U.S. Navy and merchant marine. Shufeldt argued that the Navy was "indeed the pioneer of commerce," and he held that the American merchant needed "the constant protection of the flag and the gun" because "he deals with barbarous tribes—with men who appreciate only the argument of physical force." With one eye on the still-under-exploited markets of China, Shufeldt maintained, as Mahan later did, that the "man-of-war precedes the merchantman and impresses rude people with the sense of the power of the flag which covers the one and the other."[13]

Shufeldt's thoughts were carried further in 1882 by an obscure young naval officer, Ensign William Glenn David (class of 1877). In a paper entered in the U.S. Naval Institute prize-essay competition for 1882 and published in the *Proceedings*, a paper that subscriber Mahan almost surely read, David linked the potential growth of the nation's overseas trade with the need to revive the American merchant marine and provide a respectable navy to support and protect it as it transported the surplus production of the nation's farms and factories to new markets abroad. To sustain his point, David examined briefly the history of six great maritime powers of the past and present—Phoenicia, Carthage, Constantinople, Venice, Holland, and Great Britain—and concluded that there were certain historical factors, geographical advantages, and material elements common to their maritime greatness, prosperity, and international political power. These were: the possession of extended sea coasts and good harbors; geographical position; protective (mercantilistic) trade and shipping policies written into legislation; the availability of abundant and cheap raw materials needed for a domestic shipbuilding capability; a population containing a high number of "spirited and enterprising" people with a "national aptitude for seafaring"; the maintenance of strong navies to protect merchant shipping; and the possession of numerous and rich colonies abroad. As for geographical position, these six states, at the time of their maritime greatness, were "situated between two civilizations, an old and new, between producers and manufacturers. If the state represent either extreme, that is, either manufacture or produce more than it needs for home consumption, then may it be said to fulfill this condition most perfectly." These "lessons of the past," David maintained, could be applied directly and specifically to the United States in the early 1880s. The nation possessed all the geographical and material requisites for becoming a great maritime power; all it needed to do to cross the narrow threshold separating it from that power was to pass supportive tariff, customs, and ship-subsidy legislation and otherwise stimulate the building and maintenance of a great navy and merchant marine.[14]

By the time David resigned from the service in August 1884, a number of ideas, similar to his own, were circulating in Washington, especially in Congress. These firmly linked the emerging New Navy with the desideratum that was American imperialism and commercial expansion, and did so in ways Mahan later employed in his War College lectures and in his famous book. Indeed, as early as April 1880 Representative Washington C. Whitthorne of Tennessee delivered himself of the opinion that there was obviously a relationship between sea power and history. It was axiomatic, he noted, that

> civilization is the elevation and improvement of the human race, and that commerce is the great agent of civilization. . . . I assume, again, that the wealth, progress, and improvement of a nation or people is evidenced to a large degree by its merchant marine or commerce, and that the health and wealth of the commerce of any country are supported first by its resources in production, and secondly by the means given for its defense and protection. It is singular to note what is the seeming lesson in the history of these nations which have attained the highest rank in dominion, power and civilization that they have flourished most in wealth and prosperity when they had powerful navies and commercial marine. I need not ask you, in order to establish this, to review in detail the history of Phoenicia, Carthage, Rome, Venice, Naples, Spain, Portugal, France and England. The mere mention of these names in this connection will make manifest the proposition I assert. Pause for a moment and grasp the rank and power of the civilized nations of today; and in doing so you with but an exception or two fix the rank and power of their navies and commercial marine; and thus serving as no exception to the lesson of the past history of the world.

Similarly, Senator John F. Miller of California identified Latin America in 1884 as "our India" and preached in the Senate the sermon of vigorous commercial expansion into its nearby markets as a solution to American industrial overproduction. And Representative William G. McAdoo of New Jersey, later an Assistant Secretary of the Navy under Cleveland, declared with certainty in 1887 that

> the sword has frequently made way for liberty and afterwards defended its existence against its enemies; and as against universalism in politics I am deeply impressed that the spirit of nationality has elevated and ennobled our advanced mankind and secured the freedom and

prosperity of people against the incursions of their more ignorant, debased, or vicious neighbors. The mission of nations and races has not yet ceased, much as we may desire the consummated fraternity of all mankind.[15]

In September 1889, J. R. Seeley touched on other themes that Mahan had developed in his lectures at the War College and in his *The Influence of Sea Power Upon History*, and touched on them so squarely that the Philosopher of Sea Power properly wondered whether Little, Brown and Company still wanted to publish his book. Seeley argued, for instance, that war was an inevitable concomitant of the modern state system, and that far from being a relic of a barbaric past, the practice of war had actually advanced the economic and moral concerns of civilized mankind. He argued, too, that commercial and imperial expansion by war had been inexorably and advantageously linked in British history since 1700. He also felt that as the nations of Europe had become more democratic, the greater had been popular demands within them for war, for colonies, and for empire. Like Mahan, he regarded the five Anglo-French wars of the eighteenth and early nineteenth centuries as "a single grand war, a great duel with France," and he explained the collective origins and purposes of that conflict principally in terms of England's struggle for overseas trade. "In that age it might be said that the more trade the more war, and the more war the more trade. It was for trade itself that we waged all these wars," he wrote, noting further that British policy had been "to make trade flourish by means of war." Trade, in turn, had created the British Empire, "in fact the two things grew together." With the Empire had come the concept of the standing British Army. The professional army was thus "not so much the army of England as of the British Empire." It fought the five great wars with France "in the interest of the trading classes," and it fought "just where the trade was, that is, in the New World." Only the failure of Revolutionary France to build into its navy the same degree of efficiency and menace that Bonaparte built into his army had preserved the rich fruits of British empire won from France in India and America by 1763. "And what might she not have done had her navy been regenerated as was her army?" Seeley asked. "As her regenerated army subdued almost the whole continent, so would such a regenerated navy have subverted the British Empire." It was this question that Mahan was also asking (and answering) in much the same way in the manuscript that was making its way through press in late 1889 and early 1890.

Seeley was convinced, further, that Britain had remained largely outside the war system since 1815, not because the British had become a wiser
and more civilized people, but because throughout most of the nineteenth
century there had been no powerful France to impede British commercial
expansion and colonial development in South Africa, East Africa, India,
Australia, and Asia. This did not mean, he maintained, that a millennium
of peace had suddenly arrived. It meant only that the France, Russia, and
Germany of 1889 were not yet ready to contest with the sword the imperial tidbits Britain had managed peacefully to ingest, if not fully digest,
since 1815. That day would soon come, he concluded, and British military
institutions would again be called forth to do distant battle for the Empire
while the enthusiastic British masses cheered them onward:

> England, as I have said, for special reasons, has been aloof from war,
> but in general the progress of civilization, enlightenment, and the
> preaching of Christianity have had no perceptible effect; and this seems
> a point which is constantly overlooked. I said the progress of popular
> government has had the effect of producing war instead of diminishing
> it. Is this not obvious? It is astonishing that people should suppose that
> by popularizing a Government that they would diminish war: They
> increase war—I mean to say increase the magnitude of it. Why? Na-
> poleon's last wars were conducted on a gigantic scale because he had
> the people at his back. . . . I am bound to say that one of the advances
> made in the present day, viz: the popularizing of Governments, has
> effected the popularizing of war, and therefore one of the greatest fac-
> tors of modern progress tends to increase and not diminish war.[16]

Essentially, Mahan's approach to history paralleled Seeley's in that his
The Influence of Sea Power Upon History drew significantly on the
naval, military, diplomatic, and commercial events of the several Anglo-
Dutch-French-Spanish struggles for empire in the years 1660 to 1783 to
demonstrate the proposition that the nation that had controlled the sea, or
important parts thereof, had controlled history. As Mahan's lengthy (557
pages) exposition unfolded, fleets and armies won or lost crucial battles
for empire in the degree to which they achieved or failed to achieve
tactical firepower concentration. From a strategic (as distinct from tactical) standpoint, the seventeenth- and eighteenth-century wars for empire
were seen principally as attempts to secure command of the sea and the
commerce it bore. Such command was most speedily and effectively accomplished by destroying the enemy's navy in a decisive battle (or series
of battles), stripping him of his colonies, blockading his ports, and plug-

ging the critical straits and channels through which his colonial and other commerce passed. Thus deprived of his lifeblood, he rolled over and expired. Through it all ran the theme that England, thanks to her magnificent Royal Navy, had crushed Spain, Holland, and France at sea, and had built on their ruins a prosperous and powerful empire. Why? Because Whitehall's statesmen had grasped clearly the role of sea power in history and had built the finest and largest navy on earth. Mahan's sermon was therefore clear: history proved conclusively that national power, wealth, grandeur, and security were by-products of the possession and sophisticated exercise of massive sea power.

To this thought Mahan married the contention that

> while many of the conditions of war vary from age to age with the progress of weapons, there are certain teachings in the school of history which remain constant, and being, therefore, of universal application, can be elevated to the rank of general principles. For the same reason the study of the sea history of the past will be found instructive by its illustration of the general principles of maritime war, notwithstanding the great changes that have been brought about in naval weapons by the scientific advances of the past half century, and by the introduction of steam as the motive power.

Thus the "history and experience of naval warfare in the days of sailing ships" still afforded "lessons of present application and value" because "steam navies have as yet made no history which can be quoted as decisive in its teaching." For this reason, he was certain that the

> battles of the past succeeded or failed according as they were fought in conformity with the principles of war; and the seaman who carefully studies the causes of success or failure will not only detect and gradually assimilate these principles, but will also acquire increased aptitude in applying them to the tactical use of the ships and weapons of his own day.

The successful conduct of war was thus based on strategic and tactical principles that were rooted in the "essential nature of things." These principles remained constant in spite of rapid changes in the technology of weapons.

Underlying this faith was Mahan's philosophical conviction, expressed in the book in a manner more implicit than explicit, that war, especially war for economic and commercial advantage, had been an essential part of the human condition since the emergence of the competitive state system in the sixteenth century; and the related idea that it would remain so as long as men conducted their affairs through the medium of the state. He was equally sure that nations had waxed and waned in relation to their several abilities to wage war successfully—especially war at sea. In fine, his belief in the virtual inevitability of war was based on his historical observation. This belief, repeatedly expressed in many of his later books and articles, was not an incitement to war by the author. Nor was it necessarily a moral endorsement of the institution of war, although it was so interpreted by those of his contemporaries who preferred to believe that the inevitability of human progress, especially during the late nineteenth century, increasingly excluded war as a problem-solving option available to civilized men.

If Mahan can be taken to task for viewing the conduct of victorious war as being related, tactically and strategically, to a mastery of certain immutable behavioral "principles" thought to be floating around in the universe, he is perhaps less vulnerable to criticism for his belief that war was a practical dilemma as old as society itself, one that would in all probability continue to be an integral thread in the human social fabric.[17]

Ironically, however, the section of *The Influence of Sea Power Upon History* that generated the greatest comment and speculation among American and British readers and reviewers was not the five-sixths of the book that dealt more or less with straight history and sought to document the dominant role of sea power thereon, but the one-sixth that was tacked on to the manuscript at the last minute. This was an introductory chapter titled "Elements of Sea Power," a polemical, controversial essay which resurveyed ground tilled at various times and in various ways by Shufeldt, Luce, Whitthorne, David, Seeley, and many others. It also marked the final stage in the flowering of Alfred Thayer Mahan as a mature and hardy imperialist.

Mainly, the addendum considered the natural origins of sea power, and the relationship, past and present, of the United States to sea power and to commercial expansion. It also addressed the problem of American national security as such security was said to be threatened by European commercial and imperial ambitions in 1890. This was current history, fresh as the morning newspaper, although somewhat peripheral to the broader tactical and strategic principles Mahan had discovered in his study of the history of Europe's struggles for imperial supremacy in the years 1688 to 1783. Indeed, "Elements of Sea Power" was written in a hurry, almost as an afterthought. It was designed to make the whole work, he frankly admitted to Henderson, "more popular." He knew that traditional historical exegesis was not an "attractive subject to the public."

Hence, to ensure a wide public sale and to encourage Little, Brown and Company to risk its capital in the publication of a sequel that would cover the period from 1783 to 1812, Mahan put together a one-hundred-page introduction that came to overshadow the rest of the book. What the experience ultimately taught him was that there was a great deal more fame and fortune to be had in the popularization of history than in the writing of tight little monographs whose principal readers would be other historians.[18]

At the heart of "Elements of Sea Power" was Captain Mahan's enumeration of the six basic conditions "affecting the sea power of nations," with particular emphasis on the applicability of these factors to the United States in 1890. One wonders how Ensign David reacted to this listing, if indeed he read Mahan's book. Mahan's conditions, each of which he neatly designated by a Roman numeral, were:

I *Geographical Position*: Nations situated so as not to have to defend themselves by land, or extend their territory over the land, have "by the very unity of [their] aim directed upon the sea, an advantage as compared with a people one of whose boundaries is continental." Like England, and unlike France or Holland, the United States was blessed with this condition.

II *Physical Conformation*: A nation aspiring to power on the sea must have extensive sea coasts, numerous deep and protected harbors, and large rivers penetrating a fertile agricultural interior. These physical conditions must be combined with "an inborn love of the sea . . . upon which a healthy sea power depends." The United States enjoyed these physical conformations. It needed only to rekindle among its people that love for and reliance on the sea that had characterized its early history.

III *Extent of Territory*: The total number of square miles in a nation was not as important to the development of its sea power as was the relationship of the length of coastline and character of harbors to the size and distribution of the population. "A country is in this like a fortress; the garrison must be proportioned to the *enciente*." Thus while the Confederate States of America had excellent physical conformation, it was blockaded and beaten because it had too few people and was not a nation of seamen. The Confederacy "not only had no navy, not only was not a seafaring people, but . . . its population was not proportioned to the extent of the seacoast which it had to defend." The United States, on the other hand, had the proper distribution of population along its seacoasts in 1861, and had filled its Navy with good sailors.

IV *Number of Population*:   To be or to become an effective sea power, a nation must have more than an adequate total population. "The number following the sea, or at least readily available for employment on shipboard and for the creation of naval material" must also be large. While the United States was deficient in this category in 1890, as it had not been earlier in its history, the foundation for sea-population sufficiency could best and most quickly be laid "in a large commerce under her own flag."

V *National Character*:   The people of a sea-power state must be materialistically acquisitive, have an aptitude for profitable commercial intercourse at home and overseas, and generally "love money." Americans possessed these attributes. Their government, however, stood in the way of a full expression of these desirable qualities by sponsoring "legislative hindrances," by failing to subsidize the maritime sector of the economy, and, unlike England, by an unwillingness to acquire overseas colonies.

VI *Character of the Government*:   While the form of government of several of the great sea-power states in history (Carthage, Spain) was one of despotism, it was usually desirable for maritime powers to have a participatory political structure. "In the matter of sea power, the most brilliant successes have followed where there has been intelligent direction by a government fully imbued with the spirit of the people and conscious of its true general bent. Such a government is most certainly secured when the will of the people, or of their best natural exponents, has some large share in making it." The United States, like England, enjoyed such a political system.

In sum, as Mahan looked at history and at the present from the perspective of 1890, he saw that the United States possessed all of the historical elements needed to become a great world sea power. The nation required only leadership, will, and energy to achieve its destiny.[19]

The principal sub-theme developed by Mahan in "Elements of Sea Power" turned upon the duty and destiny of American economic man as the nineteenth century drew to a close. In this vein he pointed out that the nation's traditional seaboard trading frontiers had closed in the years 1861 to 1865. The investment capital and economic energy that a distraught, endangered, and isolated America had poured into its Civil War, and into the reconstruction and further development of the nation's interior since the war, would, however, soon be available again for more profitable employment overseas. He was positive that America's foreign trade would revive and that a massive maritime capability, mercantile and naval, would soon be needed:

When the day comes that shipping again pays, when the three sea frontiers find that they are not only militarily weak, but poorer for lack of national shipping, their united efforts may avail to lay again the foundations of our sea power. . . . The tendency to trade, involving of necessity the production of something to trade with, is the national characteristic most important to the development of sea power. Granting it and a good seaboard, it is not likely that the dangers of the sea, or any aversion to it, will deter a people from seeking wealth by the paths of ocean commerce . . . . if legislative hindrances be removed, and more remunerative fields of enterprise filled up, the sea power will not long delay its appearance. The instinct for commerce, bold enterprise in the pursuit of gain, and a keen scent for the trails that lead to it, all exist; and if there be in the future any fields calling for colonization, it cannot be doubted that Americans will carry to them all their inherited aptitude for self-government and independent growth.

This, in essence, was Mahan's limited understanding of the American character, fashioned by a "tendency to trade," by an "instinct for commerce," and by a "bold enterprise in the pursuit of gain." But from this narrowly capitalist notion, rooted as it was in the teachings of Adam Smith and in the "dismal science" of classical economics, there eventually flowed many of the propositions—historical, diplomatic, and military—that he developed in his voluminous writings over the next quarter-century.

Specifically, he followed R. W. Shufeldt, W. G. David, S. B. Luce, W. C. Whitthorne, and other naval officers and congressmen in maintaining that the necessary emergence of a great merchant marine would require a strong modern navy to protect it; and that a great steam and steel navy, operated in large fleet-sized units, would in turn require numerous overseas coaling stations. Further, a national willingness and ability to carry offensive naval war to imperialist enemies who would surely threaten to halt the belated creation of America's own commercial empire would be required. His contempt for the military inefficiency and strategic inconclusiveness of single-ship privateering (*guerre de course*) —America's traditional and inexpensive substitute for a real navy—was therefore profound. He insisted that the American government, in its economic self-interest, must generously finance, sustain, and otherwise succor the nation's maritime growth; or, put his way, that the "controlling elements of the country, though it is not always easy to feel that such controlling elements are truly representative, even in a free country," must promote the legislative achievement of a maritime renaissance. More pointedly, Mahan held that the building of a canal across Central America, which was imminent, would draw foreign merchantmen and warships into American waters in great and threatening numbers, an event that could only serve to end American isolationism and hurl the United States into the maelstrom of European power politics. This alone, his book maintained, was argument enough for building a powerful navy and generally making ready for war.[20]

No sooner was the book published than the proud author began dispatching complimentary copies of it to prominent naval and political figures in England and America. Captain W. H. Henderson, Sir Geoffrey T. Phipps Hornby, and Admiral Philip H. Colomb, a noted naval historian, were among the Englishmen who received inscribed copies. Mahan explained to Henderson that the thick volume was simply the outcome of a question he had posed to himself in 1886: "How shall I make the experience of wooden sailing ships, with their pop-guns, useful in the naval present?" And his answer: "By showing the tremendous influence Naval Power, under whatever form, has exerted upon the Course of History. . . . By showing that the leading principles of war received illustration in the old naval experience, just as they did in land warfare under all its various phases during the past twenty-five centuries." He hoped Henderson would give the book a "send among your people" so that the "pecuniary results" would encourage Little, Brown and Company to publish a continuation of the study through the year 1812. The covering letter that went with the copy sent to Luce graciously thanked the admiral "for the start you gave me," and hoped, somewhat avariciously it would seem, that "you will consider what can be done to further the circulation, for the sake of the publishers and for the further continuance of the undertaking as well as for my own benefit. It is not necessarily, nor on the face, an attractive subject to the public; they must be led to the water ere they will drink." A similar letter of transmittal to Secretary Tracy emphasized the connection between the existence of the War College and the existence of the book; and one to Representative Henry Cabot Lodge of Massachusetts revealed that the author's object in writing the book was "to make the experience of the past influence the opinions and shape the policy of the future."[21]

The reviews of Mahan's book were generally excellent, although in many instances, especially the newspaper reviews, they were bland and superficial. Not so Theodore Roosevelt's. When he first read the volume he immediately wrote its author that it was "the clearest and most instructive general work of the kind with which I am acquainted. It is a *very* good book—admirable; and I am greatly in error if it does not become a classic." His review in the *Atlantic Monthly* for October 1890 publicly congratulated Mahan for his skill in "subordinating detail to mass-effects" and praised him for consulting French sources in his research. What the country needed, the Civil Service Commissioner instructed his readers, was "a large navy, composed not merely of cruisers, but containing also a full proportion of powerful battleships able to meet those of any other nation. It is not economy, it is niggardly and foolish short-sightedness, to cramp our naval expenditures while squandering money right and left on everything else, from pensions to public buildings."

Personal notes of congratulation came from such U.S. naval officers as Goodrich, Walker, Sampson, Stockton, and Luce—there was even one from Schley. All praised the book and its author. Indeed, Luce's review of the work in *The Critic* (New York) for July 26, 1890, was more a eulogy than a critical notice. He pronounced the book brilliant, "an altogether exceptional work. . . . masterful in construction, and scholarly in execution." Mahan, he held, was the first person to "weave the story of the Navy and its achievements into the affairs of State so as to bring out its value as a factor of national life." Further, his contribution was to demonstrate "the inadequacy of moral influence, such as this peace-loving country should exert, unsupported by material force." The *New York Tribune* thought the book a classic that clearly pointed the United States in the right direction and was "an honor to the author and to the United States Navy he so well serves." The *Chicago Interocean* found Mahan's argument "overwhelming" in its logic, called the book to the attention of all American statesmen, and concluded that a revival of American sea power would lead directly to a "growth in commerce and . . . the general prosperity of the whole people." The reviewer for the neighboring *Chicago Times* assured his readers that Mahan was no "crank" and confessed that it was "rather a startling thing to find that control of the sea has throughout history been the prime factor in deciding the leadership, the prosperity, and often the existence of nations, and that America not only has no navy, but by throwing away her commercial marine and the occupations related to it has deprived herself of the very means of creating a navy." Other reviewers, perhaps less startled, accepted without question Mahan's view of an endangered nation and the need for an immediate maritime rebirth. The *Cincinnati Gazette* made it clear that "though the United States at present is not the mistress of the ocean, the destiny of the country may lead in that direction. Mr. Blaine's reciprocity and the proposed subsidies for steamships point that way. . . . One thing is certain: a modern navy must have coal and supply depots in many parts of the world."[22]

By and large, then, Mahan fared extremely well at the hands of the American and British book-reviewing fraternity, several of whom called for a sequel that would carry the story through Nelson and the Battle of Trafalgar.[23] Others accepted uncritically the author's opinion that rapid and radical changes in weapons and propulsion systems in no wise compromised the known existence of certain immutable tactical principles. Some even accepted his dubious contention that wind-wafted fire ships of the Age of Sail had the same tactical function as contemporary small, swift, steam-driven, torpedo boats.[24] Only a few had the bad manners to lump Mahan's volume into a joint review with lesser books,[25] or to criticize the accuracy of his facts or his style and organization.[26] Similarly, only a handful of the reviewers were so ungenerous as to suggest that the value of the book rested principally on the fact that there were no competitors in the field.[27] More significantly, few appreciated the full import of Mahan's attack on American isolationism. The *Boston Literary World* was virtually alone in noting that the thesis of the influence of sea power on history so ably developed by Mahan, was "marred to considerable degree" by the author's "constant tendency to point a moral for fresh-water Congressmen, and to preach the gospel of American commerce and the new navy."[28]

The fact is that many American newspaper reviewers, and some foreign ones as well, seem not to have read past the controversial "Elements of Sea Power" or to have done much more than scan the chapter headings of the remainder of the volume.[29] Many of the reviews were thus little more than uncritical summaries of the arguments outlined in the "Elements" chapter.[30] If a critic did somehow manage to read past Mahan's polemical introduction, he frequently discharged his obligation to his reader with a tiresome summary of the factual content of the remainder of the book.[31] Some reviewers gave up completely and simply pirated the remarks of others.[32] But more often than not, the American commentators on *The Influence of Sea Power Upon History* jotted down a few pedestrian remarks, apparently based on its publisher's advertising copy, and let it go at that. Yet even these derivative comments served to call attention to the existence of the book and to its obscure author. Such comments also suggested that there were in 1890 few Americans, in the Navy or outside it, who were qualified to appraise such a highly technical and specialized study. As the reviewer for the *Chicago Tribune* put it: "the great theme of naval strategy and tactics is engrossing even to the landsman, and he follows Capt. Mahan's battle narratives and illustrative diagrams of sea fights with amused and amusing patience. Where he understands he sympathizes; where he does not he imagines he does."[33]

This is not to suggest that there were no perceptive American appraisals of Mahan's work. There were a few. *The Independent* (New York), for example, correctly saw that the author had really written two quite different books. The first, "Elements of Sea Power," comprising the opening hundred pages, dealt in "generalizations more or less suggestive and correct, involving questions of national policy and appealing to statesmen"; the second, "the influence of sea power on history," comprising the remainder of the work, was "a professional and historic criticism of the chief naval campaigns and battles of Europe from 1660 to 1783" that resembled the work of Jomini. While the two segments were casually related, they were "in practice . . . distinct." This produced, said *The Independent*, "a confusion in the plan of his work which must to a considerable degree neutralize its value." The *Religio-Philosophical Journal* (Chicago) noted that there had been many influences upon history in addition to sea power and chided Mahan for the philosophical narrowness of his approach. The *Christian Register* (Boston) made the same point and argued that Mahan had not measured and could not measure accurately the degree or amount of sea power that made such power either an influential or a benign factor in history at any given time. But, the reviewer confessed, "if he does not accurately measure the influence of sea power, he shows how nations without it are shorn of part of their national activity and possibilities." He also observed that a concern for the aspirations of the common man was nowhere evident in Mahan's great scheme of history, as indeed it was not.[34]

The most perceptive reactions to *The Influence of Sea Power Upon History* came from England. British reviewers were not a little put out that one of the greatest works in naval history ever to be written had come from the pen of a mere American ("Although he is an American, he can write about England with perfect civility"), particularly from an officer in the ludicrous "phantom fleet" that was the U.S. Navy in 1890. Some correctly pointed out that Mahan's idea had been foreshadowed in various discussions that had taken place at the Royal United Service Institution and in the pages of its journal between 1887 and 1889, and that both British and French naval historians had been "steadily making headway along similar lines." True, Mahan had followed those discussions; he had read the United Service Institution's publication, although precisely what he derived from its pages is not known. Nevertheless, all Britons agreed that "it was given to Captain Mahan to reach the goal first." *The Times* felt that with the possible exception of the work of Sir John Barrow and that of Professor John Knox Laughton, English historians had produced nothing to equal Mahan's *The Influence of Sea Power Upon History* or Theodore Roosevelt's *The Naval War of 1812*, an extremely well-received book emphasizing single-ship combat, published in 1882. For this reason, the Americans ("our kin beyond the sea") now stood "first in order of merit in the production of naval historical works which are truly philosophical." One ecstatic British reviewer praised Mahan's "spirit of race sympathy." Another dubbed him "one of the highest intellects in the naval world." It was also noted with approval that Mahan had heeded John R. Seeley's dictum that history properly conceived and written must do more than "merely gratify the reader's curiosity about the past. It must modify his view of the present and his forecast of the future."[35]

The lengthy review-article in the *Edinburgh Review* for October 1890 by Professor John K. Laughton, lecturer on naval history at the Royal Naval College, was perhaps the most knowledgeable and detailed analysis Mahan's book received in the English-speaking world at the time of its publication. Clearly the most qualified person in that world to undertake the task, Laughton criticized Mahan for contending that the principles of war, on land and on sea, were fixed and immutable. As for the tactical implications of changes in the propulsion and armaments of warships down through the centuries, he held, contrary to Mahan, that "the differences of motive power or of arms, are so great that points of divergence will commonly be more prominent than points of resemblance." He called attention to the relative paucity of Mahan's sources, noted that they were almost all of the secondary variety, and demonstrated that several of them on which Mahan had relied heavily were not factually accurate. He was particularly critical of Mahan's acceptance of Thomas B. Macaulay's erroneous account of the Anglo-Dutch fight off Beachy Head in 1690. Nevertheless, Laughton considered Mahan's book, on balance, to be a highly useful work. Indeed, his praise of the volume marked the beginning of a lifelong professional friendship between the two men, even though Laughton was convinced that Mahan's main motive in writing the book was "to rekindle in the hearts of his fellow-citizens some desire to contest the supremacy of the seas" with Great Britain.

Mahan considered himself "fortunate to come off so easy" at Laughton's hands since "he probably knows more naval history than any English-speaking man living." He conceded the justice of Laughton's criticism that the book was under-researched; but he accepted none of Laughton's more fundamental objections and, in a moment of pique, wished that Laughton himself would "produce a great work instead of piddling about in the byways of naval history. If he had, I need not have fallen into my mistakes and yet all that is best in my book would still have been worth writing." On the other hand, Mahan soon joined Laughton in dismissing T. B. Macaulay as a "very prejudiced" and inaccurate historian. One learns by doing.[36]

British critics, other than Laughton, were also impressed with Mahan's great book. Some were quick to borrow certain of his views, particularly his hostility to the *guerre de course* (privateering) approach to naval warfare. These were quoted in debates engaging the country in 1890 on the question of the proper size and composition of the Royal Navy in the face of a growing naval challenge from Imperial Germany. Advocates of the further expansion and technological modernization of the British fleet were, of course, delighted with Mahan's observation that England's centuries-long commercial growth, her physical security, the very existence of her rich empire, and her position as a great world power could all be traced directly to the rise of British sea power. Some English reviewers thus wondered why it was in 1890 that the government was spending more money on the army than on the Royal Navy.

Other British reviewers agreed with Laughton that Mahan's book signaled the beginning of the end of America's post-Civil War isolationism and the beginning of American imperialism, particularly in Central America and in the Gulf and the Caribbean. Some noted that America would soon be contesting with Britain the naval and commercial leadership of the world. "As an American he has looked ahead, and he sees a future for his own country of which, as yet, perhaps but few citizens of the Republic dream," said one observer. Or as the reviewer for *Blackwood's Magazine* worried:

> The arguments with which he supports his opinion, that their future welfare depends upon the adoption of what may be called a maritime policy, deserve serious attention, especially as they happen to have lately been illustrated by the action of his Government in assembling the Pan-American Conference, in greatly strengthening the navy, and in professing to claim Behring's Sea as a *mare clausum*. If we add to these the unauthenticated, but at the same time persistent reports of intended American acquisitions on the coast of Hayti, some of Captain Mahan's arguments will appear highly significant.[37]

It took the Germans a bit longer to absorb the political implications and possibilities of Mahan's doctrines and to apply his sea-power hypothesis to their own naval-building race with Great Britain. But within a few years Berlin too was toasting Mahan's sagacity. "I am," said Kaiser William in May 1894, "just now not reading but devouring Captain Mahan's book, and am trying to learn it by heart. It is a first class work and classical in all points. It is on board all my ships and constantly quoted by my captains and officers." Moreover, when Mahan was in England in August 1893 as commanding officer of the *Chicago*, he was asked to a dinner given by Queen Victoria at Osborne for the kaiser so that the German leader might meet him. In May 1894 Mahan politely declined the latter's invitation to visit Germany; his duties in the *Chicago* did not permit. But in August of that year the two men met again and conversed at dinner on board the British royal yacht at Cowes. There Mahan learned at first hand that Kaiser William was "very much interested in my books." By January 1898, when Germany's naval-building program was under a full head of steam, the Imperial German Navy ordered that a translation of the volume "be supplied to all the public libraries, schools and government institutions" in the nation. Meanwhile, in 1897, the Japanese had translated *The Influence of Sea Power Upon History* into their own language. Copies were placed in the hands of the emperor and the crown prince and were distributed throughout the school system, among government leaders, and within the officer corps of the services. Truly, the fame of Mahan had become worldwide. Moreover, it was remarked in Europe that not only had he imparted vast stimulation to the writing and study of naval history, his teachings helped increase the growth of naval armaments as well. Such were the international political implications of his popularity. As British naval historian Sir Julian S. Corbett later said of Mahan's book:

> For the first time naval history was placed on a philosophical basis. From the mass of facts which had hitherto done duty for naval history, broad generalizations were possible. The ears of statesmen and publicists were opened, and a new note began to sound in world politics. Regarded as a political pamphlet in the higher sense—for that is how the famous book is best characterized—it has few equals in the sudden and far-reaching effect it produced on political thought and action.[38]

Heady stuff this. But during the winter of 1889–1890, while waiting for the publication of the book that would change his life, Mahan prosaically went about picking up the threads of a lagging and sagging service career. He "dreaded" the thought of "hanging around Washington," knowing full well that the high cost of living in the capital would reduce him to genteel poverty, and successfully avoided being assigned to duty there. He was even successful in avoiding assignment to time-consuming duty on courts-martial. What he really wanted was another sabbatical year from active naval duty so that he could begin work on the sequel to his *Influence of Sea Power Upon History*. Thanks to Rear Admiral John G. Walker, Chief of the Bureau of Navigation, whose office assigned duty stations, Mahan got exactly what he wanted. He was ordered to "special duty" (otherwise undefined) with the Bureau of Navigation effective September 30, 1889, and was initially attached to the War College for a week as a lecturer. When the three-week session there ended on October 25 he commenced his congenial "special duty" by moving his family into his mother's home at 232 South Broad Street in Elizabeth, New Jersey, and spent a rent-free winter engaged in work on the second volume of *Influence*. He wrote occasionally to Newport about the plans and planning for the proposed new building at the War College; but for all practical purposes he enjoyed his second extended literary leave from the Navy. Under Secretary Tracy's enlightened regime in the Navy Department it was the business of at least one naval officer to write books.

Still, progress on his second volume, published in October 1892 under the title, *The Influence of Sea Power Upon the French Revolution and Empire, 1793–1812*, was very slow—mainly because for the first time in his life he was working extensively in primary sources (private letters and government documents) rather than in the more easily available secondary sources (monographs and biographies) he had used almost exclusively in his first book. By the spring of 1890 he had laboriously "accumulated a good deal of information" on the period 1793 to 1812 but had not "succeeded in reaching any generalizations upon the course and mutual bearing of events." He could only hope that "light will break through the obscurity after a while."

What broke through first, in December 1889, was Tracy's decision to restore the War College to its pre-Whitney and pre-Schley condition—a development that encouraged Mahan, in the Secretary's behalf, to run through his litany of arguments for an institution that emphasized the "Art of War" rather than mere "naval matériel." He explained to his British correspondent, W. H. Henderson, that the problem was nothing less than to "persuade our people that naval matériel is not all the battle; that first-rate men in second-rate ships are better than second-rate men in first-rate ships." Although this was distinctly a minority opinion within the New Navy, and an extreme one at that, he dismissed all contrary views as part of the evil legacy of Whitney and Schley. He therefore cheered Tracy's recommendation to Congress on December 2 to reestablish the War College as an independent facility, subordinate the Torpedo

Station to it, put both under a single commander, and have the Bureau of Navigation operate them jointly. This step he considered "gratifying not merely by the solidity of his [Tracy's] opinions, but by the decisive manner in which they are expressed. I hope much from him."[39]

Mahan cheered too soon. In March 1890 Francis M. Ramsay replaced John G. Walker, long a friend of the War College, as head of the Bureau of Navigation, the second most powerful administrative post in the Navy. Within a few weeks Ramsay ordered the college to absorb the responsibility for teaching the technical courses given at the Torpedo Station. Mahan protested this outrage to Luce, whose retirement from the service a few months earlier left him with far less leverage in such matters than he had earlier possessed:

> You know my general conviction that the admission of questions of manufacture and material is most dangerous. . . . the whole drift of the Navy is to put its trust in material development, rather than in strategic sagacity and tactical superiority. For this reason I shall favor, as far as I can, assigning to Annapolis or Washington Yard all questions of advanced instruction in ordnance and mechanics or machinery of any kind; and [given] Ramsay's antecedents I am hopeful we may thus preserve the College in the main from what would be to me a most dangerous leaven.

Mahan's fear of Ramsay's "antecedents" was well founded. Never a friend of the struggling War College, Ramsay soon became its implacable enemy. His dislike of Mahan, especially of the captain's easy access and frequent end runs to Secretary Tracy, grew steadily. His jealousy of Mahan's growing reputation as spokesman for the New Navy was pronounced. At the outset of their bureaucratic relationship, however, the two strong-willed men maintained a correct cordiality. Indeed, Mahan was flattered when Ramsay politely solicited from him in April 1890 recommendations on the exact positioning of the new college building on Coaster's Harbor Island, the arrangement of its rooms, the conveniences and equipment it should include, and the functions it should have. Mahan reciprocated in equally courteous fashion by asking Ramsay his professional opinion of the value of the lectures on international law usually given at the college. These had been delivered by James R. Soley, soon to be appointed Assistant Secretary of the Navy in President Harrison's administration.

Polite though it was, this exchange of letters with Ramsay made it known to the bureau chief that Mahan expected to run the War College in his own way. Although his official role at the institution in the spring of 1890 was a modest one—that of occasional lecturer and non-resident supervisor of construction—and although the academic work of the institution was suspended in 1890 and 1891 pending completion of the new building, the imperious captain made it clear to the short-fuzed rear admiral that he fully expected to plan the curriculum, determine the dates and length of the next session (whenever it could be held), shape the class, and engage the faculty, and all this with little more than a nominal involvement in the process on the part of his superior. "I shall keep the Bureau informed of my action by official letters," he airily notified Ramsay. With that casual dash of the pen, Mahan began his perilous trip across the thin ice that was the delicate ego and ill-tempered personality of Francis M. Ramsay. True, Ramsay was a rigid and sometimes unimaginative man, but he was also a proud, successful, and highly competent naval officer. Mahan might well have handled him with a great deal more tact than he did.[40]

Their epic battle, which raised the question of whether it was the business of naval officers to write books, was joined soon after the excellent reviews of Mahan's *The Influence of Sea Power Upon History* began to appear in the newspapers and magazines of the English-speaking world. Almost all hands regarded it as a unique, important, and influential book; and they were right. Indeed, with the possible exception of Harriet Beecher Stowe's *Uncle Tom's Cabin*, published in 1852, no book written in nineteenth-century America by an American had greater immediate impact on the course and direction of the nation. But in 1890 its principal immediate influence on Alfred Thayer Mahan was on his ego. It might well have been titled *The Influence of Sea Power Upon Mahan*.

IX

Author as Imperialist
1890-1893

The complicated administration of a large modern ship of war is a task too absorbing to admit of sustained mental effort in another direction. . . . I therefore ask that . . . the Department will rule that the contribution I may be expected to make to professional thought, by such studies [naval history] . . . outweighs the advantage that can result from the experience of two years of command, when these so shortly precede my final retirement from active service; and that the Department will for these reasons excuse me from such sea service.

Alfred Thayer Mahan to Francis M. Ramsay, March 17, 1893

It is not the business of a Naval officer to write books.

Francis M. Ramsay [April 1893]

In July 1890, Mahan and his wife moved from Elizabeth, New Jersey, into private quarters, Hall Cottage, on Merton Road, Newport. There, he spent the summer, beginning at once to carry out important new "semi-official" duties assigned him by Secretary Tracy under the direction of Francis Ramsay's Bureau of Navigation. These duties, which were secret, had to do with contingency planning for naval war with various nations, an enterprise that caused him to work closely with the Office of Naval Intelligence for the next few months. Meanwhile, he had informed the bureau of his desire to remain on shore for at least another year so that he could bring his study on the influence of sea power up to the year 1812. Thanks to the intercession of Luce with Tracy, and of a lecturer at the War College, John F. Meigs, with Ramsay, an extension of his shore duty was arranged. Arranged, too, was the Navy Department's acquiescence in Mahan's insistence that the description of his duty assignment be changed from "the vague term Special Duty" with the Bureau of Navigation to something that would permit him more flexibility to choose his work schedule and his place of residence—he could not expect government quarters at Newport. This request was also granted, and in the fall Mahan and his family took up residence in an apartment at 75 East 54th Street in New York City. Under the department's new dispensation, called simply "additional duty," he remained attached to the War College as a lecturer, it still being understood that he would supervise the construction of the new college building when that project finally got under way. The effect of the change of duty status from "special" to "additional" was that he enjoyed another extended paid leave of absence from the Navy with permission to live and work in New York. This turned out to be a highly productive period during which he virtually finished his second book on sea power, dashed off an acceptable biography of Admiral David G. Farragut, produced in a few hectic days his first and most-quoted polemical article, "The United States Looking Outward," wrote two or three contingency war plans, and supervised from afar the planning and construction of the new War College building on Coaster's Harbor Island.[1]

During the summer of 1890 Mahan was faced with his first major problem as the father of a teen-aged girl. His daughter Helen, then seventeen, had entered young womanhood, not very pretty and not very popular. A later generation would have called her a "wallflower." Her social backwardness concerned her parents greatly, as it obviously concerned her. When the children were vacationing in Bar Harbor with Elly's mother in July, a diffident Mahan took advantage of the separation to instruct Helen on the delicate subjects of social involvement, sex, and marriage; and he chose to do this in an approved Victorian manner—by mail. He wrote her that he himself was "naturally indifferent to others" and that throughout his own life he had had to fight against a tendency to social withdrawal. He assured her, however, that she could conquer her own innate shyness by performing Christian "works of kindness," and by praying "continually to God to change your nature in this respect and give you a loving heart." At the same time, he cautioned her against seeking out or consorting with companions whose "aims and principles [are] entirely worldly—living, that is, for this world, and not for the next." He was most apprehensive lest she allow herself "to attach undue importance to, and care too much for, the comforts and pleasures of this world."

Because life was short and uncertain she should, instead, concentrate only on those pleasures, "love, joy, peace," which would "endure beyond the grave." As for eventual marriage, she should not trouble herself about that at all. God, he said, provides "the marriage most suitable, to those who ask his guidance."

> Since marriage and relations with men must needs be in your thoughts [Mahan continued], let all your thoughts in such matters be referred to God. Put yourself under His care. . . . Ask Him that if He wishes you to marry He may guide you to the man to whose care He will entrust you, and whose happiness and home it may be your privilege to make. To be dwelling on and looking to marriage continually is morbid. . . . If you thus commend your future to God, He will surely direct it. You may not find all the happiness you would have, but you will have kept the course which shall bring you, yes and yours also, peace at the last. If you are to marry hereafter, the happiness of your future home, the well being of your husband and children, may depend upon the prayers you are saying and the thoughts you are thinking now.

It cannot be known what prayers Helen said, or what guidance God gave her in the matter, or what thoughts she subsequently entertained about men and about marriage. It can only be noted that she died in 1963 at the age of ninety—unmarried.[2]

Personal counseling of this sort was not Mahan's forte. He was much better at manipulating the granite for the new building at the War College. Indeed, he eventually brought it in on time and within the $100,000 appropriation allowed, even though he confessed to Ramsay that the "Bureau knows that I am absolutely without experience, public or private, in building matters." Specifically, he carried the difficult point, practically over Ramsay's supine body, that the new building must include living quarters for at least four staff officers and their families (he originally asked for six such accommodations) as well as space to house the purely educational functions of the institution. When Ramsay complained that Mahan was building "too much quarters and too little college," the captain patiently, if somewhat patronizingly, explained to him that the educational effectiveness of a college usually had something to do with the daily personal and professional associations of a resident faculty; also, that the residential feature of the institution would serve to attract superior faculty members from the officer corps as well as improve the quality of and interrelationship between various courses in the curriculum. Ramsay could never quite grasp this. Nor could he understand Mahan's opposition to providing instructional space and staff for the study of chemistry and electricity. These were practical courses which Mahan continued to feel belonged properly at the Naval Academy or at the Torpedo Station, not where the "Art of Naval War" was to be taught.

Consequently, the actual construction of the War College building, which took place between 1891 and 1892, marked a sharp deterioration, and finally an open break, in the relations between Mahan and Ramsay. Mahan complained constantly and bitterly that Ramsay's indecisiveness about plans and procedures and his unwillingness or inability to act when a decision was needed were holding up the entire timetable. Indeed they did—for at least four months. Mahan characterized him to Luce as "a desperate man to do duty with"; and he ultimately solved the problem of Ramsay's chronic "inertia" by taking his troubles directly to Secretary Tracy. These detours invariably stirred the dilatory bureau chief to action; but they also stirred his hatred of his newly prominent subordinate.[3]

It would seem in retrospect that Mahan's willingness to risk Ramsay's displeasure in the matter of construction at the War College was related to the enormous self-confidence that came with his sudden visibility in the Navy as its leading spokesman, historian, and theoretician. Also, his longtime personal identification with the institution caused him to have a proprietary attitude toward it. Seldom did he deal with his superiors on important War College business in the years ahead without linking (not always modestly) the genesis of his *Influence of Sea Power Upon History* and his worldwide reputation as its author, with the existence of the college and his concept of the institution's role and function within the Navy. The connection between the fame of the author, the importance of the book, and the usefulness of the college to the Navy was made by several reviewers. As Luce put it in his review in *The Critic*: "Such are the lessons of war as taught by the great masters; and such are the lessons that, for the three or four years last past, the author has been laying before successive classes of officers who, in the near future, are to command our ships and squadrons—some of whom, indeed, are even now in command afloat."[4]

Against Mahan's growing reputation, to say nothing of his personal access to Tracy, the stolid Francis Ramsay was small match. He therefore did what all practiced officer-bureaucrats in the Navy Department had been doing since 1798—he did nothing, and he did it very slowly. That is to say, he attempted to thwart Mahan by a policy of studied inaction. Specifically, he made little effort to arrange an instructional session at the college in 1890—there was none. He delayed Mahan's curriculum-planning for a proposed 1891 session until the possibility of having one that year had also slipped by. He would not assign or recommend the assignment of a new president to the institution; nor would he assure Mahan that student officers would be assigned to a session if one were held in 1892. He attempted to slow the construction of the new building. And he began to explore the possibility of shipping the bumptious Mahan off to sea. More peevishly, on one occasion he denied Mahan's request for a desk that cost all of $25. Francis Ramsay was a bureaucrat's bureaucrat.

As the admiral's campaign of bureaucratic suffocation became clear, Mahan's frustration reached the boiling point. "My opinion," he wrote Luce, "concerning Ramsay and the dangers of the College entirely coincides now with your own. As regards him, my expression has always been that he overlays it like a young baby." Mahan was upset, too, that his old friend J. R. Soley, appointed Assistant Secretary of the Navy in July 1890, was now so busy with larger duties in the department that he permitted Ramsay slowly to "smother" the institution to death. Mahan reluctantly decided that Soley would not or could not be bothered with the special problems of the War College. In desperation, he turned to Senator Aldrich for help on the question of assigning a senior officer to the college presidency.[5]

Mahan felt that the key to skirting various Ramsay roadblocks was to persuade Secretary Tracy to appoint a new president to the suspended institution, someone thoroughly sympathetic with his and Luce's conception of the institution, a man senior enough and tenacious enough to stand his ground against Ramsay. In December 1890 Luce suggested that Mahan himself take the post, but Mahan was then deeply involved in writing a contingency plan for war with Britain. He did not want to work directly for Ramsay ("Ramsay being what he is, I incline to think a more pushing and driving person than myself is desirable"), and he did not wish to give up his New York apartment or bear the expense of moving his family to Newport. He demurred also on the grounds that he did not think it wise to interrupt the education of his children with their New York tutors or deprive his daughters of the social poise they might gain by continued exposure to the cultural life of the city. Further, if he were called to sea in the next year or so, an event he considered likely, he would prefer to leave his family in New York rather than marooned in bucolic Newport. He therefore suggested that either Francis M. Bunce, commander of the Training Station at Newport, or French E. Chadwick might be men more suitable for the job. He leaned toward Chadwick, Chief Intelligence Officer, because of his excellent service reputation, his friendship with Soley, and his high standing with Tracy; but he thought

Bunce would be an adequate second choice since "I know him to be impressed with the fact that no attention is being paid to the question of how to fight our ships . . . and an undue amount, *comparatively*, to material." There the matter rested for nearly a year insofar as Mahan's own candidacy for the post was concerned.[6]

Mahan was certainly in no hurry to get back to sea. By December 1890 it had been nearly six years since he had left the *Wachusett* and he had enjoyed every intervening minute spent on dry land. But when Admiral J. G. Walker suggested that he might be interested in the command of the new steel cruiser *Boston*, slated to remain on the East Coast, he was inclined to pursue the idea. This, however, would mean dropping the contingency war planning, "the confidential duty" that Tracy had assigned him. Mahan therefore wrote the Secretary in early January 1891, asking for advice and noting that he had been

> sedulously engaged preparing a set of lectures upon Naval Warfare, in continuation of my former course on the same subject, since published. The very flattering opinion expressed, both here and in England, on the latter, [has] caused me to hope that I might make another substantial addition to the scanty military literature of our profession; but the prospect of sea duty that would keep me mainly on our own coast is an advantage I don't care to forego. If the *Boston* were leaving the country for two years, I should not want her. As Admiral Walker requests a *speedy* reply, may I ask you to instruct me whether to accept or decline.

Tracy suggested that he decline the command and continue writing. His suggestion was relayed to Mahan by Ramsay, who had no choice but to endorse it. "There are some things that it is neither for a man's interest nor reputation to urge," Mahan proclaimed, adding "I will not personally urge anything that looks to my remaining ashore for any considerable time." Courageous words, these, but subject to modification on scant notice.[7]

The fact was that Captain Mahan was making himself much more useful to the Navy as a writer, historian, and policy spokesman than as a sea-goer. He was certainly of little use to his service as a practical seaman. Indeed, his almost exclusive assignment to academic and literary projects from 1885 through 1892, interrupted only by his brief duty at Puget Sound, indicated that the political administrators of the New Navy valued him much more for his labors at the escritoire than for his skill on the bridge.

In December 1890, to the quiet delight of the Navy's establishment, Mahan published in the *Atlantic Monthly* the first of his popular articles on American imperialist themes. This well-received essay expanded and made more explicit several points touched upon in the "Elements of Sea Power" section of *The Influence of Sea Power Upon History*. Titled "The United States Looking Outward," the article called boldly for vigorous American competition for world trade and for the penetration of overseas markets to solve the dilemma of domestic industrial overproduction. Further, it drew attention to the nation's need to defend its existing strategic and commercial interests in Samoa, Hawaii, and at the Isthmus of Panama. It also pointed to the existence of an increasingly competitive European state system, the jungle nature of which could only endanger the security of an unarmed America. Mahan therefore demanded the building of a large and mobile combat navy (with adequate coaling stations abroad) and of powerful coastal defense systems to ensure American survival. He added the thought that neither moral superiority, international law, nor the inherent justice of a particular cause could protect the militarily weak from armed predators. As an Anglophile of long standing, he called, finally, for a "cordial understanding," not a formal alliance, between the United States and Great Britain. This last would be an understanding based on "mutual advantage" as well as on "a sense of law and justice, drawn from the same sources, and deep-rooted in . . . cordial recognition of the similarity of character and ideas." The time had come, argued Mahan, for the United States to abandon her inward-looking capitalism, dangerous isolationism, and military flabbiness, and take her rightful place in the world as a major commercial, industrial, military, and diplomatic power. With such a spirit of competitiveness would come both national prosperity and international security; without that spirit, the nation would soon be surrounded by enemies and would surely be crushed.

Such were the broad outlines of the imperialist epistle of A. T. Mahan, themes that received substantial emendation, interpretation, and application at his hands in the years ahead. "If my belief, that the United States is about to be forced out of her policy of isolation, is well founded," Mahan told Horace E. Scudder, editor of the *Atlantic Monthly*, "the age needs prophets to arouse the people. It is from gentlemen of your profession that they would naturally arise." If, however, such prophets failed to come forth from the ranks of American journalists, Mahan and various of his brother officers were ready to preach the word. "You will find," he told Scudder, "a keener sensibility to the bearing of external events upon the interests of the United States among naval officers than among the same number of men in any other profession."[8]

Mahan's widely read article demanding that the nation look outward was a recital of American imperialist arguments that had been born in the late 1870s and early 1880s and were destined for full maturation between 1898 and 1917. The unique thing about them in 1890 was that they were given expression in so broadly circulated a journal as the *Atlantic Monthly* by an active-duty naval officer; and given at a time when no leading member of the Harrison administration would have risked so blunt a statement. Mahan considered the propriety of his authorship while writing the piece in September 1890. In fact, he asked Admiral Luce to read the article in manuscript and comment on its "implicit dissent from the dominant policy." Luce suggested a few minor stylistic changes and urged Mahan to submit it as it was. "If I can have an advanced copy or two for a N.Y. paper," he said, "it is just possible they will review it at length and thus call attention to it." Mahan had already decided (foolishly as it turned out) that there "seems no reason why an officer, being also a citizen, should not express opinions on matters which are not merely politics, but affect the national interests. The connection between expansion of trade and other foreign policy seems to me natural and fitting." The thing that troubled him most about the article, once published, was that he had not had the courage to make stronger his views on the desirability of an Anglo-American connection. As he later explained to his English correspondent, George Sydenham Clarke, just after Cleveland and the Democrats had decisively won the 1892 elections,

> the time is not yet full ripe. The exigencies of politics and very particularly the Irish vote in our country, prevents clear reason from making itself felt. For it is upon a reasonable perception of our mutual interests that I would like to see policy of the two nations conjoined. Equally with yourself, I am impressed with the feeling that to work together for our mutual good and if necessary against the rest of the world, would be the highest statesmanship—for in political traditions as well as by blood we are kin, the rest alien. . . . I trust that upon the recognition of the facts, sentiments of affection may follow.[9]

While Mahan was searching for the basis of "cordial understanding" with the British, and while his "Looking Outward" article was making its way to press in November 1890, its author was secretly working on a contingency plan for naval war with those very same British. He completed the first draft of the plan in November and sent it to Rear Admirals Charles H. Davis and William M. Folger for their criticism. Davis produced his critique in December; Folger's was delayed. While waiting for

Folger's response, Mahan asked Davis to send to him in New York data "needed to take up the cases of Spain and Germany, and the West Indies generally." Ten years later he vaguely recalled having drawn up in 1890 "two [war plans] that I remember—possibly more; in the case of Great Britain and of Spain." He thought that these might have "found their way" to the Office of Naval Intelligence, but he could not be sure. In any event, only his plan for war with Great Britain has survived. Declassified in 1954, it was a naive document in that it demonstrated the certain peril of attempting to make the operations of sailing ships in 1799 analogous to the operational problems and possibilities of steel battleships in 1890. The exercise did, however, encourage Mahan to take a more realistic look at the Art of War vs. Material of War debate still raging within naval educational circles. "It is also evident," he confessed after drawing up and submitting his plan, "that, in our present condition, the development of the material, ordnance among the rest, is a more urgent necessity than these plans as to what to do when we have anything to do it with." Obviously.

Contingency war plans must necessarily be based on a series of assumptions, and their usefulness is related closely to the sophistication (probability) of the assumptions. Viewed in hindsight, Mahan's assumptions were not very sophisticated; indeed, they had something of a Mad Hatter quality about them.

With reference to the expected American situation at the moment of war with Britain, his assumptions were these: The U.S. Navy would consist of eighteen modern battleships—actually in 1890 it had the promise of but two future "sea-going coast-line" battleships—and would thus be too weak to carry the war to British waters. The naval war would therefore be fought mainly off the east coast of North America, in the New York-Halifax-Bermuda triangle. Commerce-raiding by single ships would not play a decisive role in the outcome of the war. The defenses of the major city-ports of the United States would be powerful enough to discourage bombardment by the Royal Navy (such defenses were nonexistent in 1890). American intelligence about the movements of the British fleet in American waters would be uniformly excellent, thanks to "a system of informers in Great Britain, in communication with agents on the continent, by whom information could be cabled to us of the enemy's purposes or movements." The U.S. Army would actually win the war by launching a virtually unresisted invasion of central and east central Canada, while the Navy fought a holding operation designed to bring it temporary command of the seas off the coast of North America. American naval control of Lake Ontario ("the key of the whole Lake system") and the connecting canal system would ensure the Army's speedy success in Canada, since the soft underbelly of Canada would be wholly exposed. Montreal would fall first, thus compromising the defensibility of Ottawa and all central Canada.

Conversely, Mahan's assumptions with reference to the British situation were these: Britain would deploy but thirty of her fifty-three battleships to North American waters; the remainder of her capital ships would be held in home waters and in the Far East to watch potential enemies in those sectors. British naval commanders in American waters would have generally poor intelligence, would likely "blunder," and would be "puzzled," confused, and occasionally duped by their wily American counterparts. "Worrying the opposing admiral, so as to perplex his judgment and lead him to make false dispositions, is our first effort," Mahan argued. Further, the Royal Navy could not long prosecute a war in the western North Atlantic if it were deprived of the coal deposits of Nova Scotia and Cape Breton Island and the coaling station that was Halifax. Given such deprivation, the Royal Navy would have no choice but to fall back on its base at Bermuda; it would thus effectively remove itself from the naval phase of the war. The inability of the Royal Navy to seize and maintain command of the sea in the theater of war would militate against any decision the War Office might make to send British troops to Canada.

Given these assumptions, Mahan's hypothetical Anglo-American war would proceed as follows: At the outset, the Americans would *concentrate* (a Mahanian rubric) twelve of their eighteen available battleships in New York Harbor which, because of its two accesses, would permit the U.S. fleet, or elements of it, to sortie past the British blockading squadron when necessary. "The dictum is absolute and unqualified." American torpedo vessels and other lighter craft would be deployed to New London and to Narragansett Bay, on the flank of British supply routes to New York. Meanwhile, the Royal Navy, it was assumed, would have stationed twenty-four of its thirty battleships off Sandy Hook to bottle up the American fleet concentrated in New York Harbor. With the bulk of the British naval force thus held virtually immobile at New York by an equally immobile U.S. fleet ensconced within the Narrows, the American land invasion of Canada, mainly an attack on Montreal, would move swiftly forward. Further, the British blockading force would be able to maintain itself off Sandy Hook only by shuttling its ships back and forth to Halifax for coaling.

The key to Mahan's plan centered therefore on a combined Army-Navy operation against Halifax. "Our maxim should be: Always ready to take advantage of a chance at Halifax," he wrote. "Failure, with the loss of two or three ships and ten thousand men, should not condemn such an undertaking if there should appear to be one chance in five in our favor." The fall of Halifax would seal the St. Lawrence against the possibility of reinforcements reaching the small British Army in eastern Canada and would serve also to deprive the British fleet of the coal stores collected there.

To mount this audacious operation, a division of U.S. battleships would sortie boldly from New York Harbor at the appropriate moment and would skillfully elude the British blockade in the same manner Admiral Eustache Bruix had escaped the British blockading squadron at Brest in 1799. Mahan developed this happy historical analogy at some length. Free of New York, the battleships would rendezvous with the wooden troop transports *Lancaster, Pensacola, Brooklyn,* and *Richmond* (antiquated vessels of the Old Navy) that had been secretly assembled at Boston, Portland, and Bangor, and take them under tow. The hybrid fleet would then descend with blinding speed (9 knots) and complete surprise on Halifax. The transports Mahan recognized as "old fossils," but he considered them capable of "something in an offensive move . . . laying down their lives if need be." The invasion force of 20,000 to 25,000 Army infantry and Marines would land unopposed at nearby St. Margaret's Bay, swiftly march fifteen miles overland to Halifax, and storm the Citadel which, standing 270 feet above the water, overlooks and guards the city. "The attempt on the Citadel must be made by a rush, to support which the ships of war would, having seen the landing assured, make an attack upon the forts." The Citadel, defended by 1,200 British and Canadian troops, would fall; but not before the attacking force had sustained 10,000 casualties. Having offloaded their troops at St. Margaret's Bay, the transports would then steam into Halifax Harbor and remove any mines there, presumably by the device of being blown up by them. Should any of the vessels survive the mines, they would lie in close, again kamikaze-style, and support the infantry attack on the Citadel with naval gunfire. "The weaker party," Mahan opined, "must have recourse to action vigorous to desperation. So only can he reverse the odds." The 10,000 to 15,000 surviving American combat troops would comprise an American army of occupation. Even were this force eventually overwhelmed, it would first have opportunity to destroy the city's defense works, connecting railroads, and navy yard; and especially the coaling depot on which the Royal Navy in North American waters relied. This would be a "small price" to pay for neutralizing the strategic advantages that Halifax provided the British.

Mahan confessed that the Halifax expedition would have little chance of success, even with the expenditure of some 10,000 American lives. Nevertheless, he urged it as the key to the Navy's ability to secure and maintain temporary command of the sea off the coast of New England and the Maritime Provinces. The war would thus end with the fall of Montreal and the land conquest of eastern Canada by the U.S. Army while the impotent Royal Navy would be tied to distant Bermuda, its support colliers from Britain harassed by American torpedo vessels and other commerce-destroying cruisers and raiders.

Whatever the strengths or weaknesses of Mahan's assumptions, his fanciful scenario contained the cardinal weakness of contingency war planning—entirely aside from the fact that its strategical raison d'être hung by the thread of a wild tactical gamble. The plan turned almost entirely on what he assumed the British *would* do, rather than on what the Royal Navy *would be capable* of doing. To be sure, throughout his planning document, Mahan spoke confidently of "tactical concentration" and "command of the sea," phrases on which he had built much of the theoretical thrust of his first *Influence* book. But the plan clearly underestimated the will and ability of the British government to pursue such a war with all available strength, denigrated the professional skill of British naval commanders in North American waters, and failed to take into account the impact that telegraphic communications were likely to have on fleet operations. (He still thought of fleet communications in terms of telescope-fitted observation balloons and carrier pigeons.) Further, he based much of the Nova Scotia phase of his plan on the assumption that history repeated itself and on the immutability of certain principles and practices of naval blockade. Finally, he saw naval victory—produced by limited and momentary command of the sea—emerging from a desperate throw of the dice at Halifax, which he admitted had no better chance of success than one in five.

It was well for Mahan's reputation that this plan did not see the light of day until forty years after its author's death. Charles H. Davis, who read the document in December 1890 and pronounced it admirable, inadvertently demolished it in one sentence. Calling attention to Britain's naval strength in 1890—53 battleships, 11 heavy cruisers, and 136 light cruisers, torpedo boats, and various support vessels exceeding 1,000 tons displacement—he noted that "the enemy's endeavors would be doubtless directed towards bringing the war to a speedy conclusion by doing the utmost damage in the shortest time."[10]

Mahan was much more at home with the strategy and tactics of the Age of Sail than with those of the Age of Steam. He therefore pushed ahead enthusiastically with his 1793–1812 sequel to *Influence*, pausing only to outline articles for the *Atlantic Monthly* on British admirals Jervis, Saumarez, Pellew, and Howe, and write several new lectures for his naval history course at the War College. He was beginning to appreciate what professional historians seldom have an opportunity to learn—that he could exchange his prose for hard coin. As he told Horace Scudder, in demanding payment for the four proposed articles, "I cannot afford, with the other demands upon me, to do any purely volunteer work." He insisted also that he work on the articles at his own speed, without reference to publishing deadlines ("pressure is distasteful to me"), and that all copyrights "for future publication in book form" remain with himself.[11]

The manuscript of *The Influence of Sea Power Upon the French Revolution and Empire, 1793–1812* took shape in the fall of 1891. Mahan solicited and received from J. K. Laughton in England important statistical and bibliographical information on British merchant shipping in the 1803–1815 period, wrestled with primary source materials ("I have just learned how to use the *Journals* of the House of Commons," he confessed to Luce), mastered relevant monographs sent him in New York from the War College and Redwood libraries in Newport, and drew heavily on information assembled for him by Commander Richardson Clover in the Navy's Hydrographic Office. As he had done with his first sea-power book, he began by casting the material in the form of written lectures that would be read to his classes at the War College.

He worried momentarily that Henry Adams' new *History of the United States of America*, a magisterial study of the administrations of Jefferson and Madison, paralleled his own work in several respects, but finally decided that he and Adams had approached the Anglo-American material in quite different ways, "so that upon the whole I think my treatment and subject rather gain, in interest, from the fact of his preceding me." In general, however, he found the job of writing the second *Influence* book much more difficult and complex than composing the first study had been. He decided, therefore, to "run over hastily" the concluding years (1805–1812), terminating the detailed development of the story with Nelson at Trafalgar. "When this book is done I shall want a rest," he told Bouverie Clark, "the former [was] nothing to it in point of work." By September 1891 he had four-fifths of his task finished and the quantity at that point added up to twenty-five lengthy lectures, "certainly not less." Still the labor dragged on.

In November 1892 it was finally completed and was published by Little, Brown and Company in two substantial volumes, at six dollars the set.

Mahan explained his feelings about its publication to George Sydenham Clarke:

> I shall look with interest and some anxiety to the reception of my coming book on your side. Although I attempt no controversy, I have felt the necessity of supporting my case all through, and consequently a certain amount of argument underlies the current of my story—though it does not, I hope, rise too obtrusively to the surface. It has been intensely interesting to me, but thank God! it is done. I don't think I shall ever again tackle such a task. The proofs being all read, and nothing but the binding to do, it should be out this month.[12]

He need not have worried about the reception of his second sea-power book. The reviewers, foreign and domestic, were almost universally enthusiastic. *The Times* (London) noted that "the true significance of the tremendous events of those momentous years has never been more luminously or more instructively displayed," while *The Athenaeum* remarked that Mahan had exhibited a "statesmanlike grasp of all controlling circumstances." British reviewers of the Sampson Low, Marston edition drew special attention to the author's contention that the Royal Navy had saved Britain from invasion by the French between 1803 and 1805, and that England's great war against Bonaparte had really been won not on the Peninsula or at Waterloo, but at Trafalgar. Mahan's work also gave British patriots an opportunity to eulogize Nelson in nostalgic terms and salute the Royal Navy anew. Several, including William O'Connor Morris, were pleased that in the second book Mahan had emphasized the personalities of the principal naval commanders to a greater degree than he had in the first, and that he had otherwise subordinated considerations of the machinery of war to analyses of the human factor. Others favorably compared the importance of Mahan's sea-power hypothesis with the colonial-expansion thesis found in Seeley's *Expansion of England*, and with the mercantilist theory developed by Adam Smith in his classic *The Wealth of Nations*. Much to his personal satisfaction, reviewers on both sides of the Atlantic called attention to his connection with the War College and urged the continuation of the institution. Some English reviewers could not resist the temptation again to drag Mahan's arguments into internal political debates, particularly those on Home Rule and naval building. Others complained again that a mere American, rather than an Englishman, had written such a brilliant book on the Royal Navy and understood better than Britons the role of sea power in British history. On the other hand, a few American reviewers saw the work as an ill-concealed appeal for the New Navy and for American commercial expansion. But the spirit of almost all Anglo-American reactions to Mahan's sea-power books was best expressed by Vice Admiral Sir George Tryon in an interview at Malta with a reporter of the *New York Herald* in June 1893:

> Have you read [he asked the reporter] Captain Mahan's books on The Influence of Sea Power on History and on the French Revolution? They are simply great—the best things ever written. They ought to have been written twenty years ago, and, by rights, by an Englishman. They are not only good history, written in the best and most elegant, because the simplest, diction; but they contain the most clear and comprehensive naval strategy and ship tactics in large movements that have ever been penned. You Americans ought to be proud of Mahan. We Englishmen are grateful to him. We owe him a large debt. . . . We owe Mahan a large debt.[13]

A lesser debt, surely, was owed Mahan for his quickly executed biography of Admiral David G. Farragut, a derivative book that can best be described as a potboiler that boiled no pots. Mahan took on the Farragut assignment for Appleton's publishing house in May 1891 after being assured by Secretary Tracy that his concurrent work on the second sea-power book, together with his contingency war-planning duties, had been given higher priority by the department than possible sea duty. Busy as he was with more important literary projects, Mahan felt that the Farragut book was another opportunity "to say something for the Navy," an opportunity he could not resist.

His *Admiral Farragut* was a cake-recipe approach to biography. What he did was to begin with the primary-source material in Loyall Farragut's biography of his father, a book that was published in 1879 and included many of the admiral's letters as well as his private journal. To this material, he added a number of unpublished family documents supplied by Loyall Farragut. He briskly stirred the Farragut family material into Civil War data he had included in his *The Gulf and Inland Waters* and added a dash of biographical comparison (mostly with Lord Nelson) taken from his second *Influence* manuscript, which was simultaneously in preparation. Correspondence with several participants in the Civil War rounded out the superficial research. The product was then covered with a thin icing of sea-power hypothesis. Pleas for an American maritime renaissance also found their way into the text, as did descriptions of the sad state of the U.S. Navy on the eve of the War of 1812 and the Civil

War. Not surprisingly, Mahan found in Farragut's career further evidence to support his contention that it was much more important for a commander to understand the art of war than to have mastery of the machinery of war. This point had become virtually an obsession with Mahan by 1891 and he seldom missed an opportunity in the years ahead to give voice to his strong opinions on it. Indeed, he later confessed to Admiral Sir Cyprian Bridge, RN, that he probably had gone "too far to my own extreme of exalting the Art of War, in its various branches, over the absorbing attention to matériel on the part of naval officers of the executive branch." Notwithstanding its special pleading concerning the Art of War, the 333-page work on Farragut contained but fifteen footnote references to supporting source materials. It was an extremely thin and hurried job. All the research and writing were done in bits and pieces of time borrowed over a five-month period from far more intellectually demanding labors. "The great defect in my *Farragut*," he later wrote, "was that I had no data with which to depict the *man*."

By late November 1891 the Farragut manuscript was finished, and Mahan was able to say again that he hoped "it will show as a military biography a value which I shall owe wholly to my College work." Proofreading was delayed by his brief assignment to special duty in Washington from December 1891 to January 1892, at the height of the American-Chilean war scare; and there was further delay incident to his taking over the presidency of the War College in the spring of 1892. Not, then, until early October 1892 was *Admiral Farragut* published by D. Appleton and Company. From a commercial standpoint the timing could scarcely have been worse, the book appearing as it did but a few weeks before the release by Little, Brown and Company of Mahan's brilliant *The Influence of Sea Power Upon the French Revolution and Empire*. In the wake of Nelson at Trafalgar, Farragut at Mobile sank virtually out of sight. The book eventually sold fewer than one thousand copies at $1.50 each, and for the rest of his life Mahan remained sensitive about the commercial disaster he had fathered. Five years later he glumly observed that his "experience with the *Life of Farragut*, the quality of which has been attested to me by several capable witnesses, inclines me to think that our people do not yet care for naval matters." Politically, however, it had considerable value to him in that he could send a complimentary copy to Secretary Tracy with the observation that this volume too had stemmed from his "prolonged connection with the College. . . . it is at once fitting and a pleasure to make this acknowledgment of my indebtedness to you."[14]

Useful also for Mahan was the fact that the reviews of *Farragut* appeared at about the same time as did those of the second *Influence* volume, thus allowing it to bask in the reflected glow of the vastly more important work. This was especially true in England, although there was no British edition of *Admiral Farragut*. Thus the main importance of *Farragut* was that it added to Mahan's standing as the U.S. Navy's leading literary light. It also helped the War College in that the struggling institution was again linked with the famous author who was then (1892–1893) also its president. The *New York Tribune* was certain, therefore, that the study had added to "Capt. Mahan's fame, which has been steadily widening [and] has perhaps reached a point never before touched by a writer on naval affairs. . . . The homage offered this great writer abroad surely will not lessen his influence at home." *The Academy* (London) thought it "discreditable to England that we have no biography of Blake, Hawke, St. Vincent, and, above all, Nelson, that deserves to be compared with it." The *Philadelphia Times* hailed it as an "admirable portrayal of the American Nelson's deeds," and the *London News* spoke glowingly of the author's historical methodogy: "His grasp of strategical science and mastery of tactics are not less remarkable than his faculty for accumulating facts, or the analytical power that enables him to arrange these with an accurate sense of their relative values." And so Mahan's thoroughly mediocre book slipped past the reviewers.[15]

Work on the second *Influence* volume and the Farragut biography was interrupted in December 1891 by the Chilean crisis. This event caused Mahan to be called to Washington where, ostensibly, he was set to work by Secretary Tracy "to study the military side of the question, to be ready to prepare plans, or to express opinions, as a result of my reflections." That Mahan, once arrived on the Washington scene, studied little, seems to have consulted with no one in a position of importance, prepared no naval war plan, and was generally shunted aside in the Navy Department as the crisis reached a fever-pitch in late January 1892, was a mark of the then utter amateurishness of the Navy in the field of contingency war planning. No formal board of strategy or planning was instituted; no coordination of effort was effected. America's hasty preparation for possible naval war with Chile was, instead, a one-man performance. As Mahan later recalled to Luce:

> There was no constituted Board at the time of the Chilean imbroglio in 1891–2. . . . Mr. Tracy kept matters in his own hands, consulted when he wished to consult and acted without consultation as he chose. Nor do I remember that I was ever directed to consult anyone else in

the Department; certainly very rarely, if ever. At times, I saw War Department officials by the Secretary's direction, for a specific purpose. . . . Occasionally, once or twice, I gave brief written expression to my views; but these were simply memoranda, and I do not think ever went on file.

Tracy alone ran the show for the Navy. The famous author of *The Influence of Sea Power Upon History* was brought to Washington in December 1891 largely as window-dressing, as again was the case at the time of the Spanish-American War in May 1898.

The crisis grew out of a revolution in Chile in January 1891, an event which reinforced Mahan's long-held view that the Latin-American "beggars" had an absolute "incapacity for governing themselves." This was also the attitude of Patrick Egan, the inept American minister in Chile, whose bumbling support of the losing faction had not endeared the United States to the government that took charge of the distraught nation in August 1891. While local feeling against the Americans was still running high, Captain W. S. Schley, commanding the USS *Baltimore*, the station vessel dispatched to the scene to protect American life and property, committed a grave error in judgment: he gave 24-hour shore leave in Valparaiso to 120 of his crew. Late in the afternoon of October 16, 1891, some members of the shore-leave party, apparently drunk as skunks, became involved in a bloody brawl with equally inebriated Chilean tipplers in the True Blue Saloon. It was said—more importantly it was believed in the United States—that the fight started when a Chilean seaman spat in the face of an American sailor. Whatever the cause of the explosion in the True Blue bar that afternoon, the ensuing riot was carried into the nearby streets. When it was all over, two American sailors lay dead, 17 were wounded, and 36 were badly beaten and carted off to jail, where they were further mistreated. Reportedly, the local police assisted the Chilean mob during the fracas.[16]

Public reaction in the United States was one of outrage, an emotion that increased steadily as the Chilean government studiously neglected to extend either an apology or an expression of regret to Washington. Nor was American opinion mollified when Chilean hotheads began boasting about what havoc the heroic Chilean Navy would visit on the decrepit U.S. Navy in the event of war. In his annual message to Congress on December 9, 1891, President Benjamin Harrison hinted at the possibility of just such a war if the United States did not receive full satisfaction in the matter. When satisfaction was not forthcoming, Secretary of State Blaine, on January 21, 1892, dispatched an ultimatum to Chile threatening termination of diplomatic relations and all that such action implied. Four days later, Harrison, in a special message to Congress, virtually invited that highly exercised body to declare war on Chile. "I am of the opinion that the demands made of Chile by this Government should be adhered to and enforced," thundered the president. To avoid what could only have been a suicidal engagement with the United States, the Chileans wisely capitulated. An apology was made and an indemnity of $75,000 was ultimately paid the wounded sailors and the families of the deceased. And so the crisis, fueled throughout by equal parts of American bombast and Chilean pride, passed into history.[17]

Mahan's peripheral participation in the affair began on December 17, shortly after the delivery of Harrison's annual message, when he was ordered suddenly to Washington. "What it is about," he confided to Luce, "I do not of course know." Therefore, he saw the unscheduled trip to the capital principally as a golden opportunity to discuss War College politics with Tracy and with Senator Aldrich. When he reached Washington on the 18th he discovered that both Tracy and Aldrich had already left town for the Christmas holidays. Obviously, then, there was yet no mood of impending crisis abroad in the Navy Department, and Mahan himself went back to New York for Christmas on the 24th. When he returned to Washington on the 27th he was still more concerned with the problems of the War College than with Chile. He was also in his usual state of financial difficulty. For this reason he saw Tracy on January 4, 1892, and received his permission to go home, "because my expenses were far outrunning my mileage." He had found Tracy during these eight days at the turn of the year much "occupied with the various aspects of the Chilean affair," but also "in a very happy humor." Indeed, the Secretary was in such an expansive mood as he played at making war on Chile that he agreed in principle to order a president to the War College and to assign a class of student-officers there for the 1892 session. In Mahan's behalf, Senator Aldrich had urged this course of action on Tracy.[18]

Delighted with this turn of events, Mahan made a belated attempt to immerse himself in the events that portended war with Chile. The whole business, however, seems to have interested him far less than the future of the War College. Nevertheless, on January 10 he told Luce:

> I wait impatiently and somewhat anxiously the outcome of the Chilean trouble. That their rulers are aware of the impolicy of forcing us to war, I am sure; but I doubt they may too much fear their mob. It is astounding that our government should allow matters to drag so, when there is a question of so formidable a vessel as the [Chilean battleship]

> *Prat* thus getting time to escape. We are so confident in our bigness
> and so little realize the great extra load entailed by the distance of
> Chile, in case of war. The ultimate result, I suppose can be little doubt-
> ful, but we may first get some eye openers.

Actually, he doubted that war would break out. Thus when he returned to Washington on January 14, he did so not to plan or monger a
naval war against Chile, but to press for the early selection and assignment
of the president that Tracy had promised the War College two weeks
earlier. So it was that at the height of the Chilean crisis in late January
1892 Mahan reposed quietly in the capital, calmly reading the galley proof
of his *Admiral Farragut* and assiduously pulling political strings for the
college. At no time was he involved significantly in planning for a possible war; and there is no evidence that he beat the drums for war within
the Navy Department or elsewhere. Given the kamikaze quality of the
contingency plan he had drawn up in 1890 for naval war with Britain,
perhaps his isolation from decision-making was desirable. In any event,
on January 28 he informed Luce that "the prevalent opinion here seems
to be that the war is now wholly off." He was called to Tracy's office
in mid-afternoon of that same day and assured by the Secretary that "the
war is over." He therefore promptly asked for and received permission
from Tracy to return home to New York the following morning. There
was, however, a lesson to be learned from the aborted Chilean crisis. As
Mahan reported it to Luce:

> He [Tracy] feels, and I think justly, that the energy with which he
> has pushed naval preparations has had much to do with the final pacific
> outcome. I believe myself that Chile simply temporized to see how
> much we would stand, and had our naval effort been less vigorous and
> sustained there would have been a collision.

But the high point of Mahan's interview with Benjamin F. Tracy on
Friday afternoon, January 28, came when the Secretary asked him what
he wanted to do next, now that the war with Chile was off. Mahan replied that he especially wanted to push ahead with his second *Influence*
book, delayed as it had been by his intermittent service in Washington.
Tracy then asked, "Why don't you finish it?" adding, almost as an afterthought, "Do you want to go as President of the War College?" Mahan's
answer was instant. He would take the job, "for as far as I could see there
was no one else to do it, at present." The Secretary promised to order
him to the post forthwith. When Mahan protested that he could not
afford, conveniently or financially, to leave his research or his family in

New York—there being no government quarters available for them at Newport—Tracy agreed: "We will give you orders to go to Newport as necessary," he said.[19]

The Chilean crisis, whatever else might be said of it, certainly served Captain Alfred Thayer Mahan well. His presence in Washington during the tension, if useless to the Navy in terms of war planning, had resulted in his gaining the ear of the Secretary and getting from him a commitment to reopen the War College. He also secured an official endorsement of his research and writing projects, and an assurance of continued shore assignment.

Mahan's decision to accept the presidency of the college in January 1892 was not a snap judgment. It was the only way for him to avoid sea duty (short of early retirement) and so continue his writing. He had shown no interest in the job in December 1890 when Luce suggested he take it (there was no serious threat of sea duty then facing him), preferring instead to serve the institution as its off-campus construction supervisor while he pursued the more important business of research and writing in New York. He turned down the desirable command that was the *Boston* in January 1891 when it became clear to him that Tracy was not going to exile him to sea, in any vessel, arguing on that occasion that he was far more valuable to the Navy sitting in a library than standing on a bridge. In September 1891, however, the presidency of the institution suddenly became an attractive career possibility when he learned that an assignment to sea again loomed. His numerical position on the duty roster indicated this possibility, and at one point Ramsay even told him to stand by to ship out. On September 9 he wrote Tracy that while he was prepared to go to sea he wanted definitely to know his status so that he could make housing arrangements in New York for his family for the coming winter. "My hope has been," he told the Secretary, "that I should be allowed to finish a course on Naval History I have been writing for the War College—for which about six months more will be needed—but beyond stating the fact, I have no wish to influence the Department. I have written Ramsay to the same effect." Ten weeks later he was still determined, as he told Luce, that "I will not apply *not to go to sea*, but I have said to the Secretary and to Ramsay that I should be glad to remain ashore until I have completed the course of lectures. . . . in which case if not delivered they could be published."

When Mahan heard in December 1891, on the eve of the Chilean imbroglio, that he was likely to be assigned to the command of the armored cruiser *Charleston*, his interest in the Newport job was further stimulated.

His difficulty in the matter, however, was that he had earlier recommended F. E. Chadwick for the post at the War College. He wrote Luce about his ethical dilemma in the matter on December 14:

> The step to be taken (by the Secretary) is to order a president at once.
> . . . If Chadwick is wanted for other duty, and prefers to take it, then
> let him step aside for the time at least. As regards myself, *if* Chadwick
> prefers not to take hold at once I would be willing to do so—only I
> cannot for money reasons come to live in Newport before next summer.
> But Chadwick's rights must be carefully preserved, for I myself suggested him, and the thing has gone too far for him to be cut under. On
> the other hand, he should either be ordered at once, or give it up. The
> Secretary, I think, is a real believer in the College and if Aldrich could
> see him and make the simple point that the president must be ordered
> *now* if the College is to live, I think likely he would do it; but Aldrich
> had better get from him that the orders will be issued at once, not next
> week. As regards myself, I think you will appreciate that I cannot move
> now without risk of being misunderstood—both on account of my
> advocacy of Chadwick and the imminence of my orders for sea. . . . If
> you think it would do any good for you to write to Aldrich, I see no
> other step now open—only he must go to Tracy not to Soley. The
> latter would be useless. . . . Please regard the fact of this letter as confidential. . . . Of course you are at liberty to say that you know, or
> have reason to believe, I would accept the presidency in case of Chadwick's not wishing to go.

Mahan's problem was a real one. He could not appeal to Ramsay, his immediate superior. Their personal break was complete, made final by Ramsay's foot-dragging on the construction of the War College building and on other college issues. Mahan hated him with a passion. His "greatest faculty is that of getting himself and every one else into irons; whose chief contribution to any movement not originating with himself is to tie its legs and add weight after weight till the back is broken." Nor could he risk an appeal to his former colleague, Assistant Secretary Soley, who, Mahan was convinced, was too intent upon "trying to scoop in almost all the business of the Bureaus and in so doing . . . swamps himself with business details, fears responsibility and postpones action. . . . he is too busy for any sustained interest in the College. Moreover, I think he has cooled very much toward me personally." Further, Mahan's conscience bothered him on the question of the amount of time he had already enjoyed on shore since leaving the *Wachusett* in 1885; but those twinges were stilled when he learned, during research on his biography of Farragut, that the great admiral himself had spent but twelve months at sea between the years 1843 and 1858.[20]

The only way, therefore, for Mahan to secure the War College assignment, and thereby avoid sea duty and the resultant interruption of his writing, was to mount a campaign for an extension of shore duty outside regular department personnel channels—specifically, to present his case against going to sea to Secretary Tracy through Admiral Luce and Senator Aldrich. For this reason his summons to Washington in December 1891, during the Chilean incident, was a godsend. It permitted him to press his case directly with the Secretary and with the Rhode Island senator, the essence of his argument being that a president should be appointed to the college immediately if the institution were to be saved. It was arranged that Luce would make known Mahan's personal availability for the job at the appropriate moment.

On December 24, 1891, on his way home from the capital for Christmas in New York, Mahan chanced to meet Chadwick on the train. As a result of their conversation, Chadwick, who was never particularly interested in the Newport assignment, agreed that the best solution to the problem of getting a president speedily detailed to the college "would be for me [Mahan] to take it up." As Mahan happily reported this development to Luce, "there remains no difficulty to *me* in accepting the position if the Department offers it to me. But, whosoever takes it will have an immense difficulty to encounter in Ramsay."

The ethical problem of his earlier advocacy of Chadwick having thus been resolved, Mahan, as has been noted, spoke with Tracy in Washington on January 4, 1892, and received his assurances that both a president and a class would be appointed to the college for a session to be held later in 1892. There was no mention, apparently, of Mahan's personal interest in the presidency during that interview. Three weeks passed. On the morning of January 28 Mahan was still uncertain of his future. He wrote Luce that he still knew nothing of Tracy's intentions in the matter and that "as regards myself I can not say more than that I will be willing to take the position if desired by the Department." That same afternoon, it will be recalled, Tracy summoned Mahan to his office, announced that the Chilean war was off, offered him the presidency of the college, and urged him to finish the second *Influence* book.[21]

It is quite likely that Luce or Aldrich or both had reached the Secretary on Mahan's behalf. It is also likely that Mahan himself had impressed upon Tracy the political and historical dangers of *not* sustaining the War College. During his interview with the Secretary on January 4 he had stated bluntly that "if this administration goes out . . . without putting the college on its legs then there was no telling if it ever would get on them." Tracy was already impressed with Mahan personally and with his work for the Navy and the nation, both as a historian and as an outspoken publicist for American expansion. The Chilean crisis of January 1892 had indeed found "The United States Looking Outward," a line of sight upon which Mahan had insisted in 1890. Further, the Secretary identified Mahan with the college and the college with Mahan. To advance the fortunes of the New Navy it was logical to assign Mahan to the presidency of the school. Finally, the close identification of the man with the institution and the institution with the man was the basis of the Luce-Mahan strategy to disinter the War College from the grave dug for it by Secretary Whitney and Commodore Schley and to hoist it onto the strong shoulders of *The Influence of Sea Power Upon History*. Mahan instructed Luce on the most effective technique of lobbying for the college:

> I would suggest that in speaking of my reputation, which seems at present the most obvious work of the College, it would be well to add how keenly I feel deficiencies in certain directions. . . . Also, granting I have such important attainments as some think, they are due to the College; and how absurd that with so many able men in the Navy there are not dozens who possess the same. Excuse my appearance of egotism, for I really am not vainglorious.

Vainglorious or not, Mahan carried the point and the day (January 28, 1892) with Tracy. The Secretary instructed Ramsay to order Mahan to duty as president of the Naval War College, and on February 23, 1892, the deed was done. Again, Mahan had gone successfully over Ramsay's head. But the admiral's revenge would come—and soon. "It is not the business of a Naval officer to write books," he later sputtered, as he prepared to pack Mahan off to sea.[22]

Meanwhile, Mahan informed Ramsay that until the building was finished he would administer the college from his apartment in New York, since it was "pecuniarily impossible" for him to break his lease, which was due to expire on September 30, and move his family to Newport until his quarters there were ready. He would, however, make frequent trips to the college to oversee the daily work, which was in the immediate charge of the competent Lieutenant Commander Charles H. Stockton who was on the scene. Working through Stockton, Mahan immediately began his duties as president of the institution. He ordered books and journals for the library, especially twelve copies of *The Influence of Sea Power Upon History*, which he condescendingly described to Ramsay as "a really useful book of reference for the College purposes." He ordered that maps be drawn for use in the 1892 academic session, and he recovered the records and documents of the Office of Naval Intelligence that had been removed from the college when instruction was discontinued in 1889.[23]

Similarly, Mahan wrestled with the nagging problems associated with moving into any new building—plumbing, furnishings, and landscaping. The hiring of a civilian maintenance staff and the ordering of the winter coal supply and other basic equipment produced a steady stream of routine correspondence between Mahan and Ramsay and Soley during the spring and summer of 1892. As might have been expected, Ramsay proved not a little difficult throughout this process. On one occasion he denied a requisition for thirteen pillows, referring Mahan instead to an "Allowance of Furniture, Y. & D. '88–36:224 circular." That was a big help.[24]

Throughout all this activity Mahan readied the course of instruction for the 1892 session and continued his research and writing. It was a busy time for him, made busier by his failure to duck court-martial duty in Richmond, Virginia, in March 1892. In spite of his plea that he would be better employed on War College business, Ramsay would not hear of it. He went to Richmond for three weeks.[25]

Of great importance to Mahan during these months was the need to secure a clear definition of the precise administrative relationship between the revived War College and its ancient nemesis, the Torpedo Station. The station was commanded in 1892 by Captain F. M. Bunce. Technically, Bunce was also commanding officer of the college, since Tracy had not yet formally put asunder the shotgun wedding of the two institutions solemnized by Whitney early in 1889. For this reason, Mahan made sure that he had the power personally to recruit the resident faculty he would need to assist him. Further, he insisted that these officers, like faculty members elsewhere, be permitted to wear civilian clothes while on duty at the college. Most importantly, he asked Ramsay to spell out clearly the administrative and curricular relationship between the two schools. After Ramsay had stalled on this request for a month, a frustrated Mahan again went directly over his head to Secretary Tracy. "I greatly hope that the status of the War College may receive your early attention," he wrote on July 8, 1892:

> I am so completely in the dark [he continued] that I know not what to think, but I much fear that, unless the Department soon takes some decisive action, my position will become untenable. Personally, I am quite willing to step aside—but in the interests of the College it will be neces-

sary so to define the position of its head as will ensure his self-respect as such.

Tracy hastened to the rescue. On July 16, Mahan was ordered to Newport, there to relieve Bunce of the charge of the combined War College and Torpedo School. Thus was the Torpedo School finally and formally brought under the direction of the president of the War College.[26]

The command problem at Newport having been settled to his satisfaction, Mahan finally took up residence at the college on July 21. As promised, Tracy delivered a class of students and, on September 7, the new building having barely been readied for instruction, twenty-three officers began their course of study. Faculty members assisting Mahan were Stockton, Lieutenant James H. Sears, and Lieutenant Washington I. Chambers. The 1892 session, which lasted until October 29, was a great success. Mahan even managed to include his brother Fred among the sixteen non-resident lecturers who served the college during the session, a bit of harmless nepotism that did not noticeably aid Fred's flagging career. Twenty-five years out of West Point, Frederick Augustus Mahan was still a captain in the Army's Corps of Engineers.

Mahan carefully salted the 1892 curriculum with lectures on such "practical" matters as ram and gun tactics, naval armor, electricity, torpedo characteristics, ship construction, and coaling methods. In fact, the curriculum emphasized the mechanical and logistical problems of the New Navy, rather than how that force might best someday be fought in actual combat. This did not mean that Mahan had suddenly become a convert to the gears and grease persuasion then dominant in the naval service. Far from it. It was simply a compromise course of study designed in part to heal the Art of War vs. Materials of War split in the officer corps, a division that had already done the college much damage. Indeed, Mahan wrote Lieutenant Chambers in July stating his firm conviction that there was "danger of the art of war disappearing under a deluge of machinery." He was still certain, as Chambers apparently was not, that "the trust in machinery has been pushed beyond reason, that the living human factor is more and more relegated to a position hopelessly inferior," but he was willing to admit that from a political standpoint within the Navy "one must try, not to force the current back, but to deflect it somewhat." Chambers, a bright young naval architect-engineer and ordnance technician, was not at all sure he wanted to teach at an institution where, reputedly, there was so much emphasis on the theoretical and historical. Mahan reassured him: "The usefulness of the College in the long run will result not from the predominance of my views, or your views, but from the fair collision of opinion among men connected with it." This was a major concession for Mahan, a rather sudden change of attitude.

The larger issue, suddenly made clear by the Chilean crisis, was that the U.S. Navy in 1892 was still unprepared for war, even war against such a fourth-rate power as Chile; and that without adequate materials of war the study of the Art of War was largely irrelevant. Mahan explained the reason for the Navy's weak posture to Chambers:

> It was not my purpose to ignore, much less to deny, the Navy's share in the responsibility for its material development. It is the tendency of all subordinates to shrug their shoulders, thank God it is none of their business, and disclaim responsibility; and the Navy is so thoroughly drilled into the theory of subordination, both by its military constitution and by the much-insisted-on truth of the subordination of the military to the Civil authority, that it is especially prone to this fault. I concede freely that we should be on our guard against this besetting weakness. . . . Nevertheless, responsibility ultimately is inseparable from power; and in the last analysis the *power* to remedy our deficiencies rests with the taxpayers and their representatives.

When in doubt, when shifting position, or when caught with your new cruisers still on the ways, blame the civilians and politicians.[27]

Shortly after the session of the college closed on October 29, Americans marched to the polls to elect a new president. The Democratic landslide in the mid-term 1890 congressional elections had already indicated that the Harrison administration was in deep trouble, principally because of its high-tariff policies. Mahan was convinced that the Democratic sweep of that year bode ill for future naval appropriations. But he hoped, at the very least, that Representative Hilary A. Herbert, Democrat of Alabama and Chairman of the House Naval Committee, might, as a result of the canvass, be "promoted to a more important Committee" and thus abandon his interest in harassing the Navy.

Mahan's main concern in the presidential election of 1892, however, was that a Republican defeat would remove the bountiful Secretary Tracy from office and expose him to the tender mercies of Ramsay and the related likelihood of sea duty. When the anti-expansionist Cleveland overwhelmed Harrison on November 8, returning the Democracy to power, Mahan began to see the handwriting on the bulkhead. More shocking to him was Cleveland's appointment of Herbert as Secretary of the Navy. This was not the promotion for Herbert that Mahan had had in mind in 1890. While he was persuaded that "the navy—and I may even say the country—needs a voice to speak constantly of our external interests in matters touching the navy," and while he remained certain that he himself was that voice, Cleveland's victory turned Mahan's thoughts to early retirement. Had Harrison and Tracy won, he might well have expected an "indulgence" that would keep him ashore until his regular retirement in 1896 after forty years of service. But with Cleveland and Herbert slated to take power in March 1893, he was fearful that his days as the voice and intellect of the New Navy were numbered even though "I certainly believe I could be more useful in this way than by simple sea-going."[28]

He was fully aware of the fact that Secretary Tracy's personal interest in his literary efforts for the U.S. Navy and for a muscular American foreign policy had served to keep him at his desk in New York two years past the normal tour of shore duty for officers of comparable rank and command experience. He was also persuaded, he told Bouverie Clark in May 1891, that "it is a nuisance, and I think worse, a mistake, for a man to go to sea again at fifty, after five years on terra firma." Nonetheless, he feared that the next administration would send him off anyway—this in spite of the fact, as he had often reminded the dour Ramsay without noticeable effect, that he was of far more use to the Navy as a writer than as a ship's captain. When he sent Tracy a copy of *The Influence of Sea Power Upon the French Revolution and Empire* a month after the election, he pointedly remarked that the reason he had been able to complete the manuscript was "due wholly to your support—I may say even to your protection," an observation similar to the one he made when sending the Secretary a copy of *Admiral Farragut*. Tracy, in fine, was Mahan's last best hope to avoid sea duty. In January 1893, following his return to New York from court-martial duty in San Francisco over the Christmas holidays (Ramsay struck again), he pleaded with the outgoing Secretary to intercede with Secretary-designate Herbert and arrange a continuation of his shore duty status:

> If the law remains as now, I purpose to retire at the end of my forty years—in 1896. I so intend, believing that I can achieve greater success, personally, with my pen, than by continuing on the active list; and also that I can do better work for the Navy by developing further the line of professional thought upon which I have been for seven years engaged. With retirement only three years off, I do not wish to go to sea, as that would necessarily interrupt my present studies, and break threads which, at my age, I may not be able again to unite. In fact, my whole aim may be frustrated. I wish, therefore, to continue employed as I have been through your administration.[29]

While Tracy undertook to persuade Herbert in this direction, Mahan enlisted the aid of Theodore Roosevelt, Henry Cabot Lodge, S. B. Luce, C. H. Davis, and publisher John M. Brown in his cause; indeed, he went to Washington to direct his campaign to remain on shore. Roosevelt asked him to present his case in writing so that he might circulate it among his own political friends in the capital. This Mahan did, pointing out in the statement the importance of his research, the enthusiastic reception given his books at home and abroad, and the usefulness to the Navy of the literary work he had planned for the immediate future. He concluded that the "continuance of my work depends upon my not going to sea. The absorbing administrative work of a modern large ship of war would impose an interruption, which, at my age—53—and for two years, would probably prove final. I propose, therefore, to retire, as allowed by law, after forty years service, in 1896; if, in view of that intention, I am not meanwhile ordered on sea duty." Simultaneously, Mahan wrote Ramsay along the same lines, formally requesting a stay of execution. "The complicated administration of a large modern ship of war," he told the bureau chief, "is a task too absorbing to admit of sustained mental effort in another direction." But since Ramsay was not sympathetic to naval officers who wrote books, Mahan's appeal had no effect. He was bound and determined that Mahan should go to sea, although he himself was one of the most practiced shore-huggers in the U.S. Navy.[30]

Still, Mahan received no new orders during the first month of the Cleveland administration's tenure. A rumor that he would be ordered to temporary command of the *Baltimore* proved groundless. As Roosevelt and other of Mahan's friends continued their importunities on his behalf with Secretary Herbert and with the "more civilized" William G. McAdoo, the new Assistant Secretary of the Navy, Mahan began to breathe more easily. In this mood he wrote Roosevelt in Washington on March 26:

> I thank you most gratefully for your letter and for the effort you have made on my behalf. I understand exactly the state of the case, as it now stands, i.e., no promise on the Secretary's part, but apparently a disposition to take a view favorable to my wishes. I consider it a particular piece of good fortune to have my case advocated by you. . . . I shall wait the issue quietly, though not without grave concern; but sure that in you I have all the support that I ought to desire, and a really interested friend.

Yet on April 18, 1893, some three weeks later, a shocked and bewildered Mahan was headed straight for sea. "Roosevelt writes me," he informed editor Scudder "that the new Secretary seems decidedly inclined to force me to sea, despite all arguments so far adduced to the contrary—even though I assure my retiring, as the law gives me the right, after three years more." Something in Mahan's contingency shore plan had gone wrong.[31]

What went awry was Hawaii. On January 30, 1893, Mahan had written an unsolicited letter to the editor of *The New York Times* commenting on the racial implications to the United States of the recent revolution in Hawaii. The letter, published on February 1, was a vintage "Yellow Peril" piece which argued shrilly that American control of the Hawaiian Islands, already populated by tens of thousands of restless immigrant Chinese, was necessary to discourage massive Chinese emigration across the Pacific to the West Coast. The Yellow Peril idea was one that Mahan embraced until his death. In 1893, however, he pointed out particularly that American annexation of Hawaii, the White cork in the Yellow bottle, might lead to grave complications with commercially aggressive European states, a situation that would demand "a great extension" of American naval power. "Are we ready to undertake this?" he asked rhetorically.

That Americans resident in Hawaii, with the help of armed sailors and Marines from the USS *Boston*, had seized control of the islands from Queen Liliuokalani was a fact of January 16–17, 1893. The U.S. Minister to Hawaii quickly recognized the revolutionary government, and by January 20 representatives of that government were en route to Washington to lay a formal proposal for annexation before the State Department. In mid-February a swiftly negotiated annexation treaty was submitted to the Senate for approval. Mahan's letter of February 1 to the *Times*, written while the Hawaiian emissaries were still on their way to Washington to seek annexation, had boldly advocated just that. To stem and contain the flow of the "barbaric" Yellow Tide, he declared, a "firm hold of the Sandwich Islands by a great, civilized, maritime power" would be necessary; and because of its "nearness to the scene," that hold could best be exercised by "our own country." Provocative and controversial as was his recommendation in this regard, had Mahan let it go at that he might never have been exiled to the USS *Chicago*.[32]

But no. He had to acerbate the question further. On February 2, he was asked by Walter Hines Page, editor of *The Forum*, to write an article on the "Hawaii question" for the March issue of the magazine. Page had read the letter in the *Times* and had been impressed with the outspokenness of the famous historian and the forcefulness of his arguments. Although he gave Mahan barely a week to write and submit the article, Mahan foolishly consented to undertake it. "An offer that might be made useful for the Navy I could not well decline," he remarked on February 3. The eleven-page article was hastily completed and was mailed to Page on February 10. By this time the Hawaiian emissaries had arrived in Washington and had formally made known their wishes. Thus Mahan's controversial *Forum* piece, "Hawaii and Our Future Sea Power," which appeared in print on March 1 as the magazine's lead article, was actually written between February 4 and February 9—or when it seemed likely that a quick treaty of annexation was about to be consummated by the outgoing Harrison administration.

The *Forum* article rose above the Yellow Peril demagoguery of the letter of February 1 to the *Times* and concentrated instead on the broader geopolitical advantages of annexing Hawaii. It was also a hymn to the inevitability and desirability of American imperialism:

> The issue [of annexation] cannot be dodged. . . . We can now advance, but, the conditions of the world being what they are, if we do not advance we recede. . . . Have we no right or no call to progress farther in any direction? Are there for us beyond the sea horizon none of those essential interests, of those evident dangers, which impose a policy and confer rights? . . . The Hawaiian group possesses unique importance— not from its intrinsic commercial value, but from its favorable position for maritime and military control [of the Pacific].

Mahan went on to link American possession of Hawaii with the military defensibility of the West Coast, with America's necessary domination of the trade that would ultimately funnel through an isthmian waterway ("whether the canal . . . be eventually at Panama or Nicaragua matters little"), and with American "commercial and military control of the Pacific, and especially of the Northern Pacific, in which the United States, geographically, has the strongest right to assert herself." All this added up in Mahan's mind to the need for a respectable U.S. Navy and for supportive naval coaling stations in the Pacific. He did not call for "a navy equal to the largest now existing," but he did suggest that the United States build and maintain a navy large enough to assert American "preponderance" in "our reasonable sphere of influence." This sphere included the Caribbean, the approaches to the isthmus, and the entire Pacific Basin. Further, he restated his faith in the advantages to humanity of an Anglo-American diplomatic connection knit together by "English speech and by institutions sprung from English germs." Can anyone doubt, he asked, "that a cordial, if unformulated, understanding between the chief states of English tradition, to spread freely, without mutual jealousy and in mutual support, would increase greatly the world's sum of happiness?"[33]

"Hawaii and Our Future Sea Power" could not have reached print at a less propitious moment. Within a week the anti-expansionist and Anglo-phobic Grover Cleveland was inaugurated; and on March 9, 1893, he abruptly withdrew the Hawaiian annexation treaty from the Senate, thus neatly sawing off the annexationist limb onto which Mahan had so eagerly climbed a month earlier.

Indeed, Mahan was so pleased with himself for having accomplished something "useful for the Navy" and so unaware of his impending doom, that he considered dashing off a companion piece dealing with the isthmus and American sea power. As he told editor Scudder of the *Atlantic Monthly* on March 27, "I daresay I could rush off an article similar to that I sent the *Forum* on Hawaii." But, on second thought, he decided to "let the subject mature in my mind—I am a slow thinker—and to go into print in the early fall . . . but not too long, before the meeting of Congress." It seems clear, therefore, that at this juncture Mahan expected to be reposing quietly on shore when Congress met in December. During this period of watchful waiting he toyed with a plan to incorporate the Office of Naval Intelligence into the War College and he tended scrupulously to his presidential duties at the institution. He also investigated the possibility of entering son Lyle as a boarding student in Groton School. Clearly, Mahan was counting on continued shore duty in March 1893.[34]

While he was thus anticipating a quiet future with his books, he was struck with personal sorrow. On March 8 his mother died in her Elizabeth, New Jersey, home. The passing of Mary Helena Okill Mahan was not, however, unexpected. A near-invalid for over a year, she had been bed-ridden for several months and had reached that point where "those who loved her best could scarcely desire her continuance here." Her death, at the age of 78, released Mahan's sister, Jane Leigh, from her burdensome duties as her mother's constant companion and nurse. It also provided the surviving children with small inheritances—enough for Mahan to pay for Lyle's attendance at Groton when he was matriculated there in September 1894. Mahan dutifully took his mother's body to West Point, where she was buried beside her husband, Dennis Hart Mahan.[35]

It was therefore an additional blow to him when he learned from Roosevelt in early April that all attempts to keep him on shore were likely to fail, and that sea duty was again in the offing. Ramsay's warning to this effect, dated April 17, ordered Captain Mahan to hold himself "in readiness for sea service." A last-minute effort by Roosevelt and Lodge to persuade Secretary Herbert to assign him to the antique coast-bound monitor *Miantonomah*, "which would not take him so far away as to compel him to sever all connection with his work and with libraries of reference," was launched; so too was a letter-writing campaign in his behalf, participated in by John M. Brown, that was designed to get his orders changed. The International Naval Review at New York in April, celebrating the discovery of America by Columbus four hundred years earlier, delayed Mahan's actual assignment to a ship a few days longer since no U.S. naval vessels were leaving the country during the colorful ceremonies.

On the evening of April 30, Roosevelt, Lodge, Davis, and Luce held a "solemn council of war" in Washington on Mahan's duty status and ruefully concluded, as Roosevelt put it, that "all hope for the War College (which is nothing without you) is gone; our prize idiots here have thrown away a chance to give us an absolutely unique position in naval affairs." Roosevelt reported, further, that Ramsay was "bitterly opposing" the *Miantonomah* compromise and "anything else that may help you." On May 3, Mahan's brother Fred informed him from Washington that Captain George Dewey had told him just that morning of "tremendous pressure brought to bear from naval officers themselves to keep you on shore," and that one such officer, Frederick V. McNair, had even volunteered to go to sea in Mahan's stead. Mahan quickly agreed, as he informed Brown, that any one of a "score of men are equally fit" for sea duty, whereas the Navy had in its officer corps no one else qualified to carry on his historical and literary work. McCarty Little, his colleague at the college, concurred:

> At the Union League Club in New York they call him the Jomini of the Water. *The Times* [London] . . . again speaks of him as having done for the Ocean what Adam Smith had done for the Land, and compares *Sea Power* with the *Wealth of Nations.* . . . And yet the man who wrote that book, and who thought those thoughts into it, is in danger of being taken from the War College and sent to sea!

None of this maneuvering and special pleading was to any avail. Ramsay's mind was made up. On May 3, 1893, therefore, the head of the Bureau of Navigation formally assigned Mahan to the command of the USS *Chicago*, lying at the New York Navy Yard, and on May 11 Mahan assumed that command. Admiral W. M. Folger sympathized: "I saw your orders to sea with the deepest regret and disgust. . . . I can only believe that Secretary Herbert, who is to me distinguished by his common sense, is simply misinformed as to the scope and importance of the magnificent work upon which you are engaged." Luce and Roosevelt, among others, also sent condolences. Nevertheless, the deed was done. Mahan had no choice save to attempt to arrange Lyle's entrance into Groton for the fall term and otherwise make ready for sea. He again wrote Endicott Peabody, Headmaster at Groton, about placing his son there, but was told that the lad, just turned twelve, was too young and could not be admitted into the school until September of 1894.[36]

The more he ruminated on his misfortune, the more Mahan became convinced that he was the victim of a joint conspiracy by Ramsay and Cleveland's Department of State. He was soon to learn from Archibald L. Snowden, U.S. Minister to Spain, that "what had decided my being sent abroad was my Hawaii article in the *Forum*;" he learned too that his chief executioner in the matter had been Josiah Quincy, "Cleveland's factotum in the State Department." It was all designed, he decided, "to stop my further writing." He came finally to the rueful conclusion that he had also been done in by the way "our government looks on the expression of political opinions, however general, by officers—particularly if diametrically opposed to the traditions of the party in office." His two-year assignment to the *Chicago* by the "malicious" Herbert was thus nothing less than a political "exile." It was the "pound of flesh Ramsay demands."[37]

Mahan's convictions aside, the evidence does not prove conclusively that he was dispatched to sea solely as punishment for his article on Hawaii, though it is obvious that the article was 180 degrees away from the Cleveland administration's position on annexation. It is also clear that Mahan had run afoul of the tradition in the American military fraternity that held that whatever their private political views, and their right privately to express such views, active-duty officers should not take public stances on government policy positions. Certainly they should not take contrary positions so visible and uncompromising as the stance Mahan had taken for annexation in his article on Hawaii. The imperialist views that Republicans Harrison and Tracy had tolerated (even discreetly encouraged) in 1890 when Mahan had produced his provocative essay on "The United States Looking Outward" were not tolerable to Democrats Cleveland and Herbert in 1893. It was this shifting political and policy crossfire that Mahan misjudged. Thus, when Secretary Benjamin Tracy surrendered office in March 1893, Mahan was left naked—and Ramsay was at last able, with Herbert's concurrence, to assign him to the duty that by all rights he should have pulled eighteen months earlier. Nevertheless, Mahan saw his exile almost wholly in personal terms.

> I would like you to know [he told Brown] . . . that my retention at my particular work, by Mr. Tracy, was not, as Mr. Herbert seems to think, the result of either political or social influence. I neither exerted nor possessed the one or the other. Mr. Tracy retained me simply because

he believed in my special qualifications for special work. I never entered his house, except on a New Years, we had no close mutual friends, and I knew him only at the Department. He valued me also as an adviser under some circumstances. . . . The fact is Mr. Tracy was a man of ability, used to affairs on a large scale, which Mr. Herbert is not. The latter, with the officer [Ramsay] who has the reputation of being his chief adviser, belongs to the class of men who take narrowness for principle and rigidity for firmness. Such are incapable of exceptional action.[38]

The only "exceptional action" that Ramsay managed as Chief of the Bureau of Navigation from 1890 to 1893 was to ship the outspoken Mahan off to sea. But like everything else that the testy admiral touched in his war with the troublesome captain, this too backfired. In a word, Francis M. Ramsay ordered Alfred Thayer Mahan off to worldwide fame. "It is not the business of a Naval officer to write books," he proclaimed confidently—a statement that has gone down in naval lore with Lawrence's "Don't Give Up the Ship," Farragut's "Damn the Torpedoes," and Dewey's "You May Fire When Ready, Gridley." How could Ramsay know that Mahan's duty in the *Chicago* would be in part a historical research exercise, and that his two-year European cruise would be a triumphal personal tour? The whole thing, Mahan later remarked, was "one of the luckiest things that . . . happened in my career, a boomerang for any who wished me ill."[39]

X

Author as Ship's Captain
1893-1894

You can have no idea, I had none, of the enormous increase in a captain's labors—sometimes I fear breaking down under the uncongenial load, and indeed but for the support God gives me I believe I should go to pieces.

Alfred Thayer Mahan to Ellen Evans Mahan, February 10, 1894

Secretary Hilary Herbert had no difficulty whatever defending his decision to permit Ramsay to pack Mahan off to sea. He was tired, he told one inquirer, of "soft laces" officers who avoided regular turns at sea and who employed "both political and social influence to endeavor to retain their places" on shore. As for Mahan, said the Secretary,

> It is my intention, as far as possible, to treat all officers alike. . . . I realize fully the value of the work that Capt. Mahan has been doing, and he has been assigned to one of the best ships in the service, with a good executive officer, and I hope he will be able to devote a considerable portion of his time to literary work. I should regret very much to see Capt. Mahan drop his pen, and I realize that his work is of an exceptional character, but it would be hard to explain to other officers why they should be compelled to go to sea and Capt. Mahan allowed to remain on shore.[1]

That Mahan had in Lieutenant Commander William W. Gillpatrick a good executive officer there was doubt. At least in Mahan's mind. The captain considered him "very dull . . . slow, and forgetful at times" and was distressed to learn that he had graduated only forty in a class of seventy at the Academy. That the *Chicago* might become for Mahan a floating research facility and escritoire there was also doubt, especially when the vessel was designated flagship of the European Station and Rear Admiral Henry Erben reported on board and hoisted his broad pennant as commander of the station. As Mahan remarked facetiously to James R. Thursfield, a British naval historian: "Great believer as I am in concentration of force, I am disposed to question the advisability of concentrating an admiral's command into a single ship, which is the condition of the U.S. European Squadron." The job of captain of a flagship, he told his wife, was a "nullity."

Certainly, the act of placing Mahan and Erben in the same ship was much like putting two scorpions in a bottle. The two men could scarcely have been more unlike in personality, temperament, and career backgrounds. And as will be mentioned in another place, in January 1894, their personal relations exploded into a bitter battle that rocked the inner circles of the Navy Department. The match touching off the conflagration was Erben's highly critical end-of-year fitness report of Mahan's performance as a ship's captain.

Henry Erben, six years Mahan's senior in age, was a rough seadog of the old school. A fine practical seaman under sail or steam, he was a gruff, egocentric, hot-tempered, blustering, profane, no-nonsense sailor, plagued with painful attacks of eczema. He liked his dram, and he had small toleration for those less extroverted than himself. In addition, and unlike Mahan, he had an excellent Civil War combat record, one which a jealous Mahan later derided. Indeed, he had fought with distinction at Fort Pillow, Vicksburg, Baton Rouge, and Charleston, had captured and destroyed Confederate rams on the Mississippi and Confederate blockade-runners off Texas, and had stormed and taken the Confederate naval establishment at Matagorda, Texas. He had even commanded the naval howitzer battery under General George B. McClellan during the Antietam campaign in Maryland. On land or sea, in war and in peace, Henry Erben had done almost everything a naval officer could be expected to do in a varied and colorful 45-year career; and he had done it well. True, he had not been to sea since June 1884. While he had been in the Navy eight years longer than had Mahan, he had compiled but three more years of actual sea service. His most recent duty, 1891-1893, had been as commandant of the New York Navy Yard.

One thing Erben had probably never done, or certainly had never done to excess, was read books. It is almost certain that he had never read Mahan. More certain is the fact that he came instantly to dislike the scholarly, soft-spoken, and introverted man who commanded the ship in which he patrolled his station. He had little patience with the bookish intellectual who had spent the past eight years comfortably on shore doing little more than think and write about Europe's navies in the seventeenth and eighteenth centuries. On the contrary, he liked and respected such practical offers as Francis Ramsay, a man who had also never bothered to read Mahan. The cruise of Mahan and Erben in the *Chicago* was not destined to be a pleasant one for either man.[2]

To make matters worse the *Chicago* was not much of a ship. She was, it is true, "one of the best ships in the service," as Herbert claimed. But that claim said more about the sorry state of the U.S. Navy in 1893 than it did about the *Chicago*. Nevertheless, the *Chicago* was a far better vessel, relatively, than the *Iroquois*, *Wasp*, *Wachusett*, and all the other obsolete junk heaps which Mahan had unhappily commanded or in which he had tediously served since 1859. Launched in 1885, 342 feet in length and 4,500 tons displacement, she was the most splendid of the New Navy's ABC (*Atlanta*, *Boston*, *Chicago*) protected steel cruisers. Redundantly rigged with masts to carry 14,800 square feet of sail, an arrangement Mahan thought ludicrous, she mounted four 8-inch, eight 6-inch, and two 5-inch breech-loading rifles of the latest design. Her complement was 409 officers and men. Over half of the latter were foreign-born, many of them having but "limited knowledge of English or entire inability to read or write." Not a few of them, like Irishman Michael McLaughlin, aged 48, suffered "varicose veins—consec. syphilis, defective hearing, and absence of upper teeth."

The engines of the *Chicago* were not in much better shape than McLaughlin's veins. They were wholly inadequate, even though the vessel's speed under steam was rated at 16 knots. A few weeks before Mahan took command, Rear Admiral J. G. Walker wrote that

> it will, probably, require one year to fit the *Chicago* for an extended tour of foreign service. Both boilers and engines would require such extensive repairs that it would, probably, be found more judicious to replace them with new. Two of the six boilers are now considered unsafe for general service; the others have been repaired for a short term of service, and are fairly efficient. I consider the *Chicago* in fairly good condition for eight months' duty on the North Atlantic Station. It is possible she may go for a somewhat longer period, but in her present condition she should not be sent to a distant station.

It was on this somewhat dubious piece of machinery, the best command the New Navy had to offer in 1893, that Mahan was to spend the two most frustrating years of his life.[3]

The cruise began with Mahan's usual lack of aplomb at the conn. While maneuvering the vessel into dry dock at the New York Navy Yard in Brooklyn on May 27, he managed to collide with the USS *Bancroft*, the Naval Academy training ship, damaging her slightly. Fortunately, the *Chicago* was not injured. But the incident served to unnerve Mahan, keeping intact as it did his record for having grounded, collided, or otherwise embarrassed every ship (save the *Iroquois*) he ever commanded. As one of his shipmates in the *Chicago* later wrote, "Mahan had one navigational obsession—fear of collision."

It was a happy circumstance, therefore, that Mahan managed to get his ship safely out of dry dock and down to Sandy Hook on June 17 without further mishap. And on June 18 the *Chicago*, under sail, shaped course for Queenstown, Ireland.[4]

Her commander was convinced that the passage out would afford him ample leisure for reflection and writing. Moreover, he had contracted with Scudder for an article on the isthmian canal, had suggested articles on other maritime subjects in which the *Atlantic Monthly* might be interested, and had informed John M. Brown that, when he arrived in England, he would commence research on a biography of Lord Nelson, gathering "that fund of anecdotes which is so large a factor in a biography." Prior to leaving New York, he collected and carried on board the *Chicago* the available biographies and printed letters of Lord Nelson as well as various volumes of the American State Papers series. He confidently told Brown that he might also begin research on a volume dealing with the naval aspects of the War of 1812. He was not sure whether a book on Nelson or the War of 1812 would prove "the more profitable undertaking." He was certain only that he would push on with his literary work while suffering the slings and arrows ("two years wiped out of my life") of exile at sea. Increasingly, he was becoming convinced that there was more money to be made in the writing of popular and timely magazine articles than in the writing of books. But write he would, for one audience or another.

Having equipped his cabin as a floating carrel, he made arrangements to have his expected royalty checks sent to Elly. "I shall continue reading and studying," he assured Horace Scudder, even though "ship life is unfavorable to my usually methodical habit of writing" and "what I can accomplish under these difficulties remains to be seen." What remained to be seen was Admiral Erben's displeasure with a ship's captain who viewed his command as a seagoing library. Mahan could not appreciate the admiral's possible objections to this cozy scholarly arrangement, so estranged was he in 1893 from the operational Navy and those who ran it.[5]

Painting by Anthony Battillo

The USS Chicago

He was not, however, estranged from the literary world and, as he prepared to leave his native land, it upset him to realize that his books and ideas had been far better received in England than in his own country—that they had been read by Britons of the prominence of William E. Gladstone and Arthur Balfour, men "so conspicuous not only in political standing but as men of intellectual force." He felt strongly, therefore, that he must continue writing, against all odds, if necessary, in order to help the U.S. Navy catch up with the Royal Navy in prestige, quality, and technique. He expressed some of these concerns to Luce on the eve of his departure for Queenstown:

> The lack of recognition in our own country—either official or journalistic—has been painful; not to my vanity, for that has been more than

filled by the superabundant tribute from all quarters in England, but as showing the indifference to service matters among our people. . . . Our own Navy—by its representatives, Herbert and Ramsay—has rejected both me and my work, for I cannot but think that an adequate professional opinion would have changed the issue.

It soon became apparent to the captain of the *Chicago* that Henry Erben was to be numbered among the vast majority of officers in the Navy who, in Mahan's sour view, lacked "adequate professional opinion."[6]

Further, Mahan's morale was not improved when he contemplated the personal and family problems he was leaving behind him as the *Chicago* prepared to sail. In April 1893 he and Elly had rented a small summer place in Quogue, Long Island, and had made plans to remodel it. The family, minus its head, spent a delightful summer there in 1893. The property provided a seasonal retreat from the heat of the city and served, in part, as compensation for the "horrid little flat" that Mahan had rented on East 54th Street, at the corner of Park Avenue, in October 1890 and in which the family continued to reside while the captain was abroad. Elly hated every minute she and the children spent there. Freight and passenger trains ran down the middle of Park Avenue in those days; the neighborhood was noisy and dirty. The only advantages the fifth-floor flat had were that it was cheap, it was centrally located, and there was an elevator. It had inadequate fire escapes. Several attempts in October 1893 to find something better for the same price failed, and Elly finally resigned herself to the firetrap until her husband's return to New York in March 1895. "I never believed you could much better yourself," said Mahan when he learned that his wife had reluctantly renewed the lease after spending a month with friends in Pomfret, Connecticut, looking for a more suitable residence there. Indeed, it became something of an amusing story in subsequent generations of the Mahan family that while the famous captain of the *Chicago* was being wined and dined abroad by such people as Queen Victoria and Emperor William II his family was living in what was virtually a slum apartment at home.

To support the financial burden of two residences for his family, Mahan used the income from his mother's bequest, his royalty payments from Little, Brown and Company, his earnings from several magazine articles, and the $300 monthly allotment (from his annual at-sea salary of $4,500) that he assigned to Elly while he was out of the country. During his absence these several sources provided about $500 per month income for his wife and three children. Nevertheless, Elly seriously complicated his economic position when she decided, in the fall of 1893, to give up the rented property in Quogue and build there a summer cottage on an acre of land near the water. During the winter of 1893–1894 she was therefore busy with house plans, architects, contractors, and builders—and, apparently, with the spending of part of the $6,000 of capital that Mahan had inherited from his mother. Further, some of the money he had tentatively set aside from his mother's estate for Lyle's schooling at Groton was redirected to the building of the family cottage at Quogue.

Mahan encouraged Elly in this activity, advising her on the features and appointments that should be included in the structure. He decreed, for example, the exact arrangement of his study and specified that his writing desk should be 5½ feet by 4 feet and be made of oak or ash. He vetoed a suggestion to name the place "One Acre," but he felt that if the Quogue property "should prove a little more expensive" than the earlier rental arrangement, the social "gain would be great in the intimacy year by year with the *same* pleasant people." Actually, he was "profoundly delighted at the prospect of our having a country home of our own," particularly since it was also "the first home that in any human sense can be called our own." He was less delighted to learn that Elly's initial estimate of the cost of construction and furnishing was too low and that a mortgage loan might have to be floated to see the project through in proper style.

Completed in the late spring of 1894, "Slumberside," as the cottage was called, was situated 200 yards from the ocean in a section of eastern Long Island "as flat as Holland and with nearly as many windmills—for pumping water." It was the sort of place that all socially attuned and fashionable middle-class New Yorkers, both the arrivés and the pretenders, enjoyed during the summer months. But whatever its considerable social advantages to the Mahans, "Slumberside" added up to an unexpected financial burden that gave the captain of the *Chicago* much worry. It was not surprising, therefore, that he increasingly thought of his historical and other writing as essentially a means of earning additional income. Indeed, his letters to Elly from the *Chicago* were filled with concern for the commercial prospects of his literary output.[7]

Writing for fame, fun, and profit, however, proved a difficult enterprise for him on board the *Chicago*. He did not feel professionally sure of himself in his command of the ship when she finally sailed on June 18. Nor did he make a great impression on his salty admiral, or on his officers, when, several days into the voyage, with the ship taking white water on deck in rough seas, he was "talking to the admiral in the door of his cabin when his desk pitched away and caught my leg between it and the door frame." The result of his encounter with Erben's peripatetic desk was a badly injured knee and lower leg which put the captain on the restricted-duty list, confined him to his cabin, and virtually immobilized him for the first five weeks of the cruise. The offended leg finally had to be splinted. During his period of recuperation Mahan "read very diligently" a collection titled *Sonnets of the Century* and began preliminary work on his projected biography of Nelson. There were other advantages to being placed on the restricted-duty list. As he reported to daughter Ellen ("Nellikin") from Ireland on July 9: "The doctor says I must go on the sick list for a fortnight and keep my leg perfectly quiet, so if the *Chicago* does anything amiss in that time I shall not be the culprit."[8]

The simple fact of the matter was that when it came to ships and seamanship the sonnet-reading Alfred Thayer Mahan was accident-prone. Nothing went well for him when he was at sea, and he continued to dislike every moment of the experience. The "active pursuit of the sea and its new naval monsters" should be left, he felt, to "younger men." He thought a modern ship was a "beastly thing . . . what a fool a man is who frequents one." As he later told George Sydenham Clarke: "The impatience and distaste for detail, which is at once my strong and my weak point, makes the duty of a modern captain especially onerous to me; and I have especially chafed at a multiplicity of requirements which, I am fully persuaded, tend to reduce the efficiency of modern ships, by preventing officers from concentrating their attention on the really important."

Among the "really important" was Mahan's abiding fear of colliding the *Chicago*, as he had the *Wasp* and the *Wachusett*. The *Chicago*'s brush with the *Bancroft* on May 27 had not increased his confidence in himself as a ship-handler. For this reason he often implored his wife to "pray for me, dear, that if God will this seagoing may soon cease for me." He was constantly on the bridge when other ships were in the vicinity, and these periods of self-generated tension enormously fatigued him. "We meet a great many steamers," he reported to Elly in October 1893 from off Cape Trafalgar, "which keeps me on the drive, for I have no idea of another [*Wachusett*] collision, and I off deck, to undergo again the worry of last cruise." Storms at sea continued to frighten him and turn him to God, as they had twenty-five years earlier when he served in the *Iroquois*. "You have no idea," he told his wife, "how hard it is to keep these ships straight, and how hard for me to be as hard as I ought to be. I fear trouble, indeed I do, and am constantly repeating 'in all our troubles to put our whole trust and confidence in Thy mercy.'" On another occasion, he confided to Sam Ashe that he was really in the wrong profession and had been for nearly forty years:

I am forced daily to realize that I am growing old, and especially that all charm ship life ever had is utterly gone. I am enduring, not living; and have the painful consciousness that I am expending much labor in doing what I do but indifferently, while debarred from doing what I have shown particular capacity for. It is not a pleasant feeling—especially when accompanied with the knowledge that the headstrong folly of my youth started me in a profession, which, to say the least, was not the one for which I have the best endowments.[9]

As the cruise wore on Mahan became increasingly critical of the "absurd profession" in which he was engaged. He complained incessantly to Elly of the tediousness and petty detail ("the random of pettifoggery") of a captain's daily routine, and wished he could concentrate solely on his research and writing. Minor shipboard mishaps robbed him of his "composure for days." His "simple detestation of the Navy" grew apace as his tension, frustration, and fatigue increased. He had difficulty sleeping. He was nervous, irritable, and jumpy. He alternated blaming his shipboard difficulties, real and imagined, on his two executive officers—first on W. W. Gillpatrick, then on Richardson Clover ("a great friend of Ramsay") who came on board as executive in late July 1894—and, in between, on Admiral Erben. His fear and expectation of a complete physical and mental breakdown grew as the cruise lengthened. He regularly confessed his various fears in letters to his wife and daughters:

I have not an [executive officer] who can take my burden off my hands. He is not bright nor quick. You can have no idea, I had none, of the enormous increase in a captain's labors—sometimes I fear breaking down under the uncongenial load, and indeed but for the support God gives me I believe I should go to pieces. It is to me a "vale of misery," and my one hope is that I shall so pass through it as to "go from strength to strength"—that and that only. . . . I am dead with sleep and so tired I can hardly see—harassed and driven almost to death with the conflicting duties of my position. . . . the burden seems to increase daily and I never know what it is to have a mind unpreoccupied. . . . The Station is beginning to weigh upon me as did the Pacific, and earnestly do I solicit your prayers that I may be upheld through the remnant of the cruise. At times I feel as if I must break down ere long. . . . I live as in a dream and an evil dream at that. . . . My one desire is to get home to you and the children, and to my work. I trust God will soon release me from this chastisement—this dead grind. . . . I trust [He] will strengthen me to bear the short remnant and will make it short indeed; at times I feel as if my strength might fail. . . . Pray for me, dearest, that my strength do not fail during the remaining time. I feel sometimes almost done out—mentally and morally, not physically. Pray God to hold me up through the closing days of this tribulation and bring us together for many happy days on earth, if He so will. . . . My great longing now is to get the ship off my hands, or rather off my mind, so painfully do I feel the need of rest. I am too old—too old. Pray for me that my strength fail not. . . . You must all pray for me that I may not break down.[10]

The New Navy was far too complicated for Mahan in an operational sense. It was one thing to extol its virtues and values as an arm of a vigorous American foreign policy and as the fist of American commercial expansion; it was quite another thing to command its steel and steam ships at sea. The Mahan who could cope historically and personally with the Age of Sail and its wooden ships could do neither effectively with the "new naval monsters" of the Age of Steam. So it was that out of his grim two-year experience in the *Chicago* came an irrevocable decision to retire from the Navy, possible promotion to rear admiral notwithstanding.[11]

Much of Mahan's discontent with his life on board the *Chicago* stemmed from his inability to work regularly on his proposed biography of Nelson as well as on several lucrative magazine articles to which he had tentatively committed himself prior to his departure from New York. He felt that he could and should combine his functions as naval historian and commanding officer; he also believed that the U.S. Navy should assist in effecting this marriage of his talents, a union which Herbert had blessed on the eve of Mahan's departure to sea. For this reason, he complained bitterly throughout the voyage that his multitudinous social and professional duties as the *Chicago*'s captain seriously interfered with his progress in research and writing. He complained to Horace Scudder that "in truth, I am so hampered by my work of petty administration that I have little power to do intellectual work." Faced with these interferences, he attempted to recapture the relatively relaxed study arrangements he had enjoyed in the *Wachusett* ten years earlier in Lima. "I long for the obscurity and let-aloneness of the South American ports," he wrote. Failing to achieve this on the ceremonially demanding European Station, he angrily presumed the existence of a Navy Department conspiracy to prevent his doing for the service what he was clearly best suited to do. As he brooded to Elly in October 1893:

I am very hopeless of accomplishing any further literary work until the cruise is over, but will not finally give up until we get to Nice. If I then find I can get no more chance than I do here [Lisbon] I will have to give up—it is useless. The folly of the Department is incredible—but I believe it is more that pedant Ramsay than the Secretary.[12]

His inability to move his Nelson biography along swiftly was particularly galling to him, since Lord Nelson was his hero of heroes; and since his visits to England in August and September 1893 and from August to October 1894 promised a unique opportunity for on-the-scene work in primary sources dealing with the admiral's life and times. He felt, too, that his Nelson book was likely to earn substantial royalty income. In fact, no sooner had he reached England in August 1893 than he discovered "people already interested" in the project and a reporter from the *London Chronicle* waiting to interview him on it. Also, Little, Brown and Company assured him in December 1893 that the "interest in Nelson is even greater than appears," and noted that the book would surely be a "pecuniary success" because of "the reputation I have acquired in England." The firm urged him to submit a completed manuscript by summer 1894. This he could not promise unless the company could somehow "send me a few months composed of days thirty hours long, and insure me seven hours sleep and four hours of my old inspiration daily." At times he was hopeful that the projected biography would be worth "prospective thousands of dollars," and that over the long run it would earn much more money than a series of magazine articles. But in more realistic moods he estimated that his *Nelson* would probably sell no more than 2,000 copies, on which the royalty would be 75¢ per copy.[13]

In any event, he fretted continually over his inability to execute the Nelson manuscript with dispatch and without interruption. This was because he wrote best during the morning hours—or during those very hours when he invariably had to play nursemaid to the *Chicago*. "All my previous work—*Sea Power*, etc.—has always been composed before 1 P.M.," he explained to his publishers, "and that is precisely the time which I now have to give to the infinitesimal details of the ship." Finally, however, in November 1893, while the ship was in Barcelona and Genoa, he worked out a daily writing schedule which in its precision was not unlike the prayer and meditation schedule he drew up while he was serving in the *Iroquois*. It was not an ideal arrangement for him because he was still forced to deal with the nagging problems of his command; but it promised to advance the book substantially. He explained his new system to his daughter Helen:

> I have latterly adopted a plan for my day's work to insure, if possible, doing some daily writing on Nelson. The time up to 2 p.m. I give to

the ship's work of all kinds. At 2, about, I go ashore, walk, etc. until 4:30, and when I return I lie down, giving orders not to be disturbed before 6:30, my dinner hour. I try thus for sleep as well as rest so as to be fresh as may be for an evening's work, which I try to make from 8 to 11. It is by no means the equivalent for my morning hours at home. Do what I may, my mind is jaded, and I not only fall short in quantity but am tormented with doubts as to the quality of what I do. . . . I have not that power of mustering my phrases which has before conduced much to my success.[14]

In spite of his feeling of inadequacy in the matter, the Nelson manuscript proceeded well enough. As early as September 1893 he had drafted a general outline of the book. Three weeks later he had written a "few pages on Nelson . . . wrung out of the sweat of my brow." His portrait of the admiral gradually took shape in a "correct and harmonious" way during the fall. By early December he had advanced the story to 1789 ("the part with which I was least familiar"); and by mid-January 1894 he had written "something over 160 of my usual manuscript pages, but it is very slow work." A month later the work ground to a halt when he realized that the pressure of shipboard duties would allow no further progress until he could return to New York and go on leave. This decision, as will be seen, stemmed mainly from the crisis surrounding his personal clash with Admiral Erben, a confrontation which clearly warned him that "under the circumstances I must be doubly watchful over my ship duties." He therefore sent what he had written of the "precious manuscript" home to Elly for typing—by the hand of Lieutenant Chauncey Thomas, of the USS *Bennington*, who was returning to the States in February for reassignment. His determination to stop working half-time on Nelson in favor of working full-time on the *Chicago* was done "bitterly against my will," especially since he was certain, as he told daughter Helen, that his biography of Nelson would be "the *great* work of my own life—if given by God the time and opportunity. It is a very great subject, and very hard it is for me to bear the enforced abstinence from working steadily at it. But that, too, is as God wills—so we will not complain."[15]

The interruption of work on the Nelson manuscript was also in part related to Mahan's growing financial worries and to his feeling that he had to crank out articles for the popular magazines at fees from $100 to $150 each. This additional income, along with royalties from his two *Influence* books ($870 during the first half of 1893), represented the difference between economic comfort and difficulty for the Mahan family. Mahan's chief concern in this regard was Elly, an estimable lady who had little understanding of income and outgo. Mahan was forced patiently to explain to her the simplest financial transactions involving the family budget. In addition to this, she often spent money as though there were no tomorrow. Her standard of living, her personal tastes, and her social and cultural aspirations for her children were invariably more expensive than her husband's income could be expected to sustain. She insisted, for instance, on employing two servants for the apartment on East 54th Street.

Mahan occasionally chided her about her casual attitudes toward income and expenditure but without noticeable effect. When, on one occasion, in December 1893, Little, Brown and Company reported "a satisfactory remittance for Mrs. Mahan on account of the last six months' sale" of the two *Influence* books, Mahan laughed to his wife: "Little do they know Mrs. M., I said, if they think her so easily satisfied in the matter of money —but I trust you will have the grace to seem so. . . . I did not know you would want so much money but my great desire that your mind should be easy is attained. I shall try to help myself out with magazine writing." Mahan finally gave up on the financial education of Elly, accepted her spending habits in fatalistic good humor, even encouraging them on occasion, and admitted that his own personal social expenditures on the European Station were much higher than he had anticipated. It was these unexpected costs that drove him to grind out magazine articles in 1893 and 1894, even at the expense of his Nelson biography, and at the certain risk of incurring Admiral Erben's displeasure with the way he simultaneously performed his shipboard duties.[16]

The first of these articles, the most important conceptually, was his "The Isthmus and Sea Power" which the *Atlantic Monthly* published in October 1893. It was written in anger; indeed, it was purposely designed to embarrass the isolationist Cleveland administration and repay it for having, as he believed, exiled him to the *Chicago* because of his controversial article on the annexation of Hawaii. "If they want to stop my further writing," he boasted to Elly on August 17, "the step has failed, for Isthmus and Sea Power is in type." As for Cleveland personally, Mahan remained convinced that the president was little more than a hack "civil service man," while Josiah Quincy, his hatchetman in the State Department, was "the most dangerous of party men, whose reputation for being a 'gentleman' emboldens him rather than restrains."

The article, for which Scudder paid him $100, certainly could not have pleased the timorous Cleveland people, calling as it did for American control of the isthmus and of any canal built there, as the key to American commercial expansion into the Pacific and onward to the markets of East Asia. Mahan insisted that the 1850 agreement with Great Britain, the "unfortunate" Clayton-Bulwer Treaty, which denied the United States the possibility of a unilaterally constructed, controlled, and fortified canal at the isthmus, would have to be renegotiated to assure America's "primacy of influence and control on the American continent and in American seas." Moreover, Mahan reasoned, America's domination of the isthmus was much more vital to U.S. security and interests than to existing British interests in the region, since a canal solely in American hands was fundamental to the commercial linkage of the East, West, and Gulf coasts of the sprawling nation. It would also lead naturally to U.S. geopolitical pre-eminence in the Caribbean. This benefit, in turn, would require a great American navy and acceptance of the fact that "we also shall be entangled in the affairs of the great family of nations and shall have to accept the attendant burdens. Fortunately, as regards other states, we are an island power, and can find our best precedents in the history of the people [British] to whom the sea has been a nursing mother." To one reader who felt the article had something of an anti-British ring to it, Mahan replied: "I deeply deplore any alienation between the two Anglo-Saxon states, whose interests I think largely mutual; and regret that lack of time prevented my adding a paragraph to that effect. I have, however, said the same in more than one published article." Mahan also regretted Scudder's unwillingness to buy two additional articles on related themes—one specifically on the Clayton-Bulwer Treaty, the other on the strategic and military-naval significance of the Caribbean and the Gulf. These he could have written easily, effortlessly, and profitably in late 1893. Eventually he did write them and sell them, but not to Scudder's *Atlantic Monthly*.[17]

He was pleased, however, that an article on Admiral Earl Howe, which he spun out of his *Influence* books and wrote while he was on the *Chicago's* sick list, was worth $125 to Scudder. He was disappointed when a similar piece on Admiral Lord Exmouth (Pellew) weighed in lighter on the financial scales; but he was delighted when the British *United Service Magazine* was willing to pay him $50 for an article on which he did naught but "crib it almost entire out of my old lectures on Strategy." This easily earned sum "puts me on my feet very nicely," he informed Elly from Genoa in November 1893, "for I can just about manage, fulfilling the entertaining I can scarcely avoid. I live rather better than I care to—not in quantity but in quality."

So popular and widely read were his articles becoming that by mid-1894 he had at least ten requests for topical pieces from various British and American magazine publishers. All were offering him fees in the $150 range. By this time, however, it was impossible for him longer to subordinate his shipboard duties to writing of any kind, and he was forced to decline the offers. "I have now propositions for magazine articles which would bring me in $500," he wrote Elly from Antwerp in late June 1894, "but I can't write a line—and my expenses mount. . . . It is an expensive station." It upset him that "I have now so many requests for articles it is tantalizing to be unable to comply." Nevertheless, the very existence of these attractive propositions, together with at least four solicitations for full-length books, assured him again that his pen was mightier than his sword and that his future in retirement would be economically secure. Indeed, the potential income from his writing gave him "the feeling and hope that I shall be justified in retiring at the end of my forty years—even though I do have to make this unlucky cruise; and that it will be better to do so than to waste more time waiting for promotion."[18]

The last article he was able to write on the European Station was his controversial "Possibilities of an Anglo-American Reunion." The *North American Review*, after asking him to rework his original draft of it, published it in November 1894. It was an essay produced solely for the money involved, for "I greatly need the promised $150. . . . I should never have attempted it but for the need of money." The whole experience was "painful and instructive" for him, given the fact that he had been "tempted by what seemed high pay for the amount turned out." Having written and submitted the article to editor Lloyd S. Bryce in July 1894, Mahan withdrew it in August for fear that it might do neither him nor the U.S. Navy any good. He was apparently concerned lest once again he bring down the wrath of the Cleveland administration on his head—at a time when he was hoping soon to be relieved of his unhappy command and sent home. He explained to Sir George Sydenham Clarke that the piece "might antagonize our people who must be warily converted" to the notion that the United States should broaden its role in international affairs. As was his habit when making important decisions, Mahan first prayed God for guidance and then reluctantly recalled the article. Nevertheless, he still needed the proffered $150. For that reason he assented to "some toning down" of the arguments in the original version and resubmitted it for publication, even though he was certain it would not "please the spirit of this age." Just how much "toning down" he did cannot be known, the original manuscript not having survived. The printed version, however, was certainly an exercise in shrill bellicosity.[19]

"Possibilities of an Anglo-American Reunion" was a reply to a series of three articles—by Andrew Carnegie, George Sydenham Clarke, and Arthur Silva White—published in the *North American Review* in 1893 and 1894 on the general topic of Anglo-American relations and the significance of such relations for future world peace. Carnegie ("Carnegie is nowhere—and vaporous," Mahan snorted) had advocated a formal Anglo-American political union which, he argued, would lead to universal peace and ultimately to worldwide disarmament. Clarke, in rebuttal, had proposed a loose federation of English-speaking peoples based initially on an Anglo-American naval alliance that would, among other things, police the seas in the interests of world peace and do so in such manner as to sustain and protect the property rights of neutral shippers in wartime. Clarke supported, in fine, the traditional American neutralist doctrine that free ships made free goods, and the related concept of the immunity of non-contraband neutral property on the high seas in time of war. White, somewhat more practically, had suggested a formal Anglo-American treaty of alliance as a first step toward world peace. Taken together, the several Clarke-Carnegie-White propositions added up to an idealistic vision of future universal peace (and disarmament) anchored in a bedrock of varying degrees of Anglo-American political, naval, or diplomatic union.

In response, Mahan argued heatedly that while Anglo-American cooperation was and had been in the past useful as a civilizing force among backward peoples, and was otherwise a cultural and racial desideratum, the thought of a formal union or alliance of any kind was premature and entirely unworkable. The American people simply would not accept it. Moreover, the U.S. Navy was still far too weak to participate in a naval alliance with Britain on a basis of equality.

But Mahan reacted most angrily to what he saw as dangerous proposals that would weaken nationality, advance ideas of disarmament, promote socialism, and undermine the military virtues of the civilized nations at the very moment when these states were becoming increasingly belabored by hordes of encircling barbarians. This general overview gave him an opportunity to enunciate again several of his favored themes: the need for a powerful U.S. Navy; the specter of the Yellow Peril; the strategic uselessness of *guerre de course*; and the notion that the will to fight a decisive war at sea should not be compromised by pusillanimous concern for the presumed property rights of neutrals. Continued support for the doctrine of the free ships-free goods, embraced by Americans since 1776, was to Mahan a confession of national weakness. It was favored only by small neutral states, and it would surely be disregarded by the major powers in wars involving national survival—as indeed it was in World War I and World War II. He concluded:

> It would still remain a mistake, plausible but utter, to see in the hoped
> for subsidence of the military spirit in the nations of Europe a pledge
> of surer progress of the world towards universal peace, general material

prosperity, and ease. That alluring, albeit somewhat ignoble, ideal is not to be attained by the representatives of civilization dropping their arms, relaxing the tension of their moral muscle, and, from fighting animals, become fattened cattle fit only for slaughter. . . . We may, if we will, shut our eyes to the vast outside masses of aliens to our civilization, now powerless because we still, with a higher material development, retain the masculine combative virtues. . . . Not in universal harmony, nor in fond dreams of unbroken peace, rest now the best hopes of the world. . . . Rather in the competition of interests, in that reviving sense of nationality, which is the true antidote to what is bad in socialism, in the jealous determination of each people to provide first for its own. . . . in these jarring sounds which betoken that there is no immediate danger of the leading peoples turning their swords into ploughshares are to be heard the assurance that decay has not touched yet the majestic fabric erected by so many centuries of courageous battling.

Whatever else might be said of these gory sentiments, which later historians described as "Social Darwinism," they earned Mahan the handsome sum of $150.[20]

Faced early in 1894 with the shipboard necessity of discontinuing his lucrative contributions to the popular magazines, Mahan could do little other than hope that the royalty income from his two sea-power books (10 per cent of sale price, rising to 15 per cent on all copies over 2,000) and his biography of Farragut would be sufficient to quiet Elly's demands for cash until he could decently retire from the service and take up full-time writing as a second career. His letters to his wife and children in 1893 and 1894 were filled with news, rumors, and anticipations of increased book sales and royalties, especially in England—sales stemming directly from his enthusiastic reception there by the British naval, political, and literary establishments. Each six-month royalty payment from Little, Brown and Company was anxiously awaited. His English publisher, Roy B. Marston, reported in May 1894 that Mahan's lionization in London "has reacted very favorably on the sales." So favorably, Mahan told Elly, that "I trust your cheque from Little and Brown may relieve some of your anxieties."

Needless to say, he shared her anxieties, and throughout the cruise of the *Chicago* his "most distasteful situation" was his "perpetual worry about money." When Little, Brown and Company produced a larger-than-expected royalty check for the first half of 1893 Mahan was overjoyed. "How small the little amounts are and yet how happy they make us. I felt as if I wanted to tell every one the good news." He was delighted, too, in November 1893, when the British had a political "excitement on the question of their naval supremacy" over Germany, a debate which, Mahan hoped, would "help us in our sales" during the Christmas season. In March 1894 he reckoned that 2,000 copies of each of his seapower books had been sold. "The books are booming," he happily wrote his sister Jenny in July. As he further explained this to Elly: "The large sales of the last six months were certainly due—and due only—to the furor over me in England. My exile here led to that." In January 1895 he calculated that the two *Influence* volumes had brought him $5,000 in royalties since 1891, $3,700 of which had been earned "since my reception in England." Little, Brown and Company had fared well, too, even though at times Mahan complained that the firm was "not quite enterprising enough to capture a boom." Still, Mahan "rejoiced to know" that the publisher's "generous venture of 1890 has resulted [as] favorably to you as to myself." Conversely, the Farragut book, which D. Appleton published in 1892, had brought in virtually nothing.[21]

Ironically, at the very moment when Mahan came to feel that income from his writing was all that would stand between living comfortably or living marginally in his retirement years, two deaths in the family went far toward solving his and Elly's financial problems. Ellen Kuhn Evans, Elly's mother, died early in April 1894; and Jane Leigh Okill Swift, Mahan's maternal aunt, died in September 1894. By mid-August Mahan was hoping that his wife would "soon receive some income from your mother's estate, for it is evident that I can earn nothing by my pen during this cruise." The exact amounts of the Evans and Swift bequests are not known. But, just as Mahan's inheritance from his mother in March 1893 permitted the building and furnishing of "Slumberside" in Quogue in 1894, so did the inheritance from Elly's mother pay for a fashionable four-story brownstone town house on West 86th Street in 1895. Also of great potential value to the Mahan family was the so-called "Palisades Property" which fronted on the west bank of the Hudson River across from upper Manhattan, and was located in the township of Tenafly, New Jersey. It had been inherited by Mahan's mother from her mother, Mary Jay Okill, and its market value in 1895 was thought to be in the neighborhood of $100,000. It was left in three equal shares to Mahan and his brothers Fred and Dennis.[22]

None of these windfalls meant that the Alfred Thayer Mahans became suddenly rich; it meant only that they could look forward to escalating their consumption of goods and services to a more conspicuous level, one well above that to which most retired naval captains could aspire. This later included several leisurely family tours of Europe. Nevertheless, Mahan spent the rest of his life turning a fast dollar with a faster pen in his effort to keep abreast of the increasing material wants of his family and to provide adequate inheritances for his unmarried daughters.

It would seem that Mahan's financial problems in 1893 and 1894, his abiding fear of the sea, his cordial hatred of shipboard life and routine, his literary frustrations, and his personal tension with Admiral Erben, would be enough for Poseidon to visit on any sailor, even the renowned Philosopher of Sea Power. But no. During the early months of the cruise the perennial problem of the War College returned to haunt him.

Before departing the Brooklyn Navy Yard in June 1893 in the *Chicago*, Mahan had heard that there was another move afoot in the Navy Department to turn the new War College building over to the apprentice seamen's Training Station, the argument in Washington being that the space in the building was badly under-utilized save during those few weeks in the late summer and early fall when the college was actually in session. He learned, too, correctly it proved, that Secretary Herbert was not disposed to order a class of officers to the college for a session in 1893. Mahan immediately wrote to him, pleading again that the integrity of the institution be maintained, and noting sadly that "through [a] great part of my association with the College it has been a football for sneer and prejudice." He hoped that Herbert would choose to "constitute yourself the champion of its objects." The movement to appropriate the college building to Training Station uses, he told Washington I. Chambers, was nothing more complicated than a crude space-and-power grab on the part of Captain F. M. Bunce, the station's commander. He hoped, however, that Chambers and Charles H. Stockton, the college's new president, could defeat Bunce's scheme simply by employing the proper arguments within the department. He instructed Chambers that

> one of your strongest arguments is that the College has produced, directly, one of the first, if not the first, authority on naval warfare in English, if not in any language. *I* cannot say this, but plenty have said it of me. Unfortunately, my work is made to appear as chiefly of literary excellence, when really its military value is its chief title to reputation. I enclose a circular just sent out from the publisher and if more quotations are wanted they can be found. The work is now being translated into French. It is not pleasant to be egotistic but in fact the programme and my books are the chief cards of the College—the rest is both argument and assertion which may be contested—the others cannot.[23]

On that modest note sounded in June 1893, Mahan and the *Chicago* had put to sea. Other concerns had then intervened and Mahan temporarily "washed his hands" of the college. A false rumor reaching him in London in August 1893 that the War College and the Training Station had indeed been amalgamated failed, for once, to rouse his fighting blood. He was too busy just then being feted by the British aristocracy to give the report much thought. Nevertheless, at that very moment the college was once again being saved—this time by the happy circumstance of Secretary Herbert's belated reading of Mahan's second *Influence* volume. While Ramsay apparently never read the *Influence* books, Herbert finally did.

As Mahan later learned, Herbert made an inspection tour of all Newport's training facilities in early August 1893. On his way up to Narragansett Bay in the USS *Dolphin*, he was persuaded by Lieutenant Benjamin H. Buckingham, the vessel's skipper, to read *The Influence of Sea Power Upon the French Revolution and Empire*. Buckingham's intermediary role in the matter had come at the suggestion of Captain Bowman McCalla who heard it rumored in Washington that Secretary Herbert had made up his mind at last to abolish the college root and branch, and that his inspection trip to Newport in the *Dolphin* was preliminary to the final act of execution. Mahan had heard similar rumors of the college's imminent demise during his first months in the *Chicago*, but he was in no position to do much about it. The quick-thinking McCalla could act and did, his agent in the matter being the compliant and persuasive Buckingham. So it was that after Herbert had finished reading *The Influence of Sea Power Upon the French Revolution and Empire* he decided to continue the Naval War College on a permanent basis. Mahan's books, he informed Captain McCalla, had "repaid all the money hitherto expended on the College."

The news of the Secretary's sudden conversion was eagerly transmitted to Mahan by McCalla, Chadwick, and Stockton. "I have one piece of good news for the end of my letter," Chadwick wrote on August 10. "The War College is safe. The Secretary read your last book (on Sea Power) and that convinced him. He told me sometime since he was opposed to it. He now tells me he has informed Ramsay that he has changed his mind." Mahan was overwhelmed with joy. "I scarcely knew," he told Elly, "till I got this how keenly I had felt the report of the College abolition—the tears came to my eyes of mingled relief and exultation." Further relief came with the news that Mahan's ally in earlier War College struggles, Commander Henry C. Taylor, would be ordered to the institution as its next president. This appointment was made on November 15, 1893.

Mahan now considered his victory over Ramsay complete, especially when Herbert wrote to him on October 4, 1893, "speaking of my books in the highest terms, most flattering." Said Herbert:

> Permit me . . . to tell you of my change of opinion as to the War College. . . . In my opinion, you deserve all the encomiums of the British and American press for this great work . . . by far the ablest history I have ever read of the epoch from 1792 to 1812. . . . You have conferred great honor, not only upon the American Navy, but also upon your country. I have also run over your first volume, and am particularly struck with your citations from history of the comparatively little effect of commerce destroyers in bringing the war to a successful conclusion, and expect to use in my forthcoming report the information you have therein set forth in my arguments for the building of battleships.

Mahan was pleased beyond measure. The Secretary, he noted, "so long the enemy of the College, has turned completely round and utterly routed the rest of the hostile camp at the moment they thought victory secured." Herbert even expressed the thought that Mahan should resume his historical work when he was detached from the *Chicago*. He was insistent, however, that Mahan first "see the cruise out." There would be no early homecoming for the Navy's most prominent literary figure. He would put in his full tour at sea like any other officer afloat. Indeed, Mahan felt that the malicious Ramsay would assign him straight away to another ship, were the *Chicago* to return to New York before his two-year tour was completed. "He looks upon me as one to be disciplined. I represent a movement with which he has no sympathy." Ramsay, he was positive, "will do me all the harm he can."[24]

In this Mahan was correct. His triumph, and that of his colleagues Luce, Stockton, Taylor, McCalla, and Chadwick, over Ramsay was not yet final. Within a few months of Herbert's belated though happy conversion to the faith that was the Naval War College, Mahan learned that the persistent Ramsay was at it again, this time in concert with Captain F. M. Bunce, commandant of the Newport Naval Training Station. In this instance, Ramsay and Bunce carried their campaign of destruction over Herbert's head directly to members of the House Naval Committee. They argued persuasively for the fiscal, administrative, and military efficiency that would result from consolidating the War College, the Torpedo Station, and the Training Station into a unified command that would be known as the U.S. Naval Station, Newport. As senior officer present,

Bunce would become commandant of the new station. To further his career in this regard and to undermine Taylor's independence as president of the college, Bunce circulated the argument in Washington that administrative consolidation would help put an end to the sodomy that was rampant among the apprentice seamen on board the Training Station ship in Newport because they would be moved into quarters ashore and provided greater supervision. Even Mahan admitted that the sodomy argument, however spurious, had produced a great "impression upon officials." In December 1893 he began an immediate counterattack by mail from his cabin on board the *Chicago*. A personal letter to Herbert was the major gun in this salvo.

In mid-January 1894 he learned to his dismay that the House Naval Committee had decided not to recommend a separate appropriation for the War College and that the movement toward consolidation, fueled by economy arguments related to the Panic of 1893 and the subsequent national depression, was well advanced. Mahan responded to this development with another barrage of letters—to Roosevelt, President Cleveland, Luce, Lodge, Taylor, John M. Brown, Congressman Amos J. Cummings of New York, Chairman of the House Naval Committee, Henry Saltonstall, Secretary Herbert, and other men of substance—all designed to ensure an appropriation for the college. He also urged his brother Fred, Elly's brother Hartman, "Gouv" Ogden, various family friends—even Elly herself—to bring *"direct political influence"* upon the members of the Naval Committee. The main justification for the appropriation, he pompously instructed his friends and his family, "must be the value of the College, in support of which I advance my reputation which is now worldwide in naval circles." Indeed, to secure the separate appropriation he was more than willing, he told Brown, to "stake all my reputation as an author and expert upon naval history and naval warfare." His strategy was to bring particular pressure to bear on Representative Cummings and President Cleveland and otherwise to "stir" the matter politically in Washington in such manner as to strengthen Herbert's position on the issue.[25]

Just what effect Mahan's political importunities and those of his friends and kinsmen at home had on the ultimate outcome of the matter cannot be known. What is known is that a specific budget for the college was reported out of the Naval Committee and was eventually written into the Navy Department's budget for 1894-1895. This development appealed to Mahan's "love of victory" more than to any other feeling, because, he confided to Helen, "a navy which has at its disposal the kind of work I have done so well, and can find no better use for me than commanding the *Chicago*, don't deserve much interest at my hands." Two weeks later this mood of sullen detachment had passed. "I am delighted at the turn the College affairs have taken," he informed Elly in early March. "Despite all my past experiences I can even now scarce refrain from hallooing as though it was out of the woods."

Mahan crowed too soon. Ten days later, on March 14, 1894, the other shoe dropped. On that date, a general executive order issued by the Navy Department consolidated the three Newport facilities into the new U.S. Naval Station, Newport. Bunce was made commandant. Thus Ramsay, "the arch enemy," and Bunce had prevailed over a vacillating Herbert and had finally won the game with a strategy Mahan described to Brown as "both secret and indirect." Mahan, wholly wrapped up in his struggle over the fitness report Admiral Erben had made on him, threw up his hands in disgust when he learned of the consolidation order. As he expressed his feelings to his wife in April and May:

> A letter from Stockton telling me of the order of consolidation. I shall give no notice, but in their [Stockton's and Taylor's] place I should, after a decent interval of compliance with the new orders, ask for detachment. Personally, while I cannot but regret the defeat of my policy, I feel some relief that my obligations to the College are now ended. . . .
> I hope Taylor cherishes no hope of my going back to the College. . . . my purpose is fully formed not to accept the presidency under the present conditions. I don't *want* it under the best of terms, have had more than enough of it—but to be an immediate subordinate to Bunce and work under Ramsay's wet blankets and procrastination is certainly a choice to which nothing but dire necessity will reconcile me. . . . I don't wonder the Torpedo people were disgusted—the thing is all wrong and will be worse under Bunce than under most people. My own relations with Bunce were always good, and they were, as you know, particularly nice and very hospitable to me; but he is of the aggravating kind. Besides which I feel as if my reputation now forbade my accepting such subordination in my own line.[26]

Thanks to his enthusiastic reception in England in August 1893, Mahan's reputation was by 1894 so towering that he could view a reassignment to the presidency of the college as beneath his professional station in life. Therefore when Secretary Herbert announced his willingness in February 1894 to return Mahan to the leadership of the institution after the *Chicago* cruise was over, Mahan confided to Elly that he would never work under Ramsay again and that it was his intention instead to "retire the instant the law allows me." He remained confident, however, that a word or two from his mouth or pen would always be enough to ensure a future for the school. Thus, during the fight for War College appropriations, which lasted from November 1893 to March 1894, he advised his friends to rest their cases for the college "largely upon my own now established reputation and my *positive opinion* that no one thing is so essential to the proper advance of the Navy as the maintenance of the College." Similarly, he urged his supporters in Washington to couch their pleas for the institution to President Cleveland as a "*personal* request based upon my assurance of the merits of the College."[27]

The ego of Alfred Thayer Mahan, never small, had grown to astonishing proportions during the first few months of his cruise in the *Chicago*. The very phrase "Sea Power," he told Elly, "generally means me." It was this attitude, among others, that brought on the explosion with Rear Admiral Henry Erben in January 1894.[28]

XI

With Erben in the *Chicago* 1893-1895

Capt. Mahan always appears to advantage in all that does not appertain to ship life or matters, but in this particular he is lacking in interest, as he has frankly admitted to me. His interests are entirely outside the service, for which, I am satisfied, he cares but little, and is therefore not a good naval officer. . . . In fact, Capt. Mahan's interests lie wholly in the direction of literary work and in no other way connected with the service.

Henry Erben to Bureau of Navigation (Francis M. Ramsay),
December 31, 1893

I am prone now to feel that a navy which has at its disposal the kind of work I have done so well, and can find no better use for me than commanding the Chicago, *don't deserve much interest at my hands.*

Alfred Thayer Mahan to Helen Evans Mahan, February 18, 1894

In any analysis of Mahan's conflict with Rear Admiral Henry Erben it should be noted, in fairness to Mahan, that his flattering reception in England in August and September 1893 was enough to turn the head of any mortal, Anglophile or not. The author of the *Influence of Sea Power* books suddenly found himself to be the social and literary favorite of hundreds of prominent Britons who chose to regard him as a new prophet of the Royal Navy and the great empire it stitched together. Further, his visits to England in 1893 and 1894 came at a time when questions of the morality of the British Empire and the cost of the military and naval apparatus that sustained it were being debated in Parliament and throughout the land; and at a moment when the rapid rise of Imperial Germany and the Imperial German Navy seemed to threaten England's preeminent commercial and colonial position in the world and her security in Europe.

In February 1894, Lord Rosebery replaced William E. Gladstone as prime minister partly as the result of these concerns. It was during this political transition that the words and thoughts of Mahan were pressed contentiously into service by British imperialists and big-navy advocates in their clashes with Gladstone and his so-called "Little Englanders." In truth, Mahan was cheered by those Englishmen who wished most to increase the roar of the British lion at sea and overseas. At one dinner, for example, Captain William H. Henderson of HMS *Edgar* proposed a toast to Mahan's health "in a most flattering speech speaking of my books and my distinguished reputation. He told me that the revival of interest in their navy and its fostering and right direction was mainly due to the books which had come out just in the nick of time." In fact, Henderson said, "We owe to them the £3,000,000 just voted for the increase of the navy." Flattery will get one everywhere and Mahan enjoyed each delicious minute of it. "Recognition is pleasant, particularly after the almost entire absence of it at home," he wrote his wife. "Except Roosevelt, I don't think my work gained me an entrée into a single American social circle. . . . if reputation is *any* good it is when rammed home by a certain amount of attention from people in position."[1]

The ramming-home process began on July 31, 1893, with an invitation to dinner at Osborne House with Queen Victoria and her visitor, Kaiser William, and continued through the first week in September, when the *Chicago* departed Southampton for Le Havre, Lisbon, Gibraltar, and the Mediterranean. During this heady period Mahan's views were solicited by the British press on a variety of domestic political issues (he was careful to steer clear of involving himself in these); and quotations from his *Influence* books were inserted into debates in Parliament and otherwise cited on a number of foreign-policy and armaments issues.

At the Osborne House affair Queen Victoria particularly complimented him on his books, as did numerous British generals, admirals, and aristocrats present that evening. This occasion was followed by a dinner in London given by Henry White, Secretary of the American Legation, for the specific purpose of introducing the American captain to important British political and literary figures ("the London monde")—among them Arthur J. Balfour and Herbert H. Asquith. "I can scarcely believe all that White says about my reputation here," Mahan reported excitedly. Dinner followed dinner, as members of the British military, political, social, and literary establishments vied to include the distinguished historian among their guests. Indeed, Mahan's letters home in August 1893 were virtually listings of the names of prominent Britons he had met on the dinner circuit, among them John Morley, George Trevelyan, James Bryce, John K. Laughton, Lord Spencer (reigning First Lord of the Admiralty), and former First Lords, the Marquis of Ripon, Earl Northbrook, and Lord George Hamilton. All who met him spoke highly of his *Influence* volumes. "As for naval and military men there is but one voice" of praise, Mahan noted. By mid-August the celebrated captain of the *Chicago* could report to his wife that he was "tiring a little of the racket—a quiet hour over a book suits me much better."

To be sure, Mahan found himself giving his stomach for his country. But for this sacrifice he was compensated by "a great many kind speeches about the books," and by the knowledge that his social exposure aided the sale of his histories and led to invitations to market his literary wares in various English journals. As he told Sam Ashe when the *Chicago* reached Genoa in November 1893: "It is a singular fact, due probably to the broader maritime interests of Great Britain, that I have achieved much greater standing there than at home—wherever I go I am complimented on my work by their people, while at home few know it." That observation, ironically, was all too true. It is likely that the aging Queen Victoria knew more about Mahan's histories, and knew about them earlier, than did either Secretary of the Navy Hilary Herbert or President Grover Cleveland. Certainly her admirals, generals, ministers, and historians did.[2]

More to the point, the adulation Mahan received in England during the visit of the *Chicago* there in August 1893 encouraged him to view the U.S. Navy and his superiors therein with increasing scorn, condescension, and detachment. He came even to accept the simplistic view that his difficulties with Ramsay and Bunce over consolidation of the War College and its funding could be traced to the fact that they "were almost insane in their vexation over my reception and reputation abroad." As his ego inflated, he retreated further into himself insofar as his own shipmates were concerned. He had no friends in the *Chicago* (with the possible exception of his brother Dennis' friend, the aging and much-passed-over navigator, Lieutenant Arthur P. Nazro), sought to make none, and generally held himself aloof from the other officers. His shipboard reputation was that of a testy, humorless man who lived almost entirely in a private world of historical sources and large ideas. He conveyed to his shipmates little confidence that he was a skilled seaman or that he was comfortable in handling the complicated piece of machinery that was the USS *Chicago* —as indeed he was not. But most importantly, his personal relations with

Henry Erben deteriorated in almost direct ratio to the rise of his star above the English social and literary horizon in the fall of 1893. His own sense of intellectual superiority, together with Erben's ill-disguised contempt for his daily supervision of the ship, placed the two men on a collision course.[3]

No sooner had the *Chicago* reached England and the round of dinners and receptions for Mahan begun than the captain of the *Chicago* decided that the rear admiral commanding the European Station was a crude and tasteless clown given "to stamp and to snort, to blow and to rage with many expletives"—even over such questions as what was the proper dress for dinner engagements. No, it would not be proper, Mahan patronizingly instructed him on one occasion, for the admiral to wear his blue serge coat, brown checked trousers, and brown pot hat to dinner at London's fashionable Marlborough Club. As Mahan saw him, Erben had little to do but putter around the *Chicago* and otherwise visit about on "this ridiculous station." He was, at best, "a kind of supernumerary captain" with no occupation save to "fret himself about trifles and talk shop" to the extent that "I find it almost impossible to accomplish my writing." Unfortunately, Erben left no personal record of his opinion of Mahan during their awkward service together in the *Chicago* save to refer to him on one occasion as a "pen and ink sailor." Much of the time he was insensitive to the fact that social invitations extended jointly to Mahan and himself were designed more to capture Mahan the author than Erben the admiral. Mahan thought he was downright dense in this regard.[4]

By the time the *Chicago* showed the flag at Barcelona in late October and early November of 1893, Mahan had entered upon his daily writing schedule (neatly subordinating some of his shipboard duties to it) and was busily engaged in work on his Nelson manuscript. At that moment, however, Erben chose to hold Admiral's Inspection of his flagship. What he saw of Mahan's command he did not like. And what he did not like showed up in his official semi-annual fitness report on Mahan dated December 31, 1893. That report rated his

Professional ability	Tolerable
Attention to duty	Tolerable
General conduct	Excellent
Sobriety	Excellent
Health	Good
Efficiency of men under his special control	Tolerable, except in the matter of divisional exercises where her condition is good.

He then concluded with a devastating explanation:

> Regarding my answer "Tolerable" to question No. 1—I state herewith
> that Capt. Mahan always appears to advantage to the service in all that
> does not appertain to ship life or matters, but in this particular he is
> lacking in interest, as he has frankly admitted to me. His interests are
> entirely outside the service, for which, I am satisfied, he cares but little,
> and is therefore not a good naval officer. He is not at all observant re-
> garding officers tending to the ship's general welfare or appearance, nor
> does he inspire or suggest anything in this connection. In fact, the first
> few weeks of the cruise she was positively discreditable. In fact, Capt.
> Mahan's interests lie wholly in the direction of literary work and in no
> other way connected with the service.[5]

It would certainly have been more courteous of Erben had he personally informed Mahan of his negative reaction to the condition of the
Chicago in October when he made his inspection. Instead, the admiral
gave his captain no indication of what was coming; and Mahan consequently knew nothing about it until January 22, 1894, when the ship
reached Villefranche (Nice). It thus hit him "with all the shock of a
surprise." One of the things that pained him was the fact that Erben's
concluding comment about his "tolerable" professional ability contained
more truth than venom. For, as Mahan clearly revealed in his letters
to his family and friends, he was much more interested in reading sonnets
and writing history than in the daily routine of the ship, and he neglected
the latter to embrace the former whenever conveniently he could. It was
to this proclivity that Erben principally objected.

One irony of his confrontation with Erben was that Mahan himself
was loath to give "excellent" ratings to officers for whom he wrote fitness
reports. On one occasion, in late January 1894, he bluntly informed four
young replacement officers who had just joined the *Chicago*, all "very
good men," that it was his fixed opinion that not one officer in a hundred
rated an "excellent" designation on his fitness report, and that none of the
four should expect to receive such a mark while serving under him. Indeed, the only officer in the *Chicago* who got an "excellent" rating from
Captain Mahan during the two-year cruise was Lieutenant Nazro.[6]

Mahan spent three full days drafting and polishing his official response
to Erben's critique. To assist him in this difficult endeavor, he pressed
into service Lieutenants Nazro and Thomas S. Rodgers. Both men assured their angry captain that Erben's report was unfair and "substantially
unfounded," and that the first draft of his rejoinder was both "admirable
and dignified." Perhaps the thing that outraged Mahan most as he com-

Admiral Henry Erben

posed his official explanation to Secretary Herbert (dated January 25) was the fact that the criticism had come from a man "only six years my senior and of no *particular* reputation," a man who was also "petulant, unreasonable and impulsive—thinks one thing one day and another the next." He was fearful, too, that Ramsay would use the adverse fitness report to detach him in disgrace from the *Chicago* before a proper investigation of Erben's charges could be made. "As an injury to my reputation will injure the College he will do anything he can for that," Mahan felt. On the other hand, he had faith, he told Elly, that "God will bear me clear—for I have kept my work before Him. . . . This having been really forced upon me, wholly unawares, I feel that the quarrel is none of my beginning and that I may have good hope that it is sent from above, and that I will be seen through it as shall be best for us."

His private rationalizations of these difficulties included shifting the blame to others. He told his wife that "the faults Erben found" should have been corrected earlier by Lieutenant Commander Gillpatrick, his executive officer. Gillpatrick, he charged, was "dull and slow," and as a result of his inefficiency "much was neglected" in the ship. Further, "officers of *all* services agree that the captain cannot bring his ship up to the mark with an ineffective executive." Therefore, it was mostly Gillpatrick's fault. Mahan began thus to work himself into the untenable position of complaining privately that Gillpatrick was responsible for what was wrong with the vessel, while assuring Secretary Herbert officially that all was well in the *Chicago* save Erben's unreasonable hatred of her brilliant captain.[7]

The general thrust of Mahan's formal defense of his command of the *Chicago* was that he was far too important to the Navy to have his career damaged by the inaccurate statements of a fool like Henry Erben. In fact, Mahan argued that he *was* the Navy:

> And I add [he told Herbert], with a certain proud humility, that my reputation is now so identified with that of the United States Navy, not as a mere literary man, but as one whose military opinions are quoted with respect throughout the world, that an undeserved stigma upon me will more or less hurt the service too. . . . the Department will, I am sure, feel that the statement that I am not a good naval officer can not be allowed to stand upon the say-so of any one man, merely because his rank is senior to my own. It must be substantiated from other sources. At a time when distinguished officers of other navies are saying that my treatment of naval warfare is better than anything ever yet done, to have [it] said that I am not a good naval officer gives an odd impression.

Specifically, Mahan maintained that the *Chicago* was in an excellent state of efficiency, order, and cleanliness. He demanded that his three division officers—Lieutenants James C. Cresap, Theodore G. Dewey, and T. S. Rodgers—be queried to that effect "upon [their] honor, as to my efficiency and attention as Captain of the *Chicago* and generally as a naval officer." He reminded the department that he had brought the *Wachusett* home from South America in 1885 in excellent shape, that "her efficiency was found exceptionally high," and that her decommissioning report had been "very complimentary" to him. Citing chapter and verse, he also criticized Erben for his laxness in enforcing the decisions of summary courts-martial affecting discipline on board the ship and asked the department "to form its own opinion as to the comparative disciplinary tendencies of Admiral Erben and myself." Finally, still on the offensive, he demanded "a general inquiry into the condition and efficiency of the *Chicago*, and my conduct and action as her captain."[8]

This was all well and good and persuasive. Nevertheless, the burden of Erben's criticism centered on the charge that Captain Mahan's primary interest was writing and his secondary interest was the daily operation of the vessel. This was a fact, said Erben, "he has frankly admitted to me." On this telling point, which Lodge later told him "has been made a handle for the whole business," Mahan waffled. He thought it "hardly fair" for Erben "to press a casual remark whose precise words I can not now recall, to the implication that I take no interest in my duties." He assured Herbert, who had earlier hoped that Mahan would be able to "devote a considerable time to his literary work" while on board the *Chicago*, that he never touched his pen to paper until the ship's work for the day was ended. He also informed the Secretary that there had been fewer than a dozen days during the cruise in which he had used the morning hours for his writing. "The consequence," he reported, not with complete candor, "has been that the work actually achieved is very little." Happily, he had achieved quite a bit. The writing accomplished by mid-January 1894 added up to 160 draft pages of his biography of Lord Nelson and several magazine articles. In fact, he had drawn Elly's attention to his excellent progress in this regard, even in the face of social distractions and nagging shipboard duties, as recently as a month before he learned of the admiral's hostile fitness report. Moreover, at the very moment that news reached him he had on his desk a "letter ready for mailing to Herbert, suggesting the waste of keeping me here." This embarrassing missive be pigeonholed. The clear fact of the matter was that Mahan had done a considerable amount of "literary work" during his first six months in the *Chicago*. His principal complaint to his family was that he had been unable to do more.[9]

Nevertheless, he was still faced with the necessity of parrying Erben's charges, and he was sophisticated enough in his approach to the problem to rely wholly neither on the Creator nor on his letter of January 25 to Herbert to accomplish that end. Instead, he did precisely what he had done in the fight over the War College budget two months earlier—he fired off a salvo of letters to members of his family and to his friends in New York and Washington, civilian and naval, enlisting their aid. Chief among these friends was Theodore Roosevelt whose job it would be to make certain that Herbert did not send either Ramsay or Bunce personally to conduct the shipboard inquiry Mahan had requested. It was Roosevelt to whom Mahan looked to coordinate his fight, leaving it up to him to decide whether his demand for a formal investigation should actually be pursued. Others who eventually became involved in Mahan's cause were Elly's cousin David B. Ogden, a New York lawyer who had access to Roosevelt, Captains W. T. Sampson and Henry C. Taylor, Rear Admirals S. B. Luce, C. H. Davis, and Robley D. Evans, former Secretary Tracy, and Senator Henry Cabot Lodge. Mahan felt that it would not be wise to include too many admirals in his defense group (J. G. Walker and Bancroft Gherardi were excluded), since "admirals would naturally side against an appeal against one of their number, even though the natural right of the accused was clear." Similarly, his old colleague and associate, J. R. Soley, was not to be approached, Mahan feeling that the former Assistant Secretary had drifted too close to the Ramsay clique in the department. To strengthen and document his case at home, if that became necessary, Mahan sent Elly several tributes to his genius as a naval theorist written by prominent foreign naval officers, adding the instruction: "Preserve enclosed carefully. They may become useful." Meanwhile, Erben insisted that Mahan be on board every day while the ship was in Villefranche.[10]

As the unfortunate affair progressed, Roosevelt, Lodge, and Davis took counsel on the matter. They decided that it was "a kind of conspiracy," but concluded that Mahan would be unwise to push his request for a formal investigation and risk thereby "its attendant newspaper scandal." Lodge saw Herbert privately on February 10, 1894, and the Secretary agreed with his view that Erben's charges were not substantial enough to warrant an official investigation. They agreed that nothing more should be done save hold a regular inspection of the *Chicago* when she came home. Further airing of the issue, they felt, could only harm the Navy.

This decision, T.R. told Elly, was "a practical victory for Captain Mahan." The "whole trouble arises from jealousy of Mahan," Roosevelt explained to Dave Ogden. On the afternoon of his conversation with Herbert, Lodge wrote Mahan, telling him that while he was personally indignant over Erben's action, both the captain and the Navy would be better served by a quiet interment of the conflict. He assured Mahan that the Secretary fully supported him (Herbert had instructed Lodge to convey that sentiment), and promised that Herbert would write Mahan privately to this effect later. Lodge suggested, too, that Ramsay was highly displeased with the Secretary's low-key handling of the affair. This was just the right approach to the egocentric Mahan, since Ramsay's presumed displeasure with the arrangement persuaded the captain to believe that he had achieved a great victory over his ancient enemy. It was, however, a costly triumph. In accepting Lodge's deft solution to the problem Mahan denied himself the full vindication that might have been his had a formal investigation of Erben's charges been held. The critical fitness report remained forever on his official record.

In thanking Lodge and Roosevelt for their handling of the difficulty, Mahan endorsed their argument that if the squabble reached the newspapers "unpleasant things are bound to be said." He was certain that "the natural envy of men will prompt many to make reflections upon me from the very fact of my reputation—to do what they can to drag me down." Actually, the issue was aired, generally to Erben's advantage, in the *Army and Navy Register* of April 2, 1894, and in several American newspapers. This unwanted publicity so outraged Mahan that once again he threatened to demand a formal investigation. But he soon simmered down again and his friends were finally able to defuze the crisis.

Mahan was wise in his decision to accept the Lodge-Roosevelt strategy of avoiding an investigation, lest a public explosion divide members of the officer corps "according as they like or hate the College." And while he did not necessarily consider himself the victim of a conscious Erben-Ramsay-Bunce intrigue—"I find it hard to believe in such things"—he took to heart Lodge's stern warning to bring the *Chicago* home in the highest possible state of efficiency. The warning was unnecessary. Mahan had already decided to abandon his writing and spend less time on social activities ashore, "feeling it necessary now not only that things should go well, but that I must get appearances on my side."

Erben, on the other hand, was left dangling from his own yardarm. Not until June 15, 1894, following a letter of inquiry he wrote to the department on May 13 about the status of Mahan's request for an investigation, did he learn of the decision Herbert had made on February 10. The Secretary told Erben bluntly on June 15 that there would be no investigation and that no further note would be taken of the fitness report. His tone was barely polite. Conversely, he informed Mahan on June 25 that "our whole country is proud of your reception in England. As you know . . . [from] what I thought of your books you can understand that I am not at all surprised though I am personally much gratified." In the face of such solid support for Mahan in Washington, Erben could only grumble to Herbert that he would very much have welcomed the investigation sought by the captain back in January. "Then I could have, and can now, more fully explain what I mean by the statements to which Captain Mahan objects, and could have proved that neither the service, nor the ship, nor the ship's company, have his first consideration."[11]

While Mahan won his war with Erben in Washington, his battle with the admiral continued on board the *Chicago*. From January 1894 to the time of Erben's routine replacement as commander of the station the following September, personal relations between the two men were bitter. All official shipboard business between them was conducted in writing. To be sure, Mahan's scholarly work had come to an end, since he wished to give Erben no cause for further complaint on that score. "I am doing nothing and see no hope of doing anything literary," he told daughter Helen in mid-March. "I don't suppose the Secretary wished to paralyze my activity, but he has done so effectively; as for Ramsay, his right hand man, I have little doubt that he considers that result positively a happy one." His job as ship's captain thus became even a greater "strain, work uncongenial, petty details always distasteful to me, and my liked work stopped." But the tension did not prevent him from bombarding Erben with critical observations on his handling of ship matters. Erben responded in kind. "If you are dissatisfied," the admiral finally exploded after several weeks of mutual harassment, "you have only to apply and I will send you home by the next steamer." This caused Mahan immediately to write the Navy Department and charge that the remark "shows an absolute unfitness to exercise the authority of commander-in-chief, for there was for it no adequate provocation, merely the uncontrolled temper and tongue of the person using it." He also made, for his personal files, careful memoranda of Erben's supposed failures as station commander, down to and including a notation of the fact that the admiral appeared on deck on Sunday, February 25, "without a cravat at all—and blouse one button (the 2d) only, buttoned. I make this note, not to attack him, but to defend myself if attacked, as, e.g. he has criticized much smaller matters of men's uniforms. This is not the first time." So it was that pettiness and childishness came to govern Mahan's relations with Erben during the months following the adverse fitness report. "My own belief," Mahan informed Elly, "is that he has gradually imbibed an extreme dislike to me, because I am very different from himself, and I cannot but think he feels the contempt with which I regard his ebullitions of temper. He is petulant, uncontrolled, boorish when annoyed, stamps and swears. I look on with a silent disapproval which I fancy he feels. . . . he acts like a baby of two years."

Erben did feel Mahan's contempt. Consequently, on July 1, 1894, he calmly submitted to the department another critical fitness report on Mahan. In this document he agreed that the condition and efficiency of the ship had improved since January 1, but he attributed much of the improvement to Richardson Clover, Mahan's new executive officer. Mahan protested this second attack to Herbert in late August, pointing out that he was really an excellent ship's officer, that the *Chicago* was in tip-top condition because of his excellence, and that there was no way he could now expect to receive a fair evaluation of his command from a man like Henry Erben. "I feel," he concluded, "that the perspicacity of the Department scarcely needs to be informed that the test of my work is the result, and not my liking for the work." Again the department supported Mahan. Erben's request for a hearing to explain more fully his charges against his captain was flatly denied.[12]

Mahan worked out his continuing anti-Erben hatreds and frustrations in his letters to his wife and children. Few of these flowed from the *Chicago* to 75 East 54th Street in 1894 that did not contain some biting observation on Erben's character, manners, professional behavior, or anti-intellectualism. He especially enjoyed pointing out that Erben was riding entirely on his, Mahan's, social coattails, particularly after the *Chicago* returned to England in May 1894, and he indulged in "many a sly snigger" over the admiral's insensitivity to the true social and intellectual pecking order that, in British eyes, prevailed on board the *Chicago*.[13]

The Times of London certainly understood the relative merits and importance of the two men. In an editorial on May 11, 1894, the paper noted that "the arrival of the *Chicago* bearing the flag of Rear Admiral Erben affords a fitting opportunity of paying a friendly compliment to the United States Navy, and doing honour to the greatest living writer on naval history." Mahan immediately clipped the piece and sent it to Elly with instructions to try to get it reprinted in a New York newspaper. "I hate such self-pushing," he remarked disingenuously, "and nothing but the desirability of showing the strength of my value, as a military thinker, in the face of Erben's report would lead me to it. In short, it is defence not glory I aim at."

On the other hand, Erben's anomalous position on the fringe of Mahan's literary incandescence was a difficult one for him. As the British prime minister, Lord Rosebery, put it to Mahan: "I like the way your admiral bears himself, for the position is difficult—for after all he is much in that of a chaperon to a débutante." Indeed, during the second visit of the *Chicago* to England in mid-1894 Erben deported himself admirably, carefully concealing in public his intense dislike of his socially and intellectually prominent captain. Even Mahan finally admitted that "I must say he shows no bad feeling whatever." By mid-July 1894 Mahan was also willing to call a tentative public truce. "Please also don't read or trouble about any publications concerning my affair with Erben," he instructed Elly. "Don't hunt them up. The public will have little interest in the matter unless indiscreet friends of mine warm it up. I hope Luce won't be a firebrand." But in spite of his willingness to wind down the public dimensions of the struggle (Roosevelt and Lodge advised him to do precisely that), Mahan's private little war with Erben continued virtually unabated until the admiral departed the ship on September 6, 1894. Several newspapers were aware of the tension that rode the *Chicago*.[14]

When Mahan returned to England in May 1894 for his second round of honors and eulogies, the ship had completed an eight-month swing around the station that had taken her to Barcelona, Marseilles, Genoa, Naples, Smyrna, Beirut, Alexandria, Malta, Algiers, and Lisbon. December and January were spent pleasantly in Villefranche. The voyage was filled with much formal and informal visiting, dressing of ship, mutual saluting, dining, dancing, flag-dipping, and other ceremonial chores associated with peacetime naval operations on a foreign station. Such polite activity killed young Apprentice Seaman C. F. Hill who fell to his death on the steel deck of the *Chicago* while manning yards in honor of the Prince of Wales.

Much of this activity bored and vexed Mahan because he was never certain whether the *Chicago* would be able to proceed from one pleasant Mediterranean port to another. Her boilers remained in poor condition, so bad in fact that they became the subject of critical newspaper comment at home. Fortunately, they never exploded—as had those of the *Worcester* when Mahan served in her in 1871—but they were never quite trustworthy either. Mahan's patience with modern ships' engines and the men below who tended them was sorely tried throughout the cruise. In addition to the patent combat unreadiness of a war vessel with a crippled propulsion system, there were the usual nagging problems of disease, desertion, drunkenness, and shore-leave misbehavior among the members of a polyglot, mostly illiterate, crew, more than half of whom were foreign-born. The discovery that Mahan's own mess attendant had syphilis brought no cheer to the harassed captain. Ship's courts-martial were frequent events.[15]

So it was that Mahan was pleased to conn the limping flagship of the single-ship European Squadron back to England in May 1894 where he could drink again the heady champagne that was British adulation. During his voyage in the Mediterranean the London *Times* had solemnly pronounced him to be the new Copernicus—in the sense that the American had done for naval history what the Pole had done for astronomy. The stage was thus set for another grand inflation of Mahan's considerable ego. British newspapers carried detailed stories of his arrival at Gravesend, made mention again of his books on sea power, printed more tributes to his perspicacity as a naval theorist, and saw in his visit a contribution to the peace of the world based on "a re-welding of the bonds of brotherhood between two great sections of the Anglo-Saxon race." Five of the best London clubs extended him their courtesies and facilities, while various English military and naval groups announced plans to wine and dine the famous American naval historian. Private invitations to dinner ("You will I hope be pleased to hear," he told Elly, "that I declined dinner invitations from two countesses in twenty four hours") and to weekends at various country estates piled up. It was at this juncture, excellent timing for him, really, that Poultney Bigelow, foreign correspondent of the *New York Herald*, made public the telegram he had received from the kaiser in which William II announced that he was "devouring" Mahan's books. The *Philadelphia Inquirer* proudly wrote that it was "doubtful whether any American has ever received higher honors in England than have been accorded to Captain Mahan of the United States Navy. . . . unusual honors paid to a subordinate in the presence of and to the ignoring of his ranking officer."[16]

Mahan set the professional tone of his visit to Britain in 1894 in a lengthy interview given a reporter of the *Pall Mall Gazette* on May 9, the very day the *Chicago* arrived in the Thames. In this exchange he announced that because of the steady growth of British commerce since 1800, "it is more important to Great Britain now that she should hold the command of the seas than it has been at any period of her history." He obliquely endorsed Britain's massive naval building program, designed to make the Royal Navy equal to the world's next two largest naval powers combined (the so-called "two-power naval standard"), and stated flatly that the future of naval warfare lay "decidedly with the battleship" rather than with smaller ship types. He added, carefully writing out his exact words for the reporter on the backs of two envelopes:

> Military superiority in warfare depends upon heavy blows struck at the enemy's organized fighting force. Such blows must be struck by massed forces, the units of which should be individually powerful for offence and defence, because so only can they be brought under the unity of command essential to success. The same aggregate of force in two or three different vessels will rarely be equal to that concentrated in one, because of the difficulty of ensuring mutual support. This means heavy vessels, or battleships. Of course, like all other statements, this needs limitation. . . . you need to scatter at times as well as concentrate. This involves the necessity of dividing your force into several vessels, because a ship once built cannot be divided. Between the two horns of the dilemma you must strike a mean; but always a battleship. . . . I don't mean to say that we will do without cruisers and torpedo-boats, not at all. But battleships are to a navy what infantry is to an army; the cruisers and other small vessels are the auxiliary services.

The thrust of the *Pall Mall* interview was promptly picked up by British protagonists of naval power and hurled at their opponents. "A weak Navy spells destruction for British commerce," wrote the editor of one newspaper on May 9; "we would like to have that plain truism driven home to the minds of every 'Little Englander' who is inclined to cry out against necessary Naval expenditure."[17]

It was against this background of his renewed exposure in the press that Mahan's British publishers, Messrs. Sampson Low, Marston and Co., honored the captain at a small dinner at the Langham Hotel on May 21. Roy B. Marston conducted the affair in the absence of his father, Mr. Edward Marston, senior officer of the firm. The guest list included gentlemen connected with the publishing business in London. The evening brought Mahan news that sales of his *Influence* books were brisk and afforded him an opportunity to plan future marketing strategy with Marston. At the same time, the nine other diners were promised from Mahan's pen a life of Nelson and a third and concluding volume in the *Influence* series that would incorporate the War of 1812. They heard Mahan say of that conflict that "though the Americans did splendidly, England was tired of fighting with Napoleon and was glad to get rid of the war on honorable terms." That satisfied all hands.[18]

Three days later, on Queen Victoria's birthday, May 24, a large public banquet for 300 guests, arranged by the Royal United Service Institution, was given for Erben, Mahan ("the central figure of the banquet"), and the officers of the *Chicago*. Held at St. James's Hall, it was a gala affair. Admiral Sir Nowell Salmon, who escorted Mahan to the dinner, told him that "we would have liked to make the occasion more special to you and your books, but it was impossible to overlook your Admiral." That pleased Mahan, as did the remark in the *London Spectator* that "owing to the enthusiasm for Captain Mahan's writing . . . the banquet assumed the proportions of a national demonstration." It certainly received wide coverage in the British press, all very complimentary to both Erben and Mahan, coverage that was picked up and repeated proudly in the American press.

Given the fact that the American minister, Thomas F. Bayard, shared the head table at St. James's Hall with Mahan, Erben, Lord George Hamilton, General F. S. Roberts, Lord Thomas Brassey, Admiral of the Fleet G. P. Hornby, and other high-ranking British officials, it was appropriate that the theme of the dinner was the motto "BLOOD IS THICKER THAN WATER." This sentiment was emblazoned on a large streamer hanging in the room. It was a remark made by Commander Josiah Tattnall, USN, in 1859 when he instinctively brought his ship into action in support of the Royal Navy at a difficult moment during a British attack on the Taku forts that guarded the approaches to Peking. The story of Tattnall's heroism was recounted in detail by Admiral Hornby, and it produced "great cheering for the United States Navy and the band played 'America.'" In St. James's Hall that evening Tattnall's phrase underscored the sense of Anglo-Saxon friendship that was so strongly reflected in the remarks of the participants.[19]

Erben had not wanted to attend the banquet. He was suffering a bad attack of eczema, was on heavy medication for the disorder, and would clearly be the bridesmaid at the function rather than the bride. When urged by the ship's surgeon to remain on board, he protested that he had to attend. "Mahan is going to give them a talk that will go clear over their heads. They won't know what its all about until they read it tomorrow. I've got to go and liven things up a bit." In this instance at least, "Bully" Erben's instincts were correct. Mahan read a turgid speech from a prepared manuscript which argued that in the continued strength of the Royal Navy lay one of the best hopes for the peace of the world. Similarly, he maintained that the European arms race did not threaten war. "I am not one of those who think that in the great armaments of Europe at the present time there is a threat of war; on the contrary, I think we find that they are a great maker of peace. In them, and in the expense of maintaining them, we find the alternative to those bloody and desolating wars of the last century, when each nation was ready to pitch in because it thought the other was unprepared." The speech, wrote the reporter from the *Pall Mall Gazette* gently, was delivered "in a manner that was prejudicial to enthusiasm."

Erben, on the other hand, displaying what *The Times* noted was "the genial humour of a thorough sailor," delivered a short, lively talk that evoked much laughter and good feeling among the guests. Unlike Mahan, he had served with Tattnall at the Taku Forts in China. He had fought alongside the British there. In his own experience, blood *was* thicker than water. But the high-flown speeches that evening bothered him, he said in closing, because "nobody has said a word on behalf of Jack, the man behind the gun." The remark produced loud cheers and caused *Punch* to compose a bit of doggerel titled "The Man Behind the Gun," one verse of which read:

> Captain Mahan is just the man
> To prove that Erben's right.
> Iron or oak, ships are "no joke,"
> But "flesh and blood" must fight.
> Your "hundred tonner" is a stunner,
> Yet fights will still be won,
> If won they are, by stout Jack Tar,
> "The Man Behind the Gun!"

In spite of "jolly sea dog" Erben's pointed and humorous upstaging of his scholarly captain, the entire affair was a great tribute to the U.S. Navy and to Mahan, whose work was "so overwhelmingly praised." As Mahan told his wife: "Think of Lord Roberts, one of the two first British Generals, saying in his speech last night that he wished I could be induced to do for the [British] army what I had for the navy. My darling, it is all for you all—I wish father and mother could have heard it."[20]

So lavish was the British press in praise of him and his historical works that he subscribed to Durrant's Press Cuttings service ("Contracts at Reduced Rates for 3, 6, or 12 months") and began to collect and send home the printed evidences of his triumph. As the clippings rolled in and were sent to Elly and the children, Mahan attended a formal state dinner at Prime Minister Rosebery's in celebration of the queen's birthday. This was followed by the singular honor of a dinner "nearly tête à tête," five days later, May 31, at the prime minister's home, with only Rosebery, John Morley, and himself present. The prime minister told him on that occasion that "no literary work in his time had caused such enthusiasm as *Sea Power*—to which Mr. Morley assented." The following night, it was dinner for twenty-four British and American guests at the American Embassy. There he met former Secretary of the Navy W. C. Whitney who, belatedly it would seem, complimented him on his sea-power books. Mahan replied only that "the work was pretty much all done for the War College." On June 4 it was presentation at Court, the invitation having come "by the express invitation of the Prince of Wales," followed on June 8 by a State Ball, "the Queen having commanded the Lord Chamberlain to invite me."

Mahan, meanwhile, was rapidly becoming exhausted. "The trouble is that so many things pass I can't remember all from day to day. . . . my head is a maze, I am so tired at times, and now, that I can scarcely think. . . . the deluge of letters, with the ship business, permits me no rest." He was also "tired of singing my own song even at second hand" in his letters home and asked that "God keep me in vivid recollection of my own nothingness."[21]

Perhaps no honor pleased Mahan more than his invitation to dinner at the Royal Navy Club on June 2. No foreigner had been invited to dine there since its founding late in the seventeenth century. Fortunately for Mahan, Erben was ill that evening so the *Chicago*'s captain enjoyed "The Guest" limelight alone. Admiral Sir Vesey Hamilton, president of the Naval War College at Greenwich, presided. The affair, specifically honoring Mahan, was held to commemorate Admiral Lord Howe's victory over the French on the Glorious First of June, 1794, an action about which Mahan had written extensively. In fact, Admiral Sir Houston Stewart confessed to Mahan that evening that he had never fully understood the flow of the battle "till I had explained it. He added that my last chapter was wonderful—or magnificent—I forget the exact word, but it was a large adjective." When Mahan rose to respond to a toast, the assembled throng of one hundred admirals, captains, and commanders, active and retired, gave him three cheers twice over. "If not modest, I am at least bashful," he told his sister Jenny, "so you may imagine I was somewhat overwhelmed at being thus greeted by a hundred British admirals and captains. I think it was perhaps the most spontaneous and affecting testimonial I received while in England." In response, Mahan gave a short extemporaneous speech emphasizing Anglo-American identity of interests and the need for closer ties. "While I cannot flatter myself that what I said was brilliant, it was said steadily and without embarrassment, and was well received."[22]

With the *Chicago* scheduled to depart Gravesend on June 14 to go to Antwerp for extensive repair and overhauling, Mahan was barely able to crowd in one last formal dinner at Trinity House on June 13—at "the Prince of Wales' special request." Dozens of other invitations had to be turned down. Happy and exhausted, Mahan had had scarcely a waking moment to himself since May 10. Aside from his highly visible formal dinner appearances, he had also attended some fifteen small informal luncheons or dinners with personal friends, old and new. "Well, darling," he wrote Elly on the eve of his departure for Antwerp, "it has been quite an ovation, etc etc—but it is over now and I can assure you being lionized in this way is not the real substantial enjoyment that the quiet doing the [Nelson] work was. It is like a diet of sugarplums contrasted with our simple table. My one longing now is for rest." Indeed, it was "the most fatiguing month of my life." But it was not over. Far from it.[23]

No sooner had the vessel anchored at Antwerp than Mahan took a week's leave and hastened back to England to accept honorary degrees from Cambridge and Oxford universities—an LL.D. from Cambridge on June 18, and a D.C.L. from Oxford two days later. "The trip back to Oxford will cost me $25 or 30—but I thought the honor worth it," he explained to Elly. Actually, Mahan did not know one degree from another at the time, but he rather liked the idea of so grand a laying-on of academic hands. In fact, he insisted on the degree letters being used after his name on the title pages of his later books. For the Oxford occasion he wore full dress uniform with cocked hat, no epaulettes ("they might tear my gown"), over which was draped a scarlet gown with silk sleeves. The combination of uniform and gown he thought "excessively odd." Yet two degrees in three days from two such prestigious institutions caused Lord Rosebery to tell him at Oxford, "Well, I think you have broken the record, in taking a degree from each University the same week."

So grand an academic display did Mahan make in England that there was even talk later in the British press to the effect that he would be invited to replace the deceased Sir John R. Seeley as Professor of Modern History at Cambridge. What "a glorious victory," McCarty Little wrote Elly when he heard the rumor, "and all the more bitter must be the pill for those who have sought to pooh-pooh his work." On his own part, Mahan admitted that he both craved and disliked the kind of "adulation" that the British academic community heaped upon him, confessing that his was a "kind of restlessness which defies quiet." Certainly he was pleased by Dr.

John Edwin Sandys' degree citation at the Cambridge ceremony. To a cheering company the prominent classicist delivered a warm hands-across-the-sea tribute to Mahan in which he linked the destinies of British and American sea power:

> When we read his remarkable books [said Sandys] we behold the image of our maritime empire rise from the waves made luminous by his pen. We behold the cause of, and beginnings of, our widely scattered commerce; and the need for protecting our far-off colonies. And finally we are strengthened in the determination that for the welfare of the world and for the cause of universal peace we shall never permit that glory to be snatched from us. Moreover, we prophesy that in the future our brothers across the sea will be sharers of that glory; meanwhile, thoroughly appreciating that we are of the same blood, the same language, and the same glorious history, we gladly stretch forth across the sea which happily separates us no longer our right hands in a bond of friendship which we hope is destined to be for all time.

This was all well and good until Sir Nathan Meyer, 1st Baron Rothschild, reminded Mahan at lunch a few days later, perhaps facetiously, that the books that Sandys had praised so effusively were "responsible for our increased taxation this year." This fazed the author not at all. On the contrary, he took great pleasure in the thought that Prime Minister Gladstone had fallen from power in February 1894, giving way to Rosebery, partly because of his opposition to additional naval expenditures. "If so," Mahan boasted, "I had a hand in his resignation, for all agree in telling me that the increased vote for the navy was due to the books."[24]

In any event, after passing a "very flattering pleasant week" at Cambridge and Oxford, and in London with the George Schiffs, an English family he had met at Villefranche six months earlier, Mahan returned reluctantly to Antwerp and the *Chicago* on June 24 to begin again "the grind, whose end God knoweth." Writing to his sister Jenny, he summarized his reception in England:

> Well, how do I feel about it all? Of course I have been immensely gratified and pleased. It is but human, and I cannot think wrong, so to feel; but elated, I think not. It is constantly ringing in my ears "What hast thou that thou has not received?" So feeling, withal, there has been an absence of self-consciousness or embarrassment that has fairly surprised me. . . . Except fatigue, there was scarcely a drawback to the English stay. The weather was vile—but there was no contretemps. We stayed long enough but had not I think outstayed our welcome. . . . The English publisher writes me he had an order in Boston for 500 of the first [*Influ-*

ence book] and 250 of the second, which Little & Brown could not fill till new copies were printed. They had sold in six weeks more than in six months previous. This did England for us.[25]

The English did one more thing for Mahan in July 1894. At 0730 on the 11th of that month Captain Richard Jones crashed his vessel, the collier *Azov*, into the *Chicago* as she rode at anchor in the Scheldt Estuary. The *Azov*, under way, struck the cruiser on her starboard bow, at the point of the forward sponson for the 6-inch gun, unseating the gun, buckling and otherwise damaging a number of plates, and opening in her hull a gash that extended below the waterline. But so well was the crew of the *Chicago* drilled in crash procedures that the ship's collision mats were almost instantly dropped into place. The *Chicago* was never in danger. Indeed, the officer of the deck had seen that a collision was developing and had already ordered planned countermeasures when Mahan arrived on deck, fresh from his morning bath, clad in smoking jacket and bedroom slippers. "The fault is in no way ours," he assured Elly, estimating that repair of the damage would come to about $5,000. He was mainly fearful that his wife had seen the "exaggerated account" of the incident that appeared in the American press. To be sure, the fault was in no way Mahan's or that of the *Chicago*. A Belgian team of investigators later ruled that the *Azov* was wholly to blame for the accident. The repairs to the *Chicago*, however, took nearly a month to complete and cost $23,370.[26]

Repaired and fit again for sea, the *Chicago* departed Antwerp (which Mahan hated for its dullness) on August 6, 1894, for Cowes, Isle of Wight, there to be present for "Cowes Week," the annual regatta. The Solent was alive with pleasure craft, including the kaiser's yacht *Hohenzollern*. Once more the visiting and dining began for Mahan, and on August 8 he was again invited to Osborne House to dinner with the queen and the kaiser. "The occasion was somewhat more pleasant to me than last year because I knew many more people, and so had someone to talk to all the time." Among these was Emperor William II, on board whose yacht Mahan went for dinner four days later. In the party on August 12 were the German emperor, the Prince of Wales, the Duke of York, Erben, and Mahan.

But, by and large, Mahan's second and third visits to Britain in 1894 (August 6 to September 22 and September 29 to October 20) were much less frenetic than was his previous visit in May and June of that year. London's social "season" was over by mid-September and Mahan was able to see whom he wanted when he wanted. He even spent a few days interviewing descendants of Lord Nelson and other men whose forefathers had served with the great admiral. "Now that I am back in England the compliments begin again, though of course less formal and more incidental," he reported to his family. By comparison it "seemed like a season of great quiet after our [recent] London season." Nevertheless, his personal social expenses remained relatively high, and by mid-August he hoped that Elly would soon receive some money from her mother's estate, for "I cannot live within the allowance I made myself."

In spite of the fact that he had to economize, and that "everything here is dead quiet, our friends all gone," Mahan was pleased early in October when

> The London *Times* has been calling me Copernicus again. Shall I sue for libel? I find what their meaning is—Copernicus taught that the sun was the centre of the system—not the earth as was believed before his time, and I have been the first to show that sea power is the centre around which other events move, not it around them. "In the philosophy of the subject," says my unknown friend, "we must all sit at the feet of the eminent writer—the one man who has taught us that sea power is the central factor of our national polity. *That has been done once for all.*" My dear, do you know that is your husband they are talking of?

Frankly, he missed the grand huzzah of his earlier May–June visit. "Not even a club is now open to me," he confessed sadly in October. "We are all getting bored to death with Southampton." His last social activity before leaving for Lisbon on October 20 was a five-day visit with his Royal Navy correspondent, an acquaintance from his *Wachusett* days on the South American coast, Captain Bouverie F. Clark, who was then stationed at the Royal Naval Barracks in Devonport. Actually, he would have had "nowhere to go" but for this single invitation, and he accepted it eagerly. While there, he went to dinner with the admiral commanding the facility, an event which caused Mahan to exclaim: "I am still a bit of a lion, you see." At best, however, he was a tired, lonely, and somewhat bewildered lion. The British academic, political, and naval establishments had trotted him out, cheered him lustily for their own purposes (an increase in naval appropriations), and politely deposited him back on the inhospitable decks of the *Chicago*. His vogue had passed. "I scarcely think I shall ever again see England after this leaving," he told daughter Helen. "The halo of distinction with which I was then [May 1894] greeted" had faded. He was ready to depart.[27]

One of the things that made life at all tolerable for Mahan during his sojourns in Antwerp and Southampton in 1894 was the knowledge that Erben was scheduled to be relieved of his command and would soon leave the *Chicago*. He hoped and prayed that the cruiser would be ordered home when the change of command occurred. When that hope was dashed, he blamed Herbert and Ramsay for his continued exile. Meanwhile, there was much wardroom speculation, while the ship lay repairing at Antwerp, about who might replace Erben as rear admiral on the station. In late June Mahan heard a nasty rumor that Francis Ramsay would be the replacement. "How very distasteful to me this would be you can imagine," he told Elly. "It would be out of the frying pan into the fire—with the compensation only that Ramsay is a gentleman, though a very trying one. The other [Erben] is scarcely so." So upsetting was the prospect of serving under the hated Ramsay that Mahan wrote Secretary Herbert asking to be detached immediately if Ramsay were given command of the station. Fortunately, he delayed mailing the request. A few days later he learned from an article in the Paris edition of the *New York Herald* that the command had been given to senior Captain William Ashe Kirkland, soon to be promoted to rear admiral, an officer with whom Mahan had served in the *Congress* in 1860 and who had relieved him of his command of the *Wasp* in January 1875 in Montevideo. While Kirkland as a station commander was an unknown quantity, Mahan did not see how he could possibly be worse than Erben.

Mahan was not invited to the wardroom champagne party on September 6 at which the officers of the *Chicago* bid Erben farewell. At this affair the salty admiral became nostalgic, weepy, and not a little bit drunk. He concluded the festivities by donating the remainder of his personal wine larder to the junior officers' mess. Mahan reported, caustically, that

> Erben hauled down his flag today and went ashore. He was slopping over, a thing which always rasps me, particularly when it follows a jollification and champagne, which they had in the wardroom—very nice and kindly of them all right, but one hates to see tears after wine. I was not invited, which showed Nazro's good sense. I would not have cared to refuse—yet would have had to do so, for I will do nothing that can be twisted into an acceptance of what Erben did by me.

That having been said, Mahan left the ship for a long weekend in the country—at Arlington Hall, the home of Sir Francis and Lady Jeune. There he hobnobbed with the Duke of Cambridge, Sir Redvers Buller, General Sir Baker Russell, and other people more to his refined taste than was the rough and ready "Bully" Erben.[28]

Nevertheless, Mahan was concerned lest his new commander inherit the prejudices of the old. Indeed, Erben left behind for Kirkland's guidance a mean little memorandum that criticized Mahan's performance as captain of the *Chicago*, a document which Kirkland "immediately destroyed." True, Kirkland was a fair and highly ethical officer. It was his language, temper, and health that worried Mahan. "He is irascible, profane and gouty—a warm heart, but that is of little account when the temper is violent and uncontrolled. However, we must hope for the best." Further, Kirkland had "so drenched his stomach with purgatives that it is in very bad condition. He is continually upset, and is somewhat worried especially for fear least anything should hinder his promotion." Nothing did.

Purgation and promotion aside, Mahan soon discovered that Kirkland was far less disposed to meddle in the daily routine of the ship than Erben had been, although he worried that this characteristic "may be worse if I make mistakes." Kirkland's own mistakes were, of course, another matter —as the time in Le Havre when he invited the French Minister of Marine and a large party on board to inspect the ship, quite forgetting that the *Chicago* would be in dry dock at the time. This necessitated hastily hauling the vessel out of the dock and into the stream so that the ceremonial inspection could be held. Most important to Mahan was the fact that Kirkland was entirely cordial, "kind hearted and considerate," with "no indication of the sour surliness which characterized Erben." He usually messed by himself, kept to himself, nursed his gout, tended his stomach, and let Mahan run the ship. He was, however, "extremely profane" in his language, a trait which Mahan thoroughly disliked; but since he was "disposed to make a companion of me," Mahan decided to put up with his violent cursing. As he explained this compromise to his wife: "I am determined, as far as in me lies, to avoid any occasion of coldness or dislike. I feel as if I were a bootlick, but I believe it is really right to repress that offishness which is so obstinate in me, and which perhaps had something to do with Erben's dislike of me." So ended Mahan's self-appointed task, begun on board the *Iroquois*, of attempting to clean up the language of the U.S. Navy's officer corps all by himself. His successes over the years numbered zero.

About the only fault Mahan could find with Kirkland, besides his gross profanity, was that he liked "at times to be crooked and disappoint others," and that he "seems at times to derive real pleasure that he contraries another." By this Mahan meant that the new rear admiral occasionally issued orders or invitations that interfered with Mahan's own social activities on shore and did so knowing that his captain had made other plans. A minor matter really. Indeed, Mahan's only social problem with Kirkland during the seven months they served together in the *Chicago* came in Algiers in late January 1895. There Mahan gave a small dinner honoring Prince Louis of Battenberg and debated whether to invite Kirkland since "the admiral is so dreadfully profane and at times coarse, I couldn't face the idea of his breaking out before this really very refined and sufficiently dignified gentleman." The dilemma was solved by the simple device of adding a lady to the group, Mahan knowing that "the presence of a lady would keep him in order." Fortunately, however, Kirkland declined the invitation.

Kirkland seemed to like Mahan, perhaps because the Philosopher of Sea Power gave him no cause for complaint. Thus the captain of the *Chicago*, while serving under Kirkland's relaxed command, was able to rewrite his controversial "Anglo-American Reunion" article and then sheath his pen for the rest of the cruise. Kirkland did not have to hang canary cages on his side of the bulkhead separating his cabin from Mahan's, as Erben ostentatiously had done, to drown out the late-evening scratching of the author's pen. On the contrary, as the cruise drew to a close, Kirkland took it upon himself to submit to the Navy Department an unsolicited and complimentary statement about Mahan:

> I . . . consider it an act of justice to an officer to give to the Department the result of my own personal observations in the case of Captain Mahan, based upon six months of actual service with him on board the *Chicago*, viz: Captain A. T. Mahan, U.S.N., is a careful yet bold Navigator, never afraid of his ship. He is a just and careful administrator of the Regulations and Laws of the Navy, to his officers and crew. He is indefatigable in his efforts to obtain the best results in efficiency so far as he is permitted by the Regulations. He is subordinate and cheerful in carrying out the instructions of his superiors. Of his abilities and his gentlemanly and officer-like conduct, every one is aware.

Gentleman that he was himself, Kirkland forwarded a copy of this testament to Mahan with the observation that its substance would also be included in Mahan's regular semi-annual fitness report of July 1, 1895. That, he chuckled, "perhaps may give *Your* friend F. M. R. [Ramsay] a chance to remark on the wholesale excellence of my report." Happily, a news item based on Kirkland's statement conveniently appeared in the *New York Herald* for March 24, 1895, the day the *Chicago* reached New York. Meanwhile, the department had returned the statement to Kirkland archly instructing him that if he had anything complimentary to say about Mahan he could say it in the regular fitness report. Mahan assumed this was Ramsay's doing.[29]

A rumor that upset Mahan almost as much as the prospect of Ramsay's succeeding Erben as commander of the station, had to do with sending the *Chicago* to the Far East, there to protect American lives and interests threatened by the outbreak of the Sino-Japanese War in 1894. He immediately pronounced the idea "absurd"—almost as absurd as continuing to keep the broken-down vessel on the ceremonial European Station. He again detected conspiracy. "I strongly suspect that hostility to me has much to do with our movements," he complained to Elly. He knew nothing about the distant war and thought it "curious" that on September 25 a reporter for *The Times* should bother to seek out his opinion on the Battle of the Yalu, which had been fought on September 17 and was the principal naval engagement of the conflict. With this request, however, he complied, producing for *The Times* a collection of superficial opinions on a far-away battle about which he had read practically nothing. It was an unfortunate interview, so rambling that when the editor of *Contemporary Review* asked him in October for an interpretive article on the Sino-Japanese War he wisely declined. Only when he got home seven months later did he dash off a short and lucrative ($150) piece on the Battle of the Yalu for *Century Magazine*. It was a poor effort even then.

More important to Mahan than turning a quick dollar on the war was the fact that orders to the Far East would mean a lengthy postponement of the *Chicago*'s return to New York. This prospect worried him enormously. He was suffering severe "mental fatigue and distraction which seems to increase upon me as the cruise goes on"; he was feeling the "burden" of shipboard life "more and more." Further, he was convinced that the vessel's faltering engines could not stand the 25,000-mile trip to and from the seat of conflict. The whole notion, he decided, was an "inconceivable folly."[30]

Instead of being deployed to China, the *Chicago* was sent on a second swing around the Mediterranean, departing Southampton for Lisbon on October 20, 1894. For the next four months she hopscotched between Tangier, Málaga, Gibraltar, Barcelona, and Algiers, showing the flag to ignorant natives who did not recognize it, and to sophisticated Europeans who did not fear it. All the while she was bombarded with rumors that she was soon to return to New York. This stage of the cruise was a floating social event propelled by engines as tired and worn out as was Mahan himself.

During these final months on the station, he was increasingly nervous and withdrawn; he continued to remain professionally unsure of himself when the vessel was under way. The strain of shipboard life became almost unbearable, and he worried constantly that he was on the verge of a nervous breakdown. He looked only to his homecoming. His letters home during this bleak period in his life dealt largely with the current problems and future prospects of the family he had not seen for nearly two years and with the chitchat of his experiences on shore. But with the *Chicago* tied up at Algiers from December 24 to February 21, instead of at fashionable Villefranche, where the American flagship usually put in for the winter, his social life on shore was much reduced. "I cannot feel quite certain why the admiral decided not to go to Nice," he wrote Elly; "but it seems to me he did it out of sheer crookedness" because his daughter, Florence Kirkland Noel, had come out to the Mediterranean to join her husband, Lieutenant York Noel, the admiral's secretary. Kirkland was thus demonstrating that "the ship was not be run for the convenience of the women." To daughter Helen he complained: "I . . . find continually cause to regret the strange decision of the admiral to avoid Nice where the flagship has always heretofore wintered. There I could last year count upon two or three pleasant gatherings in a week, which powerfully lightened the monotony and brushed the cobwebs out of my brain—here [Algiers] nothing, dullness even duller. My only real pleasure is climbing the hill to the English club, reading the papers there, getting a cup of *four* o'clock tea, and walking back."

It is not surprising, therefore, that with more bitterness than usual Mahan cursed the U.S. Navy and the day he entered it. His whole career, he felt, had been a "miserable blunder . . . what a shocking mistake I made." He had "suddenly . . . lost all force to bear up against the recurrent annoyances of my position" and was "incapable except of looking forward to deliverance. . . . I do my work but it wears me out." He literally counted the days until the cruiser *San Francisco* would arrive in Algiers, take Kirkland on board, assume the responsibility for the station, and release the *Chicago* for her long voyage home on a "rickety engine." That day of blessed liberation dawned at last on February 21, 1895.[31]

During his final weeks in the *Chicago* Mahan gave a great deal of thought to what duty, if any, he would request when he got home. He was certain he would not accept promotion to rear admiral if that required his staying in the Navy for any appreciable length of time after September 1896, the end of his fortieth year in the service. He also decided that he had already given too much of his life's blood to the War College, that he would do nothing more there than serve as an occasional lecturer, and that he would certainly not further empty his veins into a third tour as its president. Specifically, he would never serve under Bunce or Ramsay again. In October 1894, however, he was both "startled and . . . amused" by a rumor that he would be offered the superintendency of the Naval Academy. While he had "no intention voluntarily to assume any such nigger work as the Academy," he was willing to accept assignment there if it would shave a few months off his suffering in the floating purgatory that was the *Chicago*. He had no use for the place, and never had had, either personally or from a career standpoint. It was tolerable duty only because it was on dry land. And if he were assigned there he was determined to go to Annapolis alone. "I should for many reasons be unwilling to take the girls there," he confided to Elly. He preferred to talk these "reasons" over privately with his wife rather than spell them out in a letter that his virgin daughters might see. But one might guess that among those reasons was his dislike of the presence in Annapolis of numerous women-chasing midshipmen—the kind Mahan himself had been when he hotly pursued the local belles there in 1858 and 1859. The sealing-off of Helen and Ellen from the opposite sex, perhaps not consciously intended, was already under way in the Mahan family. They were being groomed to serve as unmarried servants of sorts in his retirement household.

When he left England for the Mediterranean in October 1894 he had tentatively decided, he announced to Elly, that he would apply for "a year's leave and then retire, that is my present aim; and I hope that with Auntie's and your mother's leavings, and my hoped-for earnings, that we may get on." The sooner he retired the sooner he could begin "more surely [to] fit myself for gaining a support independent of the Navy." While his pay during a year's leave would be only $2,800, and while he feared future cuts in the retirement pay rate ($3,375 for captains in 1895), he would risk an uncertain financial future in order to begin writing again as soon as possible. At the end of the year's leave he would again evaluate the expediency of complete retirement. By early December 1894 his mind was "fully fixed." He would retire in September 1896, at the end of forty years in the service. The business of commanding modern ships had become far too complicated. As he complained to George Sydenham Clarke in late January 1895:

> Here a little, there a little, the multitude of things to be done increases day by day—and the more of them they [Navy Department] pile together, the nearer they think they approach perfection—wherein I think they are absolutely mistaken. For myself, my mind is as bent as human purpose can be to get out of it all, when my time for retirement arrives, which will be in September, 1896. I hope that meantime they will let me take leave, in which case I hope to proceed with my life of Nelson,

and having finished that, with the War of 1812. . . . I hope to find myself sufficiently easy not to write for money chiefly. . . .

Mahan could not know at the time that Secretary Herbert was in tune
with his thinking. "I should be loath to see him [Mahan] leave the Navy,"
he wrote Henry Taylor, president of the War College. "I shall endeavor
to provide for him a place that will be agreeable to him and afford opportunities for pursuing his literary work."[32]

The leave-versus-retirement question having been settled in his mind,
Mahan turned to the last professional problem facing him in the *Chicago*
—the condition of the vessel as that would be determined formally by a
Board of Inspection when the cruiser reached New York. This was the
last act in the Mahan-Erben drama and it was important to Mahan, and to
such people as Roosevelt, Luce, and Lodge, that the inspection go extremely well. For this reason Mahan turned all hands to work for a month
to prepare for the crucial inspection. This labor was performed in Algiers
in January and February 1895. During this busy period, Little, Brown and
Company continued urging him to complete the manuscript of his Nelson
biography "while the bloom is still on the reputation of the others." Mahan agreed that the book would sell "like hot cakes," but he was in no
position in Algiers to resume his writing. The pressure of preparing for
inspection weighed heavily upon him. "Pray for your father," he implored
Helen, "during these coming anxious weeks, till I am quit of the ship."
By February 1 he was in a frightful lather about the impending inspection.
He, told Elly that

> just now my life is a constant worry, if not one thing then another.
> The approaching inspection is ever on my mind, and though I confess
> gratefully that I have so far been safely brought through every trouble,
> I cannot get rid of the fear that some censure will fall on me. People
> talk to me as if my reputation was such as to make [me] invulnerable.
> I hope it may be so, but I certainly am not presuming on it . . . . remem-
> ber me more than ever in your prayers, for very very much depends
> upon the next few weeks. I greatly need support and help. The inspec-
> tion is a terrible ordeal to me. You are, I hope, wholly reconciled to my
> intended retirement. . . . Don't forget your prayers for me, I need them
> sorely, for if God don't help me I don't know how I can manage all I
> have to do.[33]

Whether as a result of Elly's prayers or of Mahan's own competence in
seeing the matter through, the *Chicago* passed the inspection handily. But
not until her captain had endured a nervous voyage home, one that filled

him with fear and trembling lest some small mistake bring Ramsay's wrath down upon him and end his seagoing career on a sour note. "Pray for me, dearest," he again implored Elly, "that I be supported during these few remaining weeks, and may close my sea service (I trust) without discredit. How I long for repose."

He was therefore in a state of near collapse and exhaustion when, on March 27, three days after the *Chicago* dropped anchor off Staten Island, a Board of Inspection and Survey headed by Commodore Thomas O. Selfridge clambered on board and went over the ship with more than usual meticulousness. Save for some minor deficiencies in the gear in three of the ship's boats, the inspectors found the vessel to be "clean and in an efficient condition, and well drilled." Selfridge even made the unusual gesture of writing Mahan personally on the "very satisfactory condition in which I found your ship both as to cleanliness, discipline and drill. I was particularly pleased with the subordination and respect shown by the crew." What Erben had to say of Mahan's triumph, if anything, is not recorded. He was retired the moment he left the *Chicago* on September 6, 1894, and disappeared from Mahan's life until 1901.[34]

With the trying voyage and inspection at last behind him, Mahan hoped, as he told Horace Scudder, "soon to get regularly to work again at the tasks which formerly gave me so much pleasure." Herbert summoned him to Washington after the inspection for a chat about his future plans, and Mahan was confident that he would be able to persuade the Secretary "that it will be best for this Navy, as well as for myself, to have me free to work on my own lines. Now that I have a little reputation, I find that the great trouble is to resist temptations to dissipation of energy."

Mahan's confidence in Herbert was not misplaced. He remained attached to the *Chicago* until she was decommissioned on May 1, preliminary to a thorough modernization overhaul that lasted four years. Following the decommissioning ceremony the Navy gave him two months' leave and then put him on various special-duty assignments in Newport and in his own home at full shore pay of $3,500 a year until he went on the Retired List on November 17, 1896. These convenient duties again permitted him to resume his literary career at the expense of the Navy. Indeed, he told Ashe, his formal retirement eighteen months after leaving the *Chicago* introduced "no change in my recent manner of life. It only frees me from the possibility of interruption by the Department." It could not be said, therefore, that the Cleveland Democrats had treated Mahan badly.[35]

XII

A Family and Its Future
1893-1895

Recognition is pleasant, particularly after the almost entire absence of it at home. Except Roosevelt, I don't think my work gained me an entrée into a single American social circle. . . . if reputation is any *good it is when rammed home by a certain amount of attention from people in position.*

Alfred Thayer Mahan to Ellen Evans Mahan, June 14, 1893

What I shall in the future become I know not—nor do I deny that much in the conditions of those with whom I have been thrown here [England] *seems to me to be pleasant and desirable—but I have always felt the same: that the inability to mix freely with society on account of our means not being sufficient has been the chief manque in our life—depriving it of a certain variety which is very much to be wished. . . . The great defect in our family life has been the want of external social relations.*

Alfred Thayer Mahan to Ellen Evans Mahan, October 19,
November 13, 1894

Mahan's decision to retire from the Navy in 1896, forty disagreeable years after having entered it, was largely the result of his growing conviction that he was the Copernicus of History whose most important scholarly and literary accomplishments still lay ahead. This was an opinion fixed forever in his mind by the sheer misery of his two-year cruise in the *Chicago* and by the success of his sea-power books. But the decision was also motivated in part by the fact that he had a socially isolated family which he felt he could no longer neglect. Further, by 1895 he had a clear idea of the kind of retirement life he wanted for himself and his family when he came on shore for good. It was a way of life he had sampled in the gracious homes and private clubs of England in 1893 and 1894, and in the gay resort atmosphere of Villefranche during the period December 1893 to February 1894—particularly at Eze, the estate where the George Schiff family wintered. It was, therefore, mainly for social reasons that during his absence in the *Chicago* he encouraged Elly to build a summer house at Quogue and to acquire a well-situated and fashionable town house in New York City where the family would spend the winter months.

It all came down to Mahan's view of what constituted gracious living. Such living meant employing a staff of household servants and providing an impressively set table around which wealthy and attractive dinner guests would frequently gather. "Don't save on servants nor on the substantial part of your table," he instructed Elly. It also meant visits to museums and theaters, music in the drawing room after dinner, dinner dances for socially prominent friends, receptions at home for bright and intelligent people, and the entertainment of beautiful and talented women with whom Mahan might converse and flirt. "I am persuaded that my sphere in life is to have plenty of money and to talk," he told daughter Nell. A financial key to this dream was the additional income that would flow from his pen. "You will have to open your economical soul for dinners, etc.," he wrote to his wife; "I think I shall insist upon creating a dinner fund by two magazine articles per annum. The subject is really serious, for we are getting on and can't afford to lose time, but then we are all likable and if we give ourselves a chance, will, I think get on."[1]

A second key to Mahan's concept of the good life after leaving the Navy was getting to know the right people in New York and in Quogue, then pushing his reluctant family into their company. During his cruise in the *Chicago* he came to have precise notions of just who the right people were. They were, as he identified them, those pleasant, attractive, talented "nice people" with money enough to winter in New York City and summer in Quogue; or those with resources enough to live in expensive London flats during the social "season" and to winter in the south of France. Mahan felt, of course, that it would take time, money, and patience to penetrate such circles. Hence the house in Quogue was a financial and social gamble, "but I think the chances decidedly are that it will pay." It was also people like the Schiffs on whom he counted to help bring his introverted daughters into the mainstream of upper-middle-class American society. Writing from England in October and November of 1894, he explained both the problem and the opportunity to his wife:

What I shall in the future become I know not—nor do I deny that much in the conditions of those with whom I have been thrown here seems to me to be pleasant and desirable—but I have always felt the same: that the inability to mix freely with society on account of our means not being sufficient has been the chief manque in our life—depriving it of a certain variety which is very much to be wished. . . . The great defect in our family life has been the want of external social relations. In ourselves we have been most happy always; but association with others, whether they come to us or we to them, is a needful addition.

Or, as he expressed it to Elly on the eve of the *Chicago*'s return home in February 1895, "I feel that even you and I, but still more the girls, need now to establish . . . other points of contact with our kind. I have felt the benefit of it so much during the cruise."[2]

Mahan had a very active and pleasant social life ashore with "our kind" while serving in the *Chicago*, particularly at Villefranche. Indeed, it was so active an existence that he could scarcely face the prospect of returning to the relative monotony of life with his family in a dreary flat in New York. "I miss society dreadfully," he remarked after leaving the south of France; "I know how much it did for me, but scarcely realized till I fell out of it." For this reason he severely criticized Admiral Kirkland for taking the *Chicago* to dull Algiers for the winter of 1894–1895, rather than back to lively Villefranche. Meanwhile, he encouraged Elly to continue to *"reflect seriously* upon the necessity of cultivating friends."[3]

The social model Mahan selected for future emulation by his own family was Mr. and Mrs. George Schiff and their attractive daughters, Rosie and Marie. A wealthy British couple who migrated with the social and climatic seasons between London and Villefranche, the Schiffs represented in their style of living all that Mahan wanted for himself and Elly after his retirement from the Navy. He saw them often when the vessel was in Villefranche, either ashore at Eze or on board the *Chicago*, visited with them again in London in May and June 1894, and always felt relaxed and comfortable in their presence. Their daughters and Madeline Stanley, daughter of Lady Jeune by her first husband, were about the ages of Helen and Ellen. More importantly, all three of these young English ladies were pretty; they dressed fashionably, were musically talented, danced well, met new people easily and graciously, and were able to converse knowledgeably on a variety of subjects with old and young alike. Age seemed to be no barrier to them. "I have never seen young girls so cordially welcome elderly men as here," he reported to Elly in amazement. Mahan was completely captivated by them, especially by Rosie Schiff. Scarcely a letter home between December 1893 and February 1894 failed to wax rhapsodic about the beauty, charm, and social attainments of the Schiff girls; and there were few letters from London in 1894 that failed to mention Madeline Stanley and the Jeunes. Indeed, Mahan wished that Rosie Schiff were the right age for marriage to his son Lyle, so fascinated was he by her. As he confessed to Elly, "while I do enjoy the animation of a crowded room or dinner my chiefest pleasure has been—a queer confession for a graybeard—has been in watching and talking with pretty young girls, principally Rose Schiff and Madeline Stanley." Rosie, however, was his favorite. "You have very tolerable reason to be jealous of Rosie Schiff," he teased daughter Helen.

Not surprisingly, the Mahan family back on East 54th Street soon began to tire of the captain's eulogies of young Rose and suggested that he was an old fool, or that Rosie had an unnatural interest in older men. "To do Miss Rosie justice," Mahan archly assured his wife, "while she is extremely civil and attentive to me, she has no unnatural preferences for elderly gentlemen and enjoys her flirtations with the young men to the full—nor are there any absurdities going on." To make the point firmly, he revealed that she had even flirted with his old enemy Winfield Scott Schley when he too had been entertained at Eze. "I think the taste for Schley somewhat indiscriminating," Mahan noted testily, "but I believe women generally do like him, and he really is amusing."[4]

The fact of the matter was that the 43-year-old Elly became quite jealous of her bald 54-year-old husband and his new-found companions while he was abroad in the *Chicago*. Not only was it a question of his being feted officially by British royalty, statesmen, and admirals; he seemed also to be having entirely too good a time in the less formal company of attractive and talented women. "I count for nothing in the dancing," he told Helen of one party at the Schiffs, "but I rather like the meetings with the women. All are very cordial and the society is so small you feel quite at home. For the small numbers there is a remarkable proportion of pretty young women—which always is an attraction to me—as it was to my father." Elly thus began to wonder if he really wanted to come home, if he was also romantically attracted to Rosie's charming and sophisticated 50-year-old mother, and if he still planned to take care of his wife in later life. It was partly this wonder, as well as a growing feeling that she had somehow dropped out of his life, that caused her to make tentative plans to join him for a fortnight's visit at Villefranche in 1894. His teasing references to his sharp eye for a pretty face, coupled with boasts of how physically handsome he remained—"the very picture of health and as fair as a man of thirty-five. *I quite admired myself*"—did nothing to help Elly's morale. Nevertheless, when Mahan realized that she was indeed growing a bit acerbic on the subject he went to considerable lengths to assure her that their married life was "not a failure." He pointed out that Mrs. Schiff had a serious heart condition from which she would never recover, noted that "all previous fancies" in London and Villefranche were nothing compared to his enduring affection for her, and encouraged her idea of a visit to him, pointing out only that there were some practical logistical and financial problems in the scheme. "I love you and want you," he assured her. Unfortunately for Elly, the ship wintered in Algiers from December 1894 to February 1895, preliminary to being ordered home, and her proposed visit to the Mediterranean was abandoned. But Mahan clearly wanted her to join him had the ship been kept longer abroad. He wanted "the strength that women and men get from such a meeting as ours would be." Few letters went to her from the *Chicago* that did not stress his love for her, his homesickness, his need for her advice and counsel, his aspirations for their children, and his eagerness to quit the Navy and return to her side for the remainder of their natural lives. All the rest was tinsel.[5]

What was not tinsel was his campaign by mail to bring his daughters out of their social introversion, to convert them into Rosie Schiffs and Madeline Stanleys, and to reproduce in a New York City town house the sophisticated atmosphere he had so enjoyed at Eze and at Arlington, Lord and Lady Jeune's country estate near London. This fond hope for his family was complicated by the fact that he himself had never been able to make close friends. Nor had his own sense of social inadequacy been helped by his triumphal march through British society in 1893 and 1894. He lamented the loneliness of command that denied him any more than casual acquaintances in the *Chicago*'s wardroom. And while he very much wanted to be liked, and was sometimes surprised to discover people who did like him, he confessed nonetheless that "it has been the greatest error of my life to shun people, but then I am also more self-sufficing than most. . . . at best it is a loss." He still had difficulty meeting new people, as he had in the past, and he feared that in spite of his social successes in London and Villefranche, which briefly gave him some small confidence in his ability to cope with social situations, he remained the prisoner of his father's "disposition to withdraw into the background—and indeed I do." As self-appointed instructor of Ellen and Helen in the art of extroversion, he was an unfortunate choice. It was a case of the blind leading the blind.[6]

The problem was further complicated by his view of Helen and Ellen as behavioral reincarnations of the New Testament's Martha and Mary.

Elly Mahan and her daughters Ellen, left, and Helen, about 1906

Momentarily setting aside the Schiff social model in favor of one Celestial, he explained this concept to Helen in late December 1894. Speaking of a young woman's proper role in life and the acceptable ways in which such women might deal with life's many problems and setbacks, he wrote:

> I think my old rule never to be out late on Saturday one worth your consideration, for how can you bring your mind and heart clear to early Communion, if you are up and excited, late the night before? Be moderate in all things is the Bible's own teaching; and be sure that the hurry we all are in in these days is essentially faithless. For your very progress in music, in friendship, and in all innocent duties or pleasures, the promise is not to [be] careful and worried about many things, but —"They that *wait* upon the Lord shall *renew their strength*." In writing these things I am not trying to give you rules, but subject for thought and, I hope, practice. Martha and Mary are two constant types, repeating themselves from age to age. Sitting at the Lord's feet, giving yourself time to hear what He has to say, is the path, not of holiness only, but of happiness and of true success. . . . My dear child think of these things, and trust Him to show you what to do.

Having earlier ruled out marriage for Helen, short of divine intervention in the selection of a suitable mate, the thrust of Mahan's advice to his 21-year-old daughter was that she accept a life of patient servility. Both his

[313]

daughters ultimately accepted this advice and until their father's death in 1914 sat loyally and helpfully at his feet, responding to his every wish, command, and need. To be sure, Mahan occasionally recognized that the "desires of the girls seem to be summed up in the wish to be somebody, having some interest and doing some work, with an individuality of their own not merely merged in the family. I cannot but think our girls must feel that is what we have been trying to do for them." What the girls themselves felt on the matter has not been recorded.

What is known is that an attempt by Helen in June 1896 to assert a degree of personal independence outside the family circle was immediately crushed by her father. She was told bluntly that her private interests, mainly the study and teaching of music, must be subordinated to those of the family as a whole. "You should study this question and seek to find your duty in the house," he told her. "Turn therefore your mind to the fact that in the house where once you were a child—under obedience—you are now a grown woman, independent; but that, at the same time, it is your home, the scene of your primary duties, until God give you another." This direct order from the bridge was shored up with Mahan's usual barrage of selected biblical references and with the more mundane promise of making Helen "independent so far as your personal expenses are concerned . . . by making you an allowance." It was not surprising that under such heavy pressure to conform to the Martha-Mary image, Helen enjoyed little association with men her age. Her isolation from men seems to have pleased Mahan, who also carefully instructed her in the important differences between "sinful love" and "sweet love." Whatever those differences, Helen had no suitors. Instead, she was subtly being groomed to take over the daily running of the Mahan household. Even before her father returned in the *Chicago*, she was well on her way to becoming what Mahan later referred to as "my house-keeping daughter."[7]

For such a bird in such a cage music was an acceptable pastime—as it was in the drawing and music rooms of England and Villefranche. Helen had some talent at the piano and Mahan, with great reluctance, allowed her to give music lessons for money in their home. He was concerned at the time (1893–1894) that the family might not have enough income during his retirement years to live at the level to which he aspired, and, as he told Helen, taking a few students would extend her social connections as well as contribute to the family fortune. She first assisted Mrs. Morgan, her own teacher, in the instruction of students; then she began taking students of her own. Much to Mahan's amazement, by December 1893 she was earning between $50 and $75 per month in this cottage industry. When, in November 1894, she received from one of her mother's friends the gift of a baby grand piano, Mahan began seriously to consider "Helen's teaching career" in making his retirement plans.[8]

As Helen's musical career began to bloom in late 1893 and bid fair to reduce her financial dependence on her father, Mahan cautioned her to conserve her energy for more profitable use in later years. To this end he often warned her to reduce her workload, take fewer students, think less of making money, and generally to slow down. These admonitions were based on his belief, as curious as it was firmly held, that the female physique, unlike the male, did not mature fully until age 25; and that premature overwork was as dangerous to the normal development of the female anatomy as it was destructive to a woman's mental and spiritual growth. Specifically, she should husband her money-making energies against the likelihood that "the pay of retired officers will be reduced." If and when that happened it would be necessary "for us all to work and possibly pretty hard—but by then you will have your full strength if you do not impair it now." He thought two hours a day was long enough for her to work at this stage of her life.[9]

Helen heeded not. Whether it was from overwork, social isolation, or general depression, she suffered a nervous breakdown in November 1894 and took to her bed. "Try and put up with your grievance until my return," Mahan wrote, "and at any rate talk about it as little as possible." Her doctor found her "run down from the effect of the winter's drive." But when it was medically decreed that Helen should spend fourteen hours in bed daily, Mahan charged that "doctors are funny, and faddy— but I can scarcely fancy one advising so much rest for nerves." Unfortunately, Helen was destined to have another, more severe, nervous breakdown a few years later, one during which "entire rest" was ordered. Her father took her to Europe in 1905 for that purpose, convinced, as usual, that she was in "no serious trouble."[10]

The problem with Ellen ("Nellie"), on the other hand, was that she was chronically introverted during her teens; and, unlike her somewhat more self-reliant older sister, she had no artistic or other compensatory talents. Mahan worried about her "morbid feelings," and in his letters to her from the *Chicago* he attempted to encourage the sixteen-year-old to abandon her thick shell of "droopy" reserve. She suffered severe attacks of depression which Elly attributed to her childhood bout with malaria, but which Mahan chose to diagnose from afar as stemming from difficulties

less in herself than in her surroundings. The two other children [he told Elly in June 1894] are more self-sufficing, and have less need of change, etc. . . . There may possibly be physical conditions, but I doubt that. I have always thought Nellie, despite her pepperiness, to be essentially meek, lowly-minded, and self-distrustful. She has shown a lack of spirit in confronting the rubs of life. . . . the home has for her great sameness, and while she is too lowly-minded to lay the blame there (not that there *is* blame, but it is the probable cause of trouble), she feels it without knowing what ails her. My absence doubtless tells, for women somehow all feel the support of a man in the house. . . . It is then, in my opinion, the conditions of the house which unconsciously weigh upon Nellie. . . . Too monotonous, I fear, too little interest, too little variety of companionship. . . . If we can learn what kind of life and occupation best suits her, where her interest lies, provide occupation congenial, and pleasant social relations, we may solve the problem. Helen's advice and help too must be sought, and she must learn to recognize that Nellie's difficulty in gaining friends proceeds from natural peculiarities. . . . she needs change in mode of life.[11]

Mahan was no psychologist. Indeed, he had profound contempt for "psychological research and all that." But he correctly guessed that living at Quogue during the summer months, among the right people, would do young Nell a world of good. There she would make "permanent and intimate friends," as indeed she eventually did. He also urged her to bicycle, to take dancing lessons, to take walks, to join Helen in fencing and horseback riding (although he admitted that for women he had "an oldfashioned dislike" of both activities), and to "go where people gather" in search of new friends.[12]

As part of her social therapy Mahan encouraged Nellie to become a writer and an artist. Since she had dabbled in art for several years, money was made available for her to study drawing with a private tutor. It became clear in a short time, however, that she had no particular talent in the field. "Turn diligently to whatever seems next best," he instructed her. She then considered briefly the idea of undertaking the formal study of literature, this with a view toward becoming a writer. She was warned by her father that writing was an extremely difficult undertaking requiring considerable "natural gifts" of the sort he himself possessed. These gifts Nellie had not inherited and the notion died aborning.

But not before Mahan exercised his fatherly prerogative to lecture both his daughters once again on acceptable and unacceptable authors. Among the former were T. B. Macaulay, Milton, Shakespeare, Walter Scott, and James Russell Lowell. Among the latter were Mark Twain and Emile Zola. He had met Twain in England in May 1894 and had instantly disliked him. When he learned that Helen had read one of Zola's racy novels, given her by one of her more adventuresome female acquaintances, Mahan fairly exploded: "I believe he has accidentally written one or two things that are fit for decent people to read . . . but for the most part he writes, I am told, the very vilest matter, rendered none the better by his great power. I once tried to read a novel of his, but found it impossible from utter loathing—a moral feeling resembling physical nausea." Conversely, he judged innocuous books by the American authors Thomas Nelson Page and Richard Harding Davis acceptable enough to serve as Christmas presents. During his two years in the *Chicago* he recommended for the literary edification and moral elevation of his children the works of such giants in the field of nineteenth-century English literature as Julia Cartwright Ady, Thomas Stanley Treanor, and Agnes Repplier.[13]

If the personalities and emotional problems of Helen and Ellen gave small prospect of a brilliant social future for the Mahan family in New

Courtesy Alfred Thayer Mahan II

Lyle Evans Mahan

York and Quogue after the captain's projected retirement from the Navy, the otherwise harassed parents were fortunate in the molding of their son Lyle. Aged thirteen in 1894, he was a normal, outgoing American child. His home religious training seems not to have been as closely monitored as was that of his sisters, perhaps because his father was abroad as Lyle passed into puberty. "I hope you will look to Lyle's *habits* of devotion in my absence—his preparation for communion, etc.," Mahan instructed his wife shortly after the *Chicago*'s departure. "We may not expect deep vital piety in a lad of his years—it would be precocious and abnormal; but a reverent and dutiful observance of forms is an invaluable discipline and preservative. When the fire is well stacked, it is ready for the kindling when the flame falls from Heaven. I purposely and carefully appointed to him short prayers and forms." Since Mahan's letters to his only son have not survived, it is not clear whether the flame ever fell from heaven. Probably not. Mahan insisted, however, that the fire be well stacked, that the boy be rigidly disciplined in the home. He told Elly how this should be done: "he must not be allowed to take the bit between his teeth. He must obey implicitly up to the time he goes to boarding school, and so turned over. After that we may possibly gradually relax our control, but I hope that his good sense will then lead him not to distress us. But, however we may refrain from commanding, when we do command we must be obeyed in our home."[14]

Lyle entered Groton School in Massachusetts in September 1894 and his subsequent education, disciplining, and religious training passed to the responsibility of the school's legendary headmaster, Endicott Peabody. At Groton, after a shaky start, Lyle got the first-rate education, including Greek and French, that prepared him well for Columbia, which he attended from 1898 to 1902, and later for a successful financial and legal career in New York. At Groton he probably spent as much time on football, a game that mystified his father, and hunting in the nearby fields as he did on his studies. "I do not well understand these new games whose scientific character has come up since I was a boy," Mahan remarked. "Only I hope he will not make the mistake of some boys, and make them the chief instead of the secondary concern of his school. They won't help him much in life, whereas a trained mind will." In spite of this fatherly concern, or perhaps because of it, Lyle did well enough in the classroom. By and large his academic and social career at Groton was a happy and successful one, marred only by a severe case of German measles, followed by lobar pneumonia and cardiac difficulties that nearly cost him his life in

January and February 1895. Elly rushed to his side and helped nurse him back to health. She told her absent husband little of the crisis through which their son was passing and minimized the seriousness of the situation when finally she did write. After all, there was nothing he could do about it. "Everybody seems much shook up about the measles," he lectured his wife. "Don't lose your thought of others because the boy has measles." As he constantly reminded her, he had enormous problems of his own on board the *Chicago*. Once out of the home and away from his stern father young Lyle developed a "rugged aggressive independence" that both pleased and startled Mahan. "My fear was," he confessed to his wife, from Gibraltar, "that he was too timid and retiring, and shrank from intercourse with others because of the attendant collisions. That certainly is my own trouble, and sorely harassed am I here by some of my surroundings."[15]

Harassed and frustrated though he was by his unpleasant duty in the *Chicago*, Mahan was convinced that even when he was abroad he could still contribute something to the education of his children by describing for them in detail the many sites—geographical, cultural, and historical —that he visited during his excursions on shore. That culture could be acquired through travel, even travel by mail, was one of his firmly held beliefs, one that impelled him or Elly (usually both of them) to take Ellen and Helen to Europe on four occasions after his retirement—to Italy and France in 1898; to Spain, France, Italy, and Germany in 1905; to France and Germany in 1907; and on a Grand Tour in 1912. As Nellie recalled these experiences: "In Europe he would take great interest in showing us cathedrals, fortifications, and in walking with us about the streets of towns. He was tireless when it came to walking." Consequently, in 1893 and 1894, a steady stream of letters moved from his cabin in the *Chicago* to his daughters on East 54th Street describing with great vividness the sites and sights, peoples and smells, of Ireland, England, France, Portugal, Gibraltar, Spain, Italy, Turkey, Egypt, Spanish Morocco, and Algeria. Art museums, country homes, castles, fortresses, cathedrals, battlefields, shops, landscapes, even zoos ("I find a weird interest in watching lions and tigers crunching bones"), were captured by his skillful pen. From the Pyramids he wrote in March 1894:

> I could not but smile as I remembered how Napoleon said to his army, "Soldiers, from the summit of yonder pyramids forty centuries behold your actions." Now their forty centuries look down equally unmoved on British and American tourists with their bottled beers, brandy and soda, puggarees like towels tied around their hats, and other outlandish

costumes—pretty girls, sour old maids, grizzled bachelors and fin de
siècle young men and women, all assembled to astound the 40 Centuries
which, to do them justice, show no particular amazement.

Given such cultural desecration at the very navel of antiquity, it was perhaps no wonder that by July 1894 Mahan had temporarily "lost interest
in places, and in sight-seeing for the most part."[16]

At no time, however, did he lose his interest in religion or in his God
while he served in the *Chicago*, a fact clearly revealed in his many letters
home. He continued his practice of tithing his income, including his royalties. He wondered how it was that the English aristocracy and upper middle classes could be so casual about church attendance. He even felt that
the intelligent and fun-loving Schiffs were not "on the road to perfection"
and that their salvation was in doubt; and he feared that his brother Fred,
"by his mistaken abstention from church" had "lost touch with God." Not
Alfred. He regularly attended church, whether on board ship or on shore,
with the result that he had little doubt about his own salvation:

> Remember [he wrote Helen] that I, certainly a man of brains, find the
> truths of Christianity satisfying to my intellect and my only firm sup-
> port in doubt and trouble. Beware, therefore, of the nerveless doubt of
> our age. If such come to you . . . shut out doubt and refuse to listen to
> those who suggest. Remember that I, as my experience of life, tell you
> that the truth of the Gospel is my firm conviction. God is, and is the
> Rewarder of them who diligently seek Him.[17]

Armed with this simple faith, to which mechanical church attendance
and Gospel fundamentalism were important, Mahan participated regularly
in divine services on board the *Chicago*. Indeed, he insisted that Chaplain
F. F. Sherman confine his sermons to matters strictly biblical. Thus
when news reached the vessel in Antwerp on Sunday, July 7, 1894, that
President Cleveland had sent federal troops into Chicago to suppress labor
riots attendant on the bloody Pullman strike, and Sherman indicated at the
morning service that he would abandon his prepared remarks and preach
instead on the crisis at home, Mahan created a scene when he attempted
to interrupt a harmless sermon on law and order. "Sit down, Mahan. Let
him go ahead," ordered Erben. After the service Mahan told Sherman that
he must in the future avoid "dangerous political topics" and stick closely
to the Gospel. He further insisted that all the chaplain's future sermons be
cleared with him prior to delivery, an order Sherman flatly refused to
obey. Erben supported the chaplain. It puzzled the admiral that Mahan
saw so much radicalism abroad in the United States and felt that the red

germ had infected even the Navy. "Mahan is a deep thinker," he snorted, "thinks too damned much. Seems to think that subversive influences are at work in the Navy. I don't agree."[18]

Since Mahan was convinced that he was completely in the hands of God ("I have lost all faith in the power of my will, and am only thankful that I can believe in His power"), he took the position that Erben's assault on him and the travail of his duty in the *Chicago*, had somehow been arranged by the Creator to test his faith and to humble him. "God will defend the right," he assured his wife in connection with the fitness-report controversy. "How a thing like this teaches one to know God and the power of the Holy Spirit. It is worth all the trouble." As the conflict with Erben dragged into its seventh month, he took heart in the thought that "if I am able to conduct myself throughout like a gentleman and a Christian all will doubtless go well in the end." So it was that Mahan looked to God and to a literal meaning of the Gospel when he faced difficulty. Thus when he narrowly missed death in a bombing incident in Barcelona in November 1893 he attributed it to the "merciful providence of God." In the area of personal decision-making, and with reference to the meaning and impact of events on his life, he simply could not understand "how people who do not believe in God find any adequate motive for doing right. . . . I should be helpless." The cynicism of his old Naval Academy days had long since passed. His confused wrestling with the intellectual problems of scriptural higher criticism while on board the *Iroquois*, a bout triggered by Milo Mahan's involvement in the Colenso heresy, had been put aside. He had resolved the age-old faith-versus-works salvation argument in favor of faith. "Our nature is fallen," he told daughter Helen. Given that belief, he had little choice but to merge his will into the bosom of God and search for assurances of personal salvation in the ambivalent language of the Word.[19]

It was well that Mahan had this anchor of faith during his two desperate years in the *Chicago*, since it also carried him through the successive deaths of his mother, his Aunt Jane Swift, Elly's mother, and Elly's Aunt Margaret. While there was in these four departures a measure of economic benefit to Mahan, he was genuinely distressed. He was certainly made aware of his own mortality. "It surprises me to see how much I feel it [Aunt Jane's death]—my eyes quite filled with tears, especially when I thought of her freed from the burden of those sorrowful illusions which made the misery of her life and of so many others. And withal there is a sense of loneliness in that all the elders whom I knew intimately as a child have passed away and that I now stand in the front rank of the unending procession, which also is moving on to the inevitable common end." When Aunt Margaret Evans died in October 1894 he again noted sadly, "the generation before us is fast passing away."[20]

The fact that things were not going exceptionally well for the Mahans and Evanses still living further tested Mahan's religious faith and emotional composure while he languished in the *Chicago*. His brother Fred's lagging career in the Corps of Engineers was not advanced in February 1894 when, as Army representative on the Lighthouse Board, he antagonized high-ranking officers of the Corps because of his "friendly attitude toward the Navy in the Board." His brother Dennis proved to be difficult about the division of their dying Aunt Jane Swift's silver. His sister Jenny was miserable, condemned as she had been for many years to living with and taking care of her mother and her Aunt Jane, two difficult, senile, and sick old ladies. Their deaths in March 1893 and September 1894 brought her a special bequest of $5,000 from her Aunt Jane and released her from her servitude; but their passing cast the unmarried 42-year-old woman into a planless existence. Hartman Evans, Elly's brother, failed in business as a result of the Panic of 1893 and, like his father before him, fled to France in search of a more economical way of life. There he lived for several years, at first with his maternal uncle, Charles Kuhn, who maintained a home in Nice and whom Mahan saw frequently when the *Chicago* was in Villefranche.[21]

But the member of his immediate family about whom Mahan worried most was Rosalie Evans, Elly's long-suffering sister. Like Jane Leigh Mahan, Rosie had inherited the duty of living with and nursing her mother, Ellen Kuhn Evans, a senile woman who had, in her last years, a "strange aversion" to her keeper. By the time of her "merciful" death in April 1894, the strain of taking care of her had driven the 40-year-old Rosalie far "beyond her strength" and to the use of stimulants. Shortly after her release from the prison that was her mother's apartment on 34th Street, Rosie suffered a nervous breakdown. For a few months she was, according to Mahan, an "invalid." To recover from the psychological effects of her long and thankless ordeal as faithful daughter, the attractive Rosalie finally went abroad to tour and to live in Nice for a while with her brother Hartman and her Uncle Charles Kuhn, it being thought that she would probably settle permanently abroad—as indeed she eventually did. Mahan saw her briefly in Algiers in mid-January 1895, when she was en route to Nice, and reported her looking "thinner and paler than when I left home." Happily, her health rapidly improved. Within a few years she married Dr. Francis Leonard Brown, a Scots physician ten years her junior, and settled in Pau, his birthplace and home. There the Mahans often visited her when they toured Europe during the captain's retirement years. She died and was buried in Pau in 1940, at age 84, shortly after the German conquest of France. By all accounts, she was an indomitable lady.[22]

Jane Mahan and Rosalie Evans—they were the Mary and Martha of Mahan's immediate family in the 1890s. So too were Helen and Ellen until their father's death in 1914 and their mother's in 1927. Such was the fate of many well-born Victorian women in the late nineteenth and early-twentieth centuries. Rosie was relatively lucky. She escaped.

Against a background of family deaths and difficulties, the cruise of the *Chicago* nonetheless settled a number of things in Mahan's busy mind, viz.: he was a brilliant historian and intellect, destined for greatness; service in the U.S. Navy was a cruel waste of his time; he enjoyed fashionable society; his family was socially isolated and badly needed his guidance and leadership; and his unexpected inheritances made possible a comfortable future life as well as access to New York's upper crust. He would therefore retire from the Navy, purchase an appropriate house in the city, spend pleasant summers in Quogue, travel frequently abroad, participate in public affairs, and engage profitably in writing. Such was Mahan's plan for his retirement years, as the *Chicago* steamed westward from Gibraltar in February and March 1895, bound for decommissioning at the Brooklyn Navy Yard.

Important to this plan was the town house, the purchase of which Elly began working on soon after it became apparent that Aunt Jane's bequest would cover the cost. "You have stunned me with your idea of buying a house in N.Y.," Mahan wrote her in November 1894. "I have never dreamed such a thing could come within our means, nor do I now see how. . . . [even though] the advantages are obvious enough." It took him a while to get used to the idea that Elly "could get together so much money." Nevertheless, he urged her to proceed cautiously in choosing the neighborhood ("be careful about yourself and the girls in going about after dusk if the present lawlessness in N.Y. continues"), and advised her on various safe and acceptable sites as she narrowed the search. "I never smiled on the idea of going east of the bridges," he reminded her. But the prospect of genteel living in New York exicted him, and he thanked God that the social isolation of the Mahan family was at last coming to an end:

> May we remember Him in this prosperity as in the past adversity [he told Elly], and with our new money remember also the Giver. . . . I would rather pay $5,000 more and be suited in position for the reasons I give—I would even take a smaller [house] at the bigger price for the

sake of promoting social relations. . . . I feel very strongly the necessity of our having some established friends, or we really will be left quite alone. . . . The flat is impossible any longer.[23]

Mahan joined in the search for a house after the return of the *Chicago*. The property finally purchased was at 160 West 86th Street. A remodeling of the four-story structure, which took from June to December 1895, provided all hands with private bedrooms and baths (Mahan particularly insisted on "warm baths"), servants' quarters and bath on the top floor, and fireplaces throughout. Since the house was not ready for occupancy at summer's end, the Mahans moved from "Slumberside" in Quogue to a "very much exposed and flimsily built" house at 489 West End Avenue owned by their architect and loaned to them for a few months. They got into their own house during the second week of February 1896. There they lived during the winters until September 1905. Mahan considered the neighborhood, "the West Side from 72nd St." as "one of the best residence quarters of the city." But within a few years the ladies in his family came to dislike the remoteness of the 86th Street address. As Mahan explained to John Bassett Moore in 1905, just prior to leasing the property and moving out of it for good:

> The inconvenience we have found has been the distance, from the shopping and amusement centers, increased in our case by the fact that most of our friends and acquaintances are down town or Eastsiders. The subway has greatly mollified conditions, due largely to the fact we are near a station . . . nearness to a station [is] a factor of great interest to the ladies of a family. I think we have here great advantage in the air, and the width of the avenues. Personally, I should be content to remain where I am the rest of my life. The ladies had manifested great restlessness till the subway came [in 1904]. This has much reduced their complaint, but I am afraid they may yet move me in order to be nearer where friends can run in and out—rather an illusion in N.Y.[24]

Equally an illusion was Mahan's dream of using a fashionable house in town as a pad from which to launch his family into New York's high society. The blast-off was a disaster.

No sooner had the *Chicago* returned to New York than the world-famous Captain Mahan was taken up enthusiastically by what Nellie called "the Four Hundred." A succession of dinners and receptions followed, to few of which Helen and Ellen were invited. Elly attended these gala functions under duress. "Time after time she went," Nellie remembered, "never a word of complaint, just a quiet patient look, for she knew it pleased" her husband. Nor did Elly make any effort to dress for these functions as a Mrs. Schiff or a Lady Jeune might have done. She insisted on looking dowdy. Indeed, "she had only one dress, made at home, and of a material that no woman would have bought for a dress." She made no attempt to learn the names or stations in life of the fashionable people she met and her dislike of their affectations bordered on the rude. On one occasion, after dinner, a lady of quality airily announced to the assembly that "I really never see my husband until the afternoon." To which Elly archly responded, "Oh! I always get up at half past six and light the fire for mine." This "just-folks" approach was scarcely appreciated in the social circles to which Mahan aspired, and it is not surprising, as his daughter Ellen later put it, that soon "the Four Hundred got bored and went after other Lions, while we resumed the even tenor of our ways."

This is not to say that Mahan had no social life whatever in New York after the collapse of his brief experience with the Four Hundred. He did. But most of it was related to his clubs—Round Table Club, Century Club, University Club. His associates and dinner companions at these places were usually business and professional men, some well-known historians included, in New York. Few, if any, of them were numbered among the Four Hundred.

As it turned out, Mahan never reproduced Eze on West 86th Street. Nor did Helen and Ellen ever metamorphose into Rosie Schiffs. And since all the women of his family preferred the bucolic charms and informal society of Quogue to that of New York, he eventually accommodated their desire to flee the city entirely save for the four mid-winter months. Elly's respiratory problems also dictated this decision, and it was partly because of her health that 160 West 86th was leased after 1905. "Slumberside" was sold in 1908, and a much larger house, "Marshmere," suitable for year-round living, was built in Quogue in 1909. From 1905 to 1914 the winters were spent in leased houses or apartments in Woodmere, Long Island, Lawrence, Long Island, the Hotel Collingwood on 35th Street in New York, or in touring Europe.[25]

So ended Mahan's dream of high society. Neither with a bang nor with a whimper. It ended instead in "only one dress, made at home, and of a material no woman would have bought for a dress."

XIII

Beginning a Second Career
1895-1898

You can readily understand that when I have frequently had £100 for an article, the question naturally arises whether to do work I like for less, or work I don't much fancy for more. The question of time also enters, for the more I have to bestow on a special subject the less I have for my main interest.

Alfred Thayer Mahan to Leopold J. Maxse, December 26, 1901

Rid at last of the limping USS *Chicago*, Mahan turned almost immediately to the literary endeavors that had been so rudely interrupted by Henry Erben—most particularly to resumption of work on his Nelson biography. But since the completion of the manuscript lay more than a year ahead, he decided to commit himself, in the interim, to a few "potboilers." As he told John M. Brown, he hoped that royalties from his Nelson book, together with those from a projected third volume in the Sea Power series, would eventually "free me from the necessity of job-work." In the meantime, he would have to raise a few additional dollars with his pen, especially since final settlements of the family estates to which he had recently fallen heir were slow in being resolved.

Particularly galling to Mahan in the latter regard was the difficulty he and his two brothers, Fred and Dennis, were having in dividing the Palisades-Tenafly property and in deciding how best to ensure a maximum return from it. Dennis wanted a quick division and sale of the tract before he departed for China in the USS *Machias* in September 1896. He was broke and in debt. He had an invalid wife and a small daughter, a history of alcoholism, and small prospects of promotion in the Navy. "The Navy today is keen to make vacancies, and he has had one or two narrow shaves already," Mahan observed. Alfred and Fred prudently argued for holding on to the property pending a careful survey and accurate division of it, in the hope that its market value would increase. Their view prevailed and the family lawyer, Augustus T. Gillender, went to work on the legal problem, one complicated by the cloudy intent of the wills of Mahan's mother and his Aunt Jane Swift, and by the discovery of squatters on the property in May 1897. "If only I could get the thing settled, and off my mind," Mahan told Gillender. Unfortunately for Mahan's peace of mind the issue dragged on for years. Meanwhile, Mahan produced a few "potboilers."[1]

Among these was his "Lessons From the Yalu Fight," an indifferent piece of work which he dashed off in a "rush" for *Century Magazine* in June 1895. Editor Robert U. Johnson had offered him $100 for a 2,000-word comment on a perceptive eyewitness account of the action penned by Philo N. McGiffin (class of 1881). McGiffin was an American sailor of fortune who was wounded in the battle while serving as executive officer of the German-built, Chinese, armored battleship *Chen Yuen*. Mahan had known him slightly at the Naval Academy during his teaching tour there in the Department of Ordnance and Gunnery from 1877 to 1880. In spite of the pre-arranged length and price, Mahan submitted to Johnson a 3,900-word comment. This raised the payment to $150, or to about four cents a word, a rate that became his usual price for "potboilers" in the years immediately ahead.

The main issue in the debate about the Sino-Japanese fight in September 1894 off the mouth of the Yalu River was why the vastly superior Japanese fleet had not more decisively beaten the disorganized Chinese fleet. It is doubtful whether the Japanese had won a strategic victory at all. They certainly had not established command of the sea. On this point McGiffin and Mahan agreed. They agreed, too, that the inability of Japanese heavy guns to sink the two heavily armored Chinese battleships at relatively close range was an indication that armor had forged ahead of gunfire in the shifting technology of the moment. But on the clearer point of Japanese tactical supremacy in the battle, Mahan's observations constituted little more than a summary of McGiffin's. McGiffin drew attention to the superiority of Japan's rapid-fire, anti-personnel guns over the slow-firing, armor-piercing Chinese guns; to the Japanese battleships' more effective concentration of firepower; and to the superior ship-handling of the Japanese officers. From a tactical standpoint, the Japanese borrowed the concept Nelson used at Trafalgar and divided their fleet into two squadrons. One of these squadrons encircled the two armored Chinese battleships—the only vessels in the Chinese fleet worth the powder to blow them up—while the other chased off the remainder of the Chinese force. Japanese attempts to sink the two Chinese capital ships failed. Their use of two squadrons to effect a classic hit-and-hold maneuver, which McGiffin stressed as decisive, was, in Mahan's view, less significant than the fact that the entire action illustrated "general principles, operative formerly as well as now, and which were exemplified by the history and practice of the past as readily as they are by these modern instances." Since the Japanese had not massed their navy (strategic concentration) when war began, or achieved effective tactical firepower concentration at the scene of battle, or destroyed the smaller Chinese force, the "general principles" Mahan thought he saw operating at the Yalu were far from apparent. Nor did he mention the Trafalgar parallel.[2]

The Yalu article, fuzzy, superficial, and quickly written though it was, encouraged Mahan in the view that the production of popular and timely articles had distinct economic advantages over the tortuous research and laborious writing of serious history. Between 1879 and 1914 he wrote 137 articles. Eight of these were published simultaneously in two magazines; eighty-four were reprinted once, most often in his own books; and two were reprinted twice. Thus, his 137 articles appeared in 233 places. In such broad exposure he saw an excellent opportunity to supplement his income and to point public opinion in a nationalist, navalist, and imperialist direction. He felt that the public could most easily and effectively be reached if he could tie his arguments for American naval growth to contemporary domestic and foreign-policy issues.

There was also a partisan political dimension in his thinking. "I promise myself," he had written Elly from the *Chicago* in February 1894, "if I can ever get rid of my naval shackles, to . . . [advocate] one true policy by article writing. Meantime, a year of this administration [Cleveland] has convinced me, I think finally, that the future is with the Republican party. . . . the outward necessary aspirations of the U.S. will only be fulfilled by the Republicans. With rare exceptions the Democrats know nothing of Sea Power—neither by knowledge nor by instinct." For this partisan reason, and others, he searched assiduously over the years for "the best way of reaching the public ear through the press. To reach, that is, the class that thinks understandingly, and most shapes that formless thing we call public opinion." To this end, he attempted to time the appearance of his articles in such way as to assure maximum impact on public opinion; and he delighted in quoting John Seeley to the point that when "great interests are plain, and great principles of government unmistakable, public opinion may be able to judge securely even in questions of vast magnitude."[3]

He was certain, too, that the more current the event treated, the greater the impact on the reader. He had first noted this in March 1893 when his controversial article on "Hawaii and Our Future Sea Power" appeared in *The Forum*. He continued to feel that the writing of serious history was useful and challenging; but he confessed to Ashe in November 1896 that he planned to concentrate increasingly on magazine articles once he was out of the Navy and the Nelson biography was finished. This freedom would permit him to take a more "active interest in the State, Church, and social movement about me." He was also much impressed with the "immense circulation" in the United States of such illustrated magazines as *Collier's*. For these he would write "quite a little," in future years because they "pay very high." The considerable circulation of the "more weighty" journals such as *North American Review* and *The Forum* impressed him as well. Even though they paid less, they reached the right class of people. In any event, he considered his potential readership, highbrow or lowbrow, to be enormous.

He had no hesitation, therefore, in suggesting to various magazine editors the particular subjects on which he felt he was expert and on which he could quickly provide articles. Nor did it embarrass him to accommodate his output to changing editorial needs, gear his subject matter to the newspaper headlines of the moment, or produce on short notice articles that would influence public opinion in desirable ways as well as help sell the magazines involved. In August 1903, when British editor Leopold J. Maxse asked him to write a piece on the "Limits of International Arbitration" for *National Review*, Mahan replied: "I will keep the matter in mind, and also watch the papers for new developments, so as to be prepared as far as possible to write, if occasion arise. My mind once possessed with a matter, and matured, I write rapidly. I am extremely jealous of all attempts to fetter [by arbitration] a nation's—as a man's—actions by precedent promises, and there is no subject on which I would more gladly write, did circumstances demand." On several occasions he asked editors for suggestions on subject matter, as well as for bibliographical information on which a future article might be based. Like any good journalist under deadline pressure, he learned to write with great speed. Thus an article on the outbreak of the Russo-Japanese War, written for *Collier's Weekly* and published simultaneously in *The Times* (London), was put together "offhand in about three days to meet, as I thought, a question of current interest likely soon to be past."

Fastest pen in New York was A. T. Mahan. However, he was not for hire by William Randolph Hearst and other such purveyors of the sensationalist "yellow" journalism that Mahan so cordially detested—not even for the dollar per word that Hearst offered him in 1898. Mahan was adaptable, but only when the price was right and the general point of view of the magazine (or its editor) was compatible with his own. Hearst's imperialistic opinions suited Mahan. It was the poor taste in Hearst's columns that turned him off.[4]

Mahan's prices for his work in popular journals showed a lively, adjustable, and realistic appreciation of the irregular and unpredictable movements of the non-fictional literary marketplace in which he regularly sold his wares. In "estimating the value of an article," he noted, "I have, of course, to take into consideration the amount of labor which it causes me." He complained, as do all authors, that the proffered pay was seldom adequate, "not at all proportionate, in my case, to the labor I put into it"; but he understood that "many things go to the value of an article —the occasion, the writer's name, etc., as well as the mere value of the article considered alone." As he explained to Maxse in December 1901: "You can readily understand that when I have frequently had £100 for an article, the question naturally arises whether to do work I like for less, or work I don't much fancy for more. The question of time also enters, for the more I have to bestow on a special subject the less I have for my main interest." Put another way, Mahan's price was usually negotiable.[5]

As a general rule, however, Mahan charged (or asked) for his labors $50 per thousand words up to 8,000, with no additional charge for words in excess of 8,000. He liked to think that the average article was worth about $500 to him. If simultaneous publication in England and the United States could be arranged, as occasionally it was, the 8,000-word price was $250 to each journal. Prices fluctuated as his reputation waxed and waned and as nations moved toward or away from war. Mars had much to do with his income. For his first articles, those written between 1890 and 1894, he was happy to get $100 to $150 each. In January 1898, he quoted *Century Magazine* a price of $500 each for articles of 6,000–10,000 words. "You will be prepared for my expecting a higher rate than formerly as my work grows in demand," he told editor Robert U. Johnson. In October 1913, at the time of the Second Balkan War, he commanded $250 for an article of from 3,000 to 4,000 words. In May 1914, however, as general war loomed in Europe, the price he quoted to the Century Syndicate was $50 for 700 words, or 7 cents per word.

On the other hand, some professional military-naval journals in which he was occasionally published, such as the U.S. Naval Institute *Proceedings* and the Royal United Service Institution *Journal*, paid him not at all or only token amounts; and to such scholarly publications as the *American Historical Review* he gave cut rates. He seems to have charged nothing at all for his articles on various religious subjects in magazines like *The Churchman.* Conversely, he demanded and received "handsome payment" from illustrated magazines that had wide circulation. *Collier's Weekly* was one of these. Precisely how much he earned from his magazine and newspaper articles in the period 1890–1914 cannot be known. An educated guess puts the total figure at about $32,000, or an average of $1,300 annually, exclusive of whatever additional income was derived from republication.[6]

In terms of the purchasing power of the dollar and the economics of relative standards of living in the United States between 1890 and 1914, $1,300 was a substantial amount of money (as was his annual retirement pay of $3,375), especially when it is recalled that an American industrial laborer, working a 60-hour week, commanded an average annual income of $486 (19 cents an hour) in 1890 and only $682 in 1914. The average annual pay of a public-school teacher was $256 in 1890 and $564 in 1914, while a civil servant averaged $1,096 in 1892 and $1,140 in 1914. Comparatively, the Scripps-McRae newspaper chain paid Mahan $500 in 1898 for his "Distinguishing Qualities of Ships of War," and in 1907 the *National Review* paid him $500 for an article on the Second Hague Conference. By way of further comparison, royalties from Mahan's two *Influence* books in 1893 and 1894, his two best sales years for these volumes, came to about $3,400. It is doubtful that total royalty income from those of his books that were still in print in later years averaged more than $1,000 to $1,500 annually, although this figure is also an estimate. Mahan's records on his book royalties have not survived. Nevertheless, his annual income from books, articles, and retirement pay during the last two decades of his life probably came to about $6,000. The income from his and Elly's inheritances is not known. What is clear is that the Mahan family lived at a comfortable upper-middle-class level after the captain's retirement.[7]

Known too is the fact that there was black gold in Mahan's inkwell. For this reason, he had high hopes commercially for his Nelson biography, the pleasant literary task to which he returned soon after leaving the *Chicago.* While resuming this labor, he gave several lectures in late June 1895 at the War College on strategic considerations in the Gulf of Mexico and the Caribbean Sea, wrote a commentary on the college's 1895 Red (Britain) versus Blue (United States) theoretical war problem for 1895, received an honorary degree at Harvard on June 26, and then settled in seriously to the continued research and writing of *Nelson*. He remained convinced that the biography would be the "apogee" of his literary career, "after which no subject at all equal in varied interest and opportunity can offer," and that Britain would surely provide the best sales market for it because of his and Nelson's towering reputations there. Thus he informed Little, Brown and Company that he would have to have a royalty of 25 per cent (up from 15 per cent) on all copies over 2,000 sold because "I am no longer unknown, and that both reputation and the subject give this book a fair promise . . . and gives a treatment which is not likely to have a rival speedily." John M. Brown responded with a counteroffer of 20 per cent on all copies above 2,000 sold at home and 15 per cent on all sold abroad, an offer which the author accepted. Volume I of *Nelson* (100,000 words) was completed early in April 1896 and the finished manuscript (totaling 275,000 words) was delivered to the firm's Boston office during the first week of November 1896. "The work has been one of extreme difficulty," Mahan complained to Brown, "and although I am in the main satisfied with its quality, the expenditure of labor has been much greater than on the same amount of product in other books; from which I reason that biography is not an economical use of brain power for me." Difficulty aside, it should be remarked that *The Life of Nelson* was written entirely on U.S. Navy time, about one-sixth of it on board the *Chicago*, since Mahan remained on full shore-pay status until November 1896.[8]

Meanwhile, to advertise the advent of the book, aid sales, and otherwise increase his total income from the Nelson project, Mahan decided to spin out of the manuscript four articles (at $150 each) for *Century Magazine*. These were scheduled to appear just before the book itself was published. Little, Brown and Co. approved this arrangement since the articles were not verbatim passages from the manuscript. They were, said the author, "more battle and less Nelson—therefore could be adapted to an independent work." They were also designed to show that "battles are unintelligible massacres when their place in history is not indicated." A parallel attempt by Mahan to persuade *Century* to bring out the four Nelson battle articles as a separate hard-bound work, in a format similar to Edward S. Creasy's popular *Fifteen Decisive Battles of the World*, was not successful.[9]

As Mahan began the tedious task of seeing the massive Nelson manuscript through press in November 1896, three major crises came to a head —the Venezuela incident, which began in 1895 and threatened an Anglo-American war; the presidential election of 1896 which, by Mahan's lights, threatened the continued social and economic existence of the United States; and the debate on a proposed Anglo-American general treaty of arbitration, which lasted from January to May 1897. All of these events threatened to disturb the even tenor of Mahan's profitable second career.

The Venezuela affair, which stretched back to 1840, turned essentially on a boundary dispute between British Guiana and neighboring Venezuela. At stake were several thousand square miles of disputed Orinoco rain forest inhabited by 40,000 Stone Age natives who enjoyed, without being quite aware of it, the civilizing benefits of Anglo-Saxon colonial rule. Venezuela had frequently offered to arbitrate the location of the boundary, but usually on the basis of highly inflated claims; Britain had steadfastly refused such arbitration on the grounds that arbitrators invariably tended to split the difference in such matters. The United States throughout had strongly urged arbitration. The issue became a crisis on July 20, 1895, hard on the heels of a British punitive expedition against the port of Corinto, Nicaragua, when Secretary of State Richard Olney, representing the Anglophobic second Cleveland administration, dispatched a blistering note to Whitehall arguing that British refusal to arbitrate in Venezuela was a direct violation of the Monroe Doctrine. "Today," he thundered, "the United States is practically sovereign on this continent, and its fiat is law upon the subjects to which it confines its interposition. Why? . . . It is because . . . its infinite resources combined with its isolated position render it master of the situation and practically invulnerable as against any or all other powers." Maybe so. But the doctrine, as conceived in 1823, could scarcely be made applicable to the Venezuela issue by simple bombast; and Lord Salisbury, British Foreign Secretary, said so in no uncertain terms in his casually belated reply to Olney on November 26, 1895.

The antagonists, then, were Cleveland, whom Mahan personally detested, and Salisbury, whom Mahan had met on several occasions in England and very much admired. In his annual message to Congress on December 17, Cleveland threw down the gauntlet when he muttered of possible war and insisted that the dispute in the trackless jungles of South America was covered by the Monroe Doctrine and was indeed the business of the United States. In fact, an American boundary commission would be appointed by the president to draw the boundary line as it saw fit—and Britain be damned. In essence, the Cleveland-Olney position was that whatever its original meaning and scope had been, the Monroe Doctrine was now what the United States said it was—no more and no less. Representatives and senators of both parties cheered and applauded the president lustily. A wave of joyful jingoism swept the nation, fueled by the Irish-Americans on one hand and patriots such as Theodore Roosevelt on the other.

As American war fever mounted between January and April 1896, Mahan was appalled. Stroking the lion's mane was one of his favorite sports; twisting the lion's tail was not. He knew, too, that the U.S. Navy was no match whatever for the Royal Navy short of the near-suicidal approach to combat he had envisioned in the contingency plan for war with Great Britain that he drew up in 1890. Furthermore, he was scheduled for final retirement on September 30, 1896, forty years to the day after he had taken the oath in Annapolis as midshipman. But he had no choice now but to ask that this date be moved forward pending the outcome of the crisis. "I shrank from the appearance of retiring while possible trouble from an overt source remained," he later told Ashe. He informed his British acquaintance, James R. Thursfield, in January 1896, that as an officer in the U.S. Navy he could,

> of course, express no opinion upon the justice of our cause or the course of our government. In case of war it would remain to me only to do the duty for which I have been brought up. But as a matter of personal feeling, and even more of personal conviction, I am absolutely with you in the belief that no greater evil can possibly happen to either nation or to the world than such a war. My own belief has long since passed . . . from faith in and ambition for my country alone, to the same for the Anglo-Saxon race. . . . You have in your national career done things which cannot be justified, but one must be blind not to see that in the main, righteousness and good faith have been the leading motives. . . . Whether the United States is right or wrong in the Venezuelan controversy, she is at least showing fidelity to an idea [the Monroe Doctrine] which, in its inception and development, had a lofty aim.

He thought that the U.S. Boundary Commission should be given a chance to render its judgment. Critical as the situation was, he nonetheless applauded the fact that the crisis gave promise of ending American isolationism, of stimulating the building of adequate military and naval forces in the United States, and of bringing the nation around to taking "our share in the turmoil of the world."

He therefore told Bouverie Clark, his Royal Navy friend, that the Americans had finally come of age in international politics, that "we should and must count for something in the affairs of the world at large —and naturally America is our sphere." He also reminded Clark that President Cleveland had resisted "considerable popular clamor" to intervene in the Anglo-Nicaraguan clash at Corinto in April 1895 and had made no move whatever to embarrass Britain during her tension with Germany in January 1896 when the kaiser had supported the Boer settlers in South Africa in their Anglophobic postures. "I am thankful . . . that we spat before the German Emperor" did, he was pleased to note. He felt that some allowance might well be made for Grover Cleveland even though he was "a dictatorial, self-willed man, unused to diplomatic phrasing, expressing himself more strongly than he realized, or perhaps even now understands." In any event, Mahan simply could "not believe war [was] possible—if it comes, and I am in it, I think I shall have to request the admiralty to hoist on your ships some other flag than the British—for, save our own, there is none other on which I should be so reluctant to fire." To Colonel J. B. Sterling, another British correspondent, he remarked, as he had done three months earlier to Thursfield, that it would be wholly inappropriate for him, as an officer in the Navy, to comment on the crisis in British magazines or newspapers. He would have to remain silent. He assured Sterling, however, of his continuing appreciation of "the sterling qualities of your nation, and of the great part you have played and are playing in the development of civilization and righteousness throughout the world." It was a difficult time for American Anglophiles.[10]

While the crisis encouraged Mahan in the years ahead to orient the subject matter of his magazine articles to the problems of contemporary international politics, he was delighted that the particular conflict that was the Venezuelan shouting match passed without bloodshed. Actually, there was little sentiment in Britain for war with the United States over a patch of steaming jungle in distant Venezuela. British tension with the Germans and the Boers in South Africa helped stimulate demands in the House of Commons for arbitration of the boundary issue and conspired to encourage Whitehall to adopt a conciliatory line. The British thus shrewdly agreed to assist Cleveland's Boundary Commission in its study. By February 1897, after a few face-saving trips around the diplomatic mulberry bush, the pragmatic British had defused the sputtering bomb completely.

Mahan was delighted with the peaceful outcome of the crisis because it permitted the United States to focus on other areas where he felt American interests and opportunities were truly endangered. Nevertheless, the Venezuela incident permitted him, in an article titled "Preparedness for Naval War," written in December 1896 for *Harper's Monthly*, to strike a blow for the U.S. Navy. In this piece he linked the jingoistic

ALFRED THAYER MAHAN

position taken by Cleveland and Secretary Olney on what the Monroe
Doctrine purportedly covered in Venezuela, a position he privately de-
plored, to a stirring appeal for naval preparedness to maintain Olney's
bellicose stance against future European challengers in the Western Hemisphere. War in the Caribbean, he argued, was a distinct possibility for
which the nation must be instantly prepared. In truth, however, he had
little real concern that war might erupt in that region. His eyes were
focused instead on the Pacific and on Asia. As he confided to Theodore Roosevelt in May 1897: "In my opinion, rendered decisive by the
Venezuela affair, we have much more likelihood of trouble on [the
Pacific] side than in the Atlantic. . . . the real significance of the Nicaragua canal now is that it advances our Atlantic frontier by so much to
the Pacific, and that in Asia, not in Europe, is now the greatest danger
to our proximate interests."[11]

Thoughts about the Far East and other emerging problems in American foreign policy had begun seriously to occupy Mahan's mind when,
on November 11, 1896, he belatedly applied for immediate retirement
"on the reasonable certainty that the Venezuela business was out of the
way." Six days thereafter, he was officially transferred to the Retired
List. He had been on active duty in the U.S. Navy for forty years, one
month, and seventeen days. The record is clear on the point that he
had disliked virtually every minute of the experience—certainly those
unhappy thirteen years and six months at sea.

An interesting and hopeful sequel to the peaceful Anglo-American ac-
commodation of 1896 was the movement, on both sides of the Atlantic,
to provide permanent machinery for the arbitration of future disputes
between London and Washington. The Venezuelan crisis had been too
close a call. With insistence and support from American bar associations,
church congresses, university faculties, business groups, and women's or-
ganizations—substantial groups all—Secretary Olney negotiated an Anglo-
American treaty of arbitration with British Ambassador Sir Julian Pauncefote. Signed on January 11, 1897, the accord was immediately submitted
to the U.S. Senate for ratification by the outgoing Grover Cleveland
administration.

Much as he admired and respected Great Britain, deeply as he believed
in English-speaking "race patriotism," Mahan was stunned by this dangerous development. He had already made his position on arbitration clear
in February 1896, at the height of the Venezuela dispute, when he refused
categorically to lend his name to a proposal to establish a Permanent
Tribunal of Arbitration for future use by Britain and the United States.

[336]

As he explained to Colonel Sterling at the time, such a tribunal would be in the position to adjudicate "national convictions of right and wrong," and handle "questions of conscience." This was utter nonsense, said Mahan. "I do not believe in a nation, or an individual, entrusting its conscience with any other keeping than its own." Further,

> I think that while peace throughout the world is to be prayed for, I consider no greater misfortune could well happen than that civilized nations should abandon their preparations for war and take to arbitration. The outside barbarians are many. They will readily assimilate our material advance, but how long will it take them to reach the general spirit which it has taken Christianity two thousand years to put into us? What then will protect us?

As the Senate began to debate the proposed arbitration treaty in February 1897, Mahan fired off a number of angry letters in an attempt to mobilize opposition to it. Calling it a "moral disaster," and a "moral catastrophe" filled with "practical unrighteousness," he was delighted when the upper chamber, unwilling to surrender its treaty-making prerogatives under the Constitution to a mixed Anglo-American tribunal, first watered down the document with a series of amendments, and then drowned the soggy remains. Mahan hastened to explain that what American support there had been for the defeated treaty had been based on little more than a "somewhat maudlin sentimentality on the subject of war in general, and yet more upon the horrors of unsettled values and Stock Exchange derangement. Upon such a rotten basis I place no reliance for the stability of a paper convention." Such were the initial views on international arbitration held by the man who, two years later, was appointed to serve on the five-member American delegation to the First Hague Conference.[12]

Equally upsetting to Mahan in the years 1895–1896 was the bid for power of William Jennings Bryan and the Democrats. The presidential election of 1896 was one of the very few canvasses in American history that produced a sharp ideological polarization between a liberal-labor-reform movement and a conservative-business-standpat alignment. The flexible center, where political accommodations are normally made every four years in presidential campaigns, was squeezed to its narrowest girth since the Lincoln-Douglas-Breckinridge-Bell struggle of 1860. That one had led to the Civil War.

It should be kept in mind that, while Mahan often considered himself a conservative Democrat and often told Sam Ashe that he leaned toward the strict constitutional constructionism of the Democracy, he had never actually voted for a presidential nominee of that party. He might have voted for Cleveland in 1884, mainly because of his intense personal distaste for James G. Blaine; but he was abroad in the *Wachusett* at the time and did not vote at all. He certainly voted for Benjamin Harrison in 1892 instead of Cleveland or Populist Party candidate James B. Weaver. In the congressional elections of 1894 he announced his pleasure and astonishment that the Republicans had managed to carry the House of Representatives so handily in the face of the financial Panic of 1893, national depression, agrarian discontent, widespread labor unrest, inflationist free-silver agitation, the ragged march of "Coxey's Army" of jobless men on Washington, the rejection of Hawaiian annexation, and other portents of impending anarchist doom. "I myself became a Republican, I think finally, after Cleveland's action about Hawaii," he confessed to Elly in November 1894. "I became convinced that the Democrats are buried in the grave of Thomas Jefferson beyond all resurrection, and that, with all their faults, the future of the country rests with the Republicans."

Certain that the GOP had weathered the storm of 1893, the sudden rise of "Cross-of-Gold" Bryan to national political prominence in 1896 shook Mahan to the marrow. He had already become convinced that the Democrats were anti-Navy, and that they were pusillanimous isolationists as well. But the possible coming to power of Bryan, a "terrible catastrophe," meant to Mahan the flowering of the labor movement, the free coinage of silver, the disappearance of the gold standard, the rapid depreciation of U.S. currency (together with wild inflation), and the doubling of the domestic market price of his Nelson biography and his *Influence* volumes. It all added up to apprehension that his book sales in his own country tottered on the verge of collapse. "As a salaried government officer I shall be among the hardest hit, if the change comes," he told John M. Brown, "and I want to secure myself on the foreign sales—the gold sales." His feeling was that he would have to write almost exclusively for the economically stable British market, based on the gold standard, if that dangerous radical, W. J. Bryan of Nebraska, was elected. The election of 1896, he told Ashe, was thus

> the most important—even critical—election the country has ever passed through in my time; I don't except the [Civil] war. . . . I believe the Chicago [Democratic] platform to have been in the main wrong and even revolutionary; and I confess that I have not found in the *speeches* of Mr. Bryan the proof that he is both intelligent and honest. He may be the one or the other, I can't find it in his speeches that he is both. . . . My earnest prayer has been that righteousness might triumph in this

matter, not by the mere trampling of a majority upon a minority by votes, but by the persuasion of men's hearts through the manifestation of truth. In no other way can a satisfactory peace be reached.

Ashe's patient counterattempt to educate his old friend in the economic complexities of bimetalism, and to explain to him how and why the controversial silver question was favorably viewed in the depression-ridden agrarian South, was not particularly successful. Mahan confessed to him that it was "over late in life for me to turn political economist," and noted that beyond a grasp of general propositions in economics he had no "mastery of detail." He was persuaded only that the government should stay strictly out of all business, banking, and currency questions. Federal monies should be raised only by the collection of tariff revenues. As he lamented to Ashe: "The swing of the pendulum seems to me toward Socialism in the sense of the Government taking more and more into its hands—to me the insidious growth of a new slavery. I shall not live to see it, probably, but I grieve for my children and my children's children. As none of mine are either married or engaged, this is perhaps over-careful."[13]

Bryan's stunning defeat by William McKinley on November 3, 1896, permitted Mahan to return to work on his Nelson biography with some degree of equanimity, some renewed confidence that the tidal wave of socialism in America had been momentarily stayed. He was pleased, too, that Roosevelt was to become Assistant Secretary of the Navy in the McKinley administration. By the end of November he was busily at work correcting Nelson galley proofs, arranging for maps and illustrations, designing the cover of the book, worrying about who might review it when it finally appeared, and seeing the related articles for *Century Magazine* through press. A gala retirement dinner in his honor, given by former Secretary of the Navy W. C. Whitney on December 3, at which former Secretaries Tracy and Herbert and other distinguished guests were present, was gratefully attended and produced a final burying of the hatchet with his host. Whitney was careful to make no mention of the War College that evening, and Mahan concluded in turn that his ancient enemy never really "did anything to me that could possibly justify me in maintaining an attitude of personal hostility."[14]

As the year 1896 drew to a close, Mahan was distressed to learn that Professor John Knox Laughton had brought out in England his volume *The Nelson Memorial: Nelson and His Companions in Arms*. "Confound him," Mahan told Brown after glancing at the book, "he has whipped off some . . . cream—in the way of rarely quoted material. However, I trust I still have a good deal yet unpublished and more that has drifted out of memory. . . . I am glad, however, that there is a prospect of the book being out before Nelson is torn to pieces by those who are rushing in." He privately characterized Laughton's work as "sketchy—possibly hasty," but because of the "delicacy" of having a similar volume in press, he declined to review it for the *American Historical Review*. Nonetheless, the appearance of Laughton's competitive study spurred Mahan and Little, Brown and Company to faster action. In March 1897 Mahan's *The Life of Nelson*, in two volumes, was published.[15]

It was probably his best book, certainly his best-researched. It was based substantially on Nelson's own letters, on those of many of his contemporaries, on numerous eyewitness accounts, and on broad use and syntheses of the secondary sources available. No other of his historical works was so deeply rooted in primary sources.

Nelson was also his best-written book. As his British friend William O'Connor Morris generously put it, the volumes were "free from a certain stiffness visible in the *Sea Power* volumes; but a few of the author's sentences are still rather involved, and some of his words do not flow from the well of English undefiled." Given Mahan's style, which was all too often awkward and involuted, this was high praise indeed. More to the point, Morris hailed it as a "masterly work which has been justly welcomed with universal praise." David Hannay, a British naval historian of note, also found Mahan's style troublesome. He thought the book adequately researched but atrociously written. "Captain Mahan is not without something of Napier's sense of the poetry of war, but he cannot get it expressed. It is all in solution, and struggles out incoherently." On the other hand, style was less important to Douglas Sladen, writing in *St. James's Budget*, who identified *Nelson* as a study of the first rank, comprised of "wonderfully convincing pages," and destined to become "the standard work" in the field. The *Review of Reviews* found it "reverent and dignified as befits the subject . . . as vivid as it is appreciative." Spenser Wilkinson, Professor of Military History at Oxford, praised Mahan's historical methodology and factual accuracy. Francis W. Halsey, commenting in *The New York Times*, thought that "the most interesting thing about Captain Mahan's books is something which the books do not tell us—the answer to this question: How he, a naval officer, took to literature and acquitted himself in that field of action with so much honor." Praise came, too, from Admiral P. H. Colomb, J. B. Sterling, and James R. Thursfield. *The Spectator* (London), however, pulled out all stops:

This is a book which is so great—great in so many ways—that as one closes it one almost fears to review, lest one should be tempted to use language that will rather mar the effect. . . . Captain Mahan . . . has an almost Shakespearian tendency to drop as he goes along wise reflections, pithy sentences, gnomœ, many of which are, apart from their context, of almost universal application in the affairs of life. Often they are highly polished, always wholesome, and not infrequently very weighty.

Mahan was very much gratified by the first notices of his *Nelson*. Early sales were brisk—over 6,000 copies of the 36-shilling ($9.00) edition in Britain alone by mid-1897. Occasional unfriendly reviews, such as that by Hannay in *Macmillan's*, were airily dismissed: "I am sorry to say," Mahan told Brown in September 1898, "that there is lately manifested a clear disposition to jealousy of my work by a class—doubtless very small —of writers on naval history—David Hannay, etc. No naval men are mixed up in it, but I have to expect sneers from these chaps, who write for magazines as well as in books, with, I fancy, no startling success." Startling to Mahan was the fact that by mid-1898 sales had dramatically slumped, as adverse reactions to the book increased.[16]

Taken together, the belated critiques of Mahan's *Nelson* came to be known as the "Badham Contention," after Francis Pritchett Badham, a British expert in New Testament studies and amateur naval historian who led the scholarly attack on the book. Indeed, almost all the British reviewers, in greater or lesser degree, took exception to Mahan's treatment of two major controversies in Lord Nelson's life: the admiral's entirely logical behavior in the bed of Lady Emma Hamilton from 1798 to 1804 and his wholly erratic political behavior in the Kingdom of Naples (called also the Kingdom of the Two Sicilies) in June and July 1799.[17]

Mahan's attitudes toward the role of women in the home, his highly conservative views of sex and marriage, and his horror of the rampant sin of adultery, were such that he had considerable difficulty explaining the liaison between the God-fearing, hard-praying, swashbuckling Nelson and the admiral's tawdry mistress. He could not understand how a man of Nelson's heroic stature could openly abandon a dull, plain, and sexless wife for the charms of a beautiful, sensuous, amoral, and clever tart like Emma Hamilton. He could not appreciate, as reviewer Morris delicately put it, that Lady Nelson's "somewhat cold, emotionless, and commonplace nature made her no fit helpmeet for a hero of his enthusiastic character." The fact that Nelson's combat temperament expressed itself in almost identical ways on King George's quarterdecks and in Lady Hamilton's boudoir was not one that Mahan could easily absorb. One expression of that temperament was patriotic and laudable; the other was adulterous and sinful. Mahan could admit only that Nelson's good wife was possessed of a "somewhat colourless womanly affection" and that the evil Lady Hamilton, mother of Nelson's bastard daughter Horatia, enkindled in him "a singular phantasm of romantic affection." Moreover, Mahan consistently sided with Lady Nelson in the book and in his personal correspondence about the biography. "I have been careful to bring out Lady N.'s side," he told his editor. "My sympathies are greatly enlisted on behalf of Lady Nelson," he said on another occasion as he prepared a last-minute insertion in the galley sheets to make clearer that bias. The book thus said of Emma and Horatio:

> It is unreasonable to doubt he must have known of her history, there is no mistaking the profound emotions she stirred in his spirit. . . . In this contrast, of the exaltation of the hero and the patriot with the degradation of the man, lies the tragedy and misery of Nelson's story. And this, too, was incurred on behalf of a woman whose reputation and conduct were such that no shred of dignity could attach to an infatuation as doting as it was blamable.[18]

Chided even by Victorian reviewers for his rigid moralistic judgments on the Nelson-Hamilton liaison, Mahan's intellectual solution to the problem of explaining a man who was both tactical genius and sexual rake was to posit the abstract philosophical notion that, in his personality and personal behavior, Horatio Nelson was a synthesis of a dialectical contradiction. This was a philosophical concept he later developed, broadened, and related to a philosophy of history which he put forward in 1902 when he was President of the American Historical Association. Meanwhile, Spenser Wilkinson critically called attention to Mahan's convenient though somewhat superficial solution to the contradictions in Nelson's personality. He wrote in his otherwise highly favorable review of *Nelson* in *National Review* for July 1897:

> But when Captain Mahan begins a synthesis, when, having taken his hero to pieces, he puts him together again, I cannot feel quite satisfied. The question here is: How do judgment and determination come together in the same man? Captain Mahan finds the cement in the shape of "genius." This is to my mind a synonym for miracle, and amounts to giving up the problem. . . . Captain Mahan perpetually recurs to explanations that do not explain—at one time to "genius," at other times to "faith". . . . [Nelson's] determination to act when opportunity offers is the purpose of his life, the moving spring of the whole man. . . . in

him judgment and determination are inseparable; they are two sides of the same thing. If to Captain Mahan their union seems miraculous, the reason is that his career has been a different one. . . . Captain Mahan's duty in the central years of his life has been not so much to act . . . as to teach and to study in order to teach. Academical study rarely leads directly to action; it seeks principles and constructs a theory, but it is divorced from executive responsibility and authority. . . . The passionate attachment to Lady Hamilton is just what was to be expected from a man of Nelson's temperament. It matters little to us what Lady Hamilton's character seemed to be to others; to Nelson she supplied what his character absolutely required—a person from whom his devotion could meet with an expressive response.[19]

If Wilkinson's words were a harsh judgment on Mahan professionally, psychologically, and philosophically, they were far less harsh than the criticism that descended on the unsuspecting author for his exculpatory treatment of Nelson's erratic performance at Naples in the summer of 1799.

Rear Admiral Nelson first arrived in Naples with his squadron in September 1798, fresh from a great tactical victory over the French at the Battle of the Nile. There in August he had annihilated the fleet supporting Napoleon's invasion of Egypt. The conquering hero was immediately introduced into the socially relaxed and politically labyrinthian court life of the Kingdom of Naples, a life dominated by Queen Maria Carolina and by her protegée, the beautiful Lady Emma Hamilton. Emma was the 33-year-old wife of the somewhat senile, 68-year-old Sir William Hamilton, for over thirty years the British envoy to the Kingdom. Mistress to several men, including Sir William, before her marriage to Hamilton in 1791, this daughter of a Cheshire blacksmith completely captivated Nelson. Their love affair was virtually inevitable.

As the admiral came under the spell of Emma, he fell too under the political domination of the reactionary queen. The magic wands waved by these able and provocative ladies were the oldest in fairyland—sex and flattery. Within a few months the politically naive Nelson had become a confirmed Neapolitan royalist, dedicated to the repulse of the French military presence in central Italy and to the destruction of French revolutionary ideology throughout Europe. Armed with these convictions and urged by Emma and Queen Maria, Nelson unwisely persuaded Ferdinand I, King of Naples, in December 1798 to attack French garrisons of occupation in France's puppet Roman Republic to the north. Unfortunately, the march on Rome led to complete military disaster. The Neapolitans were routed, the Franco-Italian republican counterattack led to the French occupation of Naples, and the court of Ferdinand and Maria fled hastily to Palermo, Sicily, under protection of Nelson's squadron. Once in possession of Naples, the victorious French and their Italian republican allies established there the so-called "Parthenopean Republic," modeled after the revolutionary regime in Paris. Thousands of Francophile, pro-republican Neapolitans went over to the new "Jacobin" government in Naples, or actively collaborated with it. Meanwhile, Nelson, his mistress, and the exiled Queen Maria Carolina brooded in Palermo over their bad fortune.

Early in 1799, however, the reconquest of the Kingdom of Naples began. This was facilitated by the outbreak of war between France and the Austrian-Russian alliance and the related withdrawal of French military forces from central to northern Italy. By June of that year the Neapolitan royalist army, called the Army of the Holy Faith, led by the king's vicar-general, Cardinal Fabrizio Ruffo, with support from the British Royal Navy, had repossessed Naples. On June 22 the remaining Neapolitan republicans, together with a rearguard French garrison force (reduced to the defense of two strongholds) capitulated to the royalists under the terms of a generous armistice-amnesty agreement that promised safe conduct of the small garrison out of the city. This blood-saving formula had been arranged on the scene by Cardinal Ruffo and was concurred in by the senior British naval officer then present, Captain Edward J. Foote of HMS *Seahorse*. Such was the local political situation when Nelson, his squadron, and his paramour and her compliant husband arrived in Naples from Palermo on June 24.

Nelson at this juncture seems to have regarded himself as much a servant and agent of King Ferdinand I of Naples as of King George III of England. Because of this proclivity, he made the political decisions that stained his character forever and clouded his historical reputation. Aflame with anti-Jacobin sentiment, harnessed to the royalist chariot of Queen Maria Carolina and to his passion for Lady Hamilton, the hero denounced and reversed the royalist capitulation arrangement with the republicans and removed Ruffo from his command. Unfortunately, his legal authority to effect these changes did not come into his hands from the king, who was still in Palermo, until June 30, several days later. In the interim, Nelson had packed the cardinal off to Palermo and had begun urging Ferdinand to purge all Neapolitan republicans who had supported the short-lived Parthenopean government. Hundreds of prisoners were subsequently killed.

To give further point to his draconian ideological fervor, Nelson, on June 28, arrested Admiral Francesco Caracciolo, a Neapolitan officer who had collaborated with the defeated republicans and had given himself over to Ruffo under the terms of the amnesty agreement. Tried for treason on a British warship by a hastily assembled court-martial dominated by Neapolitan royalist officers, Caracciolo was hanged two days later.

Then completely beyond the effective control of his own government, the vainglorious Nelson underscored his sense of personal independence when, in July, he disobeyed the direct order of his superior, Admiral George Keith Elphinstone, Viscount Keith, to deploy some of his ships to Minorca. Encouraged in this act of disobedience by Queen Maria Carolina, through Emma, Nelson told Keith that all of his vessels were needed for the defense of Naples. Put succinctly, in June and July 1799, the Hero of the Nile seems to have considered himself but vaguely, if at all, under the orders of his own nation and navy. He was, instead, a Neapolitan royalist agent, servant of the queen, prisoner of the charms of Emma Hamilton.

In the mosaic of an otherwise consistent and brilliant career, Nelson's arrogant behavior in Naples in 1798 and 1799 simply did not fit. To be sure, Mahan sought to blame some of Nelson's passing eccentricities on the evil Eve in his Garden—That Hamilton Woman. But he made no attempt to rationalize Nelson's willful disobedience of Admiral Lord Keith, not even in the possible context of necessary naval strategy in the Mediterranean at the time. He did, however, undertake to mitigate two of Nelson's controversial actions—his repudiation of the armistice-amnesty agreement and the related embarrassment of Captain Foote, and his personal intervention in the tragic Caracciolo affair. It was his defense of Nelson's behavior in these two instances that caused Francis P. Badham in mid-May 1897 to close in on him for the scholarly kill. Even eulogistic reviewers of *Nelson* had called attention to these interpretive weaknesses, to Mahan's gentleness in judging the admiral on these matters. "The biographer has here been, I think, too lenient," said William O'Connor Morris in his otherwise friendly review of June 1, 1897.

Badham was at no time friendly. His anti-Mahan language was patronizing, snide, and condescending. In articles in the *Saturday Review* and in the *Athenaeum* throughout the remainder of 1897 and more particularly in a summary article in the *English Historical Review* for April 1898, Badham demonstrated to the satisfaction of many historians, then and now, that Mahan had indeed been much too kind to his hero. The gist of Badham's contention was that Nelson had no legal power or authority to support either his impulsive cancellation of the armistice-amnesty agreement with the beaten Neapolitan republicans, or his removal of Ruffo; and that if Nelson's role in the court-martial and hanging of Caracciolo was not technically illegal, it was, at best, cruel, vindictive, and unnecessary. To drive home his criticism, Badham cited documentary evidence reposing in the British Museum and in the Public Record Office that Mahan had either overlooked in his research or had underplayed.

Fortunately for Mahan, Badham was not always accurate or careful in his own handling of historical material. His writing was often slipshod. Some of his citations were vague, he mangled quotations, and he occasionally plowed well beyond his evidence in his eagerness to plant his interpretations. These weaknesses were emphasized by Mahan in his rebuttal and by J. K. Laughton in his defense of Mahan. But when the so-called "Badham Contention" was over and done with in late 1900, neither Mahan nor his supporters had shaken the assertion that Nelson had acted both illegally and vindictively in Naples during the week of June 24–30, 1799. By the time the argument flickered out from sheer lack of new fuel, the word *liar* had been bandied about, and both Mahan and his foe had become deeply and bitterly immersed in personalities. Indeed, the debate had degenerated to an angry exercise in textual criticism of the sort practiced by seminarians of conflicting theological persuasions. Meanwhile, in his "Nelson at Naples," published in the *English Historical Review* in October 1900, Mahan had managed to shift the focus of the argument from the strictly legal issues involved, where Badham was strong, to decisions and actions that revealed the admiral in a far better light. On several of these latter points Badham had been inaccurate, and Mahan made the most of it.[20]

As did Lord Nelson, Mahan had an ego that caused him to suffer personal criticism badly. Hence the tempest in a teapot that was the three-year war of words with Badham. It was, however, excellent training for Mahan in the technical analysis and use of archival materials and in the use of foreign-language sources. As a result of this professional education, his article on "The Neapolitan Republicans and Nelson's Accusers" in the *English Historical Review* for July 1899, while unnecessarily polemical, was successful in softening Badham's charges of illegal behavior against the hero; and his final salvo, "Nelson at Naples," published in the same journal in late 1900, while also polemical, was nonetheless an able historiographical effort. Reprinted in pamphlet form and widely distributed throughout the community of British and American specialists in English history, "Nelson at Naples," together with the Nelson biography, established its author as a full-fledged member of the exclusive club of Anglo-American historians who wrote in the period from 1890 to 1914. In 1902 Nelson's biographer was elected president of the American Historical Association.

Mahan was a realist. As the argument with Badham matured he came to the sensible, if reluctant, conclusion that he would have to rework his account of Nelson at Naples and include the revision in a second edition of the biography. This he began to do in December 1898, convinced that it was only a question of getting more material from England and Italy on which to base a rewriting of the last thirty pages of Volume I. "I am extremely anxious . . . to make a job that will last," he told Brown, as he prepared also to mount his counterattack on Badham in the magazines and historical journals. "Nothing has turned up that affects the *Life* as a *portrait*," he stoutly maintained, "the errors of fact are entirely unimportant. The pages . . . require altering not because erroneous, but in order to meet an ill-founded attack." Such bland assertions aside, in more candid moments Mahan admitted that he had made factual errors in the first edition and that they must be corrected. He also saw in the revision process an opportunity to bring out a lower-priced, single-volume edition of the work, which he thought might sell better than the original. In scholarly adversity there was commercial balm. By mid-January 1899 he was certain that Badham had shot his critical bolt and had opened himself to effective counterattack. A ten-page, 4,000-word addition to the conclusion of the first volume would be enough to rout the enemy, while a new preface to the proposed "cheap edition," to sell for three dollars, would "notice my critics sufficiently to point out the triviality or mistakes of their criticism."

Still, Mahan's revision of *Nelson* was a difficult task, and his writing of "The Neapolitan Republicans and Nelson's Accusers," the publication of which he carefully timed to coincide with the appearance of the revised *Nelson*, was even more difficult. This article he felt he was "forced" to write. It gave him "more trouble than any equal amount of result I have ever produced," since it required him to read a number of British and Italian sources that he had slighted or overlooked in preparing the first edition of the biography. But the effort eventually silenced Badham, mainly because Mahan toned down his defense of Nelson in the armistice-amnesty and Caracciolo matters. The only sour note in the finished symphony was that the author and his publishers were "disappointed pecuniarily" by the revised edition, which was published simultaneously on both sides of the Atlantic in June 1899. It did not sell well in either its single-volume economy version or in its regular, two-volume edition that sold for eight dollars in the United States.[21]

In 1896 and 1897, while Mahan was completing the first edition of his *The Life of Nelson* and seeing it through press it occurred to him that he might turn an honest dollar by accepting an earlier invitation from Augustus Lowell to deliver the annual Lowell Lectures in Boston. He presented these in ten installments between March 24 and April 24, 1897. Given the general title "Naval Warfare," Mahan's remarks were written fresh for the occasion, as required by the rules of the Lowell Institute trustees; they were, however, lifted rather freely from his *Influence* books, his published articles, and his unpublished lectures at the War College. What honorarium he received for this derivative labor is not known. But it is known that the income from the serialization of his four Nelson-in-Battle articles in *Century Magazine*, 1896–1897, together with that honorarium, "repaid me for three years of my most faithful work." As he said of a later series of lectures, also based on previously published magazine articles, it was merely a question of "turning an honest penny twice over, to nobody's harm."[22]

It was this penny-twice-over motive that persuaded Mahan in mid-1897 to arrange with Little, Brown and Company the republication in book form of eight of his articles, two of which would not be published in *Harper's Monthly* until September and October of that same year—or but a few months after he had completed his Nelson articles for *Century Magazine*. The man was tireless. He began working on the collection, titled *The Interest of America in Sea Power, Present and Future*, shortly after the first edition of his *Nelson* was in the hands of the booksellers. It was his hope, he told Thursfield, that the collected essays would help heal the Venezuelan misunderstanding and "bring before my countrymen's minds the general integrity and beneficence of the expansion of Great Britain. . . . to bring about a better mutual understanding, based upon what I believe to be a substantial identity of interests and political characteristics. . . . in the Pacific we are natural allies." He was fairly certain, in December 1897, that the next serious challenge to the security of the English-speaking peoples would come from Imperial Germany, since in Africa and in China Kaiser William II was attempting to establish new spheres of commercial and territorial influence or enlarge existing ones. Next, Mahan predicted, Berlin would likely undertake to test the Monroe Doctrine:

> The Monroe Doctrine—define it how you may—has the people unquestionably at its back. There is nothing, I believe, for which our people

would be more ready to fight at a moment's notice than any actual attempt at a European political expansion here; and I think [British] statesmen recognize the substantial justice of the position, however much they may condemn some manners of its manifestation.

Because Mahan hoped to influence both public and congressional opinion on the implications and opportunities inherent in America's emerging interest in the international issues of the day, and because "a mere trifle" of a crisis in American diplomacy "might start a run on the book, as dealing with matters of pressing present interest," he urged Brown to place advertisements for the *Interest of America in Sea Power*, which was published December 8, 1897, "where popular feeling may be strong" for Hawaiian annexation or for Cuban independence from Spain. He especially wanted the book reviewed and otherwise noticed in U.S. service journals. "Army and Navy officers cannot be great book buyers," he freely conceded, "but it may injure my works if the impression should obtain that I hold aloof from them." Whatever relations he had with his military readership, he certainly had no intention of holding aloof from the fraternity of American historians into whose midst he had been accepted. Indeed, he sent a complimentary copy of *The Interest of America in Sea Power* to James Ford Rhodes, perhaps the most distinguished practitioner of U.S. history then active, with the explanation, only half apologetic, that "my métier is that of the naval writer, not of the statesman; and if I by chance slip over the line at times, I none the less recognize that as a rule I should limit myself to stating facts—as I see them—and pointing out their military bearings."[23]

This function he accomplished effectively in two articles for *Harper's Monthly* which were included in the collection, "A Twentieth-Century Outlook," written in May 1897 and dubbed by Theodore Roosevelt "a really noble article"; and "The Strategic Features of the Caribbean Sea and the Gulf of Mexico," written in June of the same year. The first of these pieces was a survey of the major military, diplomatic, and imperialist crises of the nineteenth century which could culminate only, thought Mahan, in certain international collisions in the coming twentieth century, principally collisions between European and Asian nations. The United States, as a Christian nation, would become increasingly involved in such confrontations, as her own citizens and statesmen began to reject diplomatic isolationism, military unpreparedness, and selfish inward-looking economic development and again look outward—look toward participation in the international affairs of Europe and toward full involvement in Europe's Christian missionary activities in the Far East.

In the ebb and flow of human affairs [he wrote in the article], under those mysterious impulses the origin of which is sought by some in a personal Providence, by some in laws not yet fully understood, we stand at the opening of a period when the question is to be settled decisively, though the issue may be long delayed, whether Eastern or Western civilization is to dominate throughout the earth and to control its future. The great task now before the world of civilized Christianity, its great mission, which it must fulfill or perish, is to receive into its own bosom and raise to its own ideals those ancient and different civilizations by which it is surrounded and outnumbered—the civilizations at the head of which stand China, India, and Japan.

Since the "English-speaking family," unified by "race patriotism," would be in the vanguard of the West's ultimate collision with the East, Mahan felt that America's commercial, naval, and ecclesiastical contribution to the projected "family" enterprise could be made most effective by opening wider the nation's window on the Pacific. This would entail the securing of an isthmian canal exclusively American in construction and control, the nurturing of Anglo-American rapprochement, and the coordination of Anglo-American diplomatic and commercial objectives in East Asia. To achieve these interrelated ends, however, the United States would first have to be made secure in the knowledge and fact of her predominance in the Caribbean and Gulf. In "Strategic Features of the Caribbean Sea and the Gulf of Mexico," another perceptive article, Mahan developed at length, and with technical virtuosity, the strategical-geographical elements of such dominance from a naval standpoint.[24]

Taken together, the eight articles comprising *The Interest of America in Sea Power* represented a summary statement by Mahan of themes he had developed since 1890 and would reiterate throughout his second career in a variety of ways. These themes included: the annexation of Hawaii and the acquisition of other naval coaling stations abroad; joint Anglo-American command of the sea; the dangers of Oriental immigration to the United States; the economic desirability of American commercial expansion into overseas markets; the interpretive elasticity and war-producing potential of the Monroe Doctrine; the strategic necessities of an American-controlled canal at the isthmus; Anglo-American racial identity and superiority; American participation in Christian missionary efforts to uplift backward pagan peoples; fear of German imperialist aspirations in the Western Hemisphere and East Asia, and of Czarist Russian expansion into Manchuria and North China; the dangers inherent in international arbitration treaties; the moral necessity and historical probability of war;

and the notion that the inevitable progress and improvement of mankind resided in the hope of frequent armed combat. "Captain Mahan," *The Saturday Review* (London) correctly noted in its review of the volume, "preaches to his country the gospel of armaments, the need of aggressiveness, and the danger of a policy which looks only inward and never outward. To justify his teaching, he draws a picture of the near future which will set the votaries of the Peace Societies shuddering."

British reviews of the book were generally favorable, although Mahan's old acquaintance, George Sydenham Clarke, writing in *Nineteenth Century* in February 1898, was critical of the work, especially the author's defense of the American stance in the Venezuelan matter:

> Absurd as it may seem, there were large numbers of Americans who honestly believed that they were supporting an enlightened Republic— that of Venezuela!—against a benighted despotism. It did not occur to them that Venezuela is a Republic only in name, and that they were upholding barbarism against civilisation—gross corruption against pure government. . . . In the Venezuela dispute the United States lost, as Captain Mahan admits, and rightly lost, the sympathy of the civilised world. Why did he not fearlessly expound to his countrymen the cause of this general revulsion of sentiment? . . . The new policy [of the United States], the policy of "looking outwards," will demand radical administrative changes, the abandonment of some cherished insular ideas, and the modification of a constitution eminently unfitted to meet the requirements of expansion across the seas. It is not a question only of a navy. . . . Thus arises the vital need of statesmanlike guidance and of fearless speaking, and it is because I have failed to find such guidance so expressed in these essays that I venture to criticise the master to whose brilliant teaching Great Britain is eternally indebted.

Clarke took Mahan further to task for his misunderstanding of British attitudes toward American annexation of Hawaii and American aspirations at the isthmus. "Don't mention it," Mahan responded pleasantly. "Of course, I expect criticism unfavorable as well as favorable . . . and while I cannot concede the justice of much of your comment, and do not perceive that you have at all recognized my dominant ideas in my writing, I do not find that you have transgressed towards me either as a reviewer or as a friend."

On the other hand, *Athenaeum* cheered the book, noting only that Mahan's views were "a little more crudely put than they have been put by English writers, but defended by arguments specially adapted to the United States." The *Manchester Guardian* hailed the author as "the

Mommsen of naval history" but correctly suggested that Mahan did not have much influence on American opinion. "His book hangs as it were in mid-air and has little practical relation to present American politics." *The Times* (London) considered the collected articles "the mature fruit of his prolonged studies," and the *Naval and Military Record* described Mahan as a "genius." *Army and Navy Gazette* drew a happy contrast between the usual Fourth-of-July Anglophobic jingoism of many American orators and Mahan's "dignified and measured language" in general support of British imperial policies around the world. "No British Jingo can outdo Captain Mahan in his praise of the civilizing work of England in the East," its reviewer remarked. Indeed, the only discordant note in the madrigal of British praise was gentle criticism of Mahan's view that American possession and fortification of an isthmian canal would require Britain's willingness to abrogate the Clayton-Bulwer Treaty of 1850 and to retire gracefully from the Central American scene. "It is not likely," sniffed *The Saturday Review*, "that we should give way on a point which so vitally concerns our shipping and trade without a very distinct *quid pro quo*, and this *quid* is not indicated or suggested by Captain Mahan."[25]

As was usual with Mahan's books, *The Interest of America in Sea Power* initially attracted more attention in Britain than in his own country. A Japanese translation, under the title *The Sea Power in the Pacific Ocean*, was also soon in circulation. But with the advent of the Spanish-American War in mid-April 1898 the essays were belatedly discovered and enthusiastically reviewed by American journals caught up in the excitement of the moment. Thus the *Chicago Times-Herald* called Mahan's volume "prophetic" and found it "almost appalling to glance over these articles and recognize their startling nearness to events as they have happened." In June 1898 the *Brooklyn Citizen* was certain that even "the backwoods Congressmen" had been properly instructed by Mahan on the point that the practical ability of the nation to wage war was "essential to our national prestige and . . . to our national life." In that same month, Percival Pollard wrote in *The Criterion* (New York):

> The war with Spain has made the navy the most widely discussed subject of the day. . . . For it is the navy that must do most of the fighting in this war. It is in the navy that we must trust. . . . All the civilized world knows Captain Mahan as an expert on naval matters. His present position on the Board of Strategy, directing the American fleets, has made him even more conspicuous than usual. . . . So many of his theories have come to reality as to be positively remarkable. . . . His arguments showing the necessity for the United States becoming a great

naval power, though written long ago, have been singularly championed by recent events. . . . The policy of isolation from the general affairs of the world is no longer tenable . . . the interests of the United States as a nation are bound up with the regions beyond the sea . . . consequently a navy is an absolute necessity. . . . If Captain Mahan's practice is as fine as his theory, and as full of prophetic foresight, the success of our Board of Strategy need not be doubted by the public.[26]

It is ironic, a quirk of history, that Mahan at last became a prophet in his own land, and in his own lifetime, as the result of a war that he did not encourage, did not see coming, and for which he had made no personal or professional provision. Nor did he visualize at the outset of the wholly unequal struggle the prospect of annexing the Philippines. Indeed, in mid-1898 he had to sprint to catch up with the fast-moving events of the American imperialist crusade that he had helped launch during the 1890s.

XIV

The Splendid War
and the Naval War Board
1898

The Navy—in my opinion—wants to stop grubbing in machine shops and get up somewhere where it can take a bird's eye view of military truths, and see them in their relations and proportions. . . . I have written and talked and stormed for three months before the Board, the Secretary, and the President, and I feel now very much like the teacher who after laborious explanations, receives from one of his boys one of those answers we see in the funny columns of a newspaper.

Alfred Thayer Mahan to Stephen B. Luce, August 31, 1898

The Spanish-American War might be regarded as an internationalization of the Ten Years' War (1868–1878) in Cuba. Resumed in February 1895, the latter conflict was one in which Cuban revolutionary and patriotic forces sought political separation from the Spanish Empire. Cuba Libre! Between 1895 and 1898 it was also, to use modern terminology, a "war of national liberation," in which the United States, actuated largely by lofty moral and political motives, intervened on the Cuban side in April 1898.

Prior to American intervention, Spanish colonial authorities attempted to suppress the revolution with a brutal policy designed tactically to separate the Cuban guerrilla fighting forces from the rural civilians who helped sustain and maintain them in the field. Early in 1896, General Valeriano ("Butcher") Weyler, the Spanish governor of Cuba, began herding hundreds of thousands of Cuban civilians into unsanitary concentration camps where tens of thousands of them, mostly women and children, died.

Whatever the morality of this approach, Weyler was an energetic soldier who knew how to counteract guerrilla operations. By mid-1897 he had broken the umbilical connection between the guerrillas and the country-side and had brought the rebellion virtually to an end. It was time for peace.

In November 1897 the newly elected Práxedes Sagasta came to power in Madrid. As gestures of conciliation to the Cubans, the hated Weyler was recalled, the concentration-camp policy was modified, and Cuba was offered a large measure of self-government. This attempt to end the strife was flatly rejected by the Cuban revolutionary leadership since it had become apparent to it that there was considerable sympathy for the Cuban cause in the United States, sympathy based largely on the outrages of Weyler's policy.

It was a sympathy related also to belated American understanding of the fact that the high sugar duties built into the protectionist Tariff Act of 1894 had done much to destroy the one-crop economy of the island, bring on a sharp depression, and stimulate the revolt of desperate men against both their colonial masters and their sugar-plantation employers. Consequently, early in 1896, Congress resolved to recognize Cuban belligerency. Aided by belligerency status and by stories of Spanish atrocities in the sensational American press, Cuban exiles in the United States were able to ship a steady supply of arms and ammunition to the revolutionaries, while working assiduously to mold American public opinion to accept active U.S. intervention in the war. Only with such intervention could the Cuban revolution succeed militarily; and to provoke this reaction the guerrillas joyfully burned and pillaged American-owned properties on the island. Unfortunately for the cause of Cuba Libre, however, the crucial Bryan-McKinley election focused American attention inward during the latter half of 1896; and by the time William McKinley took office in March 1897 Weyler's military successes in the field had virtually pacified the island.

There the matter rested until January 1898 when news of Premier Sagasta's concessions to the revolutionaries triggered anti-Madrid riots in Havana by Spanish loyalists. It was these counterrevolutionary disorders that caused McKinley and his Secretary of the Navy, former Governor John David Long of Massachusetts, to dispatch the battleship *Maine* to Havana Harbor to protect American lives and property there. In early February, William Randolph Hearst added to the growing tension between Washington and Madrid when he published in his *New York Journal* an indiscreet private letter written by Dupuy de Lôme, the Spanish minister in Washington, which a Cuban agent had stolen from the mails. The letter was highly critical of McKinley's allegedly weak handling of the jingo and interventionist extremists in the Republican party. This diplomatic blunder caused de Lôme promptly to resign and return to Madrid even before Sagasta could formally recall him. But once again the "yellow" newspapers of Hearst and Joseph Pulitzer had an issue with which to beat the drums for active American involvement in the Cuba Libre movement.

The Spain to which the disgraced de Lôme returned in February 1898 was a country in crisis. Torn asunder internally for more than twenty-five years by civil war and other domestic disorders, the nation in 1898 was ruled by an incompetent queen and a corrupt parliament, or cortes, in which ministerial power was cynically rotated by arrangement. Labor strife, anarchist uprisings, and street demonstrations by nationalist students seeking the regeneration of a powerful Spain built on modern constitutional political foundations swept the nation. Further, the once-proud Spanish empire was a toothless hag administered by a venal colonial civil service. Revolution stalked Cuba and the Philippines, its only remaining major outposts.

The population of the distraught nation stood at 18,000,000. The Spanish army, however, numbered some 500,000 officers and men, nearly 150,000 of whom were stationed in Cuba. It vastly overshadowed in size and combat experience the 28,000-man standing army of the United States (a nation of 75,000,000), which was augmented by an ill-trained National Guard of some 100,000 officers and men. Nevertheless, the logistical connection between Spanish army garrisons in Cuba and the Iberian homeland was exceptionally tenuous—thanks to the virtual nonexistence of a Spanish navy worthy of the name.

The Spanish Navy in 1898 consisted of the 9,900-ton, first-class battleship *Pelayo*, which was laid up for repairs and saw no effective service during the war; the heavily armed but lightly armored 9,200-ton, second-class battleship *Carlos V*, which also played no combat role in the conflict; the new and powerful armored cruiser *Cristóbal Colón*, which had not been fitted with her main battery and sailed forth to war without it; the three relatively modern 7,000-ton armored cruisers *Infanta Maria Teresa*, *Almirante Oquendo*, and *Vizcaya*, whose 5.5-inch guns had defective mechanisms; a flotilla of poorly maintained torpedo craft in various stages of disintegration; and a laughable collection of wooden coastal vessels stationed in Cuban and Philippine waters. Several new battleships and cruisers were under construction in Spanish yards but inadequate funds and lack of administrative energy prevented their completion for war service against the United States. Madrid's desperate last-minute attempt to purchase two armored cruisers then building in British yards for the Brazilian Navy was not successful.

It was part of this pitiful force, basically the four armored cruisers, commanded by Rear Admiral Pascual Cervera that steamed westward from the Cape Verde Islands against the Americans late in April of 1898. Given the fact that, even after the loss of the *Maine*, the U.S. Navy possessed four 10,000-to-11,000-ton first-class battleships, one 6,300-ton battleship of the second-class, two 8,200-to-9,200-ton modern armored cruisers, eleven 3,000-to-7,300-ton protected cruisers, six 4,000-to-6,000-ton heavily armed and armored monitors, and a large array of lightly armed, unarmored auxiliary cruisers, gunboats, and torpedo vessels, it is not surprising that the able Cervera faced the prospect of a naval war with the United States in the distant Gulf-Caribbean with some pessimism. As he wrote in late January 1898: "We may and must expect a disaster. But as it is necessary to go to the bitter end, and as it would be a crime to say that publicly today, I hold my tongue and go forth resignedly to face the trials which God may be pleased to send me." Unhappily, God was pleased to send him the disaster he anticipated.[1]

Mahan paid little attention to the background of the war. He had small interest in the revolutionary uprising of the Cuban patriots. True, in his Lowell Lecture in Boston on March 27, 1897, he referred fleetingly to the fighting in Cuba, but only to draw an historical analogy: "The size of a sea army is of more importance than of an army on land, because the same advantage cannot be taken of position. See for instance the war in Cuba, where Spain has so much difficulty in extinguishing a rebellion which disappears when looked for." The success of guerrilla warfare activities in Cuba did not well fit his larger point of the moment. That point was that "a fundamental law of naval warfare [control of the sea] brings it into strict analogy with land warfare, which is, that armies exist to fight, but that to do this they must subsist." Further, in his article on "The Strategic Features of the Caribbean Sea and the Gulf of Mexico," written in June 1897 and published in *Harper's Magazine* four months later, he took the position that Cuba was strategically important to the United States only if it became the base of operations in the Gulf and Caribbean for a navy clearly superior to the U.S. Navy:

A superior navy, resting on Santiago de Cuba or Jamaica, could very seriously incommode all access of the United States to the Caribbean mainland, and especially to the Isthmus. . . . its nearness to the United States, and its other advantages of situation, make Cuba a position that can have no military rival among the islands of the world, except Ireland. With a friendly United States, isolation is impossible to Cuba.

At no time did he consider the Spanish Navy a "superior navy" in this regard. Nor did he think that Cuba was a territory worth seizing from Spain, as American statesmen since Jefferson had urged. He did not feel that its continued existence as a Spanish colony threatened to bring about American conflict with Madrid. Indeed, in "Preparedness for Naval War," which he wrote for *Harper's Monthly* in December 1896, he dismissed Spain as an unimportant factor in world affairs or in the Western Hemisphere. Not until the Spanish-American War was over and won did he bother to pay lip service to the notion that Spanish oppression in Cuba had brought on the conflict, and that the United States had a moral obligation to intervene in the civil war on the island and put an end to Spain's cruelties there. His, then, was a belated moral and ideological conversion to the ostensible purposes of the war. In fine, from late 1896 until early 1898 Mahan was neither a partisan of Cuba Libre nor an admirer of the yellow journals that espoused it. He was not an early advocate of American intervention in the internal Spanish-Cuban conflict and he seems to have cared little about the outcome of that internecine struggle.

He was much more concerned lest the McKinley administration not move rapidly toward the annexation of Hawaii, an act that would at last get "those islands under our wing." He was extremely conscious of the steady rise of Japanese naval power between 1895 and 1898 and saw the possibility of a future American-Japanese clash in the Central Pacific over an unannexed and dangling Hawaii. Consequently, in May 1897, he implored Roosevelt, McKinley's new Assistant Secretary of the Navy, speedily to strengthen the Pacific Squadron. "Shall two Japanese battleships appear when we have but one and a Monitor?" he asked T.R. rhetorically. "Armaments do not in this day exist primarily to fight, but to avert war. Preparedness deters the foe . . . without use of violence." Preparedness included more than ships. "Your best Admiral needs to be in the Pacific," he instructed Roosevelt. "Much more initiative *may* be thrown on him than *can* on the Atlantic man." Mahan's apparent choice for the man in the Pacific was Albert S. Barker, an excellent officer whom he had, in October 1890, recommended to editor Horace Scudder as a possible contributor to the *Atlantic Monthly*. Barker, he thought, was "an admirable man—few more so. He is extremely conscientious, and in such a case

. . . it is necessary that instructions be perfectly clear on the views of the government." Thus while many American expansionists had their eyes on Cuba and Spain in 1897, and Roosevelt had his on George Dewey for command of the Asiatic Squadron and a possible American descent upon the Spanish Philippines, in the event of war with Madrid, Mahan focused his eyes on Hawaii, Japan, and Barker.[2]

Actually, Mahan's attention was also focused at that time on writing and getting through press a 100,000-word monograph on the "Major Operations of the Royal Navy, 1762–1783." He had promised this study to Sampson Low, Marston, and Company, his British publishers, for inclusion in their projected *The Royal Navy: a History from the Earliest Times to the Present*, a seven-volume work edited by William Laird Clowes. He particularly wanted to get the manuscript written before his planned departure to Europe with his family on March 26, 1898. Since he would be out of the country for six months the writing was something of a rush job —and one reluctantly undertaken. He was persuaded that the American sales would be poor. "There is no use of a man writing what he has no reason to believe the many will read," he noted dourly. Moreover, he had agreed to sell the manuscript for £500, or for $25 per thousand words, at a time when his magazine articles were commanding twice that amount. Because of his continuing battle with F. P. Badham on judgments expressed in his *Life of Nelson* he was certain that some British reviewers would affect "a disposition to the nasty" no matter how well he handled the subject of the Royal Navy's operations in American waters during the Revolution. He felt, therefore, that he had little to gain from the enterprise, and, under forced draft, he barely got the galley sheets processed prior to his departure for Naples. Meanwhile, he had partially compensated for his financial sacrifice in the matter by spinning out of his research two related articles—one on John Paul Jones, the other on the Lake Champlain campaign of 1776—for *Scribner's Magazine*, and by selling for $500 to the Scripps-McRae Newspaper League, specifically the *New York Sun*, an 8,000-word article entitled "Distinguishing Qualities of Ships of War." The Scripps combine shrewdly held up publication of this little potboiler for a full year—or until Mahan's name had become a household word as a result of his advisory role in the great victory over Spain.[3]

It was not then a war with Spain that he had uppermost in mind as the year 1898 began. It was an approaching trip to Europe for his whole family, a jaunt he had been planning for some time and very much wanted to take. Indeed, he went to considerable effort to arrange with Headmaster Endicott Peabody for the withdrawal of son Lyle from Groton in the middle of his final semester there so that the boy could accompany the rest of the family. He was only slightly tempted to postpone the tour by a request from *Century Magazine* that he do a series of articles on great naval battles that would subsequently be issued in book form. Fortunately for the vacation aspirations of his wife and children, he could not get together with Robert U. Johnson, the editor of the magazine, on price and royalty arrangements (he demanded $500 per article and 15 per cent royalty on the book) until the very eve of his departure. Further consideration of the project was thus put off until his return. It never matured.

The vacation plan was to begin in Naples, "work slowly north through Italy and France," stopping in Pau in June for a visit with Elly's sister, Rosalie Evans Brown, then go on to England in July to visit with acquaintances he had made during his triumph there in 1893 and 1894. He would be home in early October. "It will be all new to my girls and I shall take things leisurely," he told Clarke. He needed the rest and he hoped, he told Brown, that the "respite may restore my working powers, for though I don't feel tired out, I feel near it. . . . the consciousness of work undone ahead wears on me." It would be a fine trip, especially since Navy Secretary Long had thoughtfully appointed him Honorary Representative of the United States to a gala maritime celebration to be held in Florence in honor of Amerigo Vespucci and Paolo dal Pozzo Toscanelli, cosmographic adviser to Columbus. Great was his anticipation.[4]

The mysterious explosion of the USS *Maine* in Havana on Tuesday, February 15, 1898, with a loss of 260 of her 347 officers and men, did not cause Mahan to join or condone the outburst of rage and interventionist activity that swept the nation and two months later forced a reluctant McKinley into war. While the yellow press screamed of Spanish treachery in Havana and beat the drums of war, while hot-headed expansionists such as Roosevelt and Lodge pushed the wavering president toward war, Mahan took a relatively calm and detached view of the loss of the *Maine*. As recently as the previous May he told T. R. that his primary role in great events was "only to suggest thoughts, or give information, not with any wish otherwise to influence action. . . . I have known myself too long not to know that I am the man of thought, not the man of action." His initial reactions to the sinking of the *Maine* befitted a man who for nearly a decade had been more the larynx and cerebrum of American imperialism than its sword arm. Nevertheless, he asked the Navy Department whether the *Maine* crisis would require his cancelling his European tour. He was told it would not. Obviously, then, there would be no war.

During the month following the *Maine* disaster Mahan took the stance that no conclusions on the origin or responsibility for the explosion should be reached until the naval court of inquiry, which began closed hearings on the matter on February 21 in Havana, had made its report. There were good men on the court, Captains William T. Sampson and French E. Chadwick among them, and Mahan was willing to await their judgment. He therefore worked on the galley proofs of his "Major Operations of the Royal Navy, 1762–1783," put the finishing touches on his carefully re-searched "John Paul Jones in the Revolution" for *Scribner's Magazine*, dashed off a book review for the *American Historical Review*, and looked forward to seeing old acquaintances in England. In a speech to the New Jersey chapter of the Society of the Cincinnati in Princeton on February 22, a week after the explosion, he warned his patriotic audience against "forming hasty conclusions. . . . [on] a great national crisis like this." In-stead, he devoted most of his remarks that evening to a plea that his hearers not condemn the building of U.S. battleships or lose faith in that class of vessel just because the *Maine* appeared so vulnerable to an explosive charge "from internal causes or from external" and had gone to the bottom swiftly with great loss of life.[5]

Whatever the fiery locus or cause of the *Maine*'s undoing, Mahan was gratified to receive letters of sympathy from English friends on the loss of the vessel and so many of her crew. J. B. Sterling, W. H. Henderson, G. S. Clarke, and others wrote him in this regard. The British press also took a generally sympathetic line toward America in her moment of sor-row. "The thought of treachery," Mahan told Sterling on March 4, "is not admissible until proved, and I do not myself see any indication of it as yet." At the same time, the positive value of the disaster, because of the kindly British reaction to it, was that it would stimulate further the "ten-dency . . . for our two countries to draw together, but the process is in-evitably slow, and particularly with a huge, and as yet not homogeneous, body politic as ours here, it takes a long time for a sentiment to permeate the mass."[6]

Calm as he was during the crisis, Mahan did respond to importunities from Roosevelt to consider some of the problems of naval strategy that would arise in the event hostilities with Spain should break out. Unlike Mahan, the Assistant Secretary desperately wanted a war. "I fear the Presi-dent does not intend that we shall have war if we can possibly avoid it," Roosevelt told Mahan in disgust on March 14. Indeed, during Secretary Long's absence from the Navy Department on February 25 for a few hours' rest, Acting Secretary Roosevelt, thirsting for martial glory, or-dered Dewey's Asiatic Squadron, then at Hong Kong, to "keep full of coal. In the event of declaration of war with Spain, your duty will be to see that the Spanish squadron does not leave the Asiatic coast, and then offensive operations in Philippine Islands." Such bellicose preparations notwithstanding, the Philippine dimension of Roosevelt's thinking seems to have escaped Mahan in February and March 1898.

Precisely what advice on strategy he gave the Assistant Secretary in March cannot be established fully or with certainty. At least four crucial Mahan-to-Roosevelt letters in the period March 12–March 22 have not survived, perhaps because the men destroyed some confidential letters to one another. It is known only that Mahan paused briefly in his packing, set aside writing an account of the bloody *Bonhomme Richard* and *Serapis* fight of September 23, 1779, and on March 12, 13, or 14 wrote Roosevelt on possible blockade strategy along the Cuban coast in the event of war. That letter has not survived, although the Assistant Secretary circulated it in the department at the time. However, on March 24, the thrust of it was paraphrased and incorporated in an order from Secretary Long to Commodore William T. Sampson, Commander of the North Atlantic Station.

In essence, Mahan recommended to Roosevelt a "strict blockade" of Havana, Matanzas, and the western half of Cuba pending the concentration of the entire U.S. fleet for the purpose of striking a "telling blow" at the Spanish fleet. The blockading force off Havana and Matanzas should be composed primarily of an inner circle of "small, fast vessels . . . torpedo-boat destroyers and scouts whose station shall be close to the mouth of the harbor." Three miles farther out a screen of larger unarmored or lightly armored vessels should be posted; and beyond that secondary circle, perhaps twenty-five miles distant, the heavily armed and armored battleship squadron should cruise. The key to Mahan's blockade scheme was the behavior of the small, close-in vessels. It was vitally important to him that these flea boats be commanded as intrepidly, even as suicidally, as were Lieutenant William B. Cushing's tiny longboats in the destruction of the Confederate ram *Albemarle* in the Roanoke River, North Carolina, in October 1864.

> The prime object of their being would be to prevent the egress of [Spanish] torpedo-boats. They should not only watch the latter, but should unhesitatingly attack them, no matter what the odds may be at the moment. Even if sunk they will have achieved a most useful end if they cripple a torpedo-boat. . . . The Department will give ample recognition to gallantry and efficiency displayed by the commanders of these craft, and the men in command of them will be expected to run

risks and take chances. Their duty is at all hazards to prevent the possibility of an attack by the enemy's torpedo-boats upon the battleships and squadron. . . . Each man engaged in the work of the in-shore squadron should have in him the stuff out of which to make a possible Cushing; and if the man wins, the recognition given him shall be as great as that given to Cushing, so far as the Department can bring this about.

Not only did such expected heroics smack of Passed Midshipman Mahan's romantic scheme to capture the Confederate raider *Sumter* in 1861, it also harked back to the spirit of the fanciful contingency plan he drew up in 1890 for the conquest of Halifax. Nevertheless, these kamikaze tactics appealed strongly to the reckless Roosevelt. As he thanked Mahan on March 16: "There is no question that you stand head and shoulders above the rest of us! You have given us just the suggestions we want, and I am going to show your letter to the Secretary first, and then get some members of the [Strategy] Board to go over it." In his Squadron General Order No. 2, dated March 27, 1898, Commodore Sampson noted pointedly that "attention is particularly called to that part of the memorandum which states what the Department expects of the officers in command of the scouts, picket-boats, and torpedo-boats."[7]

Mahan's recommendation that the Navy attempt a close and dangerous blockade of western Cuba, prior to the American fleet concentration that would search out and crush the enemy, represented a shift from the position he had taken in "The Strategic Features of the Caribbean Sea and the Gulf of Mexico," which he wrote the previous June. In that study he argued that the geographical distribution of Cuba's ports, its road and rail communication system, the sheer size of the island, and the extent of its coastline were such as to make virtually impossible an effective naval blockade of the island.

When he revised his blockade judgment in mid-March 1898, Mahan was probably not told that as early as March 7 the Navy Department was considering dividing the U.S. battle fleet in Atlantic waters into two independent squadrons, should there be war with Spain; that is to say, the department was prepared at the outset of hostilities to violate the principle of fleet concentration on which Mahan for a decade had based so much of his strategical thought. Given the known weakness of the Spanish Navy, however, such a division seemed to involve little tactical risk.[8]

Having solved the problem of blockading Cuba, Mahan and his family sailed in the SS *Fulda* from New York on March 26 and arrived at Naples on April 9. During their passage out, the cautious McKinley lost control of the situation in Washington and the nation skidded rapidly toward war.

On March 28, the naval court of inquiry into the loss of the *Maine* issued its report. The battleship, it held, had been destroyed "by the explosion of a submarine mine which caused the partial explosion of two or more of the forward magazines. The Court has been unable to obtain evidence fixing the responsibility for the destruction of the *Maine* upon any person or persons." Wrong-headed, in retrospect, as the court's judgment was on the cause of the explosion, it need not have been so ambivalent on the question of responsibility. To the yellow press, expansionist legislators, and jingo patriots in general, treacherous Spanish agents had blown up the *Maine*, and that was that. The call for a holy war to free Cuba from Spain became insistent and nationwide. McKinley, eyes on the political barometer, had to scramble to catch up with the vanguard of Cuba Libre sentiment running wild in the United States. On March 27 he asked Madrid to grant an armistice to the rebels and revoke what remained of the dehumanizing concentration-camp policy.

By April 9, the day the Mahan family reached Naples, the Sagasta government, after much diplomatic backing and filling, had substantially complied with the American requests, in the foolish hope that the only way to avoid war, and consequent internal disorders, was to appease the bellicose Americans. Appeasement did not work. It never has.

On April 11, as the Mahans were preparing to make their way from Naples to Rome, the distraught McKinley sent a highly moralistic message to Congress asking for authority to use the armed forces of the United States to terminate the senseless slaughter in Cuba. His words expressed the spirit of the moment:

> The forcible intervention of the United States as a neutral to stop the war, according to the large dictates of humanity and following many historical precedents where neighboring states have interfered to check the hopeless sacrifices of life by internecine conflicts beyond their borders, is justifiable on rational grounds. . . . The present condition of affairs in Cuba is a constant menace to our peace. . . . In the name of humanity, in the name of civilization, in behalf of endangered American interests which give us the right and the duty to speak and to act, the war in Cuba must stop.

Plaintively, he also asked the singing, stamping, cheering, and otherwise war-mad members of Congress to note that Spain had already capitulated to all American diplomatic demands on the Cuban question. This fact, he was sure, will have "your just and careful attention." It was like asking a hurricane to stop hurrying. On April 19, Congress declared war on Spain, pausing only to disclaim any intention of annexing Cuba. This declaration

The Naval War Board of 1898. Left to right, Captain Arent S. Crowninshield,
Captain Alfred T. Mahan, Secretary John D. Long, Admiral Montgomery Sicard.

of hostilities Madrid had no honorable choice but to accept, and reluctantly declared war on the United States on April 25.

Mahan's initial reaction to the rush of these events was a practical one. He wrote Augustus Gillender from Rome on April 20 asking him to transfer $2,000, in the form of four $500 drafts, to his Paris banker, Morgan, Harjes and Company. "My object," he explained, "is to get my money on this side, in case the value of money is affected seriously by present troubles. Therefore please buy speedily, and forward by different mails."[9]

The "present troubles" caused him within the week to abandon his barely begun European pleasures and return forthwith to the United States. On April 25, 1898, he received at the Hotel d'Italie in Rome orders to "proceed to United States immediately and report to Secretary Navy." To confuse the wily don, he therefore shaved off his moustache and beard, took the name "A. T. Maitland," and two days later slipped out of Rome bound for Paris, Le Havre, and the United States. It was all very hush-hush and exciting, save that he was easily recognized by fellow passengers on board the SS *Etruria* en route home to fight the great war. Nevertheless, he reached New York on May 7, eluded inquisitive reporters at the pier, and reported to Secretary Long in Washington on Monday morning, May 9. Long assigned him to duty on the new Naval War Board. Once in the capital, Mahan moved into the house of Theodore Roosevelt, the Assistant Secretary having resigned his post in the department and left the city to raise a volunteer cavalry outfit—the famous Rough Riders—for service in Cuba. Elly and the children continued their European trip as planned, reaching the United States again in September—or after the war had ended.

On April 29, as Mahan was making his way home, Admiral Cervera, commanding a squadron of four armored cruisers, virtually the entire operational navy of Spain, steamed westward from the Cape Verdes. His destination and the size of his force were not known to the Americans. Nor could the Americans know that his orders, issued on April 9, were to proceed via Martinique to San Juan. There he was to take coal and make necessary repairs preliminary to joining Spain's 10,000-man force in Puerto Rico in "the defense of the island." In issuing such orders, Sagasta virtually conceded that Cuba was lost before the war had fairly begun, and that, in the coming debacle, the Spanish government could hope only to salvage Puerto Rico. There would be little naval energy expended to save Cuba, even though there were some 150,000 regular army officers and men stationed throughout the island. In spite of the hopelessness of Spain's situation in the distant Gulf-Caribbean, there were anxious moments in the United States when Cervera's force managed promptly to disappear from American view for fifteen days. Not until the morning of May 14 was the phantom Spanish squadron reported to have been sighted thirty-six hours earlier (midnight May 12–13) off Martinique. Only then did a nervous U.S. Navy have any idea where Admiral Cervera was or how weak his command was.

Also on April 29, Mahan wired the Navy Department from Paris, through State Department channels, his considered opinion on what strategy the Navy should pursue until he reached home and could take his place in the nation's war councils:

FIRST   If two or three enemy's battleships enter Porto Rico, or elsewhere, they should at once be blocked by a force superior to any combination possible by the enemy at the moment.

SECOND   In such case, and in existing conditions, it seems probable that Havana could be left to light vessels, swift enough to escape if unfortunately surprised by superior force.

THIRD   It is improbable enemy fleet would seek to enter Havana adding to the burden of food subsistence, unless meaning to fight, which of course we wish.

FOURTH   M[ahan] does not think any enemy large ship would venture to enter any of our Atlantic ports. Torpedo vessels might, but they can be handled.

FIFTH   M. heartily approves naval strategy up to date, especially refusing to oppose ships to the Havana forts. He would not favor any dispersal of battleships, as he is reported to have done, to guard ports against attack.

SIXTH   M. requests secrecy as to his movements till his return.

In sum, Mahan had no idea where Cervera's squadron would turn up in the Western Hemisphere. He simply joined the guessing game going on in the Navy Department and hoped for the best. However, he did insist on concentration of the fleet, which the department had already divided into two squadrons, and he opposed Sampson's recommendation to shell the weak forts guarding Havana Harbor. Such a display at Havana would have done much for the morale of the Cubans. There is, however, no firm evidence that Mahan's recommendations reached the Navy Department. They seem to have arrived at the State Department and there been filed and forgotten until after the war. Certain it is that they had little or no effect on events.[10]

From April 30 to May 7 Mahan was at sea on board the *Etruria*, out of touch with the war. When he reached New York on Saturday, May 7, he learned that Dewey's Asiatic Squadron had heroically blown Spanish Admiral Patricio Montojo's miserable excuse for a fleet out of the waters of Manila Bay on May 1. So weak and unseaworthy was Montojo's force, so decrepit were his antiquated ships and guns, that he had no choice but to fight Dewey from anchor under the guns of the Cavite fortress. Dewey, in turn, merely steamed up and down the Spanish line and blasted away at close range, pausing for breakfast in the process of destruction. It was a glorious victory, Mahan learned. He learned, too, that Cervera's force was still "lost" at sea, insofar as U.S. intelligence was concerned. He was particularly distressed to discover that the very existence of Cervera's ghost fleet had caused widespread panic along the East Coast, and that to still the public uproar the Navy Department had created a "Flying Squadron" under the command of his longtime nemesis, Winfield Scott Schley. Formed from ships detached from Sampson's North Atlantic command, the Flying Squadron was based at Norfolk. Schley's orders were to intercept and destroy Cervera if he hove into view. His deployment to Norfolk, it was felt, would allay popular fear that Cervera's new Spanish Armada might descend on a defenseless eastern America.

Mahan was also upset to find out, upon his arrival in Washington on May 9, that the department had based its fleet dispositions in the Caribbean on the guess that Cervera would head straight for San Juan to coal. In an attempt to find the elusive Spaniard, seal him in, or bring him to battle, Sampson, with part of his force, had been ordered from his blockade position off Havana to undertake what Mahan considered to be an eccentric operation against San Juan, although he had approved such a move in his cablegram of April 29 to the Navy Department. Sampson's task force for this probe consisted of two battleships, one cruiser, two slow monitors that had to be towed, and a torpedo boat. Mahan later argued that this sortie, which lasted from May 3 to 14, further undermined the principle of fleet concentration; it also uncovered Cuba, the obvious strategic center of the war. And it did this at a time when planning for an American invasion of the island was already under way. Mahan did not consider the fact that the firepower of Sampson's task force exceeded that of Spain's operational navy; or that concentration in this instance was both unnecessary and a luxury. So enamored was he of the historical "principle" of tactical concentration that he had difficulty seeing its lack of relevance in certain real-life situations. One of these situations, as was obvious to Admiral Cervera, was the entire Spanish-American naval war in the Gulf-Caribbean in 1898.

The rub in Washington was that until May 14, when the sighting of Cervera's fleet off Martinique was reported in Washington, both Long and the Naval War Board felt that neither Sampson's squadron nor Schley's division was alone strong enough to provide safe conduct to an invasion force bound for Cuba. Consequently, no land operations could be undertaken there until command of the seas surrounding the island was firmly in American hands. Such command could not be established, it was believed in the department, until a tactically reconcentrated American naval force had found Cervera and destroyed him.

Whether this reasoning was correct or not—hindsight shows it to have been overcautious—Mahan was definitely not pleased with the course of naval events to date when he reported to the Naval War Board for duty on May 9. To be sure, the advice he himself had cabled to the Navy Department ten days earlier from Paris threw little light on the strategical, tactical, and political aspects of the problem as they were viewed by officers then on the scene in Washington. Moreover, most of that advice supported decisions already made. Where not supportive, his recommendations were general to the point of irrelevance. Nevertheless, soon after his arrival in the capital, Mahan decided that the disorganized American naval war effort could be traced to the structure and operation of the Naval War Board, the body within the department ostensibly entrusted with the overall planning of naval operations.

His first contribution to the winning of the Spanish-American War was an angry demand made on May 10 that Secretary Long abolish the board in favor of an entirely new and untried command structure. To be sure, the first two weeks of the board's existence had been shaky and purposeless. Formed in mid-April as an advisory body to the Secretary of the Navy with vaguely conceived duties in the area of naval intelligence-gathering and coordination, its original membership consisted of Assistant Secretary Roosevelt, Captains Arent S. Crowninshield and Albert S. Barker, and Commander Richardson Clover. Save for the fuzzy thought that the Secretary should have the assistance of such a group because he lacked "professional experience" and because the Navy was "without a General Staff," no specific role was officially assigned the board. It was a peculiar cross between a college debating society and a War College faculty seminar. But it was a group to which Secretary Long often listened in the months ahead. Even Mahan later agreed that while Long was not the most efficient administrator ever to occupy his post, he came to have "the sound sense to see that he was being well served by a number of capable men, in the Board and the Bureaus, and to allow them scope." But by the time Mahan joined the group, Roosevelt, Barker, and Clover had departed for more active forms of active duty and Rear Admiral Montgomery Sicard had arrived as president of the body. The Naval War Board, which functioned officially until August 24, therefore consisted of Crowninshield, Sicard, and Mahan during most of its short history. It was housed at first in a stuffy little one-window room, which was used for storing books, under the eaves of the building occupied by the Navy Department. This was not a promising situation for the world-famous theorist who was a great mover of fleets on paper and had returned incognito from Europe to move them on water.[11]

Perhaps it was a sense of frustration in this regard that caused Mahan to insist to Long that the board ("an absurd institution") be abolished and replaced forthwith by a single officer, in effect, by a chief of naval operations who, as head of a naval general staff, would have sole responsibility for advising the Secretary on the conduct of naval warfare. There is no evidence that Mahan coveted this position, although there was some newspaper speculation at the time that he would be an ideal man for the job. The point of his recommendation was that the Navy could not and should not conduct war by "majority vote". Nor did he believe that the Secretary could be served well by a committee of officers struggling toward consensual advice. Naval warfare should be conducted with the dispatch and decisiveness inherent only in highly centralized responsibility. "I offer the suggestion at once," he told Long, "before any difference with my colleagues has arisen, or could arise. Resting, as my opinion does, upon a wide study of military history, it is not liable to change, and at present it has the advantage of absolute impersonality."

Mahan returned frequently in the years ahead to his advocacy of the concept of a naval general staff headed by an officer who would later be called Chief of Naval Operations. Suffice it to say here that in May 1898 Long was unimpressed with Mahan's recommendation for a radical change in the Navy's command structure. "Has the Board as now constituted made any mistakes that you can point out?" he asked. "No," Mahan lamely confessed. But he later recalled that the board should never have approved Sampson's eccentric operation against San Juan. This operation, which he had suggested in his cable of April 29 from Paris, was actually under way when he and Long clashed on the issue of command responsibility. Mahan's recollection was, therefore, the product of twenty-twenty hindsight. In any event, from his first dealings with the famous Philosopher of Sea Power, Long got the distinct impression that Mahan might prove to be long on theory and short on the practical applications thereof. He confided to his diary that Mahan was "on the rampage again" in voicing his entire dissatisfaction with the entire Naval War Board." True, wrote Long, Mahan had "achieved great distinction as a writer of naval history, and has made a very thorough study of naval strategy; no naval officer stands higher today. Yet I doubt very much whether he will be of much value practically. He may be or he may not. That remains to be seen."[12]

One eminently practical decision made by the board came but two days after Mahan's exchange with the Secretary. This was the decision of May 12, one in which Mahan concurred, not to withdraw ships from Schley's division at Hampton Roads or from Sampson's force, which was divided between San Juan and Havana, to join the USS *Oregon*, then approaching West Indian waters at the end of her two-month voyage around the Horn from Puget Sound to fight the war in the Caribbean. That she might be intercepted at sea by Cervera's still undetected squadron the board considered unlikely. That she mounted four turreted 13-inch guns, eight turreted 8-inch guns, and four 6-inch guns, and made 16 knots was another factor in the decision.

Another practical decision made by Mahan during his first weeks in Washington was to arrange to turn a few honest pennies by writing about the war in which he had become a prominent participant. At the outset of his service on the board, he was not sure that he wanted to write anything about the conflict. At that moment he had two book offers that he thought might prove more useful historically and more lucrative. He was also deeply involved in the controversy with F. P. Badham over Lord Nelson. But the more he thought about it, the closer he moved to a decision to commit himself to writing a series of articles on the war. He had been approached by S. S. McClure, editor and publisher of the monthly *McClure's Magazine*, with the request that, should he decide to write at all, McClure be given first refusal, "at my price," of anything he produced. If McClure backed away from Mahan's price, or the arrangement fell through for other reasons, the captain agreed to sell the articles to Robert U. Johnson of *Century Magazine*. As he told Johnson on May 17, in the midst of drafting plans for Cervera's destruction, "you come second in order of application to me, and there is a third now. Of course, I am forced to know now a good deal of what goes on, and am making my mental comments on the operations, as illustrative of the theory and practice of war." Another application was from W. R. Hearst who offered his one dollar per word for whatever he would be willing to write for the *New York Journal* "on the present naval conflict." This Mahan turned down with disdain. He had no use for Hearst's kind of journalism. Nor did Hearst have much use for him. He later referred caustically to Mahan as "a stay at home naval officer" who had "made money by not going to war." McClure did not share these views and, as it turned out, he was the purchaser of Mahan's war articles. The first of five articles was published in December 1898, and a year later all were republished by Little, Brown and Company in book form under the title, *Lessons of the War with Spain and Other Articles*. It was a very successful commercial venture.[13]

Successful, too, for a week or so, was Rear Admiral Pascual Cervera. Having skillfully managed to get his little squadron across the Atlantic, his main problem upon arrival at the scene of war was to determine where he might most safely hide from the Americans. He reached neutral French Martinique early on May 12. There, not only was he denied coal, but he learned to his dismay that San Juan, his destination, was being bombarded by the Americans. Wisely deciding that it would be "madness" to proceed to Puerto Rico as ordered, he fled southwestward to the Dutch island of Curaçao, off the coast of Venezuela. At this point his options were few indeed. On the morning of May 14, at the very moment he reached Curaçao, the U.S. government heard from the American consul at Martinique that the Spanish squadron had been at that place at midnight of May 12–13. At last the Navy knew that Cervera was indeed in the Caribbean, and was not likely soon to launch a surprise attack on Charleston, Norfolk, New York, Boston, or Bangor, Maine. Armed with that knowledge, the Navy Department issued orders to Sampson and Schley to concentrate their squadrons at Key West. This concentration was effected on May 18, and the entire battle fleet came again under Sampson's command. On that same date Sampson was ordered to blockade Havana while Schley was sent with a small division to search for Cervera in Cienfuegos Bay, Cuba. Scouts were also sent to keep watch on the sea approaches to San Juan. No thought was given in Washington to Santiago de Cuba as a possible refuge for Cervera's force. Cervera, however, gave considerable thought to Santiago. Having partially coaled at Curaçao, on May 16 the harassed admiral shaped course for Santiago, 625 nautical miles to the northwest, arriving there in the early-morning hours of May 19.

Like a crippled fly, Cervera had flown blindly into a web patrolled by a dozen agile spiders, had thrashed about aimlessly for a full week, and had still managed not to be eaten. He remained safe in Santiago Harbor for ten days before the embarrassed Americans discovered him and sealed him in. Having reached Cuba, he had run out of operational orders—he had none more recent than his original instructions to make his way to Puerto Rico and assist local authorities in the defense of the island against the aggressive Yankees. He was a man without a strategic mission the day he slipped unobserved into Santiago.

Also, he was a man without much combat strength. On May 20, Ramón Blanco, the captain-general of Cuba, noted that the function of Cervera's squadron was now little more than to "elude encounter and confine itself to manoeuvers which will not compromise it and which cannot have great results." Cervera agreed. Four days later he conferred with his captains and concluded that a sortie to San Juan, "the only harbor where we could go," would be too risky an undertaking, given lack of coal and the fouled bottoms of the ships of his command. The best he could do would be to remain in Santiago and aid the army "in defense of harbor and city." He knew perfectly well that Sampson's fleet and Schley's force were "each far superior" to his own squadron, and that "few advantages" were to be derived from leaving Santiago for San Juan. He knew, too, that sooner or later he would be blockaded in Santiago by the Americans. But he hoped that this event would at least "keep the greater part of the hostile fleet busy here, which is the only effective service that can be expected of this small and poorly equipped squadron." Nevertheless, a week later, on May 26, he considered making a desperate sortie to San Juan, only to be dissuaded by his captains. By May 28 the choice was no longer his. Schley had finally discovered him and blockaded Santiago Harbor.

From May 14 to May 28, while Cervera was scurrying from Curaçao to Santiago and meditating on his dubious future, the U.S. Navy and its Naval War Board was sponsoring a guessing game as to which Spanish port in the Caribbean he would seek out and run for. Leading choices in the competition were Cienfuegos, Havana, and San Juan—in about that order of popularity. No one seems seriously to have considered Santiago, certainly not Mahan or the Naval War Board. Mahan voted first for San Juan, second for Cienfuegos. While blindman's buff was being played in the department, and while the fleet was being concentrated at Key West, the embarrassed Navy, Mahan included, blamed everything and everybody but itself for its failure speedily to locate Cervera, bring him to bay, and destroy him in the decisive manner of Dewey's victory over Montojo at Manila. Chief candidate for this blame was the American people. All of them. "I have no doubt," Mahan assured Sicard on May 19, "we have lost the first move in the game, through the Flying Squadron being kept in the Chesapeake, instead of Cuban waters. This was perhaps inevitable, owing to popular nervousness." To George Sydenham Clarke a few days later he confessed that the War Board was "the most unpopular and ridiculed body of men in the country." Cervera's squadron, he went on to explain, first appeared at Martinique ten to twelve days ago and has since amused itself "evading." That it has not already been caught and demolished is to the "public" preposterous. So far this does not move me, for I conceive my well established reputation to be that of a writer and have no ambition to be considered a great general officer, or man of action, for I know I am not either. I trust my nonchalance, thus based, may continue, for I can conceive few more pitiful sensations than that of fretting about what the public thinks. The public is an honest and in the main well-meaning fellow, but in current questions of the day a good deal of a fool.

As a man of thought, Mahan contributed to professional, if not public, enlightenment a "skeleton plan of operations" which he submitted to Sicard on May 19. This plan was based on the assumption that Cervera, wherever he was at the moment, would eventually proceed to Puerto Rico and there join forces with the so-called Cadiz Squadron which would surely be bringing fresh Spanish troops from the homeland to Puerto Rico. For this reason he advised Sicard that a "division of at least four swift cruisers" should be stationed off San Juan, "watching and following every movement of the [Spanish] division within." A junction of the Spanish fleet having been effected at San Juan, Mahan hypothesized, the Navy would cautiously lift its blockades of Cienfuegos and Havana, concentrate before San Juan, and bring the combined Spanish force there to glorious and decisive battle. The movements of the Cadiz Squadron, commanded by Admiral Manuel de la Cámara, would be known from secret agents in Spain. These people would be paid "a very large sum of money" after the "correctness of their information" had been ascertained. Tactical concentration of "our whole battle navy" off San Juan was absolutely crucial, since the combined forces of Cervera and Cámara would number at least six vessels, one of which might be the modern armored battleship *Pelayo*:

> If the enemy succeed, not only in entering Porto Rico, but quitting it, coaled and ready, with the Cape Verde [Cervera] and Cadiz [Cámara] divisions united, our perplexity will become extreme, and may lead to a vital misstep. The enemy would be stronger than either of our divisions, and either Cienfuegos or Havana must be unblockaded, which means free access to Blanco [captain-general of Cuba]; while, if either division of ours be met singly and badly beaten, they will have control of the sea till we get new ships out.

Nothing in this scenario was very realistic; nor were the Iberian actors entirely believable. "Coaled and ready" for what, Admiral Cervera might smilingly have asked the Philosopher of Sea Power. Not only did Mahan join the wrong guessers on Cervera's destination after he left Martinique, but his fears of enemy combat capabilities at sea were rooted in the assumption that something close to parity in firepower existed between the two navies in the Gulf-Caribbean. That assumption was unwarranted. The fact was that any numerical combination of American battleships and cruisers in those waters would be capable of defeating the entire Spanish Navy. Tactical concentration, a Mahanian rubric, was simply not necessary in this situation, so unequal were the contestants. True, American intelligence did not know the exact size of Cervera's squadron until May 14. But it did know the size of the entire prewar Spanish Navy; and it knew that that Navy was hopelessly weak. Indeed, Mahan himself had utter contempt for Spain as a military and naval power. As he told John M. Brown after the *Maine* disaster, it was "absurd that the U.S. should be anxious about Spain." On his way home from Europe in late April he was asked by a reporter in Rome how long the conflict would last. "About three months," he snapped. And after it was all over, he was embarrassed that the United States had been involved militarily with such a feeble power as Spain. There was little glory in winning such a lopsided contest. "We cannot expect ever again to have an enemy so entirely inept as Spain showed herself to be," he wrote shortly after the conflict.[14]

Mahan's "skeleton plan of operations" for a naval *Götterdämmerung* with Spain in the blue waters off San Juan was of little value to the Navy. All it did was document anew its author's conviction that fleet concentration, having been a fixed and efficacious principle down through the ages, must be honored and observed regardless of specific operational realities. Certainly, the plan had little to do with the war actually being fought during the third week in May 1898. That week, and the week following, found the U.S. Navy trying to locate Cervera's tiny squadron and blow it decisively out of the water. The act of location was deemed the act of destruction. The problem was no more complicated than that. Whatever its merits as a historical document, Mahan's plan of May 19 was rejected by Sicard. The captain later explained that "there were not cruisers enough available both for blockade and for such urgent occasions." Whether this was the reason for its rejection or not, the idea was given a speedy burial in the archives of the Naval War Board. Following the interment America's spiders continued to stalk the Spanish fly.

Chief stalker of the Spanish squadron was the dashing Commodore Winfield Scott Schley, whose uncharacteristically dilatory behavior during the period May 20–28 produced great embarrassment and frustration for the Navy. More importantly, it contributed significantly to the bitter recriminations that fueled the famous (or infamous) Sampson-Schley controversy, which rocked the Navy's officer corps to its foundations after the war.

When it was clear that Cervera's vessels were indeed in the Caribbean, west of Martinique, Schley and his division were ordered from Key West to Cienfuegos on May 18 to scout the area and to blockade the port if Cervera were found to be there. Once off Cienfuegos, he lingered indecisively for several days, convinced, on the basis of highly dubious intelligence, that the wily Cervera was lurking within the well-screened harbor. On May 19, Cervera had slipped quietly into Santiago Harbor, 315 nautical miles to the southeast. "The entry of the Spaniards to Santiago," Mahan later allowed, "was deemed scarcely probable, considering the inaccessibility of the place by land." Whatever that probability, Schley did not persuade himself until May 24 that Cervera was definitely not in Cienfuegos Harbor. At 6:00 p.m. on that date he finally departed for Santiago at a speed of four to five knots, towing his crippled collier *Merrimac*. He was also slowed by the presence in his force of the sluggish converted yacht *Eagle*. Still, he left Cienfuegos in the knowledge that the Spanish squadron was probably at Santiago. Indeed, he had been informed by Sampson the previous day that Cervera was almost certainly there. But by May 26, when Schley completed his run to Santiago, his ships were running dangerously low on coal.

While still twenty miles from the port, he made contact with three American scout cruisers that had been patrolling the southeastern coast of Cuba for more than a week. Ironically, these three lightly armed, converted passenger steamers, the *Harvard*, *Yale*, and *St. Paul*, had conducted their scouting operations so close to the entrance to Santiago Harbor that Cervera became convinced on May 25 that he was blockaded, a conviction that helped persuade him that it would be foolhardy to attempt escape to Puerto Rico. The scouts, however, had not detected the Spanish naval presence in the harbor. Thus when Schley asked Captain Charles D. Sigsbee of the *St. Paul* if the Spanish squadron was in Santiago he was told flatly: "No, they are not here. I have been here for a week, and they couldn't be here unless I knew it." Assured in such positive manner, Schley at 8:30 p.m. ordered his ships to return to Key West to refuel. True, he still had the crippled collier *Merrimac* in tow, and she might have done the refueling, but he deemed the seas to be running too high to permit any coaling of his vessels, whether they were under way or at anchor. Hence his decision to return to Key West.

It was at this critical point that Cervera called his captains together to consider the merits of a sortie to San Juan. At a meeting on the morning of May 26, they decided to run for Puerto Rico at 5:00 p.m. that same afternoon. But at 2:00 p.m. they again sighted the omnipresent *Harvard*, *Yale*, and *St. Paul* cruising off the harbor. Cervera summoned his seven captains for further consultation. Five of them advised staying in Santiago. One wavered. Captain Joaquín Bustamente was the only one who recommended a sortie:

> Today we are certain that they are not off this harbor [in force]. They are almost sure to be there tomorrow. . . . To go out openly and accept battle seems to me almost inhuman, because our defeat would be certain; and unwise because it would be preparing an easy triumph for the enemy. Outside of this there seems to me no other recourse than to capitulate with the city when, in a month from now or little more, we shall find ourselves without provisions, since we are completely cut off by land and sea. This last solution is to my mind even more inadmissible than any of the former.

Bustamente's opinion on how most heroically to commit suicide did not commend itself to the realistic Cervera. He therefore decided to stay in Santiago a little longer, in the hope that some miraculous change in the situation might occur. Actually, his only sensible choice in the mid-afternoon of May 26 was to sortie to San Juan, quickly take on coal and stores there, and flee home to Spain. This course of action neither his orders nor his sense of honor would permit.

At the very moment that Schley decided to turn westward, back to Key West, and Cervera decided to remain at Santiago, Sampson in Havana and Long in Washington became convinced, on the basis of reports from a number of intelligence sources, that Cervera was indeed holed up in Santiago Harbor. The Navy Department immediately dispatched a cablegram to Schley: "All Department's information indicates Spanish division is still at Santiago. The Department looks to you to ascertain facts, and that the enemy, if therein, does not leave without a decisive action. . . . As soon as ascertained, notify the Department whether enemy is there." On the morning of the 27th the scout vessel *Harvard*, bearing this dispatch, found Schley limping along at two knots and still only fifty miles to the west of Santiago. Schley replied to the message in a cable, the wording of which proved his professional undoing and condemned him for all eternity to that circle in Mahan's inferno populated by cowards:

> *Merrimac*'s engine is disabled and she is helpless; am obliged to have her towed to Key West. Have been absolutely unable to coal . . . from collier, owing to very rough seas and boisterous weather since leaving

Key West. . . . Impossible to remain off Santiago in present state of coal account of the squadron. . . . It is also to be regretted that the Department's orders cannot be obeyed, earnestly as we have all striven to that end. I am forced to return to Key West via Yucatán Passage for coal. Can ascertain nothing certain concerning enemy.

Fortunately for the disobedient Schley, unhappily for the wavering Cervera, the seas calmed a few hours after the above message was sent. The *Merrimac*'s engine was repaired and the squadron lay to and began taking on coal from her. At 8:05 the next morning (May 28) Schley decided to return to Santiago. That afternoon his force headed slowly eastward again, and, after nightfall, took close station off Santiago Harbor. On the 29th, as day broke, Schley saw the Spanish squadron with his own eyes. The elusive Cervera had at last been run to earth. A tight blockade was promptly established. On June 1 Sampson and his division arrived at Santiago from Havana. The fleet was concentrated. The bottle was firmly corked:

In my own judgment [wrote Mahan on May 30] San Juan was the proper destination of the Spanish fleet; Cienfuegos a probable one . . . but Santiago I should not at all have expected. The evidence that it was there, however, was too strong to be disregarded, and the movements of the vessels and squadrons for near a fortnight past were based upon that assumption, which is now shown to have been correct. I trust our impatient countrymen will not be wholly dissatisfied with the results up to date. They have abused us heartily enough, heaven knows.

On May 31 the War Department ordered General William R. Shafter, who was at Tampa, to make ready to proceed under naval escort with his 17,000-man expeditionary force to the Santiago area, there to occupy the high ground overlooking the harbor. Upon arrival, his dispositions would be effected in such manner as "shall best enable you to capture or destroy the garrison there, and cover the Navy as it sends its men in small boats to remove torpedoes, or, with the aid of the Navy, capture or destroy the Spanish fleet now reported to be in Santiago harbor." The date of Shafter's departure from Tampa was set for June 4. Meanwhile, Sampson was bombarding the city and its harbor defenses. "If 10,000 men were here," he wired on June 6, "city and fleet would be ours within forty-eight hours. Every consideration demands immediate army movement." Unfortunately, Army inefficiency in embarking the troops and provisioning the expedition forced Shafter to move his departure date forward to June 8. As it turned out, he did not sail until June 14.

Soon after his army waded ashore on June 20, 21, and 22 at Daiquiŕi, eighteen miles to the east of Santiago, the Army and the Navy debated how best to position the spiders that would finally finish off the enmeshed fly. In this exchange Mahan took the position, as did the Navy Department, that the first step should be for the Army to take and fortify the heights above and to the rear of the city. The Navy would then be able to "remove the mine fields and advance into the harbor." The Army's position was that the Navy should dash its ships over the minefields and shoot up the town while so doing. This would divert the defenders and allow the Army to gain the high ground behind the city without sustaining appreciable casualties.[15]

Although Mahan later said that the great trouble was "that the Army was late and not big enough," the lateness of the Army in arriving on the scene in Santiago was due in no small measure to the fact that on June 8, the day Shafter was ready to sail from Tampa, the Navy erroneously reported a Spanish naval force to be operating in the Nicholas Channel, north of Cuba. The error, which arose through U.S. ships meeting at night on June 7 and identifying each other as Spanish, further delayed the departure of the convoy from Tampa for a full week, a delay which sorely embarrassed Mahan when the facts of the matter later became known. He blamed the false report from Nicholas Channel on the negligence of the reporting officer, Lieutenant William H. H. Southerland, commanding the *Eagle*. Still, he maintained that no one on the Naval War Board "believed the report to be well-founded; but when sent by an officer of Southerland's intelligence . . . it would have been culpable to disregard it. Had that convoy been seriously injured, we had *no* army to replace the one it carried."[16]

The size of Shafter's force was unexpectedly reduced by 500 officers and men as a result of casualties sustained on July 1 in courageous but disorganized American attacks up San Juan Hill and at nearby El Caney, sites a few miles inland and to the northeast of Santiago. The spirited Spanish defense failed to save El Caney, and its loss convinced Admiral Cervera that Santiago, its back door breached, was doomed. By July 2 the Americans were entrenched within three-quarters of a mile of the eastern boundary of the city. Meanwhile, the U.S. Navy's blockading force had silenced the forts guarding the harbor, which lay to the south and west of Shafter's positions. The Spanish situation seemed hopeless.

The time had clearly come for Cervera's squadron to make a desperate run for San Juan. Better for it to die with dignity fighting at sea than to surrender supinely in the harbor when Santiago fell. Or so Captain-

General Blanco reasoned from the vantage point of Havana when he ordered Admiral Cervera into the mouth of death and into the jaws of hell on July 3. As for Cervera personally, his position had been made clear on June 25, shortly after Shafter's force had landed on an uncontested beach so near the city:

> What is best to be done? I, who am a man without ambitions, without mad passions, believe that whatever is most expedient should be done, and I state most emphatically that I shall *never* be the one to decree the horrible and useless hecatomb which will be the only possible result of the sortie from here by main force, for I should consider myself responsible before God and history for the lives sacrificed on the altar of vanity, and not in the true defense of the country. . . . It is therefore for him [Blanco] to decide whether I am to go out to suicide, dragging along with me those 2,000 sons of Spain.

As is often the case in such civilian-military differences of opinion, General Blanco, ranking Spanish official in Cuba, decided that Admiral Cervera and his sailors could best serve their distraught country by dying for it.

Thus, at 9:35 a.m. on Sunday, July 3, 1898, Cervera's squadron of four armored cruisers and two unprotected destroyers steamed, single-file, bugles blowing, battle flags streaming, into the combined firepower of the waiting battleships *Oregon*, *Indiana*, and *Iowa*, the second-class battleship *Texas*, and the cruiser *Brooklyn*. The battleship *Massachusetts* was coaling at nearby Guantánamo Bay. Sampson in his flagship, the armored cruiser *New York*, was also absent from the blockade station, having gone down the coast earlier that morning to confer with General Shafter. Otherwise, the U.S. battle fleet was intact and ready, a fact the debouching Spaniards could observe. Captain V. M. Concas of Cervera's flagship *Infanta Maria Teresa* later described the scene:

> My bugles were the last echo of those which history tells you sounded in the taking of Granada; it was the signal that the history of four centuries was ended. . . . "Poor Spain!" I said to my beloved and noble Admiral; and he answered by an expressive motion, as though to say he had done everything to avoid it, and that his conscience was clear.

Cervera's sad shrug told the story. The Battle of Santiago was no battle at all. It was, instead, a four-hour turkey shoot running westward along the Cuban coast during which all the Spanish ships were hit, set afire, and beached or sunk. It is estimated that 160 Spanish sailors were killed, 240 were wounded, and 1,800 were captured, including Cervera. American casualties were one man killed and one man wounded. No substantial damage was done any U.S. warship.

Unhappily for Sampson, he managed to scramble back to the scene barely in time to witness from a distance the final phase of the battle, the shelling and beaching of the burning *Cristóbal Colón* at 1:30 p.m. The senior American officer present during the gloriously unequal engagement was his second in command, Commodore Winfield Scott Schley, who conducted operations from his station in the *Brooklyn*. When Rear Admiral Sampson finally caught up with the action, Schley signaled him: "We have gained a great victory. Details will be communicated." Snapped Sampson in return: "Report your casualties." These were the opening shots in the Battle of Sampson-Schley. "The fleet under my command offers the nation as a Fourth of July present the whole of Cervera's fleet," Sampson boastfully reported to the Navy Department that evening. He did not mention Schley's presence at the scene.

No tactical lessons were to be learned from the Navy's "Fourth of July" present to the nation or from Dewey's target practice on Admiral Montojo in Manila Bay on May 1. Neither action was a Nile or a Trafalgar. For this reason Mahan had little to say about the unequal slaughter at Santiago, then or later. He mentioned it scarcely at all either in his *Lessons of the War with Spain* or in any of his books or articles. Indeed, the engagement was important in his mind during and after the war only insofar as the deployment of the U.S. warships involved in the blockade prior to the battle related to the merits of Sampson's case in the controversy with Schley, an argument that turned on which of the two officers was the true Hero of Santiago. Further, neither Manila nor Santiago fitted well Mahan's historical "principles" or his "art of war" concepts. Thus he confessed to Lodge that while both actions were "in a strict sense decisive battles— much more so than most naval actions of the past, they seem to give little scope for my usual treatment." It took no tactical genius to win the naval actions at Manila and Santiago, unless a form of genius is required to shoot sluggish fish in small barrels with large guns. About the best Mahan could do with those embarrassingly happy engagements was later to link them with his arguments for U.S. military and naval preparedness. As he wrote in September 1914:

> In the War with Spain, it was Spain most markedly who got that for which she prepared. The brave but unfortunate Cervera wrote some months before Santiago: "Unless I am given the means for practice I shall go to a Trafalgar"; and he went. Lack of proper preparation will not prevent war, but it is pretty sure to make war disastrous.[17]

The elimination of the Cervera annoyance at Santiago did, however, permit Mahan and the Naval War Board to turn to a threat far more dangerous to the nation's military and diplomatic interests, particularly its interests in the Philippines. This was the sortie on June 16, two days after Shafter left Tampa, of Admiral Manuel de la Cámara's squadron from Cadiz. As will be seen, it was this threat, or one aspect of it, that persuaded the McKinley administration in July to settle for something less than the unconditional surrender of the city of Santiago, which was being besieged by General Shafter. In the solution of these complicated problems, one on the sea and the other on land, Mahan played an important role. If his reaction to the strategic implications of the Cámara sortie was somewhat conservative, it had the virtue of being firmly grounded in the realities of international power politics as the war with Spain drew to a close; and certainly the bloodless formula he devised on July 13 for General José Toral's surrender to Shafter at Santiago contributed greatly to the welfare of the United States and to the safety of her Navy at a time when international complications stemming from Dewey's presence in Manila Bay were mounting.

Admiral Cámara's squadron numbered thirteen ships. Principal among these were the heavily armored 16-knot battleship *Pelayo*, mounting in turrets two 12.5-inch and two 11-inch guns, and the lightly armored, second-class battleship *Carlos V*, capable of 20 knots and mounting two turreted 11-inch and eight exposed 5.5-inch guns. The *Pelayo* was a more powerful vessel by far than anything Spain had sent to the Gulf-Caribbean with Cervera. Cámara's ships were accompanied and encumbered by two troop transports carrying 4,000 soldiers, four colliers carrying 20,000 tons of coal, and five antiquated and useless destroyers, three of which had to be taken in tow soon after the voyage began. Nevertheless, it appeared at first blush that Cámara's was at least a modestly respectable force.

In Washington it seemed that Cámara was bound eastward to Manila, via Suez, there to contest with Dewey the control of the bay. And since Dewey had in his squadron in the Philippines not a single armored cruiser, the ability of Cámara, with 12.5-inch guns, to win such a fight was granted. Dewey would have to avoid battle with the formidable *Pelayo* by fleeing the harbor, a flight that would mean abandoning the Filipino forces fighting Spain outside Manila. It would also mean virtually surrendering Luzon to the imperial mercies of a powerful German squadron of observation under Vice Admiral Otto von Diederichs that had arrived preyfully on the scene shortly after Admiral Montojo sank out of sight on May 1.

The strategic problem of the Navy and its War Board was twofold: to get some heavily armored and armed ships out to Manila to reinforce Dewey; and to create countervailing pressures that would force Madrid to order Cámara back to Spain. The diplomatic problem was to avoid war with Germany while maintaining a respectable naval presence at Manila until it had been decided what to do with the Philippines after the war with Spain had been won.

Since the Navy Department was "in constant communication with agents in Spain by cable," and since "Cámara's preparations were known, and his purposes considered," the Naval War Board reacted "instantly" to news of Cámara's sortie. It recommended that the battleships *Iowa* and *Oregon* and the cruiser *Brooklyn* be detached from Sampson's block force off Santiago and sent to Manila under the command of Commodore John Crittenden Watson. Although this decision again to divide the battle fleet was not in harmony with his historical principle of tactical concentration, Mahan supported the board, reasoning that, even without the three designated vessels, Sampson had force enough to keep Cervera bottled up in Santiago; or to defeat him if he emerged.

Further, the board urged that while Watson's task force was being provisioned and otherwise made ready for the long voyage to Manila, via Suez, the armored monitors *Monterey* (two 12-inch and two 10-inch guns) and *Monadnock* (four 10-inch guns) be dispatched to reinforce Dewey. This was done. Fortunately, the *Monterey* had left San Francisco for Manila on June 11, or five days before Cámara sailed from Cadiz. She had been sent largely for diplomatic reasons—to strengthen Dewey's posture in Manila Bay in face of the arrival there of British, German, and Japanese warships, it not then being known in London, Berlin, and Tokyo whether the United States intended permanently to retain the Philippines. Because of uncertainty over American diplomatic goals, there appeared on the Manila scene these happy harvesters of the dangling Philippine fruit.

The dispatch of the *Monadnock*, on the other hand, was directly related to Cámara's sortie. The fact that she was not ordered earlier and did not actually sail until June 25 later haunted Mahan as being "the only serious oversight chargeable to the Board." Her delayed departure should have given the board pause, since neither of the lumbering, mechanically unpredictable monitors would likely have reached Manila ahead of the *Pelayo*, had Cámara pushed on past Suez.

Mahan could not have known in mid-June, and nor could the War Board, that Cámara's journey eastward was an exercise in futility conceived in that special dream world inhabited by Spain's incompetent Ministry of Marine. American intelligence in this instance failed almost as badly as did the Spanish Navy at Santiago. It did not inform the Naval War Board, for example, that both the *Pelayo* and the *Carlos V* were unready for sea, that the remainder of the Spanish squadron was flotsam, and that Cámara's orders were to avoid combat with Dewey, in the event his force somehow managed to traverse the 6,300 miles of ocean that separated Cadiz from the Philippines. The sole purpose of Cámara's voyage was to reestablish a Spanish presence of sorts in the central and south Philippines, well clear of Dewey, in the hope of strengthening Madrid's hand at the peace table if and when the future of some or all of the islands in the archipelago was discussed. Needless to say, this modest political goal was abandoned when news of Cervera's horrendous defeat at Santiago on July 3 reached Madrid. Elements of Sampson's fleet having been freed for adventures elsewhere, including operations on the Spanish coast, Madrid considered it imperative that what was left of the Spanish Navy be hastily assembled in home waters. On July 5 Cámara, then in the Red Sea, was therefore ordered to return immediately to Spain. Two days later he passed north through the Suez Canal and on July 8 shaped course westward for Cartagena, Spain. As Mahan later wrote, "Cámara's return through the Canal, July 7, removed all possible apprehension concerning Dewey." But that was later.

On July 6, three days after Schley's triumph at Santiago, the Naval War Board, unaware of Cámara's recall to Spain, determined to push ahead with provisioning Watson's task force and dispatching it to succor Dewey at Manila. It also recommended that the main battle fleet, under Sampson, escort Watson through the Strait of Gibraltar. If, by the time Sampson and Watson arrived at the strait, the Spaniards had not seen the hopelessness of their cause and sued for peace, Sampson would be ordered to bombard the coast of Spain. Such action would, at the very least, force Cámara to return to home waters to defend the motherland.

The possibility that Spain might be bombarded was announced with great fanfare in Washington and was probably a factor in Cámara being turned around near Suez on July 5—or being kept turned around once he had started westward toward Cartagena on July 8. In any event, by July 12 Mahan could tell Lodge that "the changes in the general situation due to Cervera's defeat and to Cámara's return" had necessitated the formulation of new plans. Such plans involved nothing less than intense psychological warfare designed to force Spain to the peace table on pain of massive attacks on Cadiz, Málaga, and Barcelona. The final plan thus reaffirmed the earlier decision to send Sampson's fleet to the strait together with Watson's task force, both to bombard the Spanish coast if necessary. The Army, meanwhile, had evolved separate plans for the invasion and conquest of Puerto Rico.[18]

Mahan opposed, root and branch, the idea of coastal bombardment. On July 18 he submitted to the Naval War Board a summary of strategic and tactical options then under review in the Navy Department along with his personal assessment of the situation. Once again his abiding faith in the existence of historical principles of war, or the "art of war," dominated his analysis. He agreed, for instance, that there should be an American invasion of Puerto Rico, but he was loath to recommend any substantial naval support for it, on the grounds that it would simply require another tactically unsound division of the battle fleet. He was also reluctant to send Sampson to the Strait of Gibraltar with Watson because the Spanish Navy "under the apprehension now entertained of bombardment of coast cities" would undoubtedly concentrate all its available remaining force at Gibraltar. And even were the Spaniards to lose the engagement that would then ensue, considerable damage would surely be done to some of the participating American vessels. Mahan weighed the alternatives:

> The true solution to our present doubt, in my judgment, is this: either send the six armored ships together, seeing Watson through the Straits, or else postpone sending Watson and concentrate on Porto Rico. . . . I do not consider our force justifies the contemplated division of it. However beneficial the effect upon our diplomacy to reinforce Dewey, it is by no means equal to the injury to our diplomacy caused by a couple of armored ships being disabled.

He hoped that Spain would sue for peace before it became necessary to shell her coastal cities. Further, he argued vigorously that the nation and the Navy had little to gain by fighting another pitched fleet battle, especially one fought in hostile Spanish waters. "Their best chance against us is always in the Straits of Gibraltar. So evident is this that we surely would never dream of sending our fleet there, except to help Dewey." In effect, Mahan was recommending on July 18 that for the time being the Navy should do little or nothing beyond cautiously supporting the Army's invasion of Puerto Rico. The Navy had effected tactical concentration of the fleet—it should not risk losing it. It enjoyed command of the sea—it should not risk losing that either. These were known historical principles and they should not be tampered with. Therefore, until it acquired new battleships, the U.S. Navy should remain virtually inactive:

> I submit that the crucial feature of the whole situation, military and diplomatic, at present, is the control of the sea; and that while we unques-

tionably possess it, as against Spain, we have no such margin as justifies a risk without adequate gain. No other battleship is promised before eight months, and such promises are rarely fulfilled as to date.[19]

Besides the presumed historical principles involved, Mahan's recommendation for temporary inaction was influenced by the events of a crucial strategy meeting that had taken place at the White House on July 13. Attended by President McKinley, Secretary of War Russell A. Alger, Adjutant General Henry C. Corbin, Secretary of the Navy Long, Mahan, Sicard, Crowninshield, and others, the conference was called to resolve an Army-Navy disagreement over responsibility for the continued military stalemate in the trenches at Santiago and to consider a Spanish proposal for the conditional surrender of the city. With Cervera's squadron destroyed, General Shafter had again insisted that the Navy steam over the mines, blast its way into the harbor, and help bring about the surrender of the city.

This foolish notion was a measure of the Army's tactical frustration in Cuba in mid-July 1898. Shafter's casualties at El Caney had been relatively heavy, nearly 10 per cent of his effective force. Since then some 4,000 Spanish infantrymen from other commands on the island had slipped into the besieged city to reinforce General José Toral. Malaria had broken out in the American army, and the offshore bombardment of the city by Sampson's squadron had proven ineffective. Further, the rotund William Shafter had no stomach for leading his green troops in a banzai attack against Spanish barbed-wire defenses manned by 11,500 well-armed soldiers. Hence, in negotiations with General Toral held between the lines on July 13, he and General Nelson A. Miles accepted Toral's formula for surrender of the city—a formula that permitted the Spanish garrison to march out of Santiago, arms in hand, to Holguín or to whatever place it chose. Under this quaint arrangement, Toral would be free to join Spanish forces elsewhere in Cuba and continue fighting, were he so disposed. Mahan recalled that at first blush he had favored the proposition "considering that the place was what we then needed chiefly." In any event, "Fat Billy" Shafter had neither the force nor the will to take the city by assault. Hence his continued insistence on close Navy support in the harbor.

At the very moment the conferees gathered in the White House that day to discuss the Toral formula, Watson was coaling his task force for his voyage to Manila, Sampson was being ordered to accompany him and lead the main battle fleet to the western Mediterranean, Cámara was well on his way back to Spain from Suez, and disquieting news of arrogant German behavior in Manila Bay was reaching Washington. In fine, the Navy had better and more urgent things to do than remain longer at Santiago in the vain hope of helping the bumbling Shafter capture the city.

Because he wanted no further risk to the Navy whatever and because the "kernel of the matter—especially from the naval point of view—was to get the harbor and release our ships to other duties," Mahan was not opposed to the Toral proposal. But he took advantage of the White House meeting to object to the risky proposition that the Navy should help solve Shafter's dilemma by steaming suicidally into Santiago Harbor, guns blazing. This comment angered Secretary Alger who began abusing Sampson and the Navy for not cooperating fully with Shafter and the Army. At this point Mahan lost his temper and "sailed" into him. He pointed out that Alger had no conception whatever of the function or purpose of the U.S. Navy or of navies in general, and said he did not propose to sit silently by and hear the Navy attacked. This outburst, recalled Long, "rather amused the President who always liked a little badinage" and was "glad of the rebuke."

On the other hand, McKinley was not at all pleased with the Army's proposed concession to Toral. Mahan recalled that "the President was very emphatically opposed to it—indeed *vehemently*. . . . It was owing to the President primarily—and to no one else—that the Spanish demand was rejected." McKinley thought that acceptance of such a surrender arrangement would prolong the war and result in the impression at home and abroad that "such terms were extorted only from our sense of weakness." His answer to Secretary Alger, then, was a resounding NO. At this moment of impasse Mahan suggested that for Toral and his army "to surrender and to return to Spain would meet all our requirements and perhaps be acceptable to them." This generous compromise proved acceptable to Toral and he finally agreed to surrender Santiago on that basis—that his entire army, bearing its arms and banners, be transported free of charge by the Americans back to Spain. So pleased was Mahan with his happy solution to the problem that he asked Long a few days later: "Do you recall who it was in the Council suggested the Santiago garrison be allowed to return to Spain?" "Yes," replied the Secretary without hesitation, "it was you."

Unfortunately for Mahan's ego and for the eternal salvation of his footnote to history at Santiago, in the summer of 1899 Secretary Alger claimed Mahan's surrender compromise as his own. This upset Mahan enormously and for two years he fought for the credit he knew was his. Indeed, so few historical garlands were there to be distributed after the ludicrous Spanish-American War that his insistence on the point is understandable.

His surrender plan had saved Army lives and Navy ships, and he felt that Clio should clearly record that fact for the edification of future generations of Americans. While he wanted at times to demand that he be given his due publicly and pleaded with Long to help him set the historical record straight, he decided to confine his considerable pique in the matter to the circle of his immediate friends and correspondents. "History doubtless will do justice," he sighed to Seth Low. To Long he bitterly complained: "The credit, such as it is, belongs to me. . . . it appears to me monstrous that it should stand to the credit of a man [Alger] who, as far as I could judge him, was a monument of incapacity."[20]

Mahan's recommendation of July 18 that the Navy postpone further sea operations against Spain was influenced by his analysis of international affairs. This evaluation included the uncertainties of America's role in the Far East, the implications of the Anglo-American rapprochement that flowered in 1898, and the dangers implicit in growing Anglo-German tension.

Nothing about the onset of hostilities in April 1898 had pleased Mahan more than that it bid fair to stimulate Anglo-American rapprochement. Having convinced himself that from America's standpoint the conflict was a "just war . . . free from base alloy," and that the Constitution would somehow be reinterpreted to permit the acquisition and administration of overseas colonies ("where there is a will the Americans can find a way"), it was his happy belief, he told Clarke, that the sudden emergence of the United States onto the international political stage was "rapidly driving the people of the United States to that other pet hope of you and me, the entente with Great Britain." It was also his firm conviction that

> the United States has duties to the world outside, as well as to herself —that in a general way the extension of "Anglo-Saxon" control is a distinct benefit to the world—and, although naturally conservative, I do not think that the policy of 50 or 100 years ago is proved suitable for today, by simply calling it our tradition. Traditions wax old and useless, like other things.

At the same time, he was equally certain that Germany's attitude during the conflict was unalterably hostile to the United States. In his view, the sending of Watson's force to strengthen Dewey in the Philippines was dictated almost entirely by the appearance of von Diederichs' squadron in Manila Bay. This was taken as an indication that an opportunistic Germany might seek to fill the power vacuum that would be created by the collapse of the Spanish presence in the archipelago and a concurrent American withdrawal therefrom at war's end. It is known now that Berlin had no such acquisitive goals in the Philippines in 1898. Mahan, of course, had not the advantage of such hindsight. His thinking, therefore, turned on a genuine concern that the United States not risk war with the Imperial German Navy in the Far East until the U.S. Navy was considerably stronger. For this reason, he suggested to Secretary Long and Secretary of State William R. Day the circulation of an elaborate cover story he had concocted to mollify the aggressive Germans. The idea, never used, was to convince them that the two monitors and Watson's task group were being deployed to Manila to reestablish the prewar balance between the Atlantic and Pacific fleets, and not as the beginning of a major U.S. naval build-up in the Pacific. It was not aimed at the Germans or at any other European nation; nor did the United States have ambitions in Europe that transcended ending the war there with Spain as quickly, bloodlessly, and honorably as possible. Since Day "seemed to me a little worried about the effect of our action [Manila] in this respect upon other Powers," Mahan further advised him on July 23 that he should state "perfectly clearly" to Berlin and to all European capitals "that this country has no purpose of any territory of Spain in either Europe or Africa . . . and, further, that for the present at least we do not propose to bombard *mercantile* ports, unless forced to do [so] by some action of Spain. . . . That, of course, we must reserve bombardment as a final measure of coercion, if Spain resist beyond reasonable limit, but that we are most averse to it."[21]

The scheme to bombard Spain died aborning in the rush of events during the last week in July. By the 28th of the month news had reached Washington that Spain was informally seeking, through the French embassy in the capital, a preliminary statement of America's terms of peace. These the State Department began speedily to draft, and on July 30 they were presented to Madrid by Jules Cambon, the French ambassador in Washington. Mahan immediately suggested that the sailing of Sampson's fleet be delayed a few days longer and that this peaceful gesture be combined with a proposal for a local armistice with Spain at the Strait of Gibraltar and throughout Europe. The willingness to delay Sampson (he never did sail) would calm the fears of the Spanish people and facilitate peace talks. He recommended, however, that Watson's three-vessel task force still be sent to Manila, via Gibraltar, if Spain would give assurances that it would not be attacked en route. "I should insist," he told Long, "that those ships must go forward without delay, because we must increase our force in the Pacific; and that unless they accept this condition the [combined] fleet will sail as first proposed." The quid pro quo of this proposal was that Watson would be careful to keep clear of the Spanish coast. This freedom of passage was a "condition" Mahan insisted upon, urging that it be put in the form of a 48-hour ultimatum to Madrid. "Yes or No; in the latter event we start at once." Mahan's idea of a local armistice at the strait appealed strongly to McKinley and he instructed Long to consider the concept carefully.[22]

As matters turned out, none of these plans, suggestions, or threats was employed. On August 7, Spain accepted in principle the offer of peace made by McKinley on July 30, raising only the possibility that American demands might be made somewhat less stringent. On August 12, however, Madrid fully accepted McKinley's terms as a basis for later peace discussions in Paris. These terms included Spain's evacuation of Cuba and her relinquishment of all title to the island, cession to the United States of Puerto Rico and of one island in the Ladrones (Carolines), and continued U.S. occupation of the city and bay of Manila, pending a final decision on the future control and disposition of the Philippines at the Paris conference. This preliminary agreement did not come soon enough to suit Mahan. Five days earlier, on August 7, he urged that Long persuade McKinley to withdraw the terms he had offered on July 30 unless Spain accepted them without change within three days. If Spain did not, "let it be known that war is again on, and start Sampson's armored ships." He was fed up with the "procrastination and prevarication of the Spaniard."

His interest in swiftly forcing Spain's hand in the matter stemmed from his sudden detection of alarming signs of decay in the morale of the idle U.S. fleet, particularly among naval reservists, and his fear that "incipient demoralization," together with expiring enlistments, would soon conspire to "cripple the fleet for an appreciable time." He noted, too, that Shafter's force in Cuba, shot through with boredom and malaria, was wholly demoralized and for all practical purposes was no longer an army. Further, he was distressed with Army strategy in Puerto Rico, the invasion of which had commenced in leisurely fashion at Guánica, near Ponce, on July 25.

Mahan had viewed General Miles' operational plan in Puerto Rico "from the first with great distrust." He now noted that Miles, while actually at sea with the invasion force, had chosen to change the original plan to land his army at Cape Fajardo, a few miles to the east of San Juan. Instead, Mahan sarcastically remarked, the general had picked Guánica, "the farthest point, almost, he could find from San Juan to land." It was, Mahan said later, "a military stupidity so great, that I can account [for it] only by a kind of obsession of vanity to do a singular and unexpected thing." True, Nelson A. Miles was no Bonaparte. But neither was Alfred T. Mahan a Nelson.

Given these signs of decay, inefficiency, and dilatoriness in the armed forces, impatient with the procrastination in Madrid over bringing the war to a close, Mahan urged the resumption of all-out naval warfare against Spain; or at least a strong threat of such resumption. Probably more the latter than the former, since Cámara's squadron had returned to Spain. "Why should not the President send for M. Cambon, and civilly tell him the brute truth," he bellowed, "that we thoroughly understand that Spain is powerless before us owing to our relative naval supremacy; that she would still be so, did every man in our armies die tomorrow." Either "settled Peace or renewed War" was Mahan's solution to the "restlessness, discontent, and disorganization" that had permeated the U.S. Army and Navy. The end of the war on August 12 neatly solved the military problem. But it left unresolved the diplomatic problem of what to do with the Philippines and how to lower what Mahan viewed as a dangerous level of German-American tension at Manila.[23]

Mahan was not in the vanguard of those imperialists in 1898 who, like Roosevelt, Lodge, Senator Albert J. Beveridge, of Indiana, and others, saw in a victorious war with Spain for Cuba Libre an opportunity also to annex the distant Philippines. Mahan had seen since 1896 both the need and the opportunity for American commercial expansion in the Pacific and into the markets of China. But there is no persuasive evidence that he linked the annexation of the entire Philippine archipelago with that particular goal. The acquisition of naval coaling stations at Manila, in Guam, and at the mouth of the Yangtze he deemed entirely adequate to sustain future American commercial ambitions in China.

To be sure, he had long advocated the annexation of Hawaii, his arguments invariably centering on defense of the Pacific coast, control of Oriental immigration, and the strategic implications of Japanese expansion into the Central Pacific. He had again demanded Hawaiian annexation as recently as February 1898 when Senator James H. Kyle, of South Dakota, asked him for a statement on the strategic virtues and values of the islands. He cheered in July 1898 when the United States, almost as a national-defense reflex, blinked twice, gulped, and finally swallowed whole the Hawaiian group. As he wrote in mid-August, "In the opinion of the Board, possession of these islands, which happily we now own, is militarily essential, both to our transit to Asia, and to the defense of our Pacific coast."

His interest in the Philippines had never been as profound as his interest in Hawaii. Until Dewey's victory in Manila Bay he had scarcely given those islands a thought or a glance. His belated concern for the archipelago was related largely to his reaction to presumed German ambitions in the area, and to his desire to identify himself intellectually and politically with the leadership of the pro-annexation movement in the Republican party. By mid-July 1898, some 10,000 American soldiers were bound for Manila, the heavy monitors *Monterey* and *Monadnock* were en route there, and Watson was fitting out the task force he was to take there to reinforce Dewey. Mahan had to hurry to overtake the march of these events. He explained his uncertainty to John S. Barnes on July 21, 1898:

> Personally, I have not yet become wholly adjusted to the new point of view opened to us by Dewey's victory at Manila. It has opened a vista of possibilities which were not by me in the least foreseen, though the intimate contact of the East with the West, and a probable imminent conflict (not necessarily war-like) between the two civilizations had long been a part of my thought. As it is, I look with a kind of awe upon the passage of events in which the will of man seems to count for little.

His sense of awe did not, however, persuade him to accept Supreme Court Justice Henry B. Brown's contention that the Monroe Doctrine excluded the United States from the Philippines. That the doctrine prohibited American intervention on the European continent, Mahan conceded. It certainly did not apply to possible American intrusion into the Philippines or into China. With that observation Mahan began sprinting toward the head of the imperialist line.[24]

A week later, by July 27, he was beginning to draw abreast of the Philippine annexationists, although, as he confessed to Lodge, "I myself, though rather an expansionist, have not fully adjusted myself to the idea of taking them [the Philippines]." Nevertheless, he felt that the amount of American military and naval force being poured into Luzon was encouraging Emilio Aguinaldo and his Filipino revolutionary forces to press their war for independence from their Spanish colonial masters. These developments, Mahan thought, conferred some obligation on the United States to stay watchfully on the scene. "Can we ignore the responsibility and give them back to Spain?" he asked rhetorically. "I think not." Nor could Spain be expected "to govern justly, because she neither knows what good government is, nor could she practise it if she knew." Mahan tentatively concluded, therefore, that a "wise compromise" would be to annex Luzon and leave the rest of the archipelago to Spain, since there was still no American military presence in any of the other islands; and none was then contemplated. By mid-August, after the war had ended, and as the five American commissioners were preparing to depart for the peace conference in Paris, he had embraced the broader thought, partly theological, that

> the islands will be forced upon us by the refractoriness of the insurgents themselves. As in Cuba, so in Luzon, long before the Commissioners in Paris can act, our nation will be forced to feel that we cannot abandon to any other the task of maintaining order in the land in which we have been led to interpose. "Chance," said Frederick the Great. "*Deus vult*," say I. It was the cry of the Crusader and the Puritan, and I doubt if man ever utters a nobler.

This argument for retaining Luzon was somewhat less elaborate than was the president's subsequent explanation for annexing the entire archipelago. Indeed, McKinley later told a group of his fellow Methodists that he had prayed God long and hard for guidance on the complex question of Philippine annexation. God answered the devout president one night as he knelt in the White House, telling him in effect that the United States could not turn the islands over to France or Germany ("our commercial rivals in the Orient—that would have been bad business"); nor could the Americans leave the Filipinos to themselves since "they were unfit for self-government—and they would soon have anarchy and misrule over there worse than Spain's was." The divine recommendation on the tricky question, as McKinley reported it, was "that there was nothing left for us to do but to take them, and by God's grace do the very best we could by them, as our fellow men for whom Christ also died."

The Naval War Board, in its final report to the department in mid-August 1898, took a position on annexation far less sweeping than the one later confided to the chief executive by the Almighty. Written by Mahan, the board view was that all that was needed by the United States in the Philippines from a military and imperialist standpoint was a naval station and coaling facility at the "city and bay of Manila, or Subic Bay, if all Luzon Island be not ceded." The question of whether God truly willed so modest a territorial reward in the Philippines for the triumphant nation and its all-conquering Navy, Mahan did not address in his board report. Nor at the time had the Creator made it clear to Aguinaldo and his guerrilla soldiers that they were politically incompetent, and that Cuba Libre was not to have a Philippine branch office. As it turned out, the Filipinos were eventually asked to exchange one colonial master for another, a request that, as will be seen, pleased them not.

The resulting American-Philippine War which broke out in February 1899 was another "war of national liberation" which, like the one in Cuba, 1895–1898, Mahan had difficulty understanding. Nonetheless, it quickly drove him to advocate annexation of the entire archipelago. He was never fully convinced, however, that in strategic or geopolitical terms the islands were worth the blood and treasure the United States had to expend between 1899 and 1902 to pacify the recalcitrant Filipinos and to convert them into proper colonials, grateful for the American schools, roads, hospitals, indoor toilets, and Protestant salvation that accompanied their military suppression. He gradually shifted his view that the American entry into the islands was solely the result of "Deus vult." The United States, he told the readers of *The Independent*, February 1, 1900, was involved in a "responsibility and duty" in the Philippines which, while "troublesome," had been "committed" to the nation by God. But less than a month later, speaking extemporaneously to a college audience at the Savoy Hotel in New York, he admitted that the United States had been accidentally "pitchforked . . . into the Philippines." The continued American presence there, he noted, was more a presidential-campaign issue than a problem theological. In February 1902 he still saw something of the hand of Providence in that, by annexing the Philippines, America had been provided with stepping-stones to the markets of China. But by mid-1910 he noted that he had been a "personal witness of the extreme repugnance" with which the United States had annexed the islands. By March 1911, after Russia and Japan had skillfully squeezed American investment capital out of the Manchurian market, he felt that if the archipelago were to be separated from the American orbit by act of war its loss would be no more significant to the United States, from a purely material standpoint, than the "loss of a little finger, perhaps a single joint of it. The Philippines to us are less a property than a charge."

These distant islands, virtually indefensible by the Pearl Harbor-based squadron of a navy second to several, would come to be, in Mahan's mind, far more trouble than they were worth. Theodore Roosevelt later called them America's "heel of Achilles," a point cousin Franklin D. Roosevelt came ruefully to appreciate thirty years later. Be that as it may, Mahan from 1899 to 1902 loyally embraced the Republican party's political orthodoxy that was support for the annexation of *all* the Philippines for reasons theological, mercantile, political, ideological, or accidental. The reasons advanced by the party were interchangeable. But in his heart of hearts Mahan seems never really to have believed in the Philippine enterprise—or certainly not with great conviction.[25]

The annexation issue was not, however, the subject of Mahan's final official act as a member of the Naval War Board in 1898. That act was his perceptive study of the naval bases and coaling stations that the Navy was going to need. It was written for the Navy Department by order of the Senate during the third week in August, and it was Mahan's most thoughtful, detailed, and useful paper on the Spanish-American War. In it he called attention to the various logistical frustrations the Navy had suffered during the war in order to illustrate the point that its future requirements included no fewer than eight permanent overseas coaling stations in the Caribbean and the Pacific. "In the Pacific Ocean," he noted, "the notorious changes that are taking place in the political relations of China, the intrusion of European control upon her territory, and the consequent effect upon her trade relations, make the future of China the most interesting commercial question of the Pacific to us at the present moment." He saw American ambitions and interests in China being protected by coaling stations at Manila (or Subic Bay), at Guam in the Carolines, and, most particularly, at one of two possible places in the Chushan Islands (Chang Tau Harbor or Tai Shei Shan Harbor), which lie between Shanghai and Hangchow, near the mouth of the Yangtze River in central China. The Yangtze position, together with those at Manila and Guam, would also be desirable "for operations of war, if need be, in Eastern Asiatic waters." In addition, the existing American coaling facilities in Hawaii and at Pago Pago in Samoa should be retained and improved.

For the Caribbean, Mahan and the War Board recommended the immediate construction of a canal in Nicaragua or Panama (in 1898 Mahan leaned toward Nicaragua) and the acquisition of coaling stations near its entrances. "The right of fortification should be acquired upon cession or purchase" of these sites, he insisted. Construction of an isthmian canal should not be delayed another minute. "There follows directly the national necessity to *dig the Nicaragua Canal*. . . . the usefulness—nay, the necessity—of the Nicaragua Canal has been painfully forced upon the Navy Department during the current war, by the difficulties encountered in organizing a reinforcement of battleships for Admiral Dewey, to proceed by the Suez Canal," he argued. He also recommended the acquisition of two coaling stations in the Caribbean, one of which should be at St. Thomas, in the Danish Virgin Islands, if the United States decided to annex Puerto Rico. St. Thomas, lying on the flank of Puerto Rico, should be purchased from Denmark "to prevent some foreign power from purchasing [it] and thus acquiring a strong position near our new possessions in the West Indies."

Having thus created the logistical foundation for future American Empire in the Caribbean and the Pacific, the board rested. "Beyond these eight positions," wrote Mahan, "the Board is not prepared to recommend acquisitions." With that parting observation, the Philosopher of Sea Power returned home to Quogue, there to await the return of Elly and the children from Europe, to write a popular operational history of the naval war with Spain, and to brood over what had gone wrong in the Navy, in the Navy Department, and in the War Board during the 116 days of what Secretary of State John Hay liked to call the "splendid little war" with Spain.[26]

XV

Peace, War, and Personal Battles
1898-1901

Personally, *I consider that Schley's utter unfitness for command is conclusively demonstrated. . . . The man . . . is demonstrably unfit for
command. . . . In my judgment, as a student of military history, there
is no escape from this conclusion.*

Alfred Thayer Mahan to John D. Long, December 12, 1899

Mahan was in a less-than-joyful mood when he left Washington and
returned to Quogue at the end of August 1898. As he looked back on the
experience through which he had just passed he was appalled by the amateurish organization and operation of the Naval War Board, the Navy
Department, and the Navy in general throughout the Spanish-American
War. He was angry with Secretary of the Navy Long. His concept of
command by a general staff had been rejected; indeed, Long continued
Sicard in the presidency of the board despite Mahan's objection that the
man was "very second or third rate for what he had to do." Further, the
department had consistently dismissed Mahan's historical principles and
parallels when deciding what to do next. He described his multiple frustrations to Luce:

> We must recognize that like Popes and Czars, Secretaries pass away,
> but the Papacy and the Czardom and the Navy Department remain.
> It is with an institution, not a person, chiefly that we have to deal. . . .
> As far as a *Board* is concerned, I don't believe in it at all; and less than
> ever since I served on this. I told the Secretary so as soon as I arrived,
> and repeated it more than once. One man—a chief and subordinates—is
> needed; but I fear we can't get him because the service and the Depart-

ment don't want him. During my whole time on the Board, historical parallels to our positions were continually occurring to me. How many men in the Navy, do you suppose, know naval history, or think of naval operations, in that way; or how many, if they read this, would fail to vote me an egotistic, superannuated ass! Yet unless there can be found in the Navy a reasonable body of opinion to recognize that war may be regarded that way, I don't see how any demand for a General Staff is to arise. . . . I believe that a series of articles for a magazine I am just beginning will afford a better lever to move public opinion and naval opinion. . . . The Navy—in my opinion—wants to stop grubbing in machine shops and to get up somewhere where it can take a bird's eye view of military truths, and see them in their relations and proportions. . . . I have written and talked and stormed for three months before the Board, the Secretary, and the President, and I feel now very much like the teacher who after laborious explanations, receives from one of his boys one of those answers we see in the funny columns of a newspaper.

Mahan was never disabused of his conviction that historical precedents and analogies had eternal operational planning value. He remained convinced that the historical and theoretical work in which he had earlier been engaged at the Naval War College, and to which the college was committed, had been of enormous benefit to his labors on the Naval War Board, and to the winning of the Spanish-American War. He told Long in September 1898 that the War College was responsible for "*all* the acquirements that have underlain the reputation I have gained. Granting any natural capacity you may attribute, the fact remains that all my usefulness this summer depended upon my studies at the College, which illuminated to me every step I advocated to you." He considered the vicarious role of the college in thus helping win the war one of the few bright spots in an otherwise dreary portrait, since it was again under attack by those who failed to appreciate "the principles and methods involved in the correct Conduct of War."[1]

Mostly, Mahan was critical of a number of political, operational, and intelligence failures experienced by the nation and its armed services during the war: the fact that public ignorance and panic, shared by foolish politicians, had forced a division of the battle fleet to guard against a wholly improbable Spanish attack on coastal cities; the building of useless coast-defense monitors during the war to quiet those fears; the general incompetence of the Army leadership in almost all matters strategic, tactical, and logistical; the lack of an effective and dependable system within the Navy Department for gathering and disseminating intelligence; Army, rather than Navy, control of troop transports en route to invasion sites;

the employment of civilian merchant marine captains to command troop-ships in war zones; the inability of the armed services to maintain secrecy about their plans and movements; and the pervasive, annoying, and disruptive presence of press boats, reporters, and newspaper feature-writers who cluttered up the combat areas and leaked valuable military information to the enemy in their news releases. He called attention to these numerous failures in his *Lessons of the War with Spain* and in various postwar personal letters and official reports. "Fortunately, the war was short and simple," Mahan sighed. "Had it lasted longer, with a more efficient enemy, there could not but be mistakes, which careful previous study would have prevented."

Lack of secrecy during actual operations he considered a major failing of the war. Not only had officers in the field talked freely with reporters about current plans and operations, but the politicians in Washington thought they were entitled to know whatever the admirals and generals knew. And reporters at the scene of war passed along everything they heard—fact, rumor, and speculation. Because of this chaos, Mahan noted that a censorship system would have to be worked out and instituted in the Navy in future wars, as indeed it was. Similarly, coast and harbor defenses would have to be built to allay citizen panic in the future. "In a popular government," Mahan opined, "it is of no avail to calm people's fears by rational military considerations. They clamor to be visibly defended." He also considered the Army incompetent to provision, load, discharge, and otherwise operate troopships; and he regarded the merchant marine captains who commanded them as little better than cowards in combat situations.[2]

Some of this negativism, however constructive, could be traced to the fact that Mahan's beloved War College was again being criticized at war's end. Other dimensions of his dismay related to the fact that a penurious government, through its Department of the Treasury, refused in October 1898 to pay his travel expenses from Rome back to the United States. This patent outrage, involving the sum of $233.08, was based on the Comptroller of the Treasury's contention that Mahan was not technically on active duty from April 25, the day he received his orders in Rome to return home, until he actually set foot in New York on May 7. Only his train fare from New York to Washington was paid. Mahan, in response, contended that the comptroller was simply too stupid to understand the situation. Stupidity aside, the Treasury's position required Mahan to devote a great deal of time, energy, and correspondence to the task of searching out various public laws, administrative regulations, and related precedents—to say nothing of a personal appeal to Secretary Long—to sustain his view that he was indeed entitled to travel money home to fight in the war, a war now $233.08 less "splendid" than it had been. Long agreed with his argument, and the surviving documents in the case support Mahan's claim. But whether the Comptroller of the Treasury agreed with him and paid him the money is not known. Whatever its outcome, the incident did not improve Mahan's disposition insofar as the U.S. Navy was concerned.[3]

Nor was Mahan's immediate postwar mood improved by the flowering of his acrimonious argument with F. P. Badham over Nelson at Naples, and the direction the growing Sampson-Schley controversy was taking. Mahan's dislike of Schley was pronounced. Its roots went back to his jealousy of Midshipman Schley during their days together at the Naval Academy. It became virtually an obsession when Schley joined Ramsay and Secretary of the Navy Whitney in the attack on the Naval War College in 1888 and 1889. Conversely, Mahan's relations with Sampson, both at the Naval Academy and later, had always been cordial. Indeed, Mahan was one of the first officers to argue publicly as well as privately in July 1898 that the great victory over Cervera at Santiago had been fashioned by Sampson, who was absent, rather than by Schley, who was present. This he did in response to an editorial in the *Baltimore American* on July 6 which held that the Maryland-born Schley was the "real hero" of the battle and that Sampson had not had the grace even to mention Schley's name in his official report of victory. The main credit for the success should go to the dashing Schley, argued the Baltimore newspaper. "He was in command," said editor Felix Agnus, a friend of Schley's, "he began the destruction of the Spanish Fleet. . . . He did the work. Now give him the honors." This theme was taken up by Maryland Governor Lloyd Lowndes, by various local politicians, and by other newspapers in the Baltimore-Washington area.

Mahan's initial reaction to the pro-Schley newspaper campaign was relatively restrained. He wrote John S. Barnes from Washington on July 9:

> It is to be regretted that New Yorkers are not looking out for their man —Sampson—in the way, or rather in a more becoming way, than Maryland, her Governor and the press hereabouts are "booming" Schley. The latter is a gallant man and a good officer; but Sampson has borne the burden and the responsibility of the long watch before Santiago, and was unquestionably responsible for the disposition of the ships. The shame would have been his had Cervera escaped from bad dispositions. . . . in my judgment, from first to last, nothing has happened to deprive

Sampson of the just claim of a commander in chief to priority of consideration. . . . You are at liberty to say so, not of course for the press,
but in conversation if you choose, as my deliberate opinion.

Mahan's defense of Sampson's "priority" as the true hero of the battle,
in the face of the "shameful attempts of the Maryland press and people
to disparage" him, took the form of drumming up support for the admiral
in personal correspondence, in letters to newspaper editors, and in articles
in *McClure's Magazine* which were published between December 1898
and April 1899. In all of these, he adduced statements from various other
naval officers, Spanish included, to the effect that Sampson's skillful disposition of his blockaders outside Santiago Harbor, particularly his novel
use of searchlights to illuminate the harbor mouth at night, had won the
battle before it was fought. This tactic had intimidated Cervera into remaining within the harbor. "The attacks of the press upon Sampson, either
virulently or by constant sly innuendo, have kept my blood boiling,"
Mahan told Senator Lodge. "It is my belief that the closeness of the watch
at night largely induced the sortie by day—unwise as that was." That
argument, sound as far as it went, did not meet the main point of the pro-
Schley contention, best summarized in *The Washington Post*, that Schley
was actually present at the battle and Sampson was not. Nothing Mahan
wrote on the controversy would or could change that fact, not even comparisons between the Sampson-Schley command relationship at Santiago
and that of Nelson, as a subordinate officer, to Admiral John Jervis at the
Battle of Cape St. Vincent and to Admiral Hyde Parker at the Battle of
Copenhagen.

That the disposition of a fleet *for* battle was more important than the
direction of a fleet *in* battle, which remained Mahan's basic argument for
Sampson, was not a point all American newspaper-readers could grasp.
Few did. Nevertheless, he insisted on this view in a lengthy letter to the
New York Sun, dated August 5. In this he suggested also that while Sampson was the true hero of the Santiago engagement there was surely enough
glory for both men. He assured his readers that Schley was not "in the
least responsible" for the escalation of the controversy with Sampson, and
he cited the generous telegram Schley sent to the Navy Department on
July 10, in which he gave his commanding officer full credit for the victory. Privately, Mahan admitted that his brief for Sampson was "scarcely
popular" outside the Navy. It "involved a certain amount of trouble"
and he was disposed to let the matter drop. "There will . . . be no scandal
unless indiscreet friends of Schley . . . provoke it," he told Barnes in mid-

August 1898. "Of this I have some fear, but will use my influence against it as far as I can, unless, of course, the abuse of Sampson becomes intolerable." Barnes agreed that the issue should be dropped now that Mahan had settled "once and for all the clamor of the hero makers of the slapdash newspaper variety." He congratulated Mahan on "the clever way" he had handled the issue in his letter to the *New York Sun*.[4]

Unhappily, the controversy took on a new dimension on August 20 when President McKinley, on Long's recommendation, promoted Sampson by eight numbers on the Navy List and Schley by only six. Schley, who before the war was senior by one number to Sampson on the captains' list, suddenly became junior to him by one number on the rear admirals' list. Put another way, the man who missed the Battle of Santiago was promoted above the man who was in the thick of it.

At this point the nagging Sampson-Schley altercation split the officer corps wide open. The Sampsonites began arguing that the discrepancy in rank was entirely justified—not on the basis of anything that had happened at the Battle of Santiago, but because of Schley's tardiness in reaching Santiago and his lack of persistence in finding the Spanish squadron and in establishing the blockade that finally sealed Cervera in. Particularly emphasized in this regard was his so-called "retrograde" movement toward Key West to coal on May 26, together with his cable to the Navy Department that because he was short of fuel he could not obey its orders to remain off Santiago. There was a distinct implication in these charges that Winfield Scott Schley was either incompetent or cowardly, or both. Sampson himself had privately termed Schley's conduct in this regard "reprehensible."

Therefore, when it became in November 1898 a question of honoring Sampson, Schley, and Dewey with a Congressional Vote of Thanks, a rare honor that entitled recipients to ten additional years on the active-duty list, Mahan rejoined the fray with gusto. He told Secretary Long bluntly that Schley was incompetent and should never again be entrusted with command. Schley had, he assured Gillender, "done *nothing* to merit distinction" in the recent war. Mahan was not as harsh as this in his articles in *McClure's Magazine*, but there could be no doubt in his readers' minds that Sampson had done virtually nothing wrong in the war ("Admiral Sampson merits the highest praise") while Schley's actions preliminary to establishing the blockade at Santiago had been characterized by "uncertainty," "delay," and "mistakes" which had caused the department considerable "embarrassment."

It was soon after this, in November 1899, that Secretary Long, sick and tired of the whole business, issued a circular order prohibiting naval officers on active duty from discussing the case in public. Mahan defended Long's order in a letter dated November 15, 1899, to the pro-Schley *New York Times*, again giving it as his opinion, "as a student for many years of naval history," that "the first credit of the battle, as of the campaign, belongs to the man whose dispositions prevailed in both—to Admiral Sampson." In a private letter to Robert U. Johnson a few weeks later, Mahan charged that when Schley finally established his blockade of Santiago on June 28 he had "plucked up courage to remain nearer than 25 miles" to the harbor mouth. This remark was unworthy of Mahan. Unworthy, too, was his view, expressed to Long in mid-December 1899, that because Schley had not sought a court of inquiry to clear himself of the charges against him he was not entitled to promotion to vice admiral. On this point, he maintained, "there is no room, in my judgment, for differing opinions." Such a promotion, he told Sampson, would be a "disgrace to the Navy." In Mahan's mind, then, Schley was guilty until he proved himself innocent. As he concluded his December 12 letter to Long:

> *Personally*, I consider that Schley's utter unfitness for command is conclusively demonstrated, over his own signature, by two facts. One is the well-known telegram announcing his purpose to return to Key West; the other is the statement, in his letter of May 30, that the speed of the squadron was reduced from 7.5 to 8.5 knots to 4 or 5, going from Cienfuegos to Santiago, to allow the *Eagle* to keep up. The man who, under all the circumstances, could do those two things is demonstrably unfit for command; and I have always purposed, in case my opinion were asked, to rest it on these two statements. In my judgment, as a student of military history, there is no escape from this conclusion.[5]

Mahan's antipathy to Schley had grown mightily. Imagine then his mixed sense of pleasure and apprehension when he ran into retired Rear Admiral Henry Erben ("no friend of mine") in New York in February 1901, and received from him a spontaneous eulogy of Sampson that turned on the affirmation that numerous foreign naval officers clearly understood and valued "most highly the *operations as a whole* conducted by Sampson. They recognize what *he* did." As he told Lodge, in recounting the chance meeting with Erben, "It must be remembered that history has yet to speak in this matter. There can be no question what her verdict will be, or that it will be plainly spoken. The mere fact that under such grave imputations Schley did not ask for a court . . . will receive, can receive, but one interpretation. He dared not."

History soon spoke; and Schley, no longer able to stand above the conflict with dignity, as both he and Sampson had managed personally to do for nearly three years, was forced at last to ask for a court. The final straw came with the publication in mid-1901 of the third volume of Edgar S. Maclay's *A History of the United States Navy*, the first two volumes of which were used as a textbook at the Naval Academy. In his discussion of the Santiago campaign, Maclay flatly called Schley a coward. His retrograde turn toward Key West on May 26 to take coal was characterized as a "caitiff flight"; and a momentary maneuver of his flagship, the *Brooklyn*, away from the fleeing Spanish squadron during the Battle of Santiago, to avoid what appeared to be a ramming movement by the *Infanta Maria Teresa*, was interpreted as the "shameful spectacle of an American warship . . . deliberately turning tail and running away." Schley's total performance at Santiago, wrote Maclay, was little more than an effort to "avoid your enemy as long as possible and if he makes for you, run."

Whatever else Schley was, he was no coward. This he had demonstrated time and again during the Civil War, in the punitive operation in Korea in 1871, during the Greely Relief Expedition to the Arctic in 1884, at Valparaiso in the *Baltimore* in 1891, and at Santiago Bay in the *Brooklyn* in July 1898. But now he had no choice save to ask for a formal court of inquiry. A tribunal was convened at the Washington Navy Yard on September 12, 1901. Presided over by Admiral George Dewey and having as its members Rear Admirals Francis M. Ramsay and Andrew E. K. Benham, the body sat for forty days and amassed 2,000 printed pages of testimony and documents. When it was all over, Schley's actions near Santiago prior to June 1, 1898, were deemed by two-to-one vote to have been characterized by "vacillation, dilatoriness, and lack of enterprise." His reports on his fuel situation, as he cruised between Cienfuegos and Santiago from May 24 to May 28, 1898, were judged "inaccurate and misleading." On the other hand, his performance at the Battle of Santiago was unanimously praised. Dewey publicly took exception to the finding of "vacillation"; he also supported Schley on the fueling issue. However, Secretary Long accepted the majority report as it stood, and President Roosevelt refused Schley's appeal for relief from the court's verdict. Meanwhile, on October 9, 1901, Schley reached the statutory retirement age of sixty-two and was placed on the retired list. A few months later, on May 6, 1902, Sampson died. So ended, by acts of Dewey, Long, and God, the embarrassing and inconclusive Sampson-Schley controversy.[6]

But not by act of Mahan, even though his sour opinion of Schley was in large measure vindicated by the two-to-one vote of the court. Ironically, half of that vindication was provided by the vote of his ancient enemy, F. M. Ramsay. Mahan, however, was terribly disappointed with Dewey's stance in the matter, and he scoffed at Schley's stunned post-trial remark "I did the best I could." In December 1901, still astride his vendetta, Mahan angrily severed his relationship with *The Independent*, a popular journal in which he had published several articles, because of its vigorous pro-Schley position. He was outraged, he told Roosevelt two years after that, that "men of intelligence and position" continued to have social intercourse with a liar such as Schley. And when he wrote for the Navy Department in 1906 his short history of the Naval War Board, he again made clear his opinion that Schley's "uncertain course [and] . . . . vacillating action, as shown by his telegrams, had destroyed the confidence of the Department and of the Board in him, as a Commander-in-Chief."

Mahan's hatred of Schley continued even after the man dropped dead of apoplexy on a New York City street in October 1911. Luce, who disliked Schley as much as did Mahan, then thought the time ripe to reopen the Sampson-Schley question to the extent of petitioning the Senate to pro-claim Sampson, dead these nine years, the real victor of the Battle of Santiago Bay. Mahan was quite willing to carry on his anti-Schley crusade, but he did not go along with Luce's suggestion on the practical grounds that the Taft administration was pro-Schley. That, he felt, was evidenced by the president's public statement of sympathy when the admiral died and by the Navy Department's ordering the battalion of midshipmen to participate in the funeral ceremonies—as it had in Sampson's funeral in May 1902. "Next move?" asked Luce in obvious disappointment over Mahan's willingness to drop the matter at last. Happily, there was no next move. The participants were dead, their loyal legions had dispersed, and the bones of a fractured officer corps had begun to mend. Best to bury the controversy forever.[7]

The Sampson-Schley imbroglio had few benefits for the U.S. Navy. It did, however, bring Mahan and Secretary Long close together in the years after the war. Not only did Long take a consistently anti-Schley position during those years, but he cemented his relations with the Philosopher of Sea Power by bailing Lieutenant Dennis H. Mahan out of deep trouble in October 1898 and by assisting Mahan with his articles on the *Lessons of the War with Spain*. Mahan, in turn, was pleased to assist Long with his book *The New American Navy*, published in two volumes in 1903. This study also took an anti-Schley line in its treatment of the Santiago campaign. But it was the case of Mahan's black-sheep brother Dennis that began the rapprochement between the two strong-willed men.

Just what difficulty Dennis Mahan got into when he was serving in the

USS *Badger* at the end of the war is not known. Details of what Mahan termed "the unfortunate incident" have disappeared from the record; but Mahan traced its cause to his brother's having been ill and under the influence of an opiate at the time, and to general "mental strain and . . . sore disappointment and chagrin of losing the one opportunity of his life to do battle for his country." In any event, the incident threatened a court-martial proceeding against Dennis and clouded his chances for promotion to lieutenant commander. It was the prospect of the court-martial and "the dragging of my name and that of the family before a curious and unsympathetic public," particularly in the "carrion sheets" of Hearst's *New York Journal*, that caused the proud Mahan for the only time in his life abjectly to beg for a personal favor. This he did, unashamedly, in a poignant letter to Secretary Long, dated October 6, 1898, in which he harked back to his father's long and honorable service in the U.S. Army, to his own prominence in American and world naval circles, and to the fact that all of his father's three sons were either in the Army or the Navy. As the Mahan name

> came to us untarnished from our father, so we would all wish above every other thing to transmit it to our children. . . . No one of the name has ever asked much of the Government; and if, through the long years that cover the lives of two generations, the Country, its Army, or its Navy, is indebted to us for any service rendered, I trust that this, standing to our credit, may now serve to shield and protect the good name our father bore and gave to his children.

Long agreed and, at the risk of some criticism of himself, quashed any move in the Navy Department to bring Dennis Mahan to trial. Dennis' promotion also went through. This act of compassion Mahan interpreted as "proceeding from an unwillingness to drag a name honorably connected with the Navy through the mire of publicity, in which men never stop to really weigh the facts." It was also extremely kind, and Mahan thanked the Secretary "with my whole heart for this relief from apprehension and anxiety."[8]

The Mahan family name, thanks to Long, was secure. Thanks to President McKinley it was honored further with Mahan's appointment in March 1899 to the five-man American delegation to what became known as the First Hague Conference. Nominated as the Navy's representative on the commission by Secretary of State John M. Hay, Mahan joined Andrew D. White, historian, diplomat, and former president of Cornell University, who led the delegation; also in the group were Stanford

American delegates to the First Hague Conference. Left to right, Stanford Newel, George F. W. Holls, Andrew D. White, Alfred T. Mahan, Seth Low, William Crozier.

Newel, U.S. minister to the Netherlands, Seth Low, president of Columbia University, and Captain William Crozier of the Army. George F. W. Holls, an internationally known New York lawyer, accompanied the delegation to Holland as its non-voting secretary and legal counsel.

Not accompanying the delegation was Mahan's wife, although Mahan had considered taking her with him. Unfortunately, the cost of her passage in the liner *St. Louis* would have left him $325 out of pocket. The family decided to save this money since Elly had so recently returned from a trip to Europe. Having had unhappy experiences with the Navy Department in personal economic matters, Mahan proceeded to make arrangements with Little, Brown and Company for a $1,000 or $1,500 advance on royalties from the revised edition of his *Life of Nelson* to pay his own travel costs to The Hague. In this instance, however, the more beneficent State Department advanced him $500, took care of the cost of his stateroom, made reservations for him at the Hotel Vieux Doelen, and sent along a disbursing officer to pay the delegates' expenses as they were incurred. This efficient financial support was balanced by the inefficiency that was the State Department's failure to brief Mahan in any detail on what he was supposed to do when he got to The Hague. "I trust the Conference may realize whatever the time is ripe for," he told James Ford Rhodes on the eve of his departure, "what that is is not immediately clear to my mind." Nevertheless, Secretary Hay's instructions to the members of the U.S. delegation set general guide lines for what Mahan himself attempted to accomplish at the conference insofar as the question of arms limitation and control was concerned. Said Hay:

> It is doubtful if wars will be diminished by rendering them less destructive, for it is the plain lesson of history that the periods of peace have been longer protracted as the cost and destructiveness of war have increased. The expediency of restraining the inventive genius of our people in the direction of devising means of defence is by no means clear, and, considering the temptations to which men and nations may be exposed in a time of conflict, it is doubtful if an international agreement of this nature would prove effective.

But aside from clues such as these, Mahan's first (and last) personal venture into the practical world of international diplomacy was destined to be an exercise in on-the-job training.[9]

May 1899 was a convenient time for him to go abroad since he had reached a "good halting place" in his literary endeavors. He had completed his revision of *Nelson* as well as the first of his related articles for the *English Historical Review* on Nelson's behavior at Naples. He felt that he had the obnoxious Francis P. Badham on the run. He had also finished his Spanish-American War articles for *McClure's* and had begun negotiations on the book version for Little, Brown and Company. He was satisfied that Sampson's cause in the controversy with Schley was making progress. Further, his manuscript on "Major Operations of the Royal Navy, 1762–1783," held up at the galley stage by his unexpected service on the Naval War Board in the summer of 1898, was finished at last. In December 1898 it had been published in Volume III of W. L. Clowes' massive history of the Royal Navy. His service to American diplomacy at The Hague from May 16 to July 29, 1899, was therefore in the nature of a ten-week interlude, most of it boring to him, in a busy literary schedule. No sooner had he arrived at The Hague than he was ready to go home. The meetings, he told Ashe soon after his return to Quogue, were "interesting in a way; but ten weeks of it was rather too much." At no time was he in sympathy with the larger purposes of the conference once he came clearly to understand what these were.[10]

Called by Czar Nicholas II, the conference was attended by twenty-six nations, large and small. Its ostensible goals were to find ways of limiting or reducing armaments, of prohibiting the use of certain highly destructive new weapons of war (submarines, poison gases, balloon-launched aerial bombs), of creating additional machinery for the future arbitration and mediation of international disputes, and of extending to naval warfare the control provisions the Geneva Convention of 1864 provided for land warfare. The Hague Conference, lampooned in American political cartoons as the "Czar's Peace Picnic," met in what Andrew D. White called a spirit of "hopeless skepticism as to any good result." Russian motives in calling the charade into session were widely questioned, principally on the grounds that the czar, having fallen behind in the arms race, sought to have the other powers disarm down to Russia's level. Mahan had no sympathy whatever for any of the concepts of disarmament or arbitration bandied about at the conference and became soon convinced, as he later told Ashe, that

> Russia has not the slightest intention either of reducing her armaments, or even discontinuing the programme for their increase. . . . nor do I think any other state differs from her. . . . My own persuasion is that the immediate cause of Russia calling for the Conference was the shock of our late war, resulting in the rapprochement of the U.S. and Great Britain and our sudden appearance in Asia, as the result of a successful war. In peace, Russia's aggressive advance moves over the inert Asiatics

like a steam-roller; but the prospect of America and England, side by side, demanding that China be left open for trade, means either a change in her policy, or war. Hence she wishes peace—by pledge. . . . [a nation] should never pledge itself, by treaty or otherwise, to arbitrate before it knows what the subject of dispute is. Needless to say, I have no sympathy with those who hold that war is never imperative.

So it was that Mahan used his ten weeks of leisure at The Hague to correspond with his publishers, consider future writing projects, dine with his friends, assist the Russians (of all people) in planning the establishment of their own naval war college, urge upon Washington vigorous prosecution of the American war against the ungrateful Filipinos, and sabotage as best he could American adherence to any decision the conference threatened to reach that tended to ameliorate the harshness of war.[11]

In this last activity the smallness of Mahan's leverage within the conference as a whole was counterbalanced by the largeness of his success within the American delegation. Assigned to a relatively unimportant subcommittee charged with devising rules of neutral behavior in future war at sea, Mahan spent most of his time and energy arguing that neutral vessels, as well as both neutral and belligerent hospital ships, at the scene of a naval engagement should not be permitted to pick distressed belligerent seamen out of the water; or, if so permitted, the seamen rescued by such vessels should be handed over to the relevant belligerent as prisoners of war. This concern stemmed from his outrage that, following the defeat of the CSS *Alabama* by the USS *Kearsarge* in June 1864, the British yacht *Deerhound* had fished many of the survivors of the former out of the water off Cherbourg and carried them safely to England, where they lived to fight another day. It proceeded also from his conviction that naval warfare should not be transformed by international law, or by other rules, into a pleasant pastime. If war were ever to be abolished, it must be made a raging hell. Let those sailors who had abandoned stricken ships die in the water; or at least make sure that they became prisoners of war.

Further, Mahan took the attitude with his receptive colleagues in the American delegation that the United States should not participate formally or informally in any discussion or arrangement designed to limit the size of navies or of national naval expenditures. As he explained to Admiral Lord Fisher, "the conditions which constitute the necessity for a navy, and control its development, have within the past year changed for the United States so markedly that it is impossible yet to foresee, with certainty, what degree of naval strength may be needed to meet them." His concern, he revealed to British Colonel Charles à Court during a private conversation at The Hague, was that "the great question of the immediate future is China." Because this was so, the United States would be "compelled, by facts if not by settled policy, to take a leading part in the struggle for Chinese markets," a competition that would likely "entail a very considerable increase" in U.S. naval forces in the Pacific. In sum, Mahan felt that July 1899 at The Hague was neither the time nor the place to mortgage America's commercial and naval future with paper promises momentarily convenient to the Czar of All the Russias. His views, wrote Andrew D. White in his diary, "have been an excellent tonic; they have prevented any lapse into sentimentality. When he speaks the millennium fades and this stern, severe, actual world appears."

It should not be concluded that a bellicose and cynical Alfred Thayer Mahan single-handedly prevented eternal peace from breaking out at The Hague in June–August 1899. None of the czar's semi-utopian proposals commanded the support of the other great powers present there. In terms of positive achievement, the conference produced little more than the formation of a pie-in-the-sky Permanent Court of International Arbitration. In spite of this impressive title, the court had little power. Arbitration was not compulsory. Nor did the authority of the court extend to any question involving national honor or integrity. Even had the American delegates at The Hague gone into a collective trance and voted for compulsory arbitration, arms limitations, and weapons controls, the U.S. Senate, in its post-Spanish War wisdom, would never have accepted such international limitations on American diplomatic or military-naval sovereignty. Never. Not while the nation was spreading its commercial and imperialist wings in the Caribbean and the Far East, fighting a major war in the Philippines, and racing to catch up with the world's leading naval powers. What Mahan did at The Hague, therefore, and did most effectively, was to prevent the other members of the American delegation from making fools of themselves with the politicians, statesmen, and businessmen back home.[12]

And embarrass themselves they almost did in their parliamentary mishandling of Article 27, an attempt by France to extend and expand the principle of voluntary international arbitration. The controversial article read: "The Signatory Powers consider it their duty, in case a serious dispute threatens to break out between two or more of them, to remind these [powers] that the permanent Court of Arbitration is open to them." Innocent and innocuous as it sounded, Article 27 would have *required* all nations to involve themselves, in one degree or another, in the disputes of any two nations. Although G. F. W. Holls was a non-voting member of the American delegation, he represented his country in the subcommittee that considered Article 27, and on July 3 he voted for it there. When the article came before the entire Third Committee (Mediation and Arbitration) on July 20, Holls spoke enthusiastically for its adoption, calling it "the crown of the entire work" of the conference. He was joined by White and Low in voting for it.

Two days later, however, Mahan chanced to read an editorial in the *Manchester Guardian* which argued persuasively that, had Article 27 been operative in April 1898, mediation between the United States and Spain would have been the business of all Europe and the "splendid little war" would likely have been prevented. He immediately realized what White, Low, and Holls had missed: namely, that Article 27 was a clear violation of the original intent of the Monroe Doctrine in that it would require American interference in European tensions and European interference in the affairs of the Western Hemisphere. Mahan immediately "threw in a bomb," as White put it, and the American delegation, Holls excepted, quickly qualified its short-sighted support of the article by introducing a clause specifically exempting the United States and her Monroe Doctrine from it. Indeed, had the U.S. delegation not retreated from its initial stance, the Senate would have laughed its hapless members off Capitol Hill and out of Washington.[13]

Mahan returned to Quogue from The Hague in mid-August 1899. Once home at "Slumberside," he resumed his campaigns against Badham and Schley and launched his first attack on former Secretary of War Russell A. Alger's false contention that it was the secretary, rather than Mahan, who had amended Toral's formula for the surrender of Santiago back in July 1898. More importantly, he began a study of Far Eastern diplomatic problems as these related to Secretary Hay's recently proclaimed Open Door Policy in China. He also resumed his attempt to educate the American public on other international facts of life, particularly as he had at first hand observed some of them in action at The Hague.

He told Secretary Long that Navy Department lawyers should study carefully and critically the whole concept of applying the land-warfare rules of the Geneva Convention of 1864 to war at sea in 1899. The thought of such adaptation Mahan and the American delegation had vigorously opposed at The Hague. "I formulated certain objections . . . and proposed amendments, for which I could obtain no support," he informed Long, "but I am quite sure I was right, and I should regret to think that our Government should accept this work (formulated in 10 articles) without careful consideration of the articles themselves, and of my comments upon them. Our Delegation left them unsigned, pending the decision of our Government upon them." The decision of the Washington government was to do nothing, even though McKinley did not agree personally with Mahan on the non-applicability of some of the rules of the Geneva Convention to modern maritime warfare. He was inclined, for instance, to favor the neutrality of all hospital ships at the scene of naval battles, and he felt it would be humane to permit the neutralization of belligerent seamen picked out of the water by such vessels. Mahan finally decided that the status of neutral hospital ships at a battle scene was a minor point not worth arguing with the president.

It was far more important to Mahan that the U.S. government and its citizens have no truck whatever with the nonsense about international peace, arbitration, and arms limitation that had permeated the atmosphere at The Hague. For this reason, when he got back to Quogue, he repaired immediately to his desk and wrote for the *North American Review* his well-known, often quoted, and twice-reprinted article "The Peace Conference and the Moral Aspect of War" which was published in October 1899. In this polemical piece, for which he was paid $500, he developed at some length "general views I have long held on the subject of arbitration." Specifically, his was an angry plea "not to sign away [the] right to maintain justice by war by entering into a pledge beforehand to arbitrate, *except* on questions most strictly limited and defined," and an intellectual appeal to the proposition that men should recognize that war often had distinctly moral dimensions. He explained the larger purpose of the article to one doubting correspondent, reformer-philanthropist Grace Hoadley Dodge:

> Such an attitude toward this moral side is doubtless wholly unconscious on the part of the advocates of arbitration. The shocking evils of war have so impressed their imagination that they fail to recognize its moral character. Yet worse things can happen to a man—far worse—than to be mangled by a shell, or to a nation than to be scourged by war. It profits neither to gain the world and to lose his soul. I do not presume to read the actions of Providence, but I see not how it can fail to strike you that at the moment the very sound "Arbitration" so fills men's ears that they can listen to nothing else, their device is returned in mockery on their hands by two wars [Spanish-American and Anglo-Boer], just if ever war was just, and into which one of the parties in either case could not have refused to enter, except at the cost of dereliction to conscience. And it seems as if there were even a chance that our country would have been thus derelict, had not the inexplicable catastrophe of

the *Maine* swept our people into the decisive action, to which no such stimulus should have been needed. . . . there are contingencies which do not admit arbitration, duties which a nation must discharge even at the cost of war and suffering. . . . you may effect arbitration, but I do not believe you will have scored a step in the nation's advance. You may have made material prosperity more secure, but if the counter-vailing truth is not preached, understood, and accepted, it will have been better for the nation that it had never been born.

Aside from Mahan's belated view (expressed in the above letter) that America's march to war in 1898 upheld the correctness of anti-arbitration principles, which he had sought for some years to develop, he was perhaps on better historical ground in his article on "The Peace Conference and the Moral Aspect of War" when he argued that American success in arbitrating matters with George III in 1776 or with Jefferson Davis in 1861 would have cost the nation its soul, if not its very existence. There was, he noted, "unquestionably a Higher Law than law." Further, human conscience diligently consulted "is to the man the voice of God." Let all Americans, he declared, "especially each of us who fears God . . . ask himself how far in his personal life he is prepared to accept arbitration." The question was answered in the asking. Peace for the sake of peace, arbitration for the sake of arbitration, or the placid acceptance of rampant evil in the world—be it human slavery, political tyranny, unprovoked aggression, or religious persecution—were moral compromises Mahan feared Americans might come to embrace as the twentieth century dawned. Were these dangerous notions adopted by his countrymen, he warned Miss Dodge and others, it would be better had the United States "never been born."[14]

While there are times in history when men of conscience and decency feel they must take up arms, Mahan was apt to glorify war as an uplifting experience for all peoples and nations. He felt that war was inherently present in the fabric of international relations. But he never argued that *all* wars were good, just, necessary, or worth their costs in blood and treasure. He maintained only that *some* wars were morally necessary. These wars should never be arbitrated, he held. He was particularly pleased with himself, for example, for having managed at the First Hague Conference to insert into Article 27 the statement excluding the Monroe Doctrine from arbitration. He considered his action in this regard to have been correct and patriotic, especially when the doctrine was later cited by the United States as justification for the use of American military force in Latin America in support of causes Mahan considered decent, moral, and just.

Because of his pride in his accomplishment at The Hague, Mahan was outraged in late 1900 when George Holls published his *The Peace Conference at The Hague and Its Bearings on International Law and Policy*. In this otherwise useful book, Holls concealed the fact that within the U.S. delegation and in the subcommittee he had supported the French version of Article 27 and had voted for it enthusiastically in the Third Committee. True, he was not an official voting member of the American delegation. But he took personal credit for having persuaded the American delegation to insist upon a clause excluding the Monroe Doctrine from arbitration and for having gotten the reservation included in the final version of Article 27. Specifically, he noted that when the arbitration matter was discussed in the subcommittee (the Comité d'Examen) he had there and then reserved the right of the American delegation to make a later declaration protecting the doctrine. The paragraph on the Monroe Doctrine in the final version of Article 27, he wrote, was "the declaration for which Mr. Holls made a reservation." Similarly, the Table of Contents of his book carried the entry, "Reservation by Mr. Holls," showing the reader where he could read of the author's triumph.

Mahan considered the Holls claim to be a fabrication pure and simple, as indeed it was. Filled with righteous indignation, he immediately unsheathed his smoking pen to engage the enemy. Like Custer at the Little Big Horn, the Philosopher of Sea Power in later life collected enemies with incredible ease and regularity. In the years 1891–1901 he was variously at war with Ramsay, Erben, Badham, Schley, Alger, and Holls. In 1906 the enemy was William S. Sims. In all of these skirmishes his considerable ego became deeply involved; and in the Holls controversy it combined with his Christian sense of veracity to produce an especially violent (and ultimately tiresome) verbal attack on one of the circling Sioux. In this instance, however, there was no doubt whatever about the weight and accuracy of Mahan's artillery; his barrage virtually destroyed the pompous Holls in what was clearly a just war.

Beginning with an exceptionally blunt letter to Holls on March 13, 1901, Mahan maintained his attack on the wayward author until April 16, 1902. During this period he literally inundated his antagonist and the former members of the U.S. delegation with bitter letters of protest. These sought personal justice and credit in the matter of Article 27, demanded a retraction of the offending statements in Holls' book, and called its author various uncomplimentary names. "I purpose to get at the bottom facts, if I can, of what so far appears to me a consistent piece of dirty manoeuvring," he assured Crozier. The "bottom facts" demonstrated conclusively that soon *after* the conference adjourned Holls managed surreptitiously to have inserted into the transcript of the official record of the Comité d'Examen additional language that supported the claim he later made about the Monroe Doctrine.

In his attack on Holls' jugular Mahan was supported by former delegates Low, Newel, and Crozier. White declared neutrality. In his own defense, Holls maintained that Mahan was reading too much into his account of the history of Article 27 and that he had no intention of taking credit due the captain. He told Crozier that in the second edition of his book he would change the wording of his account to conform with Mahan's view of the matter. Unfortunately for Captain Mahan, there was no second edition.[15]

Mahan's return from The Hague also brought him face to face with the unhappy facts of the American-Philippine War, a bloody jungle conflict of three years' duration that was triggered by a decision made by the McKinley administration in October 1898 to annex the whole of the Philippine archipelago. This decision, written into the Treaty of Paris, the final accord with Spain signed on December 10, 1898, touched off one of the greatest public debates in the history of American diplomacy. Imperialists and anti-imperialists, annexationists and anti-annexationists, fought vigorously to save the nation from one another's noxious doctrines as the Senate began its debate on the treaty.

On the imperialist and annexationist side, the arguments centered on the important role of the islands in the future expansion of American commerce in the Far East; the related need for an American naval presence in the Western and Southwestern Pacific; and the moral obligation of the United States to uplift and civilize in various spiritual, material, educational, economic, and political ways, some 7,000,000 illiterate, half-naked, and near-savage Filipinos. Most often expressed was the fear that to cast the backward Filipinos adrift on the sea of political independence would be to consign them to speedy ingestion by one of the large sharks —Germany, Britain, Japan—swimming just off the Philippine shore.

On the other side, anti-imperialists and anti-annexationists pointed out that American acquisition of the distant archipelago and its culturally unassimilable natives would violate the spirit of the Declaration of Independence and the Constitution; outrage the ghosts of the Founding Fathers; compromise the hemispheric intent of the Monroe Doctrine; require an expensive two-ocean navy; and, in future years, involve the United States in the war-fraught power politics of Europe in East Asia. Also, much of the talk in anti-annexationist circles in the House and Senate equated Filipino aspirations for independence with those of American revolutionaries in 1775 and 1776.

In spite of all this imperialist and anti-imperialist rhetoric, there was very little confidence in either camp on Capitol Hill that the untutored Filipino natives could be expected to evolve democratic self-government in the rain forests of Mindanao, or that the islands of the archipelago, separately or collectively, would someday become new states in the Union. There was even less confidence among the anti-annexationists that an independent Philippine Republic would long be able to remain either independent or a republic in the fin de siècle world. This last, a highly practical point, transcended theoretical arguments for and against American imperialism as well as various tea-leaf readings on whether the United States should stride forward into an internationalist and imperialist future or remain content with its "continentalist" and isolationist past. It was, however, the basic point on which the issue of Philippine annexation was ultimately decided, since both sides agreed that, if cut adrift, the Philippine Islands would probably soon be gobbled up and digested by some major power.

On February 6, 1899, the Senate of the United States, by a vote of fifty-seven to twenty-seven (one more than the necessary two-thirds), adopted the Treaty of Paris with Spain. Since the treaty contained an annexation clause, the nation thus acquired both the Philippine Islands and an American-Philippine conflict therein which had formally begun two days earlier. This was a war that demanded a far greater military commitment than was made by the Army in Cuba and Puerto Rico in the summer of 1898, and into which the United States eventually poured 70,000 officers and men. To Mahan and other imperialists it was an embarrassing war from an ideological standpoint.

Filipino patriots, long in revolutionary opposition to their Spanish colonial masters, watched the annexation debate in the United States with great interest. At the outset of hostilities in 1898 they had been assured, informally at least, that the Spanish-American War would likely result in the liberation both of Cuba and the Philippines from Madrid. Their leader, Emilio Aguinaldo, had been transported under American auspices from his exile in Hong Kong to Manila in May 1898. On June 12, he organized a provisional Philippine government and proclaimed its independence from Spain. To this action there was no American opposition. He therefore resumed leadership of the Filipino insurrection against Spain, which had flickered out prior to Dewey's arrival on the scene on May 1, and began again to kill Spaniards—this time with U.S. backing. Troops under Aguinaldo's command assisted American infantry units in the capture of Manila in August 1898; they also carried out widespread guerrilla harassment of Spanish colonial forces in Luzon during that fateful summer. When the Spanish-American War ended in mid-August the Filipinos fought on against the Spaniards. By November 1898, Aguinaldo's forces controlled Luzon, Negros, Cebu, Panay, and other islands. His army numbered some 70,000 and the provisional government which he had proclaimed in June was functioning. For all practical purposes, an independent Philippine Republic had been conceived in the smoke of Dewey's guns at Manila Bay. Nevertheless, during the subsequent accouchement, the Americans made no formal commitments to Aguinaldo, did not recognize his government, did not officially regard him as an ally, and did not inform him as to their military plans in the islands. But neither did they oppose his revolutionary activities against Spain.

For this reason, Aguinaldo had some cause—call it the native intuition of a tutored native—to believe that a war for Cuba Libre was also a war for a free Philippines. In the light of this belief, well founded or not, he was both perplexed and angered as he watched the Senate move to its February 6 decision to annex the islands. "I shall allow myself the pleasure of congratulating you upon the ratification of the treaty," Mahan wrote Lodge the following day. "We have a long row to hoe yet, but I believe that . . . the country is now fairly embarked on a career which will be beneficent to the world and honorable to ourselves in the community of nations. I try to respect, but cannot, the men who utter the shibboleth of self-government, and cloud therewith their own intelligence, by applying it to people in the childhood stage of race development."

Unhappily for both Mahan and the United States, Emilio Aguinaldo was no child; nor was he personally in a childhood stage of race development. From his vantage point, the Spanish-American War had resulted merely in the substitution of one colonial master for another. His contempt for "those who posing as our friends and liberators, attempted to dominate us in place of the Spaniards," was profound. On February 4, 1899, using as a pretext an alleged American attack on Filipino outposts at San Juan del Monte, Aguinaldo boldly declared war on the United States of America. His war message and other statements on the reasons the Filipinos had to fight might well have been taken from the debates of the Continental Congress in 1775 and 1776; or from the pages of John Locke. He spoke of independence, national honor, the God-given rights of men, and Filipino opposition to the continuing American military presence in his country. In Aguinaldo's ringing prose, McKinley's General Elwell S. Otis in Manila in 1899 was transformed into George III's General Thomas Gage in Boston in 1775. "Be not discouraged," he told his followers. "Our independence has been watered by the generous blood of our martyrs. Blood which may be shed in the future will strengthen it. Nature has never despised generous sacrifices." Shades of Patrick Henry and Thomas Jefferson. And in the words of a Filipino propaganda leaflet issued on February 24, 1899:

> Let us therefore thank God who has willed this war. Nothing good can be expected from these people [Americans]. . . . This is the nation where honor is yet unknown; in a word, a nation hated by all other nations. . . . Are these our protectors? Better death [than] be related to a people whose evil is inborn. Away with the wretches. Destruction to the Americans. Down with the United States.

Shades of Sam Adams. It was very embarrassing, this Filipino war of national liberation. As Lodge awkwardly confessed to a stunned Senate on February 7: "I think the situation is unique in the fact that the people whom we liberated down there have turned against us."[16]

It was unique; so clearly unique that Mahan knew not quite how to regard it, especially since he had grave doubts that the American people had an inherent aptitude for colonial administration of the type, quality, and even-handedness that Great Britain had demonstrated so well for a century and a half in India. To test these doubts, in October 1898 he asked Daniel C. Gilman, president of The Johns Hopkins University in Baltimore, to undertake at the institution a study of the origins of British rule in India to ascertain the factors in the British success there. "Is . . . the great result we see now due to original developed fitness, or to germs of fitness, which have developed gradually into their present ripe efficiency by steady use at the call of duty?" he inquired of Gilman. The question was rhetorical in the sense that without any assistance whatever from Gilman or The Johns Hopkins, Mahan came soon to believe that Americans indeed had the same "natural aptitude" for colonial rule as did Englishmen. Why not? Did not the carrying of Protestant Christianity to the Filipino heathen ensure the parallel creation and maintenance of a high degree of administrative efficiency in the islands? Beneficent colonial rule, thought Mahan, was nothing more than the overseas political and administrative expression of the parable of the Good Samaritan.

Actually, Mahan had difficulty with the word *colony* in connection with the Philippines because he felt strongly that true colonials were people who could be easily, readily, and wholly assimilated into the institutions, culture, and population of the mother country. And since, at the time, the backward Filipinos were thought to be anything but assimilable, he preferred to refer to the islands as American *dependencies* and to the peoples there as *dependents* or *wards*. His search for the proper analogy in this regard led him to equate such dependents with enlisted men. He thus confidently assured the New York State Chapter of the Colonial Order in late November 1898 that

> we officers of the army and navy deal continually with men who are our dependents. . . . The American officers of the navy and army are the best possible guardians you can give to these dependencies which have come to us under the treaty of peace. We have the opportunity of bestowing upon them a beneficence which they have never known. The officers of the army and navy are better qualified to deal with these subject races than men engaged in the hard fight of ordinary existence.

He knew that it would take a while to establish and adjust the delicate mechanisms of the guardian-ward, officer-enlisted man, missionary-convert relationships that came to form the social basis of the American imperial presence in the Philippines. "The task is novel to us," he told the readers of *Engineering Magazine* in January 1899, "we may make blunders." Nevertheless, he remained optimistic. By emulating the firm, forthright, and beneficent behavior of the British in their own dependencies, and by adopting the role of the Good Samaritan, all would surely go well for the United States in the Philippines. At no time prior to February 1899 did Mahan expect America's new Filipino wards to snap at the kindly hand that stretched 8,000 miles across the Pacific to pat their empty, noble, and soon-to-be-baptized heads. They were supposed to behave like enlisted men in the U.S. Navy. Aguinaldo's declaration of war was nothing less than mutiny.

Further, the early successes he had in the field against the undermanned and inadequately trained army of his self-proclaimed guardians was a matter very much on Mahan's mind while he was at The Hague. There, rumors reached the American delegation early in June 1899 that the United States planned to terminate offensive military activities against the Filipinos and go over to a defensive strategy until more troops arrived. Mahan protested to Long that heavy pressure must be kept on Aguinaldo's force, that America's green recruits must be kept in constant motion against the enemy lest they grow soft and discouraged, and that the Army generals on the scene should be allowed to make decisions without political second-guessing from home. The best way to fight guerrilla soldiers, he reminded Long, could be learned from hundreds of campaigns against the American Indians. "Army officers used to say that our Western Indians began to be thoroughly overcome only when our troops gave up the habit of winter quarters and followed the savages through the bitter winters of the plains."[17]

Inexorably, perhaps inevitably, an augmented U.S. army gradually wore down Aguinaldo's poorly equipped, poorly armed, and poorly led troops. By the end of 1899 organized Filipino resistance in the field had virtually ceased. Guerrilla activity continued for two years, marked by senseless atrocities on both sides. Among these was the physical disfigurement of captives, ears, eyes, and noses being emphasized. The American "water cure," which exploded Filipino bellies but left no outward evidence of torture, was much criticized in anti-imperialist circles at home, as was, ironically, the effective American use of Valeriano Weyler's idea of concentration camps—camps that helped destroy the nexus between Filipino civilian and guerrilla. When Aguinaldo was captured in March 1901, what remained of his mobile government disintegrated. Meanwhile, in June 1899, the United States had announced its commitment to Philippine independence as soon as the Filipinos could be made ready for self-government. By mid-1902 the bushwhacking little war was over, the last-standing guerrillas having been hunted down and exterminated by army patrols, as the Plains Indians had been in the 1870s and 1880s. Brutal and pragmatic tactics these; scarcely splendid.

On none of these final bloody events in the American-Philippine War did Mahan comment, save to point out to President Roosevelt in January 1902 that to keep a "naturally treacherous" people like the Filipinos in good order would require a 20,000-man American army of occupation for some time to come. Earlier, in May 1901, shortly after Aguinaldo's capture, he rejoiced to Bouverie Clark that "we are pretty nearly at the end of our fighting troubles in the Philippines, but I somewhat mistrust those fellows, and hope we shan't go to sleep and stop watching them." In this letter he also equated the origin and termination of the American-Philippine War with that of the Anglo-Boer War in South Africa:

> I believe, however, that both there [Philippines] and in the Transvaal a short experience of the comforts of peace and good government, coupled with a vivid recollection of the miseries of being ever on the run, will contribute to make both Boers and Filipinos careful about quarreling with their bread and butter—their material prosperity—in the near future.[18]

"Bread and butter" issues in both wars aside, the fact of the matter was that Mahan was far more interested in the Boer War than he was in the embarrassing American-Philippine struggle. Britain's crushing of the independent Boer republics, the Transvaal Republic and the Orange Free State, was an imperialist operation he could better understand. It had a clear legal and political rationale; it was initially fought by Christian white men grouped into traditional land armies; it was conducted on relatively open terrain; it featured traditional Napoleonic infantry tactics; it outraged the anti-imperialist Bryan Democrats and their Irish-American camp followers; it struck a blow for future Anglo-American rapprochement; and it offered Mahan an opportunity to write a book on the subject for which he was paid a great deal of money. Compared with the confused and squalid struggle in the Philippines, the Boer War had everything.

It grew out of cultural, political, and economic tension between British and Dutch (Boer) settlers in South Africa that went back to the years following the Napoleonic Wars. The last of those wars saw South Africa, which had been held by Holland since 1652, pass from Dutch to British hands in the Treaty of Paris signed in 1814. Out of this transfer came a British colony centering on Cape Town (the Cape Colony) and two inland Boer republics to the north, the South African Republic (generally referred to as the Transvaal) and the Orange Free State. These last were established by Dutch migrants who, having no desire whatever to live under British rule, fled to the interior in the so-called "Great Trek," 1835–1837, to begin life anew. Almost all the Boers, then and later, were farmers and ranchers. In the 1850s the independence of both Boer republics was recognized by a London government which retained only nominal suzerainty over them. Following that, the three European political entities in South Africa, two Dutch, one English, settled down to four decades of intramural squabbling, relieved only by a common interest in expanding their respective frontiers by slaughtering the native tribes that stood in their paths. British attempts to federate the Cape Colony and the Boer republics into a single political entity by force or persuasion in the 1870s and 1880s produced more dead bodies than it did converts to federation. The discovery of diamonds and gold in South Africa stimulated British immigration to the Cape Colony and further complicated the relations between British, Dutch, and black Africans. So, too, did the rapid territorial expansion of Cape Colony in the 1890s, an expansion designed in part to deny the Transvaal Republic an outlet to the sea. The question of where British suzerainty ended and Boer sovereignty began remained a nagging and unresolved legal issue in the British-Boer tension over the years.

It was the famous (or infamous) Jameson Raid in December 1895 that brought the English-Dutch matter in South Africa to final crisis. This unauthorized and militarily disastrous British incursion into the Transvaal, led by political adventurer Leander Starr Jameson, sought to advance the political rights of British residents (called "Uitlanders" by the Dutch) in the Johannesburg area of the Transvaal by encouraging them to revolt against President Paul Kruger's government. Certain it was that the English-speaking Uitlanders of the Transvaal did not have full voting rights there; the Dutch Boers were scarcely wild-eyed democrats. But certain it also was that the Cape Colony government of Prime Minister Cecil Rhodes hoped to accomplish through support of an Uitlander revolution against the Transvaal government what his English predecessors had failed to accomplish—the crushing of Boer sovereignty and the incorporation of the Dutch settlers into a federation. The fact that the impetuous Jameson was disavowed and punished for his act did not conceal the imperialist ambitions of Cecil Rhodes. Nor did a telegram Kaiser William II sent to Kruger in January 1896, congratulating the Boers on their military victory over Jameson and their suppression of the Uitlander revolutionary movement in the Transvaal, do other than reinforce the British of Cape Colony in their growing belief that the able Kruger intended nothing less than the formation of a Boer coalition which, with foreign aid, would drive the English out of South Africa and into the sea. The so-called "Kruger Telegram" produced a major Anglo-German diplomatic crisis in Europe, one related to British appeasement of the United States on the issue of Venezuela's boundary. While the telegram may have helped the Americans, it ultimately benefitted the Boers not at all.

Out of the Jameson Raid eventually came the Bloemfontein Conference of May 31–June 5, 1899. This meeting was held against a background of continuing Uitlander agitation for extension of the suffrage in the Transvaal and an Uitlander petition to Queen Victoria for relief from political oppression. Sir Alfred Milner, British high commissioner for South Africa, demanded of Kruger an immediate grant of the franchise to all male foreigners (mainly British nationals) who had been resident in the Transvaal for five years. Existing Boer law required a fourteen-year period of residency for Uitlanders. Kruger refused and the conference abruptly ended. Later, in July, Kruger suggested a five-year residency arrangement in return for formal British abrogation of suzerainty over his nation. The British refused this trade-off and Kruger withdrew the offer. By late summer 1899 both sides were arming for the war that commenced on October 12, 1899, by Boer declaration.

At that moment the British had but 25,000 troops in South Africa to fight a combined Transvaal-Orange Free State force of some 75,000. For the first four months of the war the Boers were therefore victorious, a fact that distressed and embarrassed Mahan no end. For a brief while the power, might, and grandeur of the British Empire was humiliated by a group of rawboned Dutch farmers. "I cannot express with what deep sorrow and anxiety your checks affect me," he told Thursfield in mid-December 1899; "I cannot believe God will permit so beneficent a government to be permanently disabled; you may need chastening, but the hopes of the world rest upon you largely. . . . I don't want you beaten." Similar sentiments were expressed to General Frederick Sleigh Roberts, commanding officer of Her Majesty's forces in South Africa. Mahan failed to understand that the tenacious Boers were fighting for their very homes and their way of life. They were perfectly willing to kill Englishmen in any way they could, whether in fashion orthodox or unorthodox. "Bobs" Roberts, whom Mahan had met in England in 1894 and liked instantly, tried to explain the Boer problem to him in January 1900:

> As you write, the work here is more arduous by far than was at first supposed. We are learning how differently war must be conducted nowadays, and how impossible it is for positions, held by a determined enemy who can use their rifles with effect, to be taken by a frontal attack. We have had our lessons, and I trust we shall benefit by them. The Boers have proved themselves to be no ordinary tacticians, and the want of transport, confining us as it did to lines of railway, forced us to play into their hands. Matters are mending by degrees, and I trust you will receive good accounts of our proceedings ere very long.

The British won ere long. But before they did (in May 1902) they poured 300,000 men into South Africa and ground down the courageous Boers by sheer weight of numbers and firepower. As early as the close of 1900 the outmanned Boers were reduced to intensive guerrilla warfare, bloody tactics which Mahan dismissed as "trivial raids." Nevertheless, this desperate approach to survival in the field postponed the inevitable for eighteen months. It was finally countered by the British decision to herd 120,000 Boer women and children into concentration camps, where 20,000 of them died of disease and starvation.

As the Spanish learned in Cuba, as the Americans learned in the Philippines, and as the British learned in the Transvaal, the concentration camp was the tactical antidote to guerrilla warfare. Mahan considered Weyler's use of the camps uncivilized to the point of justifying U.S. intervention in

Cuba. He did not comment on American adoption of the policy in the Philippines or British adoption of it in the Transvaal.

The outbreak of the war in October 1899 found Mahan "painfully ignorant" of the details of the dispute in South Africa but automatically hostile to those sections of the American press and public disposed to an anti-British position. He frankly admitted that he was prejudiced in favor of Great Britain because of his "strong desire to see drawn closer our ties to the one power that stood by us 18 months ago." As he began to educate himself on the background of the war, he discovered, not to his complete surprise, that pro-Boer sentiment in the United States was concentrated heavily among Irish-American elements in the population and among those Americans ("the noisy section of our people") who were also in opposition to American imperialism in the Philippines and in the Caribbean.

In New York City, for instance, he regarded pro-Boer sentiment as little more than a reflex action of Tammany Hall. "Last night's [January 29, 1900] pro-Boer meeting here was beneath contempt in intellectual or moral weight," he informed historian James Ford Rhodes; "of course in a city that gives Tammany 250,000 votes it is never difficult to fill an auditorium of 10,000 with people who hate England." A pro-Boer meeting in Boston on January 17, 1900, attended by a number of prominent anti-imperialists and anti-Philippine annexationists, resulted in what Mahan dubbed an "impertinent resolution" in support of the Boers, one that was sent to British Prime Minister Joseph Chamberlain. This interference in European affairs Mahan angrily identified as a clear violation of the Monroe Doctrine, pointing out that the doctrine's principle of mutual non-interference in European and Western Hemispheric matters had been reaffirmed as recently as July 1899 at the First Hague Conference when the American delegation there had carefully written the concept into Article 27. For noisy pro-Boer Americans in Boston, New York, and elsewhere to undermine that diplomatic triumph so soon after its achievement could only encourage similar European interference in Latin-American and Caribbean issues near and dear to the special interests of the United States.

He hoped, therefore, that sensible men, including journalists who otherwise supported a muscular American foreign policy would soon come down decisively on the British side of the Transvaal dispute. Many did, for reasons Mahan had outlined for Thursfield in late October 1899: "The great end of checking and thwarting a factious attempt, here, to raise sympathy for 'the weaker party,' irrespective of justice, an attempt directed ultimately against the growing accord between the English-speaking states, will be rather hindered than furthered by evident partisanship. . . . advo-

cates of expansion for ourselves, though of differing political tone otherwise, will do much to guide our opinion; for expansion carries the day
here." To his English correspondents he also expressed his "profound interest and sympathy" with their cause, reminded them that great powers
had a right and duty to "put an end to gross evils at their doors," and pronounced the British support of the Uitlanders in the Transvaal "justified—
nay, imperative—upon grounds much the same as our own in Cuba. Taxation without representation is not as bad as starvation by reconcentration,
but the principle is the same."

To Mahan it was vitally important that Anglo-American rapprochement, begun so hopefully in the gracious British retreat in Venezuela in
1896, continued so steadfastly in British support of the American war with
Spain in 1898, reaffirmed in British support of American policy in China
and at the isthmus in 1899 and 1900, not founder on the rocks of American misunderstanding of the essential justice of the queen's cause in South
Africa. To the readers of *The New York Times* on January 22, 1900, he
declared flatly: "not only is the cause of Great Britain just, but to have
failed to uphold it would have been to fail in national honor." It was only a
short step from this assertion to his belief, expressed to Lodge, that Britain
had no choice militarily but to "repel [the] aggression" of a brutal "Dutch
race" bent on imposing its cultural and political stamp on all South Africa.
The Boer government, he instructed readers of *The Independent* in February 1900, was nothing less than "a corrupt and oppressive oligarchy."[19]

Mahan hung his case for the justice of the British cause in South Africa
on the technical legal argument that the Boers refused to enfranchise the
Uitlanders. Principally, he emphasized the earlier Boer decision to lengthen
the five-year residence period required by law in 1882 to the fourteen-
year period legislated by the Transvaal government in 1890. According to
Mahan, this virtual disfranchisement of the Uitlanders had produced in Johannesburg a Dutch-speaking oligarchy that heavily taxed the Uitlanders
while refusing them effective representation in the governing process. The
Boers were therefore fastening on South Africa a tyrannical political system that deserved to die forthwith. "The cause of the Uitlanders is in principle identical with that of the American Revolutionists," he told readers
of *The New York Times*, a thought that, in a somewhat different context,
had crossed the mind of Aguinaldo.

Mahan never attempted to rationalize the awkward ideological similarity between the Uitlander cause in the Transvaal and the Filipino
cause in Luzon. Instead, he insisted that neither the Boers nor the Filipinos
had any inherent right to exercise political sovereignty in the lands they

had historically occupied. He therefore called for a quick and decisive British military victory in South Africa against the Johannesburg aggressors, opposed any suggestion of American government involvement in the conflict (including the mediation suggested by the Universal Peace Union), and decided that the only way to ensure a lasting peace in the region would be to exclude the Boer leaders, their language, and their inferior institutions from the South African society of the future. When Boer emissaries visited the United States in late 1900 to rouse American public opinion to the support of their increasingly hopeless contest with Britain, Mahan disdainfully characterized their trip in a letter to the pro-Boer *New York Evening Sun* as an unmanly "whimpering to our people," a running "like babies to the nearest bystanders for comfort." "Captain Mahan in Savage Mood," said the accompanying headline. Indeed he was.[20]

The Anglo-Boer War views that Mahan expressed in his private correspondence in 1899 and 1900 were repeated in four popular articles on the subject and in his hastily written book, *The War in South Africa: a Narrative of the Anglo-Boer War from the Beginning of Hostilities to the Fall of Pretoria*, which P. F. Collier and Son of New York rushed to print in December 1900. A book of only 55,000 words, Mahan dashed it off in three months. He was frank to admit that it was little more than a "brief outline" of the war to date and that he wrote it for the "extremely high commission" offered him by the Collier organization. But he also wrote it to instruct American public opinion on the justice of the British cause in South Africa. It was exactly "the *sort* of thing the man in the street needs," he maintained. Perhaps the presumed intellectual limitations of his expected readership explain why his research seldom went beyond accounts of the fighting available in the daily newspapers. He was, however, able to secure from his old friend Bouverie Clark, who served as Director of Transports in the Admiralty, some privileged statistical information having to do with British logistical problems in the war theater. From John Bassett Moore, the prominent international lawyer and legal historian whom he had met in Washington during the Spanish-American War, he received assurances that the British had the legal right to march troops across Portuguese East Africa en route to the seat of war. Nevertheless, Mahan's *The War in South Africa* suffered the fate of most exercises in the writing of contemporary history. It was episodic and superficial. He was pleased, however, that "upon the whole, my book has received as good treatment from the press as I could have expected." Whether or not it benefited the American "man in the street," it may have proved useful to the German people. In November 1900, Major General C. Schwartz asked for, and received, permission to translate the book into German. Nobody, he wrote, "is more in want of such a book as my countrymen, where sound judgment is clouded by an Anglophobia that passes all bounds."[21]

To write his lucrative *Lessons of the War with Spain* and his quickly executed *War in South Africa*, Mahan turned down an opportunity to produce a serious biography of William B. Cushing; he was also forced to postpone the writing of a textbook on sea power for high-school students which Roy Marston, partner in Sampson Low, Marston and Company, very much wanted to publish because he thought it had great possibilities in the British schoolboy market. The Cushing biography, which the hero's widow was willing to subsidize, would have been based solidly on family papers. Nevertheless, Mahan considered it risky from a financial standpoint. His *Life of Farragut* had been such an economic disaster that he was loath to gamble his time and energy on Cushing's far more modest naval career. The sinking of the Confederate ram *Albemarle*, however intrepidly done, did not a best seller make. Mahan could do better writing articles at $500 each. Similarly, the idea of a textbook on sea power, in which Mahan's interest was "chiefly pecuniary," never got far beyond discussion of a possible title. Although he had a great deal of correspondence with Marston and with Little, Brown and Company about it, other projects that interested him more seemed invariably to materialize just in time to keep the volume from being written. A publisher's survey of British schoolmasters in March and April 1901 indicated that sales would not be as large as Marston thought and the project was shelved for good.[22]

These literary concerns notwithstanding, by the close of 1901 Mahan could rejoice in the realization that nearly all was well in the world as he saw it. British military adventures in South Africa and American military adventures in the Philippines had been brought to successful conclusions, the Anglo-American diplomatic rapprochement was far advanced, the threat of eternal peace through arms limitations and arbitration had been contained at The Hague, his personal and professional enemies—Badham, Schley, and Holls—had been routed, American Empire had been launched and was proceeding nicely in the Pacific and in the Far East, the Navy was growing rapidly, and the Republican candidates, McKinley and Roosevelt, had overwhelmed Bryan and the Democrats in the presidential election of 1900.

Mahan voted for McKinley and Roosevelt with enthusiasm. In his mind the Democracy of 1900 represented little more than an unholy alliance of urban political radicals, rural free-silverites, Aguinaldo-lovers, Boer bleeding hearts, confused anti-imperialists, small-navy advocates, fuzzy-minded peace and arbitration devotees, Irish-American Anglophobes, and Tammany crooks. He therefore gave his time, energy, and money to Republican campaigns at the local, state, and national levels. He was not as "alarmed" for the future of the Republic as he had been during the election of 1896, but a Bryan victory in 1900, he felt, would be

> a disaster, yes; and very real—but not irretrievable. Neither on the silver question, nor on imperialism, will Bryan if victorious have behind him a party sufficiently united to revolutionize. Nevertheless, in a political sense he is a bad man, a *very* bad man; all the worse if he be as honest as reported. He stands, personally, for essential revolution, and reversal of certain well-initiated advances—towards the gold standard and expansion, not to speak of the still worse attitude towards riot and the Courts. . . . Accordingly, I send my money [$200] and shall be careful to vote.

He was delighted when McKinley was swept back into the White House. He was distressed only by the fact that Roosevelt had chosen to leave the governorship of New York and bury himself in the casket that was the vice-presidency of the United States. Having charged gloriously up San Juan Hill in Cuba and straight into the Governor's Mansion at Albany, the energetic Rough Rider could now look forward, Mahan opined, to "a prolonged rest from the responsibilities and cares of office." Like St. Paul during his four years in Roman captivity, the new vice-president was approaching what the Philosopher of Sea Power saw as "a period of professional rest coupled with great intellectual advance and ripening."

The assassination of McKinley in September 1901 genuinely saddened Mahan. He had admired the president's calm firmness in his daily conduct of the Spanish-American War, especially his handling of Toral's surrender at Santiago, as well as his steadfast support of Navy in the 1898 Army-Navy game that was inter-service conflict over how best to reduce the fortifications of that city. As he told Bouverie Clark, the president's death, "at the very crown of his career," was "sad in its utter uselessness and folly." The bullet from the pistol of Leon Czolgosz "simply secured him his safe place in our history." Nevertheless, Mahan sensed that there prevailed in the nation "a general feeling that Roosevelt is even a better man for the immediate future."[23]

As Roosevelt moved from vice-president to president of the United States, Mahan moved from vice-president to president of the American Historical Association—a position that gave him a bully platform from which to expound his philosophy of history and his views on historiography.

XVI

Historian and Philosopher
of History

*Facts won't lie if you work them right; but if you work them wrong,
a little disproportion in the emphasis, a slight exaggeration of color, a
little more or less limelight on this or that part of the grouping and the
result is not truth, even though each individual fact be as unimpeachable as the multiplication table.*

Alfred Thayer Mahan, *From Sail to Steam*

According to Mahan, he became a historian by act of God. His one great concept, the influence of sea power upon history, to which all his other ideas were footnotes, addenda, and variations, came to him, he said, from above. Well it might have, although the notion of the historical importance of command of the sea dates back to Themistocles, Thucydides, and Xenophon. It had had numerous revivals in the minds of men and was again making the rounds in American naval and historiographical circles in the late 1870s and the 1880s. At various times Mahan credited Francis Bacon, Sir Walter Raleigh, Theodor Mommsen, Sir William Napier, Sir John Seeley, and Stephen B. Luce with having helped him discover, hone, and apply the idea. He claimed for himself only its rediscovery and the fact that his "habit of omnivorous though desultory reading" had led him to "the happy seizure of an idea to all intents original and unworked." His *Sea Power* books, he confessed, merely represented "old things in a new form such as may make them more cordially received, because clearer." Nevertheless, he remained certain until the end of his days that his own awareness of the influence of sea power came from *outside* of him, that it came to him from God while he was reading Mommsen in 1884.

Specifically, with God's help, it "came from within"; it dawned on his "inner consciousness." He owed the insight "to no other man." It was "one of those concrete perceptions which turn inner darkness into light—and give substance to shadow." As he confided to his wife, he was "guided to the work. . . . the gift and the call to write both came from outside—let who will, then, claim the glory." To Silas McBee, editor of *The Churchman*, he wrote: "to treat a certain range of secular subjects, imparting to them, when it can be done without straining, a coloring consistent with religious thought, is the line marked out for me by Providence."[1]

Certain that his discovery of the influence of sea power on history was a gift from above, Mahan naturally tended to view it in cosmological terms. It was a "power" he attempted to define in 1892:

> In its course and influence, this wonderful and mysterious Power is seen to be a complex organism endued with a life of its own, receiving and imparting countless impulses, moving in a thousand currents which twine in and around one another in infinite flexibility, not quite defying the investigation which they provoke, but rendering it exceedingly difficult. The Power feels and is moved by many interests; it has a great history in the past, it is making a great and yet more wonderful history in the present.[2]

Such a grand concept, "endued with a life of its own," revealed to Mahan by the Creator, clearly transcended the earth-bound limitations of mortal historians. To cope with the problem of applying such an idea to the actual writing of history, while further demonstrating the existence, importance, and grandeur of the thought, Mahan evolved a research methodology that he called "subordination." This technique involved a careful gathering and selecting of historical facts. He then applied these facts to the illustration of events that were related to the larger notion of the influence of sea power on history. Put another way, his task was to "subordinate" a group of selected facts in such a way as to prove the "truth" of an already determined conclusion. He thus rejected the inductive, more scientific alternative of proceeding from the facts to the conclusion. His approach was entirely deductive. Having reached in 1885 and 1886 what he believed to be a divine insight into sea power, he spent the next twenty-five years arranging, or "subordinating," various facts to fit it.

On a less theological level, his methodology simplified his effort to communicate with his audience. It also improved the comprehension of the average reader. In June 1897 he explained the problem of communication to the readers of *Harper's Monthly* in these terms:

In the study of a field of maritime operations, the number of available positions, whose relative and combined influence upon the whole is to be considered, should be narrowed by a process of gradual elimination to those clearly essential and representative. To embrace more confuses the attention, wastes mental force, and is a hindrance to correct appreciation. The rejection of details, where permissible and understandingly done, facilitates comprehension, which is baffled by a multiplication of minutiae, just as the impression of a work of art, or of a story, is lost amid a multiplicity of figures or of actors.

As things stood at the turn of the century, there were simply too many facts available on any historical subject to do otherwise. "The trouble of future historians," he wrote in 1908, "is going to be not the lack of material, but the super-abundance of chaff to wheat, and the labor of sifting the little valuable out of the mass of rubbish." The explosion of historical information in Mahan's lifetime made it virtually impossible for the scholar to keep abreast of the data, even in a narrow field of specialization. This was especially true in the study of contemporary history. "What is to happen to authors of the next generation, save those of fiction who spin from their own insides?" he asked in dismay. The only answer to this dilemma of factual riches, he explained to Horace Scudder in 1891, was to bring together and place "in their relation to one another and in part to history, a series of events nowhere else similarly treated, and consequently lost to sight in the mass of other more dazzling, but really less influential incidents."[3]

Whatever the merits or demerits of subordination as a research technique, Mahan was forced by his lack of formal training in history to adopt it as his way of writing history when he arrived at the Naval War College from the *Wachusett* in 1886. He knew practically no history when he reached Newport. Although he was armed with the idea of the influence of sea power, he fully recognized "the denseness of my ignorance." Even after the publication of his first *Influence* book he had to "admit disadvantages owing to no opportunity for studying" historical questions. "I bring to them no special knowledge of details, only a few general principles, and I have laboriously to apply these, and under pressure of time seek to solve difficulties, whose solution to a man who had studied before would be rapid." But he was pleased to discover that he had the kind of mind that could bypass an "abundance of minute knowledge" and quickly perceive and grasp larger concepts. This ability had permitted him mentally to outline his *Influence of Sea Power Upon History* before, in fact, he "had acquired the knowledge necessary to the full treatment of the subject." Indeed, that book was based almost entirely on hastily digested secondary sources. "Original research was not within my scope, nor was it necessary to the scheme thus outlined," he admitted. All that was required of the researcher in approaching any historical problem, then, was "a statement of general historical conditions, sufficient to understand the setting of the special incident in the mosaic of history; the sequences of cause and effect as I understand them." He had grave doubt that complete accuracy could be achieved by the most dedicated and persevering historian whatever research method he used—even in the reconstruction of the events involved in so limited a historical action as a naval battle. "Accuracy . . . in a naval battle," he decided in 1895, "is practically unattainable. The most that can be insured is a correct impression of the general and decisive features. . . . the shifting scenes of a naval action leave no adequate trace of their passage."

Given the inherent limitations of the historian's art, there was, therefore, little point in confusing and overwhelming the reader with masses of data that could only clutter up the ability of the historian to get across his main point. For this reason, the less research the better. Consequently, in 1906, when Mahan was asked to undertake a comprehensive, narrative history of the United States he flinched not at all: "Of course, I cannot contemplate exhaustive research," he told John M. Brown, "or full treatment, of our now three century record. My hope is to strike a ruling thought, like Sea Power, and to string my account so upon that as to present a more vivid and coherent whole than more elaborate and comprehensive works do—or can do." In sum, the practical beauty of the subordination method was that the use of a few carefully selected facts, and their careful grouping around a "ruling thought," permitted speed of writing and required no great knowledge of history. It was a technique perfectly suited to Mahan, who became a historian at the age of fifty and always felt that he had to write swiftly and write for money.[4]

The intellectual difficulty was that subordination was a subjective process that permitted a tiny portion of the available data to be manipulated in such a way that it appeared to document preconceived conclusions. To be sure, as Mahan once said of his account of the *Chesapeake-Shannon* fight, "I shall not make [a] comment, I only arrange the evidence." But arrange the evidence how? His answer to this question indicated that he was aware both of the temptations and opportunities that "arranging" presented:

Facts won't lie if you work them right; but if you work them wrong, a little disproportion in the emphasis, a slight exaggeration of color, a little more or less limelight on this or that part of the grouping and the result is not truth, even though each individual fact be as unimpeachable as the multiplication table.

He never admitted that he himself "worked" facts, but a reading of his complete works, historical and journalistic, clearly demonstrates that he often did. He held strong views, pro and con, on various men and nations; he held positive opinions on such subjects as war, peace, strategy, tactics, arbitration, domestic politics, imperialism, diplomacy, morality, Christianity, women, and race. Because of this, he invariably worked the facts "right" to bring his readers to share in his own biases on these matters. He had small patience with opposing points of view. At the same time, he was very aware of the intrusion of bias into the writing of history, especially when the bias was in conflict with his own. Thus he enjoyed flaying the "Whig School of historians and politicians represented by Goldwin Smith, Gladstone, Earl Russell, etc.," found Thomas B. Macaulay's histories and essays "very prejudiced," and castigated those who did not share his views of Admiral Sampson, Lord Nelson, Theodore Roosevelt, and other of his heroes. Bias, however, could sometimes be transcended. His intellectual mentor, Theodor Mommsen, for example, earned Mahan's contempt as an "old Anglo- & American-phobe." But when in 1902 Mommsen proposed the cooperation of England, Germany, and the United States in the international power politics of the day, Mahan softened momentarily: "I believe the old fellow is honest, and his historic sense compels him to recognize fundamental truths, despite his prejudices."[5]

It was Mahan's pursuit of "fundamental truths," useful to the masses, that caused him to remain wedded to his subordination method. He had little interest in history that was designed to be read solely by other historians. On the contrary, he thought that history should instruct and uplift the populace, that the ultimate measure of the value of any written history was the number of readers it attracted. "There is no use of a man writing what he has no reason to believe the many will read," he said. It was imperative, therefore, that all historians use subordination in order to reduce to essentials the quantity and complexity of their data. Indeed, he was wont to quote Sir John Seeley, who influenced him most in this regard, to the point that such simplification was absolutely essential to the public weal. Public understanding, Sir John had held, was best guided by a "few large, plain, simple ideas." The purpose of it all, thought Mahan, was to make a "general treatment" of complicated problems "more useful and more suggestive to the man in the street."

It was to reach the "man in the street" that Mahan commenced writing articles on contemporary issues shortly after his return from Europe in the *Chicago.* There was good money in it, and it also presented him with an opportunity to mold public opinion in shapes similar to those taken by his own thoughts. Popular history was thus the royal road to income and influence; and, because of this, it particularly required the clarity and simplicity that only subordination could produce. Nevertheless, Mahan recognized the transitory quality of popular history. In January 1901, a year before he became president of the American Historical Association, he half-apologized to historian James Ford Rhodes because he had been "diverted, as you know, by ephemeral work connected with the passing issues of the last few years in national policy. These seem to me to have passed now beyond my probable or necessary influence, and I wish now to resume, without distraction, my self-prescribed work."

He never denigrated the importance of his "ephemeral work" (his "potboilers"), however, and he never felt that he prostituted his considerable talent for writing history by cranking out popular articles. While his critics accused him of oversimplification, he was delighted that he had the skill, rare among professional historians, to compress his thought and research into those "simple ideas" that the average mentality could grasp. This same mentality could also be reached through the use of anecdotes. In the preparation of his biography of Nelson he noted with satisfaction that "I have got all the anecdote I could and woven it in to the best of my ability."[6]

Writing style was important to communicating easily with the reader, and Mahan had a high opinion of his competence as a writer. He was proud of the richness of his vocabulary and his mastery of the mechanics of English grammar. While he disliked writing under pressure, he was nevertheless capable of turning out reams of well-phrased manuscript at great speed to meet editorial deadlines. He boasted about his ability to do this. Occasionally, he would still be researching and writing the concluding chapters of a book, the first chapters of which were already in press. This produced death-defying races with the printer, all of which Mahan won. Sometimes, books and articles on contemporary problems would be changed in galley to reflect the latest newspaper headlines. Mahan liked to be current.

So great was his requirement for absolute silence when he was engaged in writing that he had his study at "Marshmere" soundproofed. During these periods he insisted upon being waited on hand and foot by his wife and daughters. Just as he subordinated historical facts to ruling ideas, so did he insist that the personal lives of the women in his household be subordinated to the demands of his writing routine. He felt, too, that the application of seat of trousers to surface of chair on a rigid, self-imposed daily schedule was the only way to get books written. "A consecutive and sustained attention is a large element, not only of success, but of rapidity," he once told Ramsay; "breaks lose not only their own length of time, but that which is necessary to gather up again the dropped threads." He understood the difficulty that historians engaged in writing books have in finding motivation and the time to read the books of other authors; and he experienced that sense of aloneness that all productive historians feel when a major study has been finished—that "element of sadness, which Gibbon depicted so graphically, when you and your work are parted, and it leaves your hand finally to go into the world."[7]

Mahan's effective use of subordination, his ability to popularize and simplify historical materials, and his willingness to write rapidly to satisfy changing tastes in the literary market place, did not mean that he did not understand the importance of primary sources. He knew perfectly well that personal letters and other documents contemporary with the events being described were of much greater value than secondary sources. He thought that his biography of Farragut had failed because he had had few personal letters with which to work. For the opposite reason he felt that his *Life of Nelson* was a success because it was based largely on the admiral's personal correspondence and on the inclusion of many anecdotes. Mahan had no interest, however, in gleaning or repeating anecdotes found in "intimate parts of a correspondence." In his *Nelson*, for example, he refused to include a "nasty episode" that involved Lady Nelson's holding a basin into which Lady Hamilton was vomiting while Nelson, standing nearby, was abusing his wife for her heartlessness. Material of this sort he thought irrelevant to depicting human character. Anecdotal, yes; proper, no. Nonetheless, he did believe that personal letters were vital to the historian and that a comparison of such letters was the surest road to truth. He explained this conviction to historian Andrew C. McLaughlin in January 1905:

> Public documents are necessary and invaluable; but at an early stage in my life as an attempting writer of history, I made up my mind that truth was most surely to be attained by access to private letters, subjecting them to the cross-examination of comparison with one another and with all other evidence. In private correspondence, men speak carelessly, which is against truth, but they also speak freely, which is for truth; and the gain is greater than the loss, granted reasonable insight and faculty for cross-examination. Particularly, they reveal motives

which are perhaps even more important to history than are acts. I would never rely upon the public dispatch of an unsuccessful general, and I fancy statesmen are much the same. Neither will lie, both will suppress and color; perhaps unconsciously.

Similarly, he considered the transcripts, findings, and exhibits of courts-martial to be reliable historical data, even though "liable to bias" since "the testimony of unimpeached witnesses is statement of fact, liable doubtless to error, but as near truth as we can usually get here below." On the other hand, he had little confidence in ships' logs as useful sources for research. "In reading one may strike a curious item here and there, but logs are dreary reading except to the initiated and half rations for them."[8]

Mahan's most difficult task as a professional historian was the application of his subordination method to the writing of biography. What worked so well for him in his first two *Influence* books did not work at all well in the research and writing of his *Nelson*. "I find biography, according to my aims and aspirations, far harder work than philosophizing over history," he confessed to Thursfield. Biography did not lend itself well to the arbitrary selection of a few facts designed to illustrate some already discovered truth. The influence of sea power on history simply did not equate with the influence of romance on Lord Nelson. His *Life of Nelson* involved a great deal of digging in primary sources, which resulted in the discovery of an enormous body of detail, all germane to a full and accurate portrait of the man. As his research and writing progressed, he found himself immersed in "the handling of an immense amount of detail, by the accumulation of which alone (in my judgment), and by its proper sorting and adjustment, can a life-like portrait be presented—all this greatly taxes me, for my strength has been, as far as I can judge, rather in singling out the great outlines of events, and concentrating attention upon them, than in the management of details." The work was therefore one of "extreme difficulty" for him. When he finally went to press with the book, he told Brown that "the expenditure of labor has been much greater than on the same amount of product in other books, from which I reason that biography is not an economical use of brain power for me." For this reason, he wrote no more biographies. He had no patience for the "extreme difficulty of the mosaic work" biography entailed, "mosaic, because built up of innumerable minute fragments, difficult, because necessary so to blend them as not to show the joints nor make the differences of shading conspicuous."[9]

The Nelson biography also made Mahan aware of the fact that, although he had evolved a useful interpretation of history—the influence of sea power upon it—he had no transcendent philosophy of history through which and by which he might resolve or explain apparent contradictions, irrationalities, dichotomies, and conflicts in the chronicle of mankind or in the life of a man. By March 1899 he had still not come to grips with theoretical questions then engaging historians all over the country. He had not developed a full-blown philosophy of history of the kind earlier evolved in the nineteenth century by Georg Wilhelm Hegel, Karl Marx, Henry Thomas Buckle, Herbert Spencer, and other European theorists. As he told James Ford Rhodes in some perplexity, "the line between controlling events and being controlled by them, would, I imagine, be difficult to draw; and, as in most matters, truth is best secured by holding both sides of the proposition—men both control events and are controlled by them. A mighty movement cannot be withstood, but it may be guided, or deflected. Between events and man's will there is a resultant of forces." In his *Life of Nelson* he had encountered similar philosophical difficulties. He resolved inadequately the contradictions revealed in his portrait of the personality of Nelson, as these were pointed out by friendly reviewers such as Spenser Wilkinson and hostile commentators such as F. P. Badham, explaining Nelson as a synthesis of antithetical traits. But the synthesis was unrelated to a more comprehensive philosophical system.

Many American historians were busily at work in the 1880s and 1890s trying to design philosophies of history that would explain in scientific terms in what direction the world was moving, how it moved and why—if it was moving at all. Like bloodhounds on the certain trail of rabbits, men such as Andrew D. White, George Bancroft, John Fiske, Frederick Jackson Turner, and the three brilliant Adams brothers—Brooks, Henry, and Charles Francis—sniffed the air for those "laws" of history that they hoped would rationally explain the course of human events, especially events in the United States. Some of the sniffers, Fiske, for example, applied to American history Charles Darwin's concept of evolutionary progress through the conflict of organisms and the subsequent survival of the fit. "Social Darwinism" it was later called. Charles Francis Adams toyed with the idea of the influence of railroads on American history but, drawing on Mommsen and Thomas Carlyle, concluded on the somewhat more lofty note that the fundamental law of history was that "every great, aggressive, and masterful race tends at times irresistibly towards the practical assertion of its supremacy, usually at the cost of those not so well adapted to existing conditions." And his second great commandment was like unto it: "The condition of dependency, even for communities of the same blood and race, always exercises an emasculating and deteriorating influence." With similar breadth of view Brooks Adams offered a pendulum theory of history, while brother Henry found the key to history imbedded in the laws of physics. Others among the searchers discovered the hidden and not-so-hidden hand of God in history. All of them responded in greater or less degree to Andrew D. White's call in 1884 for a "philosophical synthesis of human affairs" that would reveal

> through what cycles of birth, growth, and decay various nations have passed; what laws of development may be fairly considered as ascertained, and under these what laws of religious, moral, intellectual, social, and political health or disease; what developments have been good, aiding in the evolution of that which is best in man and society; what developments have been evil, tending to the regression of man and society.

By the time Mahan became president of the American Historical Association in 1902, Fiske had evolved an organic theory of the state based on Herbert Spencer's reading of Darwin; Turner had discovered the influence that the advancing frontier had had, through conflict, on American history, thus doing for trees and frontiersmen what Mahan had done for ships and seamen; Brooks Adams had published his *Law of Civilization and Decay*, which argued that all human societies had oscillated between barbarism and civilization, and that a sure mark of the onset of the former was the encroachment of government into the economic life of society; and Henry Adams was on the threshold of his conclusion that the Second Law of Thermodynamics, having to do with the dissipation of energy, best explained waxing and waning of states, especially the waning; indeed, he believed that the inevitable decline of civilizations brought the movement of human history into harmony with the natural laws of the universe. A few years later, in 1904, British political geographer Halford J. Mackinder presented, in what Mahan termed "really a remarkable pamphlet," the idea that the peoples who controlled the Eurasian "heartland" (Russia) would effectively control the world. In acquiring and exercising such control, said Mackinder, the existence or non-existence of sea power would not be the decisive factor. Meanwhile, Mahan himself in 1899 had evolved his "Debated Middle Strip" theory of the geopolitical future of Eurasia, one very much dependent on navies.[10]

In the United States much of this speculation on the larger meaning of history centered in the leadership and membership of the American Historical Association. It may have been for this reason that Mahan felt it necessary to provide himself with a respectable philosophy and science of history as he assumed the presidency of the association in 1902. This he did, although what he presented in his presidential address was a philosophy of historiography as well as a philosophy of history.

Mahan's career as a member of the American Historical Association was not particularly luminous prior to 1902, although he was much more active in the association at the turn of the century than he was in the U.S. Naval Institute. For the institute he did little more than pay his annual dues and let it go at that. At one point he considered dropping his membership. He was also more interested in the historical publications of the British Navy Records Society than he was in the Naval Institute and its ordnance-oriented *Proceedings*.

It is known that, through the efforts of Horace Scudder, he was elected to membership in the prestigious New-York Historical Society in 1894, but the date of his joining the AHA is not clear. It was probably about the same time, since he was one of the first subscribers to the *American Historical Review*, the association's journal, which was launched in 1895. Indeed, his first question to the editor of the *Review*, J. Franklin Jameson, when asked in July 1895 to review a book for it, was typical; he wanted to know "your proposed rates of payment." "My writing," he explained, "is a factor in my income, which I am not rich enough to disregard at a time that I am very occupied." The struggling *Review* paid nothing for book reviews in its early years and only a token $3.00 per page for articles by 1902. It did not, therefore, greatly interest Mahan as a place to publish, and he regularly turned down requests from its editors to review books on naval history. He gave various polite excuses for these declinations, usually that he was too busy with other matters, or that the book offered for review was so poor as to be unworthy of his time or notice. He properly refused to review books with which his own publishers were connected, and he preferred not to review books by men he personally disliked or deemed competitors of his in the field of naval history. Thus on one occasion he turned down a book by Clark Russell, explaining to Jameson in December 1897 that "he is in a degree a competitor of mine, and one of whom my opinion is well formed and unfavorable, as to his pre-judgment." In 1898 he did, however, respond to a request from his British friend George Sydenham Clarke ("a rather unreasonable request *from* an *author*," he admitted) to review Clarke's own *Russia's Sea-Power*; but Jameson declined to be party to such an unprofessional arrangement. Mahan also refused to consider for review books "out of my own line" that would require of him "something like very hard study"; and he avoided reviewing bad books written by people he liked. For this last reason he refused a book by the Navy Department's librarian, Edward K. Rawson, *Twenty Famous Naval Battles: Salamis to Santiago*. It was a poor book, he told Jameson, "but I should not wish to say so, being under obligation to Rawson, both for kindness and in friendship." He preferred books which, like his own, had "some general recognizable trend." In sum, during his career as a historian, Mahan chose to review but four books in the pages of the *American Historical Review*.[11]

Mahan also declined several offers to publish articles in the *Review*, arguing in one instance that a spin-off from his *Life of Nelson*, which he had already sold to *Century Magazine*, would necessarily be "more popular" than editor Jameson would wish. "I am sorry to say," he told Jameson on another occasion, "I have absolutely no time for such writing as you kindly ask." Articles for the *Review* were strictly "side issues." Moreover, "unless I resolutely practice exclusiveness of purpose," he informed Jameson in November 1900, "my short remaining time will be frittered in like trivialities." He published only one article in the *Review*, "Negotiations at Ghent in 1814," which appeared in October 1905 and was a by-product of his *The Influence of Sea Power in its Relation to the War of 1812* brought out by Little, Brown and Company that same month. For this he asked and received $100, far less than his usual price for an article, but payment nonetheless. Only about God and for God did Mahan write without compensation.

It was the question of payment, or lack thereof, that resulted in his not publishing in the *American Historical Review* the presidential address he delivered to the American Historical Association. The *Atlantic Monthly* offered him $150 for the 6,000-word piece, titled "Subordination in Historical Treatment," before it was delivered as a speech and he snapped at the offer. Other presidents of the association had done this with their speeches, so Mahan felt no obligation to favor the cash-poor *Review*. As it was entitled to do, however, the association printed a précis of the address in its *Annual Report* for 1902, paying Mahan nothing for it. The *Atlantic* retitled the essay "Writing of History" and ran it in its issue of March 1903. This effectively copyrighted the article and permitted Mahan to reprint it five years later in his *Naval Administration and Warfare*.[12]

His disinterest in the impoverished *American Historical Review* notwithstanding, Mahan was pleased to be named vice president of the American Historical Association in 1901. While he had for several years considered himself primarily a historian and incidentally a naval officer, he was delighted thus to be welcomed formally into the fraternity of professional historians. When in January 1901 Professor Albert Bushnell Hart of Harvard sent him a copy of one of his many books, Mahan was flattered. "I am always a little surprised to find I have done anything for history," he told Hart, "but such recognition as you flatter me with is very much valued." In accepting the vice-presidency of the association, however, he made it clear to Rhodes that when he moved up to the presidency, as the vice president normally did, he would have little or nothing to do with administration. "Administration has at all times been distasteful to me," he noted, because it interfered with his "proper work" as a historian. He had felt the pressure of administration while commanding the *Chicago* and he wanted no repetition of that experience while commanding the American Historical Association. Fortunately, there was no Henry Erben on board the AHA—with the result that Mahan undertook practically none of the busy work of the organization when he assumed its presidency in 1902. He cared little about the functions of the other officers of the association and never quite got their names straightened out in his mind. He opposed holding the annual meeting of December 1902 in Nashville because it would not be convenient for him to go there; and when it was convened in Philadelphia he made it known that the social calls he had planned while he was visiting in Elly's hometown were as important to him as were his duties at the convention. He did, however, manage to deliver his presidential address while he was in Philadelphia. In 1902, the American Historical Association seems to have needed Alfred Thayer Mahan more than he needed it, perhaps because he was far better known among the American people than was the organization.[13]

Nevertheless, he worked diligently on his "Subordination in Historical Treatment." Partly, this address was a justification of the subordinationist methodology he had employed in producing his first two *Influence* books; partly, it was an affirmation of the certain presence of God in history; and partly is was an attempt to show that if the historian used subordination properly, his writing of history served God. The system he presented to his colleagues in Philadelphia also contained a rationalization of conflict in human history and incorporated a dialectical process which explained historical movement (progress) in terms of a synthesis of thesis and antithesis, or the conflict of opposite thrusts in history.

There is no evidence that Mahan ever studied the dialectical system of Hegel or that he understood Karl Marx's application of Hegelian dialectics to history viewed as class struggle leading to a social and economic utopia. Nor can Mahan's philosophy of history be traced to that of Andrew D. White, with whom he had served in The Hague in 1899, of Charles Francis Adams, who immediately preceded him as president of the American

Historical Association, or of any of the other prominent American historians in the 1880s and 1890s who attempted to make some philosophical sense of the flow and ebb of the human experience. While it might be said that Mahan unconsciously absorbed some of the ideas about historical determinism that were circulating in the American Historical Association between 1885 and 1900, as he seems subconsciously to have tapped into the idea of the influence of sea power in and upon history, the fact remains that the precise paternity of the philosophical arguments Mahan expressed in "Subordination in Historical Treatment" is not known. He admitted that in preparing the address he was forced to "analyze and formulate to my own consciousness the various impressions—the 'unconscious cerebration,' to use a current phrase sufficiently vague for my purpose—which have formed my mental experience as a writer of history and have probably been reflected in my treatment of materials." What seems likely is that this mental experience, however unconscious the cerebration might have been, was shaped in part by the two men whom Mahan admitted influenced him most—the Reverend Edward Meyrick Goulburn and Mahan's own uncle, the Reverend Milo Mahan.

It will be recalled that Mahan had first encountered Goulburn when he was serving in the *Iroquois* in the late 1860s, alone there with his sense of sin and unworthiness and weighted down with depression. The Goulburn book that he read and re-read, and on which he partially modeled *The Harvest Within*, his own spiritual autobiography, was titled *Thoughts on Personal Religion, Being a Treatise on the Christian Life in its Two Elements, Devotion and Grace*. It was one of "the foundations of my best thought," Mahan confessed to daughter Helen thirty years after having first read it.

At one level, Goulburn's volume was a rather orthodox Christ-is-God, Man-is-Hopeless exercise in traditional nineteenth-century Anglican theology. It was filled with standard summonses to personal salvation and provided elaborate spiritual road maps on how best to achieve eternal life. It called for rigorous self-examination and ablution for the purpose of identifying and rooting out personal sin and tendencies thereto. It took a literal position on Scripture, argued complex theological points by analogy and with convenient references to the New Testament, recommended "ejaculatory prayer," assured the reader that he was probably damned to hell, urged a great deal of supportive Bible-reading on the off-chance that he was not so damned (Goulburn was ambivalent on predestination), criticized the pretensions and doctrines of the Roman Catholic Church, and saw Satan ever lurking in the wings of the human drama. Angels flitted hither and yon in Goulburn's pages, all of them Protestant, most of them Anglican.

But at another level, Goulburn demonstrated an awareness of science. He had a concept of biological evolution, or at least an appreciation of the evolutionary process. He knew that the human body constantly replaced its cells, that "particles of matter are continually flying off from our bodies and being replaced by others" so that "neither in mind nor in body does man ever continue in one stay." Indeed, "of each individual among us it may be said with truth at any given moment that he is either rising to, or declining from, the prime of life and the maturity of his physical powers. And the mind no less than the body is in a continual flux." The development of the microscope and its use in biology and botany told him that there was order in matter, in all nature, and that "natural growth means the gathering together of particles of matter round a single nucleus, which nucleus appropriates and assimilates those particles." He observed that a new cell was formed from particles of elements surrounding those already formed, "and then another and another, until the whole resulted at length in this magnificent mosaic of cells, so far superior to any pavement which King Solomon had in his palace or even in his temple." It was from his notion that "all growth proceeds from one nucleus, forms round one center," that Goulburn developed the related idea that "the pursuit of knowledge" was best accomplished by a process of subordination:

> The first thing to be done by a person bent upon studying any large subject of human knowledge, such as History, or Jurisprudence, or Philosophy, or Divinity, is to limit the field of his researches, and draw a circle around it. In History, for example, the attacking universal History in all its parts would make us miserable sciolists; we should take any well defined period, to which we happen to be particularly drawn, and make all our studies gather round that period as their centre. Thence our researches may extend themselves into adjacent periods systematically and on principle; and the knowledge so acquired shall be sound, not discursive. . . . begin from a centre and work outward. . . . Collect all your energies in one quarter of the field.

It was probably to this call for a subordinationist approach to historical research that Mahan responded in the 1890s. He also responded to Goulburn's view that "if we look into Nature we find that the law which pervades the whole of it is variety in unity. . . . the variety is far more apparent than the unity," even though "Science . . . is continually bringing to light an unity and simplicity of type in things which on the surface are most different." The upshot of the matter, thought Goulburn, was that "we can see tolerably clear indications that the various parts of the Universe are working together for one end. . . . The matter which is discharged from one part of the [solar] system reappears in another under a new form and there serves some other function, so that each atom seems to have its vocation and its place." His conclusion was that "such is Nature—an immense variety, knit together in unity by sameness of plan, sameness of agency, sameness of object."[14]

From Milo Mahan came additional insights into the orderly nature of the universe, how it functioned, what gave it motion, the role of God in it, and how the rise and fall of states related to it. Specifically, Milo saw historical movement (both progress and decay) in dialectical terms. Indeed, at about the time Goulburn was writing his *Thoughts on Personal Religion*, Milo published his *Palmoni; or The Numerals of Scripture. A Proof of Inspiration*. As has been indicated, this book was a direct outgrowth of his attack on the scriptural rationalism of Bishop Colenso, particularly on Colenso's heretical observation that the historical and chronological arithmetic of the Pentateuch did not scan. In *Palmoni; or The Numerals of Scripture* and in his *Mystic Numbers: A Key to Chronology; a Law of the Divine Economy; a Test of Inspiration; a Thorough Inquiry*, Milo sought to demonstrate that scriptural arithmetic did work.

He became convinced that God had thoughtfully scattered through the Bible a variety of numbers, a cryptographical code of sorts, a knowledge and proper interpretation of which held the key to an understanding of God, the Universe, and History. He noted that "a Pythagoras, a Plato, a St. Ambrose, a St. Augustine could value numbers chiefly for the *mysteries* they contained," and affirmed that the early church fathers had clearly seen that in the "*mystic* interpretation of Scriptural numbers" lay the path to great spiritual truths. An appreciation of the deeper "spiritual meaning" and interrelationships of these numbers would provide the Christian faithful not "merely the mode of explaining a few things here and there on the surface of Holy Scripture, but as the golden thread with which GOD has bound all the Ages, and the whole volume of His Word, and the entire universe of His Works, together into one inseparable Whole." It was Milo's intent, explained his biographer, the Reverend John Henry Hopkins, to study and manipulate these Divine Numbers to the end that "the whole long blood-stained story of the Ages of Man upon the earth melts into a harmonious music, with a rhythm of symmetrical motion, and a beauty of perfect harmony, and an exquisite rising swell towards the climax of future glories yet unattained, which blends in one complex whole the utmost powers of the human mind and heart and soul."

It was a grand if somewhat irrational scheme based on the idea of a whimsical God sowing cryptograms through Scripture like a farmer casting seed wheat on his fields. Nevertheless, so excited was Milo with his "wonderful discovery," with such singleness of purpose did he pursue its arithmetic, so tiresomely boring did he become on the subject, that Hopkins, his faculty colleague at General Theological Seminary in New York, noted that some of Milo's friends "became uneasy lest his mind should lose its balance." But well might Milo Mahan have been excited. He fervently believed that he had solved the ultimate mystery of Man and the Universe, had proved the existence of God, had demonstrated the Divine origin and larger Truth of Scripture, and had accomplished all this with the scientific tool that was mathematics.[15]

In *Palmoni . . . The Numerals of Scripture*, Milo developed the thesis, Pythagorean in nature, that there was symmetry, proportion, and order in nature and in history, an order revealed in the predictable mathematical relationships of various numbers found in the chronology of the Old Testament. These spiritual numbers demonstrated the existence of a rational, supernatural intelligence pervading Scripture. The philosophical implications of this pervasion were clear:

> The sacred chronology is a supernatural scheme; it is a Divinely inspired record; it has a sanction which no other can reasonably pretend to . . . . all inquiry goes to prove that everything happens according to fixed laws, nothing according to chance. . . . Upon nature and upon history there is the stamp of symmetry and proportion. But . . . we are bewildered by the multiplicity of things. In history especially, there seems at first nothing but a grand phantasmagoria of facts and dates. But were we at as great a distance from human actions as we are from the stars, doubtless we should see as much of order in the one as in the other. . . . It is science that brings order out of the seeming confusion. . . . God, indeed, is a "Wonderful Numberer". . . . Sacred chronology is full of symmetry, beauty, and significance, even in its numerals; so far we have proved, not that the Bible is in any way unhistorical, but that it is history of a vastly higher kind. . . . It is the ideal of history. It is what even common history might be, if it were written from a higher point of view, and with a more perfect knowledge of "the work that GOD maketh."

Milo based his manipulation of scriptural numbers on the belief that there were exactly 1,656 years between the Creation and the Flood, a belief that reduced all else in his system to utter nonsense. He believed, too, that specific numbers in the Bible "occur so often in connection with certain classes of ideas, that we are naturally led to associate the one with the other. This is more or less admitted with regard to the numbers *Seven, Twelve, Forty, Seventy.* . . . The [Church] Fathers were disposed to admit it with regard to many others, *and to see in it the marks of a supernatural design.*" Milo felt, for example, that the number Eight and the idea of the Resurrection were connected. At the same time, he argued that if Scripture seemed contradictory, or if the Divine Numbers therein seemed not to relate, or did not fall into a meaningful pattern, "it is because God *intended* the seeming contradiction. And if a skeptic asks me why He should so intend it, I answer that it may be for the purpose of curing us of shallow self-conceit."[16]

Possessed, indeed haunted, with the certainty that the existence and arrangement of the Divine Numbers in Scripture was the hinge on the door to all knowledge, that the "principle of sacred factors pervades all history and chronology," Milo followed his *Palmoni* with *Mystic Numbers*, a 560-page sequel written between 1863 and 1869. In this peculiar work he extended the Hebrew historical chronology treated in *Palmoni* through the New Testament period and up to the year 1865. In it Milo claimed that there was but "one principle, one grand but simple law of *Mystical Numbers,* pervading the entire Word of God, and marking with more or less distinctiveness the course of human events." He argued, and proved to his own satisfaction, that "all chronology, sacred and profane, runs in cycles of eight, thirteen, or other like terms of years: so that dates of a marked character divide evenly, without a remainder, by numbers appropriate to that character, such as 8, 13, 153, or the like." This law proved, among other things, that "the Divine Authorship of the Sacred Volume stands out a self-evident fact." Having thus inserted the Hand of God, the Wonderful Numberer, into a cyclical historical process, as well as finding it revealed arithmetically in Scripture, Milo went on to point out that there could be no element of chance or human control in the operation of these historical cycles. Like Ole Man River, they just kept cycling along.[17]

Buried in his Divine Numbers, Milo also discovered what might be termed a Pythagorean dialectic. The numbers Eight and Thirteen, in their dichotomy, held the key to all historical conflict and progress. As he explained this:

> These two, in their larger meaning, stand for two ideas which are the
> soul of history. The life of States, like the life of man, is a continuous
> manifestation of *defection, decay, apostasy, corruption, distintegration,*
> —in short, of all that is expressed in the numeral Thirteen and in its
> various multiples. On the other hand, it is equally a manifestation of

revival, renewal, reformation,—in short of that great idea, the cornerstone of Christian life, which finds its perfected reality in the Resurrection of CHRIST, and one of its most expressive symbols in the numeral Eight. History is the conflict of these two principles. Progress is the resultant of these two forces.

Milo saw further evidence of this progress of the material achievements of modern civilization, the goals of which were "to replenish the earth and to subdue it, to cover every sea with ships, and every land with cities, to bind and control the wild elements of nature, to wed religion to commerce, and by their joint influence to preach the Gospel to all nations." With none of these elements in and rationalizations for American imperialism would his famous nephew later disagree.[18]

In "Subordination in Historical Treatment," his address to his fellow guildsmen at Philadelphia, Mahan set a high goal toward which professional historians should aim. Written history, he began, should be an "artistic creation" and a "temple of truth." But most history failed to achieve these goals because most practicing historians cluttered up their minds and their written accounts of the past with a "multiplicity of details, often contradictory, not merely in appearance but in reality, [which] do not readily lend themselves to unity of treatment." This failing, widespread in the profession, posed a distinct social danger in that

> it may be difficult to see the wood for the trees . . . there may be such failure in grouping that the uninstructed reader may receive quite erroneous impressions as to the relative importance of the several incidents. . . . For the casual reader emphasis is essential to due comprehension: and in artistic work emphasis consists less in exaggeration of color than in the disposition of details . . . and in the grouping of accessories in due subordination to a central idea.

He assured his audience that the military historian came naturally and easily to an appreciation of subordination because the process was but another form of tactical concentration. Such "concentration, the watchword of military action, and the final end of all combination, reminds him that facts must be massed as well as troops if they are to prevail against the passive resistance of indolent mentality." The main social function of the practicing historian was not, therefore, to accumulate mountains of factual material. His job, said Mahan, was to marshal, arrange, and subordinate the facts already known to a "central idea," and to present them "in such wise that the wayfaring man, whom we now call 'the man in the street,' shall not err therein." Such men needed "large, simple ideas" to feed upon and historians should provide them with such concepts. They should not wait until all the evidence was in; that was to say, they should not delay writing their books. "Passion for certainty," the speaker warned, "may lapse into incapacity for decision, a vice recognized in military life and which needs recognition elsewhere. . . . The significance of the whole must be brought out by careful arrangement and exposition which must not be made to wait too long upon unlimited scrutiny." To illustrate his point, Mahan chided Lord Acton for having assiduously collected data for so many years, for having written so little, and for having taken his vast knowledge of history with him to his grave. "Had I attempted this [postponement], beginning when I did, I must have died before I lifted pen to paper." Better read than dead.

The historian who failed to see the value and social usefulness of the "artistic grouping of subordinate details around a central idea," and who failed to write history in this manner, had not, in Mahan's view, "perfectly communicated his gifts and acquirements to his brethren." If, on the other hand, the historian used Mahan's subordinationist approach, he would discover that "each particular incident and group of incidents becomes . . . a fully wrought and fashioned piece, prepared for its adjustment in its place in the great mosaic which the history of the race is gradually fashioning under the Divine overruling."

The belief that the historian could actively participate in God's work by use of proper methodology was the extension of an idea that Mahan had first expressed in an address to an Episcopal Church congregation in Connecticut in March 1899:

I no longer say, "I will do this, God helping me." I say only "I will help God do this." . . . Such is my experience which I give to you. Some distant day, perhaps, someone here [who is] young may tell a future generation that he was helped along this road—not by me but by the Spirit of God speaking through me; for unless it be the Spirit that speaks, and not I, these words are vain.

Given his supplemental view that history was nothing less than "the plan of Providence . . . in its fulfillment," it was incumbent upon Christian historians to search for, discover, and delineate those "central ideas" in history which, if subsequently verified by subordination, would comprise central themes, or foundation stones, in the fashioning of the "great mosaic" that was God's continuing revelation of Himself to man. One such theme was Mahan's own concept of the influence of sea power upon history, a central idea he had, by the proper application of subordination, verified in two major books. With overtones of Goulburn, Mahan explained the characteristics of an untested central idea en route to becoming a verified central theme of history:

> Of such artistic presentation it is of course a commonplace to say that essential unity is the primary requirement. It must be remembered, however, that such unity is not that of the simple, solitary, unrelated unit. It is organic like the human body, it finds its oneness in the due relation and proportion of many members. Unity is not the exclusion of all save one. The very composition of the word—unity—implies multiplicity; but a multiplicity in which all the many that enter into it are subordinated to the one dominant thought, or purpose, of the designer whose skill it is to make each and all enhance the dignity and harmony of the central idea.

The ultimate task of the historian-partner of God, therefore, was to strive to discover those central themes of history that permeate the cosmos and which, like Milo Mahan's Divine Numbers, are evidence of the existence of God and the involvement of God in human history. When all these themes, revealed by God, have finally been discovered and coordinated by historians

> they will present a majestic ideal unity corresponding to the thought of the Divine Architect, realized to his creatures. . . . Faith, the evidence of things not seen as yet and the needful force of every truly great achievement, may cheer us to feel that in the perfection of our particular work we forward the ultimate perfection of the whole.

Mahan devoutly believed that there would occur in some future era, effected by some future historian, a final synthesis of the numerous central themes he was certain were inherent in history and in the universe. Such synthesis would eventually bring man into harmonious oneness with God through the "majestic ideal unity" of a finished History that was nothing less than the "thought of the Divine Architect realized to his creatures." The research and writing of history, properly conceived and accomplished, was thus clearly a religious act. Its popularization for the benefit of "the man in the street" was a missionary activity. And just as Milo Mahan had felt that Divine Numbers were the "golden thread with which GOD had bound all the Ages, and the whole volume of His Word, and the entire universe of His Works, together into one inseparable Whole," so did his nephew feel that the final synthesis of central themes would mark the return of man to the bosom of God. In substituting historical themes for Uncle Milo's numbers, Mahan was certain that to some favored mind will be committed the final great synthesis; but he would be powerless save for the patient labors of the innumerable army which, stone by stone and section by section, have wrought to perfection the several parts; while in combining these in the ultimate unity he must be guided by the same principles and governed by the same methods that have controlled them in their humbler tasks. He will in fact be, as each one of us is, an instrument. To him will be intrusted, on a larger and final scale to accomplish the realization of that toward which generations of predecessors have labored.

Mahan was convinced that it would not be to his hand and mind that God would entrust the "final great synthesis." It was enough that God had led him directly to the discovery of the central theme that was the influence of sea power upon history. He could ask no more.[19]

He believed, however, that he should keep searching, that other central themes were on the verge of being discovered. In his spiritual autobiography, *The Harvest Within*, he affirmed that there existed a central theme in the realm of religion—"that man today is susceptible of an enthusiasm for Jesus Christ resembling, but surpassing that which has been shown in past times for this or that historical character in many nations." Toward the end of his life he thought that the influence of territorial expansion on U.S. history might be another central theme; but he died before he could test the thought by subordination.

Mahan was confident that conflict and progress in history through a dialectical process, like Milo's Thirteen versus Eight, might itself be a viable central theme. Such a theme, he hypothesized in 1902

may indeed be the conflict of two opposites, as in the long struggle between freedom and slavery, union and disunion in our own land; but the unity nevertheless exists. It is not to be found in freedom, not yet in slavery, but in their conflict it is. Around it group in subordination the many events, and the warriors of the political arena, whose names are household words among us to this day. All form part of the great progress as it moved onward to its consummation [in civil war].

By June 1903 he had become convinced that "the two great oppositions inherent in naval administration—civil versus military, unity of action against multiplicity of activities—are but a reflection of the essential problem of warfare. . . . the difficulty of the Art of War consists in concentrating in order to fight and disseminating in order to subsist. . . . The problem is one of embracing opposites." Similarly, he had earlier come to view Lord Nelson as a synthesis of personality opposites.[20]

Progress through synthesis of thesis and antithesis, central to the cosmic overview of Milo Mahan, was a concept fundamental also to Alfred Mahan in that it permitted him to explain the inevitability of conflict (war) in philosophical and historical terms, to argue the related need for a great U.S. Navy, to view demands for peace, disarmament, and arbitration as pusillanimous and unnatural acts, and to regard Christianity as a form of combat exercise insofar as it endorsed the fighting of just wars for the purpose of righting social wrongs. Further, his acceptance of an organic, biological interpretation of the growth and decline of states, derived in part from his Uncle Milo and in part from Edward Goulburn, allowed Mahan to swing the censer of American imperialism secure in the knowledge that states not actively expanding in size and power were, by definition, declining into senility and death.

But to Milo's observation that the "life of States" was "like the life of man," and to Goulburn's view that "the body is in a continual flux," Mahan added, in 1900, Darwin's argument that all living organisms also responded to a law of "natural selection." Among these responsive organisms Mahan included states, as had Herbert Spencer and others before him. Thus Mahan wrote in his *The Problem of Asia* that "the first law of states, as of men, is self-preservation—a term which cannot be narrowed to the bare tenure of a stationary round of existence. Growth is the property of healthful life." Growth involved struggle. "Such struggle," he noted, "as is implied in the phrase 'natural selection' involves conflict and suffering."[21]

Given Mahan's belief in the historical, philosophical, and biological probability of international conflict, it is not surprising that the subject of war—its causes, nature, purposes, prosecution, machinery, even its avoidance—dominated his writing from 1890 to 1914 as did no other single subject. It cannot be said that Mahan was a congenital war-lover. He knew the suffering, destructiveness, and horrors of war as well as did any sensitive and perceptive human being. What can be said is that his study of history and his personal observation of the events transpiring in the contentious world in which he lived, gave him little confidence that peaceableness was the natural state of man or that peace was the natural goal, thought, or desire of men organized into states. He felt that war stemmed from a natural human impulse to fight, that it was inherent in modern nationalism and that, for these reasons, it was probably inevitable. He felt, too, that it was so pervasive a phenomenon in human history that "the study of war and its illustration is . . . primarily and chiefly a study of history." As he expressed these views on various occasions:

The furor of war needs all the chastening it can receive in the human heart, to still the mad impulses towards conflict. . . . The cause of war is the human heart and its passions, more often noble than simply perverse. . . . the avoidance of war depends . . . upon a change of heart in mankind. Until that occurs War is inevitable, except by the "practical" expedient of being ready for it. . . . My aim is [to] . . . awaken public attention to the inevitable part War necessarily must play in the present state of the world.[22]

Aside from his belief that the idea of war lurked in the hearts of men, that a propensity toward it was built into the genetic structure of men, Mahan was not certain what specific historical factors could be said to cause it at a particular moment. At one point he toyed with an economic interpretation, attributing the origins of war to the "commercial wickedness" of men and nations; but on another occasion he maintained that it was "an illusion" to believe that "nations go to war for material gain chiefly." Further, his consistent position on the question of maritime neutral rights (immunity from capture) in wartime was that a denial of those rights would have the advantage of deterring or shortening wars by removing the profit motive from them. Hardly a laissez-faire capitalist observation, this. He also believed that wars might be shortened and rendered less destructive in the long run by the device of making them as swift, brutal, and total as possible. "To bring the pressure of war to bear upon the whole population," he wrote in November 1910, "and not merely upon the armies in the field, is the very spirit of modern warfare. It may safely be asserted to be least inhuman of all the inevitable inhumanities of war, because the danger of it deters from war; and because, while hostilities are proceeding, it tends most to make the war unpopular and so to hasten peace." He also applied this humane thought to modern armaments, noting, after the outbreak of World War I, that "the matter I consider interesting and demonstrative [is] that, while absence of preparation does not avert war, preparation shortens it and is so less expensive of blood and money."[23]

If Mahan was not certain just what it was in the behavior of states that actually triggered the wars to which mankind was historically subject, he was confident that the existence of armaments had not been among the factors present in the outbreak of conflicts. Conversely, he held that the absence of armaments, or national policies of disarmament, had been factors. Thus he put himself in the position of arguing from the perspective of history that the reason nations armed was to prevent those very wars that were virtually inevitable. To blur this contradiction, he argued that the existence of armaments had but side effects on wars produced by other causes. "I am not prepared to maintain that armaments never cause war," he explained in August 1914, "but . . . I should be prepared to argue that they do so only when some other exciting cause, of either interest or national feeling, comes into play. The hackneyed phrase, 'vital interests or national honor,' really sums up the motives that lead nations to war. Armament is simply the instrument of which such motives avail themselves. If there be no armament, there is war all the same."

He was persistent in his contention that American military unpreparedness had not prevented U.S. involvement in the Revolution, the War of 1812, the Mexican War, the Civil War, or the Spanish-American War. On the other hand, he held that an international balance of armaments could well lead to peaceful accommodations in time of crisis: the existence of vast armaments had preserved the peace of Europe from 1871 to 1912 and had prevented the spread of the Balkan Wars (1912–1913). In still another context, he argued that, were peace and disarmament sentiments to prevail in the Western World, they "would leave the white world weaponless before peoples of very different ideals" and would lead to the defeat of the white man in the coming "struggle between the white and yellow races in the Pacific." Ambivalent as he seems to have been on the origins of war and peace, one of the "lessons" of history to which he frequently pointed was that disarmament was no guarantor of peace.[24]

After much thought on the complicated matter, Mahan finally concluded that the historical factor that most often triggered the actual outbreak of hostilities was the moral outrage of men who, created as they were in the image of God, willingly and properly seized the sword to put an end to patent evils abroad in the world. Among these evils were political tyranny, human bondage, and religious persecution, mainly that of Christians. The necessity of the resultant "just" or "righteous" war Mahan found clearly supported in the Bible and in Christian doctrine. "War is remedial," he told an Episcopal Church gathering in Providence, Rhode Island, in November 1900:

[If] War is a remedy for greater evils, especially moral evils, War is justified. War, in short, is justified as an element of human progress, necessitated by a condition of mankind obviously far removed from Christian perfection, and, because of this imperfection, susceptible of remedy. . . . I affirm that War, under conditions that may and do arise, is righteous; and, further, that under such conditions it is distinctly an unrighteous deed to refrain from forcibly redressing evil, when it is in the power of thine hand to do so. . . . Honest collision is evidently a law of progress, however we explain its origin; whether it be in the ordinance of God, or in the imperfection of man.

To be sure, Mahan had considerable difficulty converting Jesus Christ, the "Prince of Peace," into a sword-bearing Christian soldier on the basis of biblical exegesis. " 'All they that take the sword shall perish by the sword' has always seemed to me a difficult saying," he confessed. But he managed a case of sorts for Jesus as a combat officer through the device of explaining the numerous peace and resist-not-evil statements of the Christ in terms not of what Jesus actually *said*, but what Jesus surely must have *meant*. This allowed Mahan a certain interpretive flexibility, whatever precision it lacked as an exercise in historical research or in Higher Criticism. Nevertheless, the best evidence he could muster in support of this patent caricature of the Christ was the incident of the forcible expulsion of the money-changers from the temple, and the statement in Luke 22:36–37 in which Jesus allegedly said to his disciples (as Mahan quoted the passage): "He that hath no sword, let him sell his cloak and buy one; for the things concerning me have an end." Unfortunately for his argument, however, Mahan was forced to scramble this quotation and remove it from its context to make it serve his contention that Jesus really had nothing against a little friendly swordplay in the cause of suppressing evil. Yet out of all of his semantical backing and filling there finally emerged a "King of Peace" who was "in the essence of His Being, King of Righteousness, without which true peace cannot be." As he concluded in January 1912:

> Of the Christian religion the great constituent is power; which in another shape, easily assumed, becomes force. Force is power in action. We are prone to assume that, because the personal ideal of the individual Christian, exemplified above all in the Master, is abnegation of self, therefore power and force are alien from the Christian scheme of character. The history of the Master Himself refutes this. The distinction between the Christian conception and that of its strongest rival in the outside world—Islam—is that of the entrance of the human will into the Divine accomplishment. . . . To right what is amiss, to convert, to improve, to develop, is of the very essence of the Christian ideal. Without man's responsive effort, God Himself is—not powerless—but deprived of the instrument through which alone He wills to work. Hence the recognition that if force is necessary, force must be used for the benefit of the community, of the commonwealth, of the world. . . . In the presence of evil, the genius of Christianity is aggressive.[25]

Biblical distortions notwithstanding, Mahan firmly believed that progress in history was certain. Partly was this progress fueled by conflict (war), partly by the dialectical mechanics inherent in the universe, and partly by the influence of Christianity on history.

> Things have gone on so since ere the world was [he maintained], and upon the whole men seem to be really better off than they were a hundred years ago—and God reigns. The last is the point to which I always come back. . . . The fair lessons of experience, broadly viewed, give more ground for hope as years go by; not necessarily for our particular ideals but for the general progress and welfare. . . . and that too whether we accept a personal Providence, as I do, or whether not. Surely things get better rather than worse. . . . That the race can progress, can grow better, is proved by the fact that it has grown better; I mean not in material surroundings merely, but in the accepted ideals and realized practice of justice, mercy, and truth. Through the ups and downs of two millenniums, human character has advanced; there have been failures innumerable, but there is not failure. Hence is Hope.

Human progress would accelerate even more noticeably and rapidly when all mankind became Christian since, he told his Japanese readers, "in those countries and through His followers—Christians—He has wrought the civilization, the progress, which have gathered round His Cross, and have gathered nowhere else." The sticky problem of resolving the contradiction between man's inevitable progress in history and his inherent sinful and fallen nature was one that Mahan never tackled.[26]

As a student of history, however, Mahan saw the events, policies, and options of the present and future as having been shaped decisively by the "lessons" and experiences of the past. He believed that inherent in history were numerous fundamental "principles" that had permanence as well as universal applicability to understanding and solving contemporary problems, principles that were usually best explained in analogous terms. True, he admitted and experienced the difficulty of constructively applying these principles to situations in real life (the principle of tactical concentration had not been particularly relevant during the Spanish-American War), but he never lost faith in their existence. "I fancied myself to have some appreciation of underlying principles," he wrote in 1909, "but when it comes to formulating them, and at the same time adapting them as far as possible to conservative opposition—to sugar coat the pill and get it down —the matter becomes complicated and requires much thought. The work is distasteful to me, which also makes it more wasteful of time." Nevertheless, he had a dogged faith in the existence of "principles of war," especially the principle of tactical concentration on land or at sea. Similarly, in the behavior of men through the ages he saw common and continuing patterns and cycles of thought and action. The principle that was the constancy of human nature he never doubted. "The greater motives of men, by which history is made, remain much the same from age to age, [only] the superficial details alter," he assured daughter Helen as early as 1893. Nor did he ever doubt that the modern nation state was man's noblest social edifice, and that in the conflicts between states, in their waxings and wanings, resided the key to man's gradual march from barbarism to civilization.[27]

As a historian, Mahan believed that in subordination he had found the Rosetta Stone that would eventually reveal to men the hidden truths of history. With equal assurance and fervor he averred that God had revealed to him at least one of these great truths, or central themes, of history—the influence of sea power upon it. And since man's ultimate certainty of salvation rested in an understanding of the totality of history, Mahan viewed himself as a missionary to the common man. He had helped provide these men with the "large, plain, simple ideas" that would ultimately guide all mankind to God.

As a philosopher of history, Mahan posited the existence of sweeping central themes, some already discovered and understood, others awaiting discovery, which ran like divine threads through the secular fabric of man's existence on earth. He believed in a God-centered, mechanistic universe surfeited with order, pattern, and intelligence, a universe filled with divine truths gradually being revealed by an infinite God to finite men through favored historians (such as himself) who identified and popularized the central themes that were manifestations of God's existence and handiwork. It was a universe filled also with dialectical forces, with struggle, and with war; and with the human progress related thereto.

Said Sir John Colomb of Mahan at an Imperial Federation Committee dinner in London in July 1904, to the applause of such British notables present as Sir Edward Grey, and Admirals Cyprian Bridge and Edmund Fremantle, "through his research, his power of analysis, his wonderful gifts of perspective and sense of proportion, he has rescued from the disjointed annals of the history of centuries the hidden truths of the great naval principles which have determined and will determine the operations of war in all ages. (Cheers)." Another of his admirers found far less to cheer about. Silas McBee, editor of *The Churchman*, said of him shortly after his death: "The Admiral knew the history of sea power, but did not know the philosophy of history; or perhaps I should say he did not show in his writings that he had a philosophy of history." Wrong. Mahan had a philosophy of history even though he knew little or nothing about the history of philosophy. Eclectic, composite, derivative, egocentric, parochial in its Christian stridency and narrow Anglo-Americanism, it was a philosophy of history, nonetheless. After all, "facts won't lie if you work them right," he said. Mahan always tried to work them right.[28]

XVII

Diplomatic and Naval Affairs
in the Far East
1899-1913

I have not dealt with the question of the Navy helping to resist an attack on Pearl Harbor. If the Navy be there in force, the attack will not be made; at least not until the Navy has been beaten. If the Navy is not there, the case does not arise.

Alfred Thayer Mahan to Robert U. Johnson, March 31, 1911

Whether she had been "pitchforked" into the Philippines, as Mahan argued in February 1900, or whether her "unwilling acquisition of the Philippines" had somehow been accomplished by "the hand of Providence," as he wrote in November of that year, the fact was that the United States became a major force and factor in the international power politics of the Far East as a result of the annexations stemming from the Spanish-American War.

The complete collapse of China in the Sino-Japanese War (1894–1895) and the resultant Japanese annexation of Formosa, establishment of suzerainty over Korea, and momentary acquisition of a commercial sphere of influence in the Liaotung Peninsula of Southern Manchuria, revealed clearly that the ancient and once powerful Middle Kingdom was little more than a paper dragon. And, as is the case with dragons, their presumed existence tends to encourage the emergence of St. Georges. Beginning, then, in 1896, and continuing through 1900, Germany, Russia, France, and Britain began to stake out in China mutually exclusive spheres of commercial influence, preliminary, it was feared in Washington, to an outright carving up of China territorially. This activity involved extorting various concessions from the Manchu government—naval bases, monopolistic trading rights in specified areas, exclusive mining, timber, and railroad leases, and an extension of extraterritorial legal rights. These acquisitions, many of them negotiated virtually at gun point, were written into treaties with the moribund Manchus. By 1899, Russia was ensconced in southern Manchuria (Port Arthur), Germany in Shantung (Kiaochow), Britain in northern China (Weihaiwei), and France in southern China (Kwangchowan). Having been forced by the Western Powers in 1895 to return Liaotung to defeated China, a disappointed, thwarted, imperialistic Japan waited on the sidelines for her share of the booty. China, it appeared, was finished as a nation, certainly as a nation having control over her own economic sovereignty and destiny. Physical partition loomed.

These developments severely threatened the prospects for American commercial expansion into the markets of China that Mahan and other imperialists in the United States anticipated. For this reason, in September 1899, Secretary of State John Hay issued his first Open Door Note, a polite plea to the powers that they permit equality of commercial opportunity with respect to trade, tariffs, harbor dues, railroad rates, and shipping regulations in their respective spheres of economic influence. Since the United States could not hope, alone, to penetrate monopolized markets in China, Hay asked the powers to allow America access to their leasehold areas on a competitive capitalist basis. From the capitals of the European powers that were participating in the economic rape of China came responses that were evasive to the point of rejection. Hay had little choice but to accept their evasions.

Early in June 1900, the Boxer Rebellion broke out in China. It was dedicated to the overturn of the Manchu government and to the expulsion of the Western "foreign devils" from the land. The attendant disorders culminated in the siege of the foreign legations in Peking by Boxer troops and in the formation of an American-British-French-German-Russian-Japanese relief column that was sent to raise the siege. To this international military force of 18,000 men, which fought its way from Tientsin to Peking in July and August 1900, the United States contributed 2,500 soldiers and Marines brought hastily from their war against the Filipinos to North China. If the Philippines were not proving to be a stepping-stone to the markets of Asia, as American imperialists had hoped, they did serve in mid-1900 as a military springboard for the relief of American nationals trapped with other foreigners in Peking.

On July 3, 1900, during heavy fighting near Tientsin, Secretary Hay issued his second Open Door Note to the powers. With so many foreign troops on Chinese soil he was fearful that the Europeans would use the Boxer outrages as an excuse to proceed with an outright territorial partition of China. The second note, going far beyond the first, stated that the policy of the United States was to "preserve Chinese territorial and administrative entity" as well as "safeguard for the world the principle of equal and impartial trade with all parts of the Chinese Empire." Unlike the first Open Door Note, which sought little more than unobstructed trade within the existing foreign leaseholds, the second asked for equality of commercial opportunity throughout *all* China and added the broader thought that preservation of the future territorial and administrative integrity of China was both the hope and the goal of the American government. Such an arrangement, a peculiar combination of Washington's avarice and idealism, would permit the American penetration of a market that, otherwise, would be secured to the administrative control of a weak though nominally independent China.

Hay's statement in favor of international motherhood, brotherhood, and investmenthood, may well have prevented the actual territorial partition of China following the defeat of the Boxers in August 1900, although some historians have since argued that the exigencies of European power politics, as they pertained to East Asia, most likely accomplished that end. In any event, Britain and Germany, fearful of Russia's growing ambitions in Manchuria and North China, subscribed to the principles of the second Hay declaration in their so-called Yangtze Agreement of October 16. Other powers followed suit. Only Russia paid no heed whatever to Hay. By the end of October the Czarist government had seized control of Southern Manchuria. Nevertheless, Hay's note of July 3 did slow for a time the orgy of concession-grabbing in China by the European powers. It did not, however, succeed in opening existing European spheres of economic influence to American trade.

Fearing that in the event the Open Door policy failed, America would be excluded from resumption of the Western carving of the Chinese melon, the State Department, upon the urging of the Navy Department, secretly attempted in November 1900 to secure from Peking a naval base and a sphere of economic influence at Samsah Bay, in Fukien Province, on the south-central coast of China. This move was thwarted by the Japanese who had their eyes on the same spot, and who cynically called attention to the territorial-integrity dimension of Hay's second Open Door Note. It will be recalled that the idea of a U.S. naval base on the China coast to support American merchant shipping in East Asia was one of Mahan's contributions to Naval War Board planning in August 1898. He had suggested the Chushan Islands, off the central China coast. It is not known, therefore, whether he was privy to the attempt by Secretaries Hay and Long to secure a base farther south, at Samsah Bay. Probably not, so very secret was the attempt and so enamored did Mahan continue to be of a base at the mouth of the strategically important Yangtze River. The concept of an Open Door in China as a diplomatic device to help protect and expand American commerce there, was, however, a new one to him.[1]

The proclamation of America's Open Door policy opened up a whole new literary field for Mahan, and it was to this opportunity that he turned shortly after the First Hague Conference. He had written virtually nothing on the Far East. But within a month of Hay's first Open Door Note (September 6, 1899), as American eyes began looking northward from the Philippines to the mysterious and troubled Middle Kingdom, Mahan was hard at work making himself an instant expert on China. In this effort he was encouraged by a contract with *Harper's Monthly* to produce three essays on "The Problem of Asia." Finished in December 1899, these articles were published in *Harper's* in March, April, and May 1900—or before the Boxer Rebellion started. Together with an article titled "The Effect of Asiatic Conditions Upon World Politics," written after the rebellion was over and published in *North American Review* in November 1900, they were reprinted in book form in December 1900 under the title *The Problem of Asia*. Mahan was hopeful, while he was writing the three *Harper's* articles, that the subject would "become suddenly timely," as indeed it did with the convenient eruption of the Boxer Rebellion in June 1900. Later translated into German and Japanese, *The Problem of Asia* was considered by its author to be "as good as any of my literary children." Unfortunately for Mahan's bank balance, however, the volume did not sell well. "The world has not smiled on it," he complained. Perhaps this was because he did virtually no solid research on the subject. The book was spun almost entirely out of Mahan's imaginative mind. And, as usual, he felt the need to devise a grand and comprehensive idea to explain his belief that Czarist Russia needed, and was determined to have, access to warm-water ports in East Asia.

Basically, Mahan's was a "heartland" concept of the sort Sir Halford J. Mackinder, in quite different terms, set forth in 1904. Mackinder argued that the political future of the world lay not with seagoing peoples and states, but with the landlocked peoples of a "Eurasian Heartland" that included the plains of eastern Europe, western Asia, and central Asia. Out of this inaccessible region would rise a powerful land power that would march against, and conquer, the peoples and nations situated along the littoral of the Eurasian mass. With these conquests would come possession of the resources needed for naval construction. Thus provided with great fleets, the Heartland empire would proceed to the conquest of Europe, Asia, and Africa—the "World Island"—and come eventually to dominate the whole world. During its period of initial expansion, the interior Heartland state would be virtually invulnerable to the countervailing force of sea power exercised by nations at the Eurasian littoral. That is to say, the supremacy of sea power, dominant in the world since 1500, was about to give way to massive land power rooted firmly on the steppes of Asia. Mackinder's implication was strong that Russia, by her very geography, was the likely progenitor of the coming Heartland empire.[2]

Mahan also saw Russia as the key to the future of central Asia. Writing four years before Mackinder, he outlined in his *Harper's* essays the thesis that the inexorable imperialism of Czarist Russia was the greatest threat to the stability of China and to the peace and security of the world. With broad sweeps of his geopolitical brush, Mahan painted the outlines of a politically unstable land mass lying between thirty and forty degrees north latitude and stretching longitudinally from the Mediterranean, Turkey, and the Persian Gulf in the west, to Manchuria, the China Sea, and central China in the east. This belt he called the "debated and debatable middle strip," and argued that it was destined someday to be the final great battleground between the conflicting Slavic Russian and Teutonic English civilizations. Meanwhile, it would remain a no-man's-land contested by the great "Slavic" land power that was Russia in search of ice-free ports, and by the great "Teutonic" sea powers that were Great Britain, the United States, Germany, and Japan. These four sea powers, all trading nations, would have to adopt "a common line of action" in China since no one of them alone was strong enough to dominate China; nor was any one of them alone powerful enough to check Russian imperial expansion from Eastern Siberia southward into Manchuria, Korea, and North China.

There Mahan left the matter in December 1899. Not until after the Boxer Rebellion did he seriously take note of the Open Door concept. The preliminary announcement of the idea in September 1899 seems to have had little impact on him. However, the broader version that Hay issued in July 1900, coupled with the heavy fighting at Tientsin and Peking, sent him back to his study in Quogue in August for a second look at the situation. In his "Effect of Asiatic Conditions Upon World Politics," written that month for *North American Review*, he argued that political equilibrium in his recently discovered "debated and debatable middle strip" could best be assured by assigning spheres of influence in the area. Manchuria would go to Russia, and the Middle East and the Persian Gulf to Britain. Central China, especially the rich and exploitable Yangtze Valley, would be assigned to the four-nation, Teutonic sea-power coalition. To stabilize the Yangtze sector of the "debated middle strip" and strengthen China in the process, it was important, Mahan contended, that the United States and other members of the international sea-power group prevent "preponderant political control [of China] by any external state or group of states." Further, the Teutonic coalition should insist "upon the Open Door, in a broader sense than that in which the phrase is commonly used; that is, the door should be open not only for commerce, but also for the entrance of European thought and its teachers in various branches." Among these teachers would be the Christian missionaries who would convert, educate, and otherwise uplift the backward natives of central China. In August 1900 Mahan was far more interested in the ecclesiastical penetration of China than he was in its commercial exploitation. To him the Open Door should first open into a Christian church. Once inside, the passing of the collection plate was a secondary matter. The policy did, however, harbor certain dangers. "We cannot be sure of the commercial advantages known as the 'Open Door' unless we are prepared to do our share in holding it open. . . . unless we are ready to throw . . . our physical weight into the conflict to resist an expropriation the result of which might be to exclude our commerce and neutralize our influence," he wrote. Mahan, then, was only casually interested in the purely economic aspects of the Open Door. The existence of Hay's policy was useful to him mainly as a justification for the building of a great U.S. Navy to sustain it, and for the missionary opportunities inherent in it.

To a considerable extent, Mahan hinged his predicted Russia-versus-Western Civilization confrontation in the "debated middle strip" on inherent racial contradictions pitting cruel and barbarous Slav against progressive and civilized Teuton. But to make his related concept of Teutonic Sea Power versus Slavic Land Power scan, he was obliged to recruit the Japanese into the Teutonic bloc, as did Adolf Hitler during World War II, when he designated his Asiatic cobelligerents as "honorary Aryans." Mahan's position was no less strained. He had no use for Orientals, Chinese or Japanese. He considered them culturally static, racially inferior, and intellectually backward; and he spent a good deal of his adult life working to prevent their insidious immigration to Hawaii and California. He had been a card-carrying member of the "Yellow Peril" movement since 1890. In 1900, however, he felt it appropriate to say something pleasant about the Japanese as he blandly conferred Teutonism upon them. First, he noted that Japan, "which less than four years ago notified our government of her disinclination to our annexation of Hawaii, now with satisfaction sees us in possession of the Philippines." Following that dubious assertion, he further de-orientalized them by observing that Japan's rapid Westernization—her general openness to Western technology, morality, democracy, manners, and Christianity—placed her clearly with the Teutonic coalition in its coming struggle with the brutal Slav. "In this conversion, Japan is repeating the experience of our Teutonic ancestors as they came into contact with the Roman polity and the Christian Church. . . . in Japan alone do we find the Asiatic welcoming European culture, in which, if a tree may fairly be judged by its fruit, is to be found the best prospect for the human race to realize the condition most conducive to its happiness—personal liberty." Banzai![3]

Conversely, the Russians were, in Mahan's mind, the major cause of the "Problem of Asia" at the turn of the century. Indeed, Czarist Russia was virtually the entire problem. As he looked at the map of the Eurasian continent he viewed with alarm the "vast, uninterrupted mass of the Russian Empire," dynamic, powerful, and expansive, occupying a protected geographical "central position" north of the middle strip—a nation pushing slowly and steadily toward the Persian Gulf, the Sea of Japan, and the Yellow Sea. Here was a people filled with "remorseless energy." Like a gigantic thirsty crab, the Russia that Mahan pictured was, "in obedience to natural law and race instinct," moving inexorably southward toward warm water. Her eastern claw reached down toward Korea, Manchuria, and northern China, while her other claw stretched westward toward the Persian Gulf. These giant pincers threatened to envelop the entire "debated and debatable middle strip" and drive the Teutonic trading nations out of China.

Save for having at one time thought that the Russian national anthem was rather tuneful, Mahan had never liked or trusted Czarist Russia. In 1897 he saw that American-Japanese tension about Oriental immigration to Hawaii could only redound to the benefit of Russian imperialist ambitions in Korea at the expense of a distracted Japan. For this reason he had then hoped that U.S. relations with Japan might somehow be improved. By September 1899 he was certain that the wily czar had called the First Hague Conference mainly to retard the Anglo-American rapprochement stimulated by the Spanish-American War and to undermine tentative British support for America's plea for commercial opportunity in China. Only by keeping Britain isolated, he told Sam Ashe, could Russia continue to move "over the inert Asiatics like a steam-roller."

So pronounced was Mahan's anti-Russian bias in 1899 and 1900 that he had difficulty appreciating the logic of the alliance that Paris and St. Petersburg had effected in 1894 to counterbalance the German-Austrian Dual Alliance of 1879. Concluded partly to offset France's humiliation in the Franco-Prussian War, this agreement presented Berlin with the prospect of a two-front war, should she harbor thoughts of another act of aggression in Europe. Instead, Mahan drew attention to the cultural unnaturalness of the French-Russian understanding and cheered when it nearly foundered on the rocks of the Anglo-French war scare in the Sudan in 1898. "Who was it said there are two kinds of nature—human nature and French nature?" he wrote laughingly.[4]

He did not laugh when the McKinley administration decided to withdraw American troops from northern China and return them to the Philippines after the Boxer siege of Peking had been lifted. The withdrawal order was issued on August 29, 1900, and the troops departed in late September. Mahan thought this action precipitate. It caused him great "consternation," since the aggressive Russians had taken advantage of their participation in the suppression of the Boxers to move 100,000 troops into northern Manchuria. He recognized this development when in August he added to his "debated and debatable middle strip" hypothesis a codicil that conceded all Manchuria to Russia in return for British preeminence in Persia. It was a realistic concession in that the Russians took further advantage of Chinese administrative weakness in Manchuria by militarily occupying the southern third of the province in September and October 1900. This opportunism was in direct violation of the principles of the territorial and administrative integrity of China outlined by Hay on July 3. Given ice-free water at Port Arthur on the southern tip of the Liaotung Peninsula, which they had seized in 1898, the Russians had emerged from the scramble for concessions in 1898 and 1899 and from the Boxer troubles of 1900 as the greatest gainer by far among the European imperialist powers. Further, they had chosen to deal directly with the hapless Manchu government rather than join Britain and Germany in the Yangtze Agreement or cooperate with Secretary Hay. It was clear to Mahan that Russia had no interest in helping stabilize China. Her main interest was to grab what she could get as China fell apart.

It was these multiple affronts that caused Mahan, enamored as he now was of his amended "debatable middle strip" concept, to warn President

McKinley on September 2 that "no one who has followed Russia's course about the Hague Conference, and about China, will doubt that . . . she is not only playing her own game—as all states do—but playing it with the unscrupulous craft of the Asiatic." To Vice President Roosevelt he wrote in March 1901 that

> neither we nor Great Britain, separate or combined, can adequately check Russia by main force in Northern China . . . therefore naval power always at hand and available in the Yangtze valley—the heart of China in every sense of the word—is the true counter-check. It will work in two ways: (1) It will at once humanize and strengthen China, the surest element of resistance to Russian mastery . . . and (2) its pressure will operate by force of moral assurance to Russia that, trespass as she will in our quarter, a solid core of resistance, invincible, is building up in [that] decisive field, and will be perfected before she can have strength to reach so far. If the Sea Powers . . . [providing] physical and moral support in the Yangtze, will require of China simple, but entire, liberty of entrance for European *thought*, as well as European commerce, China will in my judgment be saved, or rather, and better, will save herself.[5]

While he hoped to see the emergence of a China strong enough to serve as an anti-Slav buffer state in the middle strip, sustained in that posture by a steel spine of Western warships on or near the Yangtze, Mahan came also to appreciate the fact that Russia's primary diplomatic objective in the Far East was not so much a gigantic Slavic encirclement and ingestion of the middle strip as it was an ice-free port on her underdeveloped Pacific coast. "Russia *must* reach unfrozen water somewhere," he granted. This did not mean that he had suddenly abandoned his "deep-rooted distrust of the Slav," or his "great faith in *permanent* conditions such as Teutonism vs. Slavism," or his conviction that Russia was more dangerous to British imperial interests than was Germany. It meant only that the more closely he studied world diplomacy in 1901 and 1902, the more convinced he became that there was a "certain solidarity" inherent in the whole fabric of international relations, one that transcended his own "strong bias" against the Russians. This awareness was the beginning of his wisdom as a student of international politics, detached as it was from the racial nonsense that underpinned his idea of a "debatable middle strip."

By early 1902 Mahan had come to feel that there would be distinct advantages to British security and to American peace of mind, were London gracefully to concede Manchuria to the Russians. Such a concession would keep the czar bogged down and occupied in Manchuria, far from the Persian Gulf, and hence well removed from a flanking position on Britain's vital Suez line of communication with India. He considered the Persian Gulf to be the strategic center of that line. "It follows," he told Leopold Maxse, "that it is far better for G.B. [Great Britain] that she—Russia—should establish herself at Port Arthur, etc. She cannot for two generations be in force at both places; and in fact, as far as I can foresee, by developing her ambitions in Manchurian waters, she institutes a condition, substantially *permanent*, most favorable to you; off your flank, and committed to the maintenance of her power in a region where she meets *permanent* opposition—besides yours; to wit, Japan, the U.S., and probably Germany." Russia, he felt, could be confined in Manchuria by the four Teutonic sea powers much more easily than she could be denied access to the Persian Gulf by the power of Britain alone. For the edification of the British Foreign Office and the British people, Mahan often pointed out the basic choice that British policy had to make between the Persian Gulf and Manchuria. This he did in his personal correspondence between 1902 and 1907 and in his well-received article, "The Persian Gulf and International Relations," which appeared in the *National Review* for September 1902. Through all these comments ran the theme that Russia was Britain's natural enemy.[6]

Not until 1907, when Britain signed an entente with Russia that partitioned Persia in such a way as to block Russian access to the Persian Gulf, did Mahan drop his idea that Britain had to choose between the gulf and Manchuria. Instead, after 1907 he increasingly played the role of a journalistic Paul Revere alerting the British to the fact that the Germans were coming. So it was that the rapid and unpredictable march of world diplomatic events had a way of overtaking Mahan's historical insights and recommendations on international issues and rendering them suddenly obsolete or inappropriate. It is a problem all foreign-policy journalists face, and Mahan was no exception. He who lives by the daily headline dies by the daily headline, and the Anglo-Russian treaty of 1907 was a headline that caused Mahan radically to shift course.

Another headline that stunned Mahan was the news of an Anglo-Japanese Treaty. Concluded on January 30, 1902, primarily as a makeweight arrangement against Russia in the Far East, the agreement marked Britain's emergence from "splendid isolation" and launched her attempt to protect her imperial interests through a network of alliances, ententes, and "cordial understandings" with her erstwhile competitors. The agreement with Japan, the first alliance in modern history between a white European nation and a yellow Asian nation, provided, in effect, that if either party became involved in war with a third party (Russia) the other would remain neutral; but if a fourth party (France) should join the war the other ally would also participate. Having already accepted Japan as a surrogate Teutonic power, Mahan had no difficulty with the racial miscegenation involved in the treaty. His larger problem was that of fitting its political implications into the mosaic of international affairs that existed in 1902. As he told Maxse in February of that year, he was "at first blush inclined to applaud your recent treaty with Japan." But

> second thoughts make me rather wish you had concentred your opposition [to Russia] upon the [Persian] Gulf. For in China—Manchuria—her efforts would be naturally antagonized by Japan, and by us if trade exclusion were attempted, while, in the Persian Gulf, not only does she, if established there, flank your route to India—a much more dangerous condition to you than having her [have] sea access in Eastern Asia—but you have [there] no natural allies; none whose interests will lead them to contest Russia, unless possibly Germany. Were the latter friendly, I don't know what better condition there could be for you than to encourage her to stretch *by land* right along the western border of Russia, through Constantinople, to the Euphrates. It would entail enduring friction between her and Russia, and cripple Germany's advance to sea power—by the burden of landward defense etc. entailed. . . . I cannot bring myself to look upon Russia and France as other than your inevitable enemies, through propinquity in Europe and in Asia, and through tradition, as well as alienage of blood, etc.[7]

Mahan had a great deal more to say about the Anglo-Japanese Treaty of 1902, much of it critical, when he later considered it in the light of the American-Japanese war scare of 1907 over the immigration issue. He came to see it as a dangerous threat to Anglo-American amity and racial unity in the event of a war between the United States and Japan in the Pacific. In 1902, however, he was not sure what to make of it. Consequently, he subordinated it to the Anglo-Russian problem in the Middle East, speculated on the possibility of an Anglo-German containment of Russia in that area, and offered some general comments on traditional Anglo-French rivalry. He said nothing about it publicly at the time.

There is no evidence, however, that he considered Japan remotely the military equal of Russia in the years between 1900 and 1903. In his *The Problem of Asia* he had built Russia into an overwhelming military menace in East Asia, a "steam-roller" capable of flattening China and seizing the "debated and debatable middle strip" virtually at will. He could not and did not know that Czarist Russia was infected with a revolutionary cancer that had already metastasized into almost every cell of her domestic body politic. Because of this, he felt that to balance Russia's over-whelming land power in Asia, or contain it in its Manchurian lair, would require the combined efforts of all the Teutonic sea powers on the scene —Britain, Germany, Japan, and the United States. How surprised and pleased, then, he was when the smallest and least Teutonic of those powers boldly attacked the Russian steamroller at Port Arthur without warning on February 8, 1904, thereby starting the Russo-Japanese War.

The first Japanese strike, which Mahan called a "brilliant success," was a torpedo attack by destroyers on unsuspecting Russian warships riding at their buoys in the roadstead at Port Arthur. Two Russian battleships and one cruiser were disabled, temporarily blocking access to the harbor. The Japanese followed this by extensively mining the approaches to Port Arthur, an act that resulted in the subsequent destruction of the Russian battleship *Petropavlovsk* on April 13, 1904, with the loss of Vice Admiral S. Ossipovitch Makarov, thirty-two officers, and more than six hundred men. Meanwhile, Japanese infantry landed at Inchon, Korea, pushed northward to and beyond the Yalu River into southern Manchuria, and everywhere defeated the badly organized and outnumbered Russian Army. By June a Japanese army was besieging Port Arthur. This threat per-suaded the eighteen-ship Russian squadron lying in the harbor to sortie to freedom toward Vladivostok. Intercepted at sea on August 10, by an inferior force of the Imperial Japanese Navy, it was badly mauled and scattered in a tactically formless action that became known as the Battle of the Yellow Sea. Five (of its seven) battleships, one cruiser, and three destroyers scurried back to besieged Port Arthur. The other survivors ran for neutral ports, where they were interned.

News that Russia's Baltic Fleet had sailed from Europe for Far Eastern waters in mid-October caused the Japanese army at Port Arthur to launch massive attacks on the city in a desperate attempt to capture the port and destroy the Russian warships there before the arrival of Admiral Zinovi Petrovich Rozhdestvenski's Baltic force. For similar reasons, the Russian defense of the city was stubborn and heroic, as the czar's forces there sought to preserve a naval base into which the oncoming Baltic Fleet might repair. Theirs was a copious expenditure of blood, an investment defended by Mahan on tactical and strategic grounds. After all, control of the ice-free harbor was the key to the naval war in the Yellow Sea and the Sea of Japan and to the land war on the Liaotung Peninsula in south-ern Manchuria. Understanding this, the Japanese spent no less blood. They spent more. Much to the amazement of the Western world, their attacks on the city's defenses featured human-wave assaults against gun emplacements and other fortified strong points, human torpedo suicide attacks through barbed-wire defenses, and what in general appeared to be a total disregard for human life. On January 2, 1905, some 60,000 casualties later, the Japanese finally took Port Arthur. Russian warships in the harbor were promptly scuttled.

This deprived Rozhdestvenski of a naval force with which to "concentrate" when he reached the scene, and of an adequate port from which to conduct subsequent operations in Far Eastern waters. With Port Arthur gone, he was forced to shape course for Vladivostok. Further, by the time he reached the East China Sea in the spring of 1905 there remained in the Far East little of the Russian naval power that had existed there when the conflict began. The Japanese Navy had patiently and doggedly destroyed, or driven into neutral ports, most of the Russian warships that had been operating in Far Eastern waters in 1904. It was, as Mahan pointed out in his several articles on the war, an object lesson in what happens when a fleet fails to achieve or maintain tactical concentration. Not only did the Russians fail to concentrate their Baltic and Far Eastern squadrons, they had also failed to concentrate the segments of the latter.

When Rozhdestvenski arrived in the East China Sea in May 1905, en route to Vladivostok, after a seven-month voyage from the Baltic, his large but antiquated fleet was almost all that remained of the czar's operational navy. Unfortunately for the Russians, that residue was blown out of the water by Admiral Heihachiro Togo on May 27, 1905, at the Battle of Tsushima, a brilliantly conducted, aggressive action in which the commanders of the Japanese battle fleet thoroughly out-maneuvered, out-shot, and out-thought the Russians. Her remaining naval power thus dissipated, her single-track Trans-Siberian Railroad incapable of moving reserve armies and supplies to the Far East in sufficient quantities or with sufficient speed, her government wracked by the revolution that had broken out in January 1905, Russia sued for peace. Japan, her over-extended armies weakened by heavy casualties and her domestic economy at the point of bankruptcy, gratefully seized the opportunity to end the war. Her strategic goals had been achieved. Korea had been occupied. National "face" had been saved. The yellow man had humbled the white man.

The immediate causes of the war, conflicting Russian and Japanese imperialist ambitions in southern Manchuria and northern Korea, tensions punctuated by armed clashes along the Yalu River, did not much interest Mahan. The outbreak of the conflict caught him completely by surprise, as it did most Americans. He did not know that the Japanese sneak attack on the Russian fleet at Port Arthur on February 8, 1904, had been encouraged in part by confidential American assurances to Tokyo a month earlier to the effect that if Russo-Japanese antagonisms along the Yalu led to war, U.S. policy would be "benevolent toward Japan." Nor did he see clearly in 1904 that the Anglo-Japanese Treaty of 1902 had encouraged Japan to risk this bold adventure, since Britain would come to Japan's aid if France came to the czar's. Actually, when the attack occurred, both Britain and France declared neutrality. On April 8, 1904, the two powers signed the Entente Cordiale, which settled most of their worldwide colonial differences, reduced other tensions, and provided the basis for the Anglo-French alliance that carried the two countries together into World War I.

What Mahan did know in February 1904 was that he feared the autocratic and expansionistic Russians who threatened someday to overrun much of Asia and close the Open Door. He chortled over Russia's early defeats. Her "ludicrous inefficiency," he told Maxse, placed her "in a position as unrespectable physically as it had been morally." Further, his midshipman acquaintance from his tour at the Naval Academy from 1877 to 1880, Japanese Vice Admiral Sotokichi Uriu, class of 1881, figured prominently in the early fighting. Perhaps more important to the formation of his pro-Japanese bias in 1904 was the fact that his important works on naval history had been translated into Japanese and there was within the Imperial Japanese Navy a core of officers who counted themselves his disciples. Among these was Lieutenant Saneyuki Akiyama, who had visited Mahan in New York on the eve of the Spanish-American War and who, according to his biographers, carried on a professional correspondence with the Philosopher of Sea Power for sometime thereafter. Thus while Mahan assured readers of *The New York Times* in November that he was "no partisan in this matter," he took the unneutral position that "so far as I could understand the situation Japan had no recourse but to declare war, and at the moment she did."

Captain Mahan was very much a partisan, as were President Theodore Roosevelt, John Hay, and many other prominent Americans who took an active interest in America's Far Eastern policy in 1904. Public sentiment and newspaper commentary in the United States was heavily on the side of the Japanese "underdog" throughout the war. Privately subscribed American loans flowed to Tokyo during the conflict. Indeed, Roosevelt was delighted with Japan's opening naval victory at Port Arthur and felt Japan was basically "playing our game" in humbling the arrogant Russians in Manchuria. It was his Machiavellian hope that the combatants would exhaust themselves in a long and bloody war that would end in a stalemate and leave the two nations poised at one another's throats in Manchuria in the years ahead. "This will keep them on a war footing and reduce their appetite for other territories," reasoned the president. "Then Japan will not menace . . . us in the Philippines. Russia's attention is then diverted from her western frontier and remains concentrated upon the East." He desired a postwar situation of "balanced antagonisms" in Manchuria, with neither power strong enough to annex the territory from China or maintain rigid spheres of influence there. This would advance the prospects of American commerce in Manchuria and thereby strengthen the Open Door.[8]

The outbreak of the war was a financial godsend to Mahan, coming, as it did, on the eve of a planned trip to Europe with Elly and his daughters. They sailed on May 10, 1904, and returned early in October. Before he left, Mahan was offered "good terms" to comment on the strategy and tactics of the conflict, and he obligingly began dashing off articles to help pay for the trip. One piece he "rushed off at a sitting." In September 1905, after the war was over, he hoped it would remain a "live topic" for a while longer, since he and his family were soon going to Europe for an extended stay—they departed New York on October 28, 1905, and remained abroad until June 8, 1906—and he was eager to turn a few additional dollars by passing the collection plate in the Temple of Mars one more time. Partly because he was in and out of the country during and after the war, partly because he was forced to write in a hurry and on the move, the reading and research that went into his Russo-Japanese War articles was exceptionally thin. He did little more than scan a few newspaper and magazine articles on the subject, distilling from them whatever factual data they contained, which in most cases was not much, and recast that material to illustrate general military and naval principles that he thought must surely be operating in the war. On one occasion he asked an editor to be kind enough to send him the background information he would need to do an article.

Given this shallow approach to his task, it is not surprising that the three lucrative and "exclusive" articles on the war he did for *Collier's Weekly* between February and May 1904 were superficial and speculative. In sum, *Collier's* purchased for a good price the name "Captain Alfred T. Mahan, U.S.N., author of *The Influence of Sea Power on History*, who was a member of the Naval Advisory Strategic Board during the Spanish-American War, and is a recognized authority the world over in matters per-

ALFRED THAYER MAHAN

taining to naval strategy." Mahan, in turn, hastily filled the assigned space for the edification of readers "who have had no occasion to study the principles of war." It was strictly a business arrangement.

In these *Collier's* articles he spoke of "command of the sea," noted that the Japanese had struck while the unconcentrated Russian Navy maintained one fleet in the Baltic, one in the Black Sea, and one at Port Arthur (part of the latter deployed at Vladivostok), pointed out that Japan began the war "with the twin advantages of concentrated force and interior position between their two enemies," and speculated on what would happen if and when the Baltic Fleet reached Far Eastern waters and joined the force at Port Arthur. With appropriate quotations and analogies, he harked back to Napoleon Bonaparte and Lord Nelson. He admitted to his readers that there was little accurate information from the seat of war with which to work. Nevertheless, he assured them that the loss of the *Petropavlovsk* to a Japanese mine was something of a fluke, and he took the position that the self-propelled ("automobile") torpedo was not a decisive weapon, in spite of its apparent success at Port Arthur on February 8. The battleship was still queen. Indeed, it was high time his countrymen abandoned Mr. Jefferson's quaint notion that the Navy might safely be comprised of cheap little gunboats. "I think we may rest assured for the present that whatever modifications of armament may take place, the fleets that will control the seas will not be mosquito fleets," he told those Americans who thought economies might be achieved by building more destroyers and fewer battleships. America must continue to build battleships and cruisers, whatever the cost. His compatriots must also abandon once and for all the naive hope of "bringing an enemy to terms by commerce destruction alone, to be effected by a number of small cruisers, instead of obtaining control of the sea by preponderance of great fleets."[9]

Similarly, in his *Collier's* article on the Battle of Tsushima, written but six days after the event and based on fragmentary reports of what had happened at the southern entrance to the Sea of Japan on May 27, 1905, Mahan speculated that ordnance and ship types had most influenced the outcome of the engagement. He decided that the battleship, the armored cruiser, and the big gun had brought about the triumph at Tsushima and that Japanese torpedo-launching destroyers had played but a small role, acting "mainly the part of cavalry, rounding up and completing the destruction of a foe already routed." The articles he wrote on the battle in 1906 were somewhat more instructive, and his *Naval Strategy*, published in 1911, contained a solid analysis of it. But in the years ahead he stuck with one dubious insight expressed in June 1905: "in distributing

[474]

fleet tonnage, regard must be had to numbers quite as [readily] as to the size of the individual ship. This I say, while fully conscious of the paradox that an amount of power developed in a single ship is more efficient than the same amount in two. In part, the present Japanese success has been the triumph of greater numbers, skillfully combined, over individual ship power too concentrated for flexibility of movement." Better to have a fleet's total firepower spread among a greater number of ships than concentrated in fewer.

This observation bore small relationship to what actually happened at Tsushima the previous week. It was, instead, a salvo in Mahan's last great theoretical shoot-out within the U.S. Navy—the bitter debate with W. S. Sims over the optimum size of battleships and guns and how these might relate to tactical flexibility in combat at sea. In this debate, which Mahan lost, he opposed the concept of the all-big-gun ship. As will be seen, he favored a "balanced fleet," in terms of tonnage and ship types, and he argued vainly for capital ships that would carry guns of various calibres. What Tsushima seemed to indicate to most U.S. naval observers, however, as more detailed evidence of what had happened there became available in 1906 and 1907, was that the bigger the gun and the larger and more heavily armored the gun platform (the ship), the more effective was the total weapon system in achieving and maintaining a concentration of firepower at long ranges. Accordingly, the number of ships engaged was less decisive than the number of big guns that could be brought to bear on an enemy. Most experts agreed with Mahan that the torpedo-launching destroyer was vastly overrated and that its stellar performance on February 8, 1904, in a surprise attack against stationary targets at Port Arthur, was indicative of little. They disagreed with his contention that the all-big-gun, single-calibre ship was inferior to the mixed-battery vessel. Mahan's advice notwithstanding, the U.S. Navy favored the former type after 1905.

In his last newspaper or magazine comment on the Russo-Japanese War, written for *National Review* in March 1906, Mahan reviewed the strategy of the conflict for the purpose of making a special plea to the American people for the future tactical concentration of the U.S. Navy, noting that the entire Russian Navy on the eve of the war "outweighed decisively" the size of the Imperial Japanese Navy. Had the czar's fleets been concentrated, Russia would either have prevented the war altogether by deterring the Japanese attack or she would have won it. The politicians, however, had foolishly divided the czar's navy and, in so doing, had ensured Russia's defeat. In the light of such stupidity, it was Mahan's fear, insofar as the United States was concerned, that there is no contingency affecting the country . . . so menacing as the fear of public clamor influencing an irresolute or militarily ignorant Administration to divide the battleship force into two divisions, the Atlantic and the Pacific. . . . people do not understand the simple principle that an efficient military body depends for its effect in war—and in peace—less upon its position than upon its concentrated force. . . . It is precisely the same, in application as well [as] in principle, with the Atlantic and Pacific coasts of the United States. Both are exposed. . . . Any invader from the one side or the other must depend upon sea communications to support his army *throughout the war;* not merely for the three months needed to bring the United States fleet from one side to the other. But if the war begin with the fleet divided beween the two oceans, one half may be overmatched and destroyed, as was that of Port Arthur; and the second, on coming, prove unequal to restore the situation, as befell Rozhestvensky. That is to say, Concentration protects both coasts, Division exposes both. IT IS OF VITAL CONSEQUENCE TO THE NATION OF THE UNITED STATES THAT ITS PEOPLE, CONTEMPLATING THE RUSSO-JAPANESE WAR, SUBSTITUTE THEREIN, IN THEIR APPREHENSION, ATLANTIC FOR BALTIC, AND PACIFIC FOR PORT ARTHUR. So they will comprehend as well as apprehend.[10]

Japanese victory in the war ended Mahan's anxiety over the Russian steamroller grinding relentlessly into China and throughout the "debated and debatable middle strip." Instead, Japan suddenly emerged in Mahan's mind as America's major enemy in East Asia and in the Pacific. By the terms of the Treaty of Portsmouth (September 1905), which ended the Russo-Japanese War and was brokered by Roosevelt in the interest of his policy of "balanced antagonism" in Manchuria, Russia turned over to Japan the Liaotung Peninsula. In addition, the treaty recognized Japan's "paramount interest" in Korea. This primacy of interest, a euphemism for Japanese annexation, the United States had already recognized in July 1905 in the secret Taft-Katsura Agreement with Japan, receiving in return a Japanese disavowal of future aggressive ambitions in the Philippines. But the failure of the Japanese to obtain financial idemnity to the tune of $600,000,000 from Russia at the Portsmouth negotiations, a failure they correctly blamed on Roosevelt, set off anti-American and anti-treaty demonstrations in Tokyo that resulted in the destruction of American property there. Mahan admitted that Japan's urge to war in 1904 had stemmed in part from the shabby treatment she had received from Russia, France, and Germany in 1895, when those powers had forced her to return the Liaotung Peninsula to China at the end of the Sino-Japanese War. He therefore regarded Japan's recovery of a sphere of influence on the peninsula as the legitimate regaining of an earlier loss. On the other hand, he saw that the wave of anti-Americanism in Japan after the signing of the Treaty of Portsmouth bode ill for the future. Much of this sentiment had to do with the immigration issue.

Thanks to postwar economic distress in Japan, thousands of Japanese farmers and artisans, many of them veterans of the conflict with Russia, elected to emigrate to Hawaii and to the Pacific coast of the United States in search of economic opportunity. In 1906 close to 1,000 working-class immigrants were reaching the United States from Japan each month. A clause in a treaty concluded with Japan in 1894 gave the United States the right to exclude Japanese immigrant laborers by passing specific federal legislation to that effect, but that right had never been exercised. Given the fact that there were already more than 60,000 Japanese immigrants resident in Hawaii (40 per cent of the total population), Californians in particular became alarmed at the sudden influx of Japanese in their midst and began to agitate for the same kind of federal exclusion that had been applied to the immigration of Chinese in the 1880s.

In October 1906, the San Francisco Board of Education issued an order that provided separate and not very equal schools for Oriental students. This blatant racism provoked a major crisis in American-Japanese relations, as Japanese politicians and newspapers reacted in outrage. So tense did the situation soon become that Roosevelt ordered the Navy Department to undertake an immediate analysis of the relative strengths of the U.S. and Japanese navies. Indeed, he worried to Senator Eugene Hale, Chairman of the Senate Naval Affairs Committee, that the activities of the segregationist agitators in San Francisco "may possibly bring about war with Japan. . . . for the Japanese are proud, sensitive, war-like, are flushed with the glory of their recent triumph, and are in my opinion bent upon establishing themselves as the leading power in the Pacific."

With characteristic energy, the "Big Stick" president intervened personally in the California mess, banged together the heads of a few tin-horn politicians in San Francisco, and managed to persuade Mayor Eugene Schmitz and the local Board of Education that it was in the national interest to rescind the segregation order. This revocation occurred on March 13, 1907; but only after Roosevelt had made good a quid pro quo promise he had made to the board in mid-February to bring about an end to Japanese immigration to the United States. This he accomplished in the so-called "Gentlemen's Agreement," a series of informal arrangements concluded in 1907, strengthened in 1908, in which Japan agreed to the face-saving device of issuing no more passports to emigrant laborers bound for the

American mainland. In return for these voluntary controls, the Roosevelt administration promised to block the passage of federal legislation aimed specifically at excluding the Japanese. By mid-1907 the crisis had largely been defused. This was a signal diplomatic triumph for Roosevelt, and he celebrated it by ordering the entire American battle fleet, the Great White Fleet, on a muscle-flexing, flag-showing voyage around the world.[11]

Mahan shared the prejudices of Californians when it came right down to the question of Japanese immigration. To him, the Open Door swung only in one direction—from West to East. It must not be hinged in such manner as to permit Orientals to enter the United States. To be sure, he said he loved Japan and the "charming geniality and courtesy of her people"; but he seems to have loved them most when they remained quaintly and quietly at home in Japan. He did not want to live next door to them.

The American-Japanese crisis of 1907 caught Mahan by surprise. He was in Europe from April to June of that year. Nevertheless, he responded quickly to the situation, especially its racial dimensions, confiding to Maxse that "I feel strongly that with the black race question on our hands we must withstand a further yellow one. This, of course, implies no condonement of the blackguard conditions of San Francisco; but it does point to a time when Great Britain may have to consider her relations to Japan in the light of those to the U.S., and Australia, where the 'white' feeling also prevails." Further, he now argued that the existence of the Anglo-Japanese Treaty of 1902 ("I never believed in that treaty") seriously compromised Britain's relations with the United States, since Americans would not and could not accept unrestricted Japanese immigration—even on pain of war. He felt that the continued existence of the pact, renewed in 1905, could only have the effect of exacerbating future Anglo-American relations, perhaps even inclining the United States toward Germany "as a counterpoise." He hastened also to assure correspondents in England that the Australians, New Zealanders, and Canadians (British Columbians) fully shared American racial attitudes on the issue of Japanese immigration and that, in her continuing alliance with yellow Japan, Britain was playing dice with the cohesion and loyalty of her white Empire. "I fear, and have from the first believed, that your Government backed the wrong horse in the alliance with Japan," he told Bouverie Clark in July 1909. "It, more than anything else, may handicap us. Your own white folks in Australia etc. don't like it any better than we." And again: "Open the doors to immigration, and all west of the Rocky Mountains would become Japanese or Asiatic," he worried. "It is not a question of superior or inferior race; but of races wholly different in physical get-up. . . . The problem is yours

—through Canada—as much as ours; and with Australia backing Canada, Imperial Federation will be up against the question of Japanese alliance, *if* the Japanese insist upon freedom of immigration."

Under no conditions would Mahan accept the right of immigration for Japanese "coolies." As he told Clark on another occasion, "I for one, would accept war to-morrow rather than concede a claim which would soon fill our country west of the Rockies with another race, involving interminable trouble." He variously estimated the speed of the Japanese inundation of the underpopulated West at ten to twenty years, and noted that the competitive "economic advantage" of resident Japanese over native Americans in that section of the country was already great. He finally decided, after exhausting all other arguments, that "Asiatic immigration is against the spirit of the Monroe Doctrine because, as they don't assimilate, they colonize, and virtually annex."

His last word on the subject, however, was a flat denial that his exclusionist stance was based on a personal belief in racial superiority. Japanese immigration was more a problem of assimilation than a racial issue, he maintained, one similar to the Negro situation in the United States. As he told the readers of *The Times* (London) in June 1913:

> The question is fundamentally that of assimilation, though it is idle to ignore that clear superficial evidences of difference . . . due to marked racial types, do exacerbate the difficulty. Personally, I entirely reject any assumption or belief that my race is superior to the Chinese, or to the Japanese. My own suits me better, probably because I am used to it; but I wholly disclaim, as unworthy of myself and of them, any thought of superiority. . . . Now, while recognizing what I clearly see to be the great superiority of the Japanese, as of the white over the Negro, it appears to me reasonable that a great number of my fellow citizens, knowing the problem we have in the coloured race among us, should dread the introduction of what they believe will constitute another race problem; and one much more difficult, because the virile qualities of the Japanese will still more successfully withstand assimilation, constituting a homogeneous foreign mass, naturally acting together irrespective of the national welfare, and so will be a perennial cause of friction with Japan. . . . America doubts her power to digest and assimilate the strong national and racial characteristics which distinguish the Japanese, which are the secret of much of their success. . . .

Mahan wanted no more unassimilable citizens living in the United States. Minority groups such as the French in Canada, the Boers in South Africa, and the Slavs in Austro-Hungary caused untold internal problems for the

ALFRED THAYER MAHAN

nations in which they resided. The racially inferior Negro had already created an enormous social problem in America. The country could certainly do without the Japanese.[12]

Having just returned from Europe, Mahan was not privy to the background of the decision Roosevelt made in July 1907 to dispatch the sixteen brightly painted battleships, the Great White Fleet, under the command of Admiral Robley D. Evans, on a grand circumnavigation of the globe. Their 45,000-mile voyage, which began at Hampton Roads, Virginia, on December 16, 1907, and ended there on February 22, 1909, proudly advertised the fact that since 1898 the U.S. Navy had grown from the world's fifth or sixth in size to its second largest. Mahan was certain, however, that the president's decision was made "not in apprehension of war but merely as a matter of practice." He did not believe that the United States or Japan wanted war over the immigration issue, as hindsight shows neither did. Nor did he think that the ordering of the fleet was a provocative act. This point of view proved correct, in spite of Roosevelt's later blustering that his decision to send the battle fleet had cowed an aggressive Japan into sweet reasonableness on immigration. On the other hand, Mahan knew practically nothing about the logistical preparations for the voyage that occupied the autumn of 1907. Indeed, from September 25 to October 24 he was in the hospital for a prostatectomy, returning there early in December for the removal of adhesions.

While he was in the hospital, flat on his back, he became "greatly excited and outraged" by critical comments that Commander William S. Sims, naval aide to the president, was reputed to have made on the slowness of preparing the fleet for the voyage and on the logistical difficulties that could be expected during so extensive a trip. As noted before, Mahan had no love for the outspoken Sims. Therefore, when the *Scientific American* asked him for an article on the coming circumnavigation, Mahan could not resist the opportunity to take an oblique shot at his enemy. Soon after leaving the hospital on October 24, he dashed off a rambling piece on the proposed voyage which ranged in historical scope from Nelson to Rozhdestvenski, and in which the few relevant facts employed were gleaned from newspaper reports. *Scientific American* published the article, "The Value of the Pacific Cruise of the United States Fleet, Prospect," a few days before the fleet sailed. In it Mahan assured his readers that everything was fine insofar as preparations for the voyage were concerned, and that all would surely go well for the ships diplomatically, administratively, and logistically in the trying months ahead. The voyage could not be anything less than a valuable opportunity for practical training. In strategic terms,

[480]

he saw it as a vital exercise in moving the entire battle fleet swiftly and smoothly from one coast to the other, an operation that would demonstrate the efficacy of tactical concentration and put an end to demands in Congress and elsewhere that the battle fleet be divided between the Atlantic and Pacific coasts. Since Mahan had staked so much of his reputation and credibility on the concept of fleet concentration, it was important to him that the cruise go well.[13]

When he followed up his observations on the Great White Fleet with a second article, "The Value of the Pacific Cruise of the United States Fleet, Retrospect," he ran into criticisms from the friends of Sims. Written in July 1908, as the fleet shaped course westward from San Francisco to New Zealand, it was published in *Collier's Weekly* on August 28, 1908, when the vessels were in Australia. The article was little more than a public-relations handout on the high morale, engineering efficiency, and fighting trim of the force at the time it reached Magdalena Bay, Mexico, the previous March. It was the sort of pap the Navy Department might well have distributed to newspaper reporters. Nevertheless, said the Philosopher of Sea Power in a letter to Little, Brown and Company, the piece was based on "some interesting data of [the fleet's] experiences [which] have been furnished me." It should also be mentioned that Mahan had already committed both of his essays on the Great White Fleet to reprinting in his forthcoming *Naval Administration and Warfare*, a collection of old articles from here and there that Little, Brown and Company was scheduled to bring out early in November 1908.

He was stunned, therefore, when his colleague from save-the-War-College days, Rear Admiral Caspar F. Goodrich, wrote him from New York on September 12, 1908, with the sarcastic admonition that "had you known the real history of the trip from Trinidad to Magdalena Bay of the Atlantic Fleet, you would have framed your *Collier's* article very differently. We all look up to you as a model of accuracy. Greatness has its own responsibility you see." True, Goodrich had earlier abandoned Mahan and had gone over to the Sims camp on the all-big-gun fight of 1906 and 1907; but it was also true that Mahan, writing quickly and for good pay, knew very little more about the daily operational details of the Great White Fleet than what he read in the newspapers.

The fact of the matter was that all had not gone well during the fleet's trip around the Horn. Operational difficulties had surfaced in a number of areas, particularly in the ships' engine rooms. Coaling from the foreign colliers contracted to accompany the fleet had proved particularly difficult. Faced with Goodrich's sarcasm, Mahan could do little more than write him a testy letter demanding a list of specific misstatements in his *Collier's* article. All his contentions in that article, he insisted, were based on "what I think good and adequate authority." He asked that Goodrich be quick about responding since the article was about to be reprinted in his *Naval Administration and Warfare*. The book was already in press. Goodrich replied only that "it is for you to be sure of your facts. That's what I mean." Mahan then asked Roosevelt, through William Loeb, private secretary to the president, to intervene in the matter. Roosevelt declined the invitation to become involved in the squabble, even though Mahan informed Loeb that the report on which he had based most of his second article on the Great White Fleet had been written from Magdalena Bay by Admiral Evans' aide, Lieutenant Commander Lloyd H. Chandler, and published in the *New York Herald* on March 29, 1908.

Such was the depth of Mahan's research on the Great White Fleet. Such, too, were the "interesting data" that had been "furnished" him from the scene. They added up to little more than a published letter to a newspaper editor together with formal cruise reports and press statements from an unidentified "junior admiral" and from Admiral Charles S. Sperry, who had replaced Evans as commander of the force at San Francisco in May 1908. It was not an impressive survey of the situation. In sum, Mahan had been caught red-handed by Goodrich in a superficial piece of work. Nevertheless, when the fleet returned to the United States in February 1909 it was in excellent fighting trim. Mahan's faith in it, if not his facts about it, had not been misplaced.[14]

His shaky articles on the cruise did not disqualify him as an expert on American-Japanese naval relations in the Pacific. Two years after the battleships returned home, Mahan was asked by Rear Admiral Raymond P. Rodgers, president of the Naval War College, to comment on the college's highly secret Strategic War Plan of 1911. This plan involved a hypothetical naval war in the Pacific between Japan (Orange) and the United States (Blue), a theoretical problem that would dominate the U.S. Navy's strategic thinking and planning in the Pacific until the Imperial Japanese Navy attacked Pearl Harbor and the Philippines in December 1941. Mahan's thoughts on the subject, written in February and March 1911, as his book *Naval Strategy* was being readied for press, were realistic and incisive. Based partially on views expressed in a report on naval yards he had written for Secretary of the Navy George von Lengerke Meyer in September 1910, the paper was probably the best thing he ever wrote on naval strategy. Compared with the Alice-in-Wonderland plan for war with Britain that he wrote in 1890, it was a measure of the distance Mahan had come in his thinking about strategy in twenty years.

The War College plan, on which Mahan commented at length, argued that while Japan would enter a war with the United States with a smaller battle fleet, she would be able quickly to move by sea 100,000 soldiers of her powerful army from her home islands to the probable conquest and occupation of the Philippines, Guam, Samoa, and Hawaii. This she would do in the first three months of the war, while the U.S. Navy was laboriously moving its entire battle fleet from the Atlantic to the Pacific. The existence of an isthmian canal was not assumed; nor was a Japanese occupation of the Pacific Coast, although naval bombardment of the West Coast was anticipated. By the time the U.S. Navy reached San Francisco, the Japanese would be holding a strongly defended perimeter extending from Kiska in the Aleutians, through Hawaii, to Samoa, and on to the Philippines. Only if the U.S. battle fleet happened to be in the Pacific at the outbreak of the war, which was unlikely, could the Americans be expected to hold Hawaii. But it was assumed that Hawaii and all other American possessions in the Pacific would be lost.

The War College's scenario visualized three strategic possibilities for a counterattack across the Pacific that would bring the Navy into East Asian waters, secure to it there an advanced base of operations, and permit it to blockade and, thus, strangle the insular Japanese enemy. The first of these possibilities, the Northern Route, via the Aleutians (Kiska or Unalaska) to the Ryukyus (Okinawa), was deemed too dangerous and too uncertain from the standpoints of climate, logistics, and navigation. The second possibility, the Central Route, via Hawaii and Guam, was by far the best; but it would require unacceptable infantry casualties in the assault on and recapture of Hawaii and Guam. The third possibility, the Southern Route, via the Marquesas and the Philippines, was (virtually by default) the line of American counterattack recommended by the War College. Under this plan, the Navy would occupy a temporary base somewhere in the southern Philippines, preferably on Malampaya Sound, Palawan Island, that could be supplied via both Suez and the Pacific, and then bring in the Army. The Americans would move north by land and by sea and would seize the site for a major operational base that would be constructed in the northern part of the archipelago. From this base it would be possible to neutralize Japanese forces in Formosa and the Pescadores, sever Japanese communications and commerce, and bring Tokyo to her knees in short order. All the while, the U.S. Navy would be seeking in East Asian waters a decisive fleet action, on the Tsushima model, against the outnumbered Imperial Japanese Navy. The War College plan did not contemplate an invasion of the home islands, but it assumed that both China and Russia would enter the war on the American side in the final stages of Japan's agony. The plan conceded that there would be grave difficulties with coal supply and ship maintenance; rearguard harassment by Hawaii-based Japanese naval units during the advance along the Southern Route was also anticipated. But the authors of the plan argued that, with both Hawaii and Guam lost in the opening days of the war, the Navy would have no alternative to risking these multiple dangers.

Mahan did not agree. He did not consider the Southern Route either the obvious one or the most desirable one. "The conclusion that 'a southern approach to the Philippines would be the only practicable one,' on the supposition that Japan has so occupied Hawaii as to require a long continued direct attack to reduce it, appears to me the crux of the whole plan, and to be very disputable. Much depends upon the harborage available at Kiska, or at Unalaska, as to which my information is inadequate. I know that General [Leonard] Wood has been inclined to look favorably on Unalaska." He agreed with War College theorists that the United States should have a two-ocean Navy, that it should fortify its Pacific Coast harbors, that it should build and strongly fortify bases in Hawaii, Guam, and the Philippines, and that the Panama Canal, then building, should be rushed to completion. These were unimpeachable truths with almost all naval officers in 1911.

Mahan's main concern with the college's dubious plan centered on that part of it which considered the naval technology of the situation. In drawing attention to this point, however, he apologized for his lack of "detailed knowledge [or] . . . the familiarity with all conditions, which are essential to judicious final decisions." Still, he doubted that Japan had the transport that would enable her to occupy and fortify so much American territory with so many men so quickly. "Even granting the means and the numbers to seize all, it is to me incredible that all can also be fortified, armed, and garrisoned, before the American Fleet establishes control of the sea in the Pacific." But convinced as he was that the Japanese would not "make formal proclamation before striking, though the United States by its Constitution must do so" and assuming Japan had the transport to occupy American territory swiftly, he agreed she would be able to manage troop landings on the Pacific Coast. "But I think she will not do so, realizing that the effect would be to solidify popular feeling in the United States, and so entail upon herself a prolonged [financial] effort on a scale so huge as to be exhausting. . . . it is well understood that the advances of Japan towards peace with Russia in 1905 were attributable to a financial exigency which is not yet dispelled." He thought it more likely that the Japanese would make their major effort against Guam because Hawaii was too exposed for them successfully to resist a vigorous American counter-attack there.

To Mahan's mind, Guam was the key to the Pacific interests of the United States. He had lectured on its strategic importance at the War College in September 1910, and in that same month he had advised Secretary of the Navy Meyer that it should be at the center of all naval planning for a war with Japan:

> To . . . protect our other interests in the Pacific—the Open Door, the Philippines, Hawaii—Pearl Harbor should receive the development now contemplated, and Guam should be constituted a kind of Gibraltar.
> . . . . No situation in our possession equals Guam to protect every interest in the Pacific; nor need it be feared that Japan would attempt an invasion of the Pacific Coast, or of Hawaii, nor probably of the Philippines, with a superior or equal American navy securely based upon a point only a thousand miles from its coasts and flanking all its eastward communications.

Given the weight of Guam on his scales, it was Mahan's recommendation that U.S. naval strategy for a westward counterattack across the Pacific should be along the Northern Route and should be launched from Kiska or Unalaska in the Aleutians. The alternate Southern Route simply would not serve. He pointed out that on this route the fleet would be vulnerable to attack on its flanks, would have to steam long distances, and would have to use the coaling facilities of neutral nations in the South Pacific on its voyage to the southern Philippines. In general, the Southern Route would mean a longer war. Once the fleet was in Palawan, its alternate supply line via Suez would prove cumbersome. On the other hand, if its point of departure were at Kiska or Dutch Harbor, the fleet would outflank a Japanese-occupied Hawaii. The position in the Aleutians would serve also as an excellent springboard for a direct attack, via the Northern Route, on the Ryukyus, where it would probably be able to seize an anchorage. Kiska, he pointed out with great precision, was but 1,800 miles from Yokohama, 1,500 miles from Hakodate, and 2,700 miles from Guam. Given that the fleet's cruising radius was 4,000 miles, both the Japanese home islands and Guam would be well within operational range of the Aleutians. Kiska, therefore, was the key to the recovery of Guam, and Guam in turn would provide the Navy with the advanced base it would need to bring down Imperial Japan. "I infer, therefore, that a move of the American fleet to Kiska will compel the Japanese Fleet to fall back from Hawaii, and that it will not stop at Guam, but must retreat to home base." His strategic solution, then, was to approach the Central Route via the Northern Route, a suggestion the War College planners rejected. As for the supposed climatic disadvantages of the Aleutians, Mahan found "it difficult to admit that for white men climatic inconveniences of an over-cold climate can equal in ultimate effect those of one constantly over-warm." His larger conclusion was that

> all this elaborate and necessary scheming demonstrates only more forcibly that at a not distant date the United States fleet should be moved to the Pacific, and there remain until the opening of the Canal; that the Pacific [coast] ports be duly fortified, and Hawaii secured. There will then be no war; barring some intolerable action, which the United States as a nation will not commit.

The War College theorists responded to Mahan's criticisms and recommendations by suddenly adding new arguments to strengthen their advocacy of the Southern Route. "The latter [a fleet sortie to Palawan via Suez] not being mentioned in the Plan submitted to me, I did not consider it," Mahan replied with some testiness. The college's restatement also added a mass of technical data to its original plan. Much of this material had to do with recent ordnance developments, and almost all of it was unfamiliar to Mahan. "Many of the facts stated," he confessed, "are new to me, for my attention for several years has not kept abreast of detailed advances of naval equipment. That an advanced base can be equipped within a week for holding against a serious attempt at recapture . . . is new to me." Since the college planners in this particular were optimistic to the point of fantasy, Mahan need not have been so apologetic or deferential to "the officers on the active list" who concocted it. The college response argued further that Guam was out of range of a Kiska-based fleet. Such a force would arrive there, facing possible combat, with its bunkers two-thirds *empty*. Mahan maintained that the bunkers would be one-third *full* —or more than sufficiently supplied to meet a combat situation on arrival. Nonetheless, the college theorists contended anew that it would be better to land in the southern Philippines and work slowly northward than to accept the risk involved in seizing at the outset an attack position more central to the geography and war-making potential of the Japanese home islands. To this restatement of arguments for a cautiously mounted war, Mahan wearily responded:

> The subsequent process of gradually working northward is more secure than my suggestion, and also slower. It protracts the issue; and leaves Japan unmolested in Oahu, and for a time in Guam. Though safer, it is less decisive. My own opinion is that unless Japan is put in

tremor concerning his communications—threatened at home—he can hold out till the American people weary of the war. If the American nation does not weary, Japan will be reduced by exhaustion. . . . Even the poor Vladivostok division [in 1904] shut up the native shipping in Yokohama by appearing nearby.

Mahan did not directly respond to what was perhaps the War College's most telling criticism of the Northern Route—namely, that an American thrust from Kiska directly into the Ryukyus would expose the supply line of the attacking force to Japanese harassment on both flanks. He argued instead that the question of coal supply was a "huge administrative question, costly and intricate; but it is not insoluble to money and brains." He was sure that whatever strategy was adopted, Northern Route or Southern Route, "a [coal] depot can be secured and fortified against probable molestations by raid." His final argument for the Northern Route was, predictably, drawn from history and from the literature on strategy, as were many of the points made in his Orange vs. Blue planning papers in 1911:

> Farragut's . . . adoption as his motto of Danton's "*de l'audace, de l'audace, et encore de l'audace*," will be found in every great military achievement. . . . In this connection, I question the soundness of [Julian] Corbett's dictum of not attacking the enemy where he is strongest; and the apparent inference in the [College's] second paper that "America's security lies in an approach on Japan's weakest flank." Corbett relies mainly on Clausewitz, whose authority is of the very first; but I conceive it is not the enemy's local strength, but the chance of success and the effect produced by success which should influence.[15]

Within a few weeks of his thoughtful exchange with the War College strategists, Mahan was advising them, at their request, on how best to fortify Guam against possible Japanese incursion. Simultaneously, he instructed Secretary of the Navy Meyer, who solicited the advice, on the difficulties and theoretical considerations involved in choosing proper sites for overseas coaling depots. He recommended building fueling facilities at Guantánamo, Panama, Pearl Harbor, and Corregidor. But since he was all but certain that America's next war would be in the Pacific against Japan, he advised against accumulating substantial coal stocks at Pearl Harbor or Corregidor ("a most exposed position") until the Panama Canal was in use. To do so would only serve to hand those stores over to the Japanese while the U.S. battle fleet was making its way to the Pacific from the Atlantic. Until the canal could be used, the major deposit of coal for opening operations in the Pacific should, therefore, be made at Colón, on the Atlantic side of the Isthmus of Panama. There it could be used for operations in the Atlantic or it could be shipped by rail across the isthmus to be picked up by the fleet steaming northward to San Francisco from Cape Horn. "On war occurring in the Pacific, all military effort should be concentrated at the Isthmus, up to the utmost locally needed to hold it securely," he also advised. When the canal opened, it would be possible safely to make substantial coal deposits at Pearl Harbor, Corregidor, and Guam. In fine, the Isthmus of Panama and the canal soon to traverse it would be major factors in the next naval war in the Pacific.

In all of this Mahan saw clearly "the utter dependence of Japan upon the sea and the need of expansion room." He saw, too, that Japan, "in view of her poverty and financial needs," would abide by the Open Door policy of the United States only so long as the Russian presence in Manchuria served as a counterweight to her own imperialist ambitions there and in China. Further, Japan possessed "an excellent navy, [and] a very numerous army, highly organized." He had therefore warned Secretary Meyer and the General Board of the Navy as early as September 1910 that a Japanese "invasion of the Pacific coast" was at least a possibility, partly "because of the doubtful issue of the Open Door and the inflammable prejudice of our Pacific [Coast] population towards the Japanese resident," and partly because of the enticing vulnerability of Hawaii and the Philippines. The United States, he concluded to Meyer,

> has now two principal and permanent external policies: The Monroe Doctrine and the Open Door. The latter of these signifies that trade with Chinese territory by the world outside of China is to be regulated by China herself, and not by external powers forcibly installing themselves in possession of Chinese territory. Having reference to naval stations, the Monroe Doctrine centres around the Isthmus of Panama; the Open Door requires positions as far advanced in the Pacific Ocean as is permitted by the local advantages of points now in our possession, and by the general national willingness to maintain a navy and naval bases adequate to our avowed national policies.

He was not convinced that such Spartan willingness was present among America's "worthless leisure classes," and he feared that because of the inability of such Americans "to endure hardness . . . the Asiatics will, through this and their numbers, attain an ultimate superiority of fighting and resisting force." At best, he told Theodore Roosevelt and former Secretary of State Elihu Root in July 1913, "we have before us a long controversy with Japan, the outcome of which is in my judgment very uncertain." To old friend Sam Ashe he insisted in mid-1912 that "with Germany on one side and Japan on the other, both nations necessarily aggressive because of their need of expansion, a large navy is now our only security."

Clairvoyant as this statement proved to be in the light of December 7, 1941, Mahan made one prediction in March 1911, the logic of which seems ironic in retrospect. "I have not," he told Robert U. Johnson, editor of *Century Magazine*, "dealt with the question of the Navy helping to resist an attack on Pearl Harbor. If the Navy be there in force, the attack will not be made; at least not until the Navy has been beaten. If the Navy is not there, the case does not arise." No prophet wins them all.

By the end of 1911 the alliances that propelled Europe into war in 1914 had been fashioned. The Triple Entente of Britain, France, and Russia nervously faced the Triple Alliance of Germany, Austria-Hungary, and Italy, both groups armed to the teeth. In the Far East, Britain and Japan were allied in a regional pact. And in 1910 and 1911 Russia and Japan liquidated their long-standing differences in Manchuria—their balanced antagonisms—by the cynical though sensible device of partitioning the province into two spheres of influence, into virtual colonies, and by slamming the Open Door in Manchuria in the face of American business enterprise. Indeed, the United States inadvertently helped provide this closure when, in November 1908, Elihu Root and the Japanese ambassador Kogoro Takahira entered into an executive agreement. This understanding supplemented and expanded the Taft-Katsura arrangement of 1905, in that Washington accepted Japan's preeminent positions in Manchuria, Korea, and Formosa in return for a pious Japanese statement, entirely hypocritical, of support for the Open Door principle in China, and a second pledge that the imperial government harbored no aggressive designs on Hawaii or the Philippines.

Thus did the Roosevelt administration, in two executive agreements concluded after the unsettling Russo-Japanese War, seek to protect the Achilles heel of the United States that was the Philippine Archipelago with a mighty fortress built of Japanese paper pledges. At least André Maginot would manage to pour a little concrete. Mahan was dead right when he told Sam Ashe in June 1912 that "a large navy is now our only security." Indeed, on the eve of World War I, Imperial America, like Little Red Riding Hood in the forest, was abroad in a cruel world without an ally. Instead, she was armed with policies, doctrines, pledges, contingency war plans, and a navy second to two—Britain's and Germany's.[16]

XVIII

Mr. Monroe, Kaiser Bill, and the Balance of Power 1899-1913

International questions have now come to be my chief interest, to the subordination at least of those that are purely naval, with the details of which I have for some years past found it onerous to keep up.

Alfred Thayer Mahan to Charles Scribner, May 8, 1913

Mahan had long agitated for an isthmian canal, one that would be completely under American control. He cared little whether it pierced the isthmus through the Republic of Nicaragua or through the Republic of Colombia's revolution-prone Department of Panama. He leaned toward the Nicaraguan option, but with no fervor. He did not engage in the lively debate in Washington and within the Navy on the merits and demerits of the respective routes. It was important to him only that a canal be built somewhere in Central America because on its existence rested the maritime unification of the Atlantic and Pacific coasts, the population by white men (preferably Anglo-Saxon) of the sparsely settled West Coast, the rapid tactical concentration of the U.S. battle fleet in the event of war, American strategic control of the Caribbean, and an increased American naval role in the Pacific for the purpose of upholding the Open Door policy in China. Over the years, his arguments for a canal centered more on the strategic and naval significance of the waterway than on its commercial or economic importance. Indeed, Mahan's concept of American imperialism in the 1890s and early 1900s seldom revealed a capitalist dimension. He was scarcely a tool of Wall Street.

The legal problem associated with acquiring an American canal at the isthmus in 1900 and 1901 turned on the wording of the Clayton-Bulwer Treaty with Britain. That pact, which Mahan called "a great aberration," stated specifically in 1850 that neither of the English-speaking nations would ever fortify or attempt to exercise exclusive control over a future waterway in Central America. Nevertheless, the treaty, out of date at the turn of the century, made little sense in the context of Britain's difficulties in the Boer War and increasing American pressure to abrogate it for reasons commercial and naval. Indeed, in January 1900 Congress began to consider a bill to construct a canal in Nicaragua in open defiance of Clayton-Bulwer. This show of force on Capitol Hill resulted in the signing in February of the first Hay-Pauncefote Treaty, according to which the United States was permitted to build and own a canal. But it was also stipulated that such canal should be open to the vessels of all nations and should not be fortified.

The non-fortification clause doomed the treaty to death in the Senate, a demise that Mahan privately cheered in mid-February. He had no use whatever for the neutralization clause and he felt that to build and own a canal and not have the right to fortify it was nonsense. Imagine enemy warships sailing blithely through an American-owned canal en route to bombard American coastal cities. The very thought was preposterous. He was willing to accept the distasteful accord only "upon one condition, viz: that the country adopt a decisive policy of keeping our navy equal at least to that of Germany." Suspecting that such a condition would never be met, he could not refrain from the further observation that "the [Mc-Kinley] Administration has made a mistake if it has concluded this treaty without careful consideration with, and between, some capable officers of army and navy. . . . military considerations are, if not supreme, of very great importance. There is no indication that the opinion of any military or naval man has been asked." Certainly, Mahan himself had not been asked. The best that could be said for the first Hay-Pauncefote agreement was that it was an improvement over Clayton-Bulwer. At least it was half a loaf. Mahan felt, however, that time was on the American side in the matter; he correctly saw that Britain, beleaguered all over the world and possessing no major allies in 1900, would soon have to pull out of the Caribbean altogether.

Speaking to this point in August 1900, he called attention to Anglo-American cooperation in China, to the diplomatic rapprochement of the two powers that was then under way, and to British imperial problems that were far more vital to her national well-being than any interest she might still have in the Caribbean. Mostly he pointed to the realism and good sense of Great Britain and concluded that London was on the verge of voluntarily abandoning her position in the Caribbean to the Americans:

> Forty or fifty years ago . . . we were directly antagonized in the Caribbean by the nation having the strongest navy in the world, and convinced that our policy—in brief, the Monroe Doctrine—was irreconcilable with her interests. The events of the last half century have changed this, and, what is more important, Great Britain, though within but a very few years, now recognizes the change. . . . We find, therefore, on the part of the greatest of naval states, a politic disposition to acquiesce in our naval predominance in the Caribbean. . . . Great Britain's interests elsewhere are so great that she must unload herself of responsibility for the Caribbean.

Mahan was right. In November 1900 Britain signed the second Hay-Pauncefote Treaty which formally abrogated Clayton-Bulwer and permitted the United States to build, own, operate, and fortify a canal in Central America. Put another way, a realistic Great Britain began the process of accepting the Gulf-Caribbean as an American lake, a *mare clausum*. Within two years the Admiralty began pulling Royal Navy units out of the area. The Age of Nelson was over, at least in the Caribbean.[1]

The logic of the United States' insistence on the right to fortify a canal in Central America, whenever and wherever it was built, was made clear in December 1902 and January 1903 when a combined Anglo-German naval force intervened in revolution-ridden Venezuela to collect debts long owed to the nationals of both those nations. This combined force established a blockade and seized and sunk Venezuelan gunboats; a German warship bombarded and leveled Fort San Carlos. Cipriano Castro, the venal dictator of the distraught country, was brought to his senses and forced at naval gunpoint to accept arbitration of the claims that the British and Germans had been seeking for over a year.

This European naval intervention in the Western Hemisphere, carried out so effortlessly and so close to the Isthmus of Panama, raised the additional question of whether evil men and disorderly nations of the ilk of Castro and Venezuela might be able to hide under the skirts of Mr. Monroe's doctrine and, from that protected position, prick the capitalist conscience of civilized mankind. The answer of the new Roosevelt administration was a ringing NO: as long as the British and Germans seized no territory in Latin America they could punish the likes of Castro and his debtor compatriots without running afoul of the doctrine. Mahan concurred and explained to Leopold J. Maxse in late December 1902:

I am sorry Great Britain has associated herself with any other power in the Venezuela business. The action of the two powers does not contravene the Monroe Doctrine; but I fear the *joint* action will excite a popular sentiment here injurious to both. In this I care nothing about Germany; but I do care about Great Britain, both because I have regard for you and because *our* policy requires cordial relations. . . . However, I should not complain, for I see the facts are influencing Congress to authorize two more battle-ships.

He agreed, further, that the United States could not tolerate European infringement on the "independence or territorial integrity" of Latin-American states; nor would the United States countenance the "shirking of . . . international responsibility" by those states. Mahan did not feel, on the other hand, that the doctrine had been designed by James Monroe and John Quincy Adams to justify later American imperialist abuse of the very Latin-American nations it purported to protect from European expansionists. As he told the readers of Maxse's *National Review* in February 1903, in an article entitled "The Monroe Doctrine," the United States would not "compel" the Latin-American states to make good their international obligations to nations "other than herself," since "to do so, which has been by some argued a necessary corollary of the Monroe Doctrine, would encroach on the very independence which that political dogma defends." He also pointed out that while "the United States is inevitably the preponderant American power . . . she does not aspire to be paramount. She does not find the true complement of the Monroe Doctrine in an undefined control over [Latin] American states, exercised by her and denied to Europe."

The only thing that prevented Mahan's statement of February 1903 from being a forthright advocacy of national self-denial in Latin America was the phrase *"other than herself."* It was to this semantic loophole that he hastily repaired following Roosevelt's crude detachment of Panama from Colombia in November 1903 and his military intervention in the chaotic and bankrupt Dominican Republic in December 1904.

It was at the time of this last dramatic event, when European governments were threatening to intervene in Santo Domingo on behalf of their creditor nationals, that the president announced the so-called "Roosevelt Corollary" to the Monroe Doctrine. This sweeping reinterpretation of the doctrine argued nothing less than that "chronic wrongdoing . . . may in America, as elsewhere, ultimately require intervention by some civilized nation, and in the Western Hemisphere the adherence of the United States to the Monroe Doctrine may force the United States, however reluctantly, in flagrant cases of such wrongdoing or impotence, to the exercise of an international police power." In fine, T.R. enunciated a doctrine of preventive intervention in Latin America and wrapped it in the hoary mantle of Monroe. Just how quickly Mahan personally embraced this perversion of the original doctrine is not known. But by 1908, when he revised his article on the doctrine and reprinted it in his *Naval Administration and Warfare*, he was defending the Roosevelt Corollary root and branch, pointing out that the United States had no moral choice but to intervene in the Dominican Republic in 1904 for the precise reasons Roosevelt had then given. He argued, too, that such an act of intervention had been inherent ("evident, logical, and irresistible") in the larger purpose of the doctrine ever since the day it was written in 1823. "The interposition in Santo Domingo is not so much a corollary of the original proposition—an obvious consequence—as it is a turn in a river, or a divergence, resembling that of a new branch put forth by a tree," he maintained. He admitted, however, that comparisons between the Monroe Doctrine of 1908 and the Doctrine of Monroe of 1823 might produce certain contradictions in the minds of the uninitiated. Nonetheless, he assured his initiated readers that "to state the qualities of an apple and an apple tree is to formulate a series of paradoxes; but all the same the apple is the fruit of the tree." The doctrine, he concluded, was obviously a living, growing, and changing entity, "fruitful in consequences just because it is alive." Armed thus with vague paradoxes and pomological analogies, Mahan in 1908 sprinted to catch up with the whirring cutting edge of the American imperialist movement in the Caribbean—as he had earlier raced to overtake the imperialist implications of Philippine annexation. Captain Alfred had a habit of lagging behind the ideological vanguard of American Empire.[2]

Even though he was tutored on the subject by John Bassett Moore, Mahan had great difficulty rationalizing U.S. involvement in the events in Panama in 1903. In this instance, American lightning, partly in the form of the armored gunboat *Nashville* and the auxiliary cruiser *Dixie*, struck the tree of Manifest Destiny, causing the apple that was a legal right of way for the construction of a canal across Panama to fall into the lap of a grateful nation.

Reduced to its essentials, the background of American acquisition of a canal opportunity in Panama was this: in 1902, having decided for a variety of economic, political, and engineering reasons that a canal should be built through Panama rather than through Nicaragua, the Roosevelt administration attempted in March 1903 to purchase from the corrupt Colombian government the necessary right of way across its impoverished and inaccessible Department of Panama. The offer was $10,000,000 for a six-mile-wide strip. The venal politicians in Bogotá, led by dictator José Marroquín, held out for a better price, one in the $25,000,000-to-$40,000,000 range. It was clearly their right to do so, whatever their personal motives. However, the upshot of Bogotá's reluctance to sell at the price offered was that Roosevelt actively encouraged, smiled upon, accepted, or otherwise permitted (choose one of the above) a revolution by Panamanian separatists and patriots against the central government of Colombia.

The Panamanian freedom fighters, composed of 500 bribed Colombian garrison troops and a smattering of firemen and local barroom drifters from Panama City, were recruited by the headquarters of Panama Libre in Room 1162 of the Hotel Waldorf Astoria in New York. These patriots meandered to the barricades of human liberty on November 3, 1903, the day after the convenient arrival at the isthmus of the *Nashville* and the *Dixie*. In the Gilbert and Sullivan "revolution" that followed, an inquisitive Chinese laundryman and a stray donkey met their fates. The following day, November 4, the Republic of Panama was hastily proclaimed. It was recognized just as hastily by the United States on November 6, and on November 18 it eagerly sold to the Americans for $10,000,000 a ten-mile-wide canal right of way, together with political and administrative sovereignty over the strip. During the "revolution," American sailors and Marines prevented loyal Colombian troops in Panama from moving to suppress the uprising; and in the weeks that followed they discouraged the landing of Colombian troop transports from Buenaventura and Cartagena. A Colombian infantry force, seeking to march overland to the scene of the uprising, bogged down in the dense jungles that separate Panama from the South American body of the nation. Thus was the Colombian government prevented from putting down the bogus revolt in the manner that it had suppressed more genuine uprisings in Panama in the past, fifty-four of them in fifty-seven years by Roosevelt's count. Whether the Panamanians actually wanted political independence in 1903, and whether they were likely to be better off as citizens of an American puppet state than they had been as impoverished Colombians, remained (and remains) a moot point. They were not consulted at the time.

In any event, U.S. interference in the internal affairs of the Bogotá government in 1903 was legally, if not morally, justified on the basis of the Bidlack Treaty concluded in 1846 with New Granada, the predecessor state to Colombia. In this treaty the United States had guaranteed the neutrality of Panama, then threatened by British absorption, and the sovereignty of New Granada in the area. These guarantees were extended in return for an American right of transit across the neck and the collateral right of the United States to intervene militarily at the isthmus to ensure passage for its own and other citizens. Needless to remark, it was Article XXXV (the transit-intervention clause) of the Bidlack Treaty, rather than its neutrality-sovereignty provision, that Mahan and other apologists for the intervention stressed in their later explanations of the forced-labor birth of the Republic of Panama in 1903.

The question of the continuing validity of Article XXXV of the 1846 treaty with New Granada, a nation that had subsequently become the United States of Colombia and in 1863 had been reconstituted as the Republic of Colombia, was legally resolved within Roosevelt's cabinet by the argument that the article was a "covenant running with the land." That is to say, the transit-intervention right was perpetually inherent in the American-Colombian relationship at Panama regardless of the fact that New Granada, the nation that had originally granted the boon, no longer legally existed. International legist John Bassett Moore thought this an adequate legal rationalization of the issues and a fine phrase, although he noted with cynical humor that "it is only a question of words; that is to say, it is, indifferently, a question of the 'covenant running with the land' or a question of the 'covenant running (away!) with the land.'" The most recent of several American interventions to preserve the right of transit granted in 1846 had occurred in 1885. It will be recalled that, while commanding the *Wachusett*, Mahan had personally participated in this operation and that his experiences at that time had contributed to his abandonment of isolationism.

In 1903 he did not undertake to defend the details of the American involvement in Panama and he avoided discussion of the morality of the action for nine years, even though T.R.'s seizure of Panama from Colombia was extremely popular with the American people. Indeed, a bumbling attempt by the Democrats in the presidential campaign of 1904 to make political capital of the administration's eager intervention at the isthmus failed signally. Judge Alton B. Parker, the anti-imperialist Democratic nominee that year, was, in the words of one political humorist, "defeated by acclamation."[3]

As might be expected, Mahan was much more concerned with the strategic implications of an American canal at Panama than he was with the legal and diplomatic niceties of the acquisition of the right of way. Not until June 1912 did he confess to Moore that "my only doubt has been as to whether we violated our treaty agreement of 1846." But the more he meditated on this nagging doubt the more convinced he became that the covenant with New Granada ran with the Colombian land that was now the Republic of Panama:

> I am tenacious of the view that a national promise is as binding as a personal [he told Moore]. In 1885 we stopped fighting at the Isthmus insuring thereby transit; but then the fighting was between parties only, not sectional. Did either succeed, there was no transfer of territory. But in 1902 [*sic*] it was a sectional fight; on the one side independence, on the other subjection. We again interfere, and the result is independence of Panama, and loss of sovereignty by Colombia; but our interference in both cases assured the neutrality of the ground and the security of transit. The methods employed were different. In 1885 we used land forces as well as naval, and occupied the ground. In 1903 we used naval force only, preventing the transit of Colombian troops. . . . The endeavor to state the case to you has gone far to clarify my own mind, and to convince me of the integrity of our action. That men as keen sighted as Roosevelt and Hay should have perceived at once an opportunity, and should have purposed to embrace it, is nothing to the point of law or equity. We have to do only with the act, and that is the discharging of our guaranteed assurance of quiet.

Having confessed (and resolved) his doubts about the acquisition of a right of way in Panama to J. B. Moore, one of the best international legal minds in the United States, in October 1912 Mahan published in *North American Review* a full-blown defense of the legality and morality of American behavior at the isthmus in 1903. The United States' liberation of the Panamanians from political oppression, he argued, was ancillary to its treaty obligation to maintain the American right of transit.

Meanwhile, he had been pointing out in his letters after 1903 that the building of a canal would make the Caribbean the "central position" for the movement of a concentrated battle fleet in "any direction." He also drew attention to the strategic relationship that a canal would have with Hawaii and its defenses, and he wondered whether the American people realized that the canal "constitutes an entirely new strategic centre of the utmost world-wide importance in commercial and therefore in international conditions." Further, he was worried that the rapid growth of the Imperial German Navy threatened the American position at the isthmus and, with it, the entire fabric of the Monroe Doctrine. His larger message in all of this was a familiar one to his correspondents: the obligations assumed in the building and operation of the Panama Canal required a navy second in size only to Britain's because the very existence of the commercially and strategically vital waterway was pregnant with the possibility of conflict. Like a magnet, the isthmian canal would surely attract future wars. These thoughts he presented to the American people in a series of magazine and newspaper articles between 1911 and 1914, on the eve of the actual opening of the canal.[4]

British and German naval intervention against Castro in Venezuela, the growth of the German Navy in the decade before World War I, American intervention in Panama, and enunciation of the Roosevelt Corollary attendant upon U.S. intervention in the Dominican Republic, persuaded Mahan to study anew the theory and practice of the Monroe Doctrine. He was already proud of the fact that he had almost single-handedly "saved" the doctrine at the First Hague Conference in 1899. Still, he knew little about it historically save an awareness in October 1902 that "particular applications" of it varied with "changing circumstances." It was in this spirit of flexibility that, in 1908, in order to incorporate the Roosevelt Corollary, he shifted the stand he had taken in February 1903. He also sincerely believed, as he wrote in April 1903, that "the effect of the Monroe Doctrine [is] making for universal peace." This was a theme to which he frequently returned in the years ahead. It was rooted in his conviction that if the doctrine were supported by adequate naval force it would tend to "exclude European wars from propagation to this side of the Atlantic."

But Mahan's greatest contribution to American understanding of the doctrine in the years 1902–1914 was his insistence that Mr. Monroe's policy had no real standing in international law, as indeed it did not. It was, he said, little more than an arbitrary expression of changing American desires and ambitions in the Western Hemisphere, goals that could be sustained only by the guns of a superior navy. And because the doctrine lacked legal standing in the international community, neither its enforcement nor its non-enforcement could be the subject of international arbitration; nor could its exclusive maintenance by the United States be subordinated to the strictures of arbitration treaties in which the United States might foolishly participate:

> How do we propose to keep that national idol on its feet without a superior navy? [he asked]. . . . The question of expenditure is not that of what we are willing to pay, but whether we are willing to hold our most cherished international dogma—the Monroe Doctrine—at the mercy of a superior navy, the possessors of which may have good reason to disregard our views. . . . the Monroe Doctrine has not a leg to stand on, except the United States Navy. Eminently moral as the Doctrine is, because it makes for the peace and independence of all American states, it has not behind it a shred of sanction from international law. . . . It

contravenes particular European interests. It forbids in the American hemisphere the political transfer of territory to or between non-American states, a proceeding which has prevailed everywhere else from time immemorial, and prevails now. And this [prohibition] . . . not only has no precedent in law to show, but is without treaty support from any other nation. . . . From time to time, frequently, wretchedly disturbed social conditions recur in and about the Caribbean. Our Monroe Doctrine imposes a veto upon interposition by non-American states. Arbitration cannot uphold the Doctrine because it has no legal status. Armament alone can sustain, and to be bloodless it must be sufficient, "that the opposed be ware of thee."[5]

As early as 1900 Mahan had pointed out that America's new territorial obligations in the Pacific, her commercial ambitions, and her Open Door policy in China represented so obvious an over-extension of her naval power and related foreign-policy commitments, that a contraction of the geographic scope of the Monroe Doctrine should be considered. He suggested, therefore, that the area in which it was to be enforced be confined to the Gulf-Caribbean. Its southern boundary would be the Amazon valley. He had seen in 1890 and 1891 the logistical difficulties involved in projecting American naval power as far south as Chilean waters, and had come to believe that most of the Latin-American nations south of the valley of the Amazon were strong enough and stable enough to resist European penetration without U.S. assistance or interference. Nevertheless, his trial balloon failed. Neither Roosevelt nor Lodge supported the idea of confining the doctrine to Latin America north of the Amazon. By 1902 Mahan had abandoned the notion of narrowing the area over which the ghost of Monroe hovered and had returned to the more traditional advocacy of a navy powerful enough to sustain American interests in the Far East, the Pacific, and throughout the entire Western Hemisphere. This would have to be a Big Navy, indeed.

The credibility of the Big Navy argument as it related specifically to the Monroe Doctrine clearly required the existence (or manufacture) of a visible and viable European naval threat to Mr. Monroe's policy, particularly to the operation of the doctrine as amended by the Roosevelt Corollary, and more particularly to its operation in a hemisphere soon to be pierced by an American-owned canal at Panama. For obvious reasons, in the first decade of the twentieth century Britain and her Royal Navy no longer served the United States as a credible menace in the Western Hemisphere, as they so thoughtfully had throughout much of the nineteenth century. Tragic to relate, the Redcoats were no longer coming. Mahan knew perfectly well that Britain "has no reason now, and no disposition, to traverse our position in the matter" of the doctrine. He saw that she no longer sought to acquire territory in the Americas, and he understood that the vulnerability of Canada to American invasion effectively put to rest any casual or passing interest Whitehall might have in ever again testing the policy.

Hence Mahan hit upon Imperial Germany as the nation and naval power most likely to challenge the doctrine and perhaps even to wrest the Panama Canal from the American grasp. Berlin, of course, had no such intentions, a fact Mahan privately admitted. "I incline to think," he confessed to Bouverie Clark in March 1910, that "Germany's ambitions are not turned toward our continents, but all the same it is inexpedient for us to allow her to put us so far behind." Nonetheless, from the Spanish-American War to the eve of World War I, especially between 1909 and 1912, Mahan worked hard in the public prints to convert Germany into a respectable and acceptable naval threat to America's Monroe Doctrine and her Caribbean *mare clausum*—this, of course, as part of his broader interest in justifying the continuation and expansion of the U.S. naval building program launched at the turn of the century.[6]

As early as December 1897, he voiced the opinion that Germany was "likely soon to give us something to think about seriously on this side of the water, where the Monroe Doctrine—define it how you may—has the people unquestionably at its back." He believed that population pressure made expansion necessary for Imperial Germany, and he argued that only the Royal Navy and "we with our Monroe Doctrine threaten to stand in the way of [the emperor's] very natural (and very proper) ambition." The emperor, "a man . . . possessed of ability, imagination, and strength of character," simply had to have a great navy to support Germany's growing territorial needs. Thus the appearance of elements of his naval forces at Manila Bay in 1898 and off the coast of Venezuela in 1902 confirmed Mahan in his belief that Americans had no choice but to distrust Germany, "especially Prussians." He was persuaded, too, that Germans instinctively hated Americans because the United States stood as a roadblock to German expansion in the Western Hemisphere. But the greatest fault of Germany, he told Maxse in July 1902, was "not that she is self-interested—that her *government* ought to be—but that, having decided what her interests demand, she trusts to chicanery and twisting instead of to a straightforward course." He traced this crooked behavioral path to the character of Prussia, a state that had "a miserable back history" marked by "shameless cynicism." As he instructed President Roosevelt in August 1906, modern

Germany was "inevitably ambitious of transmarine development. I don't grudge it her. As proof, after the Spanish War I refused a suggestion to use my supposed influence against her acquisition of the Carolines [islands], etc., but her ambitions threaten us as well as Great Britain."[7]

What most worried Mahan was Germany's willingness and ability to build with great speed and determination a modern and efficient navy of all-big-gun battleships. In his opinion, Berlin's economy and social system were particularly well suited to undertaking and sustaining a vast naval building program because the nation was not burdened, as were Britain and America, with working-class discontent, irresponsible labor unions, pusillanimous peace movements, and various pension and social-welfare schemes that competed with armaments for money. "My own opinion is that Great Britain and the U.S. have a tremendous start, but that the German social framework has the better endurance," he opined.

By 1909 it appeared to him that the U.S. Navy was about to lose to Germany its second ranking among the world's naval powers, as indeed it had by 1911. It was at this time that he most effectively linked the Monroe Doctrine to the size of the Navy. He noted that unless the United States augmented its battle fleet by four battleships per year rather than by the two that Congress had authorized in February of 1909, the German Navy would by 1912 clearly surpass the U.S. Navy in modern all-big-gun vessels. "What then shall we say, upon what shall we rely, if she, on occasion arising, defy us in the Monroe Doctrine?" he asked. In "Germany's Naval Ambitions," an article in *Collier's Weekly* in April 1909, helpfully subtitled "Some Reasons Why the United States Should Wake Up to the Facts About the Kaiser's Battleship Building Program," he reminded his readers of the German intervention in Venezuela in 1902, identified it as "a condition almost sure to arise" in the future, and characterized the industrious Germans as a nation "notoriously thirsting for colonization in the supposed interest of racial development." He therefore called for four "Dreadnoughts" each year if the U.S. Navy hoped to protect the Panama Canal from German challenge. To some of his correspondents he pictured a Germany with "little temptation to acquisition" of territory in the Western Hemisphere, thanks to the "opposition of our Monroe Doctrine" and to the fact that Latin-American states south of the Amazon valley were "too strong for [German] occupation and would not accept it." But in letters to others he drew attention to an aggressive fatherland, victorious in a major European war, taking over French, Danish, and Dutch possessions (Martinique, the Danish West Indies, Curaçao) in the Caribbean. Such a challenge to the doctrine could only lead, he argued, to an American-German war. To readers of *The New York Times* in April 1912 he announced that the opening of the canal would mark the end of whatever remained of traditional American isolationism. He thereupon predicted a German victory over the United States in a future war, saw the possible landing of "a hundred thousand or more of trained troops on our coast, except for our Navy," and speculated on German terms of peace to a defeated United States:

> What terms? Well, to name three principal, omitting others: the surrender of the Panama Canal, the admission of Asiatic labor immigration, and the abandonment of the Monroe Doctrine. These may be stated as (1) the surrender of a vital link in our coastwise communications, the principal end for which the Canal has been undertaken; (2) the constitution of a population predominantly Asiatic on the Pacific slope west of the Rocky Mountains—a new race problem; and (3) the suppression of a national policy, the salutary aim of which has been to exclude foreign wars from propagation to the American Hemisphere. For example, had the strained relations between France and Germany last Summer resulted in war, Germany, naturally—and properly—desirous of a naval station near the Canal routes, because of the interest in them of her great merchant shipping, might—I believe could—have taken Martinique. The Monroe Doctrine asserts that such transfer shall not be made. With a competent American Navy it therefore would not be attempted.

A harrowing prospect, this; but one that could be avoided if the United States built four battleships a year, thereby maintaining superiority at sea over the German Navy.[8]

Mahan was equally alarmed lest Britain also permit the resurgent Germans to outbuild and outstrip her at sea; or otherwise force the Admiralty to abandon the nation's two-power naval standard, a policy that insisted on the Royal Navy being larger than the combined navies of England's two most likely European enemies in event of war. This concern, related to Mahan's belief in the desirability of Anglo-American diplomatic rapprochement and the importance to the civilized world of Anglo-American racial and cultural leadership, caused him constantly to warn his British friends that disaster would loom for them in Europe, as it would for America in the Western Hemisphere, if London dropped her naval guard against Germany or failed to strengthen the internal political bonds between the English-speaking segments of her far-flung empire.

For reasons largely strategic and racial, Mahan thus attempted to advance the concept of British imperial federation. This he defined in 1902, at the time of the meeting of the third Colonial Conference of the self-governing members of the empire, as "the strong bond of national feeling, oneness in origin and blood, joined to and inspiring the imperial conviction which involves a fundamental unity of policy." Basically, he called for a democratic United States of Britain, organized structurally in a manner similar to the American model of 1787, composed of English-speaking dominions and those colonies mature enough and British enough to warrant inclusion. Like the United States of America, this federation would "assure unified, or imperial, external action by the means of an adequate organ, common to all, while preserving the independence of the several parts in their internal affairs." Stitched together economically by preferential tariffs or no tariffs at all, and by a great navy, the Imperial Federation would represent a "power nothing short of new" in the councils of the world. Colonies not yet ready for inclusion would remain in the empire-at-large until they were ready. New territories and colonies would continue to be brought into the empire because "imperialism, the extension of national authority over alien communities, is a dominant note in the world politics of today." The foreign policy of the federation would, however, be determined by all the participating members rather than by Whitehall alone. To begin with, these members would be the United Kingdom, Canada, Australia, New Zealand, and South Africa. "In view of the spreading collision of interests throughout the world, it is hard to over-value the advantage of healthy, attached, self-governing colonies to a European country of today," Mahan noted; "blessed is the State that has its quiver full of them." He assumed that the United States, which in its Constitution had pioneered the idea of federation, would be closely associated with the international policies of the British organization because in "language, law, and political traditions there is fundamental identity." Moreover, since imperial federation also implied the maintenance of a strong Royal Navy, Mahan considered that, in advocating the idea, he was supporting the foreign-policy interests of his own country. As he told Henderson in June 1902:

> The rest, I daresay, don't see it; but for the U.S., it is to me perfectly plain that whatever makes for your naval strength works for us. Every interest of yours prompts you to be friends to us. We on the other hand profit by your navy, for you must keep it at a standard of force which we never will, in this generation, attempt; and its international weight unavoidably tells in our favor because in the great international questions of the day, your interests and ours are common. On the other hand, while I am not prepared for international federation between us

—by alliance—I hope and believe that the outside world will see in the community of interests between us a warning that by attacking one they may arouse both.

In sum, Mahan looked forward to the day when the United States would become an unofficial, silent partner of a British Empire reconstituted as a United States of Britain. In such manner would the English-speaking world be at last united against the aggressive barbarians lurking just beyond the flickering camp fires of Anglo-Saxon civilization.[9]

It was his hope for Imperial Federation, together with his firm belief in the need for an Anglo-American "community of interest" cultural, political, military, and racial, that encouraged Mahan to advise his British friends on how best they might conduct their diplomatic and naval relations with Germany. This advice took into consideration the fact that Britain's maneuverability in Europe was constricted, after 1907, by her obligations to the Triple Entente (Britain, France, and Russia) and by the likelihood that Europe's next war would pit that entente against the Triple Alliance (Germany, Austria-Hungary, Italy). For this reason, he constantly called attention to the rapidity of German naval growth, urged Britain to maintain her two-power naval standard at all costs, and pleaded that the building program designed to maintain the two-power ratio not be allowed to become a party question in British domestic politics. It was much too important for that. Simultaneously, he took a hostile view of the decision of Admiral Sir John Fisher, First Sea Lord, to put all Britain's naval building eggs into the basket that was the all-big-gun ship. But while he had small use for the *Dreadnought* and her U.S. Navy counterparts, he could not fault Fisher's reorganization of the Royal Navy, made between 1905 and 1909. This saw the incorporation of the historic Channel Fleet into the Home Fleet and the deployment of the tactically combined force to the North Sea. There, under the combat command of "one of the Sea Lords," it was highly visible from Berlin. Mahan thought all this a wonderful idea. He told Henderson that "a pet idea of mine has been that the [American] charged with Fisher's specific duties should be, ipso facto, commander in chief of the concentrated battleship force."[10]

Mainly, however, Mahan urged on his British and American correspondents the thought that the key to British victory in a future Anglo-German war in Europe would turn on the ability of the Royal Navy to maintain "positional control . . . over German commerce." By a happy accident of geography, he pointed out, "Great Britain and the British Navy lie right across Germany's carrying trade with the whole world." This position, Mahan explained, was conducive to establishing and maintaining a tight blockade of the North Sea in wartime and was thus "the strongest hook in the jaws of Germany that the English-speaking peoples have—a principal gage for peace."

To the fortunate geography of the Anglo-German naval juxtaposition in the North Sea, Mahan linked his opposition to the so-called immunity movement in international legal circles. This growing persuasion sought to expand the protection of noncontraband property at sea during wartime by excluding from capture all property, whether publicly or privately owned and whether carried in neutral or belligerent vessels. It was a capitalist idea pure and simple. The idea also involved a substantial enlargement of the eighteenth-century concept that "free ships make free goods," which had long been embraced by the United States. The original doctrine permitted neutral merchantmen to carry privately owned, noncontraband goods to belligerent or neutral ports without fear of capture by belligerent warships. It was, in other words, a limited maritime "business as usual" arrangement for the nonparticipants in Europe's eighteenth- and ninteenth-century wars. But even so limited, it was a controversial and disputed practice that had a lot to do with dragging the infant United States into the disastrous War of 1812, and one that Mahan judged to be both dangerous and unrealistic. He had opposed the whole concept of immunity at The Hague in 1899 and he was distressed to see it again stalking the seas, and the White House, as Europe and the United States prepared for the Second Hague Conference, which was to be held in 1907. In his effort to recruit British opposition to the doctrine at the coming conference, he was therefore quick to identify the "immunity of private property" issue with the problem of Anglo-German naval rivalry. He explained to Maxse:

> As our press states, the immunity of so-called "private property" has already been stated as one of our propositions. To England, the position she occupies across the approaches of all trade to north German harbors, the interdiction of all German shipping in war, makes the maintenance of the present law imperative. This view needs strong enforcement at the proper moment. As a people, *we* are interested in you, as in great measure bound to the same interests as ourselves; and we have besides our own reasons for maintaining the law. But the central reason is the grip you, our almost certain cooperator, have on German shipping. . . . I see nowhere the argument concerning maritime capture presented on the lines I have taken. Whatever it's worth, it is novel. I, of course, believe it is good. The trade policy is traditional, has never been

thoroughly searched. I am not without hopes that I may carry conviction in influential quarters which have hitherto accepted tradition without query. For your country to surrender the control over Germany's action, by your commanding position over her new merchant routes and shipping, would be madness.[11]

Into few campaigns did Mahan hurl himself with more intensity than he did into his fight to nullify in advance the possible broadening of maritime neutral rights by the Second Hague Conference. His was a belief in naval command of the sea, not in the freedom thereof; and he had long argued that to exempt private property from destruction at sea during war was to encourage the outbreak of war, lengthen wars already under way, and make a game of the serious business of war that was control of the sea. Mahan did not believe in business as usual or free enterprise at sea during wartime. Capitalism, he said in effect, should stop at the water's edge when nations began to fight. If this could be assured, the profit would be taken out of war and the maintenance of peace thereby promoted.

This curiously inverted isolationist argument did not commend itself either to Theodore Roosevelt or Woodrow Wilson, both of whom argued between 1916 and 1917, as earlier they had, that the United States had an inalienable right to trade with the belligerents engaged in World War I. It was this "right" that Berlin's submarines violently contested in March 1917 and in so doing brought America into the conflict. One can therefore speculate that had Mahan's stern view of immunity prevailed at either of the two Hague conferences, the United States might well have avoided entry into that bloody conflict and prevented the deaths of 116,516 American servicemen and the wounding of 204,002 others.

Indeed, it was Roosevelt himself who in September 1904 first proposed that a second Hague conference be held and that the exemption of non-contraband private property from capture at sea be placed high on its agenda. Mahan was appalled at the suggestion. He had just finished writing his two-volume *The Influence of Sea Power in Its Relation to the War of 1812*, in which he argued persuasively that American insistence on the doctrine of "free ships make free goods" had forced the United States into a war in which the young and ill-prepared nation was soundly whipped by Great Britain. After all, Roosevelt was a serious student of the War of 1812 and surely would understand that the whole area of maritime neutral rights needed narrowing, not broadening. For this reason, in late December 1904 Mahan sent the president a typescript of the opening chapters of his *War of 1812* with the argument that an expansion of neutral rights would be dangerous and "impolitic":

Circumstances almost irresistible are forcing us and Great Britain, not into alliance, but into a silent cooperation. . . . Our united naval strength can *probably* control the seas; but there is always a remaining chance of a combination in the East—the *Western Pacific*—which might approach an equilibrium. The future and policy of China remain uncertain. It may very well be that under such conditions the power to control commerce—the *lawful* right international precedent now confers—may be of immense, of decisive, importance. . . . There is no more moral wrong in taking "private" property than in taking private lives; and I think my point incontestable that property employed in commerce is no more private, in uses, than lives employed on the firing line are private. One is at the communications in the rear, the other at the front. The question is one of expediency; and what was expedient to our weakness of a century ago is not expedient to our strength today. Rather should we seek to withdraw from our old position of the flag covering the goods. We need to fasten our grip on the sea. . . . The question of limiting armaments is very thorny; it will not be helped, I think, by allaying fears that commerce, men's pockets, will suffer in war.

Roosevelt replied that he would think over Mahan's arguments and take up the question with Secretary of State John Hay. But his mind was principally on the Russo-Japanese War then under way. Moreover, the summoning of a second Hague conference had been postponed as a result of the outbreak of that war. The issue of neutral rights was not a pressing one in the White House in December 1904.

Finally called together by Czar Nicholas in April 1906, the Second Hague Conference, which met between June 15 and October 18, 1907, accomplished less than the first. It took place in the atmosphere of an American-Japanese war scare and in the face of an Anglo-German naval arms race that did not conduce to peace. The American delegates went to The Hague with instructions from Secretary of State Elihu Root to write a Monroe Doctrine exemption into any arbitration agreement that might be reached, and to work for the immunity of all noncontraband private property at sea. They were instructed, however, to support an extension of the abstract principle of arbitration, and to seek clarification of definitions and rules dealing with contraband, blockades, and the rights and duties of neutrals in wartime. They were not expected to support reductions of naval arms, since several American battleships had recently been authorized by Congress or were actually under construction. Other nations were also nervous about the arms-limitations dimension of the conference. The outcome was that the work of the forty-four nations present at the gathering added up to little more than a tinkering with the rules of war at sea. The arms issue was papered over, as were the controversial maritime questions of the immunity of private property, the definition of contraband, and the regulation of blockades.

Mahan labored hard to make sure that the Second Hague Conference would accomplish absolutely nothing on the questions of immunity and naval-arms reduction. Although he was in Germany when the conference was called, he immediately began badgering Roosevelt and Root, urging them to abandon the immunity issue, or at least study it to death, "before committing the nation to an irreversible step." In April 1906 he asked Root to have the General Board of the Navy, Admiral Dewey presiding, consider, before the conference convened, what implications immunity would have for the United States. He was delighted that the board supported him completely when it made its report to Secretary of the Navy Truman H. Newberry a few weeks later:

> The modern tendency has been to limit more and more the acknowledged rights of belligerents, and the present necessity is to restrain this tendency within reasonable bounds or wars may become so ineffective as to lead to long-continued struggles which would be directly contrary to the intentions of the humanitarians. Captain Mahan clearly points out, in his letter forwarded by the Secretary of State, how the fear of capture of seaborne commerce may prevent wars. . . . Germany will fear our interference with her merchant marine to some extent in case of a war with the United States single-handed, and of course if private property is immune in time of war she need not fear at all. But if the United States should secure Great Britain as an ally, Germany's shipping would be tied up no matter who Germany might secure as an ally, on account of the strategical position of England as regards German commerce, and on account of the large Navy of Great Britain. Should private property at sea be immune in time of war, this great advantage would be lost to Great Britain, as well as to the United States. . . . Germany is desirous of extending her colonial possessions. Especially is it thought that she is desirous of obtaining a foothold in the Western Hemisphere. . . . It is believed in many quarters that she is planning to test the Monroe Doctrine . . . even to the extent of war with the United States when her fleet is ready. . . . Nothing should be agreed to [at The Hague] that will . . . take away so potent and influential a factor to prevent or shorten a war, as the liability of seizure of enemy's private property at sea in time of war.

Meanwhile, Mahan wrote, for Root's edification, a position paper titled "Comments on the Seizure of Private Property at Sea." He also recommended that the Secretary read his *War of 1812*. Further, he complained that as a retired officer "military regulation forbids me recourse to the press, a rule correct in principle though with the drawback of silencing men whose profession may have led them to give special attention to a subject." Root replied that he personally harbored "serious doubts" about immunity, but explained that "the subject is no longer an open one for us. The United States has advocated the immunity of private property at sea so long and so positively that I cannot see how it is possible to make a *volte face* at The Hague."

When Mahan returned to the States in June 1906 he sought an audience with the president to urge personally his views on immunity and other issues. This interview, which took place at Oyster Bay, Long Island, on July 31 got Mahan nowhere. He argued that the United States, in its own foreign-policy interests, should help write an anti-immunity provision into international law at the coming Hague Conference, if for no other reason than that an end to immunity would help maintain the Royal Navy's geographic and strategic position astride Germany's trade routes out of the North Sea. The president could not accept Mahan's viewpoint. Nevertheless, he gave the captain a special dispensation to present his contrary position in the nation's magazines and newspapers. "You have a deserved reputation as a publicist which makes this proper from the public standpoint," T.R. told him. "Indeed, I think it important for you to write just what you think of the matter."

Mahan went immediately to work to justify President Roosevelt's confidence in him as a "publicist." Within a few weeks he had arranged for the writing and submission of two articles, at $500 each, for the British *National Review* on the subject of the second Hague conference in general and on immunity and the reduction of naval arms in particular. To reach a "wider audience," to "affect public opinion opportunely," and to "increase my total honorarium," since "my increasing years make this motive real," he saw to their simultaneous publication in the American magazine *Living Age* and their reprinting in his *Some Neglected Aspects of War*, which Little, Brown and Company published in November 1907, a month after the conference adjourned. For Mahan's crusade against freedom of the seas and for his continuing opposition to naval-arms limitations, the cash register rang thrice.

He also worked to coordinate the appearance of his *National Review* articles with the start of the conference in June 1907, and he made certain that top government officials in London and Washington received copies. He hoped particularly to puncture "some of the windbags" in the American peace movement, releasing thereby their "usual misleading mixture of truth and nonsense talked—the dangerous half-truths" and the "fizz-stuff" that characterized their opinions on war and peace. He confessed to *National Review* editor Maxse that he had "no inside knowledge" of America's preparations for the conference and preferred "not to have, in order that I may be free to speak when I write, without the fetters of confidential information." In spite of his lack of privileged information, Mahan's two anti-immunity articles "made a good impression" on several of the delegates to the conference and were quoted there by British delegate Sir Ernest M. Satow in his arguments against the immunity idea.

As the conference made its way toward the ultimate pointlessness that was inherent in it, Mahan, even though he knew that Washington "felt almost bound to do so," was pained to observe that "our Government has persisted in presenting the project of immunity." Once again, he could see nothing but catastrophe in the possibility that Britain might lose her ability to interdict German trade in the next war, were such a wild notion as the immunity of private property to prevail at The Hague. "It must be realized by our intelligent statesmen," he told Maxse, "that, in the present conditions of German ambitions and German commerce, it would be suicidal madness for England or France to surrender the control their position gives over German commerce in war." Given the obvious strategic implications of immunity in a future Anglo-German war, he doubted that Roosevelt and Root were personally or privately distressed when the idea was finally killed at the conference, even though they had publicly endorsed it for domestic political reasons. Only the small states—Switzerland, Belgium, Cuba, and so forth—supported America's eighteenth-century stand in favor of immunity; the states with large navies—Britain, France, Japan—stood solidly against it. And so it failed.

In one sense only was Mahan disappointed with the harvest of zeroes at the Second Hague Conference. He had hoped, as he explained to the readers of *National Review* in May 1906 and to Roosevelt in a letter dated October 22, 1906, that the conference would impose an "artificial limit . . . on the bigness of ships of war. Eliminate bigness beyond a certain tonnage, and men, having a limit in that direction, will turn their attention to the proper dispositions of the permitted tonnage, and to its tactical management. Bigness will no longer be a refuge from every difficulty, or a recourse from every embarrassment." Unfortunately for Mahan's losing battle within the Navy to limit battleship tonnage and his equally unsuccessful campaign against the all-big-gun ship, subjects discussed below, he was unable to muster endorsement of his views by those attending the Second Hague Conference. For reasons mainly having to do with bitter intra-service rivalries on warship design and ordnance questions, Mahan was upset that the conference had not helped him to solve one of his personal-professional problems in the Navy by imposing a limit on the tonnage of capital ships.[12]

With the conference safely out of the way, the American-Japanese war scare muted, the Great White Fleet home from its triumphant tour, the Open Door policy and the Monroe Doctrine clearly enunciated, and Roosevelt out of the White House and off to the jungles of Africa to shoot at anything that moved, Mahan cast a reflective glance back over the international events of the busy years through which he had just lived. He sat down in the quiet of his study at Quogue to write a comprehensive summary and analysis of international diplomacy during the first decade of the twentieth century, a century he had earlier predicted would be blood-soaked. His purpose was to project the rapidly moving events of the past decade into the immediate future and to draw lessons therefrom. Stern, realistic, sometimes perceptive to the point of clairvoyance, it was his best effort as a diplomatic historian. It was not, however, his best commercial effort.

His basic marketing idea was to publish four essays on contemporary diplomatic affairs in a popular magazine, then have Little, Brown and Company bring them out in book form. Designed to instruct "the average American reader" on such arcane subjects as the "balance of power" and the "concert of Europe," the articles sought also to illuminate the "existing relations between Great Britain and Germany" and to show the connection between the European alliances of 1910 and America's "two leading external policies, the Monroe Doctrine and the Open Door." Unfortunately, however, the double-pay-day approach did not work in this instance. *McClure's Magazine* turned the articles down on the grounds that they were "a little too close reading and too long." When that blow occurred, Mahan decided to skip the magazine stage altogether and go directly to the book version, even though this arrangement was "less beneficial to me pecuniarily." Much to his chagrin, he discovered that Little, Brown and Company, his publisher since 1890, was less than enthusiastic about the awkwardly written and highly theoretical essays. It would certainly not be a best seller. Indeed, it was with considerable reluctance that the Boston firm agreed to publish *The Interest of America in International Conditions* at all. But this the company finally did in October 1910, informing the author, as the volume came off the press, that his usual royalty rate was being reduced. Mahan accepted the reduction only because he was convinced that he had an intellectual obligation, indeed a patriotic duty, to instruct the American people in the complexities and dangers of international diplomacy.[13]

His principal theme in *The Interest of America in International Conditions* turned on an anti-German, pro-British analysis of contemporary world events set in the context of the historical instability of the European balance of power from 1500 to 1815. Specifically, he emphasized the inability of the balance of power to preserve international peace in moments of dire crisis. The faith that a grouping of states into two equal aggregates of power would somehow automatically produce peace, since neither bloc, by definition, could *win* a war, had simply not been sustained. Similarly, the thought that any war fought would be so debilitating to its participants that it could only end in stalemate had not lessened the will of Europe's states regularly to engage in combat over the years. Mahan attributed this failure to the fact that the balance-of-power theory had not adequately taken "human nature" into account. Furthermore, he concluded that no balance of power had ever prevented aggressive nationalism and the pursuit of "national interests." Invariably, nations had pursued their own interests without reference to the interests of their allies or enemies, and had followed their own diplomatic counsels with small regard for world peace. Witness, said Mahan, the great Anglo-French wars of the seventeenth and eighteenth centuries.

Against this historical background, Mahan carefully analyzed the power balance, the "effort towards equilibrium," thought to exist in 1910 in the confrontation of the Triple Entente and the Triple Alliance. He concluded that at best it was "an unstable and shifting balance," since the latter grouping was inherently stronger than the former—save for the factor of the British Royal Navy on the entente side of the scales. Not only were Germany and Austria great and compact land powers, but they enjoyed the strategic and military advantages of geographical contiguity and central position. Further, both nations were inherently expansive; Austria in the Balkans, and Imperial Germany in Africa, in Asia, and in the markets of the world. Germany possessed the additional advantage of having an authoritarian government that subordinated the will of the individual to the will of a highly efficient state. Therefore, the only things that made the balance of power work at all in 1910 were the superiority of the Royal Navy over the combined German, Austrian, and Italian navies, and the geographical circumstance that placed the Royal Navy athwart German trade in the North Sea and astride Austrian and Italian trade routes in the Adriatic and Mediterranean. This positioning assured command of the sea to the British Navy so long as Britain assiduously maintained her two-power naval standard. In sum, the British Navy balanced the German Army and in so doing produced, temporarily at least, an equilibrium of sorts on the European continent.

Mahan had no quarrel with German commercial and territorial imperialism, no more quarrel than he had with either British imperialism or American imperialism. He regarded it as the natural behavior of a highly industrialized twentieth-century state in desperate need of markets and raw materials abroad—to say nothing of Germany's psychological need for the prestige and grandeur that attached to colonialism. What bothered him most in 1910 was the rapid growth of the German Navy in European waters and, to a lesser extent, Austria's respectable naval building program then under way in the Adriatic. He worried that if Germany achieved naval parity with Britain the tenuous balance between the Triple Alliance and the Triple Entente would surely be upset. German sea power of such magnitude, harnessed to an enormous, concentrated Austro-German land power, would simply be too much for the Triple Entente to cope with in war, especially because Russia was an unknown factor in the European military equation after her humiliation in the Russo-Japanese War.

Mahan did not predict the outbreak of World War I. But he did predict that the 1910 balance of power would inevitably break down, as others had done; and he predicted, too, that when one of the powers in one of the alliance groups pursued national goals that brought it into conflict with a nation in the opposing group, all members of both alliances would be drawn into the fray. Such was the inherent instability in balance-of-power arrangements—with the added danger that local wars might easily become general conflagrations.

This, of course, is precisely what happened in the summer of 1914 when an Austro-Russian regional crisis in Serbia triggered the delicate treaty mechanisms within the Triple Alliance and the Triple Entente and propelled all Europe into war. At that time Mahan properly considered himself to have been unusually far-sighted in anticipating the manner in which a local crisis would escalate into world war. He was also amazingly perceptive about the critical role British sea power would play in a future Anglo-German war. Too bad he was two years in his grave at Quogue by the time the Royal Navy's tight blockade of the North Sea virtually wrecked the economy of Imperial Germany and brought Kaiser Bill to bay. He would have savored the moment.

In 1910 he argued only that the continued existence of an overwhelmingly powerful Royal Navy, watchfully poised at Germany's North Sea throat, could maintain the European balance of power and thus ensure some semblance of peace and stability on the Continent. True, such a peace would not be eternal. Nor would a shotgun wedding between the balance of power and the "artificial arrangement" that was international arbitration improve the peace-keeping potentialities of the former. Nationalism, he held, was too strong an emotional force to allow arbitration to work in situations that involved substantive national interests, whether those situations occurred within balance-of-power arrangements or outside of them.

Mahan toyed also with the idea in 1910 that a "concert of power," such as was organized at the Congress of Vienna in 1815, might be the answer to the creation and maintenance of peace between competitive states:

> In place of such balance of power [he wrote], which suggests necessarily two opposite scales, that is, an equilibrium dependent on essential antagonism, and therefore liable to frequent fluctuations, the last century witnessed the growth of the idea of concert, whereby all or some of the great states, with other communities immediately affected, act together, in accord, for the solution of questions upon a basis of right, or of compromise, which when reached has the binding force of a contract. All general treaties, in a congress of nations, partake of this character; but the present conception of "concert" applies the method of general consultation and arrangement, whether by correspondence or by congress, to particular settlements, of matters minor but important. . . . The Balance of Power is analogous to competition in industrial and commercial life, while the Concert of Europe has much in common with the operation of a Trust. Although it has not attained the feature of absorption of all into one which is the characteristic of the Trust, it does concentrate the political adjudication of Europe in the hands of a combination before which the weaker companies—I mean Powers—have to bend.

"Concert," a halfway house between eighteenth-century balance of power and twentieth-century collective security, required all or some of the great states to act together to prevent war by means of compromises that had "the binding force of contract." Concert might thus supplement, rather than replace, balance of power, if great powers normally aligned in competitive alliances would band momentarily together in a given crisis to preserve peace. Mahan noted with interest and approval that this had occurred at the Berlin Congress of 1878 when Germany, Austria, Russia, Britain, France, and Italy had come together voluntarily to arrange boundaries and delineate national spheres of influence in the Balkan Peninsula following the breakup of the Ottoman Empire in Southeast Europe. He understood that concert worked best, perhaps worked only, when great powers dealt with small powers; but he failed to take into account the fact that the rigid alliance system of 1910 did not exist in 1878.

Basically, however, Mahan had small confidence that concert was on the verge of replacing balance of power as Europe's best hope for preserving peace. He was convinced that nationalism and militarism were still the dominant political realities between the Urals and the English Channel. "The states of the world are not yet in a condition to dispense with the institution of organized force," he wrote. Moreover, "there are contentions which a state will not submit to either the deliberation of a concert or the adjudication of a tribunal."

His interest in concert, or in a congress of great powers which would enforce peace on small powers in "matters minor but important"—a temporary Pax Europa of sorts—is noteworthy in that, in 1910, he had not joined other American and European theorists of war and peace in their journey toward the idea of achieving international peace and stability through collective security. It is not likely, therefore, that Mahan would have embraced with much confidence Woodrow Wilson's grand dream of lasting peace through the League of Nations, or supported any international structure that had built into it a clause requiring all member nations to spring to the defense of a victim of aggression. There is nothing in Mahan's writing, private or public, to suggest that he would have been inclined to accept for the United States, or for Great Britain, the diminution of national sovereignty inherent in the idea of collective security. He did not believe that the idea of "arming for peace" was necessarily illogical; he accepted the idea of a state intervening militarily in the internal affairs of a neighbor in order to preserve or reestablish peace there; he believed in preventive intervention of the kind spelled out in the Roosevelt Corollary to the Monroe Doctrine; he had no difficulty with the thought that a nation might fight a war to achieve a larger and more stable peace; nor did he shrink from the thought of the "just war" fought to eradicate patent evils from the face of the earth. But he could not accept the proposition that the United States should ever surrender one iota of its national sovereignty to help achieve peace through international agencies. About as far as he was willing to go in this regard was his support of American participation in international punitive expeditions, such as the one sent to relieve the legations in Peking during the Boxer Rebellion. These were little more than necessary police actions designed by civilized nations to chastise backward natives. They involved no permanent surrender of national prerogatives or national sovereignty.

What Mahan proclaimed in 1910 was the controversial idea—a truism in hindsight—that whether Americans liked it or not U.S. foreign policy, as expressed in the Open Door policy and in the Monroe Doctrine, was inexorably bound up in the operation of the unstable balance of power in Europe. In *The Interest of America in International Conditions*, therefore, he hammered away at the argument that the maintenance of America's Open Door policy in China was related to the functioning of the Anglo-Japanese alliance and, through that alliance, to the role of the Royal Navy in sustaining the equilibrium between the Triple Entente and Triple Alliance. He saw that a war in Europe would result in the immediate recall of British and German naval forces from Far Eastern waters and would leave the U.S. Navy and the Imperial Japanese Navy facing one another in the Pacific. "The Open Door," he argued, "is but another way of expressing Balance of Power; for while conspicuously just and making for peace as the balance of power has—it means simply equal opportunity, just as balance of power means equal independence." But to maintain this "artificially sustained balance of commercial opportunity" in China against an expansion-minded Japan during the course of a war in Europe would require the creation of a regional American-Japanese balance of power in the Pacific. The United States, he told his readers, did not aspire to "supremacy in the Pacific," only to "an assured supremacy over her own possessions and over approaches to them." Even this relatively modest goal would, of course, require a great and growing U.S. Navy. The Japanese, after all, were like the Germans in that the individual citizen was wholly subordinated to an efficiently organized state. Further, the excellent military tradition that had existed in Japan's ancient feudal system still permeated Japanese society. He noted that Germany and Japan exhibited "the same restless need for self-assertion and expansion."

Mahan therefore warned Americans that the Russo-Japanese Convention of July 1910, signed partly as a result of the Triple Entente's concern over German-Russian tensions in Europe, had further delineated Russian and Japanese spheres of influence in Manchuria and was designed to close the Open Door to American investment capital there. Certainly, Secretary of State Philander C. Knox's attempt late in 1909 to "neutralize" all railroads in Manchuria by placing them in an international trust, thereby preserving some semblance of Chinese economic sovereignty in the province, had been undermined by this cynical arrangement between the former enemies. So, too, had President William H. Taft's efforts ("Dollar Diplomacy") to assist China by getting watchdog American financiers included in the international banking consortia that had forced loans upon

China in the hope that Peking would default and have to surrender the collateral. In fine, the Open Door for American trade and investment capital was rapidly closing in Manchuria and throughout China. This was the result, Mahan explained, of German pressure on Russia in Europe and Russia's consequent effort to reduce tensions in Manchuria with her recent enemy, Japan—now the ally of Russia's ally, Great Britain. These were interlocking diplomatic gears that few Americans understood at the time. Mahan did. Related as it obviously was to the European balance of power, the Open Door policy, he warned, did "not stand isolated as an unrelated doctrine but is a positive and formulated attitude affecting however unconsciously . . . the general policy of contact between the East and the West." Successful operation of the Open Door in the future, therefore, required a balance of power in both Europe and the Pacific, since only an "equilibrium will ensure [the] quiet" that the policy required if it was to function effectively.

Similarly, Mahan called attention to the American stake in Europe's balance of power because such balance affected the Monroe Doctrine. Again citing German hostility to the United States at the time of the Spanish-American War and after, he stated flatly that an America interested in her own physical security could not permit Great Britain and the Royal Navy to be defeated at sea by Germany. Should the Atlantic Ocean become a German lake, the United States would face serious defense problems, since "a German navy, supreme by the fall of Great Britain, with a supreme German army able to spare readily a large expeditionary force for oversea operations, is one of the possibilities of the future."

He did not go so far in 1910 as to advocate American intervention in a European war if that seemed necessary to bail Britain out of a losing struggle with Germany—a plea that was given strong voice in Washington in 1916 and again in 1940. He merely contended that German naval superiority in the Atlantic would be a disaster for the United States. He pointed out in this regard that the Royal Navy was an important part of the American security shield; and he argued further that such American policies as the Open Door and the Monroe Doctrine, neither of which had any standing in international law, could be maintained only by the guns of a great United States battle fleet and by a continuation of the diplomatic cooperation and cultural unity of the English-speaking world.[14]

This was strong broth to serve to Americans in 1910—so strong that few of his compatriots paid Mahan heed. But what he said was true.

XIX

The New New Navy
1900-1914

*Immense indeed has been the progress . . . within the Navy . . . since
we were shipmates in the old* Pocahontas. . . . *I have had nothing to do
with the* new *Navy, the Navy of today. I did witness the transition
from sail to steam; but my last command, though so late as 1895 (the*
Chicago*), is already* old *Navy. . . . The fleeting years have brought me
almost within touching distance of the Psalmist's term of life. I was
sixty-seven my last birthday.*

Alfred Thayer Mahan to George B. Balch, March 4, 1908

World-famous diplomatic and naval historian though he was, Mahan's
reputation within his own Navy during his last years as its most visible
spokesman turned largely on his opinions of the administration, ship-de-
sign, and ordnance of a service in rapid transition. Unhappily, his opinions
did not always command great respect or confidence in the officer corps
of what might be called the "New New Navy"—or the force that emerged
rapidly after the Spanish-American War and came principally to be comprised of all-big-gun (*Dreadnought*-type) ships. Few of the naval officers
on active duty in the period between 1900 and 1914 were particularly
interested in Mahan's thoughtful observations on the complex interrelationships of balance-of-power arrangements in Europe and the Far East.
Few sat up at night, as did Mahan, meditating upon the naval implications
of the Open Door, the Monroe Doctrine, or the immunity of private
property at sea in wartime. Fewer still gave a tinker's damn about Mahan's
abstruse thoughts on historical methodology and dialectical conflict in
the universe; or paid much attention to those of his historical "principles"

which sought to equate the tactical deployment and employment of war-ships as different as Nelson's *Victory* and Fisher's *Dreadnought*. Put succinctly, the professional advice and counsel of Alfred Thayer Mahan became increasingly irrelevant to the daily problems of the operational Navy in the decade before Jutland.

To his credit, the aging Mahan sensed this. Insofar as the writing of naval history was concerned he retreated ever more deeply into the Age of Sail. Simultaneously, his interest in the contemporary scene focused increasingly on international relations and on the theoretical dimensions of war, peace, and preparedness. More and more he turned his thoughts inward to religion and to the swiftly approaching problem of his own eternal salvation. Viewed another way, the rapid development of naval technology in the years between the Spanish-American War and World War I left Captain Mahan standing on the deck of the old *Pocahontas*, boarding saber, Bible, and voice trumpet in hand. Nowhere was this fact more apparent than in his arguments against the development of the all-big-gun-single-caliber ship and the Navy's reliance on it as its major weapon of the future.

In evaluating Mahan's strident opposition to the all-big-gun battleship, it should be kept in mind that the only steam and steel ship he had commanded or served in during his forty-year career was the armored cruiser *Chicago*, commissioned in 1883. Pride of the New Navy in the late 1880s, virtually obsolete by the time Mahan took command of her in 1893, the 16-knot *Chicago* displaced 4,500 tons and mounted but four 8-inch, eight 6-inch, and two 5-inch guns. Compared with what the world's naval architects and shipbuilders splashed into the water in the late 1890s, the *Chicago* was a veritable toy. Small and toothless though she was, Mahan found her too large and complicated for his personal and professional comfort; so much so that he had felt a distinct sense of inadequacy, even fear, while in command of her. Yet by the time of the Spanish-American War, only three years after he left the *Chicago*, the newest ships in the Navy had become much larger and more sophisticated pieces of machinery than was his last command. The battleship *Iowa*, for example, a 17-knot vessel commissioned in 1897, displaced 11,400 tons and mounted four 12-inch, eight 8-inch, and six 4-inch guns; while the *Oregon* and the *Massachusetts*, 16-knot battleships commissioned in 1896, displaced 10,300 tons and mounted four 13-inch, eight 8-inch, and four 6-inch guns. These relatively small battleships, which blew the hapless Cervera out of the water at Santiago in July 1898, were far and away more powerful than any ships with which the Philosopher of Sea Power had had personal

ALFRED THAYER MAHAN

experience. Indeed, in the areas of performance and handling, and with reference to theoretical questions of tactical maneuverability in combat, Mahan was far more comfortable with the likes of the old *Wachusett*.

President Roosevelt's 1901–1909 naval building program, which in its first four years alone produced ten first-class, 18-knot battleships in the 16,000-ton range (at costs between $6,600,000 and $7,500,000 each), was marked by bitter debates in naval circles on how large battleships could sensibly be permitted to grow, with what number and calibre of guns they should be armed, and how best to solve the design dilemma of size (weight) versus speed. Most of the battleships authorized or launched in the years 1902–1905 mounted four 12-inch guns in their main batteries and eight 8-inch guns in their secondary batteries. By 1905 the *Michigan* and the *South Carolina*, both 16,000 tons, the first of America's all-big-gun ships, had been designed and were to mount eight 12-inch guns. They dispensed with secondary batteries of 8-inch guns, as did the 20,000-ton *Delaware* and *North Dakota*. On paper, these last, laid down in November 1907, were the largest battleships in the world when Congress authorized them in 1906. Either one could have taken on the entire U.S. battle fleet of 1898 in combat. Twice the size of the intrepid *Oregon* of Round-the-Horn-to-Santiago fame, capable of 21 knots, they mounted ten 12-inch turreted guns in a main battery and fourteen 5-inch guns for use against personnel and torpedo boats. Neither was equipped with a secondary battery.

But long before the *Delaware* and *North Dakota* were finally commissioned in 1910 and 1911, respectively, indeed well before the first of the American all-big-gun battleships, *Michigan* and *South Carolina*, joined the fleet early in 1910, the British had produced the awesome HMS *Dreadnought*. Commissioned in October 1906, she was of revolutionary design, and made every other operational battleship in the world instantly obsolete. Armed with a single massive battery of ten 12-inch guns, displacing 18,000 tons, heavily armored, capable of 21 knots, the oil-fueled, turbine-driven *Dreadnought* was to be the battleship of the future, although much larger vessels than she were at sea when World War I began in August 1914. Nevertheless, her appearance on the scene forced the navies of all the great powers, particularly those of Germany, the United States, and Japan, to scurry to catch up.

In 1908 Congress therefore authorized the *Florida* and *Utah* (22,000 tons, ten 12-inch guns), and in 1909 the *Wyoming* and *Arkansas* (26,000 tons, twelve 12-inch guns). By 1910 the U.S. Navy was being authorized to build 21-knot battleships in the 27,000-to-32,000-ton range (*New York*,

[520]

Nevada, Pennsylvania, California), all mounting ten to twelve 14-inch guns. Other navies had followed suit in the 1907–1914 period. So large was the *Pennsylvania* (608 feet) in comparison with the *Chicago* (342 feet) that the latter could almost have been set down on the foredeck of the former. "The worst thing in the naval outlook—to my mind—is the increasing size of ships," Mahan wrote Henderson in dismay in February 1909, "not so much on its own account, but because of the coincident rapid scrapping of smaller ships. This is throwing money away, and must end in stopping naval preparations. Personally, I stand aghast. If absence of preparation would stop war, all right; but it won't."

The rapid movement of the world's navies toward the all-big-gun battleship, a weapon conceived and pioneered in the General Board of the U.S. Navy in 1902 and 1903, was sharply stimulated by studies made at the War College and elsewhere of the naval implications of the Russo-Japanese War. That war said to most naval theorists the world over that fleet actions of the future would probably be fought at ranges of well over 10,000 yards: therefore, the larger and more numerous the guns on a fleet's battleships, the greater would be the likelihood of that fleet achieving decisive concentration of firepower against the ships of an enemy fleet at great distances—as had the Japanese at the Battle of Tsushima. Given this hypothesis, the inclusion of medium-range secondary batteries of 6-inch or 8-inch guns on the new battleships was viewed by the all-big-gun advocates as a waste of weight (and speed) that might better be employed on protective armor.[1]

Mahan opposed the all-big-gun movement in the Navy with all the persuasiveness at his command. He argued against it within the officer corps, at the War College, with President Roosevelt, and in public. As early as 1895 he had stated flatly that "no U.S. battleship ought to draw over 24 feet." By November 1898 he had decided that battleships of 10,000 to 12,000 tons were quite large enough and that to increase their sizes to accommodate the larger steam plants necessary for ever-greater speeds was a never-ending process. Since the battleship of 1898 was an almost-perfect weapon, as was demonstrated at Santiago, why persist, he inquired, "in the adding of ton to ton, like a man running up a bill?" Fourteen months later, in January and February 1900, when asked to comment on future construction needs in the service, he told Secretary Long that while it was technically possible to build battleships of 25,000 tons, he was opposed to the Construction Board's plan to lay down vessels even of 14,000 tons—for the simple reason that such vessels would be "larger than needed, and likely to result in too few ships." He preferred to have the Navy's annual warship tonnage allotment from Congress spread over a balanced fleet comprising numerous medium-sized, dual-battery vessels; and he was highly critical of the ignorant and self-interested chiefs of the bureaus in the Navy Department who thought and willed otherwise. This he made clear to the Secretary:

> I believe that I know that one Bureau wants increased size, to attain a speed which I consider extravagant; and that another wants size, in order to insure a coal endurance which I believe unnecessary; and that both, for these ends, are willing to increase size without commensurate gain in offensive power. Both I consider distinctly contrary to sound military principle. The Navy does not exist for ships, but ships for the Navy; and correct conclusions cannot be *secured* unless you [Long] call in those who think *first*, what does the Navy need for war, and, next, what kind of ships fulfill those needs? The technologist and Bureau man necessarily thinks first of his own speciality. If such a [study] Board as I suggested affirm in the main the decisions of the Construction Board—well; if not, a serious error may be timely averted, before the country be seized with a parsimonious fit, and we be left with a few monsters, instead of a number adequate to our varied requirements.

The construction issue, he assured Long further, was simply the "old question of the two-decker and three-decker, of Nelson and his times." He remained convinced, as he explained to readers of his *Lessons of the War With Spain* in 1899 and stated personally to Roosevelt in October 1902, that naval "war depends largely upon combination [tactical concentration], and facility of combination increases with numbers. Numbers, therefore, mean increase of offensive power, other things remaining equal." What was needed, then, was not larger and larger battleships, but an agreement among seagoing naval officers all over the world, not merely among politicians and landbound naval bureaucrats, on a "conception of a *standard* battleship." By this he meant something in modern dress on the order of the workhorse 74-gun sailing ship of the line which had "represented a professional consensus reached by long experience" during the Age of Sail. Could such a consensus again be achieved, capital-ship sizes might be limited, stabilized, and equalized throughout the world's navies by the combined pressure of knowledgeable officers. Naive though this suggestion seems in retrospect, he was deadly serious in advocating it.

All through the Russo-Japanese War Mahan clung to the position that the ideal navy would consist of a mixture of battleships, cruisers, and destroyer-torpedo vessels, each class being designed, built, and armed for different operational functions, just as the sailing navies of the eighteenth century had been comprised of balanced numbers of sloops (12-18 guns), frigates (36-44 guns), and various-sized ships of the line (74s, 92s, 100s) to cope with specific tasks in, near, or removed from the order of battle. The loss of the heavy Russian battleship *Petropavlovsk* in a Japanese mine-field in April 1904 merely reminded him of the "old warning not to put too many eggs in one basket, reinforcing the military suggestion to in-crease numbers by putting some limit on size." His idea of controlling the growing tonnages of battleships in the larger interest of maintaining mixed-sized, multi-functional fleets, he again broached to Roosevelt in December 1904, linking it to the president's invitation to the powers to attend a second Hague conference. "It has occurred to me," he told the president, "as an agreement tending to lessen the expense of armaments, that nations might agree on a limitation of the tonnage of single ships." To this size-limitation theme he frequently returned, as the world's navies raced to put heavier and heavier "monsters" in the water.

To support beyond question his arguments against the single-battery all-big-gun ship, Mahan in mid-1906 glanced back at the Russo-Japanese War for another look at the fleet actions, something he had not been able to do in the five superficial articles on the war he wrote for *Collier's Weekly* in 1904 and 1905. Additional materials, primary and secondary, had since become available, among them Admiral Togo's official battle reports and Russian Captain Nikolai L. Klado's *The Battle of the Sea of Japan*. His new findings were presented to the public in the May 1906 issue of *National Review* in a popular article titled "Some Reflections Upon the Far Eastern War," which also appeared in *Living Age* for July 14, 1906. A more technical version of his point of view, centering specifically on the Battle of Tsushima, was published in the June issue of the U.S. Naval Institute *Proceedings*. It was his *Proceedings* article, written for naval officers and other experts, that launched his verbal war with William S. Sims.

In that article, "Reflections, Historic and Other, Suggested by the Battle of the Sea of Japan," he reconstructed the Tsushima engagement in a manner that explained it in terms of "Nelsonic maxims," "parallelism of principles," and analogies from the Age of Sail. He summed up his earlier views on the point that a greater number of ships carrying mixed batteries had a tactical firepower advantage over fewer ships carrying all big guns; and he indicated that the elimination of secondary 8-inch bat-teries, and the weight thereby saved, had not produced a worthwhile speed-superiority advantage in the new all-big-gun ships. Speed, he maintained, had not been a major factor at the Battle of Tsushima. "Togo by good scouting and choice of position secured beyond reasonable hazard his strategic object of bringing the Russian Fleet to battle, irrespective of speeds." Total fleet gunpower, he insisted, had played the decisive role during the battle. He particularly lauded the performance of the rapid-firing secondary batteries (the 6-inch and 8-inch guns) of the Japanese vessels at Tsushima, especially their effectiveness against Russian ship funnels. Just as gunfire into the rigging of sailing ships had ripped their canvas and reduced their speed during the Age of Sail, so had the Japanese perforation of funnels with hits from secondary batteries reduced air draft on engine-room fires and thereby slowed the speed of the Russian battleships. Further, he attributed heavy Russian ship and personnel losses at Tsushima to hits made because of the rate and volume of fire that the Japanese had been able to sustain with their secondary guns. The end result, he maintained, was that the Russians "were blinded by the volume of shells from the Japanese guns. This result, being upon personnel, goes far to establish the actual superiority of the secondary battery in which the Russians had little more than half the number possessed by the enemy; while in the heavier calibres they had more than double." Throughout his account ran the theme that the all-big-gun, single-calibre vessel had not been the decisive tactical weapon at Tsushima, that such a ship was little more than a return to the tactically outmoded Civil War monitor, and that the international race for ship and gun size, and higher speeds, was a "growing and wanton evil" since each all-big-gun vessel coming off the ways would have "no immunity from the common lot of all battleships. In a fleet, today, her speed will be that of her slower sisters; more Dreadnoughts must be built to keep up with her; and upon them in turn, according to the prevalent law of progress, she will be a drag, for her successors will excel her."

Mahan was right. That was precisely what happened in the naval arms race of 1907–1914. The ships grew steadily bigger and faster and more speedily obsolete. The problem, however, was that one of his alternatives to this financially suicidal development—Hague Conference limitations on individual battleship size—was not politically or diplomatically realistic. Nor was his other alternative—mixed-calibre batteries mounted in mixed-tonnage ships comprising "balanced" fleets—entirely persuasive in tactical terms. Further, the outcome of the Battle of Tsushima did not well sustain his contentions against all-big-gun ships. He held, for example, that fleet battles would still be decided in years ahead by ships closing to relatively close ranges and slugging it out as in days of yore, broadside to broadside, the total weight of broadsides and the bravery of the gunners being the dominant factors in the outcome rather than the calibre of guns. "All this, which is irrefutable, goes to show that the fleet which has thus placed its dependence on long-range fire has with it assumed the moral tone and temperament associated with the indisposition to close." Boarders away!

So towering was Mahan's reputation with the American public on matters naval, so respected was he in Washington legislative circles for his work in naval history, and so wrong was he in this instance, that Roosevelt had no choice but to see that the *Proceedings* article was properly and speedily answered. He himself had a high personal regard for the Philosopher of Sea Power, a man who had positively influenced, instructed, and otherwise tutored him on naval questions since the late 1880s. But Mahan's articles on Tsushima received favorable press comment and were widely quoted by the small-navy economizers in Congress and out. Aside from this political danger to his naval-building program, the president in 1906 was already leaning toward the all-big-gun ship, if indeed he had not already arrived firmly at that position when he and Mahan discussed it, among other matters, at Oyster Bay on July 31.

In any event, for the important task of countering Mahan's hostility to all-big-gun vessels, Roosevelt chose Lieutenant Commander William S. Sims, sometime Director of Target Practice, ordnance expert, and leading naval advocate of the all-big-gun ship. On August 30, 1906, he asked Sims to prepare a rebuttal to Mahan's *Proceedings* article. Roosevelt told Sims that the officers who supported single-calibre, all-big-gun batteries would have to make "headway against the great Mahan; that it was up to us to convince the public that the great Mahan was wrong." This Sims accomplished in a paper titled "The Inherent Tactical Qualities of All-Big-Gun, One-Caliber Battleships," which he finished writing on September 24. It was a well-wrought document that "convinced TR." Incidentally, it also helped earn Sims promotion to commander and appointment as naval aide to the president in 1907. Most importantly, it rallied around him a group of vocal young and not-so-young officers who believed firmly in the all-big-gun doctrine and who considered Mahan to be an out-of-date fuddy-duddy hopelessly immersed in the Age of Sail. Roosevelt personally sent a draft of the Sims paper to Mahan, which Mahan received in Quogue on or about September 29, and asked him for whatever comment or rebuttal he felt it deserved. The paper was also circulated privately among certain naval officers, army officers, and legislators in late September and early October and was published in the *Proceedings* in December.

Sims's analysis of Mahan's interpretation of the Battle of Tsushima was devastating. Mahan, he charged, had simply not kept abreast of recent developments in naval guns and gunnery, as indeed Mahan had not.

"Much of the information upon which Captain Mahan has based his conclusions is in error to a greater or less degree. The errors in some are not important, but in others they appear to be in effect diametrically opposed to the truth." He pointed out the obvious fact that had the Russians, rather than the Japanese, had the speed advantage at Tsushima there would likely have been no battle at all—the czar's ships would successfully have fled the scene and safely reached Vladivostok. Speed, therefore, had been decisive, particularly during the engagement, because Togo "had no difficulty . . . in repeatedly choosing his own position (distance and bearing) with reference to the head of the enemy's fleet, and that the battle therefore resolved itself into a competition between the fire-control officers of the two fleets as to which could make the most hits, under conditions selected by the Japanese—these conditions being of course very unequal, since the Japanese were able frequently to concentrate the fire of many ships upon a few of the Russians."

But mostly Sims gave Mahan a lecture in modern naval ordnance with emphasis on recent developments in centralized and semi-automatic gun-laying and fire-control techniques, and on the fact that 12-inch guns had greater velocity and far greater accuracy than did 6-inch guns. His conclusion, based largely on his calculations of the number of hits registered by both fleets at Tsushima, was that "at modern battle ranges an all-big-gun fleet will actually deliver a greater *volume of hitting*—a greater number of hits, twice the weight of metal hitting, and twice the weight in bursting charges—than a fleet of mixed-battery ships of the same nominal power." True, said Sims, it would be nice, and more economical for all nations, were a future Hague conference to limit the size of battleships. "But in the absence of such an agreement, we must keep pace with the increased efficiency in battleships. . . . otherwise we cannot reasonably expect to win battles. We have, indeed, no choice in the matter if we are to remain a world power." Unhappily, he was right.

The all-big-gun controversy within the U.S. Navy thus came to a head early in October 1906. By that time Congress had authorized the *Delaware* and *North Dakota*, and the keels of the *South Carolina* and *Michigan* were scheduled to be laid a few weeks hence. On October 3, HMS *Dreadnought* went to sea on her builders' trials. So it was that the all-big-gun issue had been all but decided by the march of events when Mahan responded to Roosevelt's invitation to rebut Sims's perceptive paper. This he attempted to do in two letters to the president dated September 30 and October 22. Meanwhile, early in August, in response to statements in Mahan's article in the *Proceedings*, Sims had sent to Quogue certain "confidential papers," probably documents related to the fire-control machinery being planned for the Navy's new all-big-gun ships. This professional courtesy was extended prior to Roosevelt's charge to him on August 30 to answer the "great Mahan." Mahan returned Sims's papers on October 3 with the frosty observation that "I have been able to pay little attention to it, my time is so much occupied with my other work. I had, however, read some parts, and had noted some questions which suggested themselves to me; but those I have found answered in the main in the paper prepared by you for the President, at his request, in reply to my article in the Naval Institute [*Proceedings*], which he sent to me; so that I am deprived of that evidence of interest shown by questioning." Unaware that Mahan had meanwhile written for Roosevelt two rebuttals to "Inherent Tactical Qualities of All-Big-Gun, One-Caliber Battleships," Sims later crowed that Mahan "was too busy to reply to my arguments. . . . It is now known that he was wholly mistaken. The Dreadnought type became the universal standard."

Unfortunately for Mahan's reputation in the White House, his letters to Roosevelt of September 30 and October 22 on the all-big-gun controversy were neither impressive nor persuasive; nor did they add much to the arguments displayed in his *Proceedings* article. The September 30 letter was written hastily during his family's annual fall migration from Quogue back to the New York suburbs—in this instance, to Woodmere, Long Island, where the Mahans spent the winter of 1906–1907. In this missive he criticized anew the all-big-gun group's basic tactical and fiscal contention that "the concentration of force under one hand in one ship is superior to the same force in two or three ships; while, economically, the same tonnage in big ships is more economically built and maintained than in smaller." This argument he recognized as the most important one being hurled at "those who, with me, advocate gun-power rather than speed; numbers against size; and an 'intermediate' battery in part, instead of 'primary' alone." But he countered it with the observation that "with numbers, the power of combination [concentration] increases, and combined action is the particular force of fleets." Mahan therefore called upon Roosevelt to appoint a "competent, unbiased, tribunal" to study the tactical combinations available to mixed-battery fleets. He admitted that he was not "fully equipped in tactical resource," and confessed that he presently had "neither time nor inclination for exhaustive study of tactics; and [had] besides full preoccupation in other more congenial matters." He conceded, too, that he was out of touch with modern mechanical developments in the sighting and firing of naval guns. Actually, he thought that the old-fashioned, manual way of laying and firing a gun was better than any mechanical system because the "drill ground" precision and cooperation that the process required of gun crews bred good personal and supportive habits among the men, officers and sailors alike. Certainly, it had built character on the road to Trafalgar.

In his far more detailed report to Roosevelt on October 22, 1906, Mahan attacked the superficiality of Sims's research on the Battle of Tsushima as it related to the all-big-gun issue, arguing that it was based too heavily and uncritically on Lieutenant Richard D. White's article, "With the Baltic Fleet at Tsushima." This piece, a summary of an eyewitness account of the action, White had published in the *Scientific American* for August 11, 1906. Conversely, Mahan affirmed the comprehensiveness of his own research, charged Sims with misreading or misunderstanding key points in his account of the engagement in the Sea of Japan in the June *Proceedings*, called attention to evidences of sheer speculation in Sims's "Inherent Tactical Qualities of All-Big-Gun, One-Caliber Battleships," and held, in contradiction to his earlier exposition, that Russian inefficiency in the battle was so profound that the action was scarcely instructive of anything. "The Japanese in large measure had *target* practice of them," he told the president. He denied that he was opposed to larger battleships per se and agreed that in the race for size "we must follow." But he held rigidly to his major point that a more numerous, dual-battery fleet "such as I would favor, could, by dint of numbers, effect tactical [firepower] combinations quite balancing mere weight of metal in the individual ship; could in the end enforce closing, when volume of fire would tell—probably tell also before."

He then diagrammed for Roosevelt's edification a hypothetical battle situation that sought to demonstrate his contention. This was in response to a similar diagram Sims had included in his paper, one which undertook to show that the greater the speed, the heavier the tonnage, and the more numerous and larger the guns of the individual ships in a fleet, the greater the opportunity for that fleet to achieve firepower concentration on an enemy. Mahan attempted to convince the president that exactly the opposite was the case—that a slower though more numerous fleet, equal in aggregate tonnage to its enemy, equipped with mixed (12-inch primary and 8-inch secondary) batteries, could defeat an all-big-gun opponent by the use of sophisticated tactics and by the skillful concentration of the superior total firepower of the mixed-battery vessels. The following is the diagram, clarified somewhat by the present writer, that accompanied Mahan's letter to the president:

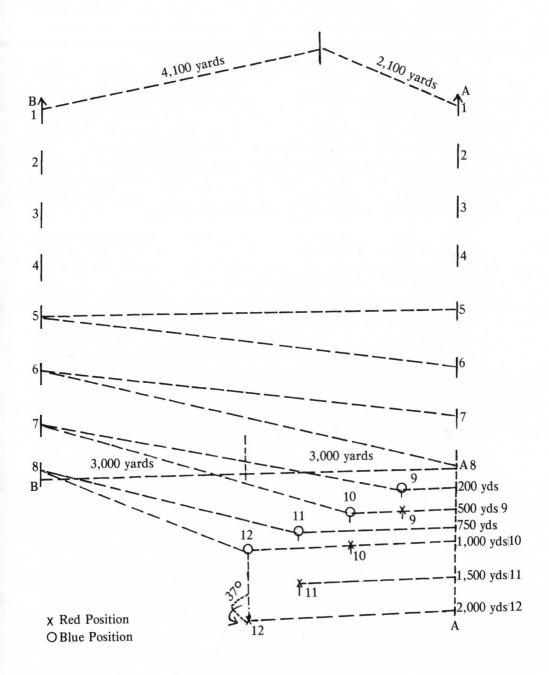

In drawing-board exercises such as these, as in contingency war planning, the assumptions built into the game are all-important. Mahan's were as follows: (1) Twelve mixed-battery ships (Fleet A) oppose eight all-big-gun ships (Fleet B); total fleet tonnages are equal; the total offensive firepower (weight of metal) of Fleet B is 75 per cent that of Fleet A; the speed of Fleet B is 3 knots faster than that of Fleet A. (2) The action is fought mainly in line-ahead formation, broadside to broadside, at 6,000 yards, or 3 nautical miles—"the range . . . now apparently favored." (3) Fleet B accepts this range since it cannot "escape from the dilemma by its superior speed, except by making its four rear ships retire. It may retire altogether; but then that is not fighting." (4) Fleet B, "to maintain position and range," that is, to fight at all, "must accommodate himself to the speed A chooses to observe." (5) Fleet B's ships, having but 3 knots greater speed, are not fast enough either to cap the head of Fleet A's column (cross the T) or to double Fleet A's column, thus bringing Fleet A's van into a concentrated cross fire. Fleet A's speed, given his interior maneuvering position, is sufficient to prevent this.

Combined with these assumptions was the fact that the maximum effective range of the 8-inch gun of 1906 was about 6,000 yards and that of the 12-inch gun was about 8,000 yards. These were the ranges at which it was then deemed that accurate fire-control solutions could be achieved in combat situations—as distinct from the far greater distances the shells were actually capable of carrying over the water at a maximum muzzle elevation of 45 degrees (18,000 yards for the 8-inch gun and 22,000 for the 12-inch).

In the "battle" that follows, ships A9, A10, A11, and A12 steer to port out of Fleet A's line-ahead formation and assume an echelon, or line-of-bearing, formation, represented in the diagram by the Red (x) positions. As Fleet A continues to steam ahead, these four vessels reach the Blue (•) positions. At these points their secondary batteries come well within range (3,600 to 5,450 yards) of B7 and B8. This maneuver allows them to concentrate their superior total firepower (both their 12-inch primary-battery guns and their secondary 8-inch guns) on B7 and B8. Meanwhile, A7 and A8 concentrate their combined fire on B6, and A5 and A6 do the same on B5. Result: Victory for Fleet A as Fleet B loses its four rear all-big-gun ships.

It was a classical massing of firepower on an enemy rear of the sort dreamed of by every Royal Navy fleet commander from Richard Howe to Horatio Nelson, but seldom, if ever, realized in actual combat. Why a fleet of all-big-gun ships mounting from eight to ten 12-inch guns would accommodate the 8-inch guns of a mixed-battery enemy fleet by fighting it at 6,000 yards (only 3,600 to 5,450 yards at its rear), rather than at

8,000-plus yards, was a question Mahan avoided. Why a faster all-big-gun fleet would not choose to break off action and open to a more advantageous range if it found itself in such an unfavorable firepower situation he did not realistically consider. Nor did he focus upon the counterstroke option open to Fleet B: namely, to effect at Fleet A's van what A was attempting to accomplish at B's rear—that is, close B1, B2, B3, and B4 to starboard in an echelon, or line-of-bearing, formation, in such a way as to concentrate the fire of B1 and B2 on A1, and that of B3 and B4 on A2.

Mahan's hypothetical firepower concentration against the all-big-gun ships *did* work mathematically as a plotting-board exercise, if his assumptions were conceded, but, to make it work in reality, Fleet B would have to fight the battle from beginning to end in the Age of Sail formation that was the line-ahead. He would also have to permit Fleet A, without challenge, to achieve firepower concentration on his rear by the tactical device of combining his line-ahead formation with an echelon deployment.

In sum, Mahan's case hung substantially on the supposition that the commanding officer of the all-big-gun fleet was a slow-thinking, albeit heroic, fellow, far less perceptive or energetic than Rozhdestvenski had been at Tsushima. Specifically, the commander of Fleet B was expected to steam blithely along in line-ahead formation, with scarcely a backward glance, 6,000 yards away from the enemy, his ships neatly positioned (targeted) equidistant within his line, while the commander of Fleet A savagely chewed up his rear. It was an interesting expectation, as practically unrealistic as it was theoretically plausible.

Indeed, his technological contentions on this subject were persuasive only if all the world's navies simultaneously abandoned their costly programs for building all-big-gun ships and agreed instead to build and fight, preferably in line-ahead formation, cheaper mixed-battery vessels of roughly the same size, speed, and firepower. Whether HMS *Dreadnought* was a cost-effective weapon or not (Mahan thought she was not), she was capable in 1907 of sinking on sight, at 8,000 to 10,000 yards, any mixed-battery ship she chanced to meet—such as the USS *Connecticut* armed with but four 12-inch guns and a secondary battery of eight 8-inch and twelve 7-inch guns. It was probably this realization among others, that caused Mahan to suggest that the Second Hague Conference should limit the size of battleships. Further, it gave rise to his vain hope, earlier mentioned, that the world's naval officers might somehow agree among themselves on a "standard" medium-sized battleship, a vessel that would serve the same function as had the 74-gun two-decker that had dominated the final decades of the Age of Sail. It was also the dilemma of ship size and spiraling construction costs that persuaded Mahan to diagram hypothetical battle situations designed to prove the unprovable, because he feared that the cost factor alone would encourage penny-pinching legislators on Capitol Hill to permit America to fall far behind the world's armaments race.

Whatever the economics of the all-big-gun ship, there is no evidence that the president was impressed with Mahan's tactical arguments, if indeed he read or understood them at all. A smattering of support from British magazines "sustaining the opinion advanced by me concerning the 8 in. and 6 in. guns at Tsushima," which Mahan personally brought to his attention, failed to move the commander-in-chief. Instead, Roosevelt went over to Sims and the all-big-gun group completely. The building of dreadnoughts in the U.S. Navy continued without pause, as it did in all the great-power navies of the world. Mahan sadly wrote William H. Henderson in January 1907:

> I am glad you liked my [June 1906] paper. You can appreciate under what sense of difficulty a man writes on that subject, unless he is one of the lucky ones who can only see one side. I am apt to be painfully conscious of the possible retorts of an opponent, and as I am not fond of argument I dislike papers that may involve it, as this did; but now that our President has come out definitely in favor of the *Dreadnought* type, and I believe that the preponderant opinion of our service goes along, I intend to withdraw from the discussion, and leave facts and experience to work out the conclusions. Somewhere, the need for numbers and the increasing cost will enforce a halt on size, if no other way [than] by bankrupting some of the competitors.

Ego wounded, Mahan withdrew for the time from public participation in the all-big-gun debate. But not before snubbing the triumphant Sims. When Sims sent him a polished version of his "Inherent Tactical Qualities," the revision that was published in the December 1906 issue of the *Proceedings*, Mahan told him that he would not be able to revert to the matter for a long time.[2]

On the other hand, friends of Sims and other proponents of all-big-gun ships were delighted by Mahan's crushing defeat on the issue. Caspar F. Goodrich, Mahan's ally in earlier battles for the War College, broke with him, noting that "I used to think with Mahan, but a couple of years ago, I changed my mind. If I remember arightly it was less through technical considerations than because I realized that nothing mechanical will stay put." Charles S. Sperry thought it "unfortunate that Captain Mahan should have fallen into the practice of making loose generalizations from insufficient or obsolete data—or both." But it was Bradley A. Fiske, who personally liked Mahan and admired his work in naval history, who put his finger on the 66-year-old Mahan's dilemma as a nineteenth-century expert on a twentieth-century Navy. He wrote to Sims:

> You see you show that Mahan fell down because he had not studied the conditions at the time, and that he applied his general principles to conditions that did not exist, and so arrived at conclusions absolutely false. I think Mahan must feel very much mortified at being dethroned from his position as the brains of the Navy; but his case is merely an illustration of the impossibility of being wise on any subject, unless you keep in practical touch with it.

Not even the faithful Luce supported Mahan during his all-big-gun aberration; and Lieutenant Ridley McLean went so far as to thank Sims for making a "back number out of Mahan" because "he's dangerous."

Mahan was not "dangerous," nor had he been "dethroned" as the Navy's leading intellectual, at least not in the public estimation. He had, however, slipped a couple of rungs on the professional Navy's caste ladder, just as he slipped still another rung because of the superficiality of his articles on the cruise of the Great White Fleet.

After 1905, then, his continuing problem, insofar as his service reputation was concerned, was his willingness (often for the sake of the money offered) to rush into print armed only with a few "general principles" and a misplaced faith that these maxims were applicable to almost any operational situation in a Navy he no longer really understood. This did not sit well with officers like Sims, Fiske, Goodrich, and Sperry. Privately, however, Mahan was quick to acknowledge, as he did in March 1908 to Admiral George B. Balch, his skipper in the *Pocahontas*, long retired, that he had had "nothing to do with the *new* Navy, the Navy of today. I did witness the transition from sail to steam; but my last command, though so late as 1895 (the *Chicago*) is already *old* Navy." He admitted, too, in moments of candor, that he had little knowledge of contemporary naval technology, and that he was unable to keep abreast of modern naval developments. "I am too old and too busy to keep up," he confessed to Clark in January 1907, "and have about made up my mind to leave it all to younger men." Operational details were really "questions for men in the prime of life; and with full knowledge abreast of modern conditions."[3]

Perhaps it was self-evaluations like these that persuaded Mahan to mute his continuing opposition to the all-big-gun ship after his defeat on the issue by Sims in 1906. For a time he held himself "aloof from professional discussion" on the difficult question and "accepted under silent protest what seemed the general verdict." His silence on this point did not, however, indicate a reversal of his long-held view that Congress should not be entrusted with the responsibility for determining technical questions of ordnance and ship design, as Senator Eugene Hale had suggested it should in May 1904; nor did Mahan think that the inefficient and civilian-dominated bureaus within the Navy Department were places where decisions on such complex matters as the all-big-gun ship should be made. The only place for such decisions, he felt, was in the hands of a Navy General Staff —if only Congress would have the good sense to reorganize the administration of the Navy to provide for such a body.

These concerns aside, the fact was that a chastened Mahan changed his views on the all-big-gun question not one whit. In November 1910 he broke his self-imposed silence on the issue when he presented a paper to the Society of Naval Architects and Marine Engineers in New York. In it he restated his arguments for mixed-battery battleships, challenged anew Sims's case for the all-big-gun vessel, and noted that neither the Japanese nor the German navy had entirely abandoned the use of secondary 8-inch batteries. Meanwhile, dreadnoughts had grown larger and larger. "Already Chesapeake Bay is too shoal for the increased draughts of battleships," he noted.

These arguments he expanded a few months later in an article titled "The Battleship of All-Big-Guns," which the widely circulated monthly magazine *World's Work* carried in its January 1911 issue. In this essay he maintained that the introduction of the foolish and expensive all-big-gun vessel had enabled the kaiser at last to dream of naval parity with Britain. Indeed, Germany had built dreadnoughts so rapidly since 1907 that she had passed the United States in total naval tonnage and had, in 1911, after the Royal Navy, the world's second largest operational navy. The U.S. Navy had slipped to third, said Mahan, "because the increased reluctance of Congress to build coincided with the advent of that type [all-big-gun]." Thanks, then, to the triumph of the all-big-gun idea, one that, ironically, had been pioneered in the U.S. Navy, America had lost ground in the naval arms race because "Britain's construction of the *Dreadnought* enabled Germany, which was hopelessly behind in numbers of smaller battleships, to start by prompt action nearly even in the class of vessel which by preponderant contemporary naval opinion is alone fit to lie in the first line of battle."

This sour observation on the international political implications of all-big-gun ships was balanced in part by Mahan's belated awareness that there had indeed been much improvement in the accuracy of naval gunfire, thanks to the new fire-control systems built into such vessels. For this development he lauded the constructive role played by his old enemy W. S. Sims. His partial volte face on Sims in 1911 may have been designed to improve his personal relations with the commander and his followers; or it may have been one aspect of his campaign to alert the American people to the growing naval menace of the German Empire, a threat he felt to be so immediate and so obvious that Congress, he held, would have to authorize annually four new battleships, all-big-gun if necessary, barely to meet it. Whatever his motives in the matter, his belated tribute to Sims did not mean that he had come suddenly to embrace the new naval ordnance. He seldom changed long-held opinions merely on the basis of new factual evidence. Historical "principles," after all, were eternal. Thus when World War I broke out in August 1914, he told a newspaper reporter that "the mooted question of the big guns will also be tested. For my own part, I have always believed that the volume of fire was the determining fact. The number of hits, and not single shots, is the most important element, I believe. However, all those things we shall soon know." Mahan never knew. He died four months later.

Nevertheless, the Battle of Jutland (May 31, 1916), fought mainly by all-big-gun ships at ranges of from 10,000 to 16,000 yards, and at speeds of 20 knots and more, did not well sustain his point of view. Big guns seem to have inflicted as many personnel casualties as did those mounted in secondary batteries; and most of the ships sunk or badly damaged at Jutland were the smaller, more lightly armored, and less-well-armed ones. Only two of the forty-four all-big-gun battleships in the 26,000-ton class that were engaged were sunk; and only four of the twenty-nine 14,000-ton armored cruisers went down. The light cruisers and the destroyers took the worst beatings by far. Nineteen of them went to the bottom of the North Sea. While, strategically, Jutland was a British victory, tactically it was a standoff. It demonstrated to many naval theorists that the slower the ship, the lighter her armor, and the smaller her guns, the less likely she was to survive fleet combat operations in the era of the dreadnought. Further, the existence or nonexistence of mixed batteries on capital ships seemed to confer neither tactical advantage nor tactical disadvantage at Jutland. In 1906 Sims had argued that the effectiveness of all-big-gun marksmanship at long ranges would be the decisive factor in fleet actions of the future. It certainly was so at Jutland, where an inferior German fleet clearly outshot the Royal Navy, sinking 111,980 tons of the king's ships while losing but 62,233 tons of the kaiser's.[4]

If Mahan had difficulty adjusting to the wave of the future that was the all-big-gun-single-calibre battleship, he experienced similar difficulties when the submarine arrived on the scene. This strange and miraculous craft, to which the Germans turned for their salvation at sea after the containment of their surface fleet at Jutland, had no Age of Sail counterpart. There were, therefore, no historical principles with which Mahan could connect the submarine when he first became aware of its existence during the Russo-Japanese War. Nevertheless, he quoted Napoleon and Nelson to the point that one should never fear the unknown in warfare, and in April 1907 he confidently analyzed the new weapon for the edification of the readers of *Collier's Weekly*, comforting them in the thought that "horizontal shell-fire in its youth was considered as dire a development as the submarine now is."

It was a poor comparison. Indeed, the submarine was well advanced technologically by the time Mahan took note of it. The French had commissioned an experimental boat into their navy as early as 1888. Inventors in the United States and in Europe had experimented with submarine designs throughout the 1890s. In 1900 the first practical American boat, the 74-ton, 54-foot *Holland*, was taken into the U.S. Navy. Carrying a crew of six, armed with a single torpedo tube, powered by gasoline on the surface and electric batteries when submerged, she had a surface cruising range of 1,500 miles (50 miles submerged) and was capable of seven knots, either surfaced or submerged. She could dive to twenty-eight feet in eight seconds and was equipped with double-hull construction, ballast tanks, hydroplanes, periscope, and conning tower. Tiny though she was, the *Holland* was the prototype of the modern submarine in almost every respect. By 1907 the Navy boasted eleven operational submarines, the newest, the *Viper*, being nearly twice the size of the *Holland*. The *Narwhal* and *Seal*, laid down in 1908 and 1909, were 337 tons and 516 tons, respectively, had four to six torpedo tubes, and carried fifteen to twenty-four men. Fascinated by this new weapon, the effervescent Theodore Roosevelt was the first American president to dive in a submarine. By 1914 all the world's major navies boasted 500- to 800-ton boats equipped with diesel engines and gyrocompasses and capable of making long voyages.

Mahan saw that the submarine, armed with invisibility, had the "power to strike a blow deadly as the rattlesnake or cobra and [with] as little warning." But he chose to compare its offensive capability and flexibility with those of a battleship or cruiser, to the clear disadvantage of the submersible. Indeed, he regarded the craft as mainly a defensive weapon, most useful against stationary targets, and not nearly so dangerous to moving targets as was the submerged mine. Quoting Lord Nelson on the strategic value of close-in blockades, Mahan thought the "highest function" of the submarine in an offensive capacity might be to seal closed an enemy port.

He failed to see that the boats might have some use as raiders against merchantmen at sea. This oversight, shared by virtually all naval observers until 1914, could in Mahan's case be traced in part to his long-standing disinterest in and distaste for single-ship commerce-raiding operations in wartime. He had lived for many years with a vision of tactically concentrated surface fleets establishing "command of the sea" by virtue of success in great battles—and in that manner ultimately bringing the commerce of an enemy to ruin. Obviously, submarines were too slow and short of range to operate with such fleets. "For long passages they will delay the fleet they accompany, and may in other ways prove embarrassing, as is the surface boat of the same size. Indeed, except in battle, they will be surface boats." In a world in which the fleet battleship was queen, whether all-big-gun or not, submarines were little more than interesting toys. "In short," Mahan told his *Collier's* readers, "I doubt the submarine finding its prey with sufficient certainty or frequency to constitute a *decisive* danger." And since he saw the logical prey of the submarine as the enemy battleship or cruiser, he was certain that in the job of delivering torpedoes to moving targets the boats would be no improvement over surface destroyer-torpedo vessels.

In fine, submarines played virtually no role in Mahan's thinking on strategy or tactics as World War I approached. In a paper he prepared in September 1910 for Secretary of the Navy George von L. Meyer and the General Board on Navy yards and stations, he paid small attention to their existence or to their special logistical needs. Commenting in February 1911 on the Naval War College's contingency plan for naval war with Japan, he recommended that the submarines and surface torpedo-boat destroyers be kept at San Francisco and Puget Sound, while the battle fleet sailed westward against the foe; and in April 1911, when he reported to Meyer on fleet fuel supply, he lumped submarines with torpedo boats and coast-defense vessels as ships that should not be included in naval fuel-supply planning. Their logistical support could best be handled by private contractors. Clearly, then, Mahan was a mixed-battery-battleship man, and he remained one until his death in December 1914. The submarine was almost as invisible in his prose and thought as it was under the sea.

For this reason, he announced confidently on August 3, 1914, that the Royal Navy's battle fleet had little to fear in the North Sea from German submarines since the kaiser's U-boats had a submerged cruising range of but 200 miles. Good scouting was all that was needed to render them ineffective. He agreed, however, that the "question of the use of the increased efficiency of the submarine is assuredly one of the most important to be tested in actual warfare." Nevertheless, he did not share the views of men like Admiral Sir Percy Scott, Britain's premier naval ordnance expert, who emphasized "the surpassing power of the submarine to the complete effacement of the battleship." Even when German submarines, a few weeks later, neatly sank the British armored cruisers *Cressy*, *Hague*, and *Aboukir*, and the Russian cruiser *Pallada*, Mahan hastened to assure his English correspondents that

> the sinking of your three cruisers did not greatly impress me from the military standpoint. I have always held that torpedo protection is a matter of scouting—watchfulness—and lapses there will occur. The result will show if I am greatly wrong. Your fleet holds the balance and I trust will be wide awake. . . . I have been surprised myself that such attempts have not been more frequent, and doubtless, if a full return of all submarine prowlings were obtainable, we should find many failures against each success. I have not shared Sir Percy Scott's dismal forebodings, believing that the question of the submarine would reduce itself to one of scouting and look-out; yet I have not ventured so positive an adverse opinion as sometimes I see attributed to me.[5]

Mahan's losing effort in the all-big-gun war within the Navy and his tardiness in adjusting to the tactical possibilities of new weapons, as well as to rapid improvements in old ones, did not destroy Roosevelt's confidence in him as a naval adviser. The stature he lost within the officer corps during the first decade of the twentieth century as the result of his backward-looking views on naval architecture and ordnance was recovered in part by his constructive role as one of the president's men in the continuing struggle for a fundamental administrative reorganization of the Navy that would lead to the creation of a naval General Staff headed by a chief of naval operations.

The General Staff concept was an idea whose time had come in the U.S. Navy. It had already been adopted in the British, German, and Japanese navies in greater or lesser degree. But to many Americans the notion smacked of German authoritarianism and militarism. It also raised searching questions about the ability of a democratic society to control so highly structured, powerful, and centralized a military organization. Fears that the administrative role of the civilian Secretary of the Navy would be eclipsed by a Chief of the General Staff were genuine, as were concerns about the possible emergence of a military dictator in time of war. Civilian America did not want a Man on Quarterdeck. The Rough Rider in the White House came too close to that image to suit many nervous Americans, what with his Big Stick diplomacy, his armed interventions in the

Caribbean, and his Great White Fleet theatrics. The next step on that escalator was a Bismarck—or so it was feared by some.

Roosevelt, it scarcely need be said, had strongly favored a General Staff organization for the Army and for the Navy since the beginning of his administration. Actually, he had embraced the idea, as it applied to the Navy, long before that. So too had Mahan, whose on-the-scene analysis of the Spanish-American War from an administrative standpoint had convinced him that operational decisions in the Navy in 1898 had been determined in a manner that was less than precise, efficient, and orderly. Only the hopeless inefficiency of a weak enemy on that occasion had saved the day. Mahan, it will also be recalled, had first attracted attention within the Navy in 1875 when he had joined with other reformers to attack the Navy Department's bureau system of administration. Hidebound, unimaginative, inefficient, overlapping in function, subject to party political manipulation, even to political corruption, the bureau system, he felt, was no way to run a navy. This observation, courageous as it was correct, had had little result other than to earn Commander Mahan temporary exile to the waiting-orders list at quarter-pay. The recommendation he made in 1876 that a high-level, policy-making, joint military-civilian "Board of Admiralty" replace the bureaus fell on deaf minds, as did his suggestion to Long in May 1898 that the Naval War Board be reorganized along General Staff lines.

Mahan had hope, however, that, under the dynamic leadership of President Roosevelt, the nation was at long last about to see the logic of reorganizing, centralizing, and modernizing the administration of the Navy in a General Staff manner. To this end, in 1908 he again joined the service reformers—"insurgents" they were called—to bring about the necessary changes in naval administration. Led by William S. Sims, Bradley A. Fiske, Cameron McR. Winslow, and others, officers with whom Mahan had fought bitterly on the all-big-gun issue, the insurgents set out to make their case against the bureaus. Singling out the particularly reactionary and vulnerable Bureau of Construction and Repair as a prime target, they attacked the architectural, structural, and engineering shortcomings of the new all-big-gun ships, especially the *North Dakota*. At the "Battleship Conference" in Newport, called by Roosevelt in July 1908 to air the whole question of battleship design and construction, the insurgents made a strong case. There were indeed serious structural defects in the *North Dakota*, then building, and in the designs of the authorized all-big-gun *Delaware*, *Florida*, and *Utah*. Almost everyone with eyes and ears open at the Newport conference became convinced of that. But the Bureau of

Construction and Repair, with faultless bureaucratic footwork, managed to paper over the findings of the conference. With only minor modifications in design, the construction of the controversial battleships went forward, much to the distress of the insurgents and to the disadvantage of the taxpayers.

Nevertheless, in the public prints, in congressional hearings, and at the War College, the insurgents continued to hammer away at the thought that the fate of the New New Navy was, from a design standpoint, in the hands of civilian and military incompetents in the Bureau of Construction and Repair. The fact that they were dead right enormously strengthened their cause within the Navy; but the fact that the alternative they offered to bureau control was a General Staff arrangement seriously weakened their influence in Congress and among the civilian population.

Although a non-reformer on most other issues in the service in 1908, the 68-year-old Mahan had no difficulty joining the insurgents. His failure to convert Secretary Long to a General Staff administrative structure in May 1898 and his contempt for the effectiveness of the Naval War Board on which he had served during the war with Spain, were reasons enough for him to enlist in their crusade. Long's creation of the General Board of the Navy in 1900 had not satisfied him. An officer-advisory body to the civilian Secretary, the General Board was, in most respects, a pallid child of the Naval War Board of 1898. Its duties were to "advise the Secretary of the Navy on war plans, bases, and naval policy and to coordinate the work of the War College and the Office of Naval Intelligence." The new board otherwise had no legal or statutory existence; nor had it the authority to implement any of its recommendations approved by the Secretary. It was hoped in 1900 that the board might gradually come to exercise some coordinative control over the eight independent and squabbling bureaus, but it had signally failed to achieve that goal. They remained separately responsible to the civilian Secretary. Had it not been for the popularity, persuasiveness, and skill of Admiral George Dewey, president of the General Board from 1900 to 1917, the group would have accomplished virtually nothing.

As it was, however, the board came to play an important role in theoretical naval planning for war, thanks to its control over the War College and the Office of Naval Intelligence. It was also effective in advancing the cause of Roosevelt's all-big-gun battleship building program with legislators on Capitol Hill. Still, it had no control whatever over ship design. That vital function remained in the hands of the Bureau of Construction and Repair. Nevertheless, the General Board was a step toward a General

Staff. It was a small step, to be sure—small in the sense that the president of the board was not expected to serve as the supreme operational commander of the battle fleet in wartime. Nor was any officer in the Navy vested with control over operational planning or made professionally responsible for victory or defeat. Power and responsibility were diffused.

That diffusion was the crux of the argument for a Naval General Staff, as was the demonstrable lack of continuity in planning for possible war. To Mahan's way of thinking, the board and the bureaus, all going their separate ways, were unable to effect the administrative concentration necessary for prudent contingency planning or to ensure speedy reaction to danger in time of national crisis. Therefore, when Roosevelt sponsored his controversial Navy General Staff bill in 1903, Mahan remarked:

> As regards the [bill], which I hope will pass in principle; it appears to me of the utmost importance that the designing of ships—their classes, numbers, and qualities—should be brought into direct relation with the naval policy and strategy of the country. This can never—in my judgment—be the case while these decisions are left to Bureau Chiefs. The General Staff, having digested what will need to be done in time of war, can best and can alone pronounce the relative importance of the several qualities, subject to the revision of the President and Secretary. This or that man's views may be more or less valuable; but an organized body can alone impart accuracy, clearness, and fixity, lasting from administration to administration.

These anti-bureau and pro-General Staff views Mahan also presented to the Anglo-American reading public in mid-1903 without noticeable effect. Although, in February 1904, the Army got legislative authorization to establish a General Staff structure, Roosevelt's attempt to secure the same thing for the Navy failed. The bureau chiefs thus remained supreme. Their preeminent position was not shaken when, in mid-1906, Admiral Dewey and Secretary of the Navy Charles J. Bonaparte asked Mahan to prepare for the General Board a short history of the Naval War Board of 1898. In his account of the dubious labors of that group, Mahan called attention to administrative and planning confusion within the Navy during the Spanish-American conflict, pointed critically to the fact that the bureaus had often worked at cross-purposes, and recommended the adoption of a General Staff structure. The Naval War Board of 1898, he concluded, operated virtually in a vacuum:

> As a body, it had had no previous connection with the preparations of the Government, nor influence upon them; and the association with

them of the individual members had been slight. The Board therefore approached the questions submitted to it without a formulated policy —other than such knowledge as its members possessed of the leading principles of war—and without previous mature consideration of the effect of this or that disposition on the whole theater of war, of the relations of the parts to the whole. Among conflicting opinions of capable men—and there were conflicts—and divers considerations of policy, the Board had only the general leading principles . . . to guide it; it began with no digested appreciation of those special conditions, in the two countries, which might modify the application of principles. . . . Fortunately, the war was short and simple.[6]

Mahan was therefore well on his way to insurgency on the question of a General Staff when the agitation for it peaked in 1908 and 1909. When Secretary of the Navy Truman H. Newberry, the sixth secretary in the seven years of the Roosevelt administration (T.R. turned secretaries over like pancakes), announced in December 1908 his intention to reorganize the Navy on the basis of modern business methods and to create a General Staff to administer the new arrangement, Mahan was in solid support. He pointed out to Roosevelt that almost every civilian Secretary of the Navy came to his duties "without military conceptions." Since neither they nor most of the civilian presidents who appointed them were equipped by experience to deal with highly technical military-naval questions or with the necessarily close relationship that should exist between the formulation of diplomatic and military policy, they were usually at the mercy of the professional officers who headed the bureaus. Hence the need for a General Staff, headed by a chief of staff, a man whose advice to the Secretary and to the White House on matters naval would be "single, not corporate." Such a person should understand clearly that "diplomatic conditions affect military action, and military considerations diplomatic measures. . . . No man is fit for Chief of Staff who cannot be intrusted with knowledge of a diplomatic situation."

At no time in his advocacy of a General Staff did Mahan question or attack the Constitutional concept of civilian control of the military. He would, he assured the president, "neither advocate nor countenance any measure tending to weaken the ultimate power of the Secretary. He should be able to overrule and upset, if necessary, every one beneath him, from Chief of Staff down." What Mahan and the other insurgents wanted in 1908 and 1909 was to centralize the Navy's advisory function on matters having to do with strategic planning, ship construction, and the development of new ordnance systems; and, incidentally, to bring administrative order out of chaos by subordinating the work of the bureaus to the General Staff. Specifically, Mahan felt that the proposed General Staff should study, consider, and advise the president and the secretary of the Navy with one voice, that of the chief of staff, on such controversial matters as the immunity of private property at sea during war and the all-big-gun-single-calibre battleship.

Mahan's leading intellectual role in the movement for a General Staff, together with the confidence Roosevelt had in him on that subject, resulted in the president appointing him to membership on the Moody Commission (sometimes called the Moody-Mahan Commission) in January 1909. The commission, which met hastily in Washington during February, was composed of former secretaries of the Navy William H. Moody and Paul Morton, former Republican Congressman Alston G. Dayton, of West Virginia, who had served on the House Naval Affairs Committee, and retired Rear Admirals Alfred T. Mahan, Stephen B. Luce, William M. Folger, Robley D. Evans, and William S. Cowles. This distinguished group, all staunch Roosevelt supporters, was given the broad charge (a hunting license, really) to study the structure, efficiency, and functions of the existing bureaus, the encroachment of civilian control in the bureaus, and the question of responsibility within the Navy Department for the planning, preparation, and conduct of naval war.

The president's known position on these matters was father to the commission's final report. What the Moody-Mahan group proposed in the recommendation it made to the White House in late February was a divisional structure for the Navy Department. Its basic idea was that the work of the existing bureaus and other department agencies should be coordinated by the chiefs of five divisions. These five men, one of them the civilian assistant secretary, the other four flag officers, would report directly to the secretary. The most important of these divisions, naval operations, would be headed by a chief of naval operations who would be the secretary's principal military adviser and would serve ex officio as the head of both the General Board and the Board of Construction. While the chief of naval operations would not have any other assigned administrative duties, his staff (a general staff) in the proposed Division of Naval Operations would be responsible for contingency war planning, the formulation of general naval policy, and the administration of the War College and the Office of Naval Intelligence.

So logical were the Moody Commission's recommendations that they had small chance of adoption in the 60th Congress, even had there been sufficient opportunity for that body to debate them. Roosevelt sent them up to the Hill during his very last week in office. There they died in the changing of the Republican guard, as the Rough Rider charged out of office on March 4, 1909, and William Howard Taft lumbered in.

Mahan approached his duties on the Moody Commission with some testiness. He disliked leaving home for the cheerless hotel rooms of Washington. He was tired, and was still feeling the effects of his prostatectomy. He had little confidence that the job could be done before Roosevelt left office; and he was distressed that the commission had been born in the spasm that was one of the president's "sudden characteristic resolutions." Further, he was then busy with the writing of two books, *The Harvest Within*, his spiritual autobiography, and *Naval Strategy*, his last will and testament to the operational Navy. He was in no mood to waste time in Washington in a lot of "desultory talk, often vague and purposeless." Nevertheless, he collected from the New York Public Library some information on the reorganization the Royal Navy had undergone in 1904 and set down for Chairman Moody's benefit, in a letter dated February 1, his long-held views on the proposed reorganization of the U.S. Navy so as "to expedite the business of the meeting" once the committee met.

He informed Moody that only a General Staff could properly coordinate the administration, war-planning, ordnance, and construction of the Navy. He warned Moody, however, that he was approaching the problem as a theorist and a principles man, not as a technician. As he explained his theoretical proclivities: "My consideration of Naval Administration hitherto has been historical and critical only, ascertaining facts and thence deducing principles. But as I have never expected to be called upon for constructive work, which is the task of the Commission, I never undertook such for my own amusement or instruction." Still, it was his opinion that, in order to save valuable time, the members of the commission should be instructed to do most of their homework on the issues before they reached Washington. All that would then be needed, he said, would be a statement on naval organization, a quickly written document "in a form that will carry weight with the public," one that either Roosevelt or Taft could use to head off "an opposition which may be conservative . . . if not actually reactionary." Speed Mahan got. Not only did he personally draft most of the commission's report, he performed the task so expeditiously and accepted suggested modifications to it so gracefully that he spent only four days and three nights in Washington in February 1909 on Moody Commission business. The rest of his work was done by mail, over the telephone, and in Paul Morton's office in New York. In this instance speed produced quality, even though the departing Congress paid scant attention to the finished product.

Nor did the Department of the Treasury especially appreciate Mahan's labors for his president and his country. His claim for reimbursement of lodging and travel expenses from Lawrence, Long Island, to New York City and to Washington, in the amount of $82.60, was disallowed. The Treasury apparently expected the aging Philosopher of Sea Power to hitch rides on freight trains and sleep on park benches while he served on the Moody Commission. The contentious Rear Admiral A. T. Mahan—he had been promoted to flag rank on the Retired List on December 20, 1906—thought otherwise. He finally hired a lawyer, Spencer Gordon, and took his case to the Court of Claims in Washington. It was both the principle and the principal of the thing.[7]

Partially redeemed in the eyes of the all-big-gun officers of the New New Navy by his effective service on the Moody Commission, in the years ahead Mahan continued to work vigorously for the concept of a General Staff. He also worked less visibly for a time against the all-big-gun idea, labored loyally for the establishment of a Council of National Defense, and, when called upon, wrote thoughtfully on various research projects of the General Board. Among these last were papers on overseas navy yards and bases, on fuel distribution and supply (particularly in the Pacific), and on a theoretical contingency plan for naval war with Japan. He had great respect for George von L. Meyer, Taft's exceptionally able Secretary of the Navy, and he responded willingly to Meyer's requests for evaluations of some of the professional issues with which the board was wrestling. But from 1909 to 1912 he worked most consistently and diligently for the Naval War College, the administration of which had become a responsibility of the General Board after the Spanish-American War. In March 1908 he wrote a short history of the early years of the institution for Meyer and, in 1909, 1910, and 1911, he lectured at the college on various aspects of naval strategy from Nelson to Togo.[8]

His most important project for the War College in those years was the writing of *Naval Strategy*, an updated and partly revised version of his lectures at the college since 1887. Published by Little, Brown and Company in November 1911, and priced at $3.50, the book emphasized once more the author's faith in the existence of general "principles of war." Frequent genuflections were again made to the proposition that the "Art of War," which "acknowledges principles and even rules," was a near-science with roots deep in history and historical analogy. Repetitiousness and special pleading ran rampant in the book. When the project was nearly completed in mid-December 1910 he discovered that "in my re-reading, which has covered all the lectures except two on the Russo-Japanese War, I have found little occasion to modify my personal opinions." At the age of seventy, Mahan was not likely to change opinions he had held for nearly twenty-five years. He merely restated them, as though he thought that wishing would make them so.

Nevertheless, most reviewers liked *Naval Strategy*. While they recognized that Mahan "has gone to the soldiers for his strategy and has applied to naval war the principles he has learned from them," and that his "theory of strategy remains in substance and in broad outline what it was at the time when he first wrote," they nonetheless regarded it as a useful volume. The knowledgeable reviewer of *The Standard* (London) compared it favorably with Julian S. Corbett's *Some Principles of Maritime Strategy*, a similar study, which appeared at the same time in England. He thought Mahan's "conclusion more interesting and his book more worth reading," if for no other reason than

> As a deep thinker, Captain Mahan will never be quite on the same plane as Mr. Julian Corbett—he is too prone to see nothing but what bears on the particular theory he wishes to demonstrate. He is the advocate, rather than the judge. But this very circumstance makes him the more dramatic, and to that extent more interesting to the general reader. . . . his intuition is never at fault.

Surprisingly, the person who seems to have liked *Naval Strategy* least was its aging author. Although it was probably the best book of its kind produced in the United States prior to World War I, Mahan considered it perhaps the worst thing he had ever written. He thought the strategy section particularly weak, as indeed it was, dubbed the entire book boring (à "perfunctory job"), and confessed that he had "come to loathe" the task of writing it. "I have never been so sick of anything I have written as I was of this before ending it," he told Roosevelt shortly after it was published. He seemed surprised to learn from the War College that "they like it there," and that people as discriminating in their judgments as TR and Bouverie Clark thought well of it. "There were very compelling reasons for undertaking it," he told Clark in March 1912, "but it alone of all my much writing was felt to be a burden. It was conscientiously done and I hope is not a bad piece of work, but it was against the grain, and I feel probably the last professional large work that I shall attempt. Enough commendation has reached me to make me hope that, with whatever faults, my reputation will not suffer seriously from it." Happily, it did not.

As early as 1893, as part of his campaign then to avoid sea duty, and again in 1897, when he was at the zenith of his literary reputation and popularity, Mahan had contemplated reworking and publishing the lectures on strategy he had delivered at the War College. But it was Luce who, in 1908, after a two-year effort, talked him into writing *Naval Strategy* as a service to the college, the Navy, and the nation. Mahan thought that a younger officer, someone active in the New New Navy, should undertake the work. He argued that he had more pressing literary commitments, and he gave Luce a variety of other excuses for not getting started on the book.

To be sure, in 1907 he was busy with the threat of the Second Hague Conference and with seeing through press his related collection of articles, *Some Neglected Aspects of War*. He was also hard at work on his naval autobiography, *From Sail to Steam*, which Harper's Brothers published in October 1907. A year later Little, Brown and Company brought out his *Naval Administration and Warfare: Some General Principles*, a hodgepodge of eleven unrelated articles which were slapped together, apparently because they had not previously been reprinted. So eclectic was this collection that he had difficulty selecting a title for it; but the project took him considerable time to organize and shepherd through press. Part of the year 1908 was also spent in planning and writing *The Harvest Within*, which was published in May 1909, at a time when he had already begun work on the four lengthy essays that eventually comprised his *The Interest of America in International Conditions*. He was, in truth, exceptionally busy in both 1907 and 1908 and was loath to obligate himself to the writing of *Naval Strategy*.

Luce, however, persisted, and Mahan's defenses finally crumbled. A pervasive sense of duty to the War College, an understanding that the institution would assist him with any research that might be involved, and an agreement that the book was to constitute a revision of materials in his files rather than be a fresh start on the topic, persuaded him at last to undertake the study.

Another element in his decision was the fact that the related financial arrangements were finally worked out by the Navy, though barely to Mahan's satisfaction. As he explained in June 1908 to Rear Admiral John P. Merrell, president of the college, "I have to consider also the pecuniary side" because "my pen has added to my income an amount of substantial importance to my family."

His automatic promotion in December 1906 to rear admiral on the Retired List, effective in June 1907, had raised his annual pension from $3,375 to $4,500. All retired captains who had served on active duty during the Civil War had been similarly advanced in rank by a special act of Congress. In Mahan's case, however, he saw small personal advantage in his final achievement of flag rank. Indeed, he became a rear admiral with reluctance, since "an officer retired and promoted, if assigned to [active] duty, gets the pay only of the grade held before retirement, in my case Captain. My duty pay as Captain is just the same as my retired pay as a Rear Admiral." He worried, too, that his new rank might hurt the sale of future books and articles. After all, the title "Captain Mahan" had become "almost a nom de plume for me, and I am a little perplexed about changing it." But in 1908 he was mostly perplexed by the fact that were he to go back on temporary active duty at the War College to write *Naval Strategy*, as Luce and Merrell suggested he might, the law required that his pay be that of an active-duty captain, the rank at which he had retired in 1896; and active-duty captains on shore that year earned a base pay of $3,500. But the law held also that no retired officer, whatever his rank at retirement, need suffer a reduction in pay by consequence of being returned to the active list. Hence Mahan could expect to receive $4,500 and no more.

At the outset of his negotiations with Admiral Merrell he refused flatly to consider such a salary arrangement. If he was going to write *Naval Strategy* at all, he would have to be compensated for it above his retirement salary, at least in the amount that he might otherwise earn with his pen "from other sources abandoned for the nonce." Thus he told Merrell in June 1908 that "if the law gave me the pay of a retired rear admiral I would begin immediately." This would have advanced his pay to $5,500, the sum paid an officer who retired in the rank of rear admiral. Mahan thought he was worth every bit of the $1,000 difference even though he had retired as a captain. Unfortunately, the law could not be repealed for Mahan's convenience and it was $4,500, take it or leave it. He took it, scarcely bubbling with joy, knowing full well that the book would probably be "too technical to be very remunerative." Indeed, the French translation rights amounted to only $50. What made the deal barely tolerable from an economic standpoint was the fringe benefit of a supplementary allowance of about $1,500 for room, board, heat, and light, since no government housing was available to him at the college.

The upshot of the matter was that the Navy Department ordered Rear Admiral A. T. Mahan to temporary active duty at the War College in October 1908 for the official purpose of revising his lectures on naval strategy for delivery at the college and for publication as "required by the public interest." He served in this duty until June 1910. In September 1911 he was brought back briefly onto active duty to work on the galleys and see the book through press. During these periods he reported only occasionally to Newport for consultation or to lecture to the class at the War

College. On two occasions his lectures were read by Captain William McCarty Little in his absence. Most of the time he lived comfortably at home with his family while he was writing *Naval Strategy* and completing the other literary projects to which he was committed.

In addition, after further negotiation, the Navy Department agreed to his publishing *Naval Strategy* through a commercial press of his choosing at whatever royalty rate he might be able to arrange as a private citizen. Moreover, the Navy promised to buy 125 copies of the book in order to "supply one copy to each ship, including the torpedo boats and destroyers, and a small number for stock." This too helped make the agreement financially more attractive. Nonetheless, Mahan complained to Rear Admiral Raymond P. Rodgers, president of the college, in September 1910 that whatever royalties the book earned "would scarcely repay me for the labor involved," and confessed that he would never have undertaken the project as a "private venture." To a great extent, therefore, *Naval Strategy* was Government Issue, as were his first two *Influence* books and his *Life of Admiral Farragut*.[9]

Financial arrangements aside, the book went badly from the start, even though college presidents Merrell and Rodgers, and Captain Little, gave the author all possible research, cartographic, and clerical assistance. So too did the Office of Naval Intelligence and the Library and Naval War Records facility of the Navy Department. Both of the latter made available to him the latest information on the Russo-Japanese War, the only subject in the book on which he did a significant amount of new research.

Still, Mahan found the research, revising, and writing to be extremely hard going, mainly because he had other pressing literary commitments simultaneously under way. Had he chosen to write a crisp, brief, original work on the subject, as Julian S. Corbett was then doing in England, based on his vast knowledge of the history and practice of naval strategy, instead of trying to rework lecture notes that dated back to the 1880s, his job would surely have been simpler and the result would likely have been more readable. The fact is he was bone tired. "I feel my years now," he told Merrell in May 1909, "and do not know how far I can stand the continuous strain." He sorely regretted having undertaken the assignment, complained in March 1910 that he was really not particularly interested in the subject, and noted that the book was not worth the "nervous strain and irritability which I have been feeling lately." He began to have difficulty sleeping. So close did he approach complete "nervous exhaustion" in the final stages of the work in October 1911 that his doctor ordered him to stop drinking tea and coffee. When *Naval Strategy* was finally finished and published he assured Roosevelt that it would probably be his "last magnum opus," and he promised himself that he would never get himself into a "like scrape again."[10]

The question might therefore be asked: What did the Navy get for its financial subsidy of *Naval Strategy*? The answer is it got little return on its investment. Certainly little that was fresh or original. Fully half of the volume, Chapters VI through XII, consisted of the lectures on strategy he had delivered at the War College. While there was "some modification in details," they were "substantially as first framed." Much of this warmed-over material had also been used in his first two *Influence* books. A chapter on naval strategy in a future war in the Gulf-Caribbean, updated from 1897, assumed "an equality of naval force between opposing sides," a situation quite different from that which had actually prevailed during the Spanish-American War there. Indeed, he continued to grouse that "from a purely professional point of view it is greatly to be regretted that the Spanish . . . showed such poor professional aptitude" during the conflict—so poor in fact that in 1898 he had been unable to apply his tactical and strategic verities to the movements of the fleets in the Gulf-Caribbean. Now he visualized a real war in the area by assuming naval parity between the contestants.

Further, naval strategy was confused with naval tactics throughout the book. And to make matters worse, two of his previous articles—"Two Maritime Expeditions," *United Service Magazine* (October 1893), and "Blockade in Relation to Naval Strategy," Royal United Service Institution *Journal* (November 1895)—were simply reprinted in the volume without change. The latter had already been reprinted in the Naval Institute *Proceedings* for December 1895. By 1911 it was a bit shop-worn. Altogether, then, *Naval Strategy* was an unoriginal, uneven, and formless book—partly written, partly rewritten, partly revised, partly pasted together, and, with one exception, almost wholly derivative. Only in the two chapters on the Russo-Japanese War was there truly fresh material.

In these chapters Mahan wisely refrained from discussing the all-big-gun issue and other tactical aspects of the Battle of Tsushima. Sims had thoroughly routed him in that debate. He noted only in passing that the guns of the Japanese secondary batteries had started fires in the "coal traps" of several Russian ships—that is, in the area of the hulls between the armor belts and the gun decks, the belts having been too deeply submerged by the weight of coal to afford adequate protection. The overloading of Russian bunkers on the eve of the engagement made the czar's vessels vulnerable to "increased danger of fire by crowding them with combustibles."

Instead of pursuing his bias against all-big-gun battleships, Mahan concentrated on the theoretical "principles" inherent in the "Fortress Fleet"-versus-"Fleet in Being" debate then under way in naval circles. He argued that both concepts were dangerous, if taken to extremes. The concept of the Fortress Fleet, a defensive force serving as an auxiliary to coastal batteries and as the protector of strategically important harbors, could lead to a defeatist attitude ("a mix-up of escape and fighting") such as Admiral Rozhdestvenski revealed at Tsushima. On the other hand, the Fleet in Being, an offensive force free to move away from its own coasts and ports toward the strategic center of the war in search of decisive combat with the enemy fleet, was more likely to achieve and exercise "command of the sea." A nation might be better served and defended by such a force. But offensive heroics could also be given too much importance, as the Japanese had shown when they succumbed to the temptation to bombard Russian coastal defenses and forts in the early stages of the war, rather than husband their strength for a showdown battle with the entire Russian Asiatic fleet. The bombardments were simply a waste of their time, energy, and resources. Japan's "greatest contribution to naval strategy in this war," wrote Mahan, "was the demonstration of exaggeration in the Fleet in Being theory."

What Mahan, ever the philosopher, advocated as an alternative solution to the problem was a dialectical synthesis of the two principles—in effect, a defensive-offensive "Fortress Fleet in Being":

> In extreme formulation, the two theories, or principles, summed up in the phrases "Fortress Fleet" and "Fleet in Being" are the antipodes of each other. They represent naval, or military, thought polarized. . . . In the case of oppositions such as that before us, truth, a correct decision, is not to be found by seeking at once a middle course, what we call compromise. Truth—that is, a right conclusion or solution—is most surely to be reached by grasping both the ideas which underlie the opposing statements. . . . Precision in allotting due weight to opposing factors can be attained only by the mental processes which first of all feel the full weight of both, and which consequently, in apportioning consideration to one, is constantly and adequately sensible of the importance of the other.

More pertinent to the usefulness of the volume than this esoteric and philosophical observation was the fact that Mahan, before preparing his manuscript, managed to read four recent secondary works in the field and to weave material in them into his revisions. Specifically, and rather proudly, he informed his readers that he had carefully studied Julian S.

Corbett's *England in the Mediterranean* (1904) and *England in the Seven Years' War* (1907), René Daveluy's *Etude sur la stratégie navale* (1905), and Gabriel Darrieus' *La guerre sur mer, stratégie et tactique* (1907). He was particularly impressed with Corbett's works.

Nevertheless, *Naval Strategy*, in its sections on land strategy and tactics, was a nostalgic voyage back to the campaigns of Bonaparte and the Archduke Charles, while, in its sections on the sea, it was a return to Jomini and the question of tactical concentration in the Age of Sail. Karl von Clausewitz, of whose doctrines he seems first to have been made aware in February 1910, received scant attention—save in the thought, shared by Jomini, that "only great tactical results can lead to great strategical results." Mahan thus insisted anew that only by a great fleet success in battle could "command of the sea" be secured; and only by the concentration of a greater part of one's own force against a lesser part of the enemy force in a close-in surface engagement could victory in battle be assured. A defeated enemy must also be relentlessly pursued, each fleeing ship hunted down and annihilated. With the hostile fleet wholly destroyed, it was then a relatively easy matter "to break up the enemy's power on the sea, cutting off his communications with the rest of his possessions, drying up the sources of his wealth and his commerce, and making possible a closure of his ports."

Basically, then, the author saw no need for any changes in the tactical and strategical interpretations he had offered his readers twenty years earlier. When a historian has hold of enduring "historical principles" he does not roll dice with the Cosmos. As Mahan wrote in his introduction to *Naval Strategy*:

> During this period [1887–1911] substantial additions have been made to the text, but there was no attempt to recast the substance of the lectures. The framework [has] continued as at first—a statement of principles. . . . Based as Naval Strategy is upon fundamental truths, which when correctly formulated are rightly called principles, these truths, when ascertained, are in themselves unchangeable; but it by no means follows that in elucidation and restatement, or by experience in war, new light may not be shed upon the principles, and new methods introduced into their application. This will constitute development, alike in the practice of Naval Strategy and in that statement of its laws and principles which we call theory. The physical sciences supply us here with apt analogies. The laws governing them, for example, electricity, are immutable; but in the application of these laws . . . great modification and progress are possible.

The appearance of such new weapons as the submarine and the long-range torpedo, and of wireless telegraphy had done little, Mahan argued, to modify or repeal these "laws." He still felt that the tactical concentration of fleets was chief among the "fundamental truths" he had discovered since 1887, a verity that remained "immutable." Indeed, in 1908 he conveniently discovered a new historical "truth," or "principle," one which said in effect that a navy of all-big-gun ships could not ensure a nation's command of the sea. For such insurance, a "second line of ships," a balanced naval posture, would also be needed—or so he assured students at the War College and the readers of his *Naval Strategy*. It would seem therefore that new "historical" principles emerged at opportune times for the Philosopher of Sea Power, principles that only he seemed capable of recognizing and capturing as they struggled upward into the realm of human consciousness.[11]

Julian S. Corbett, civilian lecturer at the Royal Naval War College in Greenwich and Mahan's chief competitor in the field of naval history and strategy, played no such philosophical games. Although the book he wrote on the subject in 1911 was titled *Some Principles of Maritime Strategy*, Corbett did not regard his particular "principles" as enduring or necessarily applicable in all circumstances. He was not locked into theory, he had small confidence that a study of history would reveal rules for the future conduct of battles or campaigns, and he eschewed the use of historical analogy to prove a point. He was certain that changes in naval weapons must bring about corresponding changes in naval tactics and strategy, and he saw little relationship between strategy and tactics on land and on sea. To him, the Art of War was largely an exercise in common sense.

In all this he differed from Mahan; yet he had for Mahan a professional admiration that was warmly reciprocated, and he frequently quoted his rival with approval. He shared Mahan's views on such questions as the importance of "command of the sea," the foolishness of immunizing private property at sea in wartime, the unimportance of *guerre de course*, the concept of a "balanced" naval force, and the all-big-gun battleship. But he was not nearly as impressed as was Mahan with the doctrine of concentration. War at sea often required flexible combinations of both massing and dispersal. For this reason, he was critical of tacticians and strategists who, like Mahan, made "a kind of shibboleth" of concentration, "so that the division of a fleet tends almost to be regarded as a sure mark of bad leadership. Critics have come to lose sight of the old war experience, that without division no strategical concentrations are possible." Although he was a close student of Jomini, as well as of Clausewitz, he was not overly impressed with the genius of Bonaparte; nor did he believe that Horatio Lord Nelson walked on water every morning before breakfast. He consistently emphasized the "far-reaching" differences, rather than the similarities and analogous relationships, between land war and sea war. His historical illustrations of naval principles were invariably derived from war at *sea*, not from the campaigns of Frederick the Great, Napoleon, or the Austrian Archduke Charles. He had grave doubts about the accuracy of the strategical rubric, embraced by Mahan, that the chief business of a navy was to "seek out the enemy's fleet and destroy it." In his opinion, this approach usually ended "in a blow in the air."

On the other hand, Corbett, unlike Mahan, made the great mistake of seeing no strategic or tactical value attaching to the convoy system once privateering had been eliminated by international treaties and conventions. The non-convoy idea, embraced by the Royal Navy at the beginning of World War I, almost ruined Great Britain, as Germany's U-boats feasted on British merchantmen running alone. As one modern English naval historian has recently and correctly observed: "By not following Mahan's example in emphasising the permanent tactical advantages of the convoy system, he [Corbett] made himself a party to the most costly mistake in British naval thinking ever made." Fortunately, the Americans, thanks largely to the persuasive powers of Admiral W. S. Sims, convinced the Royal Navy in 1917 to return to the convoy system and the error was belatedly rectified.

It should be noted also that Corbett, like Mahan, failed completely to see the tactical possibilities of the submarine. Such vessels were as invisible in his pages as they were in Mahan's. He even went so far as to dismiss the possibility of armed surface raiders operating effectively against unconvoyed merchant ships. "No Power," he said confidently, "will incur the odium of sinking a prize with all hands." Since surface raiders could not easily transfer enemy merchant seamen on board in rough weather, or function effectively as partial prison ships during their cruises, or conveniently put prize crews on board their captives and send them home, that ancient practice of war at sea virtually ceased to exist as an option in Corbett's mind.[12]

In any event, Corbett's *Some Principles of Maritime Strategy* generally overshadowed Mahan's *Naval Strategy* when both appeared in 1911. Certainly it did in England. It was succinctly and crisply written, was topically well organized, and it avoided philosophical and cosmological soarings. Whether it was actually a better book on the subject than Mahan's remains a matter of opinion.

What Mahan actually had to say about war, about strategy and tactics, and about history itself, after studying those subjects for over a quarter of a century and after writing hundreds of thousands of words about them, also remains a matter of opinion. Basically, what he seems to have said can be reduced to five abstract "principles," viz.: (1) In states inhabited by genetically aggressive men, constant war is almost inevitable. (2) Since it is constant and inevitable, the study of war is the study of history. (3) The existence and proper use of organized sea power to ensure command of the sea has mightily influenced the course of human history, certainly more than any other single factor. (4) Fleets or armies which situate themselves at geographical positions in or near the "strategic center" of a given war, thus affording themselves the greatest amount of offensive mobility or the greatest measure of defensive flexibility, usually win the battles that determine the outcome of the wars that influence the course of history. (5) A fleet or army that, in battle, can maneuver (concentrate) itself in such a way as to bring for a decisive moment a greater part of its firepower and personnel against lesser parts of the firepower and people of its enemy will invariably win the action.

These simplistic, almost obvious, precepts, supported, as they were, by dozens of sub-principles, substantially sum up Mahan's thoughts, observations, and beliefs about history, war, strategy, and tactics. All else was emendation, historical illustration, and speculation. Put another way, Mahan spent nearly thirty years as a naval and military historian discovering and rediscovering the wheel, all the while spinning it vigorously, profitably, and to the great benefit and nourishment of his self-esteem. In so doing, however, he contributed much to the regeneration and salvation of the U.S. Navy, and to the inculcation of that sense of *realpolitik* in foreign affairs that helped carry the American people safely through the first three-quarters of the twentieth century, the bloodiest and most contentious period in human history. The nation came to owe him a great and lasting debt.

On the other hand, the Department of the Treasury did not consider that it owed Mahan anything. For this reason the difficult three-year project that was *Naval Strategy* ended up in the case of *Alfred Thayer Mahan* vs. *The United States of America*—an ironic juxtaposition of litigants if ever there was one. It was a very simple case; simple, that is, from the standpoint of Mahan and the Navy; but frightfully complicated for the confused Fourth Auditor of the Treasury, who was assigned as auditor to the Navy Department, and for his superior, R. J. Tracewell, Taft's Comptroller of the Treasury. The bureaucrats in the Treasury simply could not understand how it was that Rear Admiral Mahan could be ordered to active duty at the War College in Newport on October 23, 1908, and then proceed to spend the winter of 1908–1909 writing a book in a rented house in Lawrence, Long Island, where he subsequently claimed a quarters allowance of $1,000 and reimbursement for heat and light in the amount of $481.73. To make matters more complicated for the decimal-point mentality of the Treasury, Mahan spent from May to November of 1909 at his home in Quogue, yet claimed a pro rata allowance for quarters and utilities in that residence up to September 30, 1909. It is well that he did not further confuse the issue by mentioning to the Treasury that while he was on active duty with the War College at Lawrence and Quogue, he did some private literary work, other than the writing of *Naval Strategy*.

Such was the complexity of the problem that not until April 1910 did the Comptroller of the Treasury allow the claim for $1,000 for quarters; and then only after disavowal, an appeal by Mahan, and a reversal by Tracewell. The Treasury refused, however, to allow Mahan's claim of $377.26 for fuel from October 31, 1908, to June 20, 1909, or to pay his $104.47 bill for light for the period October 31, 1908, to September 30, 1909. The total amount initially claimed by the admiral for these items was $481.73.

The claim dragged on for five dreary years, Mahan having scaled it down to $240.96 by the time he finally and wearily took it to court in 1914. Secretary Meyer and Rear Admiral Rodgers became involved in his behalf at the outset, and Mahan wrote detailed letters of explanation and entreaty probably equalling in volume and mental labor the time and effort spent on one of his better scholarly articles. It was a frightful waste of his time; but for Rear Admiral A. T. Mahan, distinguished author of *The Influence of Sea Power Upon History*, it was a matter of fairness, money, and justice. As he explained to Secretary Meyer when his battle with the Treasury was fairly joined in November 1909, "I can receive no pay at all till this question is settled or the thousand dollars worked off." Nonetheless, for several months the Treasury blocked him at every turn, sowing obscure Civil Service regulations and forms in his way like mines in the path of an oncoming enemy squadron. All were couched in the ambiguous language of the Civil Service, known as near-English.

First, the Treasury bureaucrats refused to accept the plain fact that in 1908 no quarters were available at the War College for Mahan and his family. Then they questioned the locus of his legal residence. This they followed by stating that a naval officer could not legally report for active duty "by letter." Finally, they questioned the legitimacy of a tour of active duty being granted for the purpose of writing a book, and held that the payment of a quarters allowance could not be part of such an unusual arrangement. It was not the business of naval officers to write books, they seemed to say, echoing Francis M. Ramsay. The argument reached the level of slapstick in November 1909 when the Fourth Auditor demanded to know who had supplied Mahan with heat and light in his Lawrence home and then identified Elly as the person who had. To this double-talk Mahan replied, tongue in cheek: "I enclose herewith, filled out, the blank sent me in the Auditor's letter, 4056–RSJ, November 22d, to be filled out by the party, (Mrs.) E. L. Mahan, who, I am instructed by the same letter, is the one who actually furnished me with the heat and light."

This nonsense led, however, in mid-February 1910, to payment of the quarters portion of Mahan's dual claim. Remaining was the $414.40 (Mahan's figure was $481.73) still claimed by him for heat and light. This was disallowed on the ground that "claimant's active duty was not such as would entitle him to allowances." Tracewell's logic escaped Mahan. How could it be that the nature of his War College duty had at last qualified him for a room-and-board allowance in 1908 and 1909, but not for reimbursement of the heat and light costs related thereto? Whatever the answer to that pregnant question, Mahan knew that he was claiming what he had actually spent for heat and light, not the lesser amount that the Treasury was likely to pay, if it allowed him anything at all. Allowances for fuel and light for "a captain on the active list" were clearly spelled out. The sum was $240.96, not $481.73, the amount Mahan had spent.

Angered and frustrated, he was nonetheless determined to push on. "On the general record of the Treasury Department, I have little doubt of an adverse decision . . ." he complained to Rodgers on February 17, 1910, "in view of the grave practical injustice done me, I ask that I be continued on duty with a view to lecturing the following year [fiscal 1910–1911]. I see no other way by which the Government can pay me what it justly owes me; for the work in point of time and labor is worth all that I have been receiving, and it has cut me off from the opportunities which I have heretofore used successfully." In spite of the intercession of Rodgers with the Navy Department, Mahan did not get a third year of duty (with its $1,000 worth of quarters allowances) to lecture at the college and continue his work on *Naval Strategy*. Nor did he get satisfaction on Appeal No. 18472 CCM 8 D, as his fuel-and-light claim came depressingly to be called. Tracewell was not at all impressed with Mahan's assertion that he was "accepted as an authority on the general subject" of naval strategy, "not in the United States only, but throughout the world, my other works having been translated into the principal European languages, as well as into Japanese." This stirring appeal, which Mahan admitted to Rodgers "may appear a somewhat vainglorious insistence upon my fitness for the work, as evidenced by my reputation," budged the stolid comptroller not one inch. Mahan could have built Noah's ark for all he cared. He was interested only in the fact that Mahan had reported to duty by mail, rather than in person, and that during the course of the duty concerned he had lived at home, where, had he not been on temporary active duty, he would have had to pay for his own heat and light. The nature of the duty was shaky enough, to Tracewell's way of thinking. Why should the people of the United States also pay Alfred Thayer Mahan's bill for heat and light?

The question remained unanswered until May 1914. At that point Mahan got a lawyer, Spencer Gordon, of Washington, who had represented him in his effort to get reimbursement of his travel expenses of $82.60 when he served on the Moody Commission in March 1909. Gordon promptly reactivated Mahan's claim for payment of his utilities, only to have it disallowed by the Fourth Auditor in early June 1914. The letter disallowing the claim was filled with factual inaccuracies about the nagging case. Consultations between Mahan and Gordon led to a decision to sue, it being agreed that the lawyer's fee would be a percentage of whatever was recovered. So it was that Rear Admiral Alfred Thayer Mahan, USN, took the United States of America to court for the niggling amount of $240.96. Gordon was not going to get rich on this one. "The claimant makes no claim for the amount expended by him in excess of his allowances, but claims that he is entitled to be paid the amount of his allowance, viz., $240.96 in all," explained the lawyer in his petition to the U.S. Court of Claims in the District of Columbia. Meanwhile, the Fourth Auditor of the Treasury had decided that the statute of limitations had run out, "that the time for appeal has passed, and that once having adversely decided the claim, he has no jurisdiction to reconsider it." Back to square one.[13]

And there the matter rested when Mahan himself was laid to rest in Quogue cemetery early in December 1914. "Naked came I out of my mother's womb, and naked shall I return thither," said Job. Mahan's dismay was that he returned naked minus $240.96. "The Lord gave, and the Lord hath taken away; blessed be the name of the Lord," the Old Testament patriarch concluded. In this instance, however, it was the Department of the Treasury that took away.

At least one new historical "principle" can be said to have emerged from the guerrilla warfare between Mahan and the Department of the Treasury, viz.: whatever the uncertain future of the New New Navy and its all-big-gun battleships, the future of the U.S. Civil Service was secure. It could sink a man, a cause, or an idea with a barrage of unintelligible paper at virtually any range, and do so with a tenacity of fire unequaled in the history of all the world's navies combined. Indeed, it is well that Mahan did not live into the final half of the twentieth century and witness his beloved country crushed nearly to death by the weight of millions of heavily armored, rapid-firing, tactically concentrated, all-big-gun Civil Service directives.

XX

Concerns Spiritual, Literary, and Political
1900-1914

From the look of things, I fancy some years will elapse before I again come abroad, and at our time of life a few years means a good deal. . . . the usual diversions of travel have ceased to interest me. . . . Yet what to do remains a problem. My vogue is largely over—I am less in demand, and therefore must make work for myself, without security that it will be wanted. Still, I have plans and an outlook.

Alfred Thayer Mahan to Bouverie F. Clark, March 24, 1913

In spite of his great interest in the potential clashings of powerful European alliances and the related deployments of great battle fleets, Mahan never lost sight of the fact that politics begin in one's own precinct. Nor could he forget that he was a prominent citizen of New York, one of the nation's most corruptly governed cities. Following the collapse of his dream to storm social heights ably defended by the Four Hundred, he turned his attention to the more prosaic task of helping to make the city a better place for his wife and daughters to live. After all, he had a large investment in his property on West 86th Street. To protect that investment he actively involved himself in the various reform movements that sought to overthrow Tammany Hall. It disgusted him that it was unsafe for a lady to walk the city's streets after dark, that lawlessness everywhere ran rampant, that the Police Board itself was corrupt and beyond the effective control of the mayor, and that city jobs were brokered like flounder at the Fulton Street Market. For these reasons he gave his time, money, voice, and vote to various anti-Tammany, anti-Democratic, and anti-Irish-

American causes in New York at the turn of the century. He supported such Republican reform candidates as Seth Low, the president of Columbia University, who was mayor from 1901 to 1903. But he opposed the movement, opposed also by Tammany, to remove partisan politics and party labels from city elections. Thus in 1903 he refused to support the Republican candidacy for Board of Aldermen of his friend and family solicitor, Augustus T. Gillender, because Gillender favored non-partisan municipal elections and the enthronement of non-partisan administration at City Hall. "I think it dangerous to good municipal government," Mahan told him; it "amounts to saying that considerations of what is good for the city are of less importance, *in a strictly municipal election*, than considerations of national politics." To Mahan, it was a "fundamental civil principle" that the operation of city government be related to national political issues and parties.[1]

There is no evidence that Mahan's participation in the political reform movement in New York made the smallest dent on the corruption there. Mahan had the indignation. Tammany had the votes. There is evidence, however, that he enjoyed the cultural attractions of the city, often attending the theater and the opera, and that he particularly enjoyed his membership in the Century and University clubs. In the excellent libraries of those exclusive retreats he read, studied, and wrote; and in their sitting rooms and dining rooms he met and chatted with such interesting academic, literary, and political figures as historian James Ford Rhodes, New Jersey Governor Woodrow Wilson, London *Times* writer James R. Thursfield, British editor John St. Loe Strachey, and Japanese diplomat Baron Kentaro Kaneko. He frequently entertained his own guests at the University Club, and often stayed overnight there. He enjoyed helping his friends and relatives, especially his son Lyle, to gain membership in his clubs, and he was alert in keeping people he disliked out of them. Among the latter was Frederick A. Richardson, sometime editor of *International Monthly*, who had reneged on a publishing agreement with Mahan in 1902 and thereby earned Mahan's blackball when he attempted to join the Century Club twelve years later. Similarly, Mahan was active in the discussion groups sponsored by the Round Table Club. "Here," his daughter Ellen recalled, "were always found men of distinction in their own line—indeed only such were invited to join—and they were a great stimulus to my father, he enjoying the meetings very much."[2]

But with all of its social, cultural, and intellectual attractions, New York was a city in which Mahan remained "The Cat That Walked By Himself." While the noise and flow of the crowds there stimulated him, the number of his friends was always small. Save for Sam Ashe, he had no confidant or correspondent to whom he could recite his trials and tribulations. He retained few acquaintances from his forty years in the Navy, and his opinions of his Academy classmates had improved little since 1859. He was, as he had always been, a shy and lonely man. "Individuals outside the family and its small circle of friends did not seem to be necessary to his happiness," Ellen remembered.

Perhaps it was for this reason that Mahan mounted but token opposition to the wishes of his wife and daughters to abandon the house on 86th Street in favor of suburban residences in nearby Long Island; nor did he oppose their desire to travel abroad frequently and, when in the States, to spend longer periods of time each year in Quogue. Consequently, in 1905 the town house was leased and the Mahans rented various properties during the winter months—in Woodmere, Long Island (1906–1907), and Lawrence, Long Island (1907–1911)—and they stayed at the Hotel Collingwood on West 35th Street (1911–1912 and 1913–1914). As Mahan explained to his correspondents, his flight to sylvan Long Island was dictated by "reasons of health of the women of my family." There was also the factor that West 86th Street was "a good deal to one side, so that although we had excellent public conveyance the ladies found going back and forth troublesome both as to visits and shops."

More importantly, in February 1904, Elly suffered a severe attack of influenza, followed by respiratory complications, heart strain, and gout. In May, Mahan took her to London to see a specialist; and then to Bad Nauheim, Germany, for the baths, a regime repeated in April 1905 when she returned there for "another course of baths." Thanks to the fact that she was a "most subordinate and disciplined patient," she improved rapidly. Nonetheless, it was determined that she must live always in fresh-air environments. Hence, the decision to abandon the dirt and smoke of New York City and move out to Long Island. Lawrence was but an hour's train ride from Elly's shops and Alfred's clubs, and the house they rented there had fourteen rooms and two baths. It was as commodious as it was convenient. Still, Mahan felt at first that he was "too much out of world" there. It was also troublesome for him to have to search for a new rental property near the city every October when the family closed "Slumberside" at the end of the season. The fact remained, however, that "my wife ought to sleep in fresh air, and have it all the time. I need it more and more, *feel* the need of it. My house-keeping daughter [Helen] ought to escape the nuisance of servants for a time each year. So, in short, we have a summer home, and for winters are all adrift."[3]

Mahan quickly adjusted to the peripatetic living arrangement dictated by Elly's lungs. His interest in living in the heart of the city steadily declined. He complained of being gouged by Manhattan's taxi-drivers, found the din and filth of the metropolis increasingly wearisome and unappealing, and finally decided that he liked the country better. Nor was he impressed with living in an apartment at the Hotel Collingwood, even though the hotel was conveniently and centrally situated for the lady shoppers in his family, and even though "being in the ninth story the air is much better than the street."[4]

The decision to spend six or more months of each year in Quogue also necessitated a change in the family's living accommodations in that pleasant seaside village. Accustomed as the Mahans were to a great deal of living space, they decided in 1908 to sell "Slumberside." Elly and her daughters thought it was "too small," and they wanted something closer to the ocean, "out of the way of dust and motors." Pursued by the increasingly ubiquitous automobile, the Mahans built "Marshmere" during the winter of 1908–1909. Complete with furnace, it was a year-round house that boasted seventeen rooms and five baths, and required a staff of four servants. Mahan's study was sound-proofed, and from its walls pictures of Bonaparte and Nelson gazed down upon him. The entire property was "a blaze of color from flowers, and more sunshine to the square foot and to the week than any place we know. The sea breeze blows five days out of the week, almost perpendicular to the shore, so that excessive heat is almost unknown." It was indeed a beautiful place, one in which Mahan worked out a daily way of living in his retirement years that was the envy of his friends and the dismay of his physicians. This involved working on his books or articles in the morning and brisk walks of three or four miles, vigorous bicycling, or swimming in the nearby surf in the afternoons. This strenuous exercise was followed by formal tea in the late afternoon, dinner, for which he usually donned his tuxedo, reading, and bed. Small wonder that the family's return to New York or its suburbs every November became for Mahan a less desirable migration with each passing year.

It is no wonder that he became an implacable foe of the Long Island Railroad on whose service he had to depend after 1907. Then, as now, service was terrible; moreover, the arrogance and incompetence of the company's management under Ralph Peters, its president, was exceeded only by the New York Public Service Commission's cavalier disinterest in Mahan's angry complaints about the railroad's operational inadequacies. Needless to say, however, Mahan had no more luck reforming the Long Island Railroad than he had in his attempt to purify Tammany Hall.

Alfred Thayer Mahan with Alfred Thayer Mahan II

"There is no indication of its being of the slightest use to a citizen to apply to the Commission," he complained.[5]

As Mahan and his family began changing their living pattern from urban to suburban, the head of the household published what he considered to be "the best bit of historical writing I have ever done; superior by far in research, in treatment, and in style." This was his *The Influence of Sea Power in Its Relation to the War of 1812*, a two-volume work which Little, Brown and Company brought out in October 1905. The final work in his *Influence of Sea Power* trilogy, it remains a standard work in the field.

Surprisingly, Mahan had small confidence in the book at the outset. "I am not in the least concerned about reputation, or the trilogy," he informed Brown, "believing that *1812* will not add to my reputation, though I trust it won't detract." He need not have been so pessimistic. From a research standpoint it was a superior book, although, as he confessed to his publisher in January 1907, "nothing could redeem the essential flatness of the theme. I hope the result will at best not be [financially] disastrous to you, that the prestige of the other books may have floated this enough." The author was right. There was little that was new or exciting in the book; nor did it sell well.

It was also a particularly difficult book for Anglophile Mahan to write since the "enemy" in this instance was his beloved Royal Navy. Further, American intervention in the European struggle in June 1812 came at the very moment when Britain's long and bitter struggle with Bonaparte's France reached a crescendo on the continent. Poor timing. It was, Mahan held, an unnecessary, tragic, and useless war; indeed, it was almost an accidental war, one brought on by a peculiar combination of America's proper moral opposition to Britain's impressment policy and her dogged insistence on the unrealistic doctrine that "free ships make free goods"—or the immunity of neutral noncontraband private property at sea during wartime. At the same time, Mahan saw it as a war vital to British national survival.

Faced with this interpretive dilemma, the author finally decided, as he told Luce, that "the main thesis of my *War of 1812* must necessarily be the sufferings of the country through the inadequacy of the Navy as compared with the actual power of the country to have made better preparation." The book, therefore, was essentially a plea for naval preparedness since he naively thought that a U.S. Navy numbering a bare dozen ships of the line might have curbed British pretensions in 1812. Unfortunately, author Mahan could point to few other historical lessons that might be drawn from the disaster to American naval arms that saw the Royal Navy establish near-total command of the seas on which the United States fronted, effect a tight blockade of the East Coast, burn Washington, and scatter Mr. Madison's disorganized government. Further, there were no major fleet actions to which he could easily apply his tactical and strategical "principles."

But because *War of 1812* was part of a sea-power trilogy that emphasized larger insights, Mahan gave it the old War College try. With something less than complete modesty he informed his readers that

> The present work concludes the series of *The Influence of Sea Power Upon History* as originally framed in the conception of the author. In the previous volumes he has had the inspiring consciousness of regarding his subject as a positive and commanding element in the history of the world. . . . The War of 1812 . . . represents the truth which the author has endeavored to set forth . . . recognizing clearly that the victories on Lake Erie and Lake Champlain do illustrate, in a distinguished

manner, his principal thesis, the controlling influence upon events of naval power, even when transferred to an inland body of fresh water. The lesson there, however, was the same as in the larger fields of war heretofore treated. . . . It matters not that the particular force be small. The art of war is the same throughout, and may be illustrated as really, though less conspicuously, by a flotilla as by an armada.

Maybe. On the other hand, whatever impact the Navy's successful little engagements on Erie and Champlain may have had on eventually mitigating the harshness of British peace terms at Ghent, the upshot of the matter was that the victories of Oliver Hazard Perry and Thomas Macdonough on the lakes, while strategically important in a sectional sense, did not mitigate the embarrassment of the humiliating national defeat suffered by American arms during the war. Neither did Andrew Jackson's brilliant postwar victory at the Battle of New Orleans. The glorious winning of battles during the awkward losing of wars was not one of the "arts of war" Mahan could explain deftly.

Nor did he consider or hint at various interpretations of the origins of the conflict that later historians emphasized—such as U.S. interest in territorial expansion ("On to Canada!"), the agrarian imperialism of American frontiersmen, the political role of the western "War Hawks" in bringing on the conflict, the importance to all sections of the country of the question of national honor, and the British goading of the American Indian to make war on the white man. His, instead, was almost entirely a legalistic and diplomatic approach to causality that turned heavily on technical issues of maritime neutral rights. Among these were the impressment of American seamen, the legality of broken and continuous voyages, questions of immunity from capture, distinctions between letters of marque and privateering, and blockade regulations. In other words, Mahan's was a traditional look at the maritime background of the war, although, interestingly enough, it was one to which American naval and diplomatic historians returned for another hard look some sixty years later. He concluded that the conflict had pitted the morality and justice of the American stand on impressment against the realpolitik of Britain's lonely, necessary, and desperate struggle for survival against the brute Napoleon.

In developing his theme of maritime causality, Mahan asked for and received a great deal of research assistance and advice from John Bassett Moore on the international legal and diplomatic questions involved. Luce helped him with some of the combat actions between frigates and criticized sections of the manuscript dealing with those engagements. At all times the author kept at hand Theodore Roosevelt's excellent study of the conflict as well as that of Henry Adams, on whose special insights he was careful not to trespass. Historians Andrew C. McLaughlin and J. Franklin Jameson also aided him when called upon—which was often.

At no time, however, in spite of all the assistance he received, did Mahan succeed in effectively suspending his Anglophilic biases. America's march to war and participation therein, he told Ashe, was "not a brilliant episode, nor one of which, as a whole, the United States can feel proud." American military performances on land and at sea had scarcely been impressive. A few American frigate-to-frigate victories, which gave an appearance of victory at sea, had produced nothing of the sort. All in all, it was "a very miserable showing . . . for our people," he glumly informed editor Brown early in his research. The whole sorry story told him little more than that freedom of the seas, in a commercial sense as distinct from the immorality of the British impressment of American seamen, was a dubious legal principle, one not worth contending for and certainly not one on which the nation's very existence should have been risked. Only Britain's simultaneous military involvement with Bonaparte, and her war-weariness at the end of two decades of constant struggle with France, had saved the United States from complete disaster and permitted the infant nation to crawl out of the debacle in 1815 with its independence intact. The United States had no moral choice but to fight, Mahan insisted. She should, however, have fought five years earlier, when the morality of the impressment issue was more clearly apparent. Concluded the author:

> That much of Great Britain's action was unjustifiable, and at times even monstrous, regarded in itself alone, must be admitted. . . . The conclusion of the writer is that at a very early stage of the French Revolutionary Wars the United States should have obeyed Washington's warnings to prepare for war, and to build a navy; and that, thus prepared, instead of placing reliance upon a system of commercial restrictions, war should have been declared not later than 1807, when the news of [the French victory at] Jena, and of Great Britain's refusal to relinquish her practice of impressing from American ships, became known almost coincidently. But this conclusion is perfectly compatible with a recognition of the desperate character of the strife that Great Britain was waging; that she could not disengage herself from it, Napoleon being what he was; and that the methods which she pursued did cause the Emperor's downfall, and her own deliverance, although they were invasions of just rights, to which the United States should not have submitted. If war is always avoidable, consistently with due resistance to evil, then war is always unjustifiable; but if it is possible that two nations, or two political entities, like the North and South in the

American Civil War, find the question between them one which neither can yield without sacrificing conscientious conviction, or national welfare . . . then war is not justifiable only; it is imperative. . . . Nor is this conclusion invalidated by a triumph of the unjust in war. Subjugation to wrong is not acquiescence in wrong. A beaten nation is not necessarily a disgraced nation; but the nation or man is disgraced who shirks an obligation to defend right. . . . Great Britain [in her war against Napoleon] laid her hand to any weapon she could find to save national life and independence. To justify all her measures at the bar of conventional law, narrowly construed, is impossible. Had she attempted to square herself to it she would have been overwhelmed. . . . The measures which overthrew Napoleon grievously injured the United States; by international law grievously wronged her also. Should she have acquiesced? If not, war was inevitable. Great Britain could not be expected to submit to destruction for another's benefit.[6]

As was invariably the case with Mahan, the commercial prospects of his *War of 1812* were a consideration when he first conceived the project in 1897, soon after he had finished his Nelson biography, and attempted first to market it as "a philosophical study of the causes, course, and results of the war in its broader aspects." It was his intention at the outset to avoid being pressured into "the idea of treating single ship fights." He hoped to be able to write around splinter wounds, gore in the surgical pits, and sand on bloody decks, as Britons and English-speaking Americans spoke to one another with cannon and cutlass. Moreover, the idea of a detached "philosophical study" seemed logical, given the fact that in truth he had "no faith in the paying quality of 1812." Nevertheless, as the research and writing began he tried to work out his usual pre-publication serialization arrangement between Little, Brown and Company, the publisher, and one of the popular journals of the day. He discovered, however, that *Century Magazine* was not interested in philosophical chitchat or the "broader aspects" of the conflict, but wanted "impertinent illustrations of fancy battle scenes, medallions, and the deuce knows what all." Mahan turned *Century* down. Similarly, a serialization proposal from *Atlantic Monthly* fell on fallow greenbacks when Mahan warned its editor, Walter Hines Page, that "my terms have gone up [since 1890]. . . . I hope I am not unduly mercenary, but I must begin to do less work and [get] more pay, or I shall break down."

So it was that, before it was published, Mahan's *War of 1812* was serialized in *Scribner's Magazine* in eleven parts (probably at $400 each), beginning in January 1904 and concluding in January 1905. A companion article, "Negotiations at Ghent in 1814," for which Mahan was paid $100, appeared in the *American Historical Review* for October 1905, the month Little, Brown and Company published the book in Boston. It was a handsome two-volume set. "The choice of the *Constitution* under full sail for the cover decoration was a happy thought," said Mahan, as he prepared to send complimentary copies to his British and American literary friends and his War College associates. Chief among the recipients was publisher John M. Brown himself, whose copy was inscribed "in memory of the completion of our joint Sea Power undertaking begun fifteen years ago." Attractively produced though the volumes were, it was the income from *Scribner's* serialization, together with related lecture fees, "that repaid me for three years of my most faithful work." It was "faithful" labor because Mahan found the naval subject matter with which he worked "rather dry." Indeed, he "put more heart into the [diplomatic and legal] antecedents than . . . into the war itself." The first four chapters of the first volume, comprising a 282-page discussion of the economic foreign policy and maritime neutral rights involved in the war, were by far the freshest and most useful sections of the book.[7]

The reviews were generally good, ranging from "rather colorless" on the one hand to "discriminating" on the other. None was unfavorable, save, in Mahan's opinion, that written by Gaillard Hunt, son of President Garfield's Secretary of the Navy, William H. Hunt. The younger Hunt, biographer of James Madison, was an experienced historian who had a special competence in State Department documents and other primary source material of American diplomacy in the period 1789–1820. His review of the *War of 1812*, which appeared in the *American Historical Review* for July 1906, was actually favorable, almost laudatory. He even referred to Mahan as "a skilled historical investigator and a skilled seaman." But he made two critical statements that sent Mahan into a towering rage. Whether because of his dislike of the reviewer's father for having denied him quarters at the Brooklyn Navy Yard in 1881 when he was desperately poor or because of the gun-shyness that resulted from his bitter controversy with Francis P. Badham over Nelson at Naples, the fact is that Mahan reacted violently to Hunt's remark that "the naval victories on Lake Champlain and the military victories at New Orleans are treated as events irrelevant to the objects and outcome of the war." He objected also to Hunt's opinion that he had misinterpreted in a pro-British way, which Hunt labeled an "injustice" to President Madison, the importance of an exchange of letters between Secretary of State Robert Smith and the British Minister in Washington, Francis J. Jackson, that had led to a breach in diplomatic relations between the United States and Great Britain late in 1809. Mahan considered that his scholarly honor had been traduced. In the October *American Historical Review*, he retorted:

> The statement [on Champlain and New Orleans] of your reviewer affects too seriously my sanity as an historical writer to be passed over in the silence with which an author of many years' experience learns to accept differences of opinion. But for it, I should not have written at all; but as it has drawn me out, I will say, further, that in my judgment your reviewer has failed in another respect to reach the high standard which should be expected in the *Review*. . . . This [the interpretation of the Smith letter] is simply a statement of opinion with which any one is at liberty to disagree. . . . The matter is of consequence . . . because the character of the *American Historical Review* demands on the part of its reviewers more exactness in stating the position of an author when they charge him with injustice.

In his printed rebuttal to Mahan's response, Hunt admitted that his statement on the battles was "too sweeping . . . a mistake," but still held that Mahan was "in error" in his handling of the controversial Smith-Jackson exchange. This produced another angry letter from Mahan to Jameson, editor of the *Review*, insisting that Hunt's apology was not abject enough and demanding "personal justification" on the Smith-Jackson matter. "Prejudice still stands in the way of accurate measurement of words," he charged. He claimed, further, that his handling of the Smith-Jackson correspondence was "a serious contribution to history." That Hunt was unwilling or unable to "reason closely" should not be permitted to obscure his contribution, Mahan held. Contribution to history or not, it takes two to duel and Secretary Hunt's son was apparently in no mood to take down his verbal pistols. Thus the Mahan-Hunt contention, unlike the earlier Mahan-Badham altercation, died in its crib.

Reviews and interpretations of data notwithstanding, the early sales of the *War of 1812* were at best modest—in the United States, expected to be its prime market, fewer than 1,000 copies were sold during the first four months. It reminded Mahan of his *Life of Admiral Farragut*. "Judging by the sales," he told President Roosevelt, "the book has not been very widely read in this country. Great Britain rather better." Convinced that "*1812* is in thoroughness and execution a better book than any of its predecessors," he wondered what had gone wrong. Perhaps a title "putting 1812 more forward and Sea Power more in the rear would have caught attention better." Perhaps the sale price was too high. But a reduction in price from $4.80 to $4.00 moved few copies out of Little, Brown and

Company's warehouse. Therefore, the best things that happened to the book were the author's citation of it to Roosevelt and other government officials in building his case against freedom of the seas prior to the Second Hague Conference and the president's quoting from its preface in his annual message of December 3, 1906. In that address, Roosevelt made the point that naval preparedness was the best means either to preserve peace or to sustain the nation in the event it was forced to fight a just war. "I shall be only too glad that you should use any of my writings in any manner that may be serviceable to you, or that you may think serviceable to the country," Mahan had assured him in October. "The question of credit in such connection is to me quite immaterial." Roosevelt gave him credit, but that did not help sales.[8]

Better received from a commercial standpoint, certainly a book Mahan derived more pleasure from writing, was his naval autobiography, *From Sail to Steam*, a project he had begun in June 1905, when *Harper's Magazine* asked him to "furnish them some chapters of Reminiscences." This request both delighted and flattered him, but he had to get other literary commitments out of the way before he could put his mind to it. A year passed before he seriously took up the pleasant task. "The idea seemed to me at first preposterous for so quiet a life as my own," he told John M. Brown in June 1906, "but I have begun an attempt at it, hoping thereby I may turn the few additional honest pennies that I want for current expenses." Frankly, it was "undertaken as a pot-boiler," he told Luce, one for which *Harper's* "paid a very good price." That sum was $3,000 for ten serialized articles plus a royalty of 15 per cent on the book version, it being agreed with Harper Brothers that "ultimately the carcass whole will be served in book form; the whole ox—or hog." The purpose of the book, its author explained, was to make it attractive to the public, "not for the profession." He sought "to amuse, and if possible make the book sell." He hoped also that it would help "to a certain extent to contravene erroneous ideas about naval matters, which are more dangerous in our country than in [Britain], except when we have [as president] a man like Roosevelt who really has sound military ideas." On the other hand, he did not, he assured Bouverie Clark, "fancy greatly writing about myself and hope I have minimized the ego." This he managed to do.

The nice part about *From Sail to Steam* was that it encouraged him to write old service acquaintances and ask them for recollections, anecdotes, and help. "Memory sometimes plays tricks after forty years," he noted in soliciting the assistance of Luce, Ashe, John S. Barnes, and others. He made it a particular point to discover what had happened to his Academy classmates, only three of whom were still alive, and to learn what had become of some of his old shipmates. It was a nostalgic voyage into the past, one he thoroughly enjoyed. The result was duly serialized in *Harper's Monthly* and in *Harper's Weekly*, beginning in February 1907 and concluding in December 1907. Harper's published the book version in October of that same year.

It is a charming and readable book, one containing information about Mahan obtainable nowhere else. Indeed, about all that is known of Mahan's early life at West Point, his Civil War experiences, and his first cruise as a passed midshipman in the *Congress* is found in *From Sail to Steam*. But like most autobiographies of the day it provides few insights into the personality, psyche, or intellectual predilections of its author. It does not mention his bitter fight with his Academy classmates, his fear of the sea, or his internal religious and theological turmoils. Omitted, too, is the fact of his near-helplessness as a practical and practicing seaman—save for the single humorous admission that he had never been particularly adept at fashioning nautical knots. In his retelling of it, the cruise of the *Chicago* was converted into something that was "in most ways enjoyable," annoying only in that it "necessarily suspended authorship." Erben does not exist in *From Sail to Steam*. Neither does the *Wachusett*, except as the locus of his special revelation from God about the influence of sea power on history and as the place where foreign officers, seeing the old pivot guns mounted in the decrepit vessel, had remarked: "Ah! Capitaine, les vieux canons. . . . Ou sont les neiges d'antan? Oui, oui, l'ancien système. Nous l'avons eu." His views on family, women, race, and domestic politics received no mention whatever. While admitting that there may have been some small substance in Badham's criticisms of his *Life of Nelson*, none of his other sharp personal struggles over the years, professional and literary, were deemed worthy of treatment. As portrayed in *From Sail to Steam*, his life had been a placid and happy one:

> But now I am sixty-seven [he concluded], and can recognize in myself a growing conservatism, which may probably limit me henceforth to bare keeping up with the procession in the future national march. Perhaps I may lag behind. With years, speculation as well as action becomes less venturesome, and I look increasingly to the changeless past as the quiet field for my future labors.[9]

His affirmation that the achievement of peace and quiet was all that he desired in his remaining days was actually written in the midst of his vigorous attack on Sims and the all-big-gun battleship. Some quiet.

More relevant to the fact of his mortality was the cardiac illness that visited him early in 1907 when he was seeing the manuscript of *From Sail to Steam* through press and was beginning to sound sharp alarums on the peace, arbitration, and disarmament mischief that might be done at the approaching Second Hague Conference. A physical examination in March showed that his "heart and arteries are deteriorated." His doctor ordered complete rest and urged him to join his wife and daughters, who were going to Bad Nauheim, Germany. Elly was returning there to take the baths for her respiratory difficulties; daughter Ellen was going along to take the waters in the hope of mitigating the lingering effects of the scarlatina and "inflammatory rheumatism" she had suffered on the family's last trip to Europe in 1905; Helen had had a nervous breakdown in April 1905 and was in search of a cure for her continuing nervous disposition. Alfred was instructed to take the baths for his heart condition. There were good baths in Bad Nauheim.

Mahan was also ordered to cut down on his "somewhat violent" daily exercises, reduce his brisk walking pace from four miles per hour to three, and abandon "the general plane of vigorous action" on which he had long lived. He agreed that at sixty-seven it was time for him to "slack up on the racket." This he did for a while in Germany in April and May of 1907. Nevertheless, he was frightfully bored during his stay at the Villa Albion in Bad Nauheim. It was "dull for most and crowded with cripples—like myself—bathing." He was fearful, too, that the migration to the "lively as champagne" waters at the spa was "destined to be a regular annual function during the life of my wife and myself." He dubbed the whole enterprise a "nuisance" and was certain that "one great feature of benefit to us is that the ocean lies between us and our accustomed cares and vexations. Out of sight, out of mind." Further, travel abroad did not interest him nearly as much as it had in the past. Indeed, "my girls say I am getting fussy and irritable in it, which is a good sign to quit." Fussy he was. So much so that when his cabin accommodations home from Bad Nauheim in the *Prinzess Alice*, of the North German Lloyd line, failed entirely to suit him he blasted the company in an angry letter to *The New York Times*.[10]

No sooner had he returned home than he was ordered into the Naval Hospital in New York for a prostatectomy, a serious surgical procedure in those days of cut, pray, and hope for the best. He entered the hospital on September 25, 1907, an inconvenience that slowed the production of his *Some Neglected Aspects of War*, published finally by Little, Brown and Company in November. It also forced him to postpone to March 1908 the writing of his "Reminiscences of Service at the Naval War College" for the Navy Department. He remained in the hospital for a month, emerging on October 24 "weak and somewhat sore," but with "hope for complete restoration by the new year." During his stay he gave the doctors a difficult time. Indeed, when he was taken to surgery and found the operating team had not yet arrived there he ordered himself returned to his room until the doctors had properly reported for duty. When at last they did their duty, they did it badly. "The first wound," Elly later reported, "had healed in such a peculiar way (very unusual they say) that it formed an almost impassable barrier and the last state was worse than the first." For this reason, a wan and weakened Mahan was in considerable pain when he returned to his home in Lawrence. Still, he managed somehow to write his ill-advised article, "The Value of the Pacific Cruise of the United States Fleet, Prospect," for *Scientific American* and to undertake other literary "odd jobs." By mid-November, however, he was suffering such "paroxysms of pain" and experiencing such "intense agony" from his first bout with Navy surgery that he had no choice but to submit to another operation on December 2 to remove the adhesions that were causing the difficulty. Returned home again ten days later, his brain for a time was "very weak, at times clouded and wandering." As he later told Clark, "I came out of the second [operation] pretty well shattered. For two weeks I was practically out of my head." But the second operation was a success and he began to recover slowly.

In late January 1908 he was up and about again and feisty enough to condemn Roosevelt's public support, over Secretary Victor H. Metcalf's head, of a decision by Surgeon General Presley M. Rixey, the president's personal physician, to assign surgeons to the command of the Navy's hospital ships. This act had produced the resignation in protest of Willard H. Brownson, a service favorite of Mahan's, as Chief of the Bureau of Navigation. Given what he had just passed through, Mahan took a dim view of naval surgeons commanding anything, much less ships, and a dimmer view of Roosevelt's meddling and muddling in their behalf in the administration of the department. "In my judgment," he told Luce, "the President, confident in his knowledge of naval matters and of his profound interest in the service, has made the grave mistake, since [Secretary] Moody, of filling the Secretary's chair with figureheads, expecting to run the machine himself. Necessary result: hasty and mistaken decisions, for the Navy is now so big a thing as to demand the sole attention of a first class man for a full official term. No man can run it and the Presidency together."[11]

That off his chest, Mahan turned to the problem that came most to concern him during and immediately after his illness. This was nothing less than a serious breakdown of his religious faith occasioned by the intense pain through which he had passed and his inability to bear it with the Christian fortitude he thought God demanded. As his daughter Ellen remembered, "he bore pain badly and seemed to be completely unnerved by it." Thus when it was clear to him that the first operation had not been successful, that another period of excruciating pain lay ahead, he went into deep dejection. "At present I am greatly discouraged," he confided to Luce in mid-November 1907, "my own practical piety having broken down miserably under some recent troubles. . . . the local troubles persist obstinately, taking out of me life and energy through persistent disappointment."

It was in propitiation for his weakness and as an act of contrition that he undertook to serve his God by writing *The Harvest Within: Thoughts on the Life of a Christian*, which Little, Brown and Company published in May 1909. So high a priority did it come to have on his writing schedule that he touched little else from June 1908 until the date of publication. It pushed his *Naval Strategy* project into the background and caused him to be annoyed when his service on the Moody-Mahan Commission in February 1909 interrupted his final polishing of the manuscript.

For once in his literary life, Mahan produced a book that was conceived and executed with little regard for its commercial prospects. *The Harvest Within* was a 75,000-word labor of Christian love. Indeed, he did not approach Little, Brown and Company about publishing it until he had completed the final draft. He knew that such books usually drew small and specialized audiences. Nonetheless, he attempted to interest editor James W. McIntyre in the manuscript by defining it as "a book of broadly religious character in which I think I have been governed by a leading idea similar, in its influence upon the work, to that which guided me in the Sea Power series." As for its potential sale, he could offer McIntyre little assurance beyond the observation that "last year, this year, and next year, have been and promise to be a period of sustained interest in these matters among most bodies of Christians." At the same time, however, he confessed that he had said and could say nothing new on the subject. The best he could hope to accomplish in the book was to "put old things in a new form such as may make them more cordially received because clearer." This, he noted, he had signally accomplished in his three *Influence of Sea Power* volumes.

The Harvest Within was essentially an expansion and rewriting of "The Practical in Christianity," an address given by Mahan in Holy Trinity Episcopal Church in Middletown, Connecticut, on March 22, 1899. If there was a central theme in it comparable to the influence of sea power on history, it was

> the particular thought which, by a process resembling that of natural selection, has come to be the centre around which all else groups itself,

in relation and subordination. That thought is that man today is susceptible of an enthusiasm for Jesus Christ resembling, but surpassing, that
which has been shown in past times for this or that historical character
in many nations; and that this enthusiasm is love, because it is inspired
less by His mighty deeds than by the sense of the excellence of His
Person, and by realization of personal relation to Him. . . . This unifies
all action and solves all perplexities. Nothing new? No; only always
new.

The book was nicely bound and the artfully designed monogram on the
cover consisted of an alpha superimposed on an omega, a juxtaposition of
the Beginning and the End that one of his daughters said looked like
A.T.M., the author's own initials. Embarrassing. Undaunted, A.T.M. dispatched complimentary copies of *The Harvest Within* to Randall T. Dav-
idson, Archbishop of Canterbury, and to various bishops and important
laymen in the American Episcopal Church.

In the final analysis, the volume was a dull exercise in Mahan's post-
surgery enthusiasm for Christ. True, the writing of it may have been psychologically therapeutic and may have helped restore the author's faith.
But, from a theological standpoint, it was a traditional and unoriginal piece
of nineteenth-century Anglican apologetics. Reminiscent of E. M. Goulburn's *Thoughts on Personal Religion* in organization and language, tiresome in its citation of hundreds of New Testament passages to prove his
points, freighted to the Plimsoll mark with reasoning by analogy, arrogant
in its implicit suggestion that all who believed and morally deported themselves as did Mahan would surely find eternal life, it was not the author's
most brilliant effort; nor was it his most popular, even though scattered
allusions to history in the text strongly suggested that his readers, the
English-speaking peoples of the earth, were the chosen of God.

The ecclesiastical and secular press in the United States and Great Britain
virtually ignored the book. Only *The Churchman* (Episcopal) in New
York and *The Guardian* (Anglican) in London took serious note of it.
"This . . . is as much advertisement—at least in that Church—as I could
reasonably expect," Mahan huffed. No English publisher would touch the
book on a joint-publication basis. Neither *The Times Literary Supplement*
nor *The Spectator*, British publications that had regularly and favorably
reviewed Mahan's other books over the years, paid attention to *The Harvest Within*. It particularly distressed him that his beloved London *Times*,
which had always done so well by him in the past, chose not to notice it.
So it was that *The Harvest Within: Thoughts on the Life of a Christian*

soon disappeared into that literary sepulcher reserved for ephemeral spiritual autobiographies. Requiescat in Pace.[12]

This interment did not depress Alfred Thayer Mahan. His interest in religion, personal and institutional, continued unabated until his death. He went on laboring for the Seamen's Church Institute (Episcopal) in New York as a member of its board and its lay vice president and supporting it to the tune of $100 annually. He worried often about the work of the Annual Convention of the Episcopal Church, in which he had on one occasion participated as an elected layman to the House of Delegates. He served on the church's Board of Missions from 1900 to 1910, a labor which Mahan School in Yangchow, China, came later to memorialize. And in simple language similar to that used in the nineteenth century by the Great White Father in Washington to wayward American Indian tribes, he lectured Japanese readers on the meaning of Christ and on the obvious superiority of Christianity over other religions.

He never relinquished his conviction that Christianity, and only Christianity among the world's religions, had uplifted men and nations, and was directly responsible for the advent and continuation of human civilization and progress. "If [you] will compare the conditions of the countries in which Christianity has existed with those where it has only begun to touch," he wrote *The New York Times*, "in such matters as the status of women, the administration of Justice, the conditions of settled government, [you] will find an answer. . . . The presence [of Christians] through the centuries has been the leaven which has effected what is called Christian civilization. The result, Christian civilization, is found only where the Christian leaven is found, from which may certainly be inferred that to this cause it is due." He developed this theme further in his "Twentieth Century Christianity," an article published in the April 1914 issue of the *North American Review*, wherein he also saw fit to condemn Unitarianism as a Christian aberration, no different from Judaism or Islam in its rejection of Christ. Secretary of the Navy Josephus Daniels wrote to him in agreement: "It is most helpful to the younger men to read your clear call to hold fast to the ancient landmarks our fathers set."

Most particularly, Mahan lectured the clergy of his own church on the point that it was not their business to take positions on contemporary political and diplomatic questions. The pulpit was a place for the weekly inculcation of Christian morality and decency; it was not a Union Square soap box. He was therefore greatly disturbed in November 1911, when Episcopal clergymen and laymen of the Diocese of New York, in convention, formally called for Senate passage of a proposed Anglo-American treaty of arbitration. Identifying himself as a "life-long communicant" of the Episcopal Church, Mahan told the readers of *The New York Times*:

> The Church . . . exceeds her legitimate functions, and so do the individual clergy when, as Church or as clergy, they endeavor to bring pressure to bear upon the State. . . . To use its Master's expression, the Church is intruding into the things of Caesar, the temporal power of His day. . . . On such a question the Church has no commission to speak, and no competent knowledge. The attempt of the clergy to do so is simply an intrusion into the sphere of the State, recalling the Calvinistic theocracy of Geneva and early New England, and the monstrous claims of the mediaeval Church to decide whether citizens owed allegiance to this ruler or to that. . . . All the members of that Convention, clergy and lay, are citizens as well as churchmen. As citizens it is not only their privilege, but their right, and may be their duty, to do their utmost to forward any measure of public policy that commends itself to their judgment. But when they assume—as they have—to take such action as representative of the Church, they usurp power. They do that for which they have no commission from God or man. . . . The source of the Church's authority is not the people, but Jesus Christ, and He never gave the Church, nor Himself assumed such powers. "Who made me a ruler and a judge?"

That was clear enough. But was it equally clear to all hands in the Diocese of New York when Mahan analogously equated the Christian Trinity that was the Father, the Son, and the Holy Ghost with the political trinity that was "the Executive, the Legislative, the Judiciary" of the American Constitutional system? Especially when he identified that system, in the words of St. Paul to the Romans, as an example of the "Powers that be, ordained of God?" Suffice it to say that Mahan was sometimes ambivalent on the Church-State relationship in history. "The principle of separateness of Church and States is not absolute," he assured Newton W. Rowell in September 1913, "but is conditioned by questions of expediency."[13]

He was also interested in the domestic missionary activities of the racially segregated Episcopal Church and, in addition to his work on the Church Board of Missions, was active in the affairs of the American Church Institute for Negroes, an offshoot of the board designed to "coordinate the several Church undertakings for negroes." He recognized that Negro Episcopalians were clearly discriminated against in "our Church South," but held that "the truth is that under our civilization the negro *is* advancing; the movement is upward." Be patient, he counseled his black co-religionists. But to encourage the tortuously slow advance of the race, he took an active interest in Negro educational institutions in the South, journeying in October 1906 to Raleigh, North Carolina, as the guest of George Foster Peabody to inspect the St. Augustine School. There he saw face to face for the last time his old friend and loyal correspondent from Academy days, Sam Ashe, whom he had not seen since he made a brief visit to Wilmington, North Carolina, in 1871. It was a grand reunion.

Similarly, he took a particular interest in the missionary activities of the Episcopal Church in the Philippines and in China. In 1911, for instance, he donated copies of all his books to the library of Boone University in Wuchang. On a larger scale, he consistently took the position that Christian missionaries abroad deserved, and should have, the solid backing and protection of their respective governments. He realized, of course, that such support could complicate issues relating to the separation of Church and State but, if the obligation to support were internationalized, a middle ground in Church-State relations might be reached. Let us, he said in 1913, ask

> the Governments of the various States of the Christian civilization—
> broadly, all European and American Governments, citizens of which
> may be engaged in Missions—to direct their diplomatic representatives
> to make periodical investigation into the results of Missions. . . . I can-
> not but think that it would conduce much to the cordial relations be-
> tween Missions and Governments if the better understanding of the
> benevolent work of Missions . . . were thus brought to the various
> Foreign Offices of Christian States. . . . There might even eventually
> result some check upon the tendency of the Roman Church every-
> where to complicate Christian action by ecclesiastical intrusion into the
> civil sphere. As things now stand, that separateness between the sphere
> of Missions and of the secular State . . . is permitted to entail a sense of
> mutual irresponsibility, if not alienation, which is scarcely Christian,
> and which will not aid to solve and determine their proper inter-relation.

While nothing came of Mahan's suggestion in this regard, he continued to insist, as he had in the past, that Christians of all nations were brought closer together by their labors in the mission fields, that "in the activities of the mission field, face to face with conditions alien to Christ, Christians will ultimately find the solution to the worst of our home problems— namely, our corporate separateness from one another." The coming Brotherhood of Man would thus be the creation and gift of the Christian God, not something artificially contrived by man in Hague conferences or in international disarmament and arbitration treaties.[14]

Mahan's attempt in 1913 and 1914 to halt proposed changes in the Anglican *Book of Common Prayer*, like his idea on international missions, fell on deaf pulpits, as it did on the clogged ears of the leaders of the Prayer Book Revision movement in the Episcopal Church. He was not concerned with attempts to modernize the magisterial language of the Prayer Book—that final blow to tradition was not delivered until the 1970s, to the horror of many American Episcopalians. He was interested mainly in stopping the constant "tinkering" with the Prayer Book which bore "the stamp of increased permission to the officiating minister to change at his sole discretion the features of what should be a service common to the Church at large." He held, as he explained to Bishop Frederick Burgess of the Diocese of Long Island, "that the common worship of the Church, through the length and breadth of the land, demands that in the major services of the week all should use the same order of service with one voice and one form of words." He publicly attacked those clergymen who insisted on the right to adapt the order of the Prayer Book service to meet the wishes of their congregations; and he took umbrage at those who returned his attack with the observation that interested laymen such as Mahan were not necessarily those persons best qualified to comment on the Episcopal Church's worship procedures. Indeed, he soon found himself at war once again—this time in the pages of *The Churchman*—battling over the proper order in the line of service of mixed-battery "Venites" and all-big-gun "Te Deums." But it was a lost campaign. Tinkering with the rubrics in the *Book of Common Prayer* continued to be a major indoor sport of the clergy of the Protestant Episcopal Church.[15]

Interested as he was during his last years in the internal politics of the Episcopal Church and the international politics of the Christian missionary movement, his concern for the course of American domestic politics also remained high. He felt that so long as Theodore Roosevelt was in the White House all was well in the United States. Aside from the differences of opinion they had about all-big-gun ships and about U.S. diplomatic strategy at the Second Hague Conference, the extroverted president and the introspective Philosopher of Sea Power saw eye to eye on most issues of domestic, foreign, and naval-military policy. Mahan even agreed with the trust-busting Roosevelt that monopolistic concentration of industrial wealth was as dangerous to America's capitalistic democracy and to individual liberties as was the dread disease called socialism. He had no use for the Rockefellers and their ilk, and he shared Roosevelt's belief that government regulation of socially and economically irresponsible corporations was necessary. Similarly, he argued strongly that the unions' arrogance and misbehavior in the form of strikes were as dangerous to the body politic as were the outrages of the trusts. Specifically, he had "not much faith in the capacity of a mercantile interest to take broad views, even of its own affairs."

In this social and economic sense, Mahan might be reckoned an occasional member of the Progressive movement that swept the nation in the years 1901–1914. He was, of course, no wild-eyed political reformer. The thought of women's suffrage horrified him. A woman's place was at the stove, not at the ballot box. He was loath to overhaul the existing machinery of American government—he would merely oil it better and provide more efficient and honest operators—and he believed that pension plans and other social-security schemes weakened the moral fiber of the working classes and undermined the economic resources and military postures of nations. "I don't clearly see how the naval situation of the world is going to turn out," he told Henderson in December 1910. "The increasing power of the working classes seems bent on such social expenditures as make the burden of armaments nearly insupportable. By one means or another, your [Britain's] old-age pensions, and our war pensions, etc., etc. in other countries, the resources of the countries are very mortgaged." But like most of the leaders of the Progressive movement, whether Democrat or Republican, he was an imperialist, militarist, and free-trader. To him, tariff-protection was simply a form of isolationism.[16]

The most comprehensive expression of his fears on the future of individualism in America was made to a commencement audience at Dartmouth College in June 1903:

> It will scarcely be questioned [he said] that a leading characteristic of contemporary movement . . . predominant in the political, industrial, and social activities of to-day, is the tendency to concentration; to the combination of many into one . . . . which carries with it a certain submersion of the individual, of individual initiative, and individual power of self-disposal, which are personal liberty of action. . . . In the political sphere we see this tendency in the absorption of small states, with their separate independence of action, into huge aggregations of communities, more or less closely bound together, so as to constitute a single political unit for internal or external action. . . . In the industrial sphere . . . . it will be generally conceded that the tendency, nay, even the conscious aim, of the so-called Trusts Movement, and of the antagonistic concentrations in the ranks of labor, is the elimination of the independent individual; of the small producer and the middle man in the sphere of production and distribution. . . . Competition and the middle man, it is explained, cause increased expense to the consumer, because concen-

tration of control promotes efficiency of administration, with consequent reduction of cost in the product and to the consumer. . . . [but] the same process strengthens indefinitely the political power of concentrated authority. . . . In the social order . . . I presume the supreme conception of concentration by organization is that commonly known as Socialism. This, in final analysis, if I rightly understand, proposes such subordination of the individual to the community as amounts to entire deprivation of initiative and of free action. The man's place, and sphere and scope of action, no more no less, are to be determined for him. There is no logical stopping place short of this ultimate conclusion. . . . There is, in my judgment, ground for the fears of those who see in unchecked industrial combination, the necessary and inevitable forerunner of that social concentration which, as yet an unrealized idea, we know as Socialism. . . . I discern in the various movements of the day . . . a common impulse towards concentration and organization of power, so marked and so general as to constitute a prominent, if not the predominant, tendency of the times—the spirit of the age. It is no new thing in spirit, even if it be in form. Collectivism and individualism, to use the terminology of to-day, are at another date despotism and freedom; at a third they are authority and license; they are order and anarchy at a fourth.

Mahan had no solution to this dangerous situation to recommend to Dartmouth's graduating class of 1903, save to urge its members to exercise their own personalities, to be morally and ethically true to themselves, and to consecrate their lives, actions, and thoughts to the love of God and the example of Jesus Christ with a view toward purifying their inner selves.[17]

At the same time, however, as he attached himself to the outer fringes of the Progressive movement, he was hopeful that Roosevelt and the progressive-insurgent sector of the Republican party could and would prevent the anti-individualism found in both socialism and monopoly capitalism from coming to penetrate the fabric of American life. In 1908 he voted for William Howard Taft, the Rough Rider's hand-picked successor. In so doing, he was more than ever convinced that were Bryan successful in his third try for the White House the entire American system would come apart at the seams. "He may be absolutely honest, it makes no difference," he told Ashe. "No one believes him safe, and distrust, I believe, amounts to terror." He was relieved when Taft won handily.

But then he worried that the Republican president-elect, whatever his "peculiarly eminent qualifications for the Presidency," might not have "a strong military sense." Mahan therefore urged TR to make it clear to Taft that the U.S. battle fleet, just returned from its voyage around the world, must not under any conditions be divided between the Atlantic and Pacific coasts. "As a matter of public outcry, this is a nightmare to me," Mahan explained, "and, as I see it, this is one of the most evident external dangers threatening the country." TR did Mahan's bidding in the matter and Taft accepted the recommendation. The battle fleet was not divided. It remained in the Atlantic.

What was divided in the years 1909–1911 was the Republican party. As President Taft assumed stand-pat positions on such domestic reform issues as conservation, the lowering of the protective tariff, the direct election of senators, direct primaries for the nomination of candidates for elective office, a corrupt-practices act, and the initiative, referendum, and recall, Republican progressives and insurgents began demanding his head. In November 1910 the Democrats won control of the House on a wave of popular insistence on reform, and the Senate passed into the hands of a reform-minded coalition of liberal Democrats and Republican insurgents.

In January 1911, the militant reform wing of the GOP, headed by Senator Robert M. La Follette, of Wisconsin, launched the National Progressive Republican League whose objective was to capture the party from the conservative Taft forces. This was the beginning of the formal split in Republican ranks which led in 1912 to the candidacy of Roosevelt on the third-party Progressive ("Bull Moose") ticket, a divisive act that handed the election, virtually on a silver platter, to Democrat Woodrow Wilson.

Mahan seems not to have followed closely the internal disintegration of the Republican party on issues of domestic reform in 1909 and 1910. In the November 1910 elections in New York, for example, he supported the unsuccessful gubernatorial candidacy of Republican Henry L. Stimson, neither a flaming insurgent nor a stand-pat reactionary. As he explained to Henderson, there was "nothing radical in the situation" that had brought both House and Senate under progressive-insurgent control in November 1910. He blamed the overturn instead on the "fact that the legislation of the now expiring Congress was controlled by very old men, men living in a past, unable to keep up with public opinion, or to free themselves from the 'privileged' influences which had always dominated their acts." He wished only that Taft had shown more courage in using the veto against some of the backward-looking legislation passed by the outgoing Congress. He could not believe that his friend Roosevelt harbored third-term ambitions, or that he would make another run for the White House as the leader of the rapidly growing progressive wing of the party. Still, he was much impressed with the ex-president's highly visible and successful campaign efforts for the GOP in 1910. In states where the former president had stumped for the candidates of the disintegrating party, its losses to the Democrats had been cut. "The interests and the privileges were against him," observed Mahan, but "I believe he still has a big future, for he possesses one quality which voters adore—absolute recklessness of personal consequences. The cautious man is so much in evidence that an uncautious one appeals to the people."

Mahan also favored the broad thrust of Roosevelt's speech "The New Nationalism" delivered at Osawatomie, Kansas, on August 31, 1910. There T.R. outlined the doctrines that served as the Bull Moose mating call during the presidential election two years later. New Nationalism artfully blended ideas that encompassed the building of an ever-larger Navy, the pursuit of a muscular foreign policy that included American participation in "international police work," and the humbling of the trusts and monopolies at home. "Every man holds his property subject to the general right of the community to regulate its uses to whatever degree the public welfare may require it," said the former president. With this generalization Mahan could agree. "I am a genuine radical," Roosevelt wrote a friend a few days after his Osawatomie speech. "I believe in what you would call an 'imperialist democracy.'" So did Mahan—so long as the "democracy" part of it did not become too democratic.[18]

Whatever the continuing political and personal attraction Roosevelt had for him, Mahan bore no particular animosity toward Taft in 1909 and 1910. After all, Taft had kept the battle fleet concentrated, had attempted to maintain the momentum of Roosevelt's program that called for the building of at least two battleships per year, had sought to uphold the Open Door policy in China by the device of Dollar Diplomacy, and had sustained the Roosevelt Corollary to the Monroe Doctrine in the Caribbean by making use of the U.S. Marine Corps. All this satisfied Mahan.

The break between the two men came suddenly in mid-1911 when Taft sponsored treaties of general arbitration with Great Britain and France. Signed on August 3, submitted immediately to the Senate for ratification, the treaties were designed to take advantage of a clause in the Anglo-Japanese Treaty, which had been renewed on July 13, 1911, prohibiting the signatories from going to war with a third power with which either had a general arbitration treaty. Taft's motive, obviously, was to remove from the context of continuing American-Japanese tension in East Asia the possibility that Britain might be dragged willy-nilly into an American war with Japan on the Japanese side.

Mahan scarcely believed that Taft could be so foolish as to identify himself with treaties that did not clearly exclude from arbitration the Monroe

Doctrine and the question of Asiatic immigration to the United States; or that he would number himself among those other non-exclusionists whom Roosevelt had characterized in an anti-arbitration speech on Decoration Day in May 1911 as "short-sighted, false-peace advocates." Had not Taft's sinking administration, whatever else might be said of it, supported "a strong Navy, maintained in force by the provision of two new battleships annually?" Unhappily for the bewildered Mahan, Taft favored both the Navy and the arbitration treaties, the latter without Monroe Doctrine and Oriental immigration provisions written in. When he finally realized this, Mahan hastily mounted the anti-arbitration barricade, as he had done on several occasions before.

From the standpoint of tactical verbal concentration, Mahan's return to the anti-arbitration fray in July 1911 could not have been better timed. Early in the year he had arranged to furnish *North American Review* six articles (later raised to eight) on various contemporary subjects, among them international arbitration. His "Armaments and Arbitration" had appeared in the May 1911 issue and his "Diplomacy and Arbitration" was published in July. These were followed by "The Deficiencies of Law as an Instrument of International Adjustments" (November 1911), "The Place of Force in International Relations" (January 1912), and "The Great Illusion" (March 1912). Mahan was already again in full cry against the concept of arbitration when the Senate began to debate the controversial treaties in August 1911. He regretted only that his earlier commitment to *North American Review* made it impossible for him to accept a publishing offer from Roosevelt. The latter, then editor of *The Outlook*, asked him to help fight the treaties in the pages of that widely circulated magazine. Mahan had to decline.

But the arbitration treaties brought the Roosevelt-Lodge-Mahan triumvirate briefly together again in a working alliance—as had the Mahan-Erben fight of 1894, the Hawaii and Philippine annexation debates of 1890–1899, and the various struggles to preserve the War College. Within the informal troika, it was Roosevelt's job to politicize the issue to Taft's detriment. Senator Lodge assumed the task, successfully accomplished, of loading the treaties with so many exclusions, exceptions, and insistences on Senate control of what issues would be arbitrable ("justiciable") that they would be innocuous. Mahan took on the educational duties of acting as anti-arbitration propagandist and providing Lodge and Roosevelt with historical arguments against the treaties. "I shall be glad to use the points you make," Lodge assured him on one occasion. Among those points, Mahan told TR, was that in the treaties "as I read them, the Senate parts forever with its power of advice and consent as to the determination whether a particular question is 'justiciable.' "

From an intellectual standpoint, Mahan added to his anti-arbitration broadside little ammunition that he had not fired off in 1897, 1899, and 1907. It need only be said, therefore, that he wept for the future of the Monroe Doctrine, called attention to the German menace in the Caribbean and the "Yellow Peril" in California, urged the Senate to stand fast against popular demands for the treaties and for hasty action thereon, pointed to the fact that Sir Edward Grey himself favored exclusion of the Monroe Doctrine from Anglo-American arbitration, and insisted throughout the debate that neither the doctrine nor immigration was properly or safely "justiciable."

At no point did Mahan treat fairly Taft's principal motive in sponsoring the treaties—namely, to reduce the possibility of an Anglo-American war in the Pacific growing out of American-Japanese conflict there, a precaution that would have strengthened America's diplomatic posture in East Asia vis-à-vis Japan. This exercise in White House realpolitik did not mesh with Mahan's violent anti-arbitration biases, although he was as concerned about Japanese imperialism and the future of the Open Door in China as was Taft. He was pleased, therefore, that when the treaties were finally ratified by the Senate on March 7, 1912, they specifically excluded the Monroe Doctrine and control of Oriental immigration from coverage. Going further, the agreements included clauses that permitted the Senate to determine the suitability of any question before it was submitted to formal arbitration.[19]

Although the treaties debate of 1911–1912 marked a setback for the arbitrative principle in Anglo-American councils and did little to improve Anglo-American amity, it did provide Mahan the luxury of engaging in what was to be his last great literary battle—this time with Norman Angell, a prominent British socialist. While this was not as ill-tempered a struggle as was his earlier confrontation with Angell's countryman, F. P. Badham, it was testy enough.

It began when Angell's controversial and widely read book, *The Great Illusion*, was published in the United States early in 1911. Pacifist in tone, anti-capitalist in exposition, its arguments sustained by historical references, *The Great Illusion* also included a personal attack on Mahan. Put succinctly, Angell argued that the "great illusion" stalking Europe in 1910 was the notion that war, preparation for war, and imperialism somehow ensured a nation's economic prosperity, stability, and development. He held, too, that the foreign policies of the European states, particularly those of Great Britain and Germany, were based on acquisitive material self-interest because this was foolishly considered by European statesmen to be the only realistic and measurable foundation upon which to conduct diplomatic affairs.

In developing his theme, Angell argued that the organic theory of the state (Social Darwinism) was sheer nonsense from a biological standpoint, that the aggressiveness of states and persons could not be equated with one another in behavioral terms. He was convinced, instead, "that the natural tendencies of the average man are getting more and more away from war. He is quite ready to believe in peace, once he is persuaded that it is safe to do so." As for imperialism, it merely demeaned the imperialist nations while ensuring them no long-term economic advantages. Further, Angell maintained that states did not arm for peace and international stability, as the militarists were wont to claim, but principally for aggression and war. Armaments were thus the logical expression of the "great illusion." They led not to economic prosperity; they led to war and the ultimate economic ruin of victors and vanquished alike. Therefore, no lasting advantage, not even material self-interest, could ever be obtained by the use of military force. "Is it not somewhat childish and elementary," he asked, "to conceive of force only as the firing off of guns and the launching of *Dreadnoughts*? Of struggle, as the physical struggle between men, instead of the application of man's energies to his contest with the planet? Is not the time coming when the real struggle will inspire us with the same respect and even the same thrill as that now inspired by a charge in battle; especially as the charges in battle are getting very out of date, and are shortly to disappear from our warfare?"

Angell preached an environmental alternative to war, together with the idea, as he noted in his reply to Mahan's criticism of his book, that the only sure way to achieve true economic security, disarmament, and peace was

for the nations of Europe to realize that they are a community, and that a community can only exist by virtue of the units composing it surrendering the use of force the one as against the other. . . . You cannot get communal sense enough, even in the pirate crew, unless they surrender the use of force as between themselves, act by agreement, and cooperate against their victim, their prey. The prey of civilization is Nature, the Planet, and unless the units which make up, or ought to make up, the community of Europe give up preying one upon the other, and cooperate in the attack upon their prey, that attack will by so much suffer. Inside political frontiers this general recognition that the exercise of force as between individuals composing the community, must, in the individual's own interest, be surrendered, is now fairly achieved. The next step of human progress is to render the application of that principle complete.

In *The Great Illusion* the author sarcastically quoted Mahan's belief that "like individuals, nations and empires have souls as well as bodies," and laughed at Mahan's thought that the "extension of national authority over alien communities, which is the dominant note in the world of politics today, dignifies and enlarges each State and each citizen that enters its fold." Asked Angell in reply: "Have we not come to realize that this is all moonshine, and very mischievous moonshine?"

As might be expected, Mahan did not take kindly to the "moonshine" remark, engaged then as he was in the debate on arbitration treaties. He read the book "twice attentively" in mid-January 1912, made copious notes on it, and did several careful outlines and drafts of his intended reply. As his handwritten notes on *The Great Illusion* show, he was outraged by the book and its author. He found Angell to be "shallow," inclined to "tremendous overstatement," filled with "bias," and guilty of "argument ad hominem." He decided that "this caricature of my words is so gross that it must be noted." He also accused Angell of "gross travesty" in quoting other of his sources. The entire book was, in his opinion, "essentially the opposite of my point of view that the rightful use of force (war) is remedial of Evil." It certainly was.

His printed response to Angell, which appeared in *North American Review*, March 1912, was far more polite, but it too minced few words. War, Mahan argued, as he had in the past, "proceeds from the temper of the people which, when roused, disregards self-interest." Citing his "The Place of Force in International Relations" which had appeared in the *North American Review* in January 1912, he noted that since 1860 war had "proceeded demonstrably from motives moral," not from motives of material self-interest. Its "inciting causes . . . in our day are moral." War, then, remedied evil—such evils as slavery in the American Civil War and political tyranny in the Spanish-American War. As for imperialism ("the use of power for beneficent ends"), Mahan asserted that he was "personally proud, as an American, of what America has accomplished in the late Spanish possessions and in the Panama Canal Zone; and if I were a Briton, I should feel a like pride in the benefits done to India and to Egypt." He vigorously denied Angell's contention that war invariably led its participants to economic disaster. He was quick to point out that even were Angell correct in his theory, he was shaky in his history. War often did pay, and pay handsomely, Mahan retorted. Witness England's steady economic growth during her wars with France in the eighteenth and early-nineteenth centuries and the enormous territorial, population, and economic growth that accompanied Bismarck's wars of national unification against Denmark, Austria, and France, 1864–1870. Concluded Mahan:

> The fundamental error, however, is the conception that nations maintain armaments with a view to aggression in behalf of self-interest, measured in speedy returns of dollars and cents; a view which dominates the entire book. . . . Today all recent history shows that governments are reluctant to go to war; but they recognize, and the people sustain them, that war may come, and that if it does it will expose the nation to vital injury to its "financial and industrial stability." This is quite different from the apprehension that the reason of an enemy for declaring war is to inflict such injury. . . . The entire conception of the work is itself an illusion based upon a profound misreading of human action. To regard the world as governed by self-interest only is to live in a non-existent world. . . . Yet this is the aspect under which *The Great Illusion* avowedly regards the world that now is. It matters little what the arguments are by which such a theory is advocated, when the concrete facts of history are against it.

Angell struck back in the June 1912 issue of *North American Review*, at the very moment Mahan received notification of his final detachment from all future naval duty, effective June 6, 1912. This last was in compliance with a law, dated June 1898, which increased the number of officers needed to fight the Spanish-American War in that it "authorized the employment of retired officers in peace, as well as in war, for 14 years from date." Mahan's fourteen-year period of grace was thus ended. But so intensely involved was he at the moment in single-ship combat with HMS Angell that he scarcely noticed the announcement from Secretary Meyer that his long career in the U.S. Navy was at last over—perhaps because Angell had taken the offensive in a most effective manner.

First, the Englishman denied that his thesis on material self-interest as the primary cause of war was as narrowly based as Mahan insisted, and indeed it was not. He then jumped on a statement in Mahan's *The Interest of America in International Conditions*, published in 1910, which indicated that Mahan also accepted materialism as the basis of national behavior. Angell triumphantly quoted Mahan:

> The old predatory instinct that he should take who has the power, survives . . . and moral force is not sufficient to determine issues unless supported by physical. Governments are corporations, and corporations

have not souls. . . . [Governments] must put first the lawful interests of their own wards, their own people. Such preeminence forces a nation to seek markets and where possible control them to its own advantage by preponderant force, the ultimate expression of which is possession. . . . [This produces] an inevitable link in a chain of logical sequences: Industry, markets, control, navy, bases.

True, Mahan *had* said that, as would have any self-respecting imperialist of the period. What Angell emphasized, then, was one aspect of Mahan's dual view that war was sometimes fought for moral reasons and sometimes for reasons material. Unfortunately, Mahan had never developed a workable synthesis of the morality-versus-material dichotomy, one arguing the proposition, in Angell's sarcastically helpful words, that an economic question could easily become a moral question, a question of right. "War, ineffective to achieve an economic end . . . will still be fought because a point trifling in the economic sense is all-important from the view of rights." Instead, Mahan's theory of the origin of war often varied with the historical point he was making, or illustrating, in a given book or article at a given moment.

But Mahan's greater sin, according to Angell, even more notable than his theoretical opportunism on the origin of war or his philosophical failure to synthesize the morality and materialism of war, was his failure to see the beauties of internationalism:

But Admiral Mahan, if he does not deprecate, at least does not encourage, that attitude which would make the individual . . . nation . . . part of a community. He urges that the community of nations will in some wonderful way reverse the process which has produced the communities of men; that the isolation of units employing force the one against the other is a safer road of progress than that of a completer cooperation which looks to the abandoning of force in favor of agreement and a common end determined by reason and discussion. And this, with whatever sophistry or eloquence it may be urged, is the doctrine of savagery.

In an unpublished reply to Angell's rebuttal, a stung Mahan noted only that "now no one will deny that material prosperity is a good thing, nor that up to a certain point it is essential to the moral welfare of all and should be secured. But all the same it is the least worthy of good motives and this instance shows the inability of the author [Angell] to rise above the low plane on which his argument rests throughout." That, of course, was no answer. It did, however, show that Mahan had been bested in his controversy with Norman Angell. It was well that he chose to end the game when he did, even though the ball was back in his court.[20]

Actually, he was caught up in the exciting and confusing presidential election of 1912, the outcome of which was far more important to him than rushing again to the net against the agile Angell. Needless to say, he had no interest whatever in the Democrats. In his opinion they still remained ignorantly oblivious to the needs of the Navy; they were also soft on the Monroe Doctrine and the American presence in Panama. Further, their leading candidate early in 1912 appeared to be Missouri Congressman James Beauchamp ("Champ") Clark, Speaker of the House, a man who had not endeared himself to Mahan when, in February 1911, he advocated passage of the proposed Canadian-American Reciprocity Treaty as a step toward the annexation of Canada. It was a "disgustingly indiscreet—not to say worse—utterance," Mahan declared. He decided that Clark had probably been drinking when he made that statement, because he had seen "Champ" so indulge when the two men served together for several days on the Board of Visitors at the Naval Academy in May 1903. Congressman Oscar W. Underwood, of Alabama, Democratic floor leader, struck Mahan as a reasonably sensible man but not presidential timber. He had voted wrong on the Naval Appropriation Bill for 1912. The performance of Governor Woodrow Wilson of New Jersey, who stumped the nation in 1912 in pursuit of the Democratic party's nomination, gave him "no assurance that as President personal interest will not predominate over duty to office."

In Mahan's mind, the choice came down to Taft or Roosevelt. When the Republican Convention in Chicago nominated Taft on June 22, and the party's progressive and insurgent forces walked angrily out of the hall crying "fraud" and calling for a third party headed by Roosevelt, Mahan was in a quandary. He knew that Taft's nomination had been engineered by conservative Southern Republican delegates, men who "can't deliver a single electoral vote." But he knew, too, that a Republican split would serve only to put the hated Democrats in the White House. As he explained his dilemma to Henry White on June 28:

> Personally, my views are nearer those of Taft than those of Roosevelt, but I have lost faith in the former as able to guide the ship, because he has not commanded the confidence of the people, as I think Roosevelt has. The avowed sympathies of the latter would give him greater power to influence, and to control extravagances. . . . Sick as I am of [Secretary of State] Knox, and of the diplomatic record of the administration, it is clear to me that a *party* [Democratic] which at this junc-

ture can stop building up the Navy is *ipso facto* shown to have no grasp of national—or international—issues. And look what a gang of candidates! . . . When I say my opinions are nearer Taft than Roosevelt, I refer to domestic questions chiefly. I have not been able to reconcile myself to the recall, and only partly to the initiative and referendum. His sledge hammer manner of speaking also chills me. But he is a great man; and with my principal interest in external affairs I would prefer him in the Presidential chair to any man prominently named in either party.

Mahan therefore decided on watchful waiting. If Roosevelt seemed to stand a chance as a third-party candidate, Mahan would likely vote for him; if not, he would probably go with Taft.

A few days later, July 2, the Democrats meeting in Baltimore nominated Wilson on the 46th ballot, over Clark, but only because William Jennings Bryan, not Mahan's favorite statesman, shifted his support to the New Jersey governor and former president of Princeton University. On August 5, the Progressive party convention in Chicago predictably nominated Roosevelt on a platform that called for sweeping reforms in American political and industrial life. These included the initiative, the referendum, and the recall, popular veto of judicial decisions, minimum wages for working women, and suffrage for women. There was little on the Bull Moose checklist of domestic issues that Mahan in good conscience could support. But Wilson, a fine historian in his own right, attracted him even less. As Mahan explained to one Wilson supporter, Horatio G. Dohrman, on July 15, the governor's sudden "conversion to advanced 'progressive' views has synchronized too nearly with his seeking a nomination to convince me of the purity of his motives; and his prolonged absence from his duties as governor of a state to push his personal fortunes has confirmed the unfavorable impression. I may add I am a convert away from him, having once esteemed him highly." Also, in Mahan's opinion, Wilson had waffled on the question of the battleship-building program in his acceptance speech.

Although he did not make up his mind on the question until the last minute, Mahan voted for Roosevelt on November 5. Ironically, in the last campaign he lived to see, he voted against the Republican party for the first time in his life. In doing so, he had to close his eyes to the Bull Moose platform on domestic questions and concentrate almost exclusively on foreign-policy issues. "There is really only one of the present candidates who has any large grasp of foreign policy, and that is Roosevelt," he wrote one correspondent. "I have not been able to accept his recent propositions concerning recall, etc., but believing, as I do, that our foreign policies are the most important, I am coming around to him." In the final reckoning he decided that while Taft's domestic policies "appeal more to my conservative temperament," he had made "a most disastrous muddle of our foreign policy."

Specifically, Taft had not vetoed or otherwise prevented the enactment of the Panama Canal Tolls bill of August 1912. This legislation, which discriminated economically against foreign shipping, violated the spirit of the Hay-Pauncefote Treaty of 1901, and, Mahan thought, undermined European respect for the Monroe Doctrine. Nor had Taft's attempt to maintain the Open Door in China with Dollar Diplomacy proved successful. Japan and Russia had squeezed American enterprise out of Manchuria. Further, the president's general arbitration treaties with Britain and France were palatable to Mahan only because the Senate had emasculated them. He rated Taft the equal of the Rough Rider on but one issue—"at least he, like Roosevelt, stands for [building] two battleships" each year. For reasons naval and diplomatic he therefore cast his lot with T.R., knowing that in so doing he was probably helping Wilson into the White House. "Foreign affairs," he lamented, "will almost certainly be mismanaged by the Democrats." Naval affairs would be managed by them not at all. "I have been slinging brickbats at them for months past," he told Bouverie Clark late in October, "and hope getting away [to Europe] will put them and their rottenness out of my mind. I'm sorry for the country; but if it will take what is bad for it now, it must take its medicine later like a good boy." With that sour observation, Mahan held his nose and voted. Four days later, November 9, he departed for Europe with Elly and his daughters, as though fleeing the Götterdämmerung that was soon to be visited upon the supine republic by Wilson, Bryan, Clark, and the other "doctrinaire backwoodsmen" who comprised the party of Jefferson.[21]

The family's itinerary on what proved to be Mahan's last trip abroad began with a week in London, thence to Paris for a brief visit with Mahan's brother, Frederick, who had moved there following his retirement from the Army, and then on to Pau for an extended stay with Elly's sister, Rosalie Evans Brown. From Pau the family journeyed to the French Riviera and to Palermo, Sicily. They returned home in early April 1913 on board the Cunard steamer *Saxonia*. It was a trip Mahan very much needed. "I have got into such a habit of hard monotonous work that I feel a total change necessary," he told Clark. He particularly looked forward to being freed from the "active interposition in current national naval policies which has added so much to my work this year."

It was difficult, if not impossible, for Mahan to remain inactive for more than a few days at a stretch. Indeed, when he reached Pau in mid-December 1912, he turned to the task of seeing through press his last book—*The Major Operations of the Navies in the War of American Independence* which Little, Brown and Company brought out in October 1913. It was not a new work; it was a slightly revised reprinting of the lengthy chapter he had contributed fifteen years earlier to the third volume of the seven-volume *The Royal Navy: A History From the Earliest Times to the Present* edited by William Laird Clowes. He had long believed that his naval history of the American Revolution had been buried without benefit of literary clergy in the dense and "exceedingly cumbrous" Clowes volumes, and complained that he had been badly underpaid for the piece back in 1897 ($2,500—or $25 per thousand words, half his usual rate). He considered the work important enough to stand on its own among his other naval histories, while earning a few additional royalty dollars as well. In his opinion, the book was "technically a rather unique representation of one of the most interesting naval wars of modern history."

It took him several years of acrimonious correspondence to persuade Sampson Low, Marston and Company, British publisher of the Clowes series, to release back to him the copyright on *Major Operations* so that he might republish it in the United States, perhaps as a volume in a proposed "Collected Works of Alfred Thayer Mahan," a project that aborted. Unfortunately, his friend Roy B. Marston had left the company and the new managers of the firm were loath to surrender their legal rights in the matter without more compensation than Mahan was prepared to offer. Further, they claimed he had been handsomely paid for his effort. Only after much negotiation and pleading by Mahan and by Little, Brown and Company, did the English house finally give way. In 1910 it had published as a separate volume Theodore Roosevelt's naval history of the War of 1812, which had also been entombed in the Clowes work. It could do no less for Mahan.[22]

Mahan identified *Major Operations of the Navies in the War of American Independence* as "the last work on naval history I shall ever undertake," confessed that there was nothing new in the book that had not appeared in the Clowes version, and doubted that it would sell well—as, indeed, it did not. Still, it afforded him an opportunity, in a new introduction, to develop "the general lesson to be derived from the course of the War of American Independence." That lesson was that "wars, like conflagrations, tend to spread; more than ever perhaps in these days of close international entanglements and rapid communications." It was imperative, therefore, that the governments of Europe, as they had in the First Balkan War of October 1912–May 1913, "forestall the kindling of even the slightest flame in regions where all alike are interested, though with diverse objects." It was vitally important, he later held, that "the Great Powers . . . sit down hard upon all the small states [in the Balkans] and make them . . . do as they are bid."[23]

During his entire time in Europe from November 1912 to April 1913 Mahan feared that he and his family might be caught there by the sudden escalation into general war of Turkey's conflict with the Bulgarians, Serbs, Greeks, and Montenegrins. He hated the Turks, their false religion, the atrocities and cruelties they visited on subject Christian peoples, and their senseless autocracy. He was pleased to see them defeated by the Balkan coalition. But as daughter Ellen recalled, "Papa [was] uneasy lest war break out. He considered the difficulty of getting gold at the banks a significant sign." It certainly concerned him, as he wrote from Palermo in March 1913, that "any slight slip among the diplomats might land all the fat in the fire, and the Mediterranean be a scene of war before I could get my women folk out—not to say my gray hairs, what I have of them." He was therefore much relieved to be able to get his bald pate and his family safely home before the Second Balkan War broke out in June 1913. War, he had long maintained, was an excellent stimulant to the march of human progress. He had no interest, however, in being personally inconvenienced by it, or in subjecting his own "women folk" to its ravages.[24]

The return of the Mahan family to the United States in April 1913 permitted its patriarch to survey at first hand the performance of the Wilson administration. Convinced as he already was that "for the next four years the country is in the hands of the Philistines—or worse," he did not approach the task with an open mind. Indeed, he characterized as "amateurish diplomacy" Wilson's idealistic attempt to advance democratic institutions in revolution-torn Mexico by refusing U.S. diplomatic recognition to the despotic government of General Victoriano Huerta, a brutal dictator Britain recognized and with whom she did business. Mahan admitted that he was probably being a bit unfair to Wilson in the Huerta matter; but he could not get it out of his mind that the Democrats "had refused the maintenance of a Navy" since the birth of the republic in 1789. No matter what they did or did not do, Mahan simply could not "feel secure while they are in office." For this reason, he could view the president and the secretary of state, Bryan, as little more than ideological "faddists," bumbling tyros who were hopelessly opinionated on foreign policy. In attempting to bring down Huerta's bloody regime in Mexico, they and their partisans failed to "recognize that self-government is not practicable for all peoples, merely because the English-speaking peoples have made it work." Moreover, the Wilson-Bryan crowd was even foolish enough to be "greatly captivated" by Winston Churchill's wild suggestion that the great powers observe a naval building holiday in 1913 in the interest of reducing international tensions. To Mahan, the Democrats were the "peace party," and that was that. "You may gather I am in opposition," he told Henderson, "and I am."[25]

The greatest personal question confronting Mahan on his return from Europe to Quogue in 1913 was what next to do with his career in a literary way. No major commitment hung over him, and no editor or publisher approached him with a proposal that captured his fancy. Reluctantly, he decided to begin working on a book, the idea for which he had first conceived in 1906, emphasizing the influence of territorial and commercial expansion on American history. It would be, he explained to J. Franklin Jameson, a general history of the United States in which "expansion should hold some such position as Sea Power has taken in my principal writings." But his heart was not in it, and the few manuscript pages he completed indicate that the project was well on its way to becoming a shallow and spiritless piece of work. Indeed, he knew that Henry Adams had already skillfully handled the acquisition of Louisiana and George Rives had covered thoroughly the annexation of Texas. "The ground is already very well taken up," he admitted. Knowing too that "research propagates itself like cancer," he was in no mood, nor did he have the patience or energy, to dig deeply into the vastness of the subject matter save to add to the Adams and Rives accounts "a presentation rather of motives and tendencies, which they have not neglected, but which perhaps I can the more elicit by paying less attention to the mere narrative of transactions." It is probably well that such boiler plate was never written.[26]

The fact remained, however, that Mahan required a source of income beyond his retirement pay. It was also extremely important to him that he complete the building of an estate that would support his wife and maiden daughters in comfort after his death. Because of this, he reluctantly agreed to a suggestion made by Jameson in July 1913 that he accept appointment as a research associate at the Carnegie Institution in Washington, D.C. He disliked the capital city, always had, but the formal duties of the assignment were light—little more than an informal weekly chat with Jameson and the staff of the institution "about historical matters"—and the pay was right, an honorarium of $2,400 for a six-month period scheduled to begin on November 1, 1914. In January 1914, after much backing and filling, and while still wondering what it was he was actually expected to do in the plush job, he accepted the post from Robert S. Woodward, president of the Carnegie Institution. He was slow to realize that he was expected to do very little in Washington other than lend his world-famous name to the institution and pursue his own historical research at whatever speed and on whatever topic he chose to work. He decided, therefore, to examine further his idea about the influence of expansion on American history, even though he knew that it held little promise. At no time did he exhibit any real interest in the Carnegie position "except for the feeling that I ought not to refuse the pecuniary offer." It was merely a question of "good pay, an offer not to be disregarded in these hard times."[27]

A few months before moving his family from Quogue to Washington, the event that Mahan had long assured his readers would likely never happen indeed happened. On June 28, 1914, an obscure Bosnian terrorist named Gavrilo Princip assassinated Archduke Francis Ferdinand, heir to the Austro-Hungarian throne, in an obscure little Serbian town called Sarajevo. When Austria issued an ultimatum to Serbia on July 23 and declared war on the Serbs five days later, Germany supported her. Russia, in turn, encouraged by France, supported Serbia's resistance to Hapsburg pressure. The huge European armies and navies, which Mahan had often told his readers existed only to preserve international stability and peace, were nervously mobilized and deployed to their predetermined battle stations. During the hectic first week of August the interlocked mechanisms of the Triple Entente and Triple Alliance began inexorably to grind. Germany declared war on Russia on August 1, on France on August 3, and on Belgium on August 4. Britain declared war on Germany on August 4; and Austria declared war on Russia on August 6. So highly prepared and tuned for war were the European fighting machines that the Royal Navy went instantly into action when it received the single-word order "Go" on August 4. That same evening the massive German Army smashed across the Belgian frontier, bound for France.

A relatively minor Austro-Serbian crisis thus metastasized within five confused and emotional weeks into one of the most lethal wars in human history. Of course, all the participants were quick to proclaim that they were responding only to the brutal aggression, real and potential, of their neighbors. All announced that they were fighting only to defend their territory, their sovereignty, and their national honor. And all soon agreed that the "Great War" was being waged only to achieve enduring peace.

While Mahan had occasionally warned that small regional wars could balloon into major conflagrations, thanks to complex treaty arrangements

among the great powers and to the unwillingness or inability of the statesmen of those powers to douse the sparks in time, he was surprised by the
sudden onset of World War I. But not so surprised that he was caught
without an immediate analysis of war guilt. On August 3, 1914, he gave
an interview to the *New York Evening Post* in which he maintained that
Austria, using the Serbian issue as a pretext and with German connivance
and encouragement, had wantonly launched the war to permit the Austro-
Germans ultimately to humble Russia. "The motives are to be found in
Austria's apprehension of the growing Slav power in the south and that of
Germany concerning Russia on the east," he declared. This concern also
forced Germany to launch a lightning attack on the czar's ally in the west,
"to overwhelm [France] at once by concentrated preparation and impetuous momentum" since Berlin would be unable to sustain a "prolonged
aggression" on two fronts. In this situation, Mahan concluded, Great
Britain had no choice but to "declare war at once. Otherwise, her entente
engagements, whatever the letter, will be in spirit violated, and she will
earn the entire distrust of all possible future allies." Britain declared war
on Germany the following day.

During the critical three days that were August 1–3, 1914, Mahan
dashed off an article for *Leslie's Weekly* in which he argued that the
Royal Navy could effectively blockade Germany, crushing her in the
same way that the Union blockade had crushed the South in the Civil
War. Such economic pressure would soon force the smaller German battle
fleet out of its ports and into a decisive action in the North Sea where
the Royal Navy would be able to destroy it in one grand and glorious
surface battle. Thus would Britain establish command of the sea, particularly of the North Sea, the strategic center of the naval war, and bring
Germany economically to her knees.

A few days later he was hard at work on another article, never published, which was tentatively titled "About What is the War?" In this
piece he maintained that it was not the existence of armaments or the lack
of machinery for international arbitration that had brought on the conflict; it was a spirit of intense Slav nationalism coupled with the "past
blunders" of Europe's statesmen in the Balkans. It occurred to him, somewhat belatedly it would seem, that "those little countries [should] be left
to work out their own salvation among themselves." It was at this point,
in early August, as Mahan began to blame the onset of the carnage on
factors other than those which had actually provided the fuel for the fire
storm, that he was silenced by Woodrow Wilson. But not before he
prophesied to a correspondent of the London *Daily Telegraph* that the

kaiser's war at sea would end with the Imperial German Navy steaming into English ports to surrender.[28]

It was an expensive silencing from Mahan's standpoint because the outbreak of the war brought him lucrative propositions from newspapers and magazines to comment on the diplomatic and military aspects of the conflict. Among the companies soliciting his verbal wares were the Wood Newspaper Syndicate, the Pulitzer Publishing Company, the Paul R. Reynolds & Son literary agency, Charles Scribner's Sons, *The Independent*, which sent him an advance of $100 for an article on "Naval Strategy of the War," and others. Both *The Independent* and *Leslie's* offered him $100 per week to write short commentaries on the war on a regular basis. Excellent pay, this. Little, Brown and Company sounded him out on the possibility of his writing a book on European naval operations as they developed.

Unhappily for Mahan, the president said no. As part of his naive appeal to all Americans to remain "impartial in thought as well as action" insofar as the issues and conduct of the war were concerned, Mr. Wilson, on August 6, instructed Secretary of the Navy Josephus Daniels and Secretary of War Lindley M. Garrison to gag their officer corps. All officers, "whether active or retired," were forthwith to "refrain from public comment of any kind upon the military or political situation on the other side of the water" since it "seems to me highly unwise and improper that officers of the Navy and Army of the United States should make any public utterances to which any color of political or military criticism can be given where other nations are involved."

Mahan, while complying with the order—he returned his $100 advance to *The Independent*—was much upset by it. He considered his rights as a citizen impinged upon. He felt, too, that he had an obligation to warn his countrymen that if Germany were to defeat France or England and get "full control of the continent, which is what she is trying for," elements of the kaiser's great navy would soon be ensconced in French Martinique or in some Canadian port—with consequent undermining of the Monroe Doctrine. On August 15 he therefore fired off two letters to Daniels asking that retired officers be exempt from the department's Special Order of August 6:

> Public opinion being in the last analysis the determining force in our national polity, the effect of the Order is to disable a class of men best qualified by their past occupation, and present position, to put before the public considerations which would tend to base public opinion in matters of current public interest upon sound professional grounds.

Personally, at the age of seventy-four, I find myself silenced at a moment when the particular pursuits of nearly thirty-five years, the results of which have had the approval of the naval authorities in almost all countries, might be utilized for the public. I admit a strong feeling of personal disappointment. . . . I may state that I have applications more than I could attend to, if permitted, from Great Britain and from our own country, couched in terms of strong appreciation of my particular fitness for the work, and which may consequently be assumed to indicate a popular want.

Mahan had been permitted by McKinley and Long in 1898 and 1899 to write about the Spanish-American War. In 1905 and 1906 Roosevelt had encouraged him to comment publicly on the Russo-Japanese War and on issues scheduled to come before the Second Hague Conference. But Wilson and Daniels were not moved by his appeal. Daniels replied on August 18 that Mahan's well-known Anglophilia could only "trench upon the line of American neutrality." The order stood.[29]

Thus thwarted, Mahan turned his pen to an attack on those American pacifists who were saying, with more boldness and assurance than ever, that armaments and other preparations for war clearly bred war, and conversely, that a lack of armaments usually ensured peace. *The New York Times* even went so far as to argue, in an editorial on August 29, that "the unguarded frontier between the United States and Canada suggests the real reason why the United States has for a century maintained peace with Great Britain." The advancement of this argument in the *Times* (it was doubtful history at best) dismayed Mahan no end. In a reply to the paper, which he had difficulty persuading editor Charles R. Miller to publish, he marched through American history showing that the United States had gone eagerly to war in 1812, 1846, 1861, and 1898 without attention to the deplorable state of the nation's arsenal on the eve of each of those events. "I am not prepared to maintain that armaments never cause war," he wrote. "I should be prepared to argue that they do so only when some other exciting cause, of either interest or national feeling, comes into play. . . . If there be no armament, there is war all the same."[30]

Excited by the onset of the war in Europe, agitated by the Navy Department's order that stilled his money-making pen, upset by the apparent unwillingness of *The New York Times* to publish his response to its pacifist editorial on the unguarded American-Canadian frontier, Mahan suffered, as he put it, a "rather sharp heart attack, occasioned by a pressure of work connected with the outbreak of the current war in Europe." The attack occurred on or about September 14, 1914. It forced him to suspend all thought of literary work. It did not, however, affect his strong Anglophilia. He explained his enduring bias to Bouverie Clark on October 1:

> All my entourage is strongly pro-Ally; it would be more correct to say anti-German; and I think that is the tone of our people generally, barring the "German-Americans" and some [American] Irish. Our President, in his zeal for neutrality, has forbidden army and navy men to speak or write for publication. Luckily, I had fired off my mouth all I needed before the order came out. It has done me out of dollars only, of which a good many were in sight; but it is all for the best, for the pressure to write all that was asked of me brought on a heart attack. At least I think that the cause, and I have been obliged ever since to cut down my exercise. In fact, I feel as if I have definitely turned a corner downhill, but only in the way of more careful living.[31]

Heart attack aside, he was determined to fulfill his commitment to Jameson and the Carnegie Institution. To this end, Elly began house-hunting in Washington for something in the range of $150 to $175 per month rent, something with separate bedrooms for the four family members, a study, and sufficient living space for the three or four servants they planned to take along from Quogue. She went to Washington on October 26 and soon found a suitable house at 2025 Hillyer Place. Mahan, meanwhile, closed "Marshmere" for the season and went to Haverford, near Philadelphia, to visit with Elly's cousins, Allen and Rebecca Evans, before joining his wife and daughters in Washington on November 1.

No sooner had he arrived in Washington than he fell seriously ill again. Indeed, he worked only a few days at the Carnegie Institution, during which he provided Jameson and his staff with several "illuminating talks." He had "only made a beginning," therefore, when he became too sick and weak to leave the house. "I have dragged on from day to day without energy to take up my pen," he wrote on November 10. On that day he had managed to make two calls—one at the White House, where he left his card, the other on Secretary Daniels. These were his last social excursions in Washington.

Navy physician F. M. Pleadwell was in frequent attendance on him at home from November 9 until November 28. To him Mahan complained of general weakness, shortness of breath, nervousness, stomach pains, and sleeplessness. On November 15, in one of the last letters he wrote, he explained his symptoms to the doctor:

> Last night's experience was: went to bed at 10, slept till 1:15. Then lay awake till near 4:30, much tormented by the stomach trouble and

attendant nervous restlessness. After 4 fell asleep and slept very heavily till 6. Then waked, without start, but logy, heavy and very irritable. These dispositions still hang about, even after breakfast and coffee.

Pleadwell's medical examination, in turn, showed substantial damage done to his heart by the infarction he had suffered in mid-September. His patient was in constant pain. Medication provided no relief. Thus, when Mahan learned of the death of Field Marshal Frederick S. ("Bobs") Roberts, hero of the Boer War, in mid-November, he walked to his study window, looked out, drummed his fingers on the pane, and was heard to murmur, "lucky Bobs, lucky Bobs." On Saturday, November 28, Dr. Pleadwell had him taken to the Naval Hospital in Washington. As the orderlies carried him downstairs on a stretcher, he caught daughter Ellen's eye and winked, as though to say that all would be well.

All was not well. His mind remained clear, but he went quickly and steadily downhill. Each hour he grew weaker. Conversation became an effort. His last recorded words, spoken to a nurse, as he contemplated a tree outside his hospital window, were typical: "If a few more quiet years were granted me, I might see and enjoy these things, but God is just and I am content." At 7:15 on the morning of December 1, 1914, the heart of Alfred Thayer Mahan stopped beating. His Big Battle was over.

A grateful Navy informed his grieving widow that his retirement check for November in the amount of $374.80 was being docked $1.20 for the four days that month he had spent in the hospital, but informed her that if she wanted the $10.81 due him for retirement pay earned on December 1, while he was engaged in the act of dying, she could make a claim to the Auditor for the Navy Department for that amount. There is no evidence that Elly pursued that unintentionally macabre suggestion.

There is, on the other hand, ironic evidence that the Carnegie Institution, founded and endowed by pacifist millionaire Andrew Carnegie, a man Mahan had thoroughly disliked for his wrong-headed views on arbitration and disarmament, paid his widow $400 for December. It was Mahan's full salary for that month. This sum, together with her deceased husband's bank balance in Washington, Elly contributed to the emergency fund of the Episcopal Board of Missions. This was as Mahan would have wished.

It is also known that the widow of America's Philosopher of Sea Power was denied a pension from the Navy on the grounds that her husband had died of causes not related to his active duty. "I note with keen regret," Daniels wrote her in June 1915, "that the Treasury Department has disallowed your pension." He informed her, further, that she should not publish the article Mahan had written in mid-August 1914, "About What is the War?" He pointed out that her husband had earlier submitted the piece to the Navy Department for clearance and that he, Daniels, had then given the matter his personal attention. "At that time it was thought proper to defer its publication until the end of the present European conflict, and such is my recommendation to you at this time." Having been a Navy wife for more than forty years, Elly knew what the word *recommendation* meant when it came from the Secretary of the Navy.[32]

Mahan was buried in Quogue, following simple funeral ceremonies at St. Thomas Episcopal Church in Washington, the Reverend Ernest Smith presiding. He had specifically requested that he not have a military funeral or be buried in uniform. He was going to Heaven, not to Valhalla. Eulogies on his life and work were published in hundreds of newspapers and magazines throughout the English-speaking world, in Europe, and in Asia. Only the Germans remained silent if they did not criticize him. But he had not thought highly of them, either. Elly was swamped with expressions of sympathy. Admirals and generals, statesmen and historians, politicians and poltroons, editors and publishers, kinsmen and casual acquaintances, all joined in the chorus of praise and sorrow. T.R. called him "one of the greatest and most useful influences in American life." That was the tone of most of the obituary notices, as America buried one of her great historians and her most famous naval theorist. Not surprisingly, few if any of his countrymen caught the essence of Alfred Mahan as well as did his oldest and most constant friend, Sam Ashe, one of the very few human beings—Bouverie Clark was another—he had counted a tried and true friend over the years. Said Ashe in his letter of sympathy to Elly:

> Although in late years our communication has been only desultory, yet the silken cords of affection remained strong and he was often in my thoughts—and ever in my heart. You know of our love for each other in the bright days of early manhood—and can understand my pride in his great career. . . . It was only two days ago that thinking of his increasing work, I was regretting that I had not emulated his example in Church work—for which, however, I was in no wise prepared as he was; and then, not having heard recently of him, I found myself hoping that he was now resting and enjoying repose. Alas! that it is all over. But his life presents a picture that has few equals. Hundreds of thousands will say of him, *nomen clarissimum*. Europe as well as America does him honor. The Church as well as State acknowledges its debt to him for great service. . . . it will be well with him in the world to come.[33]

And so it was that "The Cat That Walked By Himself," but always with his God and with his historical "principles," passed from the turbulent American scene. Too bad. How he would have enjoyed World War II and a ringside seat at the victorious parade of the greatest armada ever assembled—the U.S. Navy—as it crushed Germany in the Atlantic, and, following the decisive "Big Battle" of Midway, sailed inexorably westward across the Pacific against the Imperial Japanese Navy—all the way to Tokyo Bay.

Notes

References within each note are arranged to correspond with the order of the data used in the text, save that multiple citations of Mahan's letters to a single recipient are arranged chronologically.

Unless otherwise indicated, letters from Mahan cited in these notes are in Robert Seager II and Doris D. Maguire, eds., Letters and Papers of Alfred Thayer Mahan. 3 volumes. (Annapolis, Md.: Naval Institute Press, 1975). The loci of other material cited herein are given in parentheses adjacent to the citation, or are evident from the citation itself. The repositories most frequently cited are the Library of Congress (LC), the National Archives (NA), and the library of the Naval War College (NWC).

MR. MIDSHIPMAN MAHAN, 1847–1859

1. Full-length biographies and other scholarly treatments of Mahan include William D. Puleston, *Mahan: The Life and Work of Captain Alfred Thayer Mahan, U.S.N.* (New Haven: Yale University Press, 1939); Charles C. Taylor, *The Life of Admiral Mahan, Naval Philosopher* (London: John Murray, 1920); William E. Livezey, *Mahan on Sea Power* (Norman: University of Oklahoma Press, 1947); and Richard S. West, Jr., *Admirals of American Empire: The Combined Story of George Dewey, Alfred Thayer Mahan, Winfield Scott Schley and William Thomas Sampson* (Indianapolis: Bobbs-Merrill Company, 1948). Mahan's autobiography, *From Sail to Steam: Recollections of Naval Life*, was written in 1906 and published by Harper Brothers in 1907. Dozens of article-length treatments of various aspects of Mahan's life, thought, and doctrines have appeared since his death in 1914, and they continue to appear as various authors seek to apply Mahan's conceptions of sea power to the contemporary international scene. A near-complete bibliography of Mahan's printed works is found in Livezey, *Mahan on Sea Power*, 301–311, which is based substantially on George K. Kirkham, *The Books and Articles of Rear-Admiral A. T. Mahan, U.S.N.* (New York: Ballou Press, 1929). A few bibliographical items, overlooked by Kirkham and Livezey, have been included in Robert Seager II and Doris D. Maguire, eds., *Letters and Papers of Alfred Thayer Mahan.* 3 vols. (Annapolis, Md.: Naval Institute Press, 1975), III, 731–732, hereinafter cited as *Letters and Papers.*

2. John Mahan was married successively to Mary Cleary (c. 1775–1803), Mrs. Eleanore McKim (d. circa 1806) of Norfolk, and Mrs. Esther Moffitt of Norfolk. The three marriage dates were 1799 (in Ireland), 1805, and 1814. Esther Moffitt Mahan survived John, but the date of her death is not known. *See* Puleston, *Mahan*, 2–4.

3. Puleston, *Mahan*, 4–10. For D. H. Mahan's debt to Jomini, *see* Russell F. Weigley, *The American Way of War* (New York: Macmillan, 1973), 80–89. Milo Mahan's influence on his nephew is discussed in Chapters II, III, and XVI of this book. Jomini's influence on Alfred T. Mahan is discussed in Chapters VII and VIII.

4. Mahan to Samuel A. Ashe, October 29, 1858, November 21, 1858; Mahan to Helen Evans Mahan, December 25, 1893; Mahan to Ellen Evans Mahan, October 19,

1894. The revealing paragraph about Mary Mahan was omitted from a collection of Mahan's Naval Academy letters to Ashe edited and published by Rosa P. Chiles, *Letters of Alfred Thayer Mahan to Samuel A'Court Ashe (1858–1859)* (Durham, N.C.: Duke University Library Bulletin, July 1931). Other of these letters were so sharply edited by Miss Chiles that the editors of *Letters and Papers* were encouraged to work from the original manuscript letters in the Duke University Library.

5. Ellen Kuhn Mahan, "Recollections," in *Letters and Papers*, III, 719–730. This recollection was written in 1937 or 1938, probably at the urging of Captain W. D. Puleston, USN, whose biography of Mahan was then under way. Little of Ellen's revealing personal material about her father found its way, however, into the Puleston book. Ellen Kuhn Mahan (1877–1947), Mahan's second daughter and second child, died unmarried, as did her sister, Helen Evans Mahan (1873–1963).

6. Mahan to Mary Jay Okill, November 10, 1847. Mary Jay was the daughter of Sir James Jay (d. 1817). She married John Okill, an Englishman. The three children of this union were Mahan's mother, Mary Helena Okill; his aunt, Jane Leigh Okill (d. 1894), who married John L. Swift; and his uncle, James Jay Okill. For other comments on Mahan's religious upbringing *see* Puleston, *Mahan*, 15–16.

7. Mahan to Mary Okill Mahan, June 24, 1848.

8. William Whitman Bailey, "Recollections of West Point." Manuscript. John Hay Library, Brown University, n.d. [circa 1897], 8–10. For Mahan's recollection of Bailey and the steamboat disaster, *see* Mahan to Jameson, April 27, 1914.

9. Mahan, *From Sail to Steam*, vi.

10. *Ibid.*, v–vii, xiii.

11. Mahan to Ashe, January 1, 1859. The new Mrs. Milo Mahan (née Mary Griffitts Fisher) was the daughter of Redwood Fisher of Philadelphia, a political functionary in the John Tyler administration. *See* Robert Seager II, *And Tyler Too: A Biography of John and Julia Gardiner Tyler* (New York: McGraw-Hill, 1963), 221, 224. She first married Charles Smith Lewis of Baltimore on September 10, 1835, and by him had five children—two girls, Elizabeth ("Libbie") and Mary ("Maime"), and three boys, Charles, William ("Will") Fisher, and Mordecai. Milo Mahan met the widow Lewis while he was serving as Assistant Rector of St. Mark's Episcopal Church in Philadelphia in 1850. William Fisher Lewis (1843–1923) became, like his stepfather Milo, an Episcopal clergyman (General Theological Seminary, class of 1872) and was for many years (1873–1881; 1888–1923) Rector of St. Peter's Episcopal Church in Peekskill, N.Y. In 1867 he married Mary C. McGruder, a widow, and by her had three children, Charles (who also became an Episcopal clergyman), Mary, and Elizabeth. The Will Lewis–Mary McGruder union was controversial in the family. It was vigorously opposed by Will's mother and by his sister, Maime, just as Maime had also been "violently opposed" to her own mother's marriage to Milo Mahan. Libbie, on the other hand, had approved her mother's second marriage and later supported that of her brother Will. Mary C. McGruder Lewis died in 1889. Libbie, with whom Alf Mahan was so infatuated, was later married to Charles Hoppin of Providence, R.I., and had three daughters by him in rapid succession; she died young, shortly after the birth of her third child. Mary (Maime) married the Reverend Stevens Parker and moved with him to Wilmington, Del.,

where he built St. John's Episcopal Church. The various Mahans remained in touch with the various Lewises and Parkers over the years. Alfred T. Mahan referred to his Uncle Milo's wife as his "Aunt Mary," and to Libbie as having "the sweetness of the dove." Conversely, he felt that, while Maime had a "superior mind" to Libbie's, it was one that reminded him of "the wisdom of the serpent." *See* Mahan to Mary Okill Mahan, August 21, 1867, March 1, 1868; Mahan to Ellen Evans Mahan, July 21, 1893; Mahan to Ashe, January 9, 1859.

12. The full title was *A Church History of the First Three Centuries* (New York: D. Dana, 1860). An expanded treatment of this work, *A Church History of the First Seven Centuries, to the Close of the Sixth General Council* (New York: Pott, Young & Co.), was published in 1872, two years after Milo's death. The fifth edition was published in 1900. Something of the impact that the Oxford Movement had on Milo Mahan can be seen in his *The Spiritual Point of View: or The Glass Reversed; an Answer to Bishop Colenso* (New York: Pott, Young & Co., 1863). *See also* Puleston, *Mahan*, 16.

13. Only one letter from Milo to Alfred supporting this point has survived; it is dated October 3, 1864. The statement is otherwise based on the theological thrust and spiritual tone of Mahan's revealing "Iroquois Diary, 1868–1869," in *Letters and Papers*, I, 145–332. But *see also* Taylor, *Life of Admiral Mahan*, 258, 266; and Puleston, *Mahan*, 16–17; and especially *see* Mahan, *The Harvest Within: Thoughts on the Life of a Christian* (Boston: Little, Brown and Co., 1909), *passim*.

14. Mahan to Ambrose S. Murray, January 14, 1856, April 14, 1856. Murray represented the 10th Congressional District of New York. Mahan, *From Sail to Steam*, xiv.

15. *Ibid.*, xv–xvi; Puleston, *Mahan*, 17. Secretary Davis promised Congressman Murray an additional presidential appointment to West Point for his district if Murray gave Mahan the Annapolis appointment. The trade-off was thus arranged. The conditions of Mahan's appointment are found in Acting Secretary of the Navy Charles Welsh to Mahan, Navy Department, October 2, 1856 (NA); and in Taylor, *Life of Admiral Mahan*, 6. Frederick Augustus Mahan (1847–1918), USMA class of 1867, retired in the rank of major in 1900; Dennis Hart Mahan (1849–1925), USNA class of 1869, retired in the rank of commodore in June 1909. Mahan himself retired in 1896.

16. "Iroquois Diary," in *Letters and Papers*, I, entry, May 16, 1868.

17. Copy of biographical sketch in Mahan Collection (NWC); *see also* Mahan, *From Sail to Steam*, 71–72, for Mahan's own account of his advanced academic placement at the Academy.

18. Mahan to Elizabeth Lewis, October 16, 1857.

19. Green to Blake, December 7, 1857 (NA); Mahan to Blake, December 7, 1857; Blake to Mahan, December 7, 1857 (NA); Mahan to Blake, December 7, 1857; Blake Memorandum, December 8, 1857 (NA).

20. Mahan to Helen Evans Mahan, July 25, 1893; Mahan to Ashe, February 7, 1859.

21. Samuel A. Ashe, "Memories of Annapolis," *South Atlantic Quarterly* (July 1919), 203. For Mahan's performance on the 1858 training cruise *see* Captain Craven's judgment in Mahan to Ashe, November 12, 1858.

22. Mahan to Ashe, October 29, 30, 1858, November 21, 1858, January 1, 1859, February 1, 1859, February 14, 1859, March 25, 1859, June 1, 1859. Midshipman Hilary Cenas of Louisiana was one of Mahan's not overly bright classmates.

23. Mahan to Ashe, December 12, 1858. Miss Craven got her information that Mahan was "the smartest man in the class" from none other than her father, Captain Thomas T. Craven, the commandant. Mahan, however, decided that "loaf as I may I can hardly pass below [two]." He preferred to let Midshipman Wilburn B. Hall of South Carolina take the top place in the class of 1859.

24. Mahan to Ashe, February 7, 1859, December 19, 1858. For comments on the Lawrence Literary Society, its declining fortunes, and Mahan's participation in it, *see* Mahan to Ashe, October 23, 1858, November 12, 1858, February 7, 1859, March 8, 1859, April 1, 1859.

25. Mahan to Ashe, October 29, 30, 1858, February 1, 1859, January 1, 1859, December 19, 1858, February 7, 1859.

26. Mahan to Ashe, November 21, 1858, December 12, 1858, February 14, 1859, March 20, 1859, December 4, 5, 1858. For other joyful moments in chapel *see* Mahan to Ashe, January 9, 1859.

27. Mahan to Ashe, November 12, 1858, December 4, 5, 1858, December 12, 1858, March 19, 20, 1859.

28. Mahan to Ashe, March 19, 20, 1859, October 29, 30, 1858, February 7, 1859.

29. Mahan to Ashe, March 8, 1859, March 25, 1859, May 8, 1859, December 4, 5, 1858, December 12, 1858.

30. Mahan to Ashe, December 4, 5, 1858, December 19, 1858, November 21, 1858, January 1, 1859, November 7, 1858.

31. Mahan to Ashe, April 18, 1859, March 19, 20, 1859, March 2, 1859, February 20, 1859, January 23, 1859, December 4, 5, 1858. Anne Craven later married Mr. Frederick Barnard of Pittsford, N.Y., raised a large family, and died in 1915. Julia Kent later married Dr. Henry Roland Walton. Thus neither lady married former midshipmen. For Mahan's equally frustrating and unsuccessful pursuits of other Annapolis young ladies, *see* Ashe, "Memories of Annapolis," 203; Mahan to Ashe, October 23, 1858, to June 1, 1859, *passim*.

32. *See* Mahan to Ashe, October 29, 30, 1858, in which Mahan quotes for Ashe's benefit a long passage from *Charles O'Malley* which describes Lucy's fainting dead away upon a profession of love from her soldier hero. It was Victorian literature at its most saccharin. Lever (1806–1872) wrote some 37 novels. One nineteenth-century critic regarded his military novels as "a kind of parallel literature to the fine nautical novels of Captain Marryat." Percy Russell, *A Guide to British and American Novels* (London: Digby, Long & Co., 1894), 54.

33. Mahan to Ashe, November 21, 1858, November 28, 1858, December 4, 5, 1858.

34. Mahan to Ashe, November 21, 1858, December 19, 1858, January 1, 1859.

35. Mahan to Ashe, February 1, 1859, January 9, 1859, February 7, 1859.

36. Mahan to Ashe, February 20, 1859, May 1, 1859, June 1, 1859.

37. Ashe, "Memories of Annapolis," 198, 202. In those days the midshipmen were organized into "Gun Crews" of 12 to 20 men each. These small units marched to-

gether, stood formation together, ate together, and practiced together at working the 32-pounders mounted on the Academy seawall. Upperclassmen, usually from the first class, occasionally from the second class, commanded these units under the titles First Captain or Second Captain. With an attrition rate of about 50 per cent, the Academy's student body during Mahan's three years there never consisted of more than about 125 to 150 midshipmen; it was a very small college indeed. During summer practice cruises the Gun Crews were marched on board ship as functioning combat units and were assigned to service a particular gun. *See* Puleston, *Mahan*, 18–19, for the daily routine of midshipmen in the late 1850s.

38. Mahan to Ashe, October 23, 1858, October 29, 30, 1858. Ashe later reported that before he departed the Academy in August 1858 he and Mahan had made an agreement to try to raise the disciplinary standards of the class of 1859 and of the Academy as a whole. Chiles, *Letters of Alfred Thayer Mahan*, xiv; Ashe, "Memories of Annapolis," 204.

39. Mahan to Ashe, January 1, 1859. Professor Dennis H. Mahan shared the same comparative view. *See* Mahan to Ashe, December 4, 5, 1858.

40. Mahan to Ashe, October 29, 30, 1858. George Borchert of Georgia was also a member of the class of 1859.

41. Mahan to Ashe, November 28, 1858. *See also* Mahan to Ashe, March 25, 1859. Mahan had a casual attitude toward hazing, especially toward the tarring and feathering of Midshipman Henry D. Foote in April 1859, which resulted in the dismissal of the several participants. *See* Mahan to Ashe, April 18, 1859, May 1, 1859. In his autobiography, however, Mahan recalled that there was very little hazing at the Academy in his day, compared with what the evil there later became. Mahan, *From Sail to Steam*, 55–56. Mahan to Ashe, November 28, 1858, February 1, 1859, March 25, 1859.

42. In the anti-Mahan group were Midshipmen S. W. Averett, W. R. Butt, N. H. Farquhar, S. H. Hackett, W. B. Hall, A. S. MacKenzie, R. S. McCook, Roderick Prentiss, E. G. Read, C. M. Schoonmaker, B. P. Smith, and C. H. Swasey. In the positively pro-Mahan camp were George Borchert, Hilary Cenas, and H. B. Claiborne. G. C. Wiltse shifted from pro to anti. T. F. Kane, G. C. Remey, and S. D. Greene took neutral positions; and T. S. Spencer, Mahan's roommate, shifted from pro to neutral. A number of midshipmen in the second class also opposed or supported Mahan: S. D. Ames, J. L. Tayloe, and J. O'Kane were notable in their support; Silas Casey was firm in his opposition. But the real battle over the Mahan-Hackett confrontation was fought out in the first class. *See* Mahan to Ashe, October 23, 1858, to April 1, 1859, *passim.* Mahan to Ashe, October 23, 1858. *See* Mahan to Ashe, March 8, 1859; Taylor, *Life of Admiral Mahan*, 2; and Puleston, *Mahan*, 23; Mahan to Ashe, November 12, 1858. As for the position taken by Miss Nannie Craven, Mahan could only guess: "God bless her! I bet she thinks I am right in reporting the first class." Mrs. Dennis Mahan was told by Lt. Charles H. Cushman during her visit to Annapolis that Superintendent Blake, Commandant Craven, and "indeed all the officers" in the yard supported Mahan's course of action. Mahan to Ashe, November 21, 1858. Unfortunately for Mahan, this officer support, which might have been decisive, remained muted and private. Mahan was expected to fight his own battles. Mahan to Ashe, October 29, 30, 1858, November 21, 1858.

43. Mahan to Ashe, October 23, 1858, December 4, 5, 1858.

44. Mahan to Ashe, December 4, 5, 1858, December 19, 1858, March 8, 1859, December 19, 1858, March 8, 1859.

45. Ellen Kuhn Mahan, "Recollections," in *Letters and Papers*, III, 721. Miss Mahan recalled that, with the exception of Ashe and Sir Bouverie Clark (for whom "he seemed to feel a strong affection"), he had no real friends, although "he thought very highly" of John Bassett Moore. Mahan to Ashe, October 29, 30, 1858, January 9, 1859.

46. Mahan to Ashe, November 7, 1858. A. T. Mahan, *The Life of Nelson*. 2 vols. (Boston: Little, Brown and Co., 1897), II, 391–396; Mahan to Ashe, October 29, 30, 1858.

47. *Ibid*.

48. *Ibid*.; Mahan to Ashe, October 23, 1858, November 7, 1858, December 4, 5, 1858. Mahan to Ashe, October 23, 1858, to June 1, 1859, *passim*. Mahan's views on sex were traditional. His reaction to the love affair between Philip Barton Key and the wife of General Daniel E. Sickles, which led to Key's being shot to death by the jealous Sickles, prompted him to remark that all seducers should indeed be shot since "the legal punishment for such crimes will never be death." Mahan to Ashe, March 2, 1859.

49. Mahan to Ashe, April 1, 1859. Averett left behind him Averett College in Danville, Virginia. Mahan to Elizabeth Lewis, October 16, 1857. For Spencer's steady decline in Mahan's estimation, *see* Mahan to Ashe, December 4, 5, 1858, December 12, 1858, February 1, 1859, March 8, 1859, May 1, 1859. Mahan to Ashe, November 12, 1858, December 12, 1858. Some of Mahan's later critical comments on his classmates may be found in Mahan to Ashe, February 1, 1903, April 12, 1903. He came, however, to have fond recollections of "Fan" Spencer. Mahan to Ashe, February 1, 1903.

50. Alfred Thayer Mahan, "Admiral Sampson," published in *McClure's Magazine* (July 1902) and *Fortnightly Review* (August 1902) and reprinted in *Retrospect and Prospect: Studies in International Relations, Naval and Political* (Port Washington, N.Y.: Kennikat Press Reprint, 1968), 287–309. Sampson's name was not mentioned in Mahan's letters to Ashe. Nor was that of George Dewey of Vermont, class of 1858, who was the demerit king of his class and who was also famed as a prankster. *See* George Dewey, *Autobiography of George Dewey* (New York: Charles Scribner's, 1913), 13–18; West, *Admirals of American Empire*, 16–18. For comments on Schley and the Pelicans, *see* Mahan to Ashe, October 23, 1858, December 12, 1858, February 1, 1859. On Schley, *see* West, *Admirals of American Empire*, 22–24, 99; *see also* Winfield Scott Schley, *Forty-Five Years Under the Flag* (New York: D. Appleton and Company, 1904), 4, and *passim*. Schley, for example, was a fine athlete. Mahan, who enjoyed fencing with the broadsword, was near the bottom of the class in the sport. Mahan to Ashe, December 4, 1858, December 19, 1858; Ashe, "Memories of Annapolis," 204.

51. Mahan to Ashe, April 1, 1859, November 7, 1858, November 21, 1858, January 1, 1859, April 1, 1859; Mahan, *From Sail to Steam*, 80; Ashe, "Memories of Annapolis," 203; Mahan to Ashe, May 8, 1859, February 14, 1859, November 21, 1858, January 9, 1859.

52. Mahan to Ashe, February 1, 1859.

53. Mahan to Ashe, March 8, 1859, December 19, 1858.

54. Mahan to Ashe, December 12, 1858, April 18, 1859, December 4, 5, 1858.

55. Mahan to Ashe, April 1, 1859.

56. Mahan to Ashe, March 25, 1859. Mahan had inherited his father's admiration for Napoleon Bonaparte. He also shared with most of the midshipmen of his day a general contempt for mere civilians. *See* Mahan to Ashe, January 1, 1859, April 1, 1859.

57. Ellen Kuhn Mahan, "Recollections," in *Letters and Papers*, III, 722.

58. Mahan to Ashe, May 25, 1859, March 8, 1859.

THE CIVIL WAR, 1860–1866

1. Mahan, *From Sail to Steam*, 103. Mahan's interest in the *Levant* stemmed from the importunities of James C. Moseley, USNA class of 1856. Moseley, back at the Academy in May 1859 to take an examination for promotion, had been ordered to the *Levant* as master. Mahan's enemies, Midshipmen Smith, Hackett, and Averett, also applied for the *Levant* but were ordered instead to the *Wyoming*. Mahan to Ashe, May 1, 1859.

2. Mahan to Ashe, March 19, 1859, July 31, 1859. As of 1860 all the members of the 1855 graduating class of the Academy had been promoted to master, thus vacating numerous lieutenant billets. "There are now no lieutenants in the Navy not on duty," Mahan reported. Legislation was also afoot in Washington to increase the total number of lieutenant billets. For the activities of the Retiring Board, 1854–1855, *see* Mahan, *From Sail to Steam*, 19–23.

3. Mahan, *From Sail to Steam*, 103–105; Puleston, *Mahan*, 27–30; Mahan to Goldsborough, May 31, 1860; Mahan to Ashe, October 5, 1860; Mahan to Newcome, October 10, 1861; Mahan to Mary Okill Mahan, April n.d., 1868; Mahan to Ashe, July 26, 1884. Clara Villegas is not mentioned in Mahan's autobiography.

4. Mahan, *From Sail to Steam*, 150–153; Mahan to Maxse, December 26, 1901. Mahan later described himself on the eve of the Civil War as an anti-abolitionist Unionist. *See* Mahan, *From Sail to Steam*, 88–89.

5. Mahan to Newcome, October 10, 1861; Mahan, *From Sail to Steam*, 154; Puleston, *Mahan*, 29–30. Dennis H. Mahan's pro-Southern biases and his 1860 visit to Virginia are described in Mahan to Ashe, October 5, 1860. The specific purpose of his visit was to serve on an examination board for cadets of the Virginia Military Institute at Lexington, Va. For the Civil War saga of Milo Mahan, *see* John Henry Hopkins, "Memoir," [of Milo Mahan] in John Henry Hopkins, ed., *The Collected Works of the Late Milo Mahan, D.D.* 3 vols. (New York: Pott, Young and Co., 1875), III, xxviii–xxxii.

6. As he later wrote with respect to his rapid promotions during the Civil War, "Those were cheerful days . . . for the men who struck the crest of the wave." Mahan, *From Sail to Steam*, 23, 44; Mahan to Newcome, October 10, 1861.

7. Taylor, *Life of Mahan*, 15–16; Puleston, *Mahan*, 31–32.

8. Mahan to Newcome, October 10, 1861.

9. Mahan, *From Sail to Steam*, 156–159, 162–165; Puleston, *Mahan*, 33.

10. Mahan, *From Sail to Steam*, 165–171, 91; Mahan to Editor, *The Times* (London), June 25, 1913; Mahan to Editor, *New York Times*, August 31, 1914.

11. Mahan, *From Sail to Steam*, 80–81, 181–187; Puleston, *Mahan*, 35–36; Peter Karsten, *The Naval Aristocracy: The Golden Age of Annapolis and the Emergence of Modern American Navalism* (New York: The Free Press, 1972), 330.

12. Mahan, *From Sail to Steam*, 181–182; Mahan to Helen Evans Mahan, July 25, 1893. Steece died on July 15, 1864, while serving as lieutenant in the East Gulf Blockading Squadron.

13. Taylor, *Life of Mahan*, 12–13; Mahan to Ashe, January 1, 1859, January 17, 1870, March 6, 1870; Puleston, *Mahan*, 35. The apparent bowdlerization of Mahan's manuscript letter to Ashe of January 17, 1870, preserved the lady's anonymity, as well as further clues to Mahan's relationship with her.

14. Mahan, *From Sail to Steam*, 174–175, 187–188.

15. Puleston, *Mahan*, 37; Milo Mahan to Alfred Thayer Mahan, October 3, 1864 (NWC).

16. Milo Mahan, *The Spiritual Point of View. . . . An Answer to Bishop Colenso*, 170. The entire book is reprinted in Hopkins, ed., *The Collected Works of the Late Milo Mahan, D.D.*, III, 163–254. *See ibid.*, 165–186; 219–228; Milo Mahan to A. T. Mahan, October 3, 1864 (NWC).

17. Mahan to Mary Okill Mahan, April 28, 1867. "I shall make an effort to go to Capetown and see the Bishop who excommunicated Colenso. Perhaps not a very worthy motive yet I hope pardonable." *See also* Mahan to Jane Leigh Mahan, June 12, 1867; and Mahan, "Subordination in Historical Treatment" (retitled "The Writing of History"), *Atlantic Monthly* (March 1903), 289–298.

18. J. F. Green to Mahan, Morris Island, S.C., July 12, 1864 (NA). The *James Adger* at this time was at Murrell's Inlet, S.C. At the time of his assignment to the *Cimarron*, Mahan was acting commanding officer of the *James Adger*. Dahlgren to Mahan, Flag Steamer *Philadelphia*, Port Royal Harbor, S.C., October 24, 1864 (NA). Mahan recounts his service on Dahlgren's staff in *From Sail to Steam*, 189–192, 41.

19. J. M. Bradford to Mahan, November 3, 1864 (NA); Dahlgren to Mahan, November 7, 1864 (NA); February 15, 1865 (NA). While attached to Dahlgren's staff, Mahan was also assigned special reconnaissance duty, lasting but a few days, in the screw steamers *Potomska* and *Pawnee*. *See* Dahlgren to Mahan, November 10, 1864 (NA); and Mahan, *From Sail to Steam*, 193.

20. Mahan, *From Sail to Steam*, 193–194; Mahan to Drayton, June 26, 1865, July 1, 1865, July 7, 1865, July 23, 1865; Mahan to Chief, Bureau of Navigation and Detail (T. A. Jenkins), August 7, 1865, August 22, 1865, September 16, 1865, September 30, 1865.

21. Mahan to Jenkins, November 15, 1865, November 17, 1865; Mahan, *From Sail to Steam*, 194; Mahan to Mary Okill Mahan, February 16, 1867.

22. Mahan to Mary Okill Mahan, April 28, 1867; Mahan to Jane Leigh Mahan, April 17, 1868; Log of the USS *Muscoota*, 1865–1866, *passim* (NA).

23. Mahan to Jenkins, September 24, 1866, September 28, 1866, October 27, 1866, October 30, 1866.

24. "Iroquois Diary," entry for May 16, 1868; Mahan to Jenkins, December 5, 1866, January 2, 1867 (two letters).

25. Mahan to Clark, January 28, 1909, October 1, 1909; Mahan to Henderson, February 16, 1909, May 17, 1910; Mahan to Editor, *New York Times*, August 31, 1914; Mahan to Root, April 20, 1906; Mahan to Roosevelt, July 20, 1906; Mahan to Marston, October 14, 1914.

WITH GOD IN THE *IROQUOIS*, 1867–1869

1. It seems likely that both Charles C. Taylor and William D. Puleston saw Mahan's "Iroquois Diary"; *see Letters and Papers*, I, 145–332; but, for reasons not clear, neither author chose to make use of its insights. Perhaps in the 1920s and 1930s there were family objections to the use or publication of such personal materials. Alfred Thayer Mahan II, grandson of the admiral, made no stipulations about its use when he graciously made the diary available to the present writer. Mahan began keeping it on August 1, 1867, when the *Iroquois* was off the East African coast, bound for the Far East. The surviving portion of the diary, which is now in the library of the Naval War College, commences at Yokohama on April 26, 1868, and continues until September 10, 1869, the eve of Mahan's return home. On the existence of a lost segment of the diary, and on Mahan's purpose in keeping such a record, *see* the entry for April 26, 1868. Subsequent citations from the diary are designated below by date, e.g., Diary, April 26, 1868. As for the *Iroquois* herself, Mahan called her "a good seaboat but excessively wet and uncomfortable," tender in an abeam sea. Marine Lieutenant Michael Gaul said of her: "Every port in which we have touched yet, the *Iroquois* has had the name of being the prettiest vessel in the harbor." *See also* Mahan to Mary Okill Mahan, February 16, 1867, March 17, 1867; Mahan to Dennis H. Mahan, December 5, 1867; Mahan to Jane Leigh Mahan, April 28, 1867; Michael Gaul Diary, November 8, 1867 (Marine Corps Museum, Quantico, Va.). Just what the vessel mounted in the way of guns at the time Mahan served in her is not clear. In 1864, during the Civil War, she mounted 1–100#R, 2–9", 1–60#R, 4–32#. Launched in New York on April 12, 1859, and commissioned on November 24, 1859, the *Iroquois* remained in service until 1893. In that year she was transferred to the Marine Hospital Service. Renamed the *Ionie* on November 30, 1904, she was finally sold out of the Navy on October 5, 1910. *See* K. Jack Bauer, *Ships of the Navy 1775–1969*, Volume I: Combat Vessels (Troy, N.Y.: Rensselaer Polytechnic Institute, 1969), 53–54.

2. Mahan, *From Sail to Steam*, 196–265; Puleston, *Mahan*, 41–45. In writing the *Iroquois* cruise section of his autobiography in 1906, Mahan refreshed his memory by consulting the letters he wrote at the time to his father, mother, and sister Jenny (Jane Leigh Mahan). There is, however, internal evidence in his autobiography that some of these family missives have disappeared since 1907. There is no evidence in his autobiography that Mahan consulted anew his letters to Sam Ashe, or that he ever saw again any of his letters to Ashe. Captain Puleston had access to all the

Mahan-to-Ashe letters and to those that Mahan wrote his family while serving in the *Iroquois* and later in the *Chicago* (1893–1895). Those letters that have survived are in *Letters and Papers*. Readers interested in reconstructing in greater operational detail the cruise of the *Iroquois* while Mahan was her executive officer should consult a recently discovered diary kept on board the vessel by Michael Gaul, commander of the Marine detachment. The Gaul Diary covers the period October 22, 1867, to April 15, 1868, and reposes in the archives of the U.S. Marine Corps Museum at Quantico, Virginia. Unlike the Mahan diary, the Gaul journal is much interested in the political, diplomatic, and military events in which the *Iroquois* participated in Japan. The 1867–1868 log of the *Iroquois* is in the National Archives.

3. Mahan to Mary Okill Mahan, February 16, 1867, March 1, 1868; Mahan to Ashe, October 17, 1869. For similar trust in God during heavy weather, *see* Mahan to Ashe, November 19, 1868.

4. Diary, May 8, 1868, July 5, 1868, August 9, 1868, August 11, 1868, August 12, 1868, August 13, 1868, September 23, 1868, October 25, 1868, October 27, 1868, November 1, 1868, November 21, 1868, April 27, 1869. These quotations, in chronological order, are a composite of remarks found in Diary, October 26, 1868, October 27, 1868, October 28, 1868, October 31, 1868, November 16, 1868, December 17, 1868, December 18, 1868, January 20, 1869, and January 27, 1869. *See also* November 17, 1868.

5. Diary, February 8, 1869, May 11, 1868, May 26, 1868, June 6, 1868, July 13, 1868, July 14, 1868, July 22, 1868, August 6, 1868, August 22, 1868, June 22, 1868, May 21, 1868, June 22, 1868, June 4, 1868, July 20, 1868, August 3, 1868, August 4, 1868, August 10, 1868, November 1, 1868, November 24, 1868, January 25, 1869, May 18, 1869, September 18, 1868, September 3, 1868. The *Oneida* was on the station with the *Iroquois* at this time.

6. Diary, July 20, 1868, September 19, 1868; *see also* May 29, 1868, June 1, 1868, June 2, 1868, June 28, 1868, August 14, 1868, September 14, 1868, May 15, 1869. He told his sister Jenny that "the *Iroquois* is anxious to race any boat in the squadron believing that she has succeeded in beating everybody in everything else. I am afraid our pride is the precursor of a fall." Mahan to Jane Leigh Mahan, August 11, 1868.

7. Diary, July 10, 1868, July 22, 1868, July 31, 1868, August 5, 1868, December 28, 1868, July 21, 1868, March 23, 1869.

8. Diary, January 30, 1869, May 7, 1869, August 18, 1869, January 22, 1869, February 22, 1869, May 24, 1869, May 22, 1869; Mahan to Ashe, October 10, 1868, November 19, 1868; Mahan to Mary Okill Mahan, March 17, 1867, August 21, 1867. The single-screw, bark-rigged *Iroquois* was equipped with two horizontal steeple engines designed by Thomas Main, generating 1202 IHP. Solely under steam, she cruised easily at about 9 kts.; wide open, she was capable of about 11 kts. *See* Bauer, *Ships of the Navy*, I, 53–54; and Michael Gaul Diary, December 6, 1867. Mahan complained of the "rapid jar of the propeller" which caused the vessel to vibrate excessively when under steam. Mahan to Dennis H. Mahan, July 30, 1867, August 10, 1867, December 5, 1867.

9. Diary, July 22, 1868, July 23, 1868, October 16, 1868.

10. Diary, August 7, 1868, August 8, 1868.

11. Diary, July 22, 1868, July 28, 1868, April 28, 1869.

12. Diary, March 6, 1869, April 2, 1869, April 4, 1869, January 22, 1869, January 26, 1869, February 3, 1869, September 8, 1869, December 19, 1868, August 19, 1868, August 21, 1868, August 24, 1868, August 3, 1869, August 4, 1869, August 5, 1869. Of Thackeray's *The Newcomes*, Mahan wrote: "Heart a good deal touched by Thackeray's *Newcomes*—how heart answers to heart; even in my limited experience there is much like to that which he tells me." Diary, August 3, 1869, July 14, 1868, September 21, 1868, November 8, 1868, July 29, 1868. *See also* June 20, 1868, July 8, 1868, July 27, 1868, August 10, 1868, September 2, 1868, September 25, 1868, October 24, 1868, November 9, 1868, November 10, 1868, December 11, 1868, January 26, 1869, August 19, 1869, August 31, 1869, August 21, 1868, August 10, 1868, August 13, 1868, September 11, 1868, September 18, 1868, June 20, 1868, June 22, 1868, July 6, 1868, July 14, 1868, July 20, 1868, July 23, 1868, July 29, 1868, August 7, 1868, November 10, 1868. Mahan's interest in classical Greek was related to his interest in the New Testament. It should also be noted that his Uncle Milo Mahan was virtually a child prodigy in Greek, having been engaged to teach the language at the Episcopal High School in Alexandria, Virginia, at the age of 17. Mahan to Mary Okill Mahan, February 20, 1868, March 1, 1868; Mahan to Dennis H. Mahan, December 5, 7, 1867.

13. Diary, May 10, 1868, February 15, 1868, May 20, 1869, May 15, 1869, May 17, 1868, June 17, 1868, July 17, 1868.

14. Diary, November 7, 1868; Mahan, *From Sail to Steam*, 196; Diary, November 18, 1868, January 2, 1869, April 7, 1869, May 12, 1869, May 18, 1869, May 22, 1869, July 23, 1869, July 26, 1869, August 8, 1869, August 9, 1869. That the wardroom was usually noisy at all hours of the day and night was in part the fault of Lieutenant Royal B. Bradford (later a rear admiral), who was navigation officer of the *Iroquois*, and who used the space as a practice studio for his playing of the violin. Clad only in his nightshirt, Bradford invariably played for an hour or so before turning in for the night—much to Mahan's annoyance. Mahan, *From Sail to Steam*, 209.

15. Diary, July 31, 1868, August 15, 1868, August 24, 1868, May 26, 1869; Mahan to Mary Okill Mahan, April 28, 1867. In all of his correspondence there survives but one letter (to Ashe, February 12, 1860) in which Mahan uses profanity and refers to male genitals, as though to preserve the bond of masculinity between the two men that went back to Naval Academy days. Mahan apparently assumed that Ashe expected such talk from a red-blooded young American naval officer. Diary, May 24, 1869, July 12, 1868, September 17, 1868, May 29, 1868, June 5, 1868, July 19, 1868, October 29, 1868, November 24, 1868, May 7, 1868, October 28, 1868.

16. Diary, February 6, 1869, February 3, 1869, January 28, 1869, May 8, 1869, May 19, 1869, August 12, 1868, September 10, 1869, May 25, 1869, February 10, 1869, February 11, 1869. On one occasion at dinner he permitted himself to talk "about love affairs, etc. etc. perhaps somewhat foolishly." Diary, September 12, 1868.

17. Mahan to Ashe, October 10, 1868; Diary, February 8, 1869.

18. Diary, November 25, 1868, November 28, 1868, March 6, 1869, May 27, 1869, July 31, 1869; Mahan to Ashe, February 12, 1869; Mahan to Jane Leigh Mahan, April 17, 1868, January 13, 1868; Mahan to Mary Okill Mahan, April n.d., 1868. It should be noted that Mahan was not impressed with those Japanese women who ap-

peared in public "in all degrees of nudity," some of whom "were stripped to their waist making a display which we might call immodest, but hardly alluring." Or so he told Ashe in Mahan to Ashe, August 12, 1868.

19. Diary, *passim*.

20. Mahan to Jane Leigh Mahan, April 28, 1867; June 12, 1867, January 13, 1868, March 21, 1868, April 17, 1868, August 11, 1868, November 7, 1868; Mahan to Dennis H. Mahan, July 30, 1867, December 5, 1867, November 18, 1868; Mahan to Mary Okill Mahan, August 21, 1867, December 29, 1867, February 20, 1868, April 7, 1868; Mahan to Ashe, August 12, 1868, November 19, 1868; Diary, May 23, 1869, August 21, 1869, September 10, 1869. Mahan had read Sir Rutherford Alcock's *The Capital of the Tycoon: Narrative of a Three Years' Residence in Japan*, the standard work on the Japanese at that time. It should be pointed out that on the complex and controversial issue of the *Alabama* claims Mahan took a rare anti-British stance. Diary, January 14, 1869, May 29, 1868, June 27, 1868, August 16, 1869, May 2, 1868. His dislike of the U.S. minister to Japan, Robert B. Van Valkenburgh, seems to have been based on nothing but the inconvenience caused Mahan when the minister borrowed the services of the yeomen of the *Iroquois*. Diary, May 27, 1868, May 28, 1868.

21. Mahan to Ashe, October 10, 1868, August 12, 1868; Mahan to Mary Okill Mahan, December 29, 1867; Diary, May 13, 1869. Mahan made few references to the seven Negroes in the crew of the *Iroquois*. He singled them out for no special disapproval save that John H. Backus, Mahan's Negro messman, was identified on one occasion as "dilatory," and Mahan "pitched into him in my most overbearing way." Mahan had little use for the Navy's enlisted men, regardless of their color or nationality. *See* Diary, June 3, 1869, July 9, 1868, August 17, 1868, August 20, 1868, November 19, 1868; Mahan to Jane Leigh Mahan, April 17, 1868; Diary, May 12, 1868, July 31, 1868, July 15, 1868, December 28, 1868, February 21, 1869, May 12, 1869, May 18, 1869.

22. Mahan to Ashe, October 17, 1869. Both Rosa P. Chiles and T. B. Kingsbury quote a letter from Mahan to Ashe dated circa January 1867 in which Mahan noted that he had "just returned from a long cruise" (in the *Muscoota* presumably) and had saved $500. "If you have survived the war, you will need it. I would take it from you; you must take it from me." *See* R. P. Chiles, *Letters of Alfred Thayer Mahan to Samuel A'Court Ashe*, xii–xiii; and T. B. Kingsbury, "Samuel A'Court Ashe," in Samuel A. Ashe, ed., *Biographical History of North Carolina*, 70. This letter has not been found. It is known that after Mahan's death in 1914 "someone, reading one of his letters to Ashe, suggested that it be destroyed because of its intimate nature." Ashe apparently acquiesced, "with reluctance," in the destruction of a number of such highly personal letters from Mahan. Selected pages of several of Mahan's letters seem also to have been removed and destroyed by Miss Chiles or by Ashe himself. Portions of his letter to Ashe of January 17, 1870, apparently suffered this fate. *See* Kingsbury, *loc. cit.*, 69–70. Throughout 1866, Captain Samuel A. Ashe, C.S.A., who had been cited for gallantry at Cedar Run and Second Manassas, was reduced to serving as a conductor on freight and passenger trains of the Wilmington and Weldon Railroad. Just prior to leaving the employ of the railroad on December 1, 1866, he was promoted to sleeping-car porter. Mahan to Ashe, January 17, 1870. In the

state elections of 1870 Ashe was elected to the North Carolina House of Representatives where he quickly gained attention as one of the leaders of the Conservative Democrat movement to overthrow Radical Republican, Carpetbagger, and Negro rule in Raleigh. From this point forward his career in politics, law, and journalism blossomed. Kingsbury, *loc. cit.*, 70–71, and *passim*; and Mahan to Ashe, May 15, 1875, May 21, 1875, April 30, 1879, May 9, 1879.

23. Diary, May 27, 1868, May 29, 1868, June 15, 1868, June 19, 1868, July 8, 1868, July 17, 1868, August 1, 1868, August 4, 1868, September 2, 1868, December 21, 1868, December 24, 1868, December 28, 1868, January 2, 1869, January 28, 1869, February 15, 1869, August 18, 1869, December 13, 1868, December 23, 1868, December 27, 1868, January 24, 1869, August 24, 1868, November 8, 1868, November 22, 1868, February 4, 1869. On Mahan's tense relations with Fletcher, *see* Diary, May 27, 1868, May 31, 1868, June 1, 1868, June 20, 1868, July 15, 1868, July 18, 1868, July 27, 1868, July 28, 1868, August 3, 1868, August 13, 1868, September 15, 1868, September 16, 1868, September 21, 1868, November 19, 1868, January 21, 1869, January 30, 1869, February 7, 1869.

24. On Mahan's characterizations of English and his problems with English, *see* Diary, May 7, 1868, May 9, 1868, May 11, 1868, June 15, 1868, June 20, 1868, July 10, 1868, July 14, 1868, July 15, 1868, July 23, 1868, August 11, 1868, August 12, 1868, August 13, 1868, August 31, 1868, September 20, 1868, November 1, 1868, November 11, 1868, February 9, 1869, May 19, 1868, July 5, 1868, July 10, 1868, September 18, 1868, November 1, 1868, December 21, 1868, August 14, 1868, August 6, 1868.

25. Diary, June 2, 1868, August 21, 1868, December 2, 1868, December 3, 1868, December 5, 1868, December 7, 1868, December 13, 1868, May 18, 1869. Rowan replaced Rear Admiral Henry H. Bell, who was drowned in a tragic boating accident at Osaka on January 10, 1868. Bell, who began his career in the Army, had been a cadet at West Point when Mahan's father was a cadet there. Through this connection Mahan was well known to him. Mahan, *From Sail to Steam*, 238–242. The death of Bell is described in detail in Mahan to Jane Leigh Mahan, January 13, 1868. Mahan later recalled and commented on Admiral Rowan's great penchant for secrecy. *See From Sail to Steam*, 254–255. He admitted in his diary, however, that Rowan showed him great "kindness" on the station in 1869. Diary, August 10, 1869.

26. Michael Gaul Diary, December 14, 1867, December 16, 1867, February 21, 1868, and *passim*; Diary, May 22, 1868, July 4, 1868; Mahan to Ellen Evans Mahan, April 28, 1867; Diary, June 2, 1868, November 25, 1868, December 31, 1868, October 14, 1868, October 15, 1868, May 29, 1868, June 18, 1868, June 17, 1868, and *passim*.

27. Michael Gaul Diary, November 5, 1867, November 6, 1867. For Mahan's frequent courts-martial activities while serving in the *Iroquois*, *see* Diary, *passim*.

28. Diary, November 29, 1868, June 2, 1868, December 31, 1868, November 26, 1868.

29. Diary, June 3, 1868, January 3, 1869, July 3, 1868, June 17, 1868, May 7, 1869, December 2, 1868, June 18, 1868, August 1, 1868, January 2, 1869, August 17, 1868, January 13, 1869, December 24, 1868. *See also* Mahan to Mary Okill Mahan, February 20, 1868. "I had much trouble and annoyance while we had our men ashore

from their drunkenness. It is fearful to think how that great evil ruins men, body and soul alike."

30. Mahan to Mary Okill Mahan, February 20, 24, 1868, December 29, 1867, March 1, 1868; Diary, March 13, 1869, May 17, 1868; Mahan to Mary Okill Mahan, April 28, 1867.

31. Mahan to Mary Okill Mahan, March 1, 6, 1868; Diary, July 22, 1868, May 27, 1868, May 13, 1868, August 10, 1868, August 16, 1868, September 6, 1868, September 12, 1868, May 7, 1868, August 6, 1868, June 20, 1868, June 22, 1868, September 20, 1868, July 26, 1869.

32. Diary, May 12, 1868, February 17, 1869, July 3, 1868, October 23, 1868. For additional evidence of Mahan's nervousness, *see* Diary, May 8, 1868, June 4, 1868, July 6, 1868, July 8, 1868, July 31, 1868, August 10, 1868, August 18, 1868, November 23, 1868, February 9, 1869, March 9, 1869, May 21, 1869; Mahan to Jane Leigh Mahan, June 12, 1867; Diary, January 27, 1869.

33. Diary, May 2, 1868, May 7, 1868, May 9, 1868, May 14, 1868, May 15, 1868, May 16, 1868, August 17, 1868, August 19, 1868, September 17, 1868, November 20, 1868, March 9, 1869, January 22, 1869, December 17, 1868, January 23, 1869, December 22, 1868, July 4, 1868, May 16, 1869, May 15, 1869. *See also* Diary, June 17, 1868, September 7, 1868, September 13, 1868, September 23, 1868, May 5, 1869, May 13, 1869, May 16, 1869.

34. Diary, May 4, 1868, May 5, 1868, May 7, 1868, May 28, 1868, June 19, 1868, June 27, 1868, July 4, 1868, July 10, 1868, July 16, 1868, July 18, 1868, July 31, 1868, August 4, 1868, August 15, 1868, September 7, 1868, September 25, 1868, November 1, 1868, November 20, 1868, November 22, 1868, March 11, 1869, September 23, 1868. *See also* Diary, June 17, 1868 ("My falls have been grievous lately; twice in this week drinking so much that my mind refused to follow my night prayers"), and July 2, 1868, February 18, 1869.

35. Diary, August 2, 1868, August 23, 1868, September 6, 1868, September 13, 1868, November 21, 1868. The gale referred to in the quotation occurred on October 27–28, 1868, during the voyage of the *Iroquois* from Nagasaki to Hakodate, via Niigata. *See* Mahan to Jane Leigh Mahan, November 7, 1868; and Mahan to Dennis H. Mahan, November 18, 1868. Mahan's great fear during this and other gales is expressed in Diary, October 27, 1868, October 28, 1868, November 22, 1868, November 29, 1868, December 11, 1868. On that last date Mahan "broke through my rules regarding drinking. . . . Weak again I fear," when his USNA classmate Cornelius M. Schoonmaker came on board the *Iroquois* at Woosung, China, to dine. On December 17, 1868, while at sea, he became so frightened during heavy weather that he again broke his vow. Diary, December 17, 1868, January 1, 1869, New Year's Day, 1869, January 22, 1869, January 23, 1869, February 5, 1869, February 17, 1869. "More tendency toward drinking than any time during the last ten days," he wrote in May 1869. "Have displayed temper two or three times. Also somewhat morbidly depressed at times." Diary, May 26, 1869.

36. Diary, March 23, 1869.

37. Diary, May 19, 1869, May 20, 1869, August 30, 1869, February 13, 1869, March 5, 1869, April 7, 1869, April 8, 1869, March 6, 1869, April 15, 1869, April 27, 1869, April 1, 1869, May 4, 1869.

38. Ellen Kuhn Mahan, "Recollections," in *Letters and Papers*, III, 724; Diary, July 31, 1868, August 2, 1868, October 26, 1868, January 16, 1869, May 1, 1868, December 15, 1868, January 4, 1869, January 11, 1869, May 10, 1869, Mahan to Mary Okill Mahan, February 20, 1868; Diary, August 5, 1868, November 18, 1868; November 10, 1868, February 17, 1869, September 15, 1869, February 4, 1869, May 7, 1869, November 27, 1868, July 20, 1868, August 24, 1868, March 5, 1869.

39. Diary, August 23, 1868, August 5, 1869, August 15, 1869. *See also* July 9, 1868, August 16, 1868, August 22, 1868, August 30, 1868, October 23, 1868, October 26, 1868, October 27, 1868, December 6, 1868, August 1, 1869, August 3, 1869, August 7, 1869, August 8, 1869.

40. Diary, May 24, 1869, May 25, 1869, May 27, 1869, May 28, 1869, July 22, 1869, and May 1869, *passim*.

41. Mahan to Ashe, March 28, 1876, April 13, 1876; Diary, July 25, 1869, June 18, 1868.

42. Diary, June 28, 1868, November 29, 1868, December 3, 1868, December 6, 1868, January 3, 1869, February 10, 1869, February 14, 1869, February 17, 1869, February 21, 1869, March 7, 1869, March 10, 1869, May 9, 1869, and Diary, *passim*. Mahan's recording of his church attendance ashore was often accompanied by lamentations that his thoughts had wandered during the services, or that he had not been as rigidly attentive as he might have been. On one occasion (February 14, 1869), he missed getting to church on time because he "stopped and drank some whiskey which brightened me up." Diary, July 12, 1868, July 19, 1868, August 2, 1868, August 9, 1868, August 16, 1868, August 23, 1868, September 6, 1868, September 13, 1868, December 27, 1868, January 24, 1869, February 7, 1869, May 9, 1869, Diary, title page; and Diary, *passim*. Mahan was both pleased and dismayed with himself as a lay reader. "I was tempted to conceit with regard to my reading in church; it is hard to tell whether one is tempted or falls in the case of such thoughts. I can remember, however, how wretchedly and tremblingly [I] have officiated at times." Diary, December 27, 1868, August 2, 1868, August 9, 1868, August 23, 1868, October 25, 1868, November 8, 1868, January 3, 1869, January 17, 1869, April 4, 1869, May 9, 1869, May 16, 1869, May 26, 1869, July 19, 1868, February 17, 1869, March 9, 1869, March 10, 1869, May 13, 1869. Mahan was a member of the Seamen's Church Institute, an Episcopal organization sustained by the Diocese of New York and by public subscription, from 1867 until his death in 1914. Prior to 1904, its formal name was the Protestant Episcopal Church Missionary Society for Seamen in the City and Port of New York. Over the years Mahan served as one of its lay managers and as a member and officer of its governing board. He contributed money to its various fund-raising drives. When he was ashore in the New York area he faithfully supported its other spiritual and welfare activities among seamen. *See* an unpublished manuscript by the Reverend James C. Healey, "The Life of Archibald Romaine Mansfield, Apostle to Seamen: A Review of a Century of Service of the Seamen's Church Institute of New York," (n.d.), 91; and *passim*. Part of this manuscript, which can be found in the library of the institute, was written by Albert J. Nock. *See also* the annual reports of the Seamen's Church Institute, 1867–1914, also on file in the institute's library. In 1869 Mahan set aside $17.00 from his monthly salary of $195.25 for his tithe and other charitable purposes. *See* "A Set of Rules for My Life," Diary, January 1, 1869; and Ellen Kuhn Mahan, "Recol-

lections," in *Letters and Papers*, III, 723–724. Not only did he tithe throughout his life but he raised his daughters, Helen and Ellen, to do so. Later in his life, Mahan was a regular contributor to the fresh-air fund of the Protestant Episcopal City Mission Society and to other charities. Diary, July 2, 1868; Mahan to Mary Okill Mahan, April n.d., 1868. Mary Helena Okill Mahan, her husband Dennis H. Mahan, and Mrs. Mahan's sister, Jane Leigh Okill Swift, gave the land on which the Tenafly church was built, together with money and a set of altar vessels. The land was part of an inheritance from Sir James Jay through Mary Jay Okill. Mahan provided the Bible and the Prayer Book. *See* Samuel S. Vaughn, *The Little Church: The Church of the Atonement, Tenafly, New Jersey, 1868–1968* (New York: Doubleday, 1969), 30.

43. Diary, July 19, 1868, July 12, 1868, August 2, 1868, August 9, 1868, August 16, 1868, August 23, 1868, September 6, 1868, January 24, 1869, May 9, 1869; Mahan to Mary Okill Mahan, December 29, 1867. Low attendance at Protestant services on board the *Iroquois* could be explained in part by the fact that the crew contained many Irish, French, and other foreign nationals who were Roman Catholic. Michael Gaul mentioned that Roman priests came aboard the ship to say mass for the Catholics "who comprise more than half our crew." Michael Gaul Diary, November 10, 1867.

44. Diary, May 23, 1869, December 3, 1868, May 5, 1869. Mahan objected to an Anglican service he attended in Capetown because there the congregation was "too entirely precluded from its share in the services." Mahan to Jane Leigh Mahan, June 12, 1867.

45. Diary, *passim*.

46. Diary, June 15, 1868, August 30, 1869, October 23, 1868.

47. Mahan to Mary Okill Mahan, February 16, 1867, April 28, 1867; Mahan to Jane Leigh Mahan, April 28, 1867; Mahan to Ashe, October 10, 1868; Mahan to Helen Evans Mahan, June 14, 1896; Diary, May 13, 1869, August 16, 1868.

48. John Henry Hopkins, "Memoir" [of Milo Mahan], in J. H. Hopkins, ed., *The Collected Works of the Late Milo Mahan, D.D.*, III, xiv–xvi. The *Church Journal* published its first number on February 5, 1853. In the 1860s its editorial position reflected Milo Mahan's sharply anti-Vatican, pro-Anglo-Catholic stance. Mahan to Mary Okill Mahan, February 20, 1868, March 1, 1868. His mother also sent him requested religious books, among them Michael F. Sadler's *Emmanuel*. Diary, July 12, 1868, July 14, 1868, also May 11, 1869. Mahan mentioned the books and authors he read on board the *Iroquois* in his Diary, viz: (Goulburn), July 29, 1868, August 9, 1868, August 23, 1868, January 1, 1869, May 12, 1869, May 23, 1869; (Trench), June 17, 1868, June 18, 1868, June 19, 1868, June 20, 1868, August 9, 1868, August 16, 1868, January 24, 1869, January 31, 1869, April 2, 1869; (Froude), July 11, 1868, July 30, 1868; (Butler), May 20, 1868, May 29, 1868, June 4, 1868, June 17, 1868; (Sadler), July 12, 1868, July 14, 1868, May 11, 1869, May 12, 1869, May 13, 1869, May 19, 1869; (Taylor), July 4, 1868, January 15, 1869; (Putnam), June 2, 1868; (Leighton), April 26, 1868; (Dwight), August 5, 1868; (Renan), August 16, 1868; (Alford), August 21, 1868; (Smiles), May 25, 1869; (Seeley), April 5, 1869, April 6, 1869, April 7, 1869; (Robertson), May 25, 1868, January 3, 1869, June 4, 1868, August 16, 1868, April 7, 1869, July 23, 1868, July 31, 1868, August 9,

1868, February 10, 1869. Among the religious titles Mahan read were: Edward M. Goulburn, *Thoughts on Personal Religion* . . . ; Robert C. Trench, *Notes on the Parables of Our Lord*; Richard M. Froude, *Remains of Richard M. Froude*, J. H. Newman and J. Keble, eds.; Joseph Butler, *The Analogy of Religion, Natural and Revealed.* . . . ; Jeremy Taylor, *Selections from the Works of Jeremy Taylor*; Edward Putnam, *An Exposition of the Apocalypse of St. John the Apostle*; Robert Leighton, *The Whole Works of Robert Leighton*; Timothy Dwight, *Theology: Explained and Defended in a Series of Sermons.* . . . ; Ernest Renan, *The Apostles*; Henry Alford, *Meditations in Advent: Creation and Providence*; Samuel Smiles, *The Huguenots* . . . ; John R. Seeley, *Ecce Homo: A Survey of the Life and Works of Jesus Christ*; Frederick W. Robertson, *Sermons on St. Paul's Epistle to the Corinthians*.

49. Diary, May 12, 1869, March 22, 1869, January 3, 1869.

50. Diary, January 3, 1869, January 10, 1869, July n.d., 1868, September 13, 1868, July 16, 1868, July 19, 1868, January 21, 1869, January 31, 1869.

51. Diary, August 8, 1869, April 30, 1868, June 4, 1868, May 4, 1868, May 6, 1868, August 2, 1868, August 6, 1868, March 8, 1869, January 25, 1869, January 24, 1869.

52. Diary, April 2, 1869, June 20, 1868, June 21, 1868, May 13, 1868, July 31, 1869, August 2, 1869, June 20, 1868.

53. Mahan to Ashe, October 10, 1868.

54. *Ibid.*; Diary, May 9, 1868, May 10, 1868, May 11, 1868, May 14, 1868, May 16, 1868, May 17, 1868, May 19, 1868, May 22, 1868. *See also* May 29, 1868, May 30, 1868, May 31, 1868.

55. Diary, May 20, 1868.

56. Diary, May 16, 1868, June 4, 1868, June 5, 1868, June 6, 1868, June 7, 1868, June 18, 1868, June 20, 1868, June 15, 1868.

57. Diary, June 20, 1868, July 22, 1868, August 20, 1868, September 6, 1868, September 8, 1868, September 10, 1868, September 12, 1868, September 13, 1868, September 14, 1868, September 17, 1868, September 21, 1868, September 24, 1868, September 25, 1868; Mahan to Ashe, October 10, 1868.

58. *Ibid.*; Diary, December 10, 1868, May 13, 1869, July 23, 1869, July 24, 1869. The Mahan-Woolverton and Mahan-Hayes correspondence apparently has not survived. That Mahan also considered Sam Hayes a close personal friend is evident in the following remark to Ashe about both Woolverton and Hayes: "I sometimes wish very much I could get you and these two, of whom I have spoken, so associated as to know one another well, and yet not be bored; for you know a man can't stand being with his wife all the time. I feel sure you would be charmed with one another." Mahan to Ashe, October 10, 1868. Hayes shared something of Mahan's hyperactive missionary impulses. *See* Diary, May 13, 1869.

59. Diary, March 4, 1869, March 5, 1869, May 12, 1869, March 8, 1869, March 23, 1869, March 7, 1869, April 8, 1869.

60. Diary, March 6, 1869, March 10, 1869, April 2, 1869, April 1, 1869, March 22, 1869.

61. Diary, May 14, 1869, May 15, 1869, May 16, 1869, May 25, 1869, May 17, 1869, May 18, 1869, May 19, 1869, May 20, 1869. Mahan's frequent "feeling of aloneness"

on board the *Iroquois* turned his thoughts "naturally" toward the absent Woolverton, his "nearest friend." *See*, for example, Diary, May 27, 1869.

62. Diary, July 23, 1869, July 24, 1869, July 25, 1869, July 26, 1869, July 27, 1869, July 28, 1869, July 29, 1869, July 30, 1869. Woolverton was promoted to the rank of surgeon effective November 23, 1868. Hence his detachment from the *Monocacy* and reassignment. His subsequent connection with Mahan is hazy. It is known that he wrote Mahan on July 8, 1883 congratulating him on the publication of *Gulf and Inland Waters. See* Woolverton to Mahan, July 8, 1883 (NWC). Beyond this, the degree or nature of Mahan's later contact with Surgeon Woolverton remains a mystery save for the fact that Mahan received a letter from him in April 1894. *See* Mahan to Helen Evans Mahan, April 19, 1894. It is also known that Mahan wrote to him for a time after he left Yokohama for California in July 1869. This correspondence apparently has not survived. Whether Woolverton answered these letters is not known. In general, however, it would seem that the two men corresponded a few times over the years. It is known that when Woolverton departed Japan on July 29, 1869, on board the passenger steamer *China*, he left something of a mess behind him. In his eagerness to get away, he disregarded an order concerning prevention of smallpox in the *Monocacy*. One quarter of the crew subsequently came down with the disease and the vessel had to be quarantined in Nagasaki. Admiral Rowan was much exercised by Woolverton's laxity in this regard, but it seems not to have hurt the surgeon's later career.

63. Diary, August 4, 1869, August 5, 1869, August 6, 1869, August 16, 1869, August 30, 1869, September 5, 1869.

64. Diary, August 2, 1869, August 15, 1869, August 18, 1869, August 30, 1869, September 5, 1869, July 26, 1869, July 28, 1869, July 30, 1869, July 31, 1869, September 6, 1869, August 1, 1869, August 3, 1869, August 4, 1869, August 5, 1869, August 6, 1869, September 8, 1869, September 9, 1869, September 10, 1869. *See also* Mahan, *From Sail to Steam*, 264–265. Some of the details of Mahan's trip home can be found in Mahan to Ashe, September 21, 1869, March 6, 1870.

ELLY AND THE *WASP*, 1870–1875

1. Mahan to Ashe, October 17, 1869; Puleston, *Mahan*, 46–47; Mahan to Ashe, January 17, 1870, March 6, 1870; Mahan to Ellen Kuhn Mahan, January 6, 1894. A page of Mahan to Ashe, January 17, 1870, has been separated from the Mahan-Ashe correspondence at Duke University and cannot be found. Before his voyage from Hong Kong to Calcutta on the steamer *Glencartney* in October 1869, Mahan once again experienced great apprehension concerning the probability of bad weather and fortified himself for the expected agony of the journey by taking Communion. Fear of shipwreck, he told Ashe, "is a very strong argument for weekly Communions in seaport towns." Mahan to Ashe, October 17, 1869.

2. Mahan to Ashe, March 6, 1870. "Old Seager" was Edward Seager, Professor of Drawing and Teacher of the Art of Defense at the Naval Academy. He was also an artist of some talent and local reputation. Professor Seager (no kin), who retired from the Academy faculty in April 1871 and died on January 23, 1886, seems to have had small confidence in Midshipman Mahan's artistic and architectural taste.

3. Mahan to Ellen Evans Mahan, February 24, 1894; Puleston, *Mahan*, 48.

4. Mahan to Ashe, July 11, 1870, September 20, 1870.

5. Mahan to Alden, August 26, 1870, September 1, 1870, September 3, 1870, September 8, 1870; Mahan to Ashe, September 20, 1870. At Pittsburgh, Mahan reported to Commodore R. B. Hitchcock, commanding. Puleston, *Mahan*, 48, incorrectly dates Mahan's first meeting with his future wife in the "winter" of 1870–1871. She was, however, at Sharon Springs in July–August 1870.

6. Mahan to Ashe, September 20, 1870; Mahan to Alden, November 4, 1870, November 9, 1870, November 11, 1870.

7. Manlius Glendower Evans (1821–1879) married Ellen Kuhn. They had four children, viz: 1) Cadwalader Evans (1847–1880) who married Angelina Corse and had two daughters, Angelina ("Lena") and Edith; 2) Ellen Lyle Evans (1851–1927) who married Alfred Thayer Mahan and had two daughters, Helen Evans Mahan (1873–1963) and Ellen Kuhn Mahan (1877–1947), both of whom died unmarried, and a son, Lyle Evans Mahan (1881–1966), who was thrice married; 3) Rosalie Evans (1854–1940) who married Dr. Francis Leonard Brown (1864–1949) and was childless; and 4) Hartman Kuhn Evans (1860–1942) who married Mabel E. Curtis and had one son, Hartman Kuhn Evans, Jr., who died in infancy, and two daughters, Rosalie (Mrs. Van Vechten V. Burger) and Evelyn (Mrs. John B. Wright).

8. Mahan to Mary Okill Mahan, August 15, 1871; Mahan to Ellen Lyle Evans, January 6, 1871, March 10, 1871, March 22, 1871, April 3, 1871, April 5, 1871, June 12, 1871.

9. Mahan to Ashe, February 27, 1871; Mahan to Ellen Lyle Evans, March 10, 1871, March 22, 1871, April 3, 1871, April 5, 1871; Mahan to Ashe, April 25, 1871; Mahan to Ellen Lyle Evans, June 12, 1871.

10. Mahan to Ellen Lyle Evans, April 3, 1871; Mahan to Ashe, April 25, 1871; Mahan to Ellen Lyle Evans, June 12, 1871.

11. Mahan to Ashe, August 4, 1871; Mahan to Alden, August 12, 1871. Samuel A'Court Ashe (1840–1938) married Hannah Emerson Willard (1849–1892) on August 10, 1871. They had nine children, the youngest of whom was Rear Admiral George Bamford Ashe (1891–1971).

12. Mahan to Mary Okill Mahan, August 15, 1871; Puleston, *Mahan*, 50.

13. Puleston, *Mahan*, 50–51; Mahan to Alden, August 17, 1871.

14. Henry L. Abbot, *Memoir of Dennis Hart Mahan, 1802–1871*. Read Before the National Academy [of Sciences], November 7, 1878, pamphlet, (Washington, D.C., [1878]), 35. A copy of this pamphlet is in the Mahan Family Papers now in the Naval War College Library. Dennis H. Mahan was one of the founders of the National Academy of Sciences. On the question of suicide and its presumed hereditary character, *see* Mahan to Ashe, March 28, April 13, 1876.

15. Mahan to Alden, September 30, 1871; Mahan to Ammen, November 15, 1871, January 22, 1872, January 24, 1872, February 24, 1872, May 3, 1872, September 2, 1872, September 17, 1872, September 21, 1872, December 4, 1872, December 12, 1872; Mahan to Department of the Navy, Board of Examiners, September 19, 1872, September 20, 1872; Mahan to Robeson, December 2, 1872, July 1, 1873. For Mahan's marriage *see* Puleston, *Mahan*, 51.

16. Mahan to Ammen, February 15, 1873; Mahan to Robeson, February 17, 1873, February 24, 1873, May 14, 1873; Mahan to Taylor, February 17, 1873, March 6, 1873, March 21, 1873, July 7, 1873. Details of the *Wasp*'s journey from Montevideo to Asunción, December 13–22, 1874, are in the Diary of Lieutenant Commander Charles O'Neil which is in the Manuscript Division of the Library of Congress. O'Neil became executive officer of the *Wasp* on January 12, 1874. His diary covers the period January 4, 1874, to January 10, 1875. Robeson to Mahan, February 24, 1873 (NA).

17. *Letters and Papers*, I, February 1873–January 1875, *passim*. For a brief summary of the highlights of Mahan's service in the *Wasp*, *see* Puleston, *Mahan*, 52–54.

18. Mahan to Badger, August 8, 1873; Mahan to Strong, June 10, 1874; Mahan to Taylor, July 16, 1873. For the *Wasp*'s various and continuing physical maladies, *see* Mahan to Taylor, May 3, 1873, August 13, 1873, February 28, 1873, March 28, 1873, March 31, 1873, April 30, 1873, May 30, 1873, May 31, 1873, June 30, 1873, July 31, 1873, August 31, 1873, October 11, 1873, October 31, 1873, November 1, 1873; Mahan to Robeson, June 30, 1873; Mahan to Badger, July 31, 1873; Mahan to Case, March 31, 1873; Mahan to Ammen, June 30, 1873; Mahan to Strong, November 29, 1873, November 30, 1873, December 6, 1873, December 13, 1873, December 25, 1873, March 16, 1874; Mahan to O'Neil, August 18, 1874.

19. Mahan to Taylor, May 31, 1873; Mahan to Strong, December 31, 1873; Mahan to Reynolds, April 15, 1873, December 13, 1873; Mahan to Ammen, June 30, 1873 (NA); Mahan to Newman, July 7, 1873; Mahan to O'Neil, July 1, 1874; Mahan to Robeson, July 2, 1873, and June 18, 1874 (NA).

20. For the routine duties of the *Wasp* on the South Atlantic Station, *see* Mahan to Taylor, February 28, 1873, March 31, 1873, May 31, 1873, June 30, 1873, September 18, 1873, October 6, 1873, October 31, 1873, November 19, 1873; Mahan to Strong, November 30, 1873; Mahan to Caldwell, October 5, 1874; Mahan to Jacobs, September 16, 1873. For the plight of the *A. C. Bean*, *see* Mahan to Howard, May 5, 1874; and Mahan to Strong, May 6, 1874.

21. Mahan to Le Roy, October 5, 1874; Mahan to Howard, July 1, 1874; Mahan to Taylor, March 19, 1873, October 11, 1873; Mahan to Wyman, September 12, 1874; Mahan to Newman, October 8, 1873; Mahan to Strong, November 30, 1873, December 13, 1873, December 31, 1873 (two letters), March 16, 1874.

22. Mahan to Taylor, September 30, 1873, October 6, 1873, October 31, 1873; Mahan to Robeson, October 27, 1873, January 15, 1874; Mahan to Strong, December 6, 1873; Mahan to Badger, August 19, 1873. After many complaints, Mahan finally got two seaworthy ship's boats. *See* Mahan to Bacon, January 15, 1874.

23. Mahan to J. M. Muñoz, June 20, 1874, July 14, 1874; Mahan to Le Roy, October 5, 1874.

24. *See* especially Mahan to Taylor, May 30, 1873, June 14, 1873, June 30, 1873, July 16, 1873, October 6, 1873, October 8, 1873, October 11, 1873, November 19, 1873; Mahan to Strong, December 14, 1873, December 31, 1873, March 16, 1874, May 6, 1874; Mahan to Le Roy, September 28, 1874; Mahan to Caldwell, October 5, 1874, October 19, 1874; Mahan to Osborn, October 17, 1874; Ellen Evans Mahan to Mary Okill Mahan, September 13, 1874 (LC). The lecture on "Naval Battles" has not survived. Charles O'Neil, Mahan's executive officer, who carefully noted in

his own journal (and usually attended) the cultural and intellectual events taking place in Montevideo at the time, did not mention the lecture or having gone to it.

25. For Mahan's various comments and reports on the wars, threats of war, revolutions, and interventions in southeastern South America in the years 1873 and 1874, and the activities of the *Wasp* in showing the flag on the station, *see* Mahan to Taylor, May 30, 1873, June 14, 1873, June 30, 1873, July 16, 1873, October 6, 1873, October 8, 1873, October 11, 1873, November 19, 1873; Mahan to Strong, December 14, 1873, December 31, 1873, March 16, 1874, May 6, 1874; Mahan to Le Roy, September 28, 1874; Mahan to Caldwell, October 5, 1874, October 19, 1874; Mahan to Osborn, July 8, 1874, October 17, 1874; Mahan to Badger, July 29, 1873, July 31, 1873, August 1, 1873, September 11, 1873; Mahan to Silveira, February 17, 1874; Mahan to Howard, July 28, 1874. For the *Virginius* affair, *see* Mahan to Strong December 31, 1873; Mahan to Ashe, December 27, 1875; H. and M. Sprout, *The Rise of American Naval Power, 1776–1918* (Princeton, N.J.: Princeton University Press, 1944), 175.

26. Mahan to Le Roy, September 28, 1874; Mahan to Taylor, October 8, 1873; Mahan to Strong, May 6, 1874.

27. Ellen Evans Mahan to Mary Okill Mahan, October 8, 9, 1873 (LC), n.d. [early December 1873] (LC), September 13, 1874 (LC), October 12, 1874 (LC), November 10, 1874 (LC); Mary S. Hoskins to Ellen Evans Mahan, Blackmore Vicarage. Ingatestone, Essex, July 3, 1885 (NWC); Ellen Kuhn Mahan, "Recollections," in *Letters and Papers*, III, 723; Mahan to Helen Evans Mahan, August 5, 1894. Helen Evans Mahan's official godfather was the Reverend Morgan Dix of New York. Dr. Laurie is not further identifiable. Elly referred to Mahan as "Alf" and as "my own dear boy" during their Montevideo stay. For Mahan's later musical serenades to children in the Evans clan ("Where Are You Going Billy Boy?" and "Mother, Will you Buy Me a Pan of Milk?" were favorites of his), *see* Taylor, *Life of Admiral Mahan*, 285.

28. Ellen Evans Mahan to Mary Okill Mahan, n.d. [early December 1873] (LC), September 13, 1874 (LC), November 10, 1874 (LC). Dennis Hart Mahan, Jr., married Jeannette Katharine Murat.

29. Ellen Evans Mahan to Mary Okill Mahan, November 10, 1874 (LC), October 12, 1874 (LC).

30. O'Neil Diary (LC), May 9, 1874, May 25, 1874, September 15, 1874, January 18, 1874, January 25, 1874, April 5, 1874, April 12, 1874, April 19, 1874, May 10, 1874, May 14, 1874, May 24, 1874, October 18, 1874, October 25, 1874. The "very good little sermons" quotation is in O'Neil Journal, December 20, 1874. *See* entry for September 16, 1874, for the baptism of the O'Neil baby. The Reverend Mr. and Mrs. T. R. Hoskins seem to have been the only couple the Mahans saw socially in Montevideo or later kept in touch with at all. *See* Ellen Evans Mahan to Mary Okill Mahan, Montevideo, November 10, 1874 (LC); Mary S. Hoskins to Ellen Evans Mahan, Essex, July 3, 1885 (LC). When Mahan was in England, 1893–1894, he visited the widow Hoskins.

31. O'Neil Diary, April 19, 1874, May 1, 1874, May 15, 1874, July 23, 1874, November 3, 1874, November 10, 1874, December 25, 1874, January 2, 1875, January 5, 1875, January 7, 1875. It should be noted that O'Neil and Mahan got on quite well

professionally on board the *Wasp*. It was just that they seem to have had little in common socially and culturally. Their career paths crossed again in 1903 when Captain O'Neil served as Chief of the Bureau of Ordnance. *See* O'Neil Diary, *passim;* and Mahan to O'Neil, October 1, 1874, June 30, 1903, July 10, 1903.

32. Mahan to Robeson, January 1, 1875; Mahan to Kirkland, January 1, 1875.

33. Mahan to Ammen, February 7, 1875; Mahan to Mary Okill Mahan, February 1, 1875.

34. Mahan to Mary Okill Mahan, February 1, 1875.

35. Mahan to Mary Okill Mahan, February 10, 1875, March 3, 1875. As a commander on sea duty in the *Wasp*, Mahan's annual salary was $3,500.

NAVAL REFORMER, 1875–1880

1. Mahan to Ashe, June 17, 1876, May 15, 1875, May 21, 1875; Mahan to Ammen, August 27, 1875. Three years later, in April 1879, he again asked Ashe for the remainder of the monies still owing him, explaining that he needed the funds to send Elly to France to visit her parents, both of whom, he said, were in poor health and her father nearly at death's door. *See* Mahan to Ashe, April 30, 1879. Manlius Glendower Evans did indeed die later that year.

2. Mahan to Ashe, May 15, 1875, May 21, 1875.

3. Mahan to Ashe, May 21, 1875.

4. Mahan to Ashe, July 1, 1875, December 27, 1875, May 19, 1876; Mahan to Ammen, August 27, 1875, August 30, 1875, September 1, 1875; Mahan to Chandler, October 2, 1875.

5. Mahan to Ashe, December 27, 1875. It is not known how much confidential information Mahan managed to get into Senator Merrimon's hands through Ashe. It is known only that he transmitted some—specifically, the particulars of the Quackenbush case. *See also* Mahan to Ashe, March 28, April 13, 1876.

6. Mahan to Ashe, December 27, 1875, July 23, 1876.

7. Mahan to Ashe, December 27, 1875, January 27, 1876, February 1, 1876, March 28, April 13, 1876; Mahan to Bayard, March 8, 1876.

8. Mahan to Hawke, November 4, 1873; Mahan to Ashe, December 27, 1875; Mahan to Bayard, March 8, 1876. Mahan got materials he felt would be damaging to Robeson and Quackenbush to Senator Bayard through his brother-in-law, Hartman Kuhn Evans. Quackenbush unsuccessfully fought his 1874 suspension and his ultimate dismissal in 1881, within the department, in Congress, and in the courts until 1895. *The New York Times*, July 20, 1895, provides a brief history of the case.

9. Mahan to Ashe, January 27, 1876; *see also* Mahan to Ashe, March 28, April 13, 1876.

10. Mahan to Whitthorne, March 21, 1876, printed in House of Representatives, Misc. Document No. 1705, Part 8 (1876), *passim*. Whitthorne was, in the 1880s, one of the congressional founding fathers of the new steel navy. In April 1880 (*Congressional Record*, 49th Cong., 2nd Sess., Appendix, 142–143) he outlined a sea-power

hypothesis not unlike that developed later by Mahan in his *The Influence of Sea Power Upon History* (1890). *See* Robert Seager II, "Ten Years Before Mahan: The Unofficial Case for the New Navy, 1880–1890," *Mississippi Valley Historical Review*, XL (December 1953), 496–497.

11. HR, Misc. Doc. 1705, Part 8, *passim*.

12. Mahan to Ashe, March 28, April 13, 1876.

13. Mahan to Robeson, May 1, 1876. Dotty was charged with using abusive and threatening language to an officer and with drunkenness. He pleaded not guilty by reason of a previous court-martial finding of epilepsy and insanity. The Mahan court found him guilty on the abusive-language charge and sentenced him to three years' imprisonment and loss of pay; it added, however, that it doubted his sanity and for this reason recommended mitigation of the punishment. Robeson returned the record of the trial for revision, criticizing the court for not having taken the sanity question properly into account in the first place. In spite of Mahan's demurral on May 1, the court reversed its decision and declared Dotty not guilty. Robeson again rebuked the court, this time for changing its position without taking additional testimony on Dotty's sanity, and appointed a special medical board to examine Dotty. It was not Mahan's finest hour as president of a Navy court.

14. Mahan to Ashe, May 19, 1876, June 17, 1876. At this time generals of the Army received $17,000; admirals got $13,000. Navy commanders (Mahan's rank in 1876) received $3,000 ashore ($3,500 at sea) and "no allowances," while comparable rank in the Army, lieutenant colonels, received $3,000, plus longevity pay ($900), plus allowance for four rooms at $12 per month each ($576), for a total income of $4,476.

15. Mahan to Ammen, August 9, 1876; Mahan to Ashe, June 17, 1876, July 23, 1876, August 19, 21, 1876. *The Statistical History of the United States* (Stamford, Conn.; Fairfield Publishers, 1965), 90–91. The figures on wages in 1876 are little better than estimates.

16. Mahan to Ashe, July 23, 1876, August 19, 21, 1876.

17. For Mahan and the election of 1876 *see* Mahan to Ashe, June 17, 1876, July 23, 1876, August 19, 21, 1876. For his conservative view of economic, currency, and labor matters *see* Mahan to Ashe, December 27, 1875, March 5, 1878 (a long dissertation critical of the Bland-Allison Act of 1878), November 26, 1879, November 18, 1880; Mahan, "Woman's Suffrage," n.d., in *Letters and Papers*, III, 712–713. For his disgust with the "bloody shirt" policy of the GOP, *see* Mahan to Ashe, August 19, 1876, March 12, 1880.

18. Mahan to Ammen, August 30, 1876 (NA), October 11, 1876, October 16, 1876, December 5, 1876; Mahan to Church, November 25, 1876, November 29, 1876. Mahan supplied postage to have the manuscript of the first article returned to him, but it has not been found among his papers.

19. Ammen to Mahan, December 7, 1876 (NA); Mahan to Ammen, December 11, 1876; Ammen to Mahan, December 13, 1876 (NA); Mahan to Ammen, November 18, 1876 (NA); Ammen to Mahan, December 13, 1876 (NA); Mahan to Ammen, December 29, 1876. Mahan informed the bureau that his address abroad would be Villa Lébre, Pau, Basses Pyrénées, France.

20. Harold and Margaret Sprout, *The Rise of American Naval Power, 1776-1918*, 181-182; Mahan to Ammen, July 11, 1877, September 3, 1877, September 6, 1877.

21. Mahan to Ashe, October 21, 1877. Mahan was particularly interested in the local histories of Albi, Carcassonne, and Toulouse. The manuscript of his history of the region has not survived.

22. Mahan to Ashe, October 21, 1877, June 17, 1876, November 26, 1879; Mahan to Ammen, July 11, 1877.

23. Mahan to Ashe, June 16, 1878, October 21, 1877, December 2, 1877. A number of former midshipmen whom he had known at the Academy, 1856-1859, were attached to the staff there in 1877 and 1878 as officer-instructors. They were: Samuel D. Greene, John A. Howell, William T. Sampson, Henry L. Howison, and Silas W. Terry. *See* Mahan to Ashe, October 21, 1877.

24. Mahan to Ammen, January 10, 1878, March 1, 1878; Mahan to Parker, October 30, 1878; Mahan to Whiting, March 10, 1879; Mahan to Thompson, November 13, 1879; Mahan to Balch, January 8, 1880. For Mahan's hostile attitude toward the "notorious" hazing system at the Academy *see From Sail to Steam*, 54-56. For Nellie's near-fatal illness in 1880 *see* Mahan to Ashe, November 13, 1880, and his poignant letter to her dated October 18, 1884. Nellie had had scarlet fever in April 1879. *See* Mahan to Ashe, April 30, 1879, May 9, 1879.

25. Mahan, "Introduction to K. Asami's Biography of Tasuka Serata," in *Letters and Papers*, III, 688-692. *Also see* Taylor, *Life of Admiral Mahan*, 266-268. Serata was graduated very near the top of the class of 1881. The other Japanese midshipmen who were at the Academy when Mahan taught there were Yonoske Enouye, Sotokichi Uriu, and Sadanori Youchi. Uriu also became an admiral in the IJN and distinguished himself in the Russo-Japanese War (1904-1905). *See Annual Register of the United States Naval Academy . . . 1879-1880* (Washington, D.C.: Government Printing Office, 1879).

26. Mahan, "Naval Education," *The Record of the United States Naval Institute*, V, Whole No. 9 (1879), 345-376; Mahan to Ashe, May 9, 1879. Allan D. Brown won first prize in this contest and Caspar F. Goodrich won second. Like Mahan, both Brown and Goodrich went on to become prominent naval historians and publicists. All above three essays were published in the *Record* (later the *Proceedings*) of the USNI, V, Whole No. 9 (1879).

27. In this article Mahan also advocated the elimination of the controversial "line" and "staff" categories of officers. His idea was that all officers be "line," but that they be specifically trained at the Academy to perform the "staff" functions of constructor, engineer, and paymaster, just as cadet-midshipmen there were already being trained to handle such relatively narrow technical specialties as ordnance. At this time the Academy was graduating two distinct and differently trained groups of midshipmen, viz.: cadet-midshipmen (line) and cadet-engineers (staff). The class of 1879, for example, graduated 41 of the former and 23 of the latter. Mahan's forward-looking notion was that midshipmen would, in effect, major in either a "sea corps" or a "scientific corps" curriculum beginning in the junior year. But, upon graduation, all would be considered line officers.

28. Mahan to Ashe, May 9, 1879, March 12, 1880, June 16, 1878. For the role of Representatives Harris and Whitthorne in the naval regeneration of the 1880s *see* Seager, "Ten Years Before Mahan," *passim*. As foolish and inept as Mahan thought the 70-year-old Secretary Thompson to be, the Indianan had by 1880 developed a lively concept of the foreign-policy needs of a modern and expanded navy. Seager, "Ten Years Before Mahan," 501, 508.

29. Mahan to Ashe, March 12, 1880. It would seem that in March 1880 Mahan was abreast of the movement within the Navy and the Congress in the late 1870s and early 1880s that related sea power to national power and economic expansion. His absence from the country from 1883 to 1885, while in command of the *Wachusett* on the South Pacific Station, separated him from the mainstream of this movement, one he rejoined following his flag-showing experiences in Central America early in 1885 and his assignment to duty at the new Naval War College in 1886.

30. Mahan to Ashe, March 5, 1878, April 30, 1879, May 9, 1879, November 26, 1879, March 12, 1880.

31. Mahan to Ashe, November 26, 1879, November 13, 1880. Mahan took no note of the Greenback Labor Party candidacy of James B. Weaver which attracted 308,000 votes, most of them drawn from what were normally Democratic constituencies. It was these defections which likely cost Hancock the election. Mahan's theory of Tammany's "stupidity or treachery" was somewhat superficial.

A CAREER IN STAYS, 1880–1885

1. Mahan to Whiting, July 9, 1880, July 15, 1880; Mahan to Cooper, December 14, 1881. Mahan's later application for quarters at the yard was denied by Secretary William H. Hunt on April 11, 1881.

2. Puleston, *Mahan*, 62–63; Mahan to Ashe, December 21, 1882. Lyle was baptized at Trinity Episcopal Church by the Reverend Canon George William Douglas. During these years the Mahans regularly attended St. George's Episcopal Church where the Reverend William S. Rainsford was then rector. *See* Ellen Kuhn Mahan, "Recollections," in *Letters and Papers*, III, 721, 723–724.

3. *Ibid.* For Mahan's instruction of his children in history, *see* Mahan to Ashe, December 21, 1882; Puleston, *Mahan*, 63; and Taylor, *Life of Admiral Mahan*, 301–302.

4. Mahan to Helen Evans Mahan, August 22, 1884, December 31, 1884.

5. Ellen Kuhn Mahan, "Recollections," in *Letters and Papers*, III, 725. That Mahan and his wife consciously limited to zero the number of their children after the birth of Lyle in 1881 is suggested in Mahan's remark to Ashe: "It is a matter of regret to me that I cannot see myself surrounded by a larger family but it would be unjust to them [financially] situated as I am." Mahan to Ashe, December 21, 1882.

6. Mahan to Cooper, Upshur, *et al.*, Navigation Office Letters, New York, in *Letters and Papers*, I, July 1880–July 1883, *passim*.

7. Mahan to Upshur, August 31, 1882. Mahan tested and evaluated such new and allegedly superior pieces of equipment as: an invention by F. S. Barus designed to show "the deviation of a ship from her true course by the force of the wind"; var-

ious mechanisms for raising and lowering the wicks in oil lamps; a water-repellent chemical called "Neptunite"; the Walker Taffrail Log, which Mahan thought no improvement over the Bliss Taffrail Log then in use; Sir William Thomson's Navigational Sounding Machine, the tests on which were compromised by the seeming inability of the Western Electric Company to provide trouble-free glass tubes; the J. J. Walton Nickel Plated Reflector for Double Burner Cabin Lamps, which Mahan recommended for adoption and purchase; an improved speaking trumpet which Mahan felt was not much of an improvement; newly designed binocular glasses; electric bell apparatus equipment; the Bliss Metal Binnacle which Mahan thought no better or worse than existing binnacles supplied the Navy by Negus and Company. For these experiments and concerns, *see* especially Mahan to Barus, July 30, 1880; Mahan to Cooper, August 2, 1880, June 16, 1881, March 18, 1881; Mahan to Upshur, May 20, 1882, June 5, 1882, June 26, 1882, November 15, 1882, December 21, 1882, January 20, 1883, January 22, 1883 (two letters), May 9, 1883; Mahan *et al.* to Goff, January 13, 1881; and Mahan to Cooper, Upshur, *et al.*, Navigation Office Letters, in *Letters and Papers*, I, July 1880–July 1883, *passim*. Students of naval technology will find few better sources of information on the problems of naval illumination in the early 1880s than Mahan's numerous (over 50) letters on lamps and oils, wicks and prisms, found in *Letters and Papers*, I, July 1880–July 1883, *passim*.

8. Mahan to Cooper, March 16, 1882. This letter contains a detailed evaluation of existing books in the field of electricity. Mahan recommended that J. E. H. Gordon, *A Physical Treatise on Electricity and Magnetism* (1880), G. B. Prescott, *Speaking Telephone, Electric Light and Other Recent Electric Inventions* (1881), and A. P. Deschanel, *Electricity and Magnetism* (1872) be purchased for ship and shore station libraries, at a total cost of $10.05 the set. He also recommended that the Bureau of Navigation subscribe to *The Electrician*, a London weekly paper, and place it in the Navigation Office of the New York Yard, at an annual subscription cost of $5.28. *See also* Mahan to Cooper, January 19, 1882, March 16, 1882 (the second of three letters to Cooper of this date).

9. For evidence of Mahan's cautious buck-passing upward *see* Mahan to Cooper, June 4, 1881, June 13, 1881, June 24, 1881 (both letters of this date), July 12, 1881, November 12, 1881; Mahan to Upshur, July 7, 1882, August 5, 1882, August 15, 1882. The expenditure of $8.46 for plotting and drawing instruments was deemed unacceptable because Mahan had not properly processed the purchase through the purchasing paymaster. Called to task for this high crime, he explained that the improperly purchased instruments were needed immediately by the *Enterprise*, then about to sail, that similar instruments on hand and assigned to the *Enterprise* were found on inspection to be "deficient or unserviceable," and that he had quickly sent Lt. F. J. Drake into New York to buy proper instruments so that the vessel could sail on schedule. For this exercise in sensible behavior Mahan was brought to heel for violating U.S. Navy Regulation Circular No. 14. He escaped censure only because Commodore Upshur grudgingly conceded that "the necessities of the case seem to warrant" the violation. *See* Mahan to Upshur, January 9, 1883, and Upshur's forwarding note at the foot of the letter.

10. For the instances of accepting full blame for a minor error *see* Mahan to Cooper, January 7, 1882; Mahan to Upshur, June 6, 1882, December 15, 1882. For

the more usual device of shifting blame onto the shoulders of subordinates, especially his assistants, Lieutenants E. W. Bridge and F. J. Drake, *see* Mahan to Cooper, February 9, 1882, March 16, 1882, March 20, 1882; Mahan to Upshur, May 25, 1882, June 1, 1882, August 26, 1882, October 17, 1882, November 13, 1882. On one occasion, involving a tardy monthly inventory return, Mahan wrote Cooper that "because the Navigation Officer was very busy, a revision of that return was made by Ensign W. S. Benson, then attached as assistant. I do not wish to imply that Mr. Benson was in any way negligent; on the contrary, I always found him a very careful and attentive officer. But a mistake of this kind is on the face of it discreditable, and I wish to show that due care was at least attempted to be exercised." *See* Mahan to Cooper, March 16, 1882. Young Benson survived Mahan's damnation with faint praise and went on to become the Navy's first Chief of Naval Operations.

11. For evidences of Mahan's concern with efficiency and economy *see* Mahan to Cooper, Upshur, *et al.*, Navigation Office Letters, in *Letters and Papers*, I, July 1880–July 1883, *passim*; and especially *see* Mahan to Cooper, August 2, 1880, August 3, 1880, January 20, 1881, March 24, 1881, April 1, 1881, June 11, 1881, June 22, 1881, August 23, 1881, September 1, 1881, November 23, 1881, December 5, 1881, December 7, 1881 (two letters of this date), December 14, 1881, January 5, 1882, January 10, 1882, January 13, 1882 (an excellent example of Mahan's concern for and plea for proper warehousing, rational purchasing, and scientific inventory control), February 9, 1882, March 4, 1882, March 22, 1882, March 27, 1882, and Mahan to Upshur, April 1, 1882, April 13, 1882, May 9, 1882, October 6, 1882, October 16, 1882.

12. *See* especially Mahan to Cooper, June 3, 1881, November 21, 1881, March 17, 1882, March 20, 1882; Mahan to Upshur, August 17, 1882; but *see also* Mahan to Cooper, July 19, 1880, August 9, 1880, April 1, 1881, December 23, 1881, February 11, 1882, March 20, 1882 (two letters of this date); Mahan to Upshur, May 12, 1882, August 15, 1882. Mahan was able to convince the bureau that in the interests of efficiency and economy the manufacture of all flags for the Navy be centered at the New York Navy Yard. Mahan to Cooper, January 7, 1882. To push forward the hand-sewing of flags, Mahan requisitioned a stove "for the heating of irons used by women sewing flags, the need of which has been much felt." Mahan to Upshur, August 4, 1882.

13. The problem of the design, manufacture, and distribution to the Navy of foreign flags can be traced in Mahan to Cooper, July 23, 1881, December 14, 1881 (two letters of this date), December 24, 1881, January 19, 1882, March 28, 1882; Mahan to Upshur, May 12, 1882, June 5, 1882, August 2, 1882, August 12, 1882, August 26, 1882, April 3, 1883. Lt. Drake showed such great skill "in making the drawings of patterns for foreign flags" and became so important to Mahan in this regard that Mahan urged the bureau to relieve Drake of general court-martial duty so that he could push on with his task. Mahan to Cooper, March 10, 1882; Mahan to Upshur, May 8, 1882.

14. Prior to September 1882, Mahan's office had normally employed a storekeeper, a clerk, a specialman (general handyman), and a messenger. The reduction of September 15, 1882, caused him to lose his messenger. The simultaneous 20 per cent pay reduction undermined the morale of the others in his small civilian-support staff. All of which persuaded the commander to ask for a reduction in his paper-work load.

Mahan to Upshur, October 2, 1882, October 3, 1882, October 4, 1882, November 29, 1882. Mahan also had a high regard for the competence of the seamstresses he employed, apparently on a piece-work basis. The idea of women working bothered him not at all; but then working conditions at the yard were hardly of the classical sweatshop sort. Mahan requisitioned 30 pounds of bulk ice daily with which to cool his offices and work spaces during the summer months. Nevertheless, *The New York Times* of March 22, 1882, drew attention to worker discontent at the yard relating to overtime pay following the government's adoption of the eight-hour day for federal employees. Mahan to Cooper, December 14, 1881; Mahan to Upshur, May 22, 1882, May 2, 1883.

15. Mahan to Cooper, March 4, 1882; Mahan to Upshur, October 7, 1882, October 10, 1882, October 20, 1882 (one of four letters of this date), April 23, 1883. For Mahan's book requisitions *see* especially Mahan to Cooper, November 13, 1880, November 15, 1880, December 20, 1880, January 18, 1881, March 2, 1882, March 6, 1882; Mahan to Upshur, June 17, 1882, July 1, 1882, July 14, 1882, August 29, 1882, February 12, 1883, June 11, 1883, June 21, 1883.

16. Mahan to Ashe, January 10, 1881. Lt. Commander Richard L. Law, whom Mahan cordially disliked, had in some way used "his influence with the Secretary on my brother's behalf." This service by Law in no way endeared him to Mahan. Nor did Mahan suddenly become a fan of Secretary Thompson.

17. Mahan to Hunt, April 20, 1881.

18. Mahan to Ashe, March 12, 1880, December 21, 1882; July 6, 1882. *See also* Seager, "Ten Years Before Mahan," *passim*.

19. Mahan to Ashe, August 14, 1883.

20. *Ibid.* In March 1885 Mahan was the second senior commander in the Navy. Mahan to Luce, March 23, 1885.

21. Taylor, *Life of Admiral Mahan*, 23; Mahan to Ashe, July 6, 1883. Scribner's approached Mahan about doing the book on December 15, 1882. A contract offer was extended on December 26 and was immediately accepted by Mahan. Charles Scribner's to Mahan, December 15, 1882, December 26, 1882, December 30, 1882 (Scribner Collection, Princeton University Library).

22. Mahan to Ashe, July 6, 1883; Mahan to McDonald, March 10, 1883, April 28, 1883, May 2, 1883; Mahan to Charles Scribner's Sons, April 12, 1883, April 17, 1883, June 22, 1883; T. O. Selfridge to Mahan, April 30, 1883 (NA); "Memorandum of a Conversation with James E. Jouett on the Battle of Mobile Bay," in *Letters and Papers*, III, 555–556; Mahan to Stevens, May 20, 1883; Mahan to Helen Evans Mahan, August 22, 1884; Mahan to Upshur, June 21, 1883. In the requisition ordering his own book he ordered 60 copies of Daniel Ammen's *The Atlantic Coast* and 10 copies of J. R. Soley's *The Blockade and the Cruisers*, also published in the Scribner's series. It should be noted that while *The Gulf and Inland Waters* was based primarily on official reports, Mahan felt that these "omit or have lost many details that I considered essential and a large correspondence (for the subject) was entailed. I aimed at making my book both actually and apparently one upon which future writers could rely. . . . I regret that I did not state my authorities more fully but hope that the evident care I have taken may be a warrant to doubters." Mahan to Ashe, July 6, 1883.

23. T. Woolverton to Mahan, July 8, 1883; Ashe to Mahan, July 10, 1883; J. R. Soley to Mahan, July 19, 1883; *Chicago Tribune*, July 1883; John S. Cunningham to Mahan, July 9, 1883; Francis A. Roe to Mahan, July 9, 1883; James A. Greer to Mahan, June 29, 1883; Isaac N. Brown to Mahan, June 20, 1883; Francis E. Sheppard to Mahan, June 27, 1883; Thornton S. Jenkins to Mahan, June 25, 1883; Gouverneur Morris Ogden to Mahan, August 13, 1883; Cadwalader E. Ogden to Mahan, August 9, 1883. These letters to Mahan (as well as the *Chicago Tribune* clipping) are in the Mahan Family Papers at the Naval War College. The Woolverton letter to Mahan seems to indicate that the two men maintained some contact over the years. At this time Woolverton was married, had a daughter, and was stationed at the Naval Hospital in Philadelphia. *See also*, Taylor, *Life of Admiral Mahan*, 23–24.

24. Mahan to Ashe, July 6, 1883, August 14, 1883. Since there were many more commanders in the Navy in the mid-1880s than ships to command, sea-duty tours were often shortened from the usual two years so that the few commands available could be rotated.

25. Mahan to Chandler, August 6, 1883, August 10, 1883, September 9, 1883 (two letters to Chandler of this date); Mahan to Walker, August 6, 1883, August 14, 1883, September 9, 1883; Mahan to Ashe, July 26, 1884.

26. Mahan to Hughes, December 28, 1883; Mahan to Walker, December 3, 1883, July 8, 1884; Mahan to Chandler, July 9, 1884, March 5, 1885; Mahan to Upshur, December 31, 1884; Mahan to Whitney, March 22, 1885, May 4, 1885, May 15, 1885 (two letters to Whitney of this date); Mahan to Ashe, March 11, 1885; Mahan to Sicard, December 21, 1883, January 9, 1884, February 20, 1884, March 15, 1884, May 9, 1884; Mahan to English, July 15, 1884; Mahan to Ellen Kuhn Mahan, April 25, 1884. Seventy-five letters from Helen Evans Mahan and Ellen Kuhn Mahan to their father, dating from August 26, 1883, to May 29, 1885, are in the Mahan Family Papers at the Naval War College. Few of Mahan's *Wachusett* letters to his children have survived, and none of the many that surely he wrote to his wife. But *see* Mahan to Ellen Kuhn Mahan, April 25, 1884, October 18, 1884; Mahan to Helen Evans Mahan, August 22, 1884, December 31, 1884; Mahan to Lyle Evans Mahan, (summer 1884), December 29, 1884.

27. Mahan to Whitney, May 15, 1885. Rear Admiral Hughes told Secretary Chandler in March 1884 that, since September 1883, when Mahan took command and had pronounced the vessel fit, he knew "of no service done by the *Wachusett* that could have caused deterioration to the extent mentioned by Comdr. Mahan." Hughes to Chandler, March 18, 1884 (NA).

28. For Mahan's problems with enlistment expirations and crew shortages, his attempts at improvisation to secure and hold skilled seamen at the wage scales then prevailing, and his constant complaints to his superiors (principally to Commodore Earl English, his old nemesis from *Iroquois* days who headed the Bureau of Equipment and Recruiting) about enlisted-personnel problems and crew instability in the *Wachusett*, *see* Mahan to English, September 13, 1883, September 22, 1883, December 12, 1883, March 21, 1884, June 17, 1884, June 30, 1884, July 14, 1884, October 20, 1884; Mahan to Chandler, July 1, 1884, December 3, 1884; Mahan to Schley (Schley replaced English as Chief of the Bureau of Equipment and Recruiting in September 1884), October 23, 1884, November 5, 1884, December 3, 1884. For the

prohibition against recruiting Chinese nationals on the station, *see* Mahan to Walker, September 9, 1883; Mahan to Schley, December 3, 1884. For the problem of officer turnover and the shortage of certified watch officers, *see* Mahan to Chandler, September 2, 1884, December 24, 1884, March 22, 1885; Mahan to Walker, April 12, 1884.

29. Mahan to Chandler, December 11, 1883 (on Rodman's fitness as an officer); Hugh Rodman, *Yarns of a Kentucky Admiral* (Indianapolis: Bobbs-Merrill Co., 1928), 30. Mahan did young Rodman a favor by facilitating his transfer from the *Wachusett* when it became apparent that the latter's personality conflict with the executive officer was an unsolvable one. *See* Puleston, *Mahan*, 67. Mahan's favor for Rodman should not be interpreted as evidence of a general love feast between the commander and his junior officers. Quite the contrary, Mahan ran a very tight ship and was swift to put junior officers on suspension for such breaches of discipline as "disrespect to executive officer" and "provoking and profane language to another officer." Mahan to Whitney, September 9, 1885 (NA).

30. Mahan to Ashe, July 26, 1884.

31. Mahan to Walker, March 18, 1884 (two letters to Walker of this date); Mahan to Cooke, March 29, 1884; Mahan to Ashe, July 26, 1884. On Mahan's contempt for Latin-Americans *see also* Mahan to Ashe, March 11, 1885. For later pleased reactions to Cleveland's narrow victory over Blaine in the election of 1884, *see* Mahan to Ashe, March 11, 1885, February 2, 1886.

32. The early history of the War College, together with various orders, reports, and documents pertaining to its establishment, may be found in Austin M. Knight and William D. Puleston, *History of the United States Naval War College*. Unpublished manuscript (Newport, R.I., 1916), Introduction, 1–4, Chapter I, 1–15. Cited hereafter as Knight and Puleston, *Naval War College*. A typescript copy of this manuscript is in the Naval War College library.

33. Mary Edith Powel, Memorandum of a Conversation with S. B. Luce, May 7, 1897 (NA); Mahan to Luce, September 4, 1884, Footnote 2.

34. Knight and Puleston, *Naval War College*, Intro., 1–4, Chapter I, 1–15; Mahan to Luce, September 4, 1884, November 5, 1884. Mahan's executive officer in the *Wachusett*, "an efficient officer," indeed, a "quite capable" man, was Lt. Commander Abraham H. Vail, who stood at the very bottom of the class of 1864.

35. Mahan, *From Sail to Steam*, 276–277. *See also* Puleston, *Mahan*, 68–70.

36. Mahan to Luce, May 16, 1885.

37. Mahan to Ashe, March 11, 1885.

38. Mahan to Chandler, December 21, 1883; Mahan to Ashe, March 11, 1885; Taylor, *Life of Admiral Mahan*, 179–180.

39. Mahan to Luce, March 23, 1885, May 13, 1885, May 16, 1885, May 23, 1885, June 16, 1885; Mahan to Chandler, December 24, 1884, March 5, 1885, March 22, 1885; Mahan to Upshur, December 21, 1884.

40. Mahan to Chandler, February 17, 1885, March 5, 1885, March 9, 1885; Mahan to Whitney, July 25, 1885, September 5, 1885; Mahan to Ashe, March 11, 1885.

41. Mahan to Chandler, March 5, 1885; Mahan to Whitney, March 22, 1883 (third letter to Whitney of this date).

42. Mahan to Chandler, February 17, 1885, February 22, 1885; Mahan to Ashe, March 11, 1885; John Bassett Moore, *Personal Recollections of Admiral Mahan.* Pamphlet. N.P., n.d. [1940], privately printed. The diplomatic details of the Santos case are in *Foreign Relations of the United States. 1886.* (Washington, D.C.: Government Printing Office, 1887), 224–297.

43. Mahan to Chandler, March 5, 1885; Mahan to Whitney, March 22, 1885 (two letters to Whitney of this date), telegram, March 27, 1885.

44. Mahan to Whitney, March 22, 1885 (first two of three letters to Whitney of this date); Mahan to Chandler, telegram, March 18, 1885, March 22, 1885; Mahan to Luce, March 23, 1885; Mahan to Clark, February 8, 1902.

45. *Report of the Secretary of the Navy* . . . , House of Representatives, Ex. Doc. 1, Part 3, 49 Cong., 1 Sess. 2 vols. (Washington, D.C.: Government Printing Office, 1885), I, xv–xvii.

46. Mahan to Whitney, telegrams, March 27, 1885 (two telegrams to Whitney of this date).

47. Whitney to Mahan, March 17, 1885 (NA).

48. Mahan to Whitney, April 5, 1885 (two letters to Whitney of this date), April 6, 1885.

49. Mahan to Whitney, April 5, 1885 (two letters to Whitney of this date), April 6, 1885, telegram, April 8, 1885, April 10, 1885.

50. Mahan to Whitney, April 10, 1885, April 27, 1885.

51. Mahan to Whitney, May 12, 1885; Mahan to Luce, May 13, 1885, May 16, 1885, May 23, 1885.

52. Mahan to Whitney, May 14, 1885 (Mahan's emphases), May 15, 1885; *Treaties and Conventions Concluded Between the United States and Other Powers Since July 4, 1776* . . . (Washington, D.C.: Government Printing Office, 1889), 268.

53. Mahan to Whitney, May 15, 1885 (two letters to Whitney of this date), May 24, 1885, telegram, May 26, 1885, June 4, 1885, June 6, 1885, June 20, 1885, telegram, June 20, 1885, July 25, 1885, August 5, 1885, August 31, 1885; Mahan to Luce, June 16, 1885; Puleston, *Mahan*, 71. On July 30, 1887, the *Wachusett* was sold out of the service.

54. Mahan to Luce, September 2, 1885.

THE NAVAL WAR COLLEGE: SEA TACTICS AND NAVY POLITICS, 1885–1889

1. John D. Hayes and John B. Hattendorf, eds., *The Writings of Stephen B. Luce* (Newport, R.I.: Naval War College, 1975), 10–12, 47–50; Knight and Puleston, *Naval War College*, Introduction, 1–2, Chapter I, 1–13, 15–16, 18–20; Mahan to Luce, September 4, 1884. Writing in 1916 from the perspective of World War I and Mahan's fame as an authority on matters naval, Knight and Puleston sought to demonstrate that Luce's initial concept of the educational function of the War College was quite similar to Mahan's later view of the matter. The argument is not persuasive. Actually, Mahan's own early view of the college curriculum was a catholic

one. It was of an institution teaching courses "in advance of what is taught at the Naval Academy, in many branches, but most especially on the more purely professional subjects—military subjects." Mahan to Ashe, February 2, 1886.

2. Hayes and Hattendorf, *Writings of Stephen B. Luce*, 45, 53–56, 60–62, 75–76; Knight and Puleston, *Naval War College*, Chapter II (1885), 1–4. Professor Soley was Head of the Department of English, History, and Law at the Naval Academy. One of the unpaid guest lecturers was Commander Henry C. Taylor, later president of the college, who spoke on "the necessity of concentration in the formation of the naval line of battle." Another was John C. Ropes, a prominent amateur military historian. Among the nine students was Lt. Cmdr. R. B. Bradford, who had served with Mahan in the *Iroquois*.

3. Mahan to Luce, September 2, 1885, October 16, 1885, April 7, 1886; Mahan to Whitney, September 5, 1885, September 19, 1885, October 10, 1885; Mahan to Walker, October 20, 1885; Answers to Questions on Examination for Promotion to Captain, October 15, 1885, in *Letters and Papers*, III, 557–558; Mahan to Ashe, February 2, 1886.

4. Mahan to Luce, October 16, 1885, October 21, 1885.

5. Other books and articles read and sources consulted by Mahan in the preparation of his first lectures at the War College on history and tactics, 1885–1886, included: Sir Charles Ekins, *The Naval Battles of Great Britain From the Accession of the Illustrious House of Hanover to the Throne to the Battle of Navarin*, 2nd ed. (1828); John Clerk, *An Essay on Naval Tactics, Systematical and Historical. . . .* 3rd ed. (1827); John Charnock, *Biographia Navalis; or, Impartial Memoirs of the Lives and Characters of Officers of the Navy of Great Britain From the Year 1660 to the Present Time . . .* (1794–1798); Henry W. Halleck, *Treatise on International Law and the Laws of War* (1866); Sir George Augustus Elliot, *A Treatise on Future Naval Battles and How to Fight Them* (1885); Sir John Montagu Burgoyne, *A Short History of the Naval and Military Operations in Egypt From 1798–1802* (1885); M. Burrows, *Life of Edward, Lord Hawke* (1883); Sir Edward B. Hamley, *The Operations of War Explained and Illustrated* (1866); Vice Admiral J. Penhoat, *Elements of Naval Tactics* (1879); James A. Froude, *Oceana; or England and Her Colonies* (1886); William Bainbridge Hoff, *Examples, Conclusions, and Maxims of Modern Naval Tactics* (1884); Sir John Colomb, *Naval Intelligence and the Protection of Commerce* (1881); John Knox Laughton, "Notes on the Last Great Naval War," Royal United Service Institution *Journal*, XXIX (1885); S. B. Luce, "On the Study of Naval Warfare as a Science," and "On the Study of Naval History (Grand Tactics")" War College Lectures (1885), subsequently published in U.S. Naval Institute *Proceedings*, XII, No. 4 (1886), and XIII, No. 2 (1887). Mahan also read back issues of the French *Revue Maritime et Coloniale*, the *Journal* of the Royal United Service Institution, and the *Proceedings* of the U.S. Naval Institute, and read the standard biographies of British Admirals George Rodney, Augustus Keppel, James de Saumarez, John Jervis, William Sidney Smith, and others. *See* Mahan to Luce, November 3, 1885, November 19, 1885, April 24, 1886, May 31, 1886. Puleston, *Mahan*, 74–80, discusses Mahan's background reading, a discussion based on most of these same Mahan-to-Luce letters; but he blurred the point that Mahan was preparing two separate sets of lectures. He thus clouded the specific and delayed

nature of Jomini's impact on Mahan. Mahan's later dismissal of his authorship of "Fleet Battle Tactics" is found in his *From Sail to Steam*, 284–285. It was Mahan's habit, as he read, to order pertinent books for the new War College library. These he would first have sent to him for his own use. On this point, *see*, in addition to the Mahan-to-Luce letters cited above, Mahan to Luce, October 22, 1885, November 2, 1885, February 26, 1886. Mahan's own account of the scope of his research at this time may be found in *From Sail to Steam*, 278–285.

6. The high point of the battle was the fortuitous ramming and sinking of the *Re d'Italia* by the Austrian flagship *Ferdinand Maximilian*. A detailed account of this action, by James A. Arnold, may be found in Potter and Fredland, *The United States and World Sea Power*, 383–387.

7. Mahan to Luce, November 2, 1885, November 3, 1885, November 14, 1885, January 6, 1886, January 18, 1886, April 7, 1886.

8. Mahan to Luce, January 22, 1886.

9. Mahan to Luce, April 24, 1886; Mahan to Ashe, February 2, 1886.

10. Mahan to Luce, April 7, 1886, April 24, 1886, May 1, 1886; Mahan to Rodgers, April 24, 1886, April 29, 1886. Lt. R. P. Rodgers was Chief Intelligence Officer at this time. General William T. Sherman also read the lectures on strategy and tactics that Mahan was to deliver at the War College in 1887 and 1888. *See* Mahan, *Naval Strategy, Compared and Contrasted With the Principles of Military Operations on Land.* (Boston: Little, Brown and Co., 1911), 124.

11. The original manuscript of "Fleet Battle Tactics," which consists of 115 double-spaced, typed pages, is in the archives of the Naval War College. It was never published. On the title page, in Mahan's hand, is the notation: "Written in April and May 1886 and never revised." Some of the material in it, however, in revised form, found its way into Mahan's *Naval Strategy*, published in 1911. Mahan, "Fleet Battle Tactics," *passim*; but especially *see* 4–12, 14–25, 30, 32–42, 45–47, 49–52, 54, 57, 62, 64, 74, 77–80, 83, 104–105 (Jomini references are on 23, 28, 29, 52, 106); Mahan to Luce, May 6, 1886, May 31, 1886; Mahan to Rodgers, April 24, 1886; Mahan to Miles, November 22, 1888; Knight and Puleston, *Naval War College*, Chapter III (1886), 1–6. For Luce's marginalia on the original manuscript, *see* Mahan, "Fleet Battle Tactics," 32, 35, 49, 55, 59, 82, 108. For Mahan on Hoff, *see ibid.*, 79. In 1908, Mahan wrote that Hoff's lectures on tactics at the college in 1886 were little more than "a somewhat patch-work compilation of the utterances on Naval Tactics of various officers, foreign and American." *See* Mahan, "Reminiscences of Service at the Naval War College," in *Letters and Papers*, III, 663.

12. Mahan to Luce, November 3, 1885; Mahan to Ashe, January 13, 1886; Mahan to Luce, January 22, 1886.

13. Mahan to Luce, February 26, 1886, March 17, 1886; Mahan to Ashe, January 13, 1886, February 2, 1886. Mahan's brother Frederick, then a captain in the Army Corps of Engineers, was stationed in Washington at the time. He also worked on his mother's pension problem.

14. Mahan to Luce, January 18, 1886, May 6, 1886, May 31, 1886; Mahan to Walker, June 22, 1886, June 28, 1886, July 15, 1886. It should be noted that J. G. Walker, unlike Ramsay, did feel that it was the business of naval officers to write

books. Although Mahan had long since been assigned to duty at the War College, and although his annual leave expired July 26, Walker permitted him to remain in Bar Harbor until August 25 to complete the writing of the sea-power lectures. *See* Mahan to Walker, July 15, 1886. On Mahan's choice of Bar Harbor as a summer residence in 1886, *see* Mahan to Luce, January 13, 1886, January 18, 1886. The fact was he could not afford fashionable Newport's summer prices.

15. Knight and Puleston, *Naval War College*, Chapter III (1886), 1; Mahan to Luce, January 6, 1886, January 13, 1886; Mahan, "Reminiscences of Service at the Naval War College," in *Letter and Papers*, III, 663–667; Ellen Kuhn Mahan, "Recollections," *ibid.*, 725–726; Mahan to Ashe, October 3, 1886, September 8, 1887; Taylor, *Life of Admiral Mahan*, 303.

16. Knight and Puleston, *Naval War College*, Chapter III (1886), 1–6. Mahan's staff lecturers in 1886 were Commander William Bainbridge Hoff (Naval Tactics), Lieutenant John F. Meigs (Naval Gunnery), Professor James R. Soley (International Law), and Lieutenant Tasker H. Bliss (Military Strategy and Tactics). Mahan lectured on naval history. Save for Bliss and Mahan, all had primary duty elsewhere and were assigned to the college only for the September 6–November 20 session. Luce gave the opening address which was printed in the U.S. Naval Institute *Proceedings*, November 4, 1886. Mahan to Walker, October 19, 1886, October 4, 1887.

17. Mahan to Walker, October 19, 1886.

18. Mahan to Ashe, September 8, 1887; Knight and Puleston, *Naval War College*, Introduction, 5, 6, Chapter III (1886), 4; Hayes and Hattendorf, *Writings of Stephen B. Luce*, 13–14. For Mahan's view that Whitney was wholly at fault in his split with Luce (he was not), *see* Mahan to Ashe, August 10, 1888, October 3, 1886, November 14, 1887; Mahan, "Reminiscences of Service at the Naval War College," in *Letters and Papers*, III, 663–667.

19. Knight and Puleston, *Naval War College*, Chapter III (1886), 2, Chapter IV (1887), 2; Mahan to Ashe, November 14, 1887; Mahan to Walker, October 4, 1887; Mahan, "The Growth of Our National Feeling," *World's Work* (February 1902), 1764. After a one-year delay, Mahan finally delivered his "Fleet Battle Tactics" lectures in 1887.

20. Mahan to Walker, October 4, 1887; Mahan to Rodgers, June 24, 1889; Mahan to Ashe, January 12, 1888; February 20, 1888, June 14, 1888, August 10, 1888; Mahan to Ropes, February 16, 1888, February 22, 1888; Mahan to Saltonstall, May 31, 1888; Mahan, "Reminiscences of Service at the Naval War College," in *Letters and Papers*, III, 663–667. Mahan was assisted in his lobbying campaign by War College staff lecturers Commander Purnell F. Harrington (Tactics of the Ram) and Lieutenant Charles H. Stockton, later rear admiral and president of the college. *Ibid.* In 1887 Stockton lectured on "Commerce and Commercial Routes Between Europe and the Pacific" with special attention to the likely impact of an isthmian canal on such routes. Knight and Puleston, *Naval War College*, Chapter IV (1887), 2–3.

21. Mahan, "Reminiscences of Service at the Naval War College," in *Letters and Papers*, III, 663–667; Mahan to Ashe, June 14, 1888.

22. Mahan to Ashe, June 14, 1888, August 10, 1888; Knight and Puleston, *Naval War College*, Chapter V (1888), 1–2, and Chapter VI (1889), 1.

23. *Ibid.*; Mahan to Ashe, August 10, 1888.

24. *New York Times*, May 15, 1888; Mahan to Luce, November 14, 1888; Mahan to Ashe, August 10, 1888.

25. Mahan to Ashe, August 10, 1888; Mahan to Merrell, May 25, 1908; "Address of Captain A. T. Mahan, U.S. Navy, President of the U.S. Naval War College, At the Opening of the Fourth Annual Session of the College, August 6, 1888," U.S. Naval Institute *Proceedings*, XIV, No. 4 (1888), 621–639; Mahan to Walker, October 13, 1888.

26. Knight and Puleston, *Naval War College*, Chapter V (1888), 1–4; Taylor, *Life of Admiral Mahan*, 133–134; Mahan to Walker, October 13, 1888; Mahan to Henderson, October 16, 1888, November 30, 1888; Mahan to Rodgers, November 1, 1888; Mahan to Luce, November 14, 1888; Mahan to Miles, November 22, 1888. Mahan sent Henderson several copies of the address he delivered at the War College on August 6 and urged him to circulate it among officers in the Royal Navy. The 1888 session at the college was the first during which staff lecturers began to rely importantly on data secured by the Office of Naval Intelligence. Confidential materials dealing with "English Naval Manoeuvres, 1888" and "Intelligence Report on the War Resources of Canada" were asked for and received. *See* Mahan to Rodgers, August 13, 1888, September 6, 1888, September 22, 1888; Mahan to Walker, August 14, 1888. Mahan was reluctant to include in the 1888 curriculum any lectures on the U.S. Naval Reserve. Privately, he had little confidence in the Naval Reserve concept. "I confess to doubting whether the efficiency of a large part of their enormous enrolled force is not much overrated," he told Raymond P. Rodgers. "There should be a considerable nucleus of men who remain steady in service. In [a] republic there will always be wild ideas of great things to be expected from a reserve militia etc. This should be sobered by a well-informed, thoughtful, professional opinion." Mahan to Rodgers, February 22, 1888.

27. Mahan to Ashe, August 10, 1888; Mahan to Luce, November 14, 1888; Mahan to Henderson, November 30, 1888.

28. Mahan to Luce, November 14, 1888; Mahan to Whitney, December 11, 1888.

29. Mahan to Miles, November 22, 1888.

30. Knight and Puleston, *Naval War College*, Chapter VI (1889), 1–2; Mahan to Casey, December 14, 1888; Mahan to Luce, February 6, 1889, February 16, 1889; Mahan to Henderson, March 18, 1889.

THE INFLUENCE OF SEA POWER UPON HISTORY, 1888–1890

1. Mahan to Whitney, December 11, 1888, December 14, 1888; Mahan to Butler, December 14, 1888; Mahan to Harmony, December 14, 1888; Mahan to Casey, December 14, 1888; Mahan to Stockton, December 27, 1888; Tryon to Whitney, December 27, 1888 (NA); Mahan to Walker, March 24, 1889; Knight and Puleston, *Naval War College*, Chapter VI (1889), 1–3. The 1889 session began on August 5. Six of the twelve students left before the course ended on October 25.

2. Knight and Puleston, *Naval War College*, Chapter VI (1889), 1–3.

3. Mahan to Scribner's, September 4, 1888, September 6, 1888; on Scribner's rejection of Mahan's manuscript, *see* Scribner Collection, September 1889, Princeton University Library; Ellen Kuhn Mahan, "Recollections," in *Letters and Papers*, III, 725–726; Puleston, *Mahan*, 89–90, discusses Mahan's attempt to find a publisher; S. B. Luce to J. F. Meigs, October 29, 1888 (NA).

4. Mahan to Chester, June 4, 1889, May 20, 1889, September 9, 1889, September 16, 1889, September 21, 1889; Mahan to Casey, December 14, 1888; Mahan to the Mayor of Portland [Oregon] and Others, headed "Information Desired by a Commission for Selecting a Navy Yard Site Upon the North West Coast," December 15, 19, 1888; Mahan to Superintendent, Coast and Geodetic Survey, March 19, 1889, May 7, 1889; Mahan to White, March 21, 1889, September 6, 1889; Mahan to Pratt, April 23, 1889, May 17, 1889, June 27, 1889, July 11, 1889, September 28, 1889; Mahan to Colonna, June 15, 1889, July 2, 1889, August 14, 1889, August 24, 1889, August 30, 1889.

5. Mahan to Pratt, June 23, 1889, June 27, 1889; Mahan to Colonna, July 10, 1889; Mahan to Chester, July 3, 1889, September 9, 1889 (discussing commission expenditures through September 7, 1889); Taylor, *Life of Admiral Mahan*, 303; Ellen Kuhn Mahan, "Recollections," in *Letters and Papers*, III, 725; G. B. White to Mahan, November 11, 1889 (LC); Mahan to the Treasurer of the United States, November 20, 1889.

6. The Mahan-Chester-Stockton report was titled "Report of the Commission to Select a Site For a Navy Yard on the Pacific Coast North of the Forty-Second Parallel of North Latitude." It was dated September 15, 1889, and was printed in *Report of the Secretary of the Navy. 1889* (Washington, D.C.: Government Printing Office, 1890), Part 2, 124–167. Pratt estimated the hourly fresh-water outflow from Lake Kitsap at 34,200 gallons. Mahan had used the much higher figure of 337,000 gallons hourly when he sent the report to the printer. He took Pratt's figure, however, corrected it slightly, and concluded that 34,000 gallons per hour, or over 800,000 gallons per day, was "undoubtedly much more potable water than a navy yard can require." He also politely chastised Pratt for sending the revised flow figures so late, too late for inclusion in the body of the printed report. For the Lake Kitsap water-flow crisis, *see* Mahan to White, September 6, 1889; Mahan to Chester, September 7, 1889, September 9, 1889, September 13, 1889; Mahan to Pratt, September 7, 1889.

7. Mahan to Chester, June 4, 1889, July 13, 1889, July 19, 1889, September 28, 1889, October 8, 1889, October 18, 1889; Mahan to Rodgers, April 9, 1889; Mahan to Luce, October 7, 1889; John Gibbon, "Puget Sound—A Sketch of Its Defenses," *Journal of the Military Service Institution of the United States* (September 1889), 409–420.

8. Mahan to Chester, May 8, 1889, June 4, 1889, June 14, 1889, September 24, 1889, September 28, 1889, October 18, 1889; Mahan to Luce, August 1, 1889. The second site commission sent to the Puget Sound area to select a site for a dry dock (yard) was composed of Capt. Thomas O. Selfridge, USN, Lt. Ambrose B. Wyckoff, USN, Col. George H. Mendell, USA, former Secretary of the Navy Richard Thompson, and former U.S. Senator Thomas C. Platt. *See* Mahan to Chester, October 18, 1889.

9. Mahan to Luce, August 1, 1889, September 21, 1889, October 7, 1889. Mahan estimated that if every graduate of the War College course were given the book, some 20 copies could be disposed of each year. He doubted, however, that Caspar Goodrich, the "procrastinating" president of the college, could persuade the "scrupulous and slow" Montgomery Sicard, Chief of the Bureau of Ordnance, to accept such an approach to book distribution. For Mahan's earlier connection with John S. Barnes, see Mahan, *From Sail to Steam*, 58–60.

10. Mahan to Luce, October 7, 1889; Mahan to Helen Evans Mahan, July 3, 1894; Mahan to Luce, September 21, 1889.

11. Mahan to Luce, October 7, 1889; Mahan to McIntyre, January 7, 1909; Mahan to Luce, October 16, 1889; unidentified and undated newspaper clipping (probably the *New York World*) in Mahan Family Papers at the Naval War College.

12. Mahan to Little, Brown & Co., November 22, 1889; Mahan to Luce, October 7, 1889; December 3, 1889, April 4, 1890; Mahan to Chester, October 8, 1889.

13. Arnold J. Toynbee, ed., *Greek Historical Thought*. 2nd ed. (Boston: Beacon Press, 1950), 162–164; L. C. Allin, "The United States Naval Institute: Intellectual Forum of the New Navy, 1873–1889." Unpublished Ph.D. dissertation (University of Maine, 1976); Kenneth J. Hagan, *American Gunboat Diplomacy and the Old Navy, 1877–1889* (Westfield, Conn.: Greenwood Press, 1973), *passim*; and Hagan, "Alfred Thayer Mahan: Turning America Back to the Sea," in F. J. Merli and T. A. Wilson, eds., *Makers of American Diplomacy*. 2 vols. (New York: Charles Scribner's Sons, 1974), I, 279–304. Hagan develops with great skill the pre-Mahanian role of Shufeldt and other commercial-naval expansionists of the late 1870s and the 1880s. Robert Seager II, "Ten Years Before Mahan: The Unofficial Case For the New Navy, 1880–1890," *Mississippi Valley Historical Review* (December 1953), 491–512, discusses Mahanian ideas abroad in Congress and in the New Navy during the 1880s. *See also* Mahan, *From Sail to Steam*, 276–277.

14. William G. David, "Our Merchant Marine: The Causes of Its Decline and the Means to Be Taken for Its Revival," U.S. Naval Institute *Proceedings*, VIII, No. 1 (1882), 151–161. Other prize-essay entries in 1882, all carrying the same title as Ensign David's, were submitted by Lt. J. D. J. Kelley, Master C. G. Calkins, Lt. Cmdr. F. E. Chadwick, and Lt. R. Wainwright. All *ibid.*, 3–186. Kelley touched on some of the same historical elements of sea power as did David, but he did not develop them in the same detail or with the same imagination and breadth. *See ibid.*, 5–7, 9. Calkins interpreted the existence of a strong national shipping posture as evidence of the achievement of civilization (*ibid.*, 35). Chadwick argued that the stimulus for the revival of the U.S. merchant marine must come from the business and commercial community, not from federal subsidies (*ibid.*, 118). Calkins and Wainwright recommended the building of an isthmian canal as a key to the sustained growth of American overseas trade and the revival of the U.S. merchant marine (*ibid.*, 71–72, 147–148). They also called attention to a connection between the Navy and the merchant marine in terms of national defense and saw the latter as providing experienced seamen for the former in time of war (*ibid.*, 36, 67–68, 134, 145–147). Mahan later embraced all of these points and relationships in his description of the elements of sea power and in his application of these elements to his interpretations

of European and American maritime-naval history. *See also* Allin, *op. cit., passim.* The likelihood that Mahan read David's essay is a judgment based on his personal participation in the founding of the institute's annual prize-essay contest in 1878 and on the fact that he was a regular subscriber to *Proceedings*. He was not, however, an enthusiastic or particularly active member of the institute after 1885; nor, in general, did he like the emphasis on engineering and ordnance problems that he found in the columns of *Proceedings*. *See* Mahan to Ashe, May 9, 1879; Mahan to Miles, November 22, 1888; Mahan to Rhodes, October 5, 1908.

15. Washington C. Whitthorne, *Congressional Record*, 46 Cong., 2 Sess., Appendix, 142–143 (April 1880); John F. Miller, *ibid.*, 48 Cong., 1 Sess., 1454 (February 1884); William G. McAdoo, *ibid.*, 49 Cong., 2 Sess., 2341 (February 1887), all quoted in Seager, "Ten Years Before Mahan." Other legislators are quoted on similar points later treated in more detail by Mahan.

16. Mahan to Chester, October 8, 1889; Mahan to Luce, October 7, 1889; John R. Seeley, "War and the British Empire," *Journal of the Military Service Institution of the United States* (September 1889), 488–500. Seeley was also the author of *The Expansion of England: Two Courses of Lectures* (Boston: Roberts Brothers, 1883); and of *Ecce Homo: A Survey of the Life and Work of Jesus Christ* (Boston: Roberts Brothers, 1867). The latter volume, wrestling as it did with science versus religion, had impressed Mahan during his search for spiritual perfection while serving in the *Iroquois* in 1868. On Seeley as a historian, *see* Thomas P. Peardon, "Sir John Seeley, Pragmatic Historian in a Nationalistic Age," in Edward Mead Earle, ed., *Nationalism and Internationalism: Essays Inscribed to Carlton J. H. Hayes* (New York: Columbia University Press, 1950), 285–302. For Seeley's continued influence on Mahan, particularly on Mahan's fear of Russian imperialism in the Far East in the years 1899 to 1902, and on his concern that Russia menaced Britain's strategic position in the Persian Gulf and along her lifeline to India, *see* Mahan to Maxse, July 22, 1902, and Chapter XVII of this work. Mahan was fond of quoting Seeley's *Expansion of England* on these Anglo-Russian issues.

17. Mahan, *The Influence of Sea Power Upon History, 1660–1783* (New York: Sagamore Press Reprint, 1957), 1–9, 25, 71, and *passim.*

18. Mahan to Henderson, May 5, 1890; Mahan to Luce, May 7, 1890.

19. Mahan, *The Influence of Sea Power Upon History*, 25–77.

20. *Ibid.*, 23, 27–30, 34, 37, 42–43, 46, 50, 66, 72–73; Seager, "Ten Years Before Mahan," *passim.*

21. Mahan to Henderson, May 5, 1890; Mahan to Luce, May 7, 1890; Mahan to Tracy, May 10, 1890; Mahan to Lodge, May 19, 1890. Unbound sheets of the book were sent by Little, Brown & Co. to Sampson, Low, Marston and Company in London, the house that brought out a limited English edition—one speedily sold out —in August 1890. Roy B. Marston, manager of the firm, was so impressed with the book when he first read it that he wrote Mahan that the British nation and navy would always owe him a deep debt of gratitude. And as he happily confessed to Mahan several profitable printings later, "Really, the title of the book was enough!" *The Fishing Gazette*, May 26, 1894; Westminster *Budget*, reprinted in *New York Herald*, June 8, 1894; Your Correspondent, "The Naval Manoeuvres," Letter to the

Editor of *The Times* (London), August 25, 1890. *See also* Taylor, *Life of Admiral Mahan*, 45–47.

22. *Ibid.*, 45–46, 161–162. Copies of the reviews cited in the following notes, unless otherwise identified, are in the Mahan Family Papers at the Naval War College. Mahan subscribed to clipping services in Boston, New York, and London during his career as a historian. The American clippings cost five cents each. He collected hundreds of these reviews over the years and saved many of them among his personal papers. Theodore Roosevelt, "The Influence of Sea Power Upon History," *Atlantic Monthly* (October 1890), 563–567; S. B. Luce, "The Influence of Sea Power Upon History," *The Critic* (New York), July 26, 1890; *New York Tribune*, May 18, 1890; *Chicago Interocean*, June 7, 1890; *Chicago Tribune*, May 31, 1890; *Cincinnati Gazette*, October 18, 1890. *See also The Critic* (New York), May 31, 1890; *Literary Digest* (New York), July 12, 1890; *The Christian Union*, May 29, 1890; *San Francisco Sunday Chronicle*, June 1, 1890; *Boston Courier*, October 12, 1890; *Philadelphia North American*, September 18, 1890; *St. Louis Post*, October 18, 1890; *Journal of the Military Service Institution of the United States*, November 1890; *Pittsburgh Bulletin*, July 5, 1890; *New Orleans Sunday States*, May 25, 1890; *Philadelphia Inquirer*, June 9, 1890; *New York Sun*, June 8, 1890.

23. *Chicago Herald*, May 31, 1890; *The Independent* (New York), July 31, 1890; *San Francisco Argonaut*, June 9, 1890; *New York Sun*, June 8, 1890; *Philadelphia Times*, May 10, 1890.

24. *Journal of the Military Service Institution of the United States*, November 1890; *St. Louis Post*, October 18, 1890; *Boston Courier*, October 12, 1890; *Saturday Review* (London), June 21, 1890; *Army and Navy Gazette* (London), August 23, 1890; *New York Tribune*, May 18, 1890.

25. The *Boston Herald*, June 19, 1890, thought Daniel Ammen's autobiography, *The Old Navy and the New* (Philadelphia: Lippincott, 1891) a better book. On the other hand, the *Illustrated Naval and Military Magazine Monthly* (London), September 1890, compared W. Clarke Russell and William H. Jaques, *Horatio Nelson and the Naval Supremacy of England* (New York and London: G. P. Putnam's Sons, 1890) unfavorably with Mahan's work, as did the *Philadelphia Inquirer*, June 9, 1890. S. B. Luce mentioned the Russell and Jaques book in his review of Mahan in *The Critic* (New York), July 26, 1890, taking the authors to task for suggesting that Nelson's tactical genius might no longer "be serviceable . . . to a posterity whose hopes are lodged in steel plates." Noting Mahan's contrary view on this point, Luce wholeheartedly agreed with him. "The principles so ably illustrated by Nelson are just as applicable in this day of steam, steel plates, and heavy guns as they were in the days of 'tacks and sheets,' " he said.

26. *Boston Herald*, June 19, 1891; *Chicago Tribune*, June 6, 1891; *New York Sun*, June 8, 1890.

27. *Pittsburgh Bulletin*, July 5, 1890; *Boston Advertiser*, July 30, 1890; *Boston Transcript*, May 14, 1890.

28. *Boston Literary World*, July 5, 1890.

29. *Charleston* (S.C.) *News*, June 15, 1890; *Chicago Tribune*, July 20, 1890; *New England Historical Register*, October 1890; *Boston Courier*, October 12, 1890; *Phila-

delphia North American, September 18, 1890; *United Service Gazette* (London), August 9, 1890; *Admiralty and Horse Guards Gazette* (London), June 1890; *Le Yacht* (Paris), June 28, 1890; *Journal de la Marine* (Paris), June 28, 1890; *Washington* (D.C.) *Public Opinion*, July 10, 1890; *Literary Digest* (New York), July 12, 1890; *Louisville Courier Journal*, May 24, 1890.

30. *Charleston* (S.C.) *News*, June 15, 1890; *Boston Literary World*, July 5, 1890; *Alta California* (San Francisco), June 8, 1890.

31. *Chicago Herald*, May 31, 1890; *New York Times*, April 19, 1891; *The Spectator* (London), September 27, 1890; *San Francisco Sunday Chronicle*, June 1, 1890.

32. The *Charleston* (S.C.) *News* review of June 15, 1890, was based substantially on the *New York Sun* review of June 8, 1890; the *Journal of the Military Service Institution of the United States* review of November 1890 was heavily indebted to the *Illustrated Naval and Military Magazine Monthly* (London) review of September 1890; the reviews in the *Minneapolis Tribune* of July 20, 1890, and the *Milwaukee Sentinel* of the same date were virtually identical; so too were the reviews in the *Boston Transcript*, May 14, 1890, and the *Boston Advertiser*, June 30, 1890.

33. *Chicago Tribune*, June 6, 1891; *Pittsburgh Chron-Telegraph*, June 20, 1890; *Duluth Tribune*, June 15, 1890; *New York Mail and Express*, August 15, 1890; *Rochester Democrat Chronicle*, August 11, 1890; *Buffalo Courier*, May 18, 1890; *Detroit Tribune*, June 1, 1890; *Brooklyn Eagle*, June 1, 1890; *Boston Times*, June 1, 1890; *Washington Post*, May 18, 1890; *Baltimore American*, May 30, 1890; *Book Buyer* (New York), June 1890; *Buffalo Commercial*, May 2, 1890; *Cleveland Leader*, June 1, 1890; *Boston Pilot*, September 6, 1890; *Denver Republican*, October 26, 1890; *Chicago Tribune*, June 6, 1891.

34. *The Independent* (New York), July 31, 1890; *Religio-Philosophical Journal* (Chicago), July 5, 1890; *Christian Register* (Boston), August 21, 1890.

35. *Saturday Review* (London), June 21, 1890; *The Spectator* (London), September 27, 1890; *Illustrated Naval and Military Magazine Monthly* (London), September 1890; *Army and Navy Gazette* (London), quoted in the [U.S.] *Army and Navy Journal*, September 1892; *The Times* (London), October 21, 1890; *The Broad Arrow Naval and Military Gazette*, July 12, 1890; *Blackwood's Magazine* (October 1890), 576.

36. J. K. Laughton, "Captain Mahan on Maritime Power," *Edinburgh Review* (October 1890), 420–453; Mahan to Luce, December 20, 1890; Mahan to Ellen Kuhn Mahan, October 2, 1894. Another particularly able British review was by William O'Connor Morris in *The Academy*, July 26, 1890. Morris, who later became a professional friend of Mahan, stated flatly that "power at sea largely depends on commerce; but its principal element is naval force." He felt, however, that Mahan had neglected race as an element of maritime greatness; this, he argued, was more important than territory, population, government, or geographical features. It should be noted that none of the British or American reviewers, save Laughton specifically, and one or two others in passing, saw fit to comment either positively or negatively on Mahan's historical methodology. *The Broad Arrow* reviewer was virtually alone in his complaint that "Captain Mahan often quotes largely without references, and, when he gives them, they are often only general." *The Broad Arrow*, July 12, 1890.

37. *Illustrated Naval and Military Magazine Monthly*, September 1890; *The Broad Arrow*, July 12, 1890; *United Service Gazette* (London), August 9, 1890; *The Times* (London), October 21, 1890, April 6, 1891; Rear Admiral Cyprian A. G. Bridge, RN, Letter to the Editor of *The Times* (London), October 27, 1890; *Morning Post* (London), June 21, 1890; Your Correspondent, Letter to the Editor of *The Times* (London), August 25, 1890; *Admiralty and Horse Guards Gazette*, November 1, 1890; *Army and Navy Gazette* (London), August 23, 1890; *Saturday Review* (London), June 21, 1890; *The Spectator* (London), September 27, 1890; *The Academy* (London), July 26, 1890; *Admiralty and Horse Guards Gazette*, October 25, 1890; "The Influence of Sea Power Upon History," *Blackwood's Magazine* (October 1890), 576–584. For additional information on the reception of Mahan's book abroad *see* Puleston, *Mahan*, 106–110; and Taylor, *Life of Admiral Mahan*, 45–47, 134–135.

38. *New York Herald*, May 28, 1894; *The Court Journal* (London), June 2, 1894; *New York Tribune*, August 29, 1893; *New York Evening Post*, January 7, 1898; *Army and Navy Gazette* (London), quoted in [U.S.] *Army and Navy Journal*, September 1892; Editorial, *The Times* (London), April 6, 1891; Mahan to Ellen Evans Mahan, August 8, 1894; Julian S. Corbett, "The Revival of Naval History," *Contemporary Review* (November 1917), quoted in Allan Westcott, ed., *Mahan on Naval Warfare* (Boston: Little, Brown and Co., 1919), xv. *See also* Taylor, *Life of Admiral Mahan*, 114–115, 131–133.

39. Mahan to Chester, October 8, 1889; Mahan to Colonna, August 14, 1889; Mahan to Walker, August 29, 1889, September 30, 1889 (two letters to Walker of this date), October 25, 1889; Mahan to Luce, November 15, 1889, December 3, 1889, April 9, 1890; Mahan to Henderson, May 5, 1890; Knight and Puleston, *Naval War College*, Chapter VI (1889), 1–4.

40. Mahan to Luce, April 9, 1890; Mahan to Ramsay, April 15, 1890, April 28, 1890.

AUTHOR AS IMPERIALIST, 1890–1893

1. Mahan to Ramsay, July 3, 1890, June 3, 1890, June 22, 1890, September 17, 1890; Mahan to Chief Intelligence Officer, August 23, 1890; Meigs to Luce, June 1890, citing Mahan to Meigs, June 11, 1890 (in the possession of Rear Admiral John D. Hayes); Mahan to Tracy, September 6, 1890.

2. Mahan to Helen Evans Mahan, July 9, 1890, July 20, 1890.

3. Mahan to Luce, September 16, 1890, September 21, 1890, September 25, 1890, October 27, 1890, November 15, 1890, December 20, 1890, January 16, 1891, April 20, 1891; Mahan to Ramsay, September 24, 1890 (two letters of this date), October 8, 1890, November 5, 1890, May 11, 1891, May 12, 1891, May 16, 1891, June 10, 1891, June 12, 1891, June 13, 1891; Mahan to Tracy, March 14, 1891. It should be pointed out that the recommendation to reduce the number of living units from six to four was made by civil engineer George Mackay, the contractor, and concurred in by George C. Mason, Jr., of Philadelphia, the architect, in order to keep the price of the structure and its furnishings under $100,000. The cutback was not ordered by Ramsay. The building cost $82,875, the remainder of the appropriation being

expended for furnishings and equipment. Knight and Puleston, *Naval War College*, Chapter VIII (1892), 1, Chapter VII (1890–1891), 2.

4. Mahan to Tracy, March 14, 1891; Mahan to Luce, December 17, 1891, December 26, 1891; Mahan to Chambers, July 27, 1892; S. B. Luce, "The Influence of Sea Power Upon History," *The Critic* (New York), July 26, 1890. For other reviews linking Mahan, the book, and the college *see New York Herald*, October 19, 1890; Editorial, "The Naval War College," *New York Sun*, July 8, 1893 (Mahan Family Papers at the Naval War College).

5. Mahan to Luce, September 16, 1890, December 20, 1890, November 24, 1891, December 14, 1891; Mahan to Ramsay, October 8, 1890, November 7, 1890; Mahan to Clover, March 28, 1891, May 8, 1891, May 27, 1891, June 9, 1891.

6. Mahan to Luce, December 20, 1890, December 31, 1890, January 14, 1891; Mahan to Tracy, January 2, 1891.

7. Mahan to Tracy, January 2, 1891; Mahan to Luce, January 16, 1891.

8. Scudder to Mahan, August 27, 1890, in Taylor, *Life of Admiral Mahan*, 113; Mahan to Scudder, October 11, 1890. Mahan thought Commander Albert S. Barker might help in the capacity of Assistant Prophet. Barker, who had had much service experience in the Netherlands East Indies, asked Mahan (who knew him only slightly) to help him place an article speculating on the American reaction to possible German annexation of Holland and with it the vast Dutch colonial empire, including Curaçao. Would the United States accept the transfer of Curaçao to Germany under the Monroe Doctrine? Mahan passed Barker's idea along to Scudder with the observation that he did not know whether Barker could write and the suggestion that he should be given an opportunity to prove himself. Scudder, however, did not buy. Mahan to Scudder, October 8, 1890, October 11, 1890.

9. Robert Seager II, "The Progressives and American Foreign Policy, 1898–1917." Unpublished Ph.D. dissertation (Ohio State University, 1956), *passim*; Mahan to Luce, September 17, 1890, September 25, 1890; Mahan to Scudder, September 23, 1890; Mahan to Clarke, November 5, 1892. For details of the editing and the title selection of "The United States Looking Outward," *see* Mahan to Scudder, October 11, 1890, October 13, 1890. Major Clarke, later Lord Sydenham, had heard Mahan lecture at the War College in 1888. Later a colonel in the British Army, Clarke was an able military historian and analyst.

10. Mahan to Tracy, September 6, 1890, January 2, 1891; Mahan to Davis, December 23, 1890; Mahan to Luce, September 3, 1901; Mahan, "Contingency Plan of Operations in Case of War With Great Britain," in *Letters and Papers*, III, 559–576; C. H. Davis, "Critique of [Mahan] Contingency Plan of Operations in Case of War With Great Britain" (Washington, D.C.: Office of Naval Intelligence, December 13, 1890), *passim* (in Naval War College library). Mahan returned to many of these strategical ideas again in July 1895 in a comment on the War College's study problem of that year. In this account, he had the U.S. Fleet concentrated safely in Nantucket Sound, thus pinning down or "fixing" there a hostile British naval force over twice its size—while the U.S. Army invaded Canada. American naval sorties from the sound would find everything British, "from the coal mines of Nova Scotia to the West Indies," open to attack. Again he employed his-

torical analogy—Lord Nelson at Corfu in 1794—to make his point. *See* Mahan to Taylor, July 19, 1895.

11. For his negotiations and problems with the *Atlantic Monthly* on his so-called "Four Admirals" articles, *see* Mahan to Scudder, September 26, 1890, October 8, 1890, March 25, 1891, April 21, 1891, November 18, 1892, November 22, 1892, January 25, 1893, February 3, 1893, March 15, 1893, March 24, 1893, March 27, 1893. When the *Atlantic Monthly* balked at some of his conditions and rejected a proffered essay on William Pitt's war policy, Mahan calmly sold the Pitt article to the British *Quarterly Review* (July 1892), broke off negotiations with the *Atlantic*, and returned to his primary concern, which was (in 1891–1892) the completion of his second *Influence* manuscript. The negotiations with Scudder, however, were resumed in November 1892, after Mahan had finished *Influence #2*. The "Four Admirals" articles were published in the *Atlantic Monthly* in 1893 and 1894, viz.: "Admiral the Earl of St. Vincent (Jervis)" in March 1893; "Admiral Saumarez" in May 1893; "Admiral Lord Exmouth (Pellew)" in July 1893; and "Admiral Earl Howe" in January 1894.

12. Mahan to Scudder, September 26, 1890, March 25, 1891; Mahan to Luce, October 27, 1890, December 20, 1890, December 31, 1890, January 6, 1891; Mahan to Clark, May 22, 1891; Mahan to Ramsay, September 4, 1891; Mahan to Clover, March 15, 1892, March 21, 1892; Mahan to Clarke, November 5, 1892. Henry Adams' nine-volume work, published between 1889 and 1891, much impressed Mahan who came away from it with one burning observation: "Especially note," he told Admiral C. H. Davis, in recommending the book, "how a state of unpreparedness, no greater than the present caused us to fill our belly with dirt. Recommend it to every purblind Congressman you meet, and to every naval officer." Mahan to Davis, December 23, 1890.

13. Taylor, *Life of Admiral Mahan*, 50–51, 194; *New York Herald* (Paris Edition), October 20, 1893; Mahan to Helen Evans Mahan, October 28, 1893. Mahan considered Admiral Tryon's remark "a very satisfactory compliment." For a sampling of British reviews of the second sea-power book, *see Army and Navy Gazette* (London), January 28, 1893; *The Empire* (Toronto), May 26, 1894; *The National Observer* (Edinburgh), March 18, 1893; *United Service Gazette*, February 11, 1893; William O'Connor Morris, "The Influence of Sea Power Upon the French Revolution and Empire," *The Academy*, April 8, 1893, and other Morris comments printed in Taylor, *Life of Admiral Mahan*, 248–249; *The Athenaeum*, February 11, 1893; *The Saturday Review* (London), January 21, 1893; *The Daily Graphic* (London), December 27, 1892; *The Times* (London), January 5, 1893 ("This may be called the primary purpose of Captain Mahan's studies and teachings—to incite his countrymen to develop and cherish their latent sea power."); *The Daily Telegraph* (London), January 5, 1893; *The Times* (London), April 1, 1893 (a long and eulogistic review comparing Mahan with Adam Smith). American reviews, equally enthusiastic, were generally less detailed; but *see, New York Sun*, January 15, 1893; *New York Tribune*, January 22, 1893; Fletcher S. Bassett, "The Influence of Sea Power," *The Dial*, February 16, 1893; *Philadelphia Evening Telegraph*, December 31, 1892; *New York Herald* (Paris Edition), January 8, 1893, October 15, 1893; *New York Herald*, October 16, 1893. Mahan was pleased to learn that Theodore

Roosevelt liked the second sea-power book as well as he did the first. Mahan to Scudder, February 3, 1893. Copies of all the reviews cited above are in the Mahan Family Papers at the Naval War College.

14. Mahan to Tracy, May 12, 1891, October 10, 1892; Mahan to Wilson, November 17, 1891, January 26, 1892; Mahan to Luce, November 24, 1891; Mahan to D. Appleton and Co., June 8, 1892; Mahan to Bridge, September 18, 1894; Mahan to Brown, March 8, 1897, July 2, 1897, February 26, 1906. *See* also Loyall Farragut, *The Life of David Glasgow Farragut, First Admiral of the United States Navy, Embodying His Journals and Letters* (New York: D. Appleton and Company, 1879). In his own study of Farragut, Mahan acknowledged his debt to Loyall Farragut's book and to "many additional details of interest from the Admiral's journals and correspondence, and for other memoranda." He apparently corresponded with Farragut's Civil War associates, Thornton A. Jenkins, John Crittenden Watson, and James Grant Wilson (the Jenkins and Watson correspondence has not been found) "for interesting anecdotes and reminiscences." General James Grant Wilson was the editor of Appleton's Great Commander Series in which Mahan's book appeared as the first offering. The series died shortly after. On the continuing Art of War vs. Materials of War argument, *see* Mahan to Luce, September 16, 1890, November 24, 1891; Mahan to Chambers, July 27, 1892.

15. Taylor, *Life of Admiral Mahan*, 54–56; the *New York Tribune* and London *Academy* quotations are found in an otherwise unidentified *New York Evening Post* clipping in the Mahan Family Papers at the Naval War College; *Philadelphia Times*, October 30, 1892; *London News*, May 22, 1894. *See* also the favorable reviews in the *Providence* (R.I.) *Journal*, November 6, 1892; *New York Advertiser*, October 30, 1892; *New York Sun*, October 23, 1892; *Philadelphia Telegraph*, October 26, 1892; Tristram P. Coffin, "The Genius of Farragut," *Edgewood News* Wakefield, R.I.), December 7, 1892; *Chicago Tribune*, November 19, 1892; *Boston Herald*, March 10, 1893; *New York Times*, November 18, 1892; *Chicago Herald*, November 19, 1892. Copies of all of the above are in the Mahan Family Papers (NWC). The author of the *London Guardian* review of September 30, 1893, was surprised that Mahan saw fit to compare Farragut with Lord Nelson, but bravely noted that the book was "extremely instructive" once the British reader "has got over the slight shock of the juxtaposition of names." Clipping enclosed in Mahan to Helen Evans Mahan, October 28, 1893.

16. The most detailed study of the Chilean affair, particularly of the *Baltimore* dimension of it, is F. B. Pike, *Chile and the United States, 1880–1962* (Notre Dame, Indiana: Notre Dame University Press, 1963). *See also* West, *Admirals of American Empire*, 166–171, for a discussion sympathetic to Schley; and Mahan to Luce, September 3, 1901.

17. Mahan to Clark, May 22, 1891; Evans, *A Sailor's Log*, 259–260; James D. Richardson, ed., *A Compilation of the Messages and Papers of the Presidents, 1789–1902* (Washington, D.C.: Bureau of National Literature and Art, 1904), IX, 183–186, 215–226.

18. Mahan to Luce, December 17, 1891, December 19, 1891, December 26, 1891, January 5, 1892; Mahan to Tracy, telegram, December 17, 1891.

19. Mahan to Luce, January 10, 1892, January 28, 1892; Mahan to Wilson, January 26, 1892.

20. Mahan to Tracy, September 9, 1891; Mahan to Ramsay, September 4, 1891; Mahan to Luce, November 24, 1891, December 11, 1891, December 14, 1891, December 19, 1891, December 26, 1891, January 5, 1892.

21. Mahan to Luce, December 17, 1891, December 26, 1891, January 28, 1892.

22. Mahan to Luce, December 26, 1891, January 5, 1892; Mahan to Ramsay, February 24, 1892; Puleston, *Mahan*, 114–115; Taylor, *Life of Admiral Mahan*, 57. The exact date of Ramsay's often-quoted remark is difficult if not impossible to establish, but it is probably April 1893, on the eve of Mahan's assignment to the *Chicago*. Puleston implies that it was made during or shortly after the Chilean crisis. Taylor suggests that it was uttered in the early spring of 1893 when Mahan was fighting his assignment to the *Chicago*. Robert D. Heinl, Jr., ed., *Dictionary of Military and Naval Quotations* (Annapolis, Md.: Naval Institute Press, 1966), 178, quotes it as Ramsay's "endorsement of an unfavorable fitness report rendered on Mahan, 1893." Erben's first unfavorable fitness report on Mahan, however, was dated December 31, 1893, the second June 30, 1894.

23. Mahan to Ramsay, January 9, 1892, February 26, 1892, June 7, 1892, June 11, 1892, September 5, 1892, December 1, 1892, March 25, 1892; F. E. Chadwick, O.N.I. Requisition Endorsement, November 29, 1892 (NA); Mahan to Tracy, March 1, 1892; Mahan to Soley, August 4, 1892.

24. Mahan to Ramsay, March 12, 1892, June 13, 1892 (two letters of this date), June 17, 1892, June 20, 1892, July 4, 1892, August 21, 1892, August 31, 1892, December 5, 1892; Ramsay to Mahan, August 19, 1892 (NA); Mahan to Soley, August 20, 1892, October 30, 1892.

25. Mahan to Ramsay, March 23, 1892 (two letters to Ramsay of this date).

26. Mahan to Ramsay, February 26, 1892, June 24, 1892, July 18, 1892, July 21, 1892; Mahan to Tracy, July 8, 1892.

27. Mahan to Chambers, July 27, 1892; Mahan to Soley, August 19, 1892, October 29, 1892; Mahan to Ramsay, July 4, 1892; Knight and Puleston, *Naval War College*, Chapter VIII (1892), 1–3. Although invited to the opening ceremonies of the 1892 session, Secretary Tracy was unable to attend. Mahan to Soley, telegram, September 2, 1892. Mahan's opening address to the college, emphasizing the practical side of the 1892 curriculum, was published as "The Practical Character of a Naval War College," U.S. Naval Institute *Proceedings*, No. 66 (June 1893). The seven-week-long 1892 session featured lectures by Mahan on naval strategy, naval history, the naval dimensions of the War of the Pacific, and the Nicaraguan canal question.

28. Mahan to Luce, November 15, 1890; Mahan to Scudder, November 22, 1892. Mahan almost certainly voted for the Benjamin Harrison-Whitelaw Reid ticket although he never said directly that he did. He expressed no interest in the new, mildly radical People's (Populist) Party which ran James B. Weaver for president and polled over a million votes. Mahan's political and socio-economic principles were scarcely Populist. The fact that the War College was in session during September and October, together with the fact that his *Admiral Farragut* and his *The*

Influence of Sea Power Upon the French Revolution and Empire were in press during the presidential campaign likely caused Mahan to take less interest in national political events in 1892 than he might ordinarily have. In any event, he seems to have paid little attention to the campaign until after it was over and decided.

29. Mahan to Clark, May 22, 1891; Mahan to Ramsay, September 4, 1891, December 7, 1892, December 14, 1892; Mahan to Tracy, September 9, 1891, December 7, 1892, December 27, 1892, January 23, 1893; Mahan to Luce, November 24, 1891.

30. Mahan to Roosevelt, March 1, 1893; Mahan to Ramsay, March 17, 1893; Puleston, *Mahan*, 134; Mahan to Brown, May 31, 1893.

31. Mahan to Roosevelt, March 18, 1893, March 26, 1893; Mahan to Scudder, April 18, 1893; Mahan to Ramsay, April 18, 1893; West, *Admirals of American Empire*, 150–151.

32. Mahan to Editor, *New York Times*, January 30, 1893 (published February 1, 1893).

33. *Ibid.*; Mahan to Scudder, February 3, 1893; Mahan, "Hawaii and Our Future Sea Power," *The Forum* (March 1893), 1–11. For negative reactions to Mahan's article, *see* various clippings in the Mahan Family Papers at the Naval War College, especially a letter to the Editor of the *New York Herald*, dated March 3, 1893, headed "Do We Need Colonies?" and signed "X.Y.Z." XYZ decided that we did not.

34. Mahan to Sampson, February 13, 1893; Mahan to Chief Intelligence Officer, March 24, 1893; Mahan to Scudder, March 27, 1893, March 15, 1893; Mahan to Peabody, May 31, 1891, April 14, 1893.

35. Puleston, *Mahan*, 132; Mahan to Scudder, March 15, 1893; Mahan to Peabody, April 14, 1893; Mahan to Ellen Evans Mahan, April 29, 1894.

36. Mahan to Bureau of Navigation, April 18, 1893; Lodge to Herbert, April 29, 1893 (LC); Mahan to Scudder, April 8, 1893; Roosevelt to Mahan, May 1, 1893; W. M. Little statement, circa late April 1893, and F. A. Mahan to Mahan, May 3, 1893, are in Taylor, *Life of Admiral Mahan*, 57–60; Mahan to Brown, May 31, 1893, June 9, 1893; Mahan to Herbert, May 11, 1893; Puleston, *Mahan*, 134–135; Mahan to Peabody, April 14, 1893, April 20, 1893.

37. Mahan to Ellen Evans Mahan, August 17, 1893, July 22, 1894, July 29, 1894, December 2, 1894; Mahan to Clarke, July 29, 1894; Mahan to Luce, May 6, 1909.

38. Mahan to Brown, June 1, 1893.

39. Mahan to Luce, May 6, 1909.

AUTHOR AS SHIP'S CAPTAIN, 1893–1894

1. Herbert to Charles S. Fairchild, May 8, 1893 (LC). Fairchild, president of New York Security and Trust Company, had received a copy of Mahan's second *Influence* book from John M. Brown, was much impressed with it, and told Brown he had written Herbert asking that Mahan be kept ashore. Fairchild to Brown, May 6, 1893 (LC).

2. Mahan to Ellen Evans Mahan, March 23, 1894, October 22, 1893; L. R. Hamersly, *The Records of Living Officers of the United States Navy and Marine Corps*, 6th ed., 52–53; Mahan to Thursfield, May 19, 1894; Erben to Ramsay, September 17, 1894 (NA); Mahan to Herbert, January 25, 1894; Mahan to Ellen Evans Mahan, March 23, 1894. On Ramsay's failure to read his books, Mahan wrote: "Do you know that I have on the best authority [Chadwick] that the naval officer who keeps me here [Ramsay], and has most influence with the Secretary, had never (at least up to three months ago) read my works which have set all the professional men in Europe thinking and talking." Mahan to Scudder, August 12, 1894; Mahan to Ellen Evans Mahan, December 9, 1894.

3. K. Jack Bauer, *Ships of the Navy, 1775–1969*. 2 vols. (Troy, New York: Rensselaer Polytechnic Institute, 1969), I, 131–132; Mahan to Herbert, September 30, 1894, January 19, 1895; Mahan to Luce, September 1, 1893; Record (Health), Michael McLaughlin, USS *Chicago*, Gibraltar, April 19, 1894 (NA); Bureau of Navigation, # 30001, May 7, 1894 (NA); Walker to Bancroft Gherardi, March 22, 1893 (NA); Mahan to Helen Evans Mahan, July 3, 1894. Boiler repairs in Antwerp in July 1894 cost $15,000. *See* Mahan to Helen Evans Mahan, July 3, 1894.

4. Log of the USS *Chicago*, May 27, 1893 (NA); J. M. Ellicott, "With Erben and Mahan on the *Chicago*," U.S. Naval Institute *Proceedings*, (September 1941), 1236.

5. Mahan to Scudder, May 13, 1893, June 9, 1893; Mahan to Brown, May 31, 1893, June 1, 1893, June 9, 1893.

6. Mahan to Luce, May 22, 1893; Mahan to Brown, June 1, 1893.

7. Ellen Kuhn Mahan, "Recollections," in *Letters and Papers*, III, 719, 726; Log of the USS *Chicago*, June 18, 1893 (NA); Puleston, *Mahan*, 164; Mahan to Gillender, June 13, 1893, June 14, 1893; Mahan to Herbert, June 9, 1893; Mahan to Ellen Evans Mahan, October 11, 1893, October 22, 1893, October 23, 1893, October 28, 1893, November 1, 1893, November 18, 1893, November 23, 1893, November 30, 1893, March 10, 1894, August 8, 1894, October 12, 1894; Mahan to Helen Evans Mahan, October 28, 1893, November 26, 1893, April 19, 1894; Mahan to Ellen Kuhn Mahan, December 7, 1893, August 3, 1894, October 18, 1894; Mahan to Clark, June 14, 1895.

8. Mahan to Ellen Evans Mahan, June 28, 1893, July 7, 1893, July 13, 1893, July 15, 1893, July 28, 1893, August 4, 1893; Mahan to Helen Evans Mahan, July 3, 1893, July 25, 1893; Mahan to Ellen Kuhn Mahan, July 9, 1893.

9. Mahan to Ashe, November 24, 1893, November 7, 1896; Mahan to Clarke, January 29, 1895; Mahan to Ellen Evans Mahan, June 28, 1893, October 1, 1893, October 23, 1893, March 4, 1894, March 31, 1894, September 13, 1894, October 27, 1894, November 21, 1894. For further evidence of Mahan's fear of the sea, his tension in stormy weather, and the constant pressure and fatigue he felt while performing his duties as a commanding officer, *see* Mahan to Ellen Kuhn Mahan, February 26, 1894, February 8, 1895; Mahan to Helen Evans Mahan, March 16, 1894, October 28, 1894, September 18, 1894, December 25, 1894; Mahan to Ellen Evans Mahan, September 6, 1893.

10. Mahan to Ellen Evans Mahan, August 4, 1893, August 24, 1893, October 1, 1893, October 11, 1893, February 9, 1894, February 14, 1894, February 22, 1894, March 18, 1894, June 27, 1894, July 6, 1894, July 29, 1894, December 9, 1894, December 19, 1894; Mahan to Scudder, September 12, 1893. The extensive quotation on Mahan's fear of a mental and physical breakdown is a composite of comments in Mahan to Ellen Evans Mahan, February 10, 1894, September 27, 1894, October 27, 1894, November 21, 1894, December 2, 1894, December 9, 1894, March 4, 1895; Mahan to Ellen Kuhn Mahan, December 15, 1894. For other evidence of Mahan's frustration with petty shipboard administrative detail, his desire to be rid of his command, and his fear of a breakdown, *see* Mahan to Ellen Kuhn Mahan, August 21, 1893, March 29, 1894, August 3, 1894, October 18, 1894, December 15, 1894; Mahan to Helen Evans Mahan, April 19, 1894, January 29, 1895.

11. Mahan to Ellen Evans Mahan, October 22, 1893, November 18, 1893, April 14, 1894, September 6, 1894, October 19, 1894, December 2, 1894, December 9, 1894, January 13, 1895, March 4, 1895.

12. Mahan to Scudder, September 12, 1893; Mahan to Ellen Evans Mahan, September 6, 1893, October 1, 1893; Mahan to Helen Evans Mahan, September 3, 1893, November 26, 1893, December 25, 1893, February 18, 1894, August 5, 1894.

13. Mahan to Ellen Evans Mahan, August 17, 1893, December 18, 1893, January [8], 1894 (enclosure in Mahan to Ellen Kuhn Mahan, January 6, 1894), January 11, 1894, April 14, 1894; Mahan to Ashe, November 24, 1893.

14. Mahan to Helen Evans Mahan, November 26, 1893; Mahan to Ellen Evans Mahan, November 1, 1893, November 18, 1893; Mahan to Little, Brown and Co., July 24, 1894. For Mahan's complaints that the *Chicago* duty interfered with the Nelson biography and that evening work was not his cup of tea, *see* Mahan to Ellen Evans Mahan, September 1, 1893, September 15, 1893, September 22, 1893, October 1, 1893.

15. Mahan to Helen Evans Mahan, September 3, 1893, February 18, 1894; Mahan to Ellen Evans Mahan, September 22, 1893, January 11, 1894, February 19, 1894, March 10, 1894, April 4, 1894; Mahan to Ellen Kuhn Mahan, December 7, 1893; Mahan to Little, Brown and Co., July 24, 1894, January 31, 1895. It should be noted that Mahan continued occasional research into primary sources, mainly unpublished Nelson and Nelson-related letters, after he had sent the manuscript home. He also interviewed several of Nelson's descendants. Lord Radstock was particularly helpful in this regard, as was Admiral Maurice Horatio Nelson, Lord Nelson's great-nephew. So too were Lord Nelson, Sir William Parker, whose father of the same name had served with Nelson, Mr. Edgar Goble, whose father had been Captain Hardy's clerk in HMS *Victory*, and others. Mahan spent much time and energy tracking down these persons and materials when the *Chicago* returned to England in August 1894; but he lamented to his Aunt Jane Swift that it was "woeful to think how much of what I hear I lose, and that while in the midst of interest, much of which might repay research, I am so tied to the ship that I can do nothing." *See* Mahan to Ellen Evans Mahan, August 24, 1893, October 10, 1894; Mahan to Helen Evans Mahan, August 26, 1894, September 18, 1894; Mahan to Ellen Kuhn Mahan, October 18, 1894; Mahan to Jane Leigh Okill Swift, September 13, 1894; Mahan to Bridge, November 13, 1894.

16. For evidence of Elly's fiscal naiveté and Mahan's patient efforts to educate her in matters financial, *see* Mahan to Ellen Evans Mahan, August 5, 1893, August 17, 1893, August 18, 1893, November 30, 1893, December 11, 1893, July 22, 1894, October 19, 1894; Mahan to Helen Evans Mahan, October 28, 1894. For Mahan's attempts to stem Elly's spending and for his sense of fatalism in the matter, *see* Mahan to Ellen Evans Mahan, December 18, 1893, June 29, 1894; Mahan to Ellen Evans Mahan, October 19, 1894.

17. Mahan, "The Isthmus and Sea Power," *Atlantic Monthly* (October 1893), 459–472. For Mahan's correspondence and comments on this article, *see* Mahan to Helen Evans Mahan, July 25, 1893, September 3, 1893, October 28, 1893; Mahan to Scudder, July 25, 1893, September 12, 1893; Mahan to Ellen Evans Mahan, July 21, 1893, August 5, 1893, August 17, 1893, September 1, 1893; Mahan to Appleton, October 29, 1893. A year later Scudder agreed to buy proposed articles on the Clayton-Bulwer Treaty and on the strategic importance of the Caribbean and the Gulf; but by that time, August 1894, Mahan was too pressed to supply them. "I shall have to reply, as I did to Little & Brown about *Nelson*, that it is hopeless. My whole nervous system is in a state of exasperation hard to control at times." Mahan to Ellen Evans Mahan, August 8, 1894. Mahan sent his "Isthmus" and other articles written on board the *Chicago* to Elly for typing; she in turn sent the typed version to the publisher who mailed the galley proofs directly to her husband. Mahan then corrected the galleys and mailed them back to the publisher. Mahan was upset when Scudder mailed him galley with improper postage, causing him to pay the postage due. On one such occasion he made a major point over a matter of 40 cents. Mahan to Scudder, October 23, 1893. Elly, who played an important support role in her husband's literary life, also read and corrected galley from time to time. She typed almost everything he wrote, beginning with his lectures at Newport from 1886 to 1888.

18. Mahan, "Admiral Earl Howe," *Atlantic Monthly* (January 1894), 20–37. For Mahan's correspondence on the "Howe" article, *see* Mahan to Ellen Evans Mahan, June 28, 1893, July 13, 1893, July 21, 1893, July 28, 1893, August 5, 1893, August 17, 1893, September 22, 1893, January 11, 1894; Mahan to Helen Evans Mahan, July 25, 1893; Mahan to Scudder, July 25, 1893, October 23, 1893. Mahan, "Admiral Lord Exmouth (Pellew)," *Atlantic Monthly* (July 1893), 27–41. For Mahan's correspondence on the "Exmouth" article, *see* Mahan to Ellen Evans Mahan, July 21, 1893; Mahan to Helen Evans Mahan, October 28, 1893. Mahan, "Two Maritime Expeditions," *United Service Magazine* (October 1893), 1–13. For his amused comments on this little potboiler, *see* Mahan to Ellen Evans Mahan, August 17, 1893, August 24, 1893, September 1, 1893, November 21, 1893. For Mahan's refusal of various commissions to write for magazines while still on board the *Chicago*, *see* Mahan to Ellen Evans Mahan, November 18, 1893, May 22, 1894, June 1, 1894, June 29, 1894, October 5, 1894, November 1, 1894; Mahan to Sterling, July 18, 1894. He told J. B. Sterling, editor of the *Journal* of the Royal United Service Institution, that "All the best part of my days is taken up with the ship routine, which I find exhausts my brain force to a very crippling extent. I can only find opportunity to work at night—which I *never* do when ashore. This all means . . . work of inferior quality." Among the prominent magazines soliciting articles from him in 1894 were *Journal* of the Royal United Service Institution, *Fortnightly Review*, *Contemporary*,

North American Review, The Forum, Atlantic Monthly, Nineteenth Century, and *Century Magazine*.

19. Mahan, "Possibilities of an Anglo-American Reunion," *North American Review* (November 1894), 551–563. For Mahan's intellectual difficulties with and his correspondence on this article, *see* Mahan to Ellen Evans Mahan, July 6, 1894, July 12, 1894, August 8, 1894, September 20, 1894, October 5, 1894; Mahan to Sterling, July 18, 1894; Mahan to Ellen Kuhn Mahan, August 3, 1894; Mahan to Helen Evans Mahan, January 29, 1895; Mahan to Thursfield, June 7, 1894; Mahan to Little, Brown and Co., July 24, 1894; Mahan to Clarke, July 29, 1894, September 30, 1894; Mahan to Scudder, August 12, 1894, October 20, 1894.

20. Mahan, "Possibilities of an Anglo-American Reunion," *passim*. *See* also Andrew Carnegie, "A Look Ahead," *North American Review* (June 1893); George Sydenham Clarke, "A Naval Union with Great Britain: Reply to Mr. Andrew Carnegie," *ibid*. (March 1894); and Lloyd S. Bryce to George S. Clarke, New York, February 8, 1894 (LC); Andrew Carnegie to George S. Clarke, Sussex, England, April 27, 1894 (LC). Mahan was loath to enter into controversy with Clarke on these issues and fully expected that "you [Clarke] will go gunning for me when it appears, but by that time I shall be in Gibraltar and will take refuge under the guns of the fortress." He characterized his own article as "indifferent" though "suggestive," and complained to Clarke that "I am too horribly driven for any decent work." Mahan to Clarke, September 30, 1894.

21. Mahan to Ellen Evans Mahan, July 7, 1893, July 21, 1893, August 4, 1893, August 5, 1893, November 30, 1893, March 4, 1894, May 22, 1894, June 1, 1894, June 7, 1894, June 23, 1894, June 29, 1894, July 6, 1894, July 29, 1894, August 29, 1894, October 19, 1894, January 25, 1895; Mahan to Helen Evans Mahan, July 3, 1893, October 28, 1893; Mahan to Jane Leigh Mahan, July 8, 1894; Mahan to Clarke, July 29, 1894; Mahan to Little, Brown and Co., January 31, 1895, June 19, 1896.

22. Mahan to Ellen Evans Mahan, October 1, 1893, August 17, 1894, September 27, 1894, October 19, 1894, October 27, 1894, November 13, 1894, January 7, 1895; Mahan to Gillender, June 4, 1895, June 6, 1895, November 23, 1895, May 26, 1897; Mahan to Helen Evans Mahan, October 28, 1894; Mahan to Frederick A. Mahan, December 15, 1895; Ellen Kuhn Mahan, "Recollections," in *Letters and Papers*, III, 720, 728. Elly turned her mother's estate over to her husband "unconditionally," causing Mahan to note humorously: "I hope I may be trusted but greatly question if any one should be. However, I am not so young or attractive as to induce any woman to marry me for so little money as I can in any way control." Mahan to Ellen Evans Mahan, May 14, 1894.

23. Mahan to Herbert, May 30, 1893; Mahan to Chambers, June 1, 1893. For a pro-Mahan view and summary of the War College-Torpedo Station consolidation issue as seen from Newport, *see* the *Newport Daily News*, September 1, 1893.

24. Mahan to Ellen Evans Mahan, July 21, 1893, August 11, 1893, August 24, 1893, September 1, 1893, October 11, 1893; Knight and Puleston, *Naval War College*, Chapter IX (1893), 1–2; Mahan to Scudder, August 12, 1894; Mahan to Luce, August 24, 1893, September 1, 1893; Mahan to Gouverneur Morris Ogden, August 31, 1893; Mahan to Helen Evans Mahan, September 3, 1893, October 28, 1893; Herbert to Mahan, October 4, 1893, in Taylor, *Life of Admiral Mahan*, 34–35.

25. Knight and Puleston, *Naval War College*, Chapter X (1894), 1; Mahan to Luce, September 1, 1893; Mahan to Cleveland, January 13, 1894; Mahan to Ellen Evans Mahan, January 5, 1894, January 11, 1894, January 14, 1894; Mahan to Brown, January 13, 1894; Lodge to Luce, January 22, 1894 (LC); Taylor to Luce, April 27, 1894 (LC).

26. Mahan to Ellen Evans Mahan, March 4, 1894; Mahan to Helen Evans Mahan, February 18, 1894; Mahan to Brown, January 13, 1894. The extended quotation is a composite of remarks found in Mahan to Ellen Evans Mahan, April 5, 1894, and May 6, 1894.

27. Mahan to Ellen Evans Mahan, February 9, 1894, January 14, 1894, January 11, 1894.

28. Mahan to Ellen Evans Mahan, February 3, 1894.

WITH ERBEN IN THE *CHICAGO*, 1893–1895

1. Mahan to Ellen Evans Mahan, July 13, 1893, March 31, 1894.

2. *The Times*, July 10, 1893; *Pall Mall Budget*, August 17, 1893; Mahan to Ellen Kuhn Mahan, August 1, 1893, October 6, 1893; Mahan to Ellen Evans Mahan, August 4, 1893, August 11, 1893, August 12, 1893, August 24, 1893, September 1, 1893; Mahan to Luce, August 24, 1893; Mahan to Ashe, November 24, 1893. Mahan was so little known in the United States outside naval and congressional circles that the *New York Illustrated American* ran his portrait as a frontispiece to its issue of June 2, 1894, and accompanied it with a biographical article that identified him as "the greatest authority on naval tactics in the world."

3. Mahan to Ellen Evans Mahan, Febraury 3, 1894; J. M. Ellicott, "With Erben and Mahan on the *Chicago*," U.S. Naval Institute *Proceedings* (September 1941), 1235; J. M. Ellicott, "Three Navy Cranks and What They Turned," *ibid.* (October 1924), 1623. Nazro had served with Mahan at the Naval Academy in 1880 when attached to the Modern Languages Department there.

4. Mahan to Ellen Evans Mahan, August 11, 1893, September 6, 1893.

5. Ellicott, "With Erben and Mahan on the *Chicago*," 1235; [Henry Erben], Report on the Fitness of Officers, A. T. Mahan, Captain, U.S.N., Attached to U.S.S. *Chicago* . . . [December 31, 1893] (LC).

6. Mahan to Herbert, January 25, 1894; Mahan to Helen Evans Mahan, January 30, 1894; Ellicott, "With Erben and Mahan on the *Chicago*," 1235.

7. Mahan to Ellen Evans Mahan, January 22, 1894, January 23, 1894, January 25, 1894, January 26, 1894, January 28, 1894, February 9, 1894, February 10, 1894, February 14, 1894, Easter Day (March 25), 1894.

8. Mahan to Herbert, January 13, 1894, January 25, 1894 (enclosed in Mahan to Ellen Evans Mahan, January 22–25, 1894).

9. Mahan to Herbert, January 25, 1894; Mahan to Ellen Evans Mahan, January 11, 1894, January 26, 1894; Erben, Report on the Fitness of Officers, A. T. Mahan . . . (LC); Lodge to Mahan, February 10, 1894 (LC). *See also* Mahan to Scudder, September 12, 1893, in which Mahan noted that when on shore he wrote his articles

in the "forenoon, always my working period," because "in the afternoon my brain refuses to construct."

10. Mahan to Ellen Evans Mahan, January 22, 1894, January 23, 1894, January 25, 1894, January 26, 1894, January 28, 1894, February 14, 1894, February 19, 1894.

11. Roosevelt to Ellen Evans Mahan, February 10, 1894 (LC), February 12, 1894 (LC), February 14, 1894 (LC), February 22, 1894 (LC), March 4, 1894 (LC), March 10, 1894 (LC); Roosevelt to David B. Ogden, February 12, 1894 (LC); Ogden to Mahan, cablegram, February 12, 1894 (LC); Mahan to Ogden, cablegram, n.d. [February 12, 1894] (LC); Lodge to Mahan, February 10, 1894 (LC); Mahan to Lodge, February 25, 1894, June 6, 1894; Erben to Herbert, May 13, 1894 (NA), May 18, 1894 (NA); Mahan to Roosevelt, June 6, 1894; Mahan to Ellen Evans Mahan, February 9, 1894, February 14, 1894; Herbert to Erben, June 15, 1894 (LC); Herbert to Mahan, June 25, 1894 (LC); Erben to Herbert, September 1, 1894 (NA). David B. Ogden, whose office was at 111 Broadway, New York, was the son of Gouverneur ("Gouv") Morris Ogden and Harriet Verena Evans Ogden, sister to Elly's father. He was, therefore, Elly's first cousin.

12. Mahan to Ellen Evans Mahan, February 14, 1894, February 19, 1894; Mahan to Helen Evans Mahan, March 16, 1894; Mahan Memoranda, January 30, 1894, n.d. [February 15, 1894], February 25, 1894, n.d. [February 1894]; Mahan to Erben, February 17, 1894, March 8, 1894; Mahan to Department of the Navy, February 17, 1894; Mahan to Herbert, March 30, 1894, August 30, 1894; Erben to Herbert, July 20, 1894 (NA), September 1, 1894 (NA); Mahan to Lodge, June 6, 1894.

13. Mahan to Ellen Evans Mahan, February 9, 1894, February 19, 1894, March 4, 1894, March 10, 1894, March 31, 1894, April 4, 1894; Mahan to Jane Leigh Mahan, July 8, 1894.

14. Mahan to Ellen Evans Mahan, May 11, 1894, June 7, 1894, July 22, 1894, September 6, 1894; Mahan to Helen Evans Mahan, May 11, 1894; Mahan to Ellen Kuhn Mahan, August 3, 1894; *New York Times*, May 13, 1894.

15. Log of the *Chicago*, May 11, 1893, to March 29, 1895 (NA), *passim*, details the daily ceremonial functions of the vessel throughout the cruise as well as the internal life of the ship and her crew. Mahan's acerbic comments on the *Chicago*'s boilers are in Mahan to Erben, September 14, 1893; Mahan to Ellen Evans Mahan, July 6, 1894, July 29, 1894, October 12, 1894, March 17, 1895; Mahan to Herbert, August 15, 1894; Mahan to Clarke, January 29, 1895. Newspaper comment on the constant need for repair of the *Chicago*'s engines may be found among newspaper clippings in the Mahan Family Papers (NWC). Poor as Mahan generally thought the crew to be, he felt that "judging from the experience of this ship, the time is hardly yet ripe" for requiring from them an ability to read and write prior to promoting them to petty officer ratings. Mahan to Herbert, November 17, 1894. Desertion problems are treated in Mahan to Herbert, August 19, 1893 (NA). Mess Attendant Emmanuel Frendo's syphilis is the subject of Kirkland to Herbert, September 26, 1894 (NA).

16. *The Times* (London), May 11, 1894; *Hampshire*, May 19, 1894; *London Daily News*, May 22, 1894; *The Freeman's Journal* (Dublin), May 23, 1894; *New York Times*, May 13, 1894; *New York Herald*, May 27, 1894; *New York Sun*, May 26,

1894; Mahan to Ellen Evans Mahan, May 11, 1894, May 22, 1894; *Philadelphia Inquirer*, May 15, 1894. *See* Bigelow to Mahan, May 26, 1894, in Taylor, *Life of Admiral Mahan*, 131. Photocopies of all newspaper clippings cited above are in Mahan Family Papers (NWC).

17. "Our Naval Supremacy: Captain Mahan's Opinion," *Pall Mall Gazette*, May 10, 1894 (NWC). This interview, presented in somewhat different language and inflection, was also carried in the *St. James Gazette* for May 23, 1894, under the title, "A Morning on Board the *Chicago*: An Interview with Captain Mahan." (NWC).

18. Detailed accounts of the Sampson Low, Marston and Co. dinner, all flattering to Mahan, are found in (London) *Publisher's Observer*, May 26, 1894 (NWC); *London Daily News*, May 22, 1894 (NWC); and *Fishing Gazette*, May 26, 1894 (NWC). *See also* Mahan to Ellen Evans Mahan, May 22, 1894; and *New York Herald*, June 8, 1894 (NWC).

19. Mahan to Clark, January 15, 1907; detailed British accounts of the St. James's Hall affair and editorial comments on it, are in *London Standard*, May 25, 1894; *Pall Mall Gazette*, May 25, 1894; *London Morning Post*, May 25, 1894; *The Army and Navy Gazette*, May 26, 1894; *The Spectator*, May 26, 1894; *The Independent*, May 31, 1894; *The Times* (London), May 25, 1894; *United Service Gazette*, May 26, 1894; *London Globe*, May 25, 1894; *London Daily Graphic*, May 26, 1894 (a drawing of the men at the head table captioned "Hands Across The Sea"); *The Speaker* (London), May 26, 1894; Taylor, *Life of Admiral Mahan*, 63–64. Among American newspapers picking up the story were the *New York Sun*, May 25, 1894; *Chicago Tribune*, May 25, 1894; *Brooklyn Eagle*, May 25, 1894; *Ripon* (Wisc.) *Observer*, May 31, 1894; *see also* Poultney Bigelow, "Blood is Thicker Than Water," London, May 25, 1894, in *Harper's Weekly* (June 16, 1894). All these newspaper references (clippings) are in Mahan Family Papers (NWC). Seated at the head table to the left of the chairman, Lord Hamilton, were, in order: Erben, General Roberts, the Earl of Darnley, Viscount Sidmouth, Lord Leconfield, Lord Hood of Avalon, Lord Brassey, and Admiral Lord Alcester; on the chairman's right, in order, sat: Ambassador Bayard, the Earl of Carlisle, Mahan, Admiral Hornby, the Earl of Galloway, the Earl of Minto, Viscount Falmouth, and Lord de Saumarez. Among the American guests were W. C. Whitney, former Secretary of the Navy, and John Hay, who became Secretary of State in 1898. The *London Morning Post*, May 25, 1894, printed the names of some 90 of the most distinguished personages present, mostly nobles, generals, admirals, captains, colonels, and MPs. Mr. Hiram S. Maxim, of machine-gun fame, the so-called "merchant of death," was there, too. Ladies sat in the galleries.

20. Ellicott, "With Erben and Mahan on the *Chicago*," 1238; *London Morning Post*, May 25, 1894; *Pall Mall Gazette*, May 25, 1894 (article headed: "First Cousins at Dinner: The English Tar Entertains the American Tar"); *The Times* (London), May 25, 1894; Mahan to Ellen Evans Mahan, May 25, 1894. The *Newcastle Daily Chronicle* of May 24, 1894, favorably compared Mahan and the impact of his books to the work of Adam Smith and Charles Darwin. The six-verse *Punch* poem was widely quoted in Britain and the United States. A copy of it is in the Mahan Family Papers (NWC). The observation that the British Army was in need of a theorist of the stature of Mahan to give it direction as well as its historical due, was widely

commented on in the British press. *See* especially the *Army and Navy Gazette*, May 26, 1894, June 2, 1894; *Newcastle Daily Chronicle*, May 24, 1894.

21. Copies of some of Durrant's clippings are in the War College library together with copies of Mahan-related materials (mostly reviews of Mahan's books) prepared personally for Mahan in scrapbook form by his London publisher, R. B. Marston. The original scrapbook is in the possession of Alfred Thayer Mahan II. Mahan to Ellen Evans Mahan, June 7, 1894. For Mahan's dining schedule in London in late May and early June 1894, and his reactions to prominent Englishmen with whom he dined, and to their adulation, *see* Mahan to Ellen Evans Mahan, May 25, 1894, June 1, 1894, June 7, 1894; Mahan to Helen Evans Mahan, June 5, 1894; Mahan to Jane Leigh Mahan, July 8, 1894.

22. The dinner was held in the Whitehall Room of the Hotel Metropole. The Club usually met several times each year to commemorate famous British naval victories. Newspaper accounts of the affair and the list of 100 names of those in attendance are in *London Morning Post*, June 4, 1894; *London Globe*, June 4, 1894; *United Service Gazette*, June 9, 1894; *New York Herald*, June 3, 1894. All newspaper sources (clippings) are in NWC library. Mahan's reaction to his reception by the Royal Navy Club is in Mahan to Helen Evans Mahan, June 5, 1894; Mahan to Jane Leigh Mahan, July 8, 1894; Mahan to Clark, January 15, 1907.

23. Mahan to Jane Leigh Mahan, July 8, 1894. A "Plan of the Table" seating diagram for the Trinity House dinner is in Mahan Family Papers (NWC). Ninety-nine men were at table including eight members of the royal family, numerous high-ranking army and naval officers, and various prominent MPs, bankers, businessmen, barristers, and shipping magnates. Mahan sat between Vice Admiral H. Fairfax and Mr. T. H. Ismay. Erben was situated between Earl Spencer and Lord George Hamilton. Among those with whom Mahan dined, with whom he visited, or upon whom he called on a more intimate or informal basis between May 10 and June 14, 1894, were: Mrs. Beaumont, Lord Charles Beresford, Mr. and Mrs. Poultney Bigelow, Mrs. Harry Blake, Capt. Bouverie F. Clark, RN, Col. Sir George Sydenham Clarke, Mrs. Thomas R. Hoskins, Sir Francis and Lady Jeune, Mr. Shaw Lefevre, Mr. R. B. Marston, Lady Salisbury, Mr. and Mrs. George Schiff, Prof. and Mrs. James R. Thursfield, Captain John Yorke, RN. *See* Mahan to Ellen Evans Mahan, June 7, 1894, June 11, 1894.

24. Mahan to Ellen Evans Mahan, June 7, 1894, June 20, 1894, June 23, 1894; Mahan to Helen Evans Mahan, July 3, 1894; Mahan to Jane Leigh Mahan, July 8, 1894; Mahan to Brown, January 31, 1895; W. M. Little to Ellen Evans Mahan, [early February 1895], in Taylor, *Life of Admiral Mahan*, 75–76. Newspaper accounts of Mahan's honorary degree awards include *New York Herald*, June 19, 1894, and *Army and Navy Gazette* (London), June 23, 1894. *See also* Taylor, *Life of Admiral Mahan*, 68–75. Excerpts from Sandys' speech are *ibid.*, 71. George E. Belknap of Brookline, Mass., wrote a humorous little poem titled "Capt. Alfred T. Mahan, U.S.N., LL.D., D.C.L." which celebrated in patriotic tones Mahan's academic triumphs in England. Widely carried in the American press, a copy of the Belknap effort is in the Mahan Family Papers (NWC).

25. Mahan to Ellen Evans Mahan, June 23, 1894; Mahan to Jane Leigh Mahan, July 8, 1894. Rumors that Queen Victoria would bestow the Order of the Bath upon

Mahan in late June 1894 proved unfounded, although there was some speculation on this possibility in the American press. There is an unidentified and undated newspaper clipping on this point in the Mahan Family Papers (NWC).

26. The 2,300-ton *Azov*, out of Liverpool, was carrying a cargo of petroleum from Batum, Russia, to Antwerp at the time of the accident. Log of the *Chicago*, July 11, 1894 (NA); Erben to H. M. Hodges, July 11, 1894 (NA); Erben to Herbert, July 20, 1894 (NA), October 10, 1894 (NA); H. M. Hodges, A. B. Canaga, and J. B. Bernadou to Erben, July 14, 1894 (NA); Ellicott, "Three Navy Cranks and What They Turned," 1625–1626; Ellicott, "With Erben and Mahan on the *Chicago*," 1239–1240; Mahan to Ellen Evans Mahan, July 12, 1894.

27. Ellicott, "With Erben and Mahan on the *Chicago*," 1240; Mahan to Ellen Evans Mahan, August 8, 1894, August 17, 1894, September 6, 1894, September 13, 1894, September 23, 1894, October 5, 1894, October 12, 1894; Mahan to Jane Leigh Okill Swift, September 13, 1894; Mahan to Helen Evans Mahan, August 5, 1894, August 26, 1894, October 9, 1894; Mahan to Ellen Kuhn Mahan, September 10, 1894. During this period Mahan visited with, spent weekends with, entertained, or dined with Mr. and Mrs. Henry White; Mr. Edgar Goble (Nelson biography source); Sir William Parker (Nelson biography source); Admiral Maurice Horatio Nelson; the Duke of Connaught; Sir Francis and Lady Jeune; Lord Radstock (Nelson biography source); Mrs. G. M. Ogden (Elly's aunt); Mr. and Mrs. George Schiff; and Captain Bouverie Clark, RN.

28. Mahan to Ellen Evans Mahan, June 29, 1894, July 22, 1894, September 6, 1894; Mahan to Helen Evans Mahan, May 11, 1894, July 3, 1894; Mahan to Ellen Kuhn Mahan, August 3, 1894, September 10, 1894; Puleston, *Mahan*, 160.

29. Mahan to Ellen Evans Mahan, August 29, 1894, September 13, 1894, September 20, 1894, October 5, 1894, November 21, 1894, February 1, 1895, February 11, 1895; Mahan to Ellen Kuhn Mahan, October 2, 1894, December 15, 1894; Mahan to Helen Evans Mahan, December 25, 1894, January 29, 1895; Puleston, *Mahan*, 151, 164; Kirkland to Herbert, February 28, 1895 (LC); *New York Herald*, March 24, 1895. This unsolicited Kirkland recommendation of Mahan caused one American newspaper to comment, in mock horror, that the tribute "appears to have excited a spasmatic distress in the part of some officer of the Navy Department." Clipping in Mahan Papers (LC).

30. Mahan to Ellen Evans Mahan, July 29, 1894, August 17, 1894, September 23, 1894, October 5, 1894, October 12, 1894; Mahan, "The Battle of the Yalu: An Interview with *The Times*, London, September 25, 1894," in *Letters and Papers*, III, 583–585; Mahan, "Lessons From the Yalu Fight," *Century Magazine* (August 1895), 629–632. Mahan's opinions on the Sino-Japanese War may have been solicited as the result of a remark by Captain John Ingles, RN, carried in *The Standard* (London), August 18, 1894. Ingles, just returned to England from a six-year tour as an adviser to the Imperial Japanese Navy, was quoted as saying that "Japanese naval officers are much impressed with the advantage in a land war of superiority at sea. They have been, I know, faithful students of the American naval historian, Captain Mahan." *See* Mahan Family Papers (NWC).

31. *See*, variously, Mahan to Ellen Evans Mahan, Helen Evans Mahan, and Ellen Kuhn Mahan, October 28, 1894 to February 24, 1895, in *Letters and Papers*, II,

352–405; but especially *see* Mahan to Ellen Evans Mahan, November 13, 1894, November 21, 1894, January 7, 1895, February 1, 1895; Mahan to Ellen Kuhn Mahan, December 15, 1894; Mahan to Helen Evans Mahan, January 9, 1895.

32. Mahan to Ellen Evans Mahan, October 5, 1894, October 19, 1894, December 9, 1894; Mahan to Helen Evans Mahan, September 18, 1894; Mahan to Clarke, January 29, 1895; Herbert to Taylor, February 23, 1895 (LC).

33. Mahan to Ellen Evans Mahan, December 2, 1894, February 1, 1895; Mahan to Helen Evans Mahan, January 29, 1895.

34. Mahan Memorandum, March 6, 1895, in *Letters and Papers*, III, 589; Mahan to Ellen Evans Mahan, February 24, 1895; Herbert to Mahan, April 10, 1895 (LC); Selfridge to Mahan, March 29, 1895 (LC). Almost as an afterthought, the Board of Inspection wondered also why there had been no target practice on board the *Chicago* after July 1, 1894. Mahan replied simply that target practice might have proved dangerous in the crowded English Channel; that the weather had been too rough on the voyage to Lisbon and later in the western Mediterranean; that no ammunition was available for such activity; and that there was difficulty in finding suitable anchoring ground outside the three-mile limit for the target-observation boats. Mahan to Herbert, April 17, 1895. As for Erben, the few of his papers of the *Chicago* period that have survived are deposited in the New-York Historical Society. Of a formal character, they throw no light whatever on Erben's personal relations with Mahan. Indeed, Mahan is not mentioned in them in any significant way. With the outbreak of the Spanish-American War, Erben came briefly out of retirement to command the Patrol Fleet on the coast of the United States from Galveston to Bar Harbor, with headquarters in New York. He saw no sea duty or combat. He met Mahan again in February 1901. *See* Mahan to Lodge, February 19, 1901.

35. Mahan to Scudder, March 25, 1895; Navy Department, Bureau of Navigation, *Service of Rear Admiral Alfred Thayer Mahan, U.S. Navy, Retired, Deceased*. September 21, 1935 (LC); Mahan to Bureau of Navigation, May 1, 1895, May 7, 1895, June 29, 1895; Mahan to Ashe, January 3, 1897.

A FAMILY AND ITS FUTURE, 1893–1895

1. Mahan to Ellen Evans Mahan, December 11, 1893, December 18, 1893, January 7, 1895; Mahan to Ellen Kuhn Mahan, September 10, 1894.

2. Mahan to Ellen Evans Mahan, November 2, 1893, December 11, 1893, April 29, 1894, October 19, 1894, November 13, 1894, January 13, 1895; Mahan to Helen Evans Mahan, February 18, 1894.

3. Mahan to Ellen Evans Mahan, December 2, 1894, January 7, 1895; Mahan to Helen Evans Mahan, January 11, 1895.

4. For Mahan on the Schiff family, particularly the Schiff daughters, and on his social life on shore in Villefranche from December 1893 to February 1894, *see* Mahan to Ellen Evans Mahan, December 18, 1893, January 1, 1894, February 3, 1894, February 10, 1894, May 9, 1894, December 9, 1894; Mahan to Helen Evans Mahan, December 25, 1893, January 31, 1894, February 18, 1894; Mahan to Ellen Kuhn Mahan, January 6, 1894. For Madeline Stanley, who "quite won my heart" in London, *see*

Mahan to Jane Leigh Okill Swift, September 13, 1894; Mahan to Ellen Evans Mahan, September 13, 1894, September 20, 1894, October 19, 1894, December 9, 1894; Mahan to Helen Evans Mahan, October 9, 1894.

5. Mahan to Helen Evans Mahan, December 25, 1893; Mahan to Ellen Evans Mahan, May 9, 1894, June 7, 1894, September 13, 1894, September 20, 1894, October 27, 1894, January 25, 1895. Mahan's continued appreciation of a pretty female face is in Mahan to Helen Evans Mahan, October 28, 1893, November 23, 1893, December 25, 1893, June 5, 1894. His self-admiration is in Mahan to Ellen Evans Mahan, October 19, 1894; Mahan to Ellen Kuhn Mahan, January 4, 1895. Elly's proposed trip to join her husband on the station is treated in Mahan to Ellen Evans Mahan, February 10, 1894, August 10, 1894, August 29, 1894, October 12, 1894, October 19, 1894, October 27, 1894, November 1–2, 1894, November 13, 1894. Mahan's professions of love for Elly, his loneliness, and his homesickness from 1893 to 1895 are in Mahan to Ellen Evans Mahan, July 15, 1893, May 25, 1894, June 11, 1894, August 10, 1894, September 13, 1894, October 12, 1894, October 19, 1894, November 24, 1894, December 2, 1894; Mahan to Helen Evans Mahan, July 3, 1894, January 29, 1895.

6. Mahan to Ellen Evans Mahan, September 6, 1893, February 10, 1894, October 5, 1894; Mahan to Helen Evans Mahan, May 11, 1894, July 3, 1894, December 25, 1894; Mahan to Ellen Kuhn Mahan, December 7, 1893; Mahan to Jane Leigh Mahan, July 8, 1894.

7. Mahan to Helen Evans Mahan, July 3, 1893, July 25, 1893, September 3, 1893, December 26, 1894, June 14, 1896; Mahan to Ellen Evans Mahan, September 6, 1893, March 10, 1894, October 11, 1894; Mahan to Clark, July 23, 1909.

8. Mahan to Helen Evans Mahan, October 28, 1893, November 26, 1893, September 18, 1894, December 25, 1893; Mahan to Ellen Evans Mahan, December 18, 1893, January 11, 1894, October 20, 1894, December 9, 1894.

9. Mahan to Ellen Evans Mahan, September 6, 1893, January 11, 1894, August 27, 1894; Mahan to Helen Evans Mahan, November 26, 1893, December 25, 1893, May 11, 1894, June 5, 1894, September 18, 1894, December 26, 1894.

10. Mahan to Helen Evans Mahan, November 17, 1894, December 26, 1894; Mahan to Ellen Evans Mahan, January 25, 1895; Mahan to Brown, April 9, 1905; Mahan to Maxse, September 14, 1905.

11. Mahan to Ellen Kuhn Mahan, October 6, 1893, December 15, 1894; Mahan to Ellen Evans Mahan, September 6, 1893, September 22, 1893, June 15, 1894.

12. Mahan to Helen Evans Mahan, August 26, 1894; Mahan to Ellen Kuhn Mahan, December 7, 1893, January 4, 1895; Mahan to Ellen Evans Mahan, April 29, 1894, May 9, 1894, May 25, 1894.

13. Mahan to Ellen Evans Mahan, June 15, 1894, August 29, 1894, December 11, 1893; Mahan to Ellen Kuhn Mahan, August 3, 1894, November 8, 1894, November 27, 1894, January 1, 1894; Mahan to Helen Evans Mahan, October 28, 1893, October 28, 1894, December 25, 1893.

14. Mahan to Ellen Evans Mahan, August 24, 1893, October 11, 1893, November 1, 1893.

15. Mahan to Peabody, April 14, 1893, April 20, 1893, February 18, 1898; Mahan to Ellen Evans Mahan, January 1, 1894, August 17, 1894, September 20, 1894, Octo-

ber 5, 1894, November 21, 1894, December 19, 1894, February 6, 1895, February 11, 1895, February 24, 1895; Mahan to Helen Evans Mahan, November 26, 1893, November 17, 1894, January 9, 1895; Mahan to Clark, June 14, 1895. *See also* Ellen Kuhn Mahan, "Recollections," in *Letters and Papers*, III, 727.

16. *Ibid.*, 721; Mahan to Ellen Kuhn Mahan, July 9, 1893, September 11, 1893, October 6, 1893, November 10, 1893, December 7, 1893, February 26, 1894, March 29, 1894, November 8, 1894; Mahan to Helen Evans Mahan, September 28, 1893, October 28, 1893, March 16, 1894, July 3, 1894; Mahan to Ellen Evans Mahan, October 17, 1893, November 18, 1893, February 14, 1894, February 22, 1894, March 23, 1894.

17. Mahan to Helen Evans Mahan, January 31, 1894, June 5, 1894, August 26, 1894. Mahan's habit of tithing and making other charitable donations from 1893 to 1895 is in Mahan to Ellen Evans Mahan, August 5, 1893, November 1, 1893, January 11, 1894, March 4, 1894; Mahan to Helen Evans Mahan, September 3, 1893; Mahan to Ellen Kuhn Mahan, November 4, 1893, January 4, 1895.

18. Mahan to Erben, October 19, 1893; Ellicott, "Three Navy Cranks and What They Turned," 1623–1625; Ellicott, "With Erben and Mahan on the *Chicago*," 1237, 1240.

19. Mahan to Ellen Evans Mahan, November 10, 1893, November 18, 1893, January 25, 1894, February 9, 1894, June 1, 1894, June 29, 1894, July 22, 1894, October 18, 1894; Mahan to Helen Evans Mahan, July 9, 1890.

20. Mahan to Ellen Evans Mahan, September 27, 1894, October 27, 1894.

21. Mahan to Ellen Evans Mahan, November 1, 1893, February 23, 1894, March 4, 1894, April 29, 1894, September 27, 1894, November 1, 1894, December 9, 1894, December 30, 1894; Mahan to Helen Evans Mahan, December 25, 1894; Mahan to Ellen Kuhn Mahan, January 4, 1895; Mahan to Gillender, December 26, 1895. Jane Leigh Mahan traveled in Europe and lived in France for a few years after Mahan returned to the United States in the *Chicago*. Born August 16, 1852, she lived until August 28, 1945.

22. Mahan to Ellen Evans Mahan, December 18, 1893, April 13, 1894, April 29, 1894, December 9, 1894, December 30, 1894, January 13, 1895, January 16, 1895, February 19, 1895; Mahan to Helen Evans Mahan, January 9, 1895, January 29, 1895; Mahan to Ellen Kuhn Mahan, February 8, 1895; Mahan to Clark, October 28, 1912; Ellen Kuhn Mahan, "Recollections," in *Letters and Papers*, III, 719.

23. Mahan to Ellen Evans Mahan, October 8, 1894, November 1, 1894, November 13, 1894, December 30, 1894, January 7, 1895, January 13, 1895, January 25, 1895; Mahan to Ellen Kuhn Mahan, January 4, 1895; Mahan to Helen Evans Mahan, January 9, 1895.

24. Mahan to Gillender, June 4, 1895, June 6, 1895; Mahan to Herbert, November 18, 1895; Mahan to Clark, January 17, 1896; Mahan to Moore, April 20, 1905; Ellen Kuhn Mahan, "Recollections," in *Letters and Papers*, III, 719.

25. Ellen Kuhn Mahan, "Recollections," in *Letters and Papers*, III, 727–728, 729. For the housing arrangements of the Mahans in 1905–1914, *see* Mahan to Clark, December 14, 1906; Mahan to Little, Brown and Co., October 28, 1907; Mahan to Luce, May 6, 1909.

BEGINNING A SECOND CAREER, 1895–1898

1. Mahan to Brown, June 19, 1896, June 29, 1896; Mahan to Frederick A. Mahan, December 15, 1895; Mahan to Gillender, November 23, 1895, December 26, 1895, March 1, 1896, July 1, 1896, August 5, 1896, May 26, 1897, June 12, 1897, June 28, 1897, April 27, 1901, June 15, 1901, July 16, 1901.

2. Mahan to Johnson, May 14, 1895, June 2, 1895, June 11, 1895, June 14, 1895; Mahan, "Lessons From the Yalu Fight," *Century Magazine* (August 1895), 629–632; *see also* Mahan, "The Battle of the Yalu: An Interview with *The Times*, London, September 25, 1894," in *Letters and Papers*, III, 583–585. McGiffin's account, "The Battle of the Yalu," also appeared in the August 1895 issue of *Century Magazine*, 585–604. Mahan read it in galley prior to writing his own article, which he sub-titled, "Comments on Commander McGiffin's Article by the Author of *Influence of Sea Power Upon History*." In a later view of the Yalu action, presented in a lecture in Boston on April 3, 1897, Mahan argued that the rapid-fire Japanese guns were so effective in killing Chinese sailors in their turrets and on their decks that "it would seem that the verdict was for guns against ram or torpedo since the force of the latter two is directed against the ship." *Boston Journal*, April 4, 1897 (NWC).

3. Mahan to Ellen Evans Mahan, February 23, 1894; Mahan to Low, March 28, 1900; Mahan to Maxse, January 22, 1907, March 5, 1907, May 30, 1907; Mahan to McIntyre, July 30, 1910; Mahan to Little, Brown and Co., May 21, 1908.

4. Mahan to Scudder, November 22, 1892, February 3, 1893; Mahan to Ashe, November 7, 1896; Mahan to Johnson, December 7, 1895, March 31, 1911; Mahan to Page, September 10, 1897; Mahan to Thursfield, December 1, 1897; Mahan to Maxse, December 26, 1901, January 24, 1902, January 30, 1902, February 21, 1902, July 25, 1902, October 3, 1902, April 28, 1903, August 21, 1903, January 15, 1906; Mahan to Chambers, May 8, 1897; Mahan to Choate, August 19, 1898; Mahan to Long, October 6, 1898.

5. Mahan to Johnson, August 6, 1895; Mahan to Ashe, January 3, 1897; Mahan to Scudder, November 22, 1892; Mahan to Brown, June 9, 1893, July 24, 1898, September 8, 1899; Mahan to Clarke, December 19, 1902; Mahan to Maxse, December 26, 1901, January 28, 1902, January 30, 1902, October 9, 1905, August 21, 1906.

6. Mahan to Ellen Evans Mahan, June 1, 1894, June 29, 1894; Mahan to Scudder, September 26, 1890; Mahan to Brown, March 8, 1897, July 24, 1898; Mahan to Mitchell, April 29, 1904; Mahan to Maxse, December 26, 1901, April 10, 1902; Mahan to Johnson, January 17, 1898; Mahan to de Camp, October 25, 1913; Mahan Memorandum, May 1914. The estimate of $32,000 is based on known income ($7,225) from 26 articles in representative magazines, and the fact that he wrote 137 articles, at least 14 of which produced no income, or virtually none, and 8 of which were published simultaneously in England and the United States.

7. *The Statistical History of the United States from Colonial Times to the Present* (Stamford, Conn.: Fairfield Publishers, 1965), 90–92, presents data on wages and hours in the United States between 1890 and 1914.

8. Mahan to Clark, June 14, 1895; Mahan to Brown, June 20, 1895, April 11, 1896, June 19, 1896, June 29, 1896, August 31, 1896; Mahan to Ramsay, June 22, 1895, June

29, 1895; Mahan to Taylor, July 19, 1895; Mahan to Henderson, May 21, 1897; Mahan to Ashe, November 7, 1896.

9. The four Nelson battle articles were: "Nelson at Cape St. Vincent," *Century Magazine* (February 1896); "Nelson at the Battle of the Nile," *ibid.* (January 1897); "The Battle of Copenhagen," *ibid.* (February 1897); "Nelson at Trafalgar," *ibid.* (March 1897). Mahan to Johnson, July 9, 1895, July 27, 1895, August 6, 1895, August 8, 1895, October 23, 1895, February 27, 1896, March 6, 1896, June 9, 1896, June 13, 1896; Mahan to Brown, July 18, 1895, April 11, 1896, June 19, 1896, August 31, 1896. For Mahan's unsuccessful attempt to persuade *Century* to republish the four Nelson battle articles in book format similar to Edward S. Creasy, *Fifteen Decisive Battles of the World, see* Mahan to Johnson, April 4, 1895, October 23, 1895, March 6, 1896.

10. Mahan to Ashe, January 3, 1897; Mahan to Brown, November 13, 1896; Mahan to Thursfield, January 10, 1896; Mahan to Clark, January 17, 1896; Mahan to Sterling, April 17, 1896. There is no evidence that Mahan viewed an Anglo-American war in 1896 as possibly having a harmful impact on the sales of his forthcoming Nelson biography. He was fearful, however, in early March 1897, that the approaching Greco-Turkish War, which commenced April 17, 1897, over the nagging problem of Crete might well trigger a general European conflagration and thus "affect sales, and certainly direct from the book attention, which if favorable, is the most important factor to success." Mahan to Brown, March 1, 1897. For Mahan's opinion of the Greco-Turkish War, *see* Mahan to Sterling, April 27, 1897.

11. Mahan to Sterling, April 17, 1896; Mahan to Brown, November 13, 1896; Mahan to Ashe, January 3, 1897; Mahan to Roosevelt, May 1, 1897; Mahan, "Preparedness for Naval War," *Harper's Monthly* (March 1897), 579–588.

12. Mahan to Sterling, February 13, 1896, April 27, 1897; Mahan to Low, March 10, 1896, March 12, 1897. On Mahan's decision to retire, *The New York Times*, November 18, 1896, wrote: "The announcement was received at the Navy Department with astonishment, as Capt. Mahan would have been promoted to the rank of Commodore in a few months, and could then have retired with increased pay. It is thought that he must have been forced to act now by reason of his pressing literary engagements."

13. Mahan to Ellen Evans Mahan, November 13, 1894; Mahan to Brown, August 31, 1896, September 8, 1896; Mahan to Ashe, November 7, 1896, January 3, 1897. In a commencement address at Dartmouth College in June 1903, Mahan returned to his attack on socialism; but he equated it with the equally dangerous assault on freedom and individualism inherent in the capitalist movement toward trusts and industrial concentration. Said he: "There is, in my judgment, ground for the fears of those who see in unchecked industrial combination the necessary and inevitable forerunner of that social concentration, which, as yet an unrealized idea, we know as Socialism." Mahan, "Personality and Influence: A Commencement Address at Dartmouth College . . . June 24, 1903," in *Letters and Papers*, III, 611. *See also*, Chapter XX of this work.

14. Mahan to Brown, October 31, 1896, November 9, 1896, November 30, 1896, December 15, 1896, December 28, 1896, February 8, 1897, February 10, 1897. For details of the Whitney-sponsored retirement dinner, *see* Mahan to Luce, December 5, 1896. Also present at the dinner were former Governor Levi P. Morton, Mayor W. L. Strong, General John M. Schofield, Rear Admirals M. Sicard, and R. D.

Evans, popular novelist Silas W. Mitchell, and statesmen Charles Francis Adams, Henry White, and Elihu Root. Newspaper clippings calling attention to Mahan's retirement from the Navy are found in the Mahan Papers (LC). The *New York Herald*, November 18, 1896, carried a particularly full account of the retirement.

15. Mahan to Brown, December 10, 1896, December 15, 1896, December 17, 1896; Mahan to Jameson, December 16, 1896.

16. William O'Connor Morris, "Captain Mahan's Nelson," *Fortnightly Review* (June 1, 1897); Douglas Sladen, "Captain Mahan's Life of Nelson," *St. James's Budget*, July 23, 1897; *The Review of Reviews* (May 1897); Spenser Wilkinson, "The New Nelson," *National Review* (July 1897). *The Sketch*, May 12, 1897, liked the book but held that it "starts very few new theories, and disturbs very few old conclusions." Copies of these and other reviews are in the Mahan Family Papers at NWC. For still other reviews, and sales information, *see* Taylor, *Life of Admiral Mahan*, 81–84, 86–87, 206, 252–255; and Mahan to Brown, April 22, 1897, April 26, 1897, May 31, 1897, July 14, 1897, January 18, 1898, September 10, 1898; Mahan to Sterling, April 27, 1897; Mahan to Thursfield, May 21, 1897; Mahan to Henderson, May 21, 1897; David Hannay, "Nelson and His Biographers," *Macmillan's* (June 1897).

17. The extensive literature on the Badham vs. Mahan controversy includes the following: from the pen of F. P. Badham, "Nelson at Naples," *Saturday Review* (May 15, November 3, 1897); comments in *Athenaeum* (July 1, July 15, August 5, 1899); "Nelson and the Neapolitan Republicans," *English Historical Review* (April 1898), 261–282; *Nelson at Naples: A Journal for 10–30 June, 1799*, pamphlet, (London: David Nutt, 1900). Mahan responded with comments in various publications: *Athenaeum* (July 8, July 22, August 12, 1899); "The Neapolitan Republicans and Nelson's Accusers," *English Historical Review* (July 1899), 471–501; "Nelson at Naples," *ibid.* (October 1900), 699–727; *Nelson at Naples*, pamphlet, (London: Spottiswoode and Company, 1900); and in the 2nd Edition, Revised, of his *The Life of Nelson* (1900). John K. Laughton's defense of Mahan in the controversy with Badham is found in his "Life of Nelson," *English Historical Review* (October 1897), 801–805, and in "Nelson at Naples," *Athenaeum* (August 26, 1899).

18. Morris, "Captain Mahan's Nelson," *Fortnightly Review* (June 1, 1897), 898; Wilkinson, "The New Nelson," *National Review* (July 1897), 708; *Review of Reviews* (May 1897), 492. References to Lady Nelson's goodness and blamelessness are in Mahan to Helen Evans Mahan, September 18, 1894; Mahan to Brown, December 17, 1896, January 13, 1897, February 10, 1897.

19. Wilkinson, "The New Nelson," *National Review* (July 1897), 703, 705, 708.

20. Details of Nelson's actions in Naples are in the sources cited in Note 17 above, as are additional insights into Mahan's struggle with F. P. Badham.

21. Mahan to Brown, September 10, 1898, December 20, 1898, December 30, 1898, January 13, 1899, January 18, 1899, April 7, 1899, April 15, 1899, July 20, 1901; Mahan to Greene, April 5, 1899; Mahan to Thursfield, June 17, 1899; Mahan, "The Neapolitan Republicans and Nelson's Accusers," *English Historical Review* (July 1899), 471–501; Mahan, "Nelson at Naples," *ibid.* (October 1900), 699–727. The pamphlet version of this article, published by Spottiswoode and Company of London in November 1900, was designed to counteract Badham's pamphlet of the same title published by David Nutt of London a few months earlier. For additional Italian

sources purchased and consulted by Mahan in responding to Badham, *see* Mahan to Billings, December 20, 1902, February 13, 1905. These books and pamphlets Mahan later donated to the New York Public Library.

22. Mahan to Lowell, April 1, 1895, May 9, 1895, February 13, 1896, February 28, 1896, November 29, 1896; Mahan to Roosevelt, May 6, 1897; Mahan to Clark, May 16, 1904. Mahan delivered the Lowell Lectures in Huntington Hall, Boston, on consecutive Wednesdays and Saturdays. For summaries of the contents of several of these lectures, and extended quotations from them, *see* the *Boston Post*, April 4, 1897, April 8, 1897; *Boston Globe*, April 4, 1897; *Boston Journal*, March 28, 1897, April 1, 1897, April 4, 1897; *Boston Transcript*, April 1, 1897, April 8, 1897; *Boston Herald*, April 1, 1897, April 4, 1897, April 8, 1897; *Boston Advertiser*, April 1, 1897. Clippings from these Boston newspaper accounts of the lectures are in the Mahan Family Collection (NWC). They were supplied to Mahan by The Authors' Clipping Bureau of Boston. A few other clippings describing Mahan's Lowell Lectures are in the Mahan Collection (LC).

23. Mahan to Brown, March 8, 1897, August 17, 1897, December 13, 1897, December 26, 1897; Mahan to Thursfield, December 1, 1897; Mahan to Rhodes, December 9, 1897.

24. Mahan, "A Twentieth Century Outlook," *Harper's Monthly* (September 1897), 521–533; Mahan, "Strategic Features of the Caribbean Sea and the Gulf of Mexico," *ibid.* (October 1897), 680–691. Both of these articles were reprinted in Mahan, *The Interest of America in Sea Power, Present and Future* (Boston: Little, Brown and Company, 1897). The eight articles, in order and place of publication were: "The United States Looking Outward," *Atlantic Monthly* (December 1890); "Hawaii and Our Future Sea Power," *The Forum* (March 1893); "The Isthmus and Sea Power," *Atlantic Monthly* (September 1893); "Possibilities of Anglo-American Reunion," *North American Review* (November 1894), "The Future in Relation to American Naval Power," *Harper's Monthly* (October 1895); "Preparedness for Naval War," *ibid.* (March 1897); "A Twentieth-Century Outlook," *ibid.* (September 1897); and "The Strategic Features of the Caribbean Sea and the Gulf of Mexico," *ibid.* (October 1897). *See also* William E. Livezey, *Mahan on Sea Power* (Norman: University of Oklahoma Press, 1947), 118–120.

25. George S. Clarke, "Captain Mahan's Counsels to the United States," *Nineteenth Century* (February 1898); Taylor, *Life of Admiral Mahan*, 202–203; Mahan to Clarke, February 22, 1898; "Aggressive America," *The Saturday Review* (January 15, 1898); *Athenaeum* (January 1, 1898); *Manchester Guardian*, January 18, 1898; *The Times* (London), October 13, 1897; *Naval and Military Record* (January 8, 1898); *Army and Navy Gazette*, December 18, 1897. For other favorable British reviews, *see*, *Review of Reviews* (January 1898); *Western Morning News* (Plymouth), December 31, 1897; *London Daily Graphic*, December 13, 1897; *London Daily Chronicle*, December 13, 1897. Copies of these reviews are in the Mahan Family Papers at NWC. *See also* Mahan to Brown, December 13, 1897, Footnote 1, December 26, 1897; and Livezey, *Mahan on Sea Power*, 124–125.

26. Taylor, *Life of Admiral Mahan*, 116–117, 119; Henry E. Bourne, "America and Sea Power," *The Citizen* (Brooklyn, N.Y.), March 1898; *Chicago Times-Herald*, June 4, 1898; *Brooklyn Citizen*, June 19, 1898; Percival Pollard, "Mahan on American Sea Power," *The Criterion*, June 1898.

THE SPLENDID WAR AND THE NAVAL WAR BOARD, 1898

1. The American debate over the advent of the Spanish-American War, and the territorial annexations to which it subsequently led, can be traced in Leslie E. Decker and Robert Seager II, eds., *America's Major Wars: Crusaders, Critics, and Scholars, 1775–1972*. 2 vols. (Reading, Mass.: Addison-Wesley Publishing Company, 1973), II, 21–70. Relevant diplomatic and congressional documents are included. For the onset and prosecution of actual hostilities *see also* Walter Millis, *The Martial Spirit* (New York: The Literary Guild of America, 1931), *passim*; and Frank Freidel, *The Splendid Little War* (Boston: Little, Brown and Co., 1958), *passim*.

2. *Boston Journal*, March 28, 1897; Mahan, "The Strategic Features of the Caribbean Sea and the Gulf of Mexico," in Mahan, *The Interest of America in Sea Power, Present and Future* (Port Washington, N.Y.: Kennikat Press Reprint, 1970), 289, 303, 310, 312–313; Mahan, *Lessons of the War with Spain and Other Articles* (Freeport, N.Y.: Books For Libraries Press Reprint, 1970), 26, 88, 225–227, 229; Mahan to Henderson, March 7, 1898; Mahan, "Preparedness for a Naval War," in *Interest of America in Sea Power*, 184; Livezey, *Mahan on Sea Power* 123; Mahan to Roosevelt, May 1, 1897, May 6, 1897; Mahan to Scudder, October 8, 1890, October 11, 1890.

3. Mahan's contribution to the Clowes project, *A History of the Royal Navy*, which was published by Sampson Low, Marston and Company in London late in 1898, appeared as Chapter 31 in Volume III, 353–565. The publication of Volume III was somewhat delayed by reason of Mahan's service on the Naval War Board in 1898 and his consequent inability to finish work on the page proofs of his monograph. *See* Mahan to Wingate, May 23, 1897, Footnote 2. Mahan to Brown, March 8, 1897, July 14, 1897, February 25, 1898, September 16, 1898, March 16, 1907; Mahan to Marston, December 9, 1897; Mahan to Craig, February 11, 1898; Mahan to Wingate, May 23, 1897; Mahan to Page, July 23, 1897; Mahan to Mitchell, December 4, 1897; Mahan to Burlingame, July 5, 1897, July 11, 1897, July 14, 1897, July 26, 1897, July 31, 1897, August 3, 1897, August 23, 1897, September 6, 1897, September 27, 1897, September 30, 1897, February 13, 1898; Mahan, "The Naval Campaign of 1776 on Lake Champlain," *Scribner's Magazine* (February 1898); Mahan, "John Paul Jones in the Revolution," *ibid.* (July 1898, August 1898), 22–36, 204–219; Mahan, "Distinguishing Qualities of Ships of War" (written in November 1897 for Scripps-McRae Newspaper League and published in November 1898), reprinted in Mahan, *Lessons of the War with Spain*, 257–273.

4. Mahan to Johnson, January 17, 1898, February 14, 1898, March 25, 1898; Mahan to Clarke, February 22, 1898; Mahan to Peabody, February 18, 1898, June 20, 1898; Mahan to Brown, March 21, 1898; Mahan to Burlingame, March 24, 1898. Mahan received from Peabody in June a refund of $308 on Lyle's room, board, and tuition for the period March–June 1898. Lyle entered Columbia College the following September.

5. Mahan to Roosevelt, May 6, 1897; Puleston, *Mahan*, 186; Mahan to Peabody, February 18, 1898; Mahan to Clarke, February 22, 1898; Mahan to Brown, February 25, 1898; Mahan to Burlingame, February 28, 1898, March 4, 1898, March 16, 1898; Mahan to Jameson, March 10, 1898; Mahan, "The Sinking of the USS *Maine*," Princeton, N.J., February 22, 1898, in *Letters and Papers*, III, 592–594.

6. Mahan to Sterling, March 4, 1898; Mahan to Henderson, March 7, 1898.

7. Between March 10 and March 24, Roosevelt wrote Mahan at least five times, viz., on March 10, 14, 16, 21, and 24. Mahan seems to have replied to those of March 10, 14, 16, and 21 in letters now lost but probably dated March 12, 14, 19, and 22. The known Roosevelt-to-Mahan correspondence of March 10–24 has been ably summarized by William E. Livezey in his excellent *Mahan on Sea Power*, 133–134. For evidence of the contents of the lost Mahan letter to Roosevelt dated March 12, 13, or 14, *see* Long to Sampson, Enclosure, March 24, 1898, in F. E. Chadwick, *The Relations of the United States and Spain: The Spanish-American War*. 2 vols. (New York: Charles Scribner's Sons, 1911), I, 21–22. Hereafter cited as *The Spanish-American War*. Chadwick's first volume is in large measure an operational naval history of the war with considerable emphasis on Spanish operations.

8. Mahan, "The Strategic Features of the Caribbean Sea and the Gulf of Mexico," in *Interest of America in Sea Power*, 289; Chadwick, *The Spanish-American War*, I, 11, 16.

9. Millis, *The Martial Spirit*, 127–128; Decker and Seager, *America's Major Wars*, II, 30–32; Mahan to Gillender, April 20, 1898. H. G. Rickover, *How the Battleship Maine Was Destroyed* (Washington, D.C.: Government Printing Office, 1976), *passim*, argues persuasively that the explosion was caused by spontaneous combustion and that the Navy's Court of Inquiry was not competent to judge the evidence.

10. Taylor, *Life of Admiral Mahan*, 88; Mahan to Long (via Ambassador Porter to Secretary Day), April 29, 1898; Chadwick, *The Spanish-American War*, I, 51–53, 71–76, 87; Richard S. West, *Admirals of American Empire* (Indianapolis, Ind.: Bobbs-Merrill Company, 1948), 212–213, 215; Mahan, "The Work of the Naval War Board of 1898," in *Letters and Papers*, III, 629.

11. Mahan to Long, May 10, 1898; Mahan, "The Work of the Naval War Board of 1898," in *Letters and Papers*, III, 627–628; Mahan to Luce, August 31, 1898.

12. Mahan to Long, May 10, 1898; Mahan to Clarke, May 24, 1898; Mahan, "The Work of the Naval War Board of 1898," in *Letters and Papers*, III, 630; Lawrence S. Mayo, *America of Yesterday as Reflected in the Diary of John D. Long* (Boston: Atlantic Monthly Press, 1923), 191, 194; Livezey, *Mahan on Sea Power*, 134–135.

13. Chadwick, *The Spanish-American War*, I, 15–16, 28; Mahan to Johnson, May 17, 1898, May 22, 1898, June 5, 1898. Hearst to Mahan, telegram, [April 1898], in Mahan Family Papers (NWC); *New York Journal* to M. F. Ihmsen, telegram, August 7, 1898, in Mahan Family Papers (NWC).

14. Chadwick, *The Spanish-American War*, I, 308, 311–312, 315–316; Mahan, "The Work of the Naval War Board of 1898," in *Letters and Papers*, III, 631, 643; Mahan to Sicard, May 19, 1898; Mahan to Clarke, May 24, 1898; Mahan to Brown, February 25, 1898; Puleston, *Mahan*, 186; Mahan, *Lessons of the War with Spain*, 157–158.

15. Mahan, "The Work of the Naval War Board of 1898," in *Letters and Papers*, III, 633; Chadwick, *The Spanish-American War*, I, 313, 314–318, 351–352; West, *Admirals of American Empire*, 240–242, 247, 249; Ellery Clark, "The Spanish-American War," in E. B. Potter and C. W. Nimitz, eds., *Sea Power* (Englewood

Cliffs, N.J.: Prentice-Hall, Inc., 1960), 366–377; Mahan to Barnes, May 30, 1898, July 9, 1898.

16. Mahan to Long, January 16, 1899, January 19, 1899, February 26, 1899; Mahan, "The Work of the Naval War Board of 1898," in *Letters and Papers*, III, 635–636.

17. Chadwick, *The Spanish-American War*, II, 117, 124, 129–157; Clark, "The Spanish-American War," in Potter, *Sea Power*, 374–376; Millis, *The Martial Spirit*, 307–308, 312–313; Mahan to Lodge, October 18, 1898; Mahan to Editor, *New York Sun*, circa September 7, 1914.

18. Puleston, *Mahan*, 193–194, 196–197; Chadwick, *The Spanish-American War*, II, 382–390; Mahan, "The Work of the Naval War Board of 1898," in *Letters and Papers*, III, 637, 638–641; Mahan to Brownson, July 7, 1898; Mahan to Lodge, July 12, 1898; Mahan to Kittelle, November 7, 1906.

19. Mahan to Naval War Board, July 18, 1898; Mahan, "The Work of the Naval War Board of 1898," in *Letters and Papers*, III, 640–641.

20. Mahan to Long, August 21, 1899, November 16, 1898, April 25, 1901, June 17, 1901; Mahan to Low, August 7, 1900, June 28, 1900; Mahan, "The Work of the Naval War Board of 1898," in *Letters and Papers*, III, 637; Millis, *The Martial Spirit*, 322–324; Margaret Leech, *In the Days of McKinley* (New York: Harper and Brothers, 1959), 265–267.

21. Mahan to Clarke, May 24, 1898; Mahan to Unidentified Addressee, May 29, 1898; Mahan to Long, July 23, 1898.

22. Mahan to Long, July 28, 1898, July 29, 1898.

23. Puleston, *Mahan*, 198–199; Mahan to Long, August 5, 1898, August 7, 1898, November 16, 1898.

24. Mahan to Kyle, February 4, 1898; Mahan to Long, August 15–20, 1898; Mahan to Sterling, December 23, 1898; Mahan to Barnes, July 21, 1898; *see also* Livezey, *Mahan on Sea Power*, 157–181.

25. Mahan to Lodge, July 27, 1898; Mahan to Clarke, August 17, 1898; Mahan to Long, August 15–20, 1898; Mahan, "The Transvaal and the Philippines," *The Independent* (February 1, 1900), 290; Mahan, "The Navy and the Philippines: Remarks to the Associate Alumni of the College of the City of New York," February 24, 1900, in *Letters and Papers*, III, 603; Mahan, *The Interest of America in International Conditions* (Boston: Little, Brown and Co., 1910), 86; Mahan, "Why Fortify the Panama Canal?," *North American Review* (March 1911), in Mahan, *Armaments and Arbitration* (Port Washington, N.Y.: Kennikat Press Reprint, 1973), 182. See also Livezey, *Mahan on Sea Power*, 182–187.

26. Mahan to Long, August 15–20, 1898. The naval stations that Mahan and the War Board recommended for acquisition or retention in mid-August 1898 were: In the Pacific, four: Manila or Subic Bay in the Philippines; Guam; Chang Tau or Tai Shei Shan in the Chushan Islands; and Pago-Pago in Samoa. At the isthmus, two: one on the west coast either at Punta Sacate in El Salvador, or at Port Elena or Salinas Bay, or Port Culebra in Costa Rica; the other on the east coast at Almirante Bay in Colombia's Department of Panama. In the Caribbean, two: one either at Guantánamo Bay, east of Santiago, or at the Bay of Nipe on the northeast coast

of Cuba; the other either at St. Thomas, or Samaná Bay in the Dominican Republic, or Culebra Island off the east coast of Puerto Rico. The board thus recommended a choice of eight of sixteen possible locations, Hawaii not considered.

PEACE, WAR, AND PERSONAL BATTLES, 1898–1901

1. Mahan to Luce, August 31, 1898; Mahan to Long, September 14, 1898; Mahan to Unidentified Addressee, October 12, 1898; Mahan to Kittelle, November 7, 1906.

2. Mahan, "The Work of the Naval War Board of 1898," in *Letters and Papers*, III, 636, 637, 642–643; Mahan to Clark, May 16, 1904; Mahan to Luce, January 27, 1908; Mahan, *Lessons of the War with Spain and Other Articles* (Boston: Little, Brown and Co., 1899), *passim*.

3. Mahan to Comptroller of the Treasury, October 18, 1898; Mahan to Long, October 26, 1898; Mahan, "Expenses Incurred While Traveling Under Orders from Rome, Italy, to New York, April 27–May 7, 1898," in *Letters and Papers*, III, 595.

4. West, *Admirals of American Empire*, 286–302; Mahan to Barnes, July 9, 1898, August 10, 1898; Mahan to Edith Kermit Carow Roosevelt, July 17, 1898; Mahan to Lodge, July 27, 1898, July 29, 1898; Mahan to Editor of *New York Sun*, August 5, 1898; Barnes to Mahan, August 9, 1898, in Taylor, *Life of Admiral Mahan*, 92. *See also* F. J. Higginson to Mahan, August 27, 1898, *ibid.*, 91–92.

5. Mahan to Long, November 16, 1898, December 12, 1899; Mahan to Gillender, December 27, 1898; Mahan to Editor, *New York Times*, November 15, 1899; Mahan, *Lessons of the War with Spain*, 33, 81, 177–182; Mahan to Johnson, December 3, 1899; West, *Admirals of American Empire*, 288–289, 291, 299–300.

6. Mahan to Lodge, February 19, 1901; West, *Admirals of American Empire*, 262–263, 300–302; Chadwick, *The Spanish-American War*, I, Appendix C, 409–414.

7. Mahan to Holt, December 22, 1901, January 3, 1902, January 6, 1902; Mahan to George, January 3, 1902; Mahan to Long, January 16, 1902; Mahan to Roosevelt, September 7, 1903; Mahan, "The Work of the Naval War Board of 1898," in *Letters and Papers*, III, 634–635; Mahan to Luce, October 17, 1911, October 20, 1911.

8. John D. Long, *The New American Navy*. 2 vols. (New York: The Outlook Company, 1903), I, 276–277; Mahan to Long, October 6, 1898, October 10, 1898.

9. Mahan's role in the First Hague Conference of 1899 is ably treated in Puleston, *Mahan*, 203–217, and Taylor, *Life of Admiral Mahan*, 94–101; Livezey, *Mahan on Sea Power*, 241–252, also summarizes Mahan's personal participation in the conference; Mahan to Brown, April 16, 1899; Mahan to Rhodes, April 28, 1899.

10. Mahan to Wingate, May 23, 1897, Footnote 2; Mahan to Johnson, April 8, 1899; Mahan to Brown, April 15, 1899, May 26, 1899; Mahan to Ashe, September 23, 1899.

11. Mahan to Ashe, September 23, 1899; Mahan to Brown, May 26, 1899, June 27, 1899; Mahan to Long, June 7, 1899 (two letters); Mahan to Rhodes, June 10, 1899; Mahan to Thursfield, June 17, 1899.

12. Mahan to *Comité d'Examen*, June 20, 1899; Mahan to Fisher, June 21, 1899, July 18, 1899 (three letters to Fisher of this date); Mahan to U.S. Commission, July 26, 1899, late July 1899; Puleston, *Mahan*, 208–210; Taylor, *Life of Admiral Mahan*, 158–159.

13. Puleston, *Mahan*, 210–214; Livezey, *Mahan on Sea Power*, 244–245; Mahan to Roosevelt, September 9, 1905; *see also* Mahan-Holls correspondence, Note 15 below.

14. Mahan to Long, August 21, 1899, September 27, 1899; Mahan to Rideing, August 20, 1899; Mahan to McBee, September 23, 1899; A. T. Mahan, "The Peace Conference and the Moral Aspect of War," *North American Review* (October 1899), 433–447, reprinted in *Lessons of the War with Spain* (1899) and in *Some Neglected Aspects of War* (1907); Mahan to Brown, September 23, 1899; Mahan to Ashe, September 23, 1899; Mahan to Thursfield, October 28, 1899; Mahan to Dodge, January 4, 1900. For supportive British reactions to Mahan's article, *see* the *London Morning Post*, October 17, 1899, and *The Public* (London), November 4, 1899, in Mahan Family Collection (NWC). Grace Hoadley Dodge (1856–1914) was the great-granddaughter of merchant prince David Low Dodge (1744–1852), early American pacifist and founder of the New York Peace Society, the first organization of its kind in the United States.

15. G. F. W. Holls, *The Peace Conference at The Hague and Its Bearings on International Law and Policy* (New York: The Macmillan Company, 1900), xxi, 268–271; Mahan to Holls, March 13, 1901; Mahan Memorandum, March 14, 1901; Mahan to Holls, March 25, 1901, April 9, 1901, December 10, 1901, December 23, 1901, March 12, 1902, March 17, 1902; Mahan to Crozier, December 31, 1901; Mahan to Long, April 25, 1901; Mahan to Low, April 4, 1901; Mahan to White, March 15, 1901, March 26, 1901, April 11, 1901, January 2, 1902, March 13, 1902; Mahan to Jarousse de Sillac, [late March 1901], August 20, 1901; Mahan to Moore, April 9, 1902, April 16, 1902. Copies of Holls's letters to Mahan, March 15, 1901, March 30, 1901, April 10, 1901, are in the Mahan Collection (LC).

16. Mahan to Lodge, February 7, 1899; Decker and Seager, *America's Major Wars*, II, 21–70; Robert Seager II, "The Progressives and American Foreign Policy, 1898–1917," Unpublished Ph.D. dissertation (Ohio State University, 1956), Chapter I; Millis, *The Martial Spirit*, 370–402.

17. Mahan to Gilman, October 23, 1898, October 27, 1898; Mahan to Editor, *The Churchman*, [early September 1899]; Mahan, "A Distinction Between Colonies and Dependencies," in *Letters and Papers*, III, 596; Mahan, "The Relation of the United States to Their New Dependencies," *Engineering Magazine* (January 1899), reprinted in *Lessons of the War with Spain* (1899), 241–253; Mahan to Long, June 7, 1899.

18. Mahan to Clark, May 3, 1901; Mahan to Roosevelt, January 25, 1902.

19. Mahan to McBee, September 23, 1899, October 13, 1899; Mahan to Thursfield, October 28, 1899, December 15, 1899; F. S. Roberts to Mahan, January 23, 1900, in Taylor, *Life of Admiral Mahan*, 187–188; Mahan to Rhodes, January 30, 1900; Mahan, "The Boer Republic and the Monroe Doctrine," *The Independent* (May 10, 1900), 1101–1103; Mahan to Editor, *New York Times*, January 20, 1900;

Mahan, "The Transvaal and the Philippine Islands," *The Independent* (February 1, 1900), 291; Mahan to Lodge, December 8, 1900.

20. Mahan to Thursfield, December 15, 1899; Mahan to Editor, *New York Times*, January 20, 1900, January 25, 1900; Mahan to Lodge, December 8, 1900; Mahan to Low, November 18, 1899; Mahan to Maxse, October 17, 1902; Mahan to Editor, *New York Evening Sun*, n.d. [late 1900] in Mahan Family Collection (NWC).

21. Mahan's Boer War articles were: "The Transvaal and the Philippine Islands," *The Independent* (February 1, 1900); "Merits of the Transvaal Dispute," *North American Review* (March 1900), 312–326, reprinted in his *The Problem of Asia and Its Effect Upon International Policies* (1900); "The Boer Republic and the Monroe Doctrine," *The Independent* (May 10, 1900); "The Influence of the South African War Upon the Prestige of the British Empire," *National Review* (December 1901), reprinted in his *Retrospect and Prospect: Studies in International Relations, Naval and Political* (1902). The unillustrated English edition of *The War in South Africa*, published by Sampson Low, Marston and Company, Ltd., of London, in December 1900, was titled *The Story of the War in South Africa, 1899–1900*. Mahan to Brown, April 9, 1900, April 15, 1900; Mahan to Rawson, May 31, 1900; Mahan to Clark, December 19, 1900; Mahan to Moore, May 7, 1900, May 11, 1900 (two letters to Moore of this date); C. Schwartz to R. J. Collier, [November 1900], and R. J. Collier to Mahan, November 21, 1900, in Taylor, *Life of Admiral Mahan*, 118–119.

22. Mahan to Brown, July 2, 1897, June 21, 1898, July 24, 1898, August 2, 1898, September 4, 1898, September 10, 1898, September 16, 1898, June 27, 1899, September 8, 1898, January 16, 1900, April 15, 1900, January 22, 1901, April 15, 1901, May 9, 1901. A proposed children's history of the United States was similarly considered and abandoned. *See* Mahan to Brown, May 9, 1901.

23. Mahan to Greene, August 12, 1900, September 17, 1900; Mahan to Fairchild, October 28, 1900; Mahan to Rhodes, November 9, 1900; Mahan to Roosevelt, March 12, 1901; Mahan to Clark, February 8, 1902.

HISTORIAN AND PHILOSOPHER OF HISTORY

1. Mahan, *From Sail to Steam*, 276–277; Puleston, *Mahan*, 68–70; Julius W. Pratt, "Alfred Thayer Mahan," in William T. Hutchinson, ed., *The Marcus W. Jernegan Essays in American Historiography* (Chicago: University of Chicago Press, 1937), 208–209; Mahan to Luce, July 20, 1907; Mahan to McIntyre, February 16, 1909; Mahan to Ellen Evans Mahan, May 25, 1894, June 7, 1894, August 29, 1894; Mahan to McBee, September 8, 1899. In the Lowell Lecture he delivered in Boston on March 31, 1897, Mahan stated that Raleigh and Bacon had been particularly "farseeing in asserting that the control of the sea meant the control of the wealth of the world." *See, Boston Herald*, April 1, 1897. The *Boston Advertiser* of April 1, 1897, quoted Mahan in the same lecture as saying that "The idea of controlling the sea came from the lips of Bacon, who saw the influence of sea power quite as well as we today."

2. Mahan, *The Influence of Sea Power Upon the French Revolution and Empire*, II, 372–373.

3. Mahan, *The Interest of America in Sea Power*, 284–285; Mahan to Ashe, December 9, 1908; Mahan to Stewart, May 23, 1908; Mahan to Billings, December 5, 1904; Mahan to Scudder, March 25, 1891. On subordination, *see also* Mahan to Clarke, January 29, 1895; Mahan to Thursfield, January 10, 1896.

4. Mahan to Luce, December 26, 1891; Mahan to Marston, February 19, 1897; Mahan, *From Sail to Steam*, 277; Mahan to G. W. Stadley and Co., October 14, 1895; Mahan to Johnson, March 25, 1898; Mahan to Brown, June 18, 1906. *See also* Mahan to Scudder, September 26, 1890.

5. Mahan to Luce, August 10, 1903; Mahan, *From Sail to Steam*, 168; Mahan to Scudder, September 26, 1890; Mahan to Brown, December 17, 1896, February 10, 1897; Mahan to Maxse, April 10, 1902.

6. Mahan to Wingate, May 23, 1897; Mahan to Little, Brown and Co., May 21, 1908, June 6, 1908, July 16, 1908; Mahan to Maxse, May 23, 1902; Mahan to Rhodes, January 3, 1901; Mahan to Brown, January 13, 1897.

7. Mahan to Ellen Kuhn Mahan, August 3, 1894; Mahan to Ellen Evans Mahan, August 29, 1894; Mahan to Scudder, October 8, 1890, February 3, 1893, March 27, 1893, May 13, 1893; Mahan to Maxse, August 21, 1903; Mahan to Brown, March 30, 1905, April 9, 1905, July 22, 1905, July 28, 1905; Mahan to Little, Brown and Co., September 13, 1910, September 15, 1910, September 26, 1910; Ellen Kuhn Mahan, "Recollections," in *Letters and Papers*, III, 729; Mahan to Ramsay, March 23, 1892; Mahan to Page, October 28, 1902; Mahan to Rhodes, May 20, 1906.

8. Mahan to Brown, June 9, 1893, December 17, 1896, July 2, 1897; Mahan to McLaughlin, January 17, 1905, April 28, 1905; Mahan to Kittelle, November 7, 1906; Mahan to Billings, February 13, 1905; Mahan to Jameson, December 24, 1899.

9. Mahan to Thursfield, November 21, 1895, January 10, 1896; Mahan to Brown, April 11, 1896, August 31, 1896.

10. Mahan to Rhodes, March 26, 1899; Herman Ausubel, *Historians and Their Craft: A Study of the Presidential Addresses of the American Historical Association, 1884–1945* (New York: Columbia University Press, 1950), 189–202; Hutchinson, *The Marcus W. Jernegan Essays in American Historiography*, 191–206, 252–270; Mahan to Maxse, June 17, 1904.

11. Mahan to Rhodes, October 5, 1908; Mahan to Scudder, August 12, 1894; Mahan to Jameson, July 11, 1895, July 22, 1895, July 26, 1895, October 14, 1895, October 20, 1896, December 12, 1896, December 16, 1896, January 9, 1897, March 8, 1897, June 1, 1897, December 27, 1897, April 21, 1898, November 1, 1898, January 3, 1899, April 8, 1899, October 2, 1899, November 2, 1899, December 24, 1899, September 1, 1906, September 10, 1906, October 13, 1909, February 18, 1910, November 14, 1913; McLaughlin to Mahan, March 31, 1902 (LC). Among the books declined by Mahan for review in the *American Historical Review* were: James Anthony Froude, *English Seamen in the Sixteenth Century. . . .* (1895); J. K. Laughton, ed., *Journal of Rear-Admiral Bartholomew James, 1752–1828* (1896); Robert A. P. H. Duncan, Earl of Camperdown, *Admiral Duncan* (1898); Edward Field, *Esek Hopkins. . . .* (1898); Charles de la Roncière, *Histoire de la marine française* (1899); William A. Fraser, *Hic et Ubique* (1893); James Barnes, *David G. Farragut* (1899); T. S. Jackson, ed., *Logs of the Great Sea Fights, 1794–1805* (1899); Edward K. Rawson, *Twenty Famous Naval Battles: Salamis to Santiago*

(1899); A. R. Colquhoun, *The Mastery of the Pacific* (1902); Charles P. Lucas, *The Canadian War of 1812* (1906); William Wood, ed., *The Logs of the Conquest of Canada* (1909); Charles O. Paullin, *Commodore John Rodgers. . . .* (1910); Julian S. Corbett, ed., *Private Papers of George, Second Earl Spencer, First Lord of the Admiralty, 1794–1801* (1913). Books reviewed by Mahan for the *American Historical Review* were: James Barnes, *Naval Actions of the War of 1812. . . .* (1896); M. Oppenheim, *History of the Administration of the Royal Navy and of Merchant Shipping in Relation to the Navy, 1509–1660* (1896); John Randolph Spears, *History of Our Navy from its Origin to the Present Day, 1775–1897* (1897); M. E. Matcham, *The Nelsons of Burnham Thorpe: A Record of a Norfolk Family* (1910); these reviews were published, respectively, in the *Review* for April 1897; July 1897, October 1897–January 1898, and October 1911. Mahan agreed to review Julian S. Corbett's *Drake and the Tudor Navy* (1898), but other obligations interfered.

12. Mahan to Jameson, October 14, 1895, December 12, 1896, November 6, 1900, January 18, 1901, July 27, 1905, August 11, 1905, October 9, 1905, October 23, 1905, July 25, 1906, July 31, 1906, May 18, 1908; Mahan to McLaughlin, December 17, 1902, January 11, 1903, January 17, 1905, February 21, 1905, April 28, 1905; Mahan to Perry, December 17, 1902, December 19, 1902, January 13, 1903; Mahan to Putnam, May 9, 1903; Mahan to Little, Brown and Co., May 9, 1908.

13. Mahan to Helen Evans Mahan, December 25, 1894; Mahan to Clarke, January 29, 1895; Mahan to Hart, January 5, 1901; Mahan to Rhodes, January 3, 1901, December 24, 1901; Mahan to Jameson, January 8, 1902; Mahan to A. H. Clark, November 1, 1902; Mahan to Haskins, December 2, 1902; Mahan to McLaughlin, May 9, 1905. It should be noted that from 1903 to 1914 Mahan served as a councilor of the American Historical Association as well as of the association-initiated federal government Committee on Documentary Historical Publications (in 1908). For his service and duties on this last, *see* Mahan to Stewart, April 9, 1908; Mahan to Turner, May 9, 1908; Mahan to Jameson, April 20, 1910; Mahan, "Testimony Before the House Committee on the Library," *Letters and Papers*, III, 676. He insisted, unsuccessfully, that the members of the Committee on Documentary Historical Publications be paid for their service thereon. In 1911 he served also on the AHA's committee on the Federal Archives Building.

14. Mahan, "Subordination in Historical Treatment," in *Naval Administration and Warfare*, 248–249; Mahan to Helen Evans Mahan, June 14, 1896; Mahan, *The Harvest Within: Thoughts on the Life of a Christian* (Boston: Little, Brown and Co., 1909); Edward M. Goulburn, *Thoughts on Personal Religion, Being a Treatise on the Christian Life in its Two Elements, Devotion and Grace*. First American from the Fifth London Edition (New York: D. Appleton and Co., 1865), 15, 23, 52, 177, 267–268, 282–283, 345–346.

15. Milo Mahan, *The Spiritual Point of View*, in Hopkins, ed., *Collected Works of Milo Mahan*, III, 219–228. Milo's *Palmoni . . . The Numerals of Scripture* (1862) and his *Mystic Numbers* (1875) are also reprinted in Hopkins, ed., *Collected Works of Milo Mahan*, the former in Vol. II, 7–154; the latter in Vol. II, 155–715. To this collection Hopkins contributed a "Memoir" of Milo Mahan, *ibid.*, III, xx–xxxii. The Hopkins quotations are in "Memoir," *ibid.*, III, xxiii, xxvi, and *ibid.*, II, 155. Palmoni, an obscure Hebrew spirit or angel, is identified by translators of the

King James version, in marginal exposition of a reference in Daniel 8:13, as "the numberer of secrets or the wonderful numberer." In this passage Daniel hears Palmoni speak to him while he is in a dream or trance. Milo Mahan equated Palmoni with God, *ibid.*, II, 135.

16. Hopkins, *Collected Works of Milo Mahan*, II, 125, 134–135, 135–136, 23, 60, 117, 122.

17. *Ibid.*, II, 207, 207–208, 209, 214–215, 217, 346, 347. The cardinal or key numbers (dates) in early U.S. history, Milo argued, were 1765 (Stamp Act Congress), 1776 (Declaration of Independence), 1778 (Franco-American Alliance), and 1789 (Federal Union). All these numbers, he marveled, were multiples of Thirteen. "It is curious that the Christian era date gives the *condition* on which alone human liberty can be achieved," he wrote. "1776 is twice 888 or eight times 222, numbers of JESUS and the Incarnation. 'If the SON shall make you free, ye shall be free indeed.'" *Ibid.*, II, 254. For the "Thirteen-ness" of the American Civil War, *see also, ibid.*, II, 345.

18. Hopkins, *Collected Works of Milo Mahan*, II, 255, 265, 330. The most pervasive of all of Milo Mahan's Divine Numbers was the number 153. "It shows," he maintained, "the reality and certainty of the numerical plan, that in every place where I have been led to look for the number 153, I have invariably found it." *Ibid.*, II, 612. God the Father, God the Son, and God the 153; or seek and ye shall find.

19. Mahan, "Subordination in Historical Treatment," in *Naval Administration and Warfare*, 251, 248, 264–265, 260, 261, 263, 252, 267, 254–255, 271, 272; Mahan, "The Practical in Christianity: An Address Delivered in the Church of the Holy Trinity, Middletown, Connecticut, March 22, 1899," in Mahan, *The Harvest Within*, 275–276, 279.

20. Mahan to McIntyre, February 16, 1909; Mahan to Brown, June 18, 1906; Mahan to Moore, June 1, 1912; Mahan, "Subordination in Historical Treatment," in *Naval Administration and Warfare*, 256–257; Mahan, "The Principles of Naval Administration," *National Review* (June 1903), *ibid.*, 20; Mahan, "The Strength of Nelson," *National Review* (November 1905), *ibid.*, 275–280. For a discussion of *The Harvest Within*, see Chapter XX.

21. Mahan, *The Problem of Asia and Its Effect Upon International Policies* (Boston: Little, Brown and Co., 1900), 29–30, 46.

22. Mahan to Merrell, December 20, 1908. The quotation is a composite of sentiments found in Mahan to Roosevelt, December 27, 1904; Mahan, "About What is the War?," in *Letters and Papers*, III, 703; Mahan to Luce, July 8, 1907; and Mahan to Corbett, August 12, 1907.

23. Mahan to Clarke, October 1, 1909; Mahan to Maxse, December 24, 1912; Mahan to Editor, *New York Times*, November 2, 1910; Mahan, "Comments on the Seizure of Private Property at Sea," in *Letters and Papers*, III, 626; Mahan, "The Work of the Naval War Board of 1898," *ibid.*, III, 638; Mahan to Reynolds, September 11, 1914; Mahan to Henderson, May 17, 1910.

24. Mahan to Editor, *New York Times*, August 31, 1914; Mahan to Clark, January 28, 1909, October 1, 1909; Mahan to Henderson, February 16, 1909, May 17, 1910; Mahan to Little, Brown and Co., June 7, 1913; Mahan, "About What is the

War?," in *Letters and Papers*, III, 703; Mahan, "Why Not Disarm?," *ibid.*, III, 685–686; Mahan to Stein, November 10, 1906; Mahan to FitzHugh, January 18, 1913.

25. Mahan to Ashe, September 23, 1899; Mahan to Thursfield, October 28, 1899; Mahan to Dodge, January 4, 1900; Mahan, "Thoughts on the Righteousness of War," in *Letters and Papers*, III, 683; Mahan, "Why Not Disarm?," *ibid.*, III, 686; Mahan, "War From the Christian Standpoint," in *Some Neglected Aspects of War* (Boston: Little, Brown and Co., 1907), 97–114; Mahan, "A Twentieth Century Outlook," in *The Interest of America in Sea Power*, 268; Mahan, "The Place of Force in International Relations," in *Armaments and Arbitration* (Port Washington, N.Y.: Kennikat Press Reprint, 1973), 116–117, 119. In arguing his contention that the Bible supported the concept of Christ as a man on horseback, and Christianity as the onward march of Christian soldiers, Mahan variously cited Romans 13:4; Luke 19:45, 22:36–37; John 2:15, 18:10–11, 36; Matthew 21:12, 26:52–54; and Mark 9:15.

26. The quotation is a composite of remarks found in Mahan to Ashe, January 3, 1897; Mahan to Clarke, February 22, 1898; Mahan, "Personality and Influence," in *Letters and Papers*, III, 616, 619; and Mahan to FitzHugh, January 18, 1913. Mahan, "Introduction to K. Asami's Biography of Tasuka Serata," in *Letters and Papers*, III, 690. On man's fallen nature, *see* Mahan to Helen Evans Mahan, July 9, 1890.

27. Mahan to Merrell, May 31, 1909; Mahan to Little, Brown and Co., February 20, 1911; Mahan to Moody, February 1, 1909; Mahan to Henderson, February 16, 1909; Mahan to Kittelle, November 7, 1906; Mahan to Helen Evans Mahan, December 25, 1893.

28. The Colomb remark is in *The Times* (London) for July 7, 1904. Mahan attended the dinner. Silas McBee to Theodore Roosevelt, January 25, 1915 (Univ. of North Carolina).

DIPLOMATIC AND NAVAL AFFAIRS IN THE FAR EAST, 1899–1913

1. Mahan, "The Navy and the Philippines," *Letters and Papers*, III, 603; Mahan, "The Effect of Asiatic Conditions Upon World Policies," *North American Review* (November 1900), in Mahan, *The Problem of Asia* (Port Washington, N.Y.: Kennikat Press Reprint, 1970), 41, 65, 120, 175, 176; *Foreign Relations of the United States* (1899), 299; *ibid.* (1915), 114–115; P. J. Treat, *Diplomatic Relations Between the United States and Japan, 1895–1905* (Palo Alto, Calif.: Stanford University Press, 1938), 109–112.

2. Mahan to Craig, October 30, 1899; Mahan to Brown, April 9, 1900, April 15, 1900, January 22, 1901, July 28, 1905; Mahan, *The Problem of Asia* (Boston: Little, Brown and Co., 1900), viii. For a discussion of Mackinder and Mahan in a geopolitical context, *see* Livezey, *Mahan on Sea Power*, 286–289.

3. Mahan, *The Problem of Asia*, 1–146; Mahan, "The Effect of Asiatic Conditions Upon World Policies," *ibid.*, 147–202; Livezey, *Mahan on Sea Power*, 191–199.

4. Mahan, *The Problem of Asia*, 25–26, 56, 63, 105–106; Mahan to Ellen Evans Mahan, December 30, 1894; Mahan to Roosevelt, May 1, 1897; Mahan to Ashe, September 23, 1899; Mahan to Sterling, December 23, 1898.

5. Mahan to McKinley, September 2, 1900; Mahan to Roosevelt, March 12, 1901.

6. Mahan to Maxse, February 21, 1902, March 7, 1902, May 27, 1902, July 22, 1902, July 25, 1902, May 14, 1904, June 17, 1904, November 22, 1904, July 30, 1907; Mahan to Clark, September 6, 1907. Mahan's most complete public statement on this question was his article, "The Persian Gulf and International Relations," *National Review* (September 1902), in Mahan, *Retrospect and Prospect* (Port Washington, N.Y.: Kennikat Press Reprint, 1968), 209–251.

7. Mahan to Maxse, February 21, 1902.

8. Edward H. Zabriskie, *American-Russian Rivalry in the Far East: A Study in Diplomacy and Power Politics, 1895–1914* (Philadelphia: University of Pennsylvania Press, 1946), 101–130; Mahan to Editor, *New York Times*, November 14, 1904; Mahan to Maxse, June 17, 1904, August 20, 1904, November 22, 1904. Mahan argued that the strategic center of the land war was Newchwang (now Yingkow), key to a Japanese incursion into the Liaotung Peninsula from the north. The author is indebted to Professor Mark R. Peattie for information on the Mahan-Akiyama relationship in 1898. Neither Dr. Peattie nor the present writer has been able to find any Mahan-Akiyama correspondence. Akiyama served on the staff of the Japanese Naval Staff College at the time of the Russo-Japanese War and later helped develop tactical doctrine in the Japanese Navy, a doctrine that increasingly veered away from Mahan's emphasis on tactical concentration and toward the concept of enveloping an inferior enemy force with divided (though mutually supportive) squadrons.

9. Mahan to Clark, May 16, 1904; Mahan to Maxse, November 22, 1904, September 14, 1905, November 9, 1905, January 15, 1906; Mahan, "Appreciation of Conditions in the Russo-Japanese War," Two Parts, *Collier's Weekly*, February 20, 1904, and April 30, 1904; Mahan, "Torpedo Craft vs. Battleships," *ibid.*, May 21, 1904. Similar concerns and observations, also rather superficial and speculative, found their way into Mahan, "Principles Involved in the War Between Japan and Russia," *National Review* (September 1904), in *Naval Administration and Warfare* (1908), 89–129. The article, written in Switzerland in August 1904, was an attempt, in part, to minimize the combat importance of torpedo vessels.

10. Mahan, "The Problems That Rojestvensky and Togo Must Solve," *Collier's Weekly*, May 13, 1905; Mahan, "The Battle of the Sea of Japan," *ibid.*, June 17, 1905; Mahan, "Retrospect Upon the War Between Japan and Russia," *National Review* (May 1906) and *Living Age* (July 14, 1906), in *Naval Administration and Warfare*, 133–173. For similar views on his opposition to dividing the battle fleet, see Mahan to Editor, *New York Sun*, January 28, 1907; Mahan to Perkins, January 11, 1911.

11. Mahan to Henderson, May 17, 1910; Mahan to Clark, September 11, 1908; A. Whitney Griswold, *The Far Eastern Policy of the United States* (New York: Harcourt, Brace and Co., 1938), 344–359.

12. Mahan to Maxse, May 30, 1907, June 28, 1907, July 30, 1907; Mahan to Luce, July 8, 1907; Mahan to Clark, September 6, 1907, July 23, 1909, March 10, 1910, March 12, 1912; Mahan to Roosevelt, June 19, 1911, December 2, 1911; Mahan to Editor, *The Times* (London), June 13, 1913.

13. Mahan to Clark, September 6, 1907; Mahan, "The Value of the Pacific Cruise of the United States Fleet, Prospect," *Scientific American* (December 7, 1907); and

Mahan, "The Value of the Pacific Cruise of the United States Fleet, Retrospect," *Collier's Weekly* (August 28, 1908), combined and reprinted in *Naval Administration and Warfare*, 307–353; Mahan to Luce, November 18, 1907; William R. Braisted, *The United States Navy in the Pacific, 1897–1909* (Austin, Texas: University of Texas Press, 1958), 223–232. *See also* Elting E. Morison, *Admiral Sims and the Modern American Navy* (Boston: Houghton Mifflin Co., 1942), 182–184.

14. Mahan to Little, Brown and Co., June 6, 1908, July 16, 1908, July 19, 1908, July 24, 1908, September 30, 1908, October 5, 1908, October 6, 1908; Goodrich to Mahan, September 12, 1908 (LC), September 15, 1908 (LC); Mahan to Goodrich, September 14, 1908; Mahan to Loeb, September 30, 1908; Mahan, "The Value of the Pacific Cruise of the United States Fleet, Retrospect," in *Naval Administration and Warfare*, 339–340, 341–344, 353; Mahan to Clark, September 11, 1908.

15. Mahan to Rodgers, February 22, 1911, March 4, 1911, March 17, 1911; Mahan to Meyer, April 21, 1911; Mahan to Andrews, September 24, 1910; *Notes on Comments of Rear Admiral Mahan* (War College Response to Mahan's February 22 Critique of Strategic War Plan of 1911), circa February 25–March 1, 1911 (NWC). In the discussion supported by these notes the word "Orange" has been rendered as Japan or Japanese; the word "Blue" has been rendered as United States, America, or American; William R. Braisted, *The United States Navy in the Pacific, 1909–1922* (Austin, Texas: University of Texas Press, 1971), 30–35.

16. Mahan to Rodgers, April 14, 1911, May 13, 1911; Mahan to Meyer, April 21, 1911; Mahan to Andrews, September 24, 1910; Mahan to Henderson, March 28, 1912; Mahan to Roosevelt, July 8, 1913; Mahan to Root, July 9, 1913; Mahan to Ashe, June 7, 1912; Mahan to Johnson, March 31, 1911.

MR. MONROE, KAISER BILL, AND
THE BALANCE OF POWER, 1899–1913

1. Livezey, *Mahan on Sea Power*, 143–156; Mahan to Clark, February 8, 1902; Mahan to Moore, November 27, 1902; Mahan to Low, February 15, 1900; Mahan, "The Effect of Asiatic Conditions Upon World Policies," *North American Review* (September 1900), in Mahan, *The Problem of Asia*, 180–186; Mahan to Editor, *New York Evening Post*, November 8, 1911; Mahan to Maxse, December 24, 1912; Mahan to Editor, *New York Times*, June 2, 1911, December 7, 1911. Mahan's thoughts on the fortification of a canal were later summarized in "Why Fortify the Panama Canal?," *North American Review* (March 1911), reprinted in his 1912 *Armaments and Arbitration; The Place of Force in the International Relations of States* (Port Washington, N.Y.: Kennikat Press Reprint, 1912), 181–195.

2. Livezey, *Mahan on Sea Power*, 144–145; Dexter Perkins, *The Monroe Doctrine, 1867–1907* (Baltimore, Md.: Johns Hopkins University Press, 1937), 333–335; Mahan to Maxse, October 3, 1902, December 22, 1902, February 7, 1903; Mahan, "The Monroe Doctrine," *National Review* (February 1903), reprinted (with a 1908 addendum) in Mahan, *Naval Administration and Warfare* (1908), 395–396; Addendum (1908), 397–409. Several paragraphs of the "Monroe Doctrine" article, for which Mahan received $500 from Maxse, were cabled by the *National Review* to

the *New York Sun*, where they were reprinted and commented upon. As Mahan had hoped, the article exhibited the "characteristic of opportuneness" which he worked to achieve in his pieces on foreign policy. Mahan to Maxse, February 7, 1903. In 1909 he was pleased to be told by a former U.S. Supreme Court justice that "the article contained in compact form *all* that the ordinary man needed to know about the Monroe Doctrine." Mahan to Little, Brown and Co., October 28, 1911.

3. In the extensive literature on the subject, there is no more accurate (or humorous) account of American intervention in Panama in 1903 than that in Thomas A. Bailey's standard text, *A Diplomatic History of the American People*, 8th edition (New York: Appleton-Century-Crofts, 1969), 486–498; *see also* Seager, "The Progressives and American Foreign Policy," 93–108; Mahan to Moore, November 27, 1902.

4. Mahan to Moore, June 1, 1912; Mahan, "Was Panama 'A Chapter of National Dishonor'?," *North American Review* (October 1912), in *Armaments and Arbitration*, 218–250; Mahan to Taylor, December 7, 1903; Mahan to Clark, July 23, 1909; Mahan, "Germany's Naval Ambition," *Collier's Weekly* (April 24, 1909), 12–13; Mahan to Editor, *New York Times*, April 2, 1912, May 22, 1912; Mahan, "The Panama Canal and Sea Power in the Pacific," *Century Magazine* (June 1911), in *Armaments and Arbitration*, 155–180; Mahan, "The Panama Canal and the Distribution of the Fleet," *North American Review* (September 1914), 406–417. Mahan opposed the Panama Canal Act of August 1912, which exempted U.S. coastwise shipping from paying tolls, as a violation of the 1901 Hay-Pauncefote Treaty, which held that the canal should be open to "all nations" on the basis of "entire equality." He described it as "obnoxious" legislation which "has demonstrated the need of a navy by bringing all Europe down on the Monroe Doctrine." Mahan to Dohrman, September 2, 1912; Mahan to FitzHugh, January 18, 1903; Seager, "The Progressives and American Foreign Policy," 212–223.

5. Mahan to Maxse, October 3, 1902, April 28, 1903; Mahan to Moore, February 26, 1912; Mahan to Henderson, March 28, 1912; Mahan to Editor, *New York Times*, May 22, 1912. The quotation on the Monroe Doctrine is a composite of observations found in Mahan to Stewart, March 19, 1909; Mahan to Editor, *New York Times*, May 22, 1912; and Mahan, "Why Not Disarm" (September 1913), in *Letters and Papers*, III, 687. On aspects of these same points, *see* Mahan to Henderson, May 17, 1910; Mahan to Roosevelt, June 19, 1911; Mahan to Lodge, January 8, 1912; Mahan to Maxse, February 26, 1912.

6. Mahan, "The Monroe Doctrine," *National Review* (February 1903), in *Naval Administration and Warfare*, 357–409; Mahan, "The Problem of Asia," *Harper's Monthly* (March and April 1900), in *The Problem of Asia*, 16–17, 85–86; Mahan, "The Effect of Asiatic Conditions Upon World Policies," *North American Review* (November 1900), in *The Problem of Asia*, 202; Livezey, *Mahan on Sea Power*, 146–147; Mahan to FitzHugh, March 9, 1912; Mahan to Stewart, March 19, 1909; Mahan to Clark, March 10, 1910.

7. Mahan to Thursfield, December 1, 1897, January 25, 1898; Mahan to Maxse, June 12, 1902, July 14, 1902, July 22, 1902, July 25, 1902; Mahan to Roosevelt, August 14, 1906 (misdated circa July 20, 1906 in *Letters and Papers*, III, 164).

8. Mahan to Henderson, December 26, 1910; Mahan to Stewart, March 19, 1909; Mahan, "Germany's Naval Ambitions," *Collier's Weekly* (April 24, 1909), 12–13; Mahan to Editor, *The Daily Mail* (London), June 1910 (published July 4 and 6, 1910); Mahan to Johnson, February 8, 1911 (Enclosure); Mahan to Lodge, January 8, 1912; Mahan to FitzHugh, June 7, 1911, March 9, 1912; Mahan to Moore, February 26, 1912; Mahan to Editor, *New York Times*, April 2, 1912.

9. Mahan, "Motives to Imperial Federation," *National Review* (May 1902), in Mahan, *Retrospect and Prospect*, 89–135; Mahan to Henderson, June 1, 1902. For Mahan's interest in and advocacy of imperial federation *see* Mahan to Maxse, December 26, 1901, March 7, 1902, August 21, 1903; Mahan to Henderson, June 18, 1904, Footnote 1; Mahan to Thursfield, January 22, 1906; *see also* Mahan's remarks on the subject at the Imperial Federation Committee dinner in London on July 6, 1904, as reported in *The Times*, July 7, 1904; Mahan, "Personality and Influence: A Commencement Address at Dartmouth College" (June 24, 1903), in *Letters and Papers*, III, 609. For Mahan's support of the British imperial preferential tariff system, *see* Mahan to Maxse, August 21, 1903, November 9, 1905; Mahan to Thursfield, January 22, 1906.

10. Mahan to Maxse, June 11, 1903; Mahan to Stewart, March 19, 1909; Mahan, "Germany's Naval Ambitions," *Collier's Weekly* (April 24, 1909); Mahan to Clark, September 11, 1908, July 23, 1909, October 1, 1909, March 10, 1910; Mahan to Editor, *New York Times*, May 22, 1912; Mahan to Henderson, January 19, 1907, February 16, 1909. Fisher's reforms on fleet distribution and the dreadnought issue in the Royal Navy are treated in Arthur J. Marder, *The Anatomy of British Sea Power* (New York: Alfred A. Knopf, 1940), 483–545.

11. Mahan to Root, April 20, 30, 1906; Mahan to Roosevelt, July 20, 1906. The quotation on immunity is a composite taken from Mahan to Maxse, November 9, 1906, April 30, 1907. *See also* Mahan to Maxse, January 22, 1907, May 10, 1907, May 30, 1907; Mahan to Henderson, February 16, 1909; Mahan to Editor, *New York Times*, November 2, 1910.

12. Mahan to Roosevelt, December 27, 1904, August 14, 1906 (misdated circa July 20, 1906, in *Letters and Papers*, III, 164); Livezey, *Mahan on Sea Power*, 249–252; Mahan to Root, April 20, 1906; Taylor, *Life of Admiral Mahan*, 149–152; Mahan, "Comments on the Seizure of Private Property at Sea," in *Letters and Papers*, III, 623–626; Mahan to Dewey, July 29, 1906; Mahan to Sims, August 6, 1906; Mahan to Maxse, August 21, 1906, April 30, 1907, May 30, 1907, June 28, 1907, July 30, 1907; Mahan, "The Hague Conference: The Question of Immunity For Belligerent Merchant Shipping," *National Review* (June 1907) and *Living Age* (July 6, 1907); Mahan, "The Hague Conference and the Practical Aspect of War," *National Review* (July 1907) and *Living Age* (July 27, 1907), both reprinted in Mahan, *Some Neglected Aspects of War* (Boston: Little, Brown and Co., 1907), 157–193, 57–93; Mahan to Roosevelt, October 22, 1906; Mahan, "Retrospect Upon the War Between Japan and Russia," *National Review* (May 1906), in *Naval Administration and Warfare*, 133–173. The all-big-gun-ship controversy is discussed in Chapter XIX.

13. Mahan to McIntyre, July 30, 1910, August 13, 1910, August 26, 1910; Mahan to Little, Brown and Co., August 29, 1910, September 13, 1910, October 1, 1910, October 8, 1910.

14. The articles were titled, in order, "The Origin and Character of Present International Groupings in Europe," in Mahan, *The Interest of America in International Conditions* (Boston: Little, Brown and Co., 1910), 3–68; "The Present Predominance of Germany in Europe—Its Foundations and Tendencies," *ibid.*, 71–124; "Relations Between the East and the West," *ibid.*, 127–185; and "The Open Door," *ibid.*, 189–212. Page references in *The Interest of America in International Conditions* specifically supporting this discussion of the book are 23, 26, 35–37, 39–40, 47–48, 53–56, 61–68, 74–80, 89–94, 102–104, 110–114, 117–123, 130–131, 144, 146–148, 162–174, 178–179, 182, 184–185, 189–192, 198–199, 204–206, 209–210. There was a good deal of repetition and redundancy of argument in these four essays, written as they were initially for separate publication as articles. *See also* Mahan, "Britain and World Peace," *The Daily Mail* (London), October 31, 1910; Mahan, "The International Significance of German Naval Development," *ibid.*, July 4, 1910, July 6, 1910; Mahan to Editor, *The Daily Mail* (circa June 1910).

THE NEW NEW NAVY, 1900–1914

1. Harold and Margaret Sprout, *The Rise of American Naval Power*, 259–285; Marder, *The Anatomy of British Sea Power*, 515–545; Bauer, *Ships of the Navy*, 93–101; Mahan to Henderson, February 16, 1909.

2. Livezey, *Mahan on Sea Power*, 231; Mahan to Taylor, July 19, 1895; Mahan, "Distinguishing Qualities of Ships of War" (November 1898), in *Lessons of the War with Spain*, 261–265; Mahan to Long, January 31, 1900, February 15, 1900; N. L. Klado, *The Battle of the Sea of Japan. . . .* (London: Hodder and Stoughton, 1906); Mahan to Editor, *New York Sun*, May 9, 1904; Mahan to Roosevelt, October 16, 1902, December 27, 1904, August 14, 1906 (misdated circa July 20, 1906, in *Letters and Papers*, III, 164), September 30, 1906 (misdated circa October 8, 1906, in *Letters and Papers*, III, 178), October 22, 1906, January 10, 1907; Mahan to Sims, August 6, 1906, Footnote 2, October 3, 1906, November 16, 1906; Mahan to Alger, January 10, 1907; Mahan to Henderson, January 19, 1907; Mahan, "Some Reflections Upon the Far Eastern War," *National Review* (May 1906), retitled "Retrospect Upon the War Between Japan and Russia," in *Naval Administration and Warfare*, 133–173; Mahan, "Reflections, Historic and Other, Suggested by the Battle of the Sea of Japan," U.S. Naval Institute *Proceedings* (June 1906), 447–471; W. S. Sims, "The Inherent Tactical Qualities of All-Big-Gun, One-Caliber Battleships of High Speed, Large Displacement and Gunpower," *ibid.*, (December 1906), 1337–1366; E. E. Morison, *Admiral Sims and the Modern American Navy* (Boston: Houghton Mifflin Co., 1942), 156–175. *See also* Puleston, *Mahan*, 272–274.

3. William S. Sims Collection (LC). *See* especially letters to Sims from C. F. Goodrich, B. A. Fiske, C. S. Sperry, S. B. Luce, J. Hood, H. B. Gillman, C. S. Stanworth, C. J. Bailey, and Admiral Sir John Fisher in support of Sims's position against Mahan in the all-big-gun fight; Mahan to Balch, March 4, 1908; Mahan to Roosevelt, October 22, 1906; Mahan to Alger, January 10, 1907; Mahan to Clark, January 15, 1907; Mahan to Rodgers, March 4, 1911.

4. Mahan to Henderson, February 16, 1909, May 17, 1910; Mahan to Clark, May 16, 1904; Mahan to Roosevelt, January 13, 1909; Mahan, "Comments on the Arma-

ment of Battleships," in *Letters and Papers*, III, 679–681; Mahan, "The Battleships of All-Big-Guns," *World's Work* (January 1911), 13898–13902; Mahan, "The Origins of the European War: Interview with the *New York Evening Post*, August 3, 1914," in *Letters and Papers*, III, 700; Holloway H. Frost, *The Battle of Jutland* (Annapolis, Md.: U.S. Naval Institute Press, 1936), 102, 506–509, 539–542.

5. Mahan, "The Submarine and Its Enemies," *Collier's Weekly* (April 6, 1907), 17–21; Bauer, *Ships of the Navy*, 246–249. In 1914 Britain had 97 boats built and building, France had 86, the United States had 49, and Germany had 45. *See* E. B. Potter and J. R. Fredland, eds., *The United States and World Sea Power* (Englewood Cliffs, N.J.: Prentice-Hall, Inc., 1955), 465–466; Mahan to Andrews, September 24, 1910; Mahan to Rodgers, February 22, 1911; Mahan to Meyer, April 21, 1911; Mahan to Clark, October 1, 1914; Mahan to Marston, October 14, 1914; Mahan, "Sea Power in the Present European War," *Leslie's Illustrated Weekly* (August 20, 1914) [written August 1–3, 1914], in *Letters and Papers*, III, 706–710.

6. H. and M. Sprout, *The Rise of American Naval Power*, 276–280; Morison, *Admiral Sims and the Modern American Navy*, 198–234; Ronald Spector, *Admiral of the New Empire: The Life and Career of George Dewey* (Baton Rouge, La.: Louisiana State University Press, 1974), 122–128; Puleston, *Mahan*, 287–292; Mahan to Roosevelt, September 7, 1903; Mahan, "The United States Navy Department," *Scribner's Magazine* (May 1903), 567–577, and Mahan, "Principles of Naval Administration," *National Review* (June 1903), 546–565, both reprinted in Mahan, *Naval Administration and Warfare* (1908); Mahan to Bonaparte, June 26, 1906; Mahan to Luce, July 11, 1906; Mahan to Dewey, July 13, 1906, July 19, 1906, September 5, 1906; Mahan, "The Work of the Naval War Board of 1898," in *Letters and Papers*, III, 627–643. Details of the Newport (Battleship) Conference of 1908 are in Knight and Puleston, *Naval War College*, Chapter XXIV (1908).

7. Taylor, *Life of Admiral Mahan*, 109–111; Mahan to Roosevelt, January 13, 1909; Mahan to Root, April 20, 1906; Mahan to Moody, January 28, 1909, February 1, 1909, February 3, 1909, February 22, 1909; Mahan to Billings, January 30, 1909, February 2, 1909; Mahan to Luce, February 2, 1909, February 11, 1909, Footnote 1; Mahan to Henderson, February 16, 1909; Mahan to Gordon, n.d. [March 1909].

8. Mahan to Meyer, February 1, 1911, April 21, 1911; Mahan to Andrews, September 24, 1910; Mahan, "Reminiscences of Service at the Naval War College," in *Letters and Papers*, III, 663–667. *See also* Mahan, "The Advantages of Subig Bay Over Manila as a Base in the Philippine Islands" (October 25, 1907), in *Letters and Papers*, III, 658–662; Mahan to Merrell, May 22, 1909; Mahan to Rodgers, April 30, 1910, May 25, 1910, August 23, 1910, August 31, 1910, September 15, 1910, February 22, 1911, April 14, 1911; Mahan to Little, Brown and Co., February 1, 1911, June 14, 1911, July 8, 1911.

9. Mahan, *Naval Strategy, Compared and Contrasted With the Principles and Practice of Military Operations on Land* (Westport, Conn.: Greenwood Press Reprint, 1975), 299–302, 346–347, 383–431, and *passim*; *Morning Post* (London), January 26, 1912 (NWC); *The Standard* (London), January 21, 1912 (NWC); Taylor, *Life of Admiral Mahan*, 127–128; Mahan to Roosevelt, March 1, 1893, July 1, 1911, December 2, 1911, December 23, 1911; Mahan to Clark, January 15, 1907, Decem-

ber 15, 1911, March 12, 1912; Mahan to Luce, September 30, 1897, July 11, 1906, December 15, 1906, December 21, 1906, July 8, 1907, November 18, 1907, June 17, 1908; Mahan to Merrell, June 5, 1908; Mahan to Brown, November 24, 1898; Mahan to Stewart, May 16, 1908; Mahan to Rodgers, October 22, 1909, September 28, 1910, Footnote 2, October 19, 1910, December 15, 1910, Footnote 2, July 26, 1911; Mahan to Little, Brown and Co., March 8, 1913; *Register of the Commissioned and Warrant Officers of the Navy of the United States and of the Marine Corps to January 1, 1907* (Washington, D.C.: Government Printing Office, 1907), 231–233; *Ibid.* . . . *to January 1, 1914* (Washington, D.C.: Government Printing Office, 1914), 295–297; R. P. Rodgers to Chief of Bureau of Navigation, July 31, 1911 (NWC).

10. Mahan to Luce, June 17, 1908; Mahan to Stewart, May 16, 1908, May 23, 1908, December 23, 1910, March 11, 1911; Mahan to Merrell, November 17, 1908, November 30, 1908, December 20, 1908, May 22, 1909, May 31, 1909, July 23, 1909, July 31, 1909, August 26, 1909; Mahan to Clark, October 1, 1909, March 10, 1910, October 27, 1911; Mahan to Little, December 15, 1910; Mahan to Rodgers, January 20, 1910, February 3, 1910, March 18, 1910, April 16, 1910, May 11, 1911, May 13, 1911, June 19, 1911, June 26, 1911, July 26, 1911, August 12, 1911; Mahan to Roosevelt, August 25, 1911. Mahan sent inscribed complimentary copies of *Naval Strategy* to S. B. Luce, R. P. Rodgers, W. McC. Little, Gen. William Crozier, Gen. Leonard Wood, J. K. Laughton, and to his brother-in-law in Pau, France, Dr. F. Leonard Brown. *See* Mahan to Little, Brown and Co., October 31, 1911.

11. Mahan to Merrell, November 30, 1908, December 20, 1908; Mahan to Meyer, Ferbruary 1, 1911; Mahan to Stewart, July 22, 1911; Mahan to Rodgers, August 12, 1911; Ellen Evans Mahan to Luce, December 12, 1907; Mahan to Luce, April 6, 1908; Mahan, *Naval Strategy*, 1–3, 7–10, 15–18, 279, 386, 391–393, 415, 422–423, 428–429. The Russo-Japanese War is treated *ibid.*, 383–431. *See also* Puleston, *Mahan*, 307–317, for a less critical view of Mahan's *Naval Strategy* book and its subject matter. It should also be noted in this regard that Puleston's attempts to identify Mahan's strategic and tactical concepts with those set forth by Clausewitz in his essay *On War* are not persuasive. Indeed, there is no certain evidence that Mahan read Clausewitz's book, although it is likely that he did in 1910 while preparing *Naval Strategy* for press. *See* Puleston, *Mahan*, 295–298.

12. Julian S. Corbett, *Some Principles of Maritime Strategy*, new impression (Annapolis, Md.: Naval Institute Press, 1972), viii, x–xiii, xv–xvi, 1–2, 5–7, 8, 79, 89–90, 92–97, 99, 113–116, 123–126, 128–135, 157–163, 170–172, 268–273. The excellent foreword (vii–xvi) to this edition, written in August 1971, is by B. McL. Ranft, Professor of History at the Royal Naval College, Greenwich.

13. Mahan to Fourth Auditor of the Treasury, October 11, 1909, October 28, 1909, November 3, 1909 (two letters), November 19, 1909, November 30, 1909, December 10, 1909; Mahan to Tracewell, February 16, 1910, March 9, 1910; Mahan to Meyer, November 3, 1909, March 9, 1910; Mahan to Rodgers, February 17, 1910, March 9, 1910, April 17, 1910, May 3, 1911; Mahan to Gordon, May 20, 1914, June 19, 1914, June 25, 1914, June 29, 1914, July 24, 1914, August 7, 1914; Gordon, Petition in Court of Claims, Washington, D.C. in *Alfred T. Mahan* vs. *The United States*, circa August 5, 1914 (LC); Book of Job, 1:21.

CONCERNS SPIRITUAL, LITERARY, AND POLITICAL, 1900–1914

1. Mahan to Editor, *New York Times*, November 1, 1899; Mahan to Low, March 10, 1896; Mahan to Ellen Evans Mahan, October 8, 1894; Mahan to Greene, August 12, 1900; Mahan to Gillender, February 21, 1896, July 1, 1896, October 15, 1903. Gillender (the Mahans occasionally saw him socially in New York) who Mahan nominated for membership in the Century Club, soon after this developed paresis, dropped out of Mahan's life, and gave up his law practice. *See* Mahan to Demarest, July 15, 1913.

2. Mahan to Clark, March 12, 1912. For Mahan's club life in New York, *see* Mahan to Gillender, July 1, 1896; Mahan to Rhodes, November 9, 1900, December 12, 1904, April 8, 1908, July 4, 1908, January 26, 1909; Mahan to Thursfield, January 12, 1899; Mahan to Low, June 9, 1902, November 17, 1902; Mahan to Billings, January 17, 1903; Mahan to Moore, December 26, 1901, January 28, 1902, January 30, 1902, May 23, 1902, February 3, 1905; Mahan to Little, Brown and Co., November 11, 1908, April 11, 1913; Mahan to Henderson, February 16, 1909; Mahan to Merrell, April 24, 1909; Mahan to Clark, July 23, 1909; Mahan to Stewart, March 11, 1911; Mahan to Rodgers, May 3, 1911; Mahan to Committee on Admissions, Century Club, circa August 1914; Ellen Kuhn Mahan, "Recollections," in *Letters and Papers*, III, 721, 728. The University Club was first at the corner of Madison Avenue and 26th Street, then moved to Fifth Avenue and 54th Street. An overnight lodging there cost Mahan $3.00 in 1908. Mahan considered the University Club superior to the Century Club. *See* Mahan to Rhodes, July 4, 1908. For Mahan's activities in the Round Table Club, *see* Mahan to Ropes, February 6, 1898; Mahan to Billings, February 2, 1909; Mahan to Choate, March 15, 1912; Ellen Kuhn Mahan, "Recollections," in *Letters and Papers*, III, 728.

3. Ellen Kuhn Mahan, "Recollections," in *Letters and Papers*, III, 721; Mahan to Ashe, February 1, April 12, 1903; Mahan to Billings, September 8, 1905; Mahan to Henderson, June 18, 1904, February 16, 1909; Mahan to Clark, May 16, 1904, May 20, 1907, July 23, 1909, December 15, 1911; Mahan to Brown, March 30, 1905, February 26, 1906; Mahan to Maxse, September 14, 1905.

4. Mahan to Clark, October 31, 1907, December 15, 1911; Mahan to Editor, *New York Times*, October 13, 1913; Mahan to Henderson, November 7, 1913; Mahan to Jameson, April 27, 1914.

5. Mahan to Luce, May 6, 1909, Footnote 1; Mahan to Clark, July 23, 1909, October 1, 1909, October 6, 1913; Mahan to Gordon, May 20, 1914; Mahan to Jameson, October 6, 1914; Ellen Kuhn Mahan, "Recollections," in *Letters and Papers*, III, 729–730; Puleston, *Mahan*, 291, 295, 337–338; Mahan to New York State Public Service Commission, September 30, 1912, October 7, 1912.

6. Mahan to Luce, January 13, 1903, June 17, 1903; Mahan to Ashe, February 1, April 12, 1903; Mahan to Brown, January 1, 1907; Mahan to Moore, March 1, 1904, March 6, 1904, November 22, 1904, December 3, 1904, January 2, 1905, February 20, 1905, March 2, 1905, March 5, 1905, March 20, 1905, April 20, 1905; Mahan to Brown, May 9, 1901; Mahan, *Sea Power in Its Relations to the War of 1812* (London: Sampson Low, Marston and Company, 1905), I, v, vii, viii–ix. For evidence of

the extensive research in primary and secondary sources undertaken by Mahan for this book, *see* Mahan to Rawson, June 13, 1902, July 21, 1902; Mahan to Luce, May 12, 1903, June 17, 1903, July 29, 1903, August 3, 1903, August 10, 1903; Mahan to Stewart, June 26, 1903, August 4, 1903, December 2, 1903, April 14, 1904 (misdated October 14, 1904 in *Letters and Papers*, III, 103–104), December 5, 1904; Mahan to O'Neil, June 30, 1903; Mahan to Gauss, July 23, 1903; Mahan to Jameson, February 10, 1904; Mahan to McLaughlin, January 3, 1905, January 17, 1905, March 29, 1905, April 2, 1905, April 28, 1905, May 9, 1905, June 19, 1905; Mahan to Billings, February 26, 1905, June 15, 1905; Mahan to Putnam, January 28, 1905, June 29, 1905. Mahan's research on *War of 1812* took him to Washington and Ottawa to work the archival materials in the national libraries there. On this point, *see* Mahan to Brown, December 13, 1903; and Mahan to McLaughlin, January 17, 1905, February 21, 1905, March 5, 1905, March 20, 1905.

7. Mahan to Brown, February 15, 1897, June 21, 1898, September 14, 1905, October 19, 1905; Mahan to Little, Brown and Co., October 8, 1905, January 1, 1907; Mahan to Page, August 2, 1897; Mahan to Thursfield, January 31, 1906; Mahan to Maxse, September 14, 1905, November 5, 1905. For his problems in seeing the prepublication installments of his *War of 1812* through press at *Scribner's*, *see* Mahan to Chapin, November 5, 1903, November 9, 1903, November 22, 1903, December 27, 1903, December 28, 1903; Mahan to *Scribner's Magazine*, December 29, 1903, December 30, 1903, February 11, 1904. Similarly, for the author's labors in seeing the book version of *War of 1812* through press, *see* Mahan to Brown, April 9, 1905, July 22, 1905, July 28, 1905, September 14, 1905.

8. Mahan to Little, Brown and Co., January 9, 1906, December 6, 1906, January 1, 1907, August 1, 1911; Mahan to Jameson, July 25, 1906, July 31, 1906, August 13–14, 1906; G. Hunt, review of Mahan, *Sea Power in Its Relation to the War of 1812*, in *American Historical Review* (July 1906), 924–926; Mahan to Editor, *American Historical Review*, July 26, 1906 (published in the *American Historical Review* for October 1906, pp. 183–185; with Hunt rebuttal on p. 185); Mahan to Ashe, November 13, 1880, and Footnote 4; Mahan to Brown, February 26, 1906; Mahan to Roosevelt, October 24, 1906; Richardson, *Messages and Papers of the Presidents*, X, 7446–7447. For the reviews of Mahan's *War of 1812*, *see*, further, Mahan to Luce, March 29, 1904; Mahan to Little, Brown and Co., June 20, 1906, December 6, 1906. For other favorable reviews and comments on *War of 1812*, *see* Taylor, *Life of Admiral Mahan*, 125, 165–166. "It is the best of all your writings," said Goodrich, "I am immensely proud of you."

9. Mahan to Brown, June 18, 1906, August 31, 1906; Taylor, *Life of Admiral Mahan*, 123–124; Mahan to Clark, December 14, 1906, September 6, 1907, October 31, 1907; Mahan to Luce, July 8, 1907, July 15, 1907, July 20, 1907; Mahan to Barnes, August 3, 1907; Mahan to Ashe, September 9, 1907; Mahan to Stewart, July 8, 1907; Mahan to Balch, March 4, 1908, and Footnote 1; Puleston, *Mahan*, 281; Mahan, *From Sail to Steam: Recollections of Naval Life* (New York: Da Capo Press Reprint, 1968), 80–81, 197, 275–278, 316–317, 322–323, 326, and *passim*.

10. Mahan to Clark, May 20, 1907; Mahan to Ashe, September 9, 1907; Mahan to Maxse, January 15, 1906, May 30, 1907; Mahan to Editor, *New York Times*, June 8, 1907.

11. Mahan to Corbett, August 12, 1907; Mahan to Little, Brown and Co., September 3, 1907, September 5, 1907, September 11, 1907, September 21, 1907, September 23, 1907, September 24, 1907, October 28, 1907; Mahan to Brown, August 30, 1907, September 20, 1907, September 23, 1907; Mahan to Merrell, November 16, 1907, March 13, 1908; Mahan to Clark, October 31, 1907, September 11, 1908; Ellen Kuhn Mahan, "Recollections," in *Letters and Papers*, III, 729; Ellen Evans Mahan to S. B. Luce, December 3, 1907, December 12, 1907, in *Letters and Papers*, III, 235; Mahan to Luce, January 27, 1908, and Footnotes 1 and 2. For other details of Mahan's prostatectomy and his recovery therefrom, *see* Mahan to Rhodes, April 11, 1908; Mahan to Maxse, May 7, 1908; Mahan to Clark, September 11, 1908, January 28, 1909 ("I continue very well, though the surgeon still has to tinker at me"); Mahan to Henderson, February 16, 1909, May 17, 1910; Mahan to Gordon, March 1909; Mahan to Ashe, November 30, 1908. "I will give you the warning the surgeon gave me," he told Ashe. "If you have to rise, habitually, to urinate, more than once in an ordinary seven or eight hours bed period, see a doctor."

12. Mahan to Luce, November 18, 1907; Ellen Kuhn Mahan, "Recollections," in *Letters and Papers*, III, 724; Mahan to Merrell, June 5, 1908; Mahan to McIntyre, January 7, 1909, February 16, 1909; Mahan, *The Harvest Within: Thoughts on the Life of a Christian* (Boston: Little, Brown and Co., 1909), vi, and *passim*; Mahan to Little, Brown and Co., May 22, 1909, June 3, 1909, June 28, 1909, July 2, 1909, August 31, 1909; "Captain Mahan's Interpretations of the Faith," *The Churchman* (August 21, 1909), 272; "Faith in Action," *The Guardian* (August 18, 1909). The 1909 edition of *Harvest Within* incorporated the text of an address he had delivered at Holy Trinity Episcopal Church, Brooklyn, in March 1899. This is also printed in *Letters and Papers*, III, 598–602. A later edition of *Harvest Within*, published after Mahan's death, added his "War From the Christian Standpoint," an essay dated November 15, 1900, previously printed in *Some Neglected Aspects of War* (1907); also added in the posthumous edition were "The Apparent Decadence of the Church's Influence," *The Churchman*, April 25, 1903; "Freedom in the Use of the Prayer Book," *The Churchman*, November 8, 1913; "Prayer Book Revision," *The Churchman*, October 10, October 17, 1914; and "Twentieth Century Christianity," *North American Review* (April 1914).

13. Taylor, *Life of Admiral Mahan*, 263, 264–265; Mahan, "A Statement on Behalf of the Church Missionary Society to Seamen in the Port of New York," in *Letters and Papers*, III, 590–591; Mahan, "Presentation to the Annual Meeting of the Church Missionary Society to Seamen in the Port of New York," *ibid.*, III, 597; Mahan, "The Well Being of the Seaman in Port," *ibid.*, III, 605–607; Mahan to Ashe, September 23, 1907; Mahan, "Introduction to K. Asami's Biography of Tasuka Serata," in *Letters and Papers*, III, 688–692; Mahan to FitzHugh, January 18, 1913; Mahan to Editor, *New York Times*, August 14, 1914 (Christian Progress), and November 21, 1911, (concerning Church and State); Mahan, "Twentieth Century Christianity," *North American Review* (April 1914), 589–598; Daniels to Mahan [April 1914], in Taylor, *Life of Admiral Mahan*, 263; Mahan, "The Christian Doctrine of the Trinity," in *Letters and Papers*, III, 714–716; Mahan to Rowell, September 27, 1913. *See also* Mahan, "The Mediatorial Office of the Church Toward the State," *The Churchman* (August 29, 1914).

14. Mahan to McBee, November 27, 1898; Mahan to Ashe, January 3, 1897, October 25, 1906; Mahan to Long, February 9, 1902; Mahan to Little, Brown and Co., August 1, 1911, August 3, 1911; Mahan to Rowell, July 9, 1913, September 27, 1913; Mahan, "Excerpt From a Statement to the American Movement," in *Letters and Papers*, III 657.

15. Mahan to Burgess, April 6, 1914; Mahan to Editor, *The Churchman*, July 28, 1914 (published September 8, 1914); Mahan to Gilbert (editor of *The Churchman*), September 10, 1914. For Mahan's controversy on Prayer Book reform in *The Churchman*, see Walker Gwynne, "Sources of the Church's Strengths and Weaknesses," *The Churchman* (July 25, 1914); Mahan, "Freedom in the Use of the Prayer Book," *ibid.* (November 8 1913); Mahan, "Prayer Book Revision," *ibid.* (October 10 and October 17, 1914).

16. For a detailed discussion of the relationship between the attitudes of Progressive movement leaders on domestic reform and foreign policy, see Seager, "The Progressives and American Foreign Policy, 1898–1917," *passim.* For various Mahan opinions that link him tangentially to the Progressive movement, or at least to Theodore Roosevelt's version of progressivism, see Mahan to Ashe, August 10, 1888; Mahan to Clark, January 17, 1896, March 12, 1912; Mahan to Rhodes, April 26, 1897; Mahan to Thursfield, January 22, 1906; Mahan to Stein, November 10, 1906; Mahan to Maxse, May 7, 1908; Mahan to Henderson, December 26, 1910; Mahan to Dohrman, September 2, 1912; Mahan, "Woman's Suffrage," in *Letters and Papers*, III, 712–713; Mahan, "Personality and Influence: A Commencement Address at Dartmouth College" (1903), *ibid.*, 609, 611–612, 618.

17. *Ibid.*, 608–619.

18. Mahan to Ashe, November 30, 1908; Mahan to Roosevelt, March 2, 1909, December 23, 1911; Mahan to Editor, *New York Times*, October 25, 1910, June 2, 1911; Mahan to Henderson, December 26, 1910; Seager, "The Progressives and American Foreign Policy," 189–190.

19. Mahan to Editor, *New York Times*, June 2, 1911, November 21, 1911, December 7, 1911; Mahan to Roosevelt, June 19, 1911, August 11, 1911, August 25, 1911, December 2, 1911, December 13, 1911, December 23, 1911; Mahan to Lodge, January 6, 1912, January 8, 1912; Mahan to Moore, February 26, 1911.

20. Norman Angell, *The Great Illusion* (New York: G. P. Putnam's Sons, 1911), *passim*, but particularly 4–5, 19, 28–29, 262–263, 273–274, 280–281, 308–309, 320–321, 336–337, 370–371; Mahan, "The Great Illusion," *North American Review* (March 1912), 319–332; Angell, "The Great Illusion: A Reply to Rear Admiral A. T. Mahan," *ibid.* (June 1912), 754–772; Meyer to Mahan, May 24, 1912 (NA); Mahan to Choate, March 15, 1912, and Footnote 2. Mahan's notes on *The Great Illusion* and a handwritten outline and draft of his March 1912 response to Angell are in the Mahan Papers (LC). Angell replied to Mahan in June 1912; also in the Mahan Papers (LC) is the draft of Mahan's unpublished answer to that reply. For Mahan's final detachment from all naval duty, see Meyer to Mahan, May 24, 1912 (NWC); Mahan to Rodgers, May 30, 1912; Mahan to Ashe, June 7, 1912.

21. Mahan to Clark, March 12, 1912, October 27, 1911, October 28, 1912; Mahan to Johnson, February 23, 1911; Mahan to Editor, *New York Times*, May 22, 1912,

August 20, 1912; Mahan to Ashe, June 7, 1912; Mahan to Dohrman, June 6, 1912, July 15, 1912, September 2, 1912; Mahan to White, June 28, 1912; Mahan to Parrish, June 13, 1912; Taylor, *Life of Admiral Mahan*, 199, 203–204.

22. Mahan to Clark, October 28, 1912; Mahan to Little, Brown and Co., December, 18, 1912. For Mahan's struggle to disinter *Major Operations* from the Clowes volumes and prepare it for republication in the United States, *see* Mahan to Brown, November 27, 1898, September 29, 1906, January 1, 1907 (two letters of this date), March 16, 1907, April 6, 1908; Mahan to Little, Brown and Co., October 10, 1906, February 9, 1911, February 20, 1911, July 17, 1911, May 30, 1912, June 20, 1912, August 1, 1912, August 2, 1912, August 7, 1912, October 1, 1912, October 12, 1912, October 14, 1912, October 19, 1912, October 21, 1912, October 22, 1912, January 10, 1913, January 16, 1913, April 1, 1913, April 23, 1913, June 25, 1913, September 25, 1913, October 4, 1913; Mahan to McIntyre, April 12, 1909, April 16, 1909; Mahan to Stewart, August 10, 1912, August 15, 1912. Roosevelt's contribution to the Clowes volumes was separately republished by Sampson Low, Marston under the title, *The Naval Operations of the War Between Great Britain and the United States, 1812–1815* when the former president visited England in 1910.

23. Mahan to Clark, October 23, 1913, March 12, 1914; Mahan to Henderson, November 7, 1913; Mahan to Little, Brown and Co., July 17, 1911, June 7, 1913; Mahan, *The Major Operations of the Navies in the War of American Independence* (New York: Greenwood Press Reprint, 1969), Preface, Introduction, 2.

24. Mahan, *Major Operations*, Introduction, 2; Mahan to Little, Brown and Co., June 7, 1913; Ellen Kuhn Mahan, "Recollections," in *Letters and Papers*, III, 720; Mahan to Clark, March 24, 1913; Mahan to Editor, *New York Times*, July 23, 1913. For Mahan's hatred of the Turks, *see* Mahan to FitzHugh, January 18, 1913; Mahan to Clark, October 6, 1913; Mahan, "Thoughts on the Righteousness of War," in *Letters and Papers*, III, 683–684; Mahan, "Why Not Disarm?" *ibid.*, III, 686.

25. Mahan to Roosevelt, July 8, 1913; Mahan to Clark, October 23, 1913, March 12, 1914; Mahan to Henderson, November 7, 1913.

26. Draft pages of and notes for Mahan's manuscript on the influence of expansion are in the Mahan Papers (LC). For the development of his interest in the concept, *see* Mahan to Brown, June 18, 1906; Mahan to Moore, June 1, 1912; Mahan to Dohrman, September 2, 1912; Mahan to Jameson, July 22, 1913, April 27, 1914; Mahan to Clark; March 12, 1914.

27. Mahan to Jameson, July 22, 1913, September 11, 1913, January 22, 1914, February 6, 1914, April 27, 1914; Mahan to Woodward, January 29, 1914; Mahan to Putnam, February 2, 1914; Mahan to Clark, October 1, 1914. Jameson headed the Research Department of the Carnegie Institution from 1913 to 1914. He assured Woodward that while Mahan had lately been writing popular articles and doing no serious research, "his thinking is of a very high quality and would do me much good. He is a good talker, lucid, penetrating, interesting." Woodward was willing to appoint Mahan, but wondered about his advanced age. *See* Jameson to Woodward, July 3, 1913 (LC); Woodward to Jameson, July 7, 1913 (LC).

28. Taylor, *Life of Admiral Mahan*, 141, 209; Mahan, Interview with the *New York Evening Post*, August 3, 1914, in *Letters and Papers*, III, 698–700; Mahan, "Sea Power in the Present European War," *Leslie's Weekly* (August 20, 1914),

reprinted in *Letters and Papers*, III, 706–710; Mahan, "About What is the War?" *ibid.*, 702–705; Puleston, *Mahan*, 340–347.

29. Mahan to Otis F. Wood Company, August 6, 1914; Mahan to Pulitzer, August 7, 1914; Mahan Memorandum, August 11, 1914; Mahan to Reynolds, September 11, 1914; Mahan to Brownell, September 21, 1914; Mahan to Little, Brown and Co., October 23, 1914; Mahan to Daniels, August 15, 1914 (two letters of this date). *See also*, Puleston, *Mahan*, 341–342; Taylor, *Life of Admiral Mahan*, 277–280.

30. Editorial, "The American Example," *New York Times*, August 29, 1914; Mahan to Editor, *New York Times*, August 31, 1914 (published September 10, 1914 under heading "Unguarded Frontiers: Not Factors in Preventing Wars, Admiral Mahan Says"); Mahan to Miller, September 6, 1914, September 12, 1914; Mahan to Editor, *New York Sun*, September 7, 1914 (unpublished), in *Letters and Papers*, III, 545; Mahan to Reynolds, September 11, 1914.

31. Mahan to Brownell, September 21, 1914; Mahan to Clark, October 1, 1914. That Mahan's heart attack and subsequent death were the fault of Wilson and Daniels was an opinion that passed quickly into Mahan family history. Frederick A. Mahan wrote to Theodore Roosevelt on February 11, 1915 (LC): "My sister [Jane] writes me that there is no doubt in her mind that his death was hastened by the worry caused through not being able to show our people, as this wretched war goes on, the necessity for preparedness, by illustrating the subject from the events of the day, his mouth being closed and his pen being stopped by the Executive Order forbidding our officers of the army and navy to express their opinions in public or through the medium of the press."

32. Puleston, *Mahan*, 352–354; Mahan to Jameson, September 26, 1914, October 6, 1914, November 21, 1914; Mahan to Little, Brown and Co., October 23, 1914; Ellen Evans Mahan to Rebecca Lewis Evans, November 10, 1914 (LC); Mahan to Rebecca Lewis Evans, November 10, 1914; Mahan to Pleadwell, November 15, 1914 (LC); Jameson to C. F. Adams, December 14, 1914 (LC); Jameson to Bernard Moses, November 17, 1914 (LC); Mahan to Greene, November 6, 1914; Ellen Kuhn Mahan, "Recollections," in *Letters and Papers*, III, 730; Ashe to Ellen Evans Mahan, December 2, 1914 (NWC); H. H. Balthis (Paymaster, Washington Navy Yard) to Ellen Evans Mahan, December 19, 1914 (NA); Alfred Harding to Ellen Evans Mahan, December 21, 1914 (LC); Carnegie Institution to Ellen Evans Mahan, December 21, 1914 (LC); Daniels to Ellen Evans Mahan, June 25, 1915 (LC). A few months earlier, on December 1, 1914, Daniels had written Elly a saccharine letter of sympathy in which he described the departed Mahan as "possessed of a lovable character that endeared him to all with whom he came in contact," noted that "what he so ably and convincingly wrote was accepted at home and abroad as authority," and assured her that "your grief is shared not only by the Service he loved and long and nobly worked for, but by the Nation." *See* Taylor, *Life of Admiral Mahan*, 289.

33. Puleston, *Mahan*, 355–358, summarizes numerous obituaries of Mahan and letters of sympathy, as does Taylor, *Life of Admiral Mahan*, 284–295; Ellen Kuhn Mahan, "Recollections," in *Letters and Papers*, III, 721; Ashe to Ellen Evans Mahan, December 2, 1914 (NWC). *See also* John Bassett Moore, *Personal Recollections of Admiral Mahan: Address Made at the Grave of Rear Admiral Alfred Thayer Ma-*

han at Quogue, Long Island, on September 27, 1940, at a Ceremony in Celebration of the 100th Anniversary of His Birth. Pamphlet. Privately printed, N.P., N.D. [October 1940] (copy in NWC). Among the expressions of sorrow, condolence, and eulogy were those from Seth Low, William S. Sims, Theodore Roosevelt, Cecil Spring-Rice, John Bassett Moore, Bouverie Clark, Henry White, David H. Greer, Josephus Daniels, Raymond T. Rodgers, James Ford Rhodes, Roy B. Marston, the U.S. Naval Institute, the Seamen's Church Institute, the American Church Institute for Negroes, the Department of the Navy, the Vestry of Trinity Episcopal Church in New York, the Navy League of Great Britain, the Navy Records Society (Great Britain), *The New York Times,* the *New York Press,* and the London *Morning Post.* For these and others, *see* Taylor, *Life of Admiral Mahan,* 100–101, 135–136, 169–170, 171, 189, 225–226, 240–241, 243–244, 265–266, 271, 283, 284, 286–294.

Index

As regards the Index, laborious though it is, I prefer to give both the labor and the time myself—for it is scarcely less a factor of a book than the text itself.

Alfred Thayer Mahan to John M. Brown, July 22, 1905

For the complete range of Mahan materials and references on a given point, users of this index may find it helpful to consult the more extensive index, compiled by Caroline P. Seager, in Robert Seager II and Doris D. Maguire, eds., *Letters and Papers of Alfred Thayer Mahan*. 3 Volumes. (Annapolis, Md.: Naval Institute Press, 1975), III, 755–873.

M. articles on annexation, 248–250, 329;
M. banished to sea for article on annexa-
tion, 248, 252; Japanese opposition to U.S.
annexation, 465; relationship of isthmian
canal to, 497
Hay, John Milton, 396, 406, 408, 412, 460,
461, 462, 463, 464, 466, 472, 497, 507, 657.
See also Open Door policy
Hay–Pauncefote treaties. *See* Isthmian canal
Hayes, Rutherford B., 115, 116, 117, 121, 122
Hayes, Sam, 76, 78, 81, 621
Hearst, William Randolph, 329, 355, 356,
371, 372, 406
Hegel, Georg Wilhelm, 438, 442
Henderson, William H., 160, 187, 190, 191,
205, 209, 216, 279, 361, 459, 503, 504, 521,
532, 581, 583, 596, 639
Henry Clay (M), 7
Herbert, Hilary A., 180, 182, 246, 247, 250,
256, 263, 264, 275, 276, 280, 284, 285, 289,
307, 339, 651; shifting attitude toward
NWC, 179, 181, 245, 272, 273; sends M.
to sea, 248, 252, 254; lauds M. books, 273,
274; opinion of M., 288, 306; M. opinion
of, 181, 245, 253, 259, 274, 300; defends M.
in Erben controversy, 286–287, 288. *See
also* Erben, Henry; U.S. Navy, Naval
War College
Heroine (Br), 152
History: M. early interest in, 2, 8, 94; early
study of, 50, 134–135, 166, 168–169; USN
support of M. as historian, 137, 166, 216,
219–220, 307, 332, 549, 637–638; USN opposition to M. as historian, 137 (*see* Ramsay, Francis M.); M. more useful to USN
as historian than seaman, 224, 239, 246,
247; economic motives and rewards for
writing, 135, 205–206, 209, 231, 257, 259,
260, 264, 265–266, 267–268, 270, 271, 272,
280, 292, 297–298, 303, 305, 309, 326–327,
328, 329, 330–331, 332, 341, 348, 349, 359,
360, 371–372, 413, 422, 427, 428, 435, 440,
441, 473, 509, 547, 549, 568–569, 570, 571,
594, 599, 601, 647, 663, 678; warriors must
study, 186, 452; study of war is study of,
555; purpose of, 209; bias in, 434, 437;
facts in, 430, 433–434; truth in, 434, 436–
437; anecdotes in, 435, 436; God in, 439,
442, 449, 457; progress in, 442, 452, 456;
M. as biographer, 257, 437; M. as geopoli-
tician, 439; M. emphasis on contemporary
foreign-policy issues in, 328, 335; as tool
to mold public opinion, 328, 329, 330, 349,
434, 435, 448–449, 457; primary source materials of, 136, 437, 632; M. writing style,
136, 329, 340, 435; research techniques,

135–136, 213, 216, 231, 233, 298, 329, 340,
433, 632; M. methodology in research and
writing (subordination), 235, 431–434, 436,
442, 444, 448–450, 457, 575–576, 644; search
for laws in, 438–439, 446–447; M. on general principles of war and, 167, 173, 186,
191, 204, 205, 209, 213, 328, 381, 385, 386,
397, 398, 434, 454, 456–457, 474, 533, 535,
545, 551, 552, 553, 604; origin of M. philosophy of, 442–448; M. philosophy of, 437–
438, 439–440, 457–459; dialectical forces in,
342, 438, 442, 445, 447–448, 451, 456, 551.
See also Books (by Mahan); Sea-power
hypothesis; War
Hitchcock, R. B., 623
Hitler, Adolf, 464
Hoff, William Bainbridge, 173, 637, 638
Hohenzollern (Ger), 298
Holland, 536
Holland, 200, 204, 206, 260, 408, 442, 646
Holls, George F. W., 407, 408, 411, 412, 671;
M. conflict with on Hague Conference,
416–417, 428
Honduras, 130, 153, 155
Hong Kong, China, 52, 53, 55, 57, 62, 76, 77,
81, 361, 417, 622
Hopkins, John Henry, 445, 446, 674
Hopkins, William F., 12
Hornby, Geoffrey T. Phipps, 209, 293, 657
Hoskins, Reverend and Mrs. Thomas R., 96,
97, 625, 658
Hotel Collingwood (New York), 325, 562,
563
Howe, Richard, 167, 181, 295, 530
Howell, John A., 628
Howison, Henry L., 628
Huerta, Victoriano, 595
Hughes, Aaron K., 138, 633
Hunt, Gaillard: M. controversy with on
War of 1812, 569–570
Hunt, William H., 131, 132, 569, 629

Imperialism: M. opposition to, 121, 132–133,
140–141; M. conversion to, 132, 141, 146–
147, 180, 205, 494, 496; M. imperialist
themes, 350–351; overseas colonies, 208;
colonial administration, 419–420; U.S. economic expansion into foreign markets,
121, 132, 180, 207, 208, 225, 226, 350, 391,
410–411, 460, 461, 490, 629; M. articles on,
180, 220, 225, 226, 242, 267. *See also* Boer
War; Hawaii; Isthmian canal; Open Door
policy; Philippine annexation
Independent, The, 212, 405, 426, 599
India, 81, 201, 202, 350, 419, 468, 469, 588,
622, 642

Schley, Winfield Scott (*cont.*)
  William T.; Spanish-American War; U.S. Navy, Naval War College
Schoonmaker, Cornelius Marius, 23, 609, 618
Schwartz, C., 427–428
Scientific American, 480
Scott, Sir Percy, 538
Scott, William Lawrence, 182
Scribner, Charles, 490
Scribner's Magazine, 359, 568, 569
Scribner's Sons, 135, 137, 192, 198, 199, 599, 632, 640
Scudder, Horace, 225, 231, 248, 250, 257, 263, 266, 267, 307, 358, 432, 440, 646, 647, 653
Seager, Edward, 82, 622
Seahorse (Br), 344
Seal, 536
Seamen's Church Institute of New York, 65–66, 576, 619, 690
Sea-power hypothesis: origin of concept, 135, 141, 145–146, 165, 174, 191, 430–431, 443, 451, 457, 572, 641–642, 672; development of concept, 166, 174–175, 205, 206–207, 208, 209; precursors of M. on, 199–203, 205, 206, 208, 430, 626–627; M. lectures on, 156, 166–167, 173–174, 175, 178, 187; relevance of, 146; discovery of converts M. to imperialism, 180; M. books and articles on, 173–174, 197–199, 430. See *also* History
Sears, James H., 244
Seeley, John R., 68, 205, 296, 328, 430, 434, 621; anticipates M. ideas, 199, 202–203; influence on M., 213, 232, 328, 642
Selfridge, Thomas O., 307, 640
Seminole: M. service in, 36, 38, 39, 40
Serata, Tasuka, 119, 628
Serbia, 513, 597, 598; war with Turkey, 106
Seward, William H., 43
Shafter, William R., 378, 379, 380, 382, 386, 387, 390
Sharon Springs, N.Y., 83, 85, 86, 87, 90
Shenandoah, 49
Sherman, F. F., 320
Sherman, William T., 3, 41, 637
Shufeldt, Robert W., 199–200, 205, 208
Sicard, Montgomery, 143, 365, 370, 373, 374, 375, 386, 397, 641, 664
Sigsbee, Charles D., 376
Sims, William S., 481, 534, 539, 554, 572, 690; M. conflict with, 415, 480, 523, 525–526, 527, 528, 532, 533, 550, 572; M. lauds, 535. See *also* U.S. Navy, technology
Singer, Isaac M., 129
Sino-Japanese War (1894–1895): M. ignorance of, 303; M. on Yalu battle, 303,

327–328, 659, 663; outcome of, 459–460, 476
Slamm, Jefferson A., 33
"Slumberside" (Quogue), 260, 271, 324, 325, 412
Smith, Adam, 208, 251, 647, 657
Smith, B. P., 609, 611
Smith, Goldwin, 434
Smith, Melancthon, 85
Smith, Robert, 569, 570
Snowden, Archibald Loudon, 252
Socialism, 269, 270; M. sees in USN, 320–321; the new slavery, 339; anti-individualism, 582, 664
Society of the Cincinnati, 361
Society of Naval Architects and Marine Engineers, 534
Soley, James Russell, 136–137, 163, 175, 197, 198, 217, 223, 240, 243, 286, 632, 636, 638
South Carolina, 520, 526
Southerland, William H. H., 379
Spain, 38, 95, 105, 122, 129, 133, 201, 204, 207, 227, 252, 264, 281, 290, 303, 319, 321, 349, 354, 355, 356, 357, 358, 359, 361, 362, 363, 364, 366, 374, 375, 377, 380, 381, 382, 383, 384, 385, 386, 387, 388, 389, 390, 391, 392, 393, 396, 412, 416, 417. See *also* Spanish-American War
Spanish-American War (1898), 352, 406, 411, 426, 427, 429, 454, 456, 459, 466, 472, 473, 500, 501, 517, 518, 519, 541, 545, 588, 589, 600, 660, 667; causes of, 354–356, 357, 358, 360–361, 363–364, 414, 421, 424, 668; outbreak not foreseen by M., 353, 359, 560; M. no jingo prior to, 358, 359, 361, 362; weakness of Spain, 357, 358, 363, 366, 368, 373, 374–375, 377, 380, 381, 383–384, 391, 399, 539, 550; unequalness of, 353, 356–357, 381, 387; movements of Cervera, 357, 366–367, 372, 376–377; strategic dimensions of, 357–358, 362–363, 367, 369, 374, 375, 382–383, 384, 388, 389, 390; M. recalled to active duty in, 366, 399–400; USN tactics in, 363, 367, 372, 374, 375; USN errors during, 376, 378, 379, 383; M. criticism of USN strategy and tactics, 368, 373, 398; work of Naval War Board, 371, 373–374, 382, 383, 384, 393, 395–396, 461–462; M. criticism of Naval War Board, 369–371, 397, 539, 540, 541–542; M. surrender formula for Santiago, 386–387, 388; Army operations in, 378, 379, 382, 385, 390–391, 398; Army-Navy disagreements during, 379, 386, 387; naval intelligence during, 383, 384, 398; Sampson-Schley controversy, 376, 381, 397, 400–405, 409, 412; plan for bombardment of